THE CULTURES AND GLOBALIZATION SERIES 4

HERITAGE, MEMORY & IDENTITY

THE CULTURES AND GLOBALIZATION SERIES 4

HERITAGE, MEMORY & IDENTITY

Edited by

HELMUT ANHEIER
YUDHISHTHIR RAJ ISAR

Guest Editor
Dacia Viejo-Rose

Los Angeles | London | New Delhi
Singapore | Washington DC

SAGE Publications Ltd
1 Oliver's Yard
55 City Road
London EC1Y 1SP

SAGE Publications Inc.
2455 Teller Road
Thousand Oaks, California 91320

SAGE Publications India Pvt Ltd
B 1/I1 Mohan Cooperative Industrial Area
Mathura Road
New Delhi 110 044

SAGE Publications Asia-Pacific Pte Ltd
33 Pekin Street #02-01
Far East Square
Singapore 048763

Library of Congress Control Number: 2010925734

British Library Cataloguing in Publication data

A catalogue record for this book is available from the British Library

ISBN 978-0-85702-389-6
ISBN 978-0-85702-390-2 (pbk)

Typeset by C&M Digitals (P) Ltd, Chennai, India
Printed and bound in Great Britain by Ashford Colour Press Ltd
Printed on paper from sustainable resources

CONTENTS

Foreword   ix
Pierre Nora

Acknowledgements   xii
Contributors   xv
List of boxes, figures, photos and tables   xxiii

Introduction   1
Yudhishthir Raj Isar, Dacia Viejo-Rose and Helmut K. Anheier

PART 1   CONFIGURATIONS OF HERITAGE, MEMORY, IDENTITY   **21**

Global Approaches   **23**

1   The Role of Narratives in Commemoration: Remembering as Mediated Action   25
     James V. Wertsch and Doc M. Billingsley

2   UNESCO and Heritage: Global Doctrine, Global Practice   39
     Yudhishthir Raj Isar

3   Destruction and Reconstruction of Heritage: Impacts on Memory and Identity 53
     Dacia Viejo-Rose

4   The Political Economies of Heritage   70
     Tim Winter

5   Unsettling the National: Heritage and Diaspora   82
     Ien Ang

6   Territorialization and the Politics of Autochthony   95
     Jean-Pierre Warnier

7   Grassroots Memorials as Sites of Heritage Creation   106
     Cristina Sánchez-Carretero and Carmen Ortiz

8   Sites of Conscience: Heritage of and for Human Rights   114
     Liz Ševčenko

9   'Not Just a Place': Culture Heritage and the Environment   124
     Benjamin Morris

Regional Realities   **137**

10 Living Sacred Heritage and 'Authenticity' in South Asia   139
Jagath Weerasinghe

11 A Contested Site of Memory: The Preah Vihear Temple   148
Aurel Croissant and Paul W. Chambers

12 Memory and Identity as Elements of Heritage Tourism in Southern Africa   157
Susan Keitumetse, Laura McAtackney and Gobopaone Senata

13 Multiple Heritages, Multiple Identities: The Southwest Indian Ocean   169
Rosabelle Boswell

14 Remembering and Forgetting Communist Cultural Production   177
Dragan Klaic

15 Post-socialist Recollections: Identity and Memory in Former Yugoslavia   187
Zala Volcic

16 Contemporary Creativity and Heritage in Latin America   199
Lucina Jiménez López

Fields and Issues   **211**

17 The Manipulation of Memory and Heritage in Museums of Migration   213
Julie Thomas

18 Heritage, Memory, Debris: Sulukule, Don't Forget   222
Asu Aksoy and Kevin Robins

19 Knowing the City: Migrants Negotiating Materialities in Istanbul   231
Yael Navaro-Yashin

20 Divided Memories, Contested Histories: The Shifting Landscape in Japan   239
Akiko Hashimoto

21 Memorialization and the Rwandan Genocide: The Use of Theatre   245
Ananda Breed

22 Narrating Shared Identity   252
Brian Schiff, Carolina Porto de Andrade and Mathilde Toulemonde

23 Listening Voices: On Actualizing Memories   262
Esther Shalev-Gerz

Commentaries   **271**

24 Intangibles: Culture, Heritage and Identity   273
Henrietta L. Moore

25 From the Tower of Babel to the Ivory Tower   281
David Lowenthal

PART 2 INDICATOR SUITES   285
Michael Hoelscher and Helmut Anheier

Indicator Suites for Heritage, Memory, Identity   287
Michael Hoelscher

Heritage   297

   World Heritage Sites, Ryan Weafer, designer   298
   Legal and Political Frameworks, George Michael Brower, designer   304
   Museums, Camile Orillaneda, designer   310
   Intangible Heritage, Fei Liu, designer   314
   Tourism, Everett Pelayo, designer   318
   Sustainability, Ryan Weafer, designer   322

Memory   331

   Memoralization, Donnie Luu, designer   332
   Contested memories, Donnie Luu, designer   336
   Global Collective Memories, Roxane Zargham, designer   340
   Places, George Michael Brower, designer   346
   Media, Camile Orillaneda, designer   350
   Migration and Diaspora, Everett Pelayo, designer   354
   Education, Everett Pelayo, designer   358

Identity   363

   Geographical identities, Ryan Weafer, designer   364
   Internet Identities, Roxane Zargham, designer   370
   Multiple Citizenship and Naturalization, Roxane Zargham, designer   374
   Popular Culture, Fei Liu, designer   378
   Identities in the Economy, Camile Orillaneda, designer   382
   Religion, Fei Liu, designer   386

References & Source Materials   392

Index   409

Pierre Nora

A constellation of three terms – heritage, memory and identity – has dominated ideological thinking for some thirty years now. This is the phenomenon that the contributors to the present volume have set out to examine, each from a different geocultural perspective; together, their essays provide an invaluable overview that looks set to become the standard work on the subject.

What is particularly striking is the way in which all three terms have shifted, over the same period and in the same manner, from the individual to the collective. They echo and complement one another. *Heritage* traditionally referred to the goods and properties you inherited from your father or your mother; today, it refers to the goods and properties of a group which help define the identity of that group. The meaning of the word has been enormously extended, in fact, since we readily speak today of a linguistic, cultural or genetic heritage. *Memory*, strictly speaking a phenomenon linked to the psychology and physiology of an individual person, now encompasses a broad spectrum of meanings relating to the different forms of presence, real or imaginary, of the past in the present; it could almost be said to have replaced the word 'history', which by definition refers to a social and collective phenomenon. *Identity* traditionally expressed the unique character of a person in an administrative or police sense, the latter being the context in which it was most frequently used, as in 'identity papers' (a card or a passport). Today, it is the broadest of the three terms: at one end of the spectrum we speak of the 'identity' of this or that group or minority; at the other, of 'national identity', as in the Ministry of Immigration and National Identity, a government department set up in France in 2007 that continues to provoke much discussion and hostility.

The emergence of this constellation is linked to a number of fundamental changes in contemporary society. To understand these changes, we can draw on a distinction the German philosopher Walter Benjamin made between 'transmitted' memory and 'acquired' memory, that he also calls 'lived' memory. Transmitted memory is everything that is handed down from one generation to the next – how we exist in the world, how we conduct our lives, how we think and reason – and is thus an educational heritage that includes history and the manner in which it is taught. Acquired memory is everything that has happened, or is felt to have happened, to ourselves alone. It is obvious that, as a result of certain developments in the world over the last third of the twentieth century, there is less and less transmitted memory and more and more acquired memory.

The main cause of this is the rapidly increasing pace of history, which obliges everyone to live under the banner of the new and, consequently, of loss. Another factor is the major historical and political upheavals that have affected the entire globe. In one place it might be the brutal transition from the Communist world to the free world; in another, the transition from colonial rule to the ups and downs of independence. Everywhere it means mass urbanization and the disruption this causes to the mechanisms of collective stability in rural societies. In industrial and democratic societies, it means internal changes to the conditions of social life.

And then there are the major conflicts of the last century, which have certainly weighed heavily on those changes. War, totalitarianism, genocide and the crimes humanity has perpetrated against itself have become the dominant image of the age of memory. The Shoah has become a sort of commemorative matrix for the twentieth century, the calamity by which it was radically transformed. It was Auschwitz, moreover, that gave rise to the 'obligation to remember'. For the West, it was the defining trauma. And the fact that the genocide in question concerned the 'people of memory' only reinforces, no doubt, the link between the Shoah and the rise of memory. The Shoah has conferred quasi-historical status on the figure of the victim, whose image is now so powerful that the whole of past history is reinterpreted in its light, together with all human rights and laws – the rights of men, women, children, animals, even of nature itself.

This threefold constellation of memory, heritage and identity signals a new form of democratization that manifests itself first and foremost in the liberation and emancipation of all forms of minority group – social, sexual, religious or ethnic. The movement is world-wide; the forms it takes are by definition myriad and infinitely varied. In principle, however, they are governed by the same mechanism.

Memory, heritage, identity: we can understand how the three terms have come to overlap, to the point where they have become all but synonymous. The fact remains, however, that each word conveys a specific set of meanings. What we are now in the habit of calling 'memory' is in reality the history of those who have been forgotten by History, those who have been excluded from official history because they live on the margins of society; hence the founding connection between memory and minority groupings. The word itself was spontaneously adopted to describe the emergence of self-awareness on the part of these minorities, but is today widely misused. In relation to history it has even taken on an aggressive, polemical, protest-driven dimension. There are two reasons for this, no doubt: on the one hand, it represents the side of history that the official version – the version set down by officials, the victors of history – had deliberately concealed; on the other, it embraces all that history is unable, by definition, to embrace: the affective and the emotional, the warmth and the sorrows of lived experience.

The notion of heritage, meanwhile, has been so over-extended that it now means the opposite of what it originally described. In the past it referred to the finest, most elevated and most ancient creations of human genius; today, it has come to denote the most traditional forms of the mundane. By definition, it referred to what was non-utilitarian and shielded from the world of commerce, what was made on the margins of society and preserved in archives and museums; today, it plays a leading role in the tourist and industrial economies of democratic societies. Formerly, it was the embodiment, not merely of culture but of high culture; today, it has been extended to nature itself, henceforth our most treasured and most vulnerable possession. In short, whereas formerly it referred to a narrow selection of the most remarkable tokens of the past, it now refers to the sum total of all traces of the past *as past*. The notion of heritage, that is, has cast off its historical, material and monumental moorings and embarked on an age of memory, society and identity.

The kaleidoscope of meanings attached to the term 'identity' is richer still, but more difficult to define. The notion of identity is being reconfigured in a novel and extraordinary dialectic of outer and inner. An attachment to identity is symptomatic of a profound transformation of subjectivity and self-awareness and implies an unusual degree of psychic activity: the internalizing of an outer imperative which is immediately transformed into a spontaneous conviction; an 'ought-to-be' dictated from without which is then transformed into an ineradicable individual belief. This emergent new sense of plural identities obviously implies a radical redefining of forms of being-together, in conjunction with a society of individuals, in a society hitherto regulated by traditional forms of being-together – that is, by religious and political structures that for the last two centuries, in the West at least, have been subsumed under the figure of the nation.

Ever since the eighteenth century, the nation has been the principal frame of reference for the collectivity of individuals. A multiplicity of identity markers above or below that of the nation, or transgressive of national boundaries, also existed – religions and ideologies, for example, or languages. The fact remains, however, that in the movement of history the nation was the primary vehicle of progress, civic and social identification, and respect for common rights and obligations. It wasn't only of France that Ernest Renan was speaking when, in his famous lecture at the Sorbonne in 1882, he defined the nation in terms of a collective programme: 'to have done great deeds together, and to wish to perform still more'. Such a programme describes rather well what a public memory, a common heritage, an identity which takes priority over all others, might and ought to consist of.

It is the erosion of traditional forms of identity, beginning with that of national identity, that has fostered the emergence of individualised forms of identity. And that is why the rise of our threefold constellation – memory, identity and heritage – far from being a momentary fad or crisis, having only a superficial effect on history and society, is the profound expression of a radical mutation.

It has only just begun.

[Translated from the French by Mark Hutchinson]

ACKNOWLEDGEMENTS

The *Cultures and Globalization Series* has benefited from the advice, support, and contributions of many individuals and organizations. We endeavour to acknowledge and thank all of them here. In the ultimate analysis, however, the co-editors alone are responsible for this final version of the publication.

International Advisory Board

Hugo Achugar (Uruguay)
Arjun Appadurai (India/USA)
Benjamin Barber (USA)
Hilary Beckles (Barbados)
Tony Bennett (United Kingdom)
Craig Calhoun (USA)
George Corm (Lebanon)
Masayuki Deguchi (Japan)
Mamadou Diouf (Senegal)
Yehuda Elkana (Israel/Hungary)
Yilmaz Esmer (Turkey)
Sakiko Fukuda-Parr (Japan/USA)
Mike Featherstone (United Kingdom)
Nathan Gardels (USA)
Anthony Giddens (United Kingdom)
Salvador Giner (Spain)
Xavier Greffe (France)
Stuart Hall (Jamaica/United Kingdom)
Seung-Mi Han (Korea)
David Held (United Kingdom)
Vjeran Katunaric (Croatia)
Nobuku Kawashima (Japan)
Arun Mahizhnan (Singapore)
Achille Mbembe (Cameroon/South Africa)
Candido Mendes (Brazil)
Henrietta Moore (United Kingdom)
Catherine Murray (Canada)
Sven Nilsson (Sweden)
Walter Santagata (Italy)
James Allen Smith (USA)
Prince Hassan bin Talal (Jordan)
David Throsby (Australia)
Jean-Pierre Warnier (France)
Margaret Wyszomirski (USA)
Yunxiang Yan (China/USA)
George Yúdice (USA)

Additional Support

Text Boxes
Ien Ang, Fabrice de Kerchove, Milena Dragićević Šešić, Michael Francis, Yudhishthir Raj Isar, Marta de Magalhães, Benjamin Morris, Chandra Morrison, Marie Louise Sørensen, Lina G. Tahan, Dacia Viejo-Rose, Gabriele Woidelko

Research Coordination for Indicator Suites
Michael Hoelscher

Research Assistance
Meghan Corroon, Antje Groneberg, Martin Hölz, Anael Labigne, Thomas Laux, Manar Nidah, Anubha Prakash, Simon Scholtz, Johannes Sonnenholzner, Filip Zielinski, David Zimmer

Design and Production
Indicator suites were designed by alumni of the UCLA Design and Media Arts programme under the direction of Ryan Weafer.

Designers: George Michael Brower, Camile Orillaneda, Fei Liu, Everett Pelayo, Donnie Luu, Ryan Weafer, Roxane Zargham

Cover and divider artwork
Emilia Birlo

Administration
Jocelyn Guihama

Financial Support

We gratefully acknowledge the financial support of the following institutions:

ARC Centre of Excellence for Creative Industries and Innovation
Asia Research Fund
The Bank of Sweden Tercentenary Foundation
Compagnia di San Paolo
The Fritt Ord Institute
Heidelberg University
Hertie School of Governance
The London School of Economics
The Prince Claus Fund for Culture and Development
The Sasakawa Peace Foundation
Swedish International Development Agency
UCLA International Institute
UCLA School of the Arts and Architecture
UCLA School of Public Affairs

We would also like to acknowledge the support of:

- Professor Henrietta Moore and the Culture and Communication group of Centre for the Study of Global Governance at the London School of Economics.
- The faculty and staff of the Centre for Social Investment at Heidelberg University, especially Ursula Fischer.

CONTRIBUTORS

Asu Aksoy teaches in the Cultural Management Programme at Istanbul Bilgi University, where she was also involved in the setting up of Santralistanbul, a new cultural complex at the site of Istanbul's first electricity power plant. At Santralistanbul, she has managed a number of projects and international collaborations. She also contributed to preparing Istanbul's successful bid to become a European Capital of Culture in 2010. She is currently in charge of a major citywide project, *Cultural Mapping of Istanbul*. She has researched the changing media consumption practices in Europe of Turkish-speaking migrants, and has authored and co-authored many articles on this topic.

Ien Ang is Distinguished Professor of Cultural Studies at the Centre for Cultural Research, University of Western Sydney. Her wide-ranging interdisciplinary work deals broadly with patterns of cultural flow and exchange in our globalized world, focusing on issues such as the formation of audiences and publics, the politics of migration, identity and difference, and issues of representation in contemporary cultural institutions. Her influential books include *Watching Dallas: Soap Opera and the Melodramatic Imagination*, *Living Room Wars*, and *On Not Speaking Chinese: Living Between Asia and the West*.

Helmut K. Anheier (PhD, Yale) is Dean of the Hertie School of Governance in Berlin. Professor Anheier holds a chair of Sociology at Heidelberg University and serves as Academic Director of the Center for Social Investment. From 2001 to 2009, he was Professor of Public Policy and Social Welfare at UCLA's School of Public Affairs and Centennial Professor at the London School of Economics. Professor Anheier founded and directed the Centre for Civil Society at LSE and the Center for Civil Society at UCLA. Before embarking on an academic career, he served as social affairs officer to the United Nations. He is currently researching the nexus between globalization, civil society, and culture and is interested in policy analysis and methodological questions.

Doc M. Billingsley is a PhD candidate in Anthropology at Washington University in St. Louis, USA. His forthcoming dissertation research examines networks of Guatemalan Maya intellectuals and activists who are combining memory and literacy practices to develop alternative narratives about their histories and to imagine new forms of indigenous citizenship in Guatemala's future. Address: Department of Anthropology, Washington University in St. Louis, St. Louis, MO 63130, USA. [email: dmbillin@artsci.wustl.edu]

Emilia Birlo (artwork) is a visual artist and fashion designer who divides her time between Berlin and Los Angeles. Her art designs can be viewed at www.birlos.de.

Kara Blackmore is a curator, archaeologist and photographer who is particularly interested in how local communities relate to or use heritage. This has been the body of her recent work in Zanzibar's Stone Town, where she has attempted to understand divisions among souvenir artists, vendors and shop owners.

Rosabelle Boswell is an Associate Professor of Anthropology at Rhodes University in South Africa. She is author of *Le Malaise Creole: Ethnic Identity in Mauritius and Challenges to Identifying and Managing Intangible Cultural Heritage in Mauritius, Zanzibar and Seychelles*. She has done fieldwork in Mauritius, South Africa, Seychelles, Madagascar and Zanzibar and is particularly interested in the dynamics of culture, heritage and identity in these countries.

Ananda Breed, PhD, is Senior Lecturer at the University of East London and has conducted research in Rwanda, Congo, and Burundi into justice and reconciliation. In addition to theatre in relation to conflict, Ananda has co-directed a participatory theatre project based on domestic violence in Rwanda which was funded by the Ministry of Justice and toured within the country. She has trained theatre practitioners in participatory theatre methodology in a number of different settings in Africa and Asia and has worked with a number of UN-sponsored theatre and peace-building initiatives.

Paul Chambers, PhD, is Senior Research Fellow at the Institute of Political Science, Heidelberg University and at Payap University, Thailand. His research interests focus on comparative politics and international relations in Southeast Asia. His articles have appeared in *Asian Journal of Political Science* and *Party Politics*, among others.

Aurel Croissant, PhD, is Professor and Head of the Institute of Political Science at the Ruprecht-Karls-University, Heidelberg. His main research focus is on the comparative politics of East and Southeast Asia, democratic theory, democratization studies, culture and conflict, and political violence and extremism.

Milena Dragićević Šešić, PhD, is a former President of the University of Arts, Belgrade and now holds the UNESCO Chair in Interculturalism, Art Management and Mediation and is professor of Cultural Policy and Cultural Management. She is the President of the Jury of the European Cultural Foundation's Cultural Policy Research Award. She has published 15 books and more than 100 essays, including *Art Management in Turbulent Times: Adaptable Quality Management*, *Culture: Management, Animation, Marketing and Intercultural Mediation in the Balkans*.

Michael Francis is Assistant Professor of Anthropology at Athabasca University. His undergraduate degree in Anthropology was from the University of Alberta (2001). He then moved to South Africa where he earned his MA (2003) and PhD (2007) from the University of KwaZulu-Natal in Durban, where he was also a post-doctoral research fellow in 2008–09. He currently works on issues of San identity and Indigenous rights in the Kalahari and is turning his attention to the nature and understanding of landscapes, aesthetics and livelihoods in the Canadian north.

Akiko Hashimoto is Associate Professor of Sociology and Asian Studies at the University of Pittsburgh. Earlier, she was Research Associate at the United Nations University in Tokyo. She was educated at the University of Hamburg, the London School of Economics, and Yale University. Her publications include *Imagined Families, Lived Families: Culture and Kinship in Contemporary Japan* (SUNY Press, 2008, with J. Traphagan), *The Gift of Generations: Japanese and American Perspectives on Aging and the Social Contract* (Cambridge University Press, 1996), and *Family Support for the Elderly: The International Experience* (Oxford University Press, 1992). She is currently working on a book-length study of cultural identity and national memory in post-World War II Japan.

Michael Hoelscher is a lecturer at the Department of Sociology, Heidelberg University, Germany, and Senior Research Fellow at the University of Oxford. His main fields of interest are cultural sociology, economic sociology, globalization processes, especially European integration, higher education and quantitative comparative methods. His publications include 'Wirtschaftskulturen in der erweiterten EU' (2006).

Yudhisthir Raj Isar is Professor of Cultural Policy Studies at The American University of Paris and *Maitre de Conférences* at the *Institut d'Etudes Politiques de Paris (Sciences Po)*. An independent cultural adviser and public speaker, he also serves on the boards of several international cultural institutions and writes on a range of cultural topics. From 2004 to 2008 he was President of the International Association Culture Action Europe. Previously, at UNESCO, he was Executive Secretary of the World Commission on Culture and Development, and in 1986–87 he was Executive Director of The Aga Khan Program for Islamic Architecture at Harvard University and the Massachusetts Institute of Technology.

Lucina Jiménez Lopéz has a PhD in anthropology from the Metropolitan Autonomous University at Iztapalapa (UAM-I), Mexico. She is a specialist in cultural policy, cultural management and arts education, themes on which she has lectured and published widely. She has also been a consultant on these topics in the Americas and Spain. In 2001–05 she was Director-General of the National Center for the Arts, where she coordinated the creation of five new arts centres across the country. She is currently Director-General of the International Consortium for Art and School (CONARTE), an association that promotes education through the arts in public schools.

Susan Keitumetse has a background in Archaeology and Environmental Sciences from the University of Botswana. Her PhD focused on sustainable development and cultural heritage management. She is currently employed as a research fellow in Cultural Heritage Tourism at the University of Botswana's Harry Oppenheimer Okavango Research Centre, where she conducts research within the Okavango Delta region as well as the Kalahari desert region. She also sits on the Board of Directors of Botswana Tourism Board.

Dragan Klaic is a theatre scholar and cultural analyst. He serves as a Permanent Fellow of Felix Meritis Foundation in Amsterdam and is a professor of the arts and cultural policy at the University of Leiden's Faculty of Creative and Performing Arts. He lectures widely at various universities, speaks at conferences and symposia and serves as adviser, editor, researcher and trainer. His fields of engagement are contemporary performing arts, European cultural policies, strategies of cultural development and international cultural cooperation, interculturalism and cultural memory.

David Lowenthal, Emeritus Professor of Geography and honorary research fellow at University College London, formerly secretary of the American Geographical Society, has taught at a score of universities in America, Europe, Australia, and the Caribbean, and has been a Fulbright, a Guggenheim, a Leverhulme, and a Landes Fellow. Among his books are *West Indian Societies*, *Geographies of the Mind*, *The Past is a Foreign Country*, *Landscape Meanings and Values*, *The Politics of the Past*, *The Heritage Crusade and the Spoils of History*, *George Perkins Marsh, Prophet of Conservation*, and *Paysage du temps sur le paysage*. He is currently working on small-island survival strategies, on the links between cultural and physical heritage conservation, and on the troubled relations between the sciences and the humanities.

Marta de Magalhães is a post-doctoral fellow at the Centre of Latin American Studies, University of Cambridge. She completed her PhD in social anthropology at Cambridge, with a dissertation on urban transformation, cosmopolitanism and violence in contemporary Bahia (Brazil). Her research interests include legal anthropology, ethnography of the state, memory, cities and space and critical theory.

Laura McAtackney is a post-doctoral fellow at the John Hume Global Institute, University College Dublin, where she is researching issues of identity and memory through iconic landscapes in Ireland. She has a background in historical archaeology and heritage studies and her PhD explored the complexities of understanding contemporary political imprisonment at the Long Kesh/Maze Prison, Northern Ireland. She is on the standing committee for CHAT (Contemporary and Historical Archaeology in Theory), recently co-organized the most recent CHAT conference in Oxford and is co-editing the proceedings.

Henrietta L. Moore holds the William Wyse Chair of Social Anthropology at the University of Cambridge and is Director of the Culture and Communications programme at the LSE's Centre for the Study of Global Governance. She is a leading theorist of gender in Social Anthropology and has developed a distinctive approach to the analysis of the interrelations of material and symbolic gender systems, embodiment and performance and identity and sexuality. Her long-term research programme with Africa has focused on gender, livelihood strategies, social transformation and symbolic systems. She is a Fellow of the British Academy, a Fellow of the Royal Society of Arts and Academician of the Learned Societies for the Social Sciences.

A native of Mississippi, **Benjamin Morris** recently completed his PhD in the Department of Archaeology at the University of Cambridge, where his research examined the rebuilding of New Orleans after Hurricane Katrina. He is the co-convener, with Bradon Smith, of the Cultures of Climate Change research group, originally founded at the Centre for Research in the Arts, Social Sciences, and Humanities at Cambridge, and a member of the Creative Climate Initiative at the Open University. Writer, curator and editor (at Forest Publications in Edinburgh, Scotland), his creative work has been published widely and has won recognition in both the USA and the UK.

Chandra E.F. Morrison is a PhD candidate at the Centre of Latin American Studies, University of Cambridge, where she also received her MPhil (2007) specializing in visual arts and anthropology of Latin America. Her doctoral thesis explores street art, urban space, and social agency in São Paulo, Brazil, and Santiago, Chile. She served as 2008–09 President of PILAS, the postgraduate affiliate of the Society of Latin American Studies (SLAS) for the UK.

Yael Navaro-Yashin is Senior Lecturer in Social Anthropology at the University of Cambridge and a Fellow of Newnham College and is the author of *Faces of the State: Secularism and Public Life in Turkey*. She has also worked on displacement, materiality and affect in post-war Cyprus, out of which a book is forthcoming. Her chapter in this volume is based on recent fieldwork she conducted in Istanbul with a research grant from the Arts and Humanities Research Council (AHRC) of the UK.

Pierre Nora is a historian who divides his professional life between academia and publishing. He has been a member of the *Académie Française* since 2001. He was the initiator of the internationally celebrated memory studies project *Les Lieux de mémoire* (published in English as *Realms of Memory*). He is *directeur littéraire* at Éditions Gallimard where, three decades ago, he founded the journal *Le Débat*. He is also president of the association *Liberté pour l'Histoire*, which in particular seeks to combat the proliferation of legislation in France that encourages selective readings of the past, and thereby impedes historical research.

Carmen Ortiz is senior researcher at the Spanish National Research Council (CSIC). She is currently working in the CSIC Research Group 'The Anthropology of Heritage and Popular Cultures'. Her fields are history of anthropological ideas and practices in the modern period, especially in Spain and Spanish America, and popular culture and manners of expression in urban contexts, use of public space and the social construction of the cultural heritage. (carmen.ortiz@cchs.csic.es)

Carolina Porto de Andrade received her BA in Psychology with honours from The American University of Paris and is currently pursuing her Masters in Clinical Psychology at the University of Paris V.

Kevin Robins is a Visiting Fellow at Goldsmiths, University of London, working within the Goldsmiths Leverhulme Media Research Centre. In this programme he has been concerned with questions of European media and cultural policy. In recent years, he has worked extensively on issues of media and migration, with particular respect to transnational Turkish migrants. In the context of the Council of Europe's programme on Cultural Policy and Cultural Diversity, he was the author of a report on *The Challenge of Transcultural Diversities*. At present, he is working on Roma culture, with particular reference to wider questions of European identity.

Cristina Sánchez-Carretero is a staff researcher at the Heritage Laboratory (LaPa), Spanish National Research Council (CSIC) in Santiago de Compostela, Spain. She was awarded a PhD in ethnology by the University of Pennsylvania (2002). Her areas of interest are: processes of traditionalization and heritage formation and the role of rituals and expressive culture in contemporary societies. She co-edited, with Jack Santino, *Holidays, Ritual, Festival, Celebration, and Public Display* (2003), and with Peter Jan Margry, *Grassroots Memorials: The Politics of Memorializing Traumatic Death* (2011). (cristinas.sanchez-carretero@iegps.csic.es)

Brian Schiff received his PhD from the Committee on Human Development at The University of Chicago. He was a Lady Davis Postdoctoral Fellow at the Hebrew University of Jerusalem and a Mellon Fellow at Wellesley College. He is currently Associate Professor and Chair of the Department of Psychology at The American University of Paris. Schiff's research uses life-story interviews in order to study the social and cultural dynamics of identity formation. He is also interested in culture and human development, the individual's connection to collective memory and the contribution of narrative theory to psychological science.

Gobopaone Senata is a graduate student at the Harry Oppenheimer Okavango Research Centre, University of Botswana where he undertook his thesis research on totems and taboos relating to one of Botswana's protected areas, Moremi Game Reserve, under the supervision of Dr Susan Keitumetse, who leads the broader research on the subject. He is currently registered as a student at the History Department, University of Botswana.

Liz Ševčenko is founding Director of the International Coalition of Sites of Conscience, a network of historic sites that foster public dialogue on pressing contemporary issues. Before launching the Coalition, she developed public history projects for museums and communities. As Vice-President at the Lower East Side Tenement Museum, she developed exhibits and activities that used the neighbourhood's stories of immigration past and present to inspire dialogue on cultural identity, labour relations, housing, welfare, and other issues. She has a BA from Yale University and is completing her PhD in History at New York University.

Esther Shalev-Gerz was born in Lithuania, was raised in Israel and has lived in Paris since 1984. Her art practice explores the nature of democracy, citizenship, cultural memory and spatial politics. Her installations, photography, video and public sculpture are developed through active dialogue, consultation and negotiation with people whose participation provides an emphasis to their individual and collective memories, accounts, opinions and experiences, which then become both represented and considered.

Marie Louise Stig Sørensen is a University Senior Lecturer in Archaeology at the University of Cambridge where she created and now coordinates the postgraduate degree in 'Archaeological Heritage and Museums'. She is a partner on several research projects, including the EU-funded initiative she describes in this volume. Within Heritage Studies her principal interest has been the link between heritage and identity with specific attention to gender and nationalism. She has recently investigated the impact of slavery in the Cape Verde Islands. She co-edited, with John Carman, the 2009 volume entitled *Heritage Studies: Methods and Approaches.*

Lina Gebrail Tahan completed a PhD in archaeology from the University of Cambridge. She is currently a Senior Research Fellow at the Centre for Tourism and Cultural Change at Leeds Metropolitan University and an affiliated scholar at the department of Archaeology, University of Cambridge. Her research and teaching interests relate to representation issues within Middle Eastern museums and the role of museums in fostering understanding in divided societies. She is an active member of the International Council of Museums (ICOM), mainly working for promoting museums in the Arab World.

Julie Thomas (MA Harvard, MLitt. Trinity College, Dublin, PhD University of London) is Associate Professor of Global Communications at The American University of Paris, where she teaches courses on Fashion, Material Culture, the Museum as Medium, and Colour. She writes on colour in cultural space, digital interactivity (guest editor with Claudia Roda of the special issue on 'Attention Aware Systems' of *Computers in Human Behaviour*), the museum and cultural identity, and in 2004 organized the international conference *Mediating Fashion, Mediating Paris* at The American University of Paris.

Mathilde Toulemonde received her BA in Psychology with honours from The American University of Paris and is currently pursuing her Masters in Clinical Psychology at the University of Paris V.

Dr Dacia Viejo-Rose is a Research Associate at Jesus College, Cambridge and a post-doctoral researcher on the project 'Cultural Heritage and the Reconstruction of Identities after Conflict' (CRIC) based at the McDonald Institute for Archaeological Research. Her PhD (2009) from the University of Cambridge focused on the reconstruction of cultural heritage after civil war and its long-term impacts on societies. Her interest in this field began in 1997 when she interned at the United Nations Department for Humanitarian Affairs. In 2006 she founded the Cambridge Post-Conflict and Post-Crisis Group and has been running it ever since. She was coordinator of the European Cultural Foundation's UK National Committee (2003–05) and worked at UNESCO's Division of Cultural Policies (2000–02) where she managed the Cities for Peace Prize.

Zala Volcic is a post-doctoral fellow at the Centre for Critical and Cultural Studies, and a Senior Lecturer at the School of Journalism at the University of Queensland, Australia. In her research she focuses on international communication, media and cultural identities. She has recently published articles in *Discourse and Society*, *Critical Studies in Media Communication*, *Information Communication & Society*, and *Canadian Journal of Communication*.

Jean-Pierre Warnier (PhD in Anthropology, University of Pennsylvania) has taught anthropology in Nigeria, Cameroon and, since 1985, at the University Paris-Descartes. He is now Professor Emeritus and associated researcher at the Centre d'études africaines, Paris. His latest books include *La mondialisation de la culture* (Paris, La Découverte, 2007), *The Pot-King: The Body and Technologies of power* (Leiden & Boston, Brill, 2007) and *Régner au Cameroun: Le Roi-pot* (Paris, CERI-Karthala, Coll. 'Recherches internationales', 2009).

Ryan Weafer is a Graphic Designer and Art Director whose independent practice focuses on cultural and non-profit clients as well as self-initiated works. He is a current Yale MFA candidate in Graphic Design and has a BA in Design Media Arts from UCLA where he studied under W. Henri Lucas.

Jagath Weerasinghe is an artist and is also a professor at the Postgraduate Institute of Archaeology, University of Kelaniya, Sri Lanka. He obtained a BFA (Hons) from the Institute of Aesthetic Studies, University of Kelaniya in 1981 and then an MFA from The American University, Washington, DC in 1990. He has been a Visiting Fellow at the Institute of Archaeology, University of London and a fellow at ICCROM. He is also a recipient of the Hirayama Silk Road Fellowship.

James V. Wertsch is the Marshall S. Snow Professor in Arts and Sciences at Washington University in St. Louis, USA, where he is also Director of the McDonnell International Scholars Academy. His research interests include collective memory and national narratives in the USA, Russia, Georgia, Estonia and elsewhere. Recent publications include *Enough! The Rose Revolution in the Republic of Georgia in 2003* (edited with Z. Karumidze, Nova Science Publishers, 2005), *Memory in Mind and Culture* (edited with P. Boyer, Cambridge University Press, 2009), and 'Creating a New Discipline of Memory Studies' (with H.L. Roediger III, *Memory Studies* 1(1), 2008). He is a Fellow in the American Academy of Arts and Sciences, an honorary member of the Russian Academy of Pedagogical Sciences, and holds visiting professorships at the University of Oslo, Fudan University and Tsinghua University. Address: Department of Anthropology, Washington University in St. Louis, St. Louis, MO 63130, USA. (jwertsch@wustl.edu)

Tim Winter is Senior Research Fellow at the Centre for Cultural Research, University of Western Sydney. He is author of *Post-conflict Heritage, Postcolonial Tourism, Culture, Politics and Development at Angkor*, and editor of *Expressions of Cambodia: The Politics of Tradition, Identity and Change* and *Asia on Tour: Exploring the Rise of Asian Tourism*, and the forthcoming *Heritage in Asia: Converging Forces, Conflicting Values*. A consultant for the World Bank, Getty Conservation Institute and World Monuments Fund, he is also editor of the ICOMOS journal *Historic Environment*.

Gabriele Woidelko joined the Körber Foundation after graduating from Hamburg University in History, Slavonic and Turkish Studies in 1996. In 2000 she became responsible for the EUSTORY project and led the team that developed it into an international non-profit association (AISBL) registered in Brussels under Belgian law. She now directs the EUSTORY International Office in Hamburg.

LIST OF BOXES, FIGURES, TABLES AND PHOTOS

Boxes

I.1   Cultures and globalization – the knowledge gap, Helmut Anheier and Yudhishthir Raj Isar   1
I.2   EUSTORY – the History Network for Young Europeans, Gabriele Woidelko   6
1.1   Forgetting: an overview, Benjamin Morris   27

2.1   The intergovernmental elaboration of global norms, Yudhishthir Raj Isar   40
2.2   Return or restitution of cultural property, Yudhishthir Raj Isar   41

3.1   Armistice Day in France, Dacia Viejo-Rose   63
3.2   Cultural Heritage and the Re-construction of Identities after Conflict, Marie Louise Stig Sørensen   65
3.3   Memory and its absence in two Lebanese museums, Lina G. Tahan   66

4.1   Saturated by souvenirs: art and identity in Zanzibar's Stone Town, Kara A. Blackmore   71
4.2   The margin of a centre: heritage, space and memory in Salvador, Marta de Magalhães   77

5.1   Transnational initiatives, Ien Ang   84

8.1   Gulag Museum at Perm-36, Russia, Liz Ševčenko   117
8.2   Corporación Parque por la Paz Villa Grimaldi, Chile, Liz Ševčenko   118
8.3   Constitution Hill, South Africa, Liz Ševčenko   122

12.1   The secret San, Michael Francis   163

15.1   Dah Theatre of Belgrade, Milena Dragićević Šešić   193

16.1   Monumento al Che: participatory memorial and collective heritage, Chandra E.F. Morrison   202

Figures

2.1   Number of World Heritage properties (both cultural and natural) inscribed each year by region   45
2.2   Number of World Heritage properties (cultural and mixed) by region   46

12.1   Totems practised by Sankuyo people of Northwest Botswana   162
12.2   Perceived past roles of taboos and totems in Sankuyo settlement area   163

Tables

3.1   Truth and Reconciliation Commissions (TRCs)   62

12.1a   Gender of respondents   161
12.1b   Education level of respondents   161
12.1c   Age of respondents   161
12.2   Taboos practised in Sankuyo area   162

Photos

23.1 *White Out – Between Telling and Listening*, Installation view, Historiska Museet, Stockholm, Sweden 2002, Christer Ahlin — 264

23.2 *The Place of Art*, Video installation view, Gothenburg Konsthall, Sweden, 2007, Dorota Lukianska — 265

23.3 *The Place of Art*, Video installation view, Gothenburg Konsthall, Sweden, 2007, Courtesy Esther Shalev-Gerz — 265

23.4 *The Place of Art*, Video installation view, Gothenburg Konsthall, Sweden, 2007, Courtesy Esther Shalev-Gerz — 267

23.5 *D'eux* (On two), Video projection detail, Jeu de Paume, Paris, France, 2010, Courtesy Esther Shalev-Gerz — 268

23.6 *D'eux* (On two), Video projection detail, Jeu de Paume, Paris, France, 2010, Courtesy Esther Shalev-Gerz — 268

INTRODUCTION
Yudhishthir Raj Isar, Dacia Viejo-Rose and Helmut K. Anheier

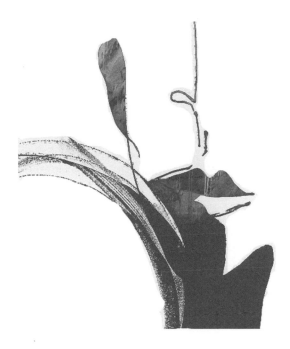

The concepts of identity and heritage long antedate the conjoined usage of these terms today. In the past, identity referred not to self-consciousness but to likeness, and heritage was mainly a matter of family legacies. In the present, these terms swim in a self-congratulatory swamp of collective memory. Heritage is now that with which we all individually or collectively identify. It is considered the rightful (though sometimes unwelcome) legacy of every distinct people.
(Lowenthal 1994: 41)

Rationale

The relationships between cultures, cultural change and globalization remain inadequately understood. Often reduced to the seemingly one-way impact of globalization processes on the world's cultures, these relationships, and the changes they involve, are in reality reciprocal and far more complex and multifaceted: cultures do shape globalization processes and patterns, and vice versa; what is more, the relationships in turn involve many further interactions with social, economic and political forces. Addressing the richness of these relationships is the main purpose of *The Cultures and Globalization Series* (see Box 1.1 for further details).

Various readings of the multiplexity of 'culture' have informed all the preceding volumes in the *Series* and each one has privileged a particular interpretation. Our common denominator and point of departure was an understanding broad enough to reconcile several such readings, in any case embracing both the 'arts and heritage' sense of the term and a more capacious social science interpretation of culture as the social construction, articulation and reception of meaning.[1] As for the notion of globalization, we should underline that we mean contemporary *accelerated* globalization, for the process as such has a long history, that long predates our epoch. For this we borrowed from Held et al. (1999) a straightforward definition, namely the intense and instantaneous time–space compression created by the movement of objects (goods, services, finance and other resources, etc.), meanings (language, symbols, knowledge, identities, etc.) and people across regions and intercontinental space.

Box I.1   Cultures and globalization – the knowledge gap

While a substantial evidence base has been developed on the economic, political and social aspects of globalization, the cultural dimension continues to be the object of many unsubstantiated generalizations and *unquestioned* assumptions. This is the key knowledge gap the *Series* is designed to fill. The complex, two-way relationships between cultural change and globalization have remained largely uncharted empirically and under-analyzed conceptually.

One reason for this dual neglect at the global level is that conventional understandings of culture are still connected principally to the sovereign nation-state. However, today, this nexus of culture and nation no longer dominates: the cultural dimension has become constitutive of collective identity at narrower as well as broader levels. What is more, cultural processes take place in increasingly 'deter-ritorialized' and transnational contexts, many of which are beyond the reach of national policies. Mapping and analyzing this shifting terrain, in all regions of the world, as well as the factors, patterns, processes, and outcomes associated with the 'complex connectivity' (Tomlinson 1999) of globaliza-tion, is therefore a main purpose of this *Series.*

In so doing, the *Series* aims to meet three further goals: to highlight key contemporary cultural changes and their policy implications; to channel and encourage cutting-edge research; and to con-tribute to the development of information systems in the field of culture. In this way, it will seek to build bridges between the social sciences, the arts and the humanities, and policy studies. Indeed, our approach is based on our awareness that the social sciences and the humanities have become too compartmentalized – a state of affairs that we seek to overcome by the kind of inter and cross-disciplinary thinking required for a project of the kind proposed here that seeks to explore the nexus of cultures and globalization. We therefore encourage 'out of the box' thinking and approaches that cut across established disciplines and methods.

Each volume is more than a compilation of separate conceptual chapters. An analytical framework and a set of over-arching questions spell out organizing principles and substantive priorities to authors in advance. Each volume is also more than a compendium of country or 'area' studies. While such aspects are important, they take second place in this project to a pronounced transnational, comparative and evidence-based perspective that is our key signature.

The knowledge gap in the field of cultures and globalization stems from the paucity of com-parative information. It is for this reason that, alongside the 'narrative' chapters, all of which rely upon freshly-observed empirical phenomena, each volume includes a significant data section. Departing from conventional approaches, we have developed a new way compiling, analyzing and presenting quantitative data on specific aspects of the cultures and globalization relation-ship. These 'indicator suites' make up Part II of the volume and are based on the premise that much information on many facets of the cultures and globalization nexus is already 'out there', but is not being processed in appropriate ways. Another point of departure is that for most read-ers interpretative information graphics are far easier to understand than 'raw' data in tabular form.

Initiated in 2007, the indicator approach has been refined with each successive volume. More details will be provided in Part II, which, among other topics, presents indicator suites on topics such as contested memories; museums, memory and heritage; territorial identities; internet identities; work-related identities; World Heritage Sites and Intangible Heritage.

Heritage, memory, identity: what do we mean?

This fourth volume in the *Series* is devoted to a triad of contemporary keywords, namely 'Heritage', Memory' and 'Identity'. These notions are articulated principally around the notion of culture as 'ways of life'.[2] As different human groups define certain objects and practices as 'heritage'; as they envision heritage to reflect some form of collective memory, either lived or imagined; and as they combine both to construct composite cul-tural identities, the potency of the triad becomes evident. Today, the three terms raise conjoined issues of practice, policy and politics. Together they have come to constitute 'global scripts', to borrow a term deployed by Lily Kong in volume 3 (Kong 2010).

Heritage, memory and identity have each been abundantly discussed from the perspective of different disciplines. The vast majority of these treatments have concerned the local, the sub-national and the national levels. Our purpose here is not to rehearse or augment these existing debates (the bibliography alone would be interminable!), but to shed light on the ways in which the tropes of heritage, memory and identity intertwine at *the transnational and global levels.* This interface is at the core our project. Some of the issues germane to it were taken up in previous volumes of the *Series*, but neither centrally nor explicitly.[3] So in conceiving this volume, we asked contributors to focus on the following sorts of questions:

- Is contemporary accelerated globalization challenging the ways in which heritage, memory and identity hitherto functioned in and for nation-states in a Westphalian world?
- Is globalization driving and shaping the triad in new directions?
- How are the terms of the triad interacting in response to increased mobilities, flows and space–time compression?
- Specifically, how are heritage, memory and identity affecting, and how are they, in turn, impacted by, the dynamics of globalization?

These broad questions were, in turn, broken down in more specific interrogations. However, before taking these up, it would be useful to present the general conceptual framework in which we placed the notions of heritage, memory and identity.

Among the three terms, the one that is recognized across the world as a domain of public *cultural policy* (in the sense of the remit assigned to ministries or departments of culture) is *heritage*, or, more precisely, *heritage preservation*. This consists of the valorization and preservation by individuals and groups of traces of the past that are thought to embody their cultural identities.[4] At the societal level, heritage preservation has become a quasi-habitus; as Stuart Hall reminds us, 'we should think of The Heritage as a discursive practice' (Hall 2005: 25). The field has grown much in recent years, testifying to the cultural self-consciousness of our time, as a result of which the concept of 'culture' itself has become ever more protean, its forms,

usages and repertoires increasingly complex and diverse. Some of the expansion was metaphorical (Samuel 1994), but in real terms the idea of heritage has also been doubly expansive: extending both to the entirety of what anthropologists call 'material culture' – structures, sites, artefacts – and to immaterial cultural manifestations now celebrated as 'intangible heritage' (see also Smith 2006).

The values and practices of heritage preservation – and revitalization – are prominent in contemporary cultural life, demanding major economic and political trade-offs in determining what sites and properties are to be preserved, restored, rebuilt, documented or not. The narrative that binds these societal decisions together also shapes the social meanings and symbols that are central to the construction of collective memories and identities. The latter, in turn, shape collective perceptions of 'selves' and 'others' and, therefore, also influence the ways in which societies perceive and interact with one another. Paradoxically, when rhetorically invoking these notions of heritage, as they do today with increasing vigour and remarkable unanimity, nation-states lay claim to 'patrimony' that was very often created long before they themselves came into being and/or by members of societies that no longer exist. What is more, this patrimony is valorized because it is taken to be universal, 'the shared heritage of humanity'. But instead of becoming a true global public good, it becomes the 'cultural property' of a national (or sub-national) unit (Appiah 2006). Archaeological sites, monuments, etc., all become instruments for territorial self-fashioning, providing a symbolic terrain on which imaginaries compete and battles for the future are fought, e.g., the 'facts on the ground' revealed by the study of archaeological practice in Israel (Abu El-Haj 2001).

In this context, the fraught issue of conceptualizing 'culture' as the fixed property of particular groups also arises (cf. Moore's concluding commentary in this volume). For example, anthropologists working in Eastern Europe have observed the ambivalent branding role played by representations of 'heritage' in tourism agendas (Urry 1990). In the Balkans, a region with highly diverse cultures and histories, and where the past has recently been drawn upon to justify present violence and war, heritage tourism employs the (ancient) past as a restructuring element for the future. The emphasis on heritage seeks both to selectively rewrite histories and to reshape an image for tourists, as when the former Yugoslav Republic of Macedonia focuses on its 'Alexander the Great' period in order to be perceived as a locus of key historical events… Indeed the very fact that Greece refuses to allow that country to call itself Macedonia *tout court* is a wry illustration of the manner in which Alexander's Macedonia has become a memorial stake in national identity-building today…

The contemporary cult of heritage has produced the 'inflation' of which Françoise Choay has written (1992, 2009) and that David Lowenthal has described as follows:

> *Like identity, heritage is today a realm of well-nigh universal concern. It betokens interest in manifold pasts – family history, buildings and landmarks, prehistory and antiques, music and paintings, plants and animals, language and folklore – ranging from remote to recent times. So widespread and fast-growing is such interest that heritage defies definition. Indeed, the term celebrates every conceivable thing and theme: anchorites and anoraks, Berlin and Bengal, conkers and castles, dog breeds and dental fillings, finials and fax machines, gorgonzola and goalposts are topics typical of a thousand recent books entitled* Heritage of _____. *Pervading life and thought as never before, heritage suffuses attitudes toward everything.* (Lowenthal 1998: 42)

These attitudes have generated various practices of identification, classification, preservation, exhibition and *mise en valeur*. Once taken at their face value, these practices are now recognized as constituting a new mode of cultural production in the present that simply has recourse (principally but not exclusively) to the resources of the past. As Barbara Kirshenblatt-Gimblett (1998) has argued, the discourses and practices of preservation, restoration, reclamation recovery, re-creation, recuperation, revitalization and regeneration need to be seen against the reality that there is really 'no there, there' prior to what somebody has to do to identify, evaluate, conserve and celebrate. This applies most aptly perhaps to the notion of 'intangible heritage', as defined by the Convention for the Safeguarding of the Intangible Cultural Heritage, adopted in 2003 by UNESCO: 'the practices, representations, expressions, knowledge, skills … as well as the instruments, objects, artefacts and cultural spaces associated therewith – that communities, groups and, in some cases, individuals,

recognize as part of their cultural heritage.' Unlike the preservation of the tangible heritage, which is conserved in its extant materiality, the preservation of the intangible heritage consists of recording and documentation, in other words, a sort of materialization of the immaterial. The 2003 Convention requires each State Party to 'identify and define the various elements of the intangible cultural heritage present in its territory' and to 'draw up, in a manner geared to its own situation, one or more inventories of the intangible cultural heritage present in its territory'. Identifying, inventorying: what kind of 'safeguarding' is taking place here? In the oral history perspective, for example, safeguarding would mean maintaining such traditional forms alive by adding items to the repertoire today, not just ensuring the survival of existing histories. In the case of traditional music, it would be to ensure the continuation of these forms and their use – and the list could be extended considerably.

But real practice does not and indeed cannot keep all these forms 'alive'. What is being engaged upon, rather, is a 'metacultural' process (Kirshenblatt-Gimblett 2004), one that does not, indeed cannot, actually ensure that the knowledge embodied in those who possess and 'are' the intangible heritage may actively enact or perform itself. The library metaphor frequently cited in this context actually gives the game away: the reasoning behind the famous statement attributed to Amadou Hampâté Ba – 'Africa loses a library when an old man dies' – actually confuses an archive for an active repertoire. Yet the intangible heritage is essentially repertoire embodied, manifested and transmitted in performance; it is not documentation in an archive. Any repertoire is based on embodied knowledge and requires active social relations for its creation, enactment, transmission and reproduction. When compared with the objects typically displayed in the museum showcase, intangible cultural forms can be less easily detached from the persons who embody them (Isar 2005a).

Yet this kind of 'museal sensibility' in Andreas Huyssen's words, 'seems to be occupying ever larger chunks of everyday culture and experience', including 'the electronic totalization of the world on data banks', making the museum far more than a mere cultural institution but 'a key paradigm of contemporary cultural activities' (Huyssen 1995: 14). As collective pasts are increasingly mobilized in a museum complex, as it were, heritage has necessarily become an arena for conscious choice, justification and representation. This has led to a form of fetishization, as dramatizations and ritual enactments of cultural traditions are celebrated in the form of dress, music, dance, handicrafts. The process, however, is not new. What is happening across the global South today already occurred in Europe and North America decades ago, as industrialization gradually eliminated entire peasant cultures. Today, such 'museumization' is part and parcel of heritage politics. Thus dominant national populations often impose their idea of heritage on minority groups, whose cultures are then in turn preserved like specimens in jars. In this process, the 'cultures' ostensibly valorized in their fetishized forms may be the site of a double violence. In Ecuador, for example, in festivals where indigenous culture is celebrated, Spanish-speaking *mestizos* don Indian costumes, perform pre-Columbian dances, and play 'Indian' music, while the very people whose 'cultures' are being performed are not allowed to participate (Isar 2005b). Phenomena such as these challenge the process of heritage valorization. What is the point of preserving in the museum, or as performance for the tourist, what has been wiped out in the community? As Richard Kurin warns (2004: 74–75), this is to miss the

> *intricate and complex web of meaningful social actions undertaken by individuals, groups and institutions. … Whether they survive or flourish depends upon so many things – the freedom and desire of culture bearers, an adequate environment, a sustaining economic system, a political context within which their very existence is at least tolerated. Actions to safeguard 'tangibilized' inventoried items of cultural production are unlikely to safeguard adequately the larger, deeper, more diffuse cultural patterns and contexts.*

Clearly also 'The Heritage' is neither inherently nor exclusively positive. It can be a receptacle of meanings whose content can be positive or negative, constructive or destructive. Indeed, it is often accompanied by a complex and often discordant array of identifications and potential conflicts, not least when heritage places and objects are involved in legitimating power structures. The invention or creation of any heritage potentially disinherits or excludes those who do not subscribe to, or are not

embraced within, the terms of meaning attending that heritage; this quality is exacerbated when it is implicated in the same zero-sum definitions of power and territoriality that attend the modernist notion of the nation-state and its allegories of exclusive membership. That landscapes of tourism consumption are simultaneously other people's sacred places is another cause of heritage contestation on a global scale – the processes of sacralization and sacralizing also involve the exercise of profane forces (Ashworth, Graham and Tunbridge 2007). Hence the increasing salience of concepts such as 'heritage that hurts', 'negative heritage', or 'dissonant heritage' (Ashworth, et al. 2000).

In the 2007 volume of this *Series*, Viejo-Rose argued that heritage both tangible and intangible 'has become central to contemporary perceptions of collective memory' and that 'an increasing number of cultural groups now articulate their struggles for rights and recognition around the ownership and representation of their cultural heritage. … And these representations – or negations of them – have often become conflictual, yoking history and culture to the purposes and acts of war' (Viejo-Rose 2007: 102). Spatial or temporal disruptions – war, conflict or crisis – have an impact on a collective's sense of continuity, and are remembered differently by different groups, who might uphold divergent accounts of the 'historical truth' or 'authentic memory' of the event. The idea of 'dissonant heritage' relates to the conflicts that arise from divergent interpretations of heritage or from opposing memories or visions of identity. These, in turn, bring up questions of authenticity, ownership and representation. Whose heritage is it? Whose voice is more authentic, or more legitimate in claiming the right to 'interpret' a site? Who has the right to publicly remember and be remembered?

For with the 'cult of heritage' comes the 'memory boom'. The notion of *collective memory*, our second term, not yet institutionalized as a public policy field,[5] but almost equally prevalent as heritage, was first theorized by the French sociologist Maurice Halbwachs in the 1930s and has been refracted since then in many different ways (Wertsch 2002; also Wertsch and Billingsley in this volume). For Halbwachs, collective memory is always selective; different human groups elaborate different collective memories, which in turn give rise to different modes of behaviour. He explored, for example, how pilgrims to the Holy Land over the centuries had evoked very different images of the life of Jesus Christ; how wealthy old families in France had a memory of the past that diverged sharply from that of the *nouveaux riches*; and how working-class constructions of past reality differed from those of their middle-class counterparts. A particularly influential recent addition to this tradition was made by the historian Pierre Nora and the colleagues, with whom he conceived the massive collaborative work entitled *Les lieux de mémoire* (1994). In relation to the memorializing function of cultural heritage (in its original meaning, derived from the Latin verb *monere*, a monument was something designed to remind, as an anamnesic device, a deliberate memorial), the collective memory of a nation or ethnic group can be represented in part by the memorials it chooses to erect. Forgetting is closely linked to anamnesis. As pointed out by the historian Ernest Renan as long ago as 1882, forgetting is not just a negation or absence of memory; it is a means of remembering otherwise (1990). Both what a collectivity chooses to memorialize, physically or otherwise, and what is chooses *not* to memorialize are significant. Such choices are integral to the way collectives deploy memory 'in the service of providing a usable past' (Wertsch 2002: 37) and can therefore be conceptualized as mnemonic communities that forge mnemonic traditions and often engage in mnemonic battles with one another (Zerubavel 2003).

In recent years, many different readings of memory have been articulated alongside the 'memory boom' that has emerged most strongly in Euro-American discursive space. The term has enjoyed considerable purchase in French academic thought for some decades and is in fact commonly used in that country by more people than just the intelligentsia.[6] In other European settings as well, the notion of memory seems to have been pressed into service as a form of collective Freudian 'work' on atrocious historical events such as massacres and genocides, notably the Holocaust (Todorov 2004). It has considerable currency in Germany, where memories of the Nazi era are prominent in public debates.[7] Post-Communist memory work abounds in Central and Eastern Europe, documented in archives of repression built up in certain countries.[8] Other regions have seen horrific events as well, but in India and Pakistan, for example, the massacres of the 1947 Partition and the mass-scale ethnic cleansings that took place are rarely evoked as issues of memory as such. Yet, as the notion of collective memory has been appropriated by diverse streams of socio-cultural research and commentary, it has perhaps become the most protean of the three terms, often used in rather muddled ways. Andreas Huyssen, a literary scholar, uses the term 'cultural memory as it is articulated in institutions, in public debates, in theory, in art, and in literature' (1995: 4). He observes that its broad use, 'the newest obsession with memory', also poses the 'paradox that novelty in our culture is ever more associated with memory and the past rather than with future expectations'.[9] He also notes that 'memory as a concept rather than merely material for the historian seems increasingly to draw literary critics, historians and social scientists together' (1995: 5–6). The textbox below is about the work of EUSTORY, a pan-European initiative on 'historical images and patterns of remembrance'.

Box I.2 EUSTORY – the History Network for Young Europeans

The early twenty-first century winds of change that swept across Europe confronted Europeans with major challenges. One of these is the issue of European identity and how this is shaped by our common, but conflicted, European past. How much history still matters in Europe has become visible in many recent debates, disputes and even conflicts at the highest political level. For example, the Polish–German confrontation about the commemoration of forced migration and expulsion, the heated debate about the North-Stream gas pipeline and the different perceptions of the year 1989 as a major European turning point, to mention just a few. 'Peace and freedom in Europe are still put to the test today by hatred and violence. If we Europeans want to establish a peaceful common future, we have to talk openly about our past' said Nobel Peace Prize Winner and former Finnish President

Martti Ahtisaari when asked about his reason for supporting EUSTORY, the History Network for Young Europeans (www.eustory.eu). This international association of non-governmental organizations from 22 European countries is based on the common aim of understanding differences and overcoming divisions in Europe by enabling young Europeans to look critically at their past in order to understand the present. Instead of using history as an ideological weapon against others, EUSTORY emphasizes a European perspective on history that recognizes the vast diversity of historical experience and promotes understanding instead of exclusion. All EUSTORY member organizations share the same basic tool: they promote self-regulated work among young Europeans (school students) with national historical research competitions. In these competitions, the young people learn to view history from the grassroots by doing research in their own villages, communities and families. This research makes them understand how history has affected their surroundings, how it has shaped the lives of people in their community and in their family. With this approach, EUSTORY aims at the democratization and social reintegration of history, which is very important especially (but not only) in societies where memories have long been manipulated and suppressed. The topics of the EUSTORY competitions are usually very broad, i.e. 'Migration in History', 'The History of my Family', 'Borders' or 'Labour'. These broad topics allow the participants to find their own relevant sub-topics in their surroundings. Despite the fact that some of the topics do not seem to be political at all, the results of the competitions reveal a variety of different aspects of political European history. Twentieth-century family history in Russia cannot be dealt with without tackling the legacy of Stalinism. And looking at Spanish young people in the 1950s means asking questions about the Franco era as well. Since the Körber Foundation initiated EUSTORY in 2001, more than 115,000 students from Wales to the Eastern border of Russia, between the North Sea and Sicily have participated in its competitions.

But there is more to EUSTORY than national historical research competitions. It also enables its laureates to work together with their peers from other countries on topics of the European past and present by organizing regular international youth seminars. These seminars create space for encounters and facilitate dialogue on issues that are difficult and disputed within European societies today. These seminars deal with topics such as exclusion, discrimination and persecution in Europe, e.g. in Berlin on the sixtieth anniversary of the 1938 'Kristallnacht' pogrom that took place Germany and Austria, on stereotypes and prejudices within and towards the Balkans (Belgrade) and the legacy of the Soviet past in the Baltic States (in Tallinn and Tartu/Estonia).

The seminars give participants the opportunity to see history from different angles and understand that different perspectives and interpretations have to be taken into account before drawing any conclusions about the past and its relevance for the present. The seminars are the first steps the young prize winners actually take at the pan-European level. As a second step, EUSTORY has developed international e-learning projects for alumni (i.e. prize winners who took part in at least one international seminar) on topics of European remembrance, memory and identity. Using the internet as a tool and lasting between four and six months each, these projects provide the opportunity both for the participants as well as for EUSTORY as an organization to work in more depth on challenging themes of European relevance. Usually, these projects are linked to anniversaries and commemorations of major European historical events in order to provide a bottom-up perspective to the official discourses of remembrance.

For example, in 2005, when Europe celebrated the sixtieth anniversary of the end of the Second World War, EUSTORY asked 40 young Europeans, most of them prize winners of national history competitions, to research the legacy of the conflict in Europe and develop ideas for the future of remembrance. What will be the future of memories about the Second World War once there are no more eyewitnesses left who can keep the memories alive? How is the story of the War told in the different European countries, in families, in history textbooks at school and, last but not least, in the media? The project proved to be a practical lesson in multiple perspectives. One element was a comparative analysis of history textbooks from different countries: Bulgaria, Germany, France, Great Britain, Latvia, Poland, Russia and Sweden. Each of these countries were affected by the Second World War in very different ways, and looking at these ways made the participants aware of how strongly images of history are formed by the narrative that is taught and learned at school. And it also made them understand how much the official narrative is still dominated by the national outlook. It was astonishing to see how united the participants were in their evaluation of the 'history culture' in their countries. They gave low marks to history teaching at school and were all in favour of an active form of dealing with history and strengthening of cross-border discussions about it. In summary, they all agreed that working on memory can only be successful if it does not end with the passive receipt of information, but allows each generation to enjoy the freedom of asking their own questions of history and of connecting the answers to their own reality.

In 2006 and 2007, when Europe officially celebrated the anniversaries of the Hungarian Uprising and the adoption of the Treaties of Rome, EUSTORY again used the opportunity to question the official politics of memory. Young Europeans from 12 different countries researched and debated the different ways in which protest, resistance and civil disobedience are remembered in Europe today. They compared definitions of these three terms in their respective national contexts, looked at the perceptions of the Hungarian Uprising of 1956 and presented events of protest, resistance and civil disobedience that are important for the remembrance in their countries. As a result, they questioned the official perception of the 1956 events as a precursor to European unification (as stated during the jubilee celebrations in spring 2007), but underlined instead how much this interpretation is a component of the European self-image in the twenty-first century. These two examples show that although Europe is struggling with global challenges, it is still vitally important for us Europeans to learn about our respective historical images and patterns of remembrance, to continually scrutinize them and to discuss them together. Above all, young people in particular must play an active role in this dialogue, never losing an opportunity to grapple critically with the Europe of yesterday and today. To do so would to demonstrate responsible European citizenship in the best sense of the word.

Gabriele Woidelko

Yet the very idea of collective memory is also contested – and not only by psychologists like Schiff, who in this volume observes that the concept is as metaphorically potent as it is empirically inaccurate. The influential German historian Reinhard Koselleck had long been highly critical of the concept, and the late Susan Sontag was even more dismissive:

all memory is individual, unreproducible – it dies with each person. What is called collective memory is not a remembering but a stipulating: that this is important, that this is the story about how it happened, with the pictures that lock the story in our minds. Ideologies create substantiating archives of images, representative images, which encapsulate common ideas of significance and trigger predictable thoughts, feelings. (Sontag, 2003: 85–86)

Yet Assmann herself, although she cites this severe judgment does not believe that the idea of collective memory is spurious, but that 'it is much too vague to serve as a critical term' (2008: 55). She stresses the need to disaggregate this abstract, umbrella notion, to distinguish – as indeed do the contributors to this volume – among the different formats in which memory processes operate 'such as family memory, interactive group memory, and social, political, national and cultural memory' (2008: 55). While the first three are grounded in lived experience and will vanish with their carriers (like 'intangible heritage'), political and cultural memory must be 'grounded on the more durable carriers of external symbols and representations'. Designed for long-term use, these vehicles include libraries, museums, archives, monuments – all repositories of the discursive formation termed 'The Heritage' – as well as educational and artistic institutions, ceremonies and commemorative dates and practices. But it is important to heed Assmann's call to 'the memory discourse to develop its own stance of critical vigilance and to develop criteria for probing the quality of memory constructions, distinguishing more 'malign' from more 'benign' memories – that is, memories that perpetuate resentment, hatred and violence from those that have a therapeutic or ethical value' (Assmann, 2008: 54).

In global mediascapes, processes of transmission of such cultural memory generate flows of, and productions of, memories in which particular narratives and images are reproduced and reframed, yet also questioned and contested through new images. Mediated memories are central in the creation of both individual and collective identities. Van Dijck has explored the shifts in new media technologies as they influence how we remember the past, and argues that 'media and memory, as cultural concepts, form the metaphors we live by: present technologies invariably and inherently shape our memories of past and present life' (2004: 272). Also, today, people are called upon to construct new memories better suited to increasingly 'post-national' cultural complexities. In many cases, the 'nation' is no longer the principal site or frame of memory. As compulsive consumers of the past, people now shop for what best suits their own sense of self at a given moment, and construct multiple identities out of a great variety of materials, times and places. The old *lieux de mémoire* seem to have lost much of their power to forge and sustain a single vision of the past, but they remain useful as sites where people with very different memories of the same events can communicate, appreciate and negotiate their respective differences. As Nora reminded us (1989: 13), after tracing the pre-national, national and post-national phases in the history of memory, 'modern memory is, above all, archival (cf. earlier remarks on the intangible heritage concept). It relies entirely on the materiality of the trace, the immediacy of the recording, the visibility of the image.' Or, as Huyssen suggests, for whom 'the media are the hidden veil through which I am looking at the problem of cultural memory', 'our mnemonic culture rejects the idea of the archive while depending on the archive's contents for its own sustenance' (1995: 6).

Whatever forms they take, collective memories are now yoked to the pervasive notion of *identity,* a

central keyword of our time. There is a vast and multi-faceted literature on the topic. Identity understood as a set of distinctive features inherited, assumed and asserted by different social formations – nations, ethnic groups, professions, age-sets or groups with shared sexual orientation – has been discussed in a great variety of ways. In previous volumes of this *Series,* we too have analyzed the contemporary avatars of identity in their relationships to the forces of globalization. We have foregrounded the play of identity politics, in both its beneficent and malevolent aspects, the latter being particularly toxic in the form of what Appadurai (2006: 51) has called 'predatory identities', whose 'social construction and mobilization require the extinction of other, proximate social categories', or when wars are waged in their name (Maalouf 2003), or when they are reduced to what Amartya Sen (2006) calls their single, 'solitarist' understandings. For this reason, instead of discussing the term in some depth, as we have done with the preceding two, suffice it to say here that the focus in this volume will be placed on the particular ways in which, driven by the forces globalization and their responses to them, social groups deploy the resources of heritage and memory to identify themselves and cope with the 'uncertainties' about 'us' and 'them' that, as Appadurai also argues (2006: 6), globalization so often exacerbates. Although the myriad social constructions of identity in and by today's nation-states are rarely recognized as major questions of public policy, references to the notion of identity are on all politicians' lips. France, for example, was for several years endowed with a Ministry of Immigration and National Identity (*Ministère de l'Immigration, de l'Intégration, de l'Identité nationale et du Développement solidaire*). The concatenation of terms tells its own eloquent story. It represents anxieties that are encountered in other countries as well, significant aspects of which will be explored by the contributors to this volume.

Globalization and the triad of terms

Today, having a heritage is indispensable to having an identity and cultural memory; losing a heritage is like losing a key bit of both. Heritage has come to be used as 'proof' of past, tradition, belonging, and therefore proof also of rights to place, representation and political voice. To what extent does globalization modify these interactions? As people become more mobile, and connect more frequently and widely, has there been a shift in trends towards valuing forms of heritage that are equally moveable and with higher connectivity? Could it be that the identities of both individual subjects and their collective cultural worlds may now be shifting and fragmented rather than unified and stable; composed, not of a single, but of several, sometimes contradictory or unresolved, strands? Do the migratory flows of our time, when churning up the relatively 'settled' character of many populations and cultures, also construct multiple identities across different, often intersecting and antagonistic, discourses, practices and positions? Is Hall correct to think that

> although they appear to invoke an origin in a historical past with which they continue to correspond, actually identities are about questions of using the resources of history, language and culture in the process of becoming rather than being: not 'who we are' or 'where we came from', so much as what we might become, how we have been represented and how that bears on how we might represent ourselves. Identities are therefore constituted within, not outside representation. They relate to the invention of tradition as much as to tradition itself, which they oblige us to read not as an endless reiteration but as 'the changing same': not the so-called return to roots but a coming-to-terms-with our 'routes'. (Hall 1996: 3–4)

Against this backdrop, the terms heritage-memory-identity form a conceptual troika, in which both the concepts and the practices lead parallel as well as contrapuntal lives. They have become performative in their very utterance, 'doing things' (Austin 1962) rhetorically and concretely in the public sphere. They form composite discursive practice, as heritage serves as one of the ways in which 'the nation slowly constructs for itself a sort of collective social memory' as well as an identity 'by selectively binding its chosen high points and memorable achievements into an unfolding "national story"' (Hall 2005: 25). They are ever-changing as well. They deploy processes of domination and suppression, inclusion and exclusion: as these unfold, people tend to reify both identity and memory, referring to both as if they were material objects – memory as something to be retrieved; identity as something that can be lost or found. But neither identities nor memories are *things*. Rather, they are *constructions* or *representations*, and as such, they are embedded in power and class relations that determine what is remembered (or forgotten), what is valued or deemed valueless – what is defined as heritage and what isn't – by whom and for what end. Just as history is written by the 'winners,' so too are the definitions and boundaries of heritage. Is globalization intensifying these multiple interpenetrations of heritage-memory-identity? These intersections are sometimes potentially explosive, as a result of both internal fissures and imaginings, but also under the impact of global pressures, e.g. *Hindutva*'s claims on 'authentic Indian Hindu heritage', the kinds of memories that it constructs and the schizophrenic identities it is forced to assume. Along with this scenario, as Rustom Bharucha observes, there are counter-identity formations, with different memory restructurings, as in secular activism, which is not without its own violence and sanitization of pain.[10] In taking up these sorts of issues in different settings, this volume would also echo earlier explorations in the 2007 volume of the *Series*, entitled *Conflicts and Tensions*.

There is a politics of heritage and a politics of memory just as there is a politics of identity. Heritage, memory and identity are central to 'invented tradition'.[11] They are not just constructs that individuals and groups think *about*; they are also constructs they think *with*. Every assertion of identity/heritage represents not only difference but also the elimination of difference. So too with any kind of commemorative activity that involves the deployment of individual and group memories together (Connerton 1989). Commemoration is often the product of intense contest and struggle. There are cases too of outright annihilation, as the persisting destruction of heritage in armed conflict sadly indicates, or instances of manipulation and suppression, of deliberate erasures of memory which lead to the construction of counter-memories, of 'memory-as-struggle', 'memory-as-resistance', counter-memories, and the re-emergence of submerged memories. Indeed, many different struggles for group rights – 'cultural rights' – are now organized as issues of memory as much as of identity, targeting the taboos and the exclusions. As Huyssen observes, 'monolithic notions of identity, often shaped by defensiveness or victimology, clash with the conviction that identities, national or otherwise, are always heterogeneous and in need of such heterogeneity to remain viable politically and existentially' (1995: 5).

There is much social science investigation of the processes of cultural invention whereby peoples across the world 'are creating pasts, myths of ancestral ways of life that serve as powerful political symbols. In the rhetoric of postcolonial nationalism (and sometimes separatism) and the struggles of indigenous Fourth World peoples, now minorities in their own homelands, visions of the past are being created and evoked' (Keesing 1989: 19). Indeed, as Keesing puts it, anybody, whether scholar or activist, who is sympathetic to these political struggles and quests for identity, would be in a contradiction-ridden position in relation to these processes, for the ancestral ways of life evoked rhetorically may bear little relation to those documented historically, recorded ethnographically, and reconstructed archaeologically. Yet their symbolic power and political force are undeniable. To distance ourselves from them 'is a politically delicate task', as Richard Handler (1994: 38) observes, for the protagonists may well be peoples whose struggles we *want* to support. Deconstructing such notions 'at precisely the moment when the disempowered turn to them may aid the reactionary social forces who seek to reassert the validity of homogeneous 'mainstream' collective identities against proponents of 'multicultural' diversity'.

A decalogue of questions … and a range of answers

In summary, the global cultural landscape is marked by a triple and conjoined proliferation: of heritages, of memories, of identities. This proliferation is highly fluid; it is sometimes irenic, sometimes conflictual; and it is highly diverse and ever-changing. Yet there are also shared trends in the ways the three elements interact with one another in the context of globalization. How are the forces of globalization inflecting the discourses and practices of heritage, memory and identity? In what new directions is globalization taking these discourses and practices? Are globalization processes facilitating them, or are their impacts rather more constraining? What happens to these knowledges and practices in an age of transnational migrations and networks (Ashworth et al. 2007)? What happens to boundaries and continuities as the smooth equivalence between national identity, national memory and national heritage is challenged? Guided by this conceptual envelope, we initially set out ten sets of questions to articulate the content and structure of the volume:

1 *Heritage conservation as a global doctrine and practice*: What forces have been in play as preserving heritage has been made global doctrine by international standard-setting by organizations such as UNESCO? What local, national and regional discrepancies have arisen? Are these discrepancies accentuated by globalization or not?

2 *Deliberate destruction of heritage, memory and identity and their reconstruction*: As the reverse of the preservation medal, or counter-script, what transnational factors encourage or discourage deliberate defacement and destruction of heritage, memory and identity? What ideas are woven into the post-conflict reconstruction rhetoric? How, by whom, and with what intentions are certain elements and forms selected and others ignored? How do rewriting, revisioning, and reinterpreting heritage, memory and identity become explicit in policy and discourse?

3 *From the national to the sub-national*: How is heritage becoming an allegory for memories and identities at regional, sub-cultural and class levels? In other words, how is the concept becoming untied from the nation-state? What is the role of globalization in such processes? What role do the media play?

4 *Contemporary creativity and cultural heritage*: Following up on some of the questions explored in the 2009 volume, what are the interdependencies between artistic creation and heritage? How does artistic practice 'de-freeze', uncover or recover memories and identities? How does it shape or alter them?

5 *The cultural economy and heritage*: Heritage and commemoration are tied increasingly to the tourism industry. How is globalization accentuating the commodification of heritage and memory in different settings? How does the tourism industry impact upon the notions of authenticity and identity – of objects, performances and experiences?

6 *Diasporic heritage*: Are there manifestations of collective memory, identity and heritage among diasporic communities that are detached or different from nation-state-based manifestations?

7 *Multiple identities and multiple heritages*: How are multiple identities leading to the construction of mixed or hybrid heritage? Are 'intercultural' forms emerging? What are the implications?

8 *Memorializing practice and its sites*: What forms is memorializing practice taking in diverse socio-cultural settings? What deliberate or other forms of forgetting are taking place? What borrowings or transfers are being facilitated by globalization?

9 *Manipulated, erased and suppressed memories*: What forms of manipulation and suppression of historical memories are taking place today, e.g. as in Communist and post-Communist regimes, and the resulting 'counter-memories', 'memories of struggle' and 'memory wars'?

10 *Policy implication*: Finally, what are the policy implications that follow from the questions above, and what policy recommendations can be made?

Global approaches

As in previous volumes of this series, the first section explores cross-cutting themes that are global in scope or at least generic enough to manifest themselves in a very wide range of geo-cultural settings. We have chosen to open this section with a stage-setting essay by a leading scholar in the field of memory studies, James Wertsch, whose intellectual groundings span several disciplines. This chapter, written jointly with anthropologist Doc Billingsley, provides a framework for grasping the term 'collective memory'. Rather than review diverse theories, the authors suggest that a fruitful method of engaging memory and of establishing its connections with heritage and identity in an era of globalization is to focus on *remembering* as an active process. So the authors present an understanding of collective remembering based on mediation, particularly on narrative frameworks that mediate our understanding of the past, and their effects on our present identities. They argue that attention to the cultural mediation allows for a more coherent exploration of the relationship between identity projects that call upon the notion of memory and globalization. The latter may encourage the perpetuation of old mnemonic nationalisms and the emergence of new forms. In this perspective, we should see commemorative practices and

artefacts as examples of intangible and tangible heritage being used as resources to construct and legitimate representations of the past. In their most effective form, these representations take on characteristics of collective remembering, influencing people's understandings of their personal and group identities. It is also important to explore the impacts that national narratives and schematic narrative templates have on how people relate to the past and draw on memory for understanding the present. This is what the authors set out to do as they analyze the links between globalization and memory-related identity projects. Their case study is an ethnographic analysis of contemporary cultural revitalization movements among Maya communities in Guatemala.

'The Heritage' as a discursive practice has been central to cultural revitalization everywhere and the role played by international organizations, principally UNESCO, in propelling an intergovernmental discursive process is well known. Two major global scripts have emerged: 'World Heritage' and 'Intangible Heritage'. Isar's chapter, entitled 'UNESCO and Heritage: Global Doctrine, Global Practice' (see Chapter 2), explores the ways in which the UNESCO-led expansion of the heritage concept (appeals to *national* memories and identities are its ever-accompanying tropes) has evolved. Nation-states are the stakeholders here, as the owners of the symbolic capital they aptly term 'cultural property', and their ambitions in the heritage arena feed into a global political economy of prestige. Hence the need to deconstruct the identitarian stakes that lie behind the proliferation of World Heritage Sites. The discursive paradigm to which 'World Heritage' belongs was elaborated originally in Europe and North America. It may have been thoroughly globalized, but in the process, it has been contested in other geo-cultural settings, leading at once to ever-broader definitions of what is heritage, notably in the form of 'intangible heritage', but also to different notions of how all kinds of heritage should be preserved.

But what about more malevolent ways of affirming difference, such as the deliberate destruction of heritage, especially during war-time? What impacts does such destruction have in turn on notions of memory and identity? Dacia Viejo-Rose's chapter, entitled 'Destruction and Reconstruction of Heritage: Impacts on Memory and identity' (see Chapter 3), explores these questions. She also takes up the positive and negative consequences of reconstruction or neglect. She discusses the more salient of these consequences, including those that we are only now beginning to appreciate, including the ways in which war creates new heritage even as it destroys. Memory and memorials are also put to diverse uses in the aftermath of war; their ever-changing nature makes it easy to deploy them for political ends. Mediated and transformed into global icons, destructive acts also acquire formidable symbolic dimensions. Part of this impact, as discussed in this chapter, is visible in ways the 'international community' has responded through reconstruction programmes and policies and in the creation of Truth and Reconciliation Commissions around the world that seek to acknowledge the firm grip in which the long arm of memory can hold societies. As these programmes are salient in cultural policies today, the author highlights some of the key policy implications of her findings and arguments.

The 'heritage industry' that accompanies contemporary tourism has been widely analyzed in many publications. Tim Winter's essay, 'The Political Economies of Heritage', places it within the global economic frameworks that condition the interplays among heritage, memory, identity and capital. These are not always recognized or adequately understood. Commodification (as discussed in Throsby 2008) is certainly involved, but there is more. Supposed losses of 'authenticity' are bemoaned, as the global dollar destroys, pollutes or erases, but Winter argues that the casual use of that term as a generic way of understanding the cultural–economic dyad masks the real complexities of the interaction. While the many instances in which heritage resources have been either endangered or lost give validity to such accounts, more nuanced, multi-vector understandings of this relationship are needed. In recent years much attention has been paid to how heritage, memory and identity are socially actualized in both material and non-material ways in the light of globalization. Winter considers how heritage and memory are being produced and shaped in particular contexts through a series of global political and economic processes, and highlights how such processes involve the privileging of certain forms of expertise and cultural knowledge. More specifically, he explores how heritage, memory and identity can come to be constituted and reconstituted through a highly complex, highly interconnected set of political economies.

The pulls and pressures of today's migratory flows complexify notions of heritage, memory and identity in different ways. Some of these are explored in Ien Ang's 'Unsettling the National: Heritage and Diaspora' (see Chapter 5). The relationships between heritage and diaspora are complex and problematic. Bringing them together in a cultural studies perspective therefore opens up a range of tensions which trouble the intimate interrelationship that presumably exists among (national) identity, memory and heritage. A diasporic perspective cracks open the nationalist narrative of seamless national unity, highlighting the fact that nations today inevitably harbour populations with multiple pasts, bringing memories and identities into circulation that often transcend or undercut the homogenizing image of nationhood and national heritage. At the same time, the heritage lens reveals some of the internal tensions and contradictions in the very idea of diaspora, which exemplify the multifaceted complexities of identity formation in the contemporary globalized world. These complexities cannot be contained within the cultural and geographical confines of the nation-state. Ang focuses on new institutions of memorial culture in the diasporic space, in particular museums, a concern that is echoed further on in the volume by Julie Thomas's ethnographic exploration of museums of immigration.

But primordially rooted peoples relate to territory in rather different ways, invoking the resources of heritage, memory and identity in reference to a *single* place to which they claim privileged belongingness. This perspective is addressed by anthropologist Jean-Pierre Warnier's chapter, entitled 'Territorialization and the Politics of Autochthony' (see Chapter 6). This politics has emerged around the claims of 'autochthonous' (or 'Indigenous') peoples who claim to be born on a territory occupied by their ancestors from time immemorial and with which they maintain a specific economic and spiritual relationship. Their territorial rootedness was recognized in the 'Declaration on the Rights of Indigenous Peoples', adopted by the United Nations in 2007. Elaborated in the wake of fifty years of activism on the part of non-governmental organizations and Indigenous movements, this international standard-setting treaty was designed to protect *inter alia* the heritage, memory and identity of the latter. Indigenous Peoples justify their activism on the grounds of their autochthony. They claim fundamental and special rights to territories. Yet a closer examination of their movements around the world shows that they can have diverse and sometimes conflicting agendas. This has not prevented them from converging on a global scale and confronting the top-down policies of states, which all have a key stake in territorializing their populations and controlling migratory flows. As a result, Indigenous People's politics of heritage, memory and identity are intertwined with complex global issues.

The passion for memorialization has also created a specific contemporary and global expression in the ritual forms that include mourning and protest that have emerged recently in public spaces where particular deaths are considered unjust and traumatic, either because a famous person or because anonymous citizens the victims of a massacre. These improvised memorials have been dubbed 'grassroots memorials' in order to highlight both their political dimension and their non-institutionalized character. There appears also to be a global pattern in the ways these memorials are formed and organized. In their chapter, entitled 'Grassroots Memorials as Sites of Heritage Creation' (see Chapter 7), Cristina Sánchez-Carretero and Carmen Ortiz explore this phenomenon with particular reference to the *Archivo del Duelo* (Archive of Mourning) research project created by the Spanish National Research Council (CSIC) in response to the terrorist attacks of 11 March 2004 in Madrid.

Yet in the global memory culture, formal institutions have long existed as well, e.g. as museums and heritage sites. In 1999, the directors of nine historic sites across the world came together to explore a common question: how could their sites promote human rights? They imagined a new type of space, a 'Site of Conscience'. These entities work at the intersection of historic preservation, human rights, citizen engagement, education, and the arts. To achieve their vision, they wrestle with a variety of critical issues. What does a heritage practice for human rights look like? What is required to promote a lasting culture of human rights and civic participation in a society? And what role can heritage play in that process? These are some of the difficult questions raised by Liz Ševčenko, who is the founding Director of the International Coalition of Sites of Conscience, in her chapter, entitled 'Sites of Conscience: Heritage for Human Rights' (see Chapter 8).

It has become inconceivable today to use any of the three cultural notions we are discussing in this volume – particularly heritage – independently of

the concept of 'nature'. A passionate advocate of environmental conservation, writer and researcher Benjamin Morris, takes us through the many diverse relationships between cultural heritage and the natural environment. Beginning with the premise that conventional divisions between nature and culture can no longer be maintained, Morris explores the multiple forms of heritage that the natural world has occasioned, such as protected spaces and conservation movements. How have natural events, such as disasters, been memorialized into heritage? How has the natural world been invoked in the construction and/or representation of local and national identities? Looking to the future, Morris also allows us to round off this first section of the volume on a future-oriented note of interrogation. Will anthropogenic global warming serve as a context in which changes in natural processes that simultaneously impact cultural heritage sites and traditions provide an opportunity to reconnect societies fragmented by the forces of globalization?

Regional realities

This section, as its title indicates, brings together essays that explore issues specific to or characteristic of different world regions. It is not designed to be an exhaustive 'state of the art' for each region, but merely to provide a selection of regionally-specific perspectives or problem areas. We are aware of the potential risk of essentialization in reverse, as if such abstractions as 'Africa' or 'Asia' are ever effective platforms for commonalities rather than internal difference. Yet we still recognize the value of treatments that bring to the fore families of cultural and societal realities distinctly different from those of the 'West'. Under the conditions of globalization, it surely behooves us to contribute to the latter's 'provincialization', to borrow Chakrabarty's provocative term (2000). The contestation of Western ideas of universalism has characterized the expanding heritage discourse, as Isar's chapter has argued. Jagath Weerasinghe's 'Living Sacred Heritage and "Authenticity" in South Asia' (see Chapter 10) explores how different forces in South Asia – states, civil societies and the corporate world – articulate ideas and practices in opposition to norms originating in the erstwhile 'central' countries. His focus is on South Asian understandings of the notion of 'authenticity' and the way these influence heritage preservation practice.

The lens remains focused on Asian conditions as sociologists Aurel Croissant and Paul Wesley Chambers analyze the acrimonious dispute between Cambodia and Thailand over an eleventh-century Hindu temple situated along the Thai–Cambodian border. Their focus is on the way Thais perceive and talk about this contested site of collective memory. As in many other local cases, the inter-state heritage and memory-based conflict has taken on special salience in the context of globalization, as it is linked to the spread of new concepts of identity, boundary, and territory and their links to distinguished architectural heritage. The contested temple site and the surrounding area are registered in recent Thai memory as land wrested away from them by Westerners.

The viewpoint then shifts to the African continent, focusing on Southern Africa. Heritage tourism is developing here at a rapid pace. As archaeologists Susan Keitumetse, Laura McAtackney, and Gobopaone Senata argue, these developments heighten the need for the communities concerned to clarify the ways in which local cultural identities can be positively expressed thereby. Archaeological remains, monuments and cultural landscapes are readily available for heritage marketing and consumption. But intangible and/or invisible aspects of heritage also exist, as storehouses of memory that can provide significant resources. Formulating identities on the basis of the latter is necessarily varied and often will not conform to conventional heritage management methods. The authors explore the potential for alternative approaches in Botswana and South Africa. While their concerns echo and amplify those expressed earlier by Winter with regard to the hegemonic political economies within which heritage tends to be exploited for tourism purposes, their judgement of heritage tourism itself is more positive (however, Box 12.1 by Michael Francis on the San people that accompanies the chapter is less sanguine about its benefits (see page 163)).

Such concerns are also tied to the ways in which *multiple* and shifting notions of heritage and identities are being elaborated. Anthropologist Rosabelle Boswell explores these dynamics in the three island nations of southern Africa: Mauritius, Zanzibar and Madagascar. In these countries, heritage, memory and identity are categories of practice. In other words, they are constructed by the actors themselves for their own purposes. However, the deployment of heritage for tourism, nation-building and ethnic memorialization is turning heritage into a category of analysis. Moreover, the formalizing of heritage risks homogenizing identity and recasting heritage and memory as uncomplicated reflections on the past. Globalization is complicating the process of abstraction: identity and memory are becoming more deterritorialized, ordinary people are actively engaged in the casting of their own identities and new spaces are challenging the continued salience to identity of heritage and memory-making.

We alluded earlier in this Introduction to the many debates about history and memory taking place in post-Communist Europe. As these societies turn their backs on the 1945–89 years, is the material and immaterial culture left behind from that period condemned to total destruction? Is there an historical responsibility to preserve the cultural production of the discredited 'socialist' order? And what of the principles that characterized its cultural policies, apparently so beneficial and benevolent – at least to those who trod the ideological line? Arguing that the cultural production of that era was much more diverse and multifaceted than is commonly assumed, Dragan Klaic sets out his case by examining the uses of heritage policy – under Communism and after it. In the latter case, heritage and memory have been appropriated by governments for national representation and promotion. They have also been swept into the maw of the global neo-liberal political economy. In fact, Klaic argues, there is an ongoing tension between nationalist and neo-liberal motivations, and the case studies of some 'radical interventions', as he calls them, are there to prove it. Nostalgia is part of the 'structure of feeling' here. Many groups experience forms of 'aesthetic nostalgia' that lead them to venerate an 'authentic' collective past. A particularly salient form of the latter is the 'Yugo-nostalgia' that Zala Volcic analyzes in her chapter entitled 'Post-socialist Recollections: Identity and Memory in Former Yugoslavia' (see Chapter 15). This collective phenomenon harks back to a shared cultural history yet also provides the raw material for new forms of distinct national identities for each of the former Yugoslav republics. Symbolic spaces and 'flows' of people, capital and products form particular routes of memorizing, determining the ways in which discourses of memory and nostalgia circulate. Memories of the Yugoslav past come together with nationalist affirmations of identity to create a distinctive cultural arena. As in many settings across the world, the combination also provides content for the global commercial communication order.

Whereas in an earlier age heritage was the artist's principal source of inspiration, the grounding for the continuity of cultural identity, twentieth-century modernism held that contemporary art must oppose or negate tradition. Postmodern sensibility has led us to challenge this dichotomy. Indeed, contemporary attempts to build continuity between heritage and creativity were among the topics taken up in the previous volume, entitled *Cultural Expression, Creativity and Innovation.* Globalization bears upon these attempted syntheses between past and present in many different ways. Analyzing the recent experience of Latin America, where public policies have tended to privilege 'high culture' forms, Lucina Jiménez López explores both Latin American popular culture and contemporary artistic practice marked by blurred boundaries and new genres. She analyzes how globalization has impacted these different repertoires and draws some strong conclusion for policy-making in the countries of the region.

Fields and issues

This section brings together chapters covering particular issues that arise with regard to heritage, memory, identity or relevant phenomena. Complementing Ien Ang's treatment of conceptual issues pertaining to museums as public sites, Julie Thomas provides an ethnographic analysis of the permanent exhibitions of two national museums of immigration in France and the United Kingdom. This museography structures the interplay between diasporic heritage and identity and nation-state heritage and identity. In response to the pressures of globalization, 'memory' and 'identity' have been manipulated in the display in ways that allows the 'heritage' in these two countries to be subtly redefined not in terms of plural content but in terms of civic 'process'.

The city of Istanbul has two chapters devoted to it. This is not because it was declared a 'European Capital of Culture' for the year 2010, but because it is an exceptionally germane laboratory for the heritage/memory/identity problematic, as well as embodying such an evocative palimpsest of heritage and memory for artists and writers. In 'Heritage,

Memory, Debris: Sulukule, Don't Forget' (see Chapter 18), Asu Aksoy and Kevin Robins explore the sociological interactions between political economy and ethnic discrimination, as they relate the recent destruction of Sulukule, a predominantly Roma district located in the historical peninsula of Istanbul. They describe the process by which the local municipality initiated a programme of radical urban 'redevelopment' in the cause of gentrification in the historic, central zone of the city. They situate the developments in Sulukule in the context of the longer-term cultural imaginary through which the city's historical trajectory has come to be conceived, as elaborated in the literary texts of Ahmet Hamdi Tanpınar and, later, Orhan Pamuk. Finally, they explore the evolving new conceptual and ideological frame that is serving as a rationale for the reinvention, in the name of development, of Istanbul's cultural heritage and identity. In her essay, 'Knowing the City: Migrants Negotiating Materialities in Istanbul', Yael Navaro-Yashin deploys the ethnographer's gaze on the ways in which migrants into two districts of Istanbul come to know and interpret the built environment which they inhabit. Weaving through migrants' ways of negotiating the materialities around them, the author discovers that the city is known to its contemporary inhabitants in fragmentary and partial terms. As if collecting pieces of a puzzle or assembling units of debris, migrants attempt to understand the past and the future of the built environment left behind by Greek and Jewish exiles or emigrés. Their stories form another distant layer of memory by removal in the record of Istanbul's history.

A very specific type of memory work is connected with the remembering (or not) of traumatic or shameful collective experiences. Sociologist Akiko Hashimoto's chapter, 'Divided Memories, Contested Histories: The Shifting Landscape in Japan' (see Chapter 20), examines the way Japanese society treats traumatic memories of the Second World War and includes comparisons with the German approach in her discussion. Her essay adds to the broad sweep of Ian Buruma's classic treatment of the topic (2009). As she observes, winners and losers remember wars differently. For every victor who remembers a good, honourable war, there is a vanquished counterpart who remembers a humiliating failure. If winners accept victory as a mostly uncomplicated affair, losers, by contrast, face a predicament of living with a discredited past that stains national history. Hashimoto's exploration illuminates the impact of this quandary in post-Second World War Japan, and its search for a renewed identity in the global world at the turn of the century. The last years of the twentieth century proved to be a critical time for Japan to revise its national goals, yet at this pivotal time of social transition, Japanese citizens remain deeply divided in their vision of the future between progressive and conservative directions.

Ananda Breed looks at a very specific genre of memory work in her treatment of the use of theatre in relation to the Rwandan mass killings of 1994. The use of theatre to memorialize and commemorate that terrible genocide is illustrated by a case study of *Rwanda My Hope*, a production written and performed by survivors of the genocide. While initially recognizing the usefulness of theatre to embody survivor testimonies and human rights discourses, the author actually questions its performative dimension and considers some of the ethical implications of 'genocide theatre' when presented to international audiences and donor agencies in the context of globalization.

Given the metaphoric nature of the very notion of memory itself, the stipulated or fictive aspect we alluded to earlier, we thought it would be appropriate to include a contribution from psychologists or social psychologists whose work is grounded in empirically observable *individual* memories. Schiff, Porto de Andrade and Toulemonde have analyzed the narrations of Arab–Jewish couples living in France. On this basis, they argue that collective memories can be understood as individual narratives that are negotiated in concrete social relationships. Here, in the context of globalization, the task of establishing a coherent and sustaining couple identity has become more problematic. On the basis of life-story conversations with Arab–Jewish mixed couples, they discover how couples create, or fail to create, a coherent story of their identity.

It also seemed indispensable to hear from a contemporary artist who directly addresses memory in her work. Paris-based Esther Shalev-Gerz develops photographs and installations in public space through active dialogue, consultation and negotiation with people whose participation places the emphasis on their individual and collective memories. In her essay, entitled 'Listening Voices: On Actualizing Memories', she comments on how

globalization brings together people who have very different modes of both conceiving and communicating what memory, identity and heritage mean for them. Some of these modes are not even thinkable for others. Language/s become elements of identification and translation through voice and listening (the person's body and image). Yet many meanings remain wordless. How can art create a place that does not depend only on concepts and words, but acts as a platform that opens up new encounters and thus unlocks new openings into memories and heritage, she asks?

To close Part I, we invited two eminent scholars to contribute commentaries on the heritage-memory-identity triad and globalization in the light of perspectives brought to bear by other contributors to the volume. In her commentary, anthropologist Henrietta L. Moore interrogates the notion of 'intangible heritage' in the context of the broader claims of identity and culture that are abroad in the world today. What are the links between the notion of intangibility and ideas of culture as assets? To address such questions it is necessary to deconstruct the value assigned to cultural distinctiveness and/or diversity, to revisit the taken-for-granted dichotomy between the traditional and the modern and thence to analyze, as does Moore, the entanglements between the 'modernities' that have emerged in different parts of the world. Here is the argument is based on the entanglements between Western and Japanese modernity. Finally, Moore explores how globally shared technologies abet the elaboration of new worlds of meaning that engage in new ways with notions of heritage, memory and identity. The closing essay, entitled 'From the Tower of Babel to the Ivory Tower', by the doyen of heritage scholars David Lowenthal, echoes the axiological note struck in the Foreword by Pierre Nora. The 'Tower of Babel' is a metaphor for the ways in which, as demonstrated by various contributions to the volume, obsessive emphasis on exclusive, unique and fiercely acquisitive identities suffuses the heritage debate with tension and conflict; the 'Ivory Tower' for the utopian vision of a truly cosmopolitan heritage, hence for a truly global trust in heritage stewardship that might curb 'the reckless present with the elevated lessons of the past'.

These observations bring us back to the abiding purpose of this *Series*, which is to shed light on the ways in which issues of culture, together with the complex and often loose understandings characteristic of contemporary 'culture talk', have generated such a range of expectations, anxieties and illusions across the world. As with ideas of the 'cultural conflict', 'cultural economy' or 'creativity and innovation', the expectations with regard to heritage, memory and identity are tied to their paradigmatic usage in our societies today. The anxieties arise from their frequent overuse and abuse, while the illusions are the result of overblown visions, of simplifications that are reductive, and readings that are instrumental. We can only reiterate our conviction that the expectations can be justified, the anxieties allayed and the illusions dispelled by the patient and methodical marshalling of evidence in informed and conceptually sensitive ways. It is our hope that this volume too, like its predecessors, will contribute meaningfully to that task.

Notes

1   For the purposes of the Series, we take 'culture' to be both the lived and creative experience for individuals and a body of artifacts, symbols, texts and objects; in other words, both heritage and contemporary creation, involving both enactment and representation. In this broad yet bounded vision, culture embraces art and art discourse, the symbolic world of meanings, the commodified output of the cultural industries as well as the spontaneous or enacted, organized or unorganized meaning-linked expressions of everyday life, including social relations. It is constitutive of both collective and individual identity.

2   As was the 'conflicts and tensions' dyad of the first volume, which explored the ways in the exponential growth in affirmations of, or claims to, cultural difference in the face of the forces of globalization have given rise to multiple conflicts and tensions in recent years. As we put it, 'behind the concern for "culture" that is increasingly evoked in contemporary public debate lurks the specter of conflict: the cultural dimensions of conflict on the one hand, and the conflictual dimensions of culture on the other' (Anheier and Isar 2007: 19). By contrast, the 'cultural economy', our theme in 2008, related rather more to the 'arts and heritage' understanding of culture or, more precisely, to the ways in which a global political economy of goods and services based on cultural content, commonly referred to as the 'cultural' or the 'creative' industries, was fraught by global imbalances and/or divides. This we followed up with the third volume, entitled *Cultural Expression, Creativity and Innovation*, a theme chosen precisely because the reigning 'creative economy' discourse tends to ignore the core resources

of individual or collective creativity and innovation in artistic practice. It appeared necessary to redress the balance.

3   For example, in the inaugural *Conflicts and Tensions* volume, the politics of identity was linked to 'memory wars' and the deliberate destruction of historic monuments was also discussed. The role of cultural industries as vectors of group identity was highlighted in *The Cultural Economy*, the second volume, while attention was paid to heritage conservation as a form of meta-cultural production and as an 'industry'. The third volume, *Cultural Expression, Creativity and Innovation*, explored the dialectics of twenty-first century cultural expression based on both inherited and emerging forms and traditions.

4   While *valuing* means simply appreciating existing value, *valorizing* is the process of adding value through intervention and interpretation, a process that 'begins when individuals, institutions or communities decide that some object or place is worth preserving, that it represents some worth remembering, something about themselves and their past that should be transmitted to future generations' (Avrami, Mason and de la Torre 2000: 8).

5   Only a few countries, for example, have official institutes devoted to questions of national memory. Spain is rare in having adopted in 2007 a Historic Memory Law (see chapter by Sánchez-Carretero and Ortiz, page 106). Its full official title is the following: *Ley por la que se reconocen y amplían derechos y se establecen medidas en favor de quienes padecieron persecución o violencia durante la Guerra Civil y la Dictadura.*

6   As these lines are being written, the 2010 *Monumenta* exhibit in the historic *Grand Palais* exhibition hall in Paris is a massive audiovisual commemoration mounted by the French artist Christian Boltanski. In a parallel project he calls *The Heart Archives*, Boltanski is recording millions of heartbeats. An explanatory panel that 'the sound of a beating heart, a symbol of life to oppose time's passage to oblivion, becomes one part of a vast living memory, in which each may find his or her place, concretely and individually, while also participating in creating a modern myth…'.

7   For example, on 13 February 2010, two memory scholars contributed an Op-Ed piece to the *New York Times* linking historical memory and built form. The piece, entitled 'A Damnation of Memory', was about the construction by the Bavarian Monument Protection Agency of a roadside chapel near the town of Berchtesgaden using stones from Adolf Hitler's nearby alpine retreat on the Obersalzberg (Ryback and Beierl 2010).

8   See István Rév's masterful treatment in *Retroactive Justice: Prehistory of Post-Communism* (Stanford: Stanford University Press, 2005). Also Richard S. Ebenshade, 'Remembering to Forget: Memory, History, National Identity in Postwar East-Central Europe' in *Representations*, Special Issue 49, Winter 1995.

9   He speaks of the West.

10 In email comments made to the co-editors about the initial *Brief* sent to contributors.
11 See the classic definition in E.J. Hobsbawm and Terence Ranger, *The Invention of Tradition* (1983: 1): '"Invented tradition" is taken to mean a set of practices, normally governed by overtly or tacitly accepted rules and of a ritual or symbolic nature, which seek to inculcate certain values and norms of behaviour by repetition, which automatically implies continuity with the past ... However, insofar as there is such reference to a historic past, the peculiarity of 'invented' traditions is that the continuity with it is largely factitious.'

REFERENCES

Abu El-Haj, N. (2001) *Facts on the Ground: Archaeological Practice and Territorial Self-Fashioning in Israeli Society*. Chicago: The University of Chicago Press.

Appadurai, A. (2006) *Fear of Small Numbers. An Essay on the Geography of Anger*. Durham, NC: Duke University Press.

Appiah, K.A. (2006) *Cosmopolitanism: Ethics in a World of Strangers*. New York: W.W. Norton and Co.

Ashworth, G.J., Graham, B. and Tunbridge, J.E. (2000) *A Geography of Heritage: Power, Culture and Economy*. London: Hodder Arnold.

—— (2007) *Pluralising Pasts: Heritage, Identity and Place in Multicultural Societies*. London: Pluto Press.

Assmann, A. (2008) 'Transformations between History and Memory', *Social Research*, Vol. 75, No. 1, Spring, pp. 49–72.

Austin, J.L. (1962) *How To Do Things with Words: The William James Lectures Delivered at Harvard University in 1955*. Oxford: Clarendon Press.

Avrami, E., Mason, R. and de la Torre, M. (2000) 'Report on Research' in E. Avrami and Mason (eds) *Values and Heritage Preservation*. Los Angeles: The J. Paul Getty Trust.

Buruma, I. (2009) *The Wages of Guilt: Memories of War in Germany and Japan*. London: Grove Atlantic (revised edition).

Chakrabarty, D. (2000) *Provincializing Europe: Postcolonial Thought and Historical Difference*. Princeton, NJ: Princeton University Press.

Choay, F. (1992) *L'allegorie du patrimoine*. Paris: Editions du Seuil.

—— (2009) *Le patrimoine en questions: Anthologie pour un combat*. Paris: Editions du Seuil.

Connerton, P. (1989) *How Societies Remember*. Cambridge: Cambridge University Press.

Halbwachs, M. (1980) *The Collective Memory*. New York: Harper & Row/Colophon Books.

Hall, S. (1996) 'Introduction: Who Needs Identity?', in S. Hall and P. du Gay (eds), *Questions of Cultural Identity*. London: Sage.

—— (2005) 'Whose Heritage', in J. Littler and R. Naidoo (eds), *The Politics of Heritage: The Legacies of 'Race'*. London: Routledge.

Handler, R. (1994) 'Is "Identity" a Useful Concept?', in J.R. Gillis (ed.), *Commemorations: The Politics of National Identity*. Princeton, NJ: Princeton University Press.

Held, D., McGrew, A., Goldblatt, D. and Perraton, J. (1999) *Global Transformations: Politics, Economics, and Culture*. Cambridge: Polity Press.

Hobsbawm, E. and Ranger, T. (1983) *The Invention of Tradition*. New York and Cambridge: Cambridge University Press.

Huyssen, A. (1995) *Twilight Memories: Marking Time in a Culture of Amnesia*. New York: Routledge.

Isar, Y.R. (2005a) 'Tangible and Intangible Heritage: Are They Really Castor and Pollux?', in *INTACH Vision 2020* (Proceedings of the conference INTACH 2020, organized by the Indian National Trust for Art and Cultural Heritage, INTACH, November 2004). New Delhi: INTACH.

Isar, Y.R. (2005b) 'The Mobilization of Cultural Identity and Difference: Some Conceptual Perspectives', paper presented at the Sixth Mediterranean Social and Political Research Meeting, Robert Schuman Centre for Advanced Studies, European University Institute (March).

Keesing, R. (1989) 'Creating the Past: Custom and Identity in the Contemporary Pacific', *The Contemporary Pacific*, Vol. 1, Nos. 1 and 2, Spring and Fall, pp. 19–42. Honolulu: University of Hawaii Press.

Kirshenblatt-Gimblett, B. (1998) *Destination Culture: Tourism, Museums and Heritage*. Berkeléy: University of California Press.

Kirshenblatt-Gimblett, B. (2004) 'Intangible Heritage as Metacultural Production', *Museum International*, Nos 221–222 (May): 52–65. Paris: UNESCO/Blackwell Publishing.

Kong, L. (2010) 'Creative Economy, Global City: Globalizing Discourses and the implications for Local Arts', *Cultural Expression, Creativity and Innovation. The Cultures and Globalization Series, 3*. London: Sage, pp. 166–175.

Kurin, R. (2004) 'Intangible Cultural Heritage in the 2003 UNESCO Convention', *Museum International*, Nos 221–222 (May): 66–76. Paris: UNESCO/Blackwell Publishing.

Lowenthal, D. (1985) *The Past is a Foreign Country*. Cambridge: Cambridge University Press.

—— (1998) *The Heritage Crusade and the Spoils of History*. Cambridge: Cambridge University Press (first paperback edition).

—— (1994) 'Identity, Heritage and History', in J.R. Gillis (ed.), *Commemorations. The Politics of National Identity*. Princeton, NJ: Princeton University Press.

Maalouf, A. (2003) *In the Name of Identity: Violence and the Need to Belong*. London: Penguin Book.

Nora, P. (1989) 'Between Memory and History: *Les Lieux de Mémoire*', *Representations*, No. 26 (Spring), pp. 7–25.

—— (1994) *Les lieux de mémoire*. Paris: Gallimard.

Renan, E. (1990) 'What is a Nation?', in H. Bhabha (ed.), *Nation and Narration*. New York: Routledge (English translation of lecture delivered in 1882).

Ryback, T.W. and Beierl, F.M. (2010) 'A Damnation of Memory', *The New York Times*, 13 February, 2010.

Samuel, R. (1994) *Theatres of Memory*. London: Verso.

Smith, L. (2006) *Uses of Heritage*. New York: Routledge.

Sontag, S. (2003) *Regarding the Pain of Others*. New York: Picador.

Throsby, D. (2008) 'Globalization and the Cultural Economy: a Crisis of Value', in H.K. Anheier and Y.R. Isar (eds), *The Cultural Economy: The Cultures and Globalization Series*, 2. London: Sage.

Todorov, T. (2004) *Les abus de la mémoire*. Paris: Arléa.

Tomlinson, J. (1999) *Globalization and Culture*. Cambridge: Polity Press.

Urry, J. (1990) *The Tourist Gaze: Leisure and Travel in Contemporary Societies*. London: Sage.

van Dijck, J. (2004) 'Mediated Memories: Personal Cultural Memory as an Object of Cultural Analysis', *Continuum: Journal of Media and Cultural Studies*, Vol. 18, pp. 261–277.

Viejo-Rose, D. (2007) 'Conflict and the Deliberate Destruction of Cultural Heritage', *Conflicts and Tensions: The Cultures and Globalization Series, 1*. London: Sage, pp. 102–118.

Wertsch, J.V. (2002) *Voices of Collective Remembering*. Cambridge: Cambridge University Press.

Young, J.E. (1993) *The Texture of Memory: Holocaust Memorials and Meaning*. New Haven, CT: Yale University Press.

Zerubavel, E. (2003) *Time Maps: Collective Memory and the Social Shape of the Past*. Chicago and London: The University of Chicago Press.

PART 1   CONFIGURATIONS OF HERITAGE, MEMORY, IDENTITY

GLOBAL APPROACHES

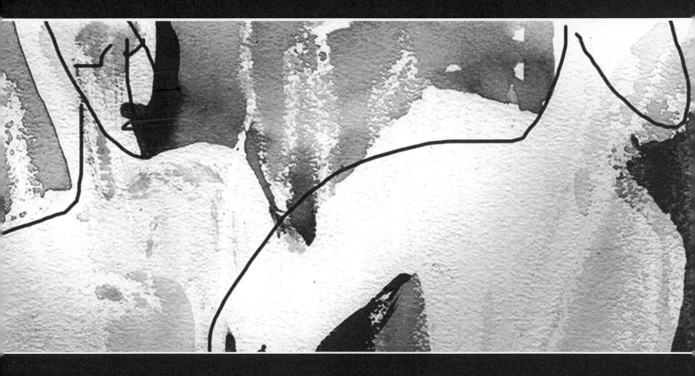

CHAPTER 1

THE ROLE OF NARRATIVES IN COMMEMORATION: REMEMBERING AS MEDIATED ACTION

James V. Wertsch and Doc M. Billingsley

This opening chapter presents a framework for conceptualizing collective memory that focuses on the ways in which cultural tools mediate collective remembering. The authors begin by evoking recent conflicts that illustrate the powerful links between heritage, memory and identity. They see commemorative practices and artifacts as examples of intangible and tangible heritage that are used as resources to construct and legitimate representations of the past. In their most effective form, these representations take on characteristics of collective remembering, influencing people's understandings of their personal and group identities. The fundamental impacts that national narratives and schematic narrative templates have on how people relate to the past and draw on memory for understanding the present are then explored. Linking globalization on mnemonic identity projects, they conclude with an ethnographic view of contemporary cultural revitalization movements among Maya communities in Guatemala.

The objects and the stakes of commemoration

The great encyclopedic museums of industrially advanced countries typically are composed of displays of treasured works of art from virtually every region of the world, drawn from the whole of the human past. The curators of these artifacts argue that they are the cultural patrimony of all humankind, representations at once of our diversity and unity. Consequently, the mission of these institutions revolves around exhibiting these remarkable objects for the enrichment of all who would enter and behold. This cosmopolitan turn in the museum world, following earlier historical objectives of glorifying the geographic and cultural diversity of imperial patrons, would seem to reflect an emerging consensus for the celebration of world heritage.

Yet the consensus has failed. Nations and groups around the world have initiated renewed calls for the repatriation of art and artifacts that originated within their territorial borders. This booming demand for the return of ancient 'loot' has led to high-profile cases such as Marion True's ongoing series of trials in Rome for allegedly trafficking in stolen artifacts (Cuno 2008). Egypt's Secretary General of Antiquities, Zahi Hawass, has made repeated demands for museums throughout the world to return ancient Egyptian artwork, including high-publicity demands for such iconic pieces as the Rosetta Stone (presently displayed at the British Museum), a bust of Nefertiti (at Berlin's Neues Museum), and the Ka-Nefer-Nefer funerary mask (at the St. Louis Art Museum) (Waxman 2008; Hawass 2009; Kimmelman 2009).

However high the stakes may be in international debates over the repatriation of cultural patrimony (see also Isar's chapter in this volume), the consequences rarely equal the violent toll that can accompany civil ruptures over heritage objects and sites. The violent demolition of the Babri Masjid in Ayodhya, India, offers a flashpoint example of the ferocity that these conflicts can entail. A crowd of as many as 150,000 Hindu nationalists demolished the Mogul-era building on December 6, 1992, leading to violent riots that left over 2,000 people dead (Romey 2006). At the heart of this conflict was an assertion by hard-line nationalists that the mosque was built upon the ruins of a Hindu temple marking the birthplace of the god Rama. With scant visible evidence of this earlier building, and no historical records of its existence until the eighteenth century, the basis of proponents' belief in the Rama temple appears to have been predominately memorial, motivated by the political and religious exigencies of the present (Romey 2004). In a move to settle once and for all the conflict over competing collective interpretations of the site, the Indian courts ordered the Archaeological Survey of India to excavate the site and determine whether there was sufficient evidence of a Hindu temple beneath the ruins of the mosque. However, the controversies reflected in and engendered by the archaeologists' final report cast doubt upon the ability of these professional scientists to provide a perspective on the past that transcends the clashing narratives that prompted their involvement (Romey 2004, 2006).

Adding new monuments to public spaces can also engender conflicts – as happens virtually every time a new memorial or museum is erected on the United States' 'most sacred space', the National Mall in Washington, DC (Ellis 1997). Erika Doss argues that the placement of the National World War II Memorial directly in between the monuments to Washington and Lincoln threatens to transform the public memory of those presidents by redefining their leadership as a matter of warfare (the Revolutionary and Civil Wars, respectively) and thus to glorify American militarism (Doss 2008). She contrasts the purpose of this memorial, which is used to 'bury memories, essentialize historical narratives and coerce public feeling', with alternative memorials that prompt viewers to question the purpose and consequences of warfare (2008: 247).

In other instances the origin of conflict may involve neither the addition nor demolition of a monument, but simply a change in its location. The unrest surrounding the movement of a monument

in Tallinn, Estonia, in April 2007 is illustrative of this type of conflict (Wertsch 2009a). In this case, a bronze statue of a soldier, officially known as the 'Monument to the Liberators of Tallinn', was erected in 1947 in a small park at the city's center and stood above the graves of several unidentified Soviet soldiers. For Russians, and for Estonia's sizeable Russian minority, the monument represents the sacrifices made by Soviet forces in their triumph over the Nazi invaders, and celebrates the larger theme of liberation that characterizes Russian narratives about the 'Great Fatherland War' of 1941–1945. However, for many ethnic Estonians the monument holds a very different meaning, evocatively expressed in private references to the statue as 'the unknown rapist.' For them, the monument is a reminder of Stalin's annexation of Estonia under the secret protocols of the Molotov – Ribbentrop Pact and the subsequent interruption of their national independence for the next five decades. The central location of the statue, and the occasion of pilgrimages to the site by ethnic Russians – at times by schoolchildren bearing portraits of Stalin and red flags – were regarded as provocations that could lead to violent confrontations between Estonian and Russian communities. In response, the Estonian government decided to relocate the monument and the soldiers' remains to a military cemetery on the outskirts of town.

As the government prepared to move the statue, mounting tensions erupted into two nights of violent rioting, leaving up to a thousand people in police custody, hundreds injured, and one young Estonian resident with Russian citizenship, Dmitry Ganin, slain by stabbing wounds. The uproar extended into Russia as well: hundreds of protestors besieged the Estonian embassy in Moscow as members of the Russian Duma demanded the resignation of Estonian officials. Although the rioting in Estonia quickly subsided, a wave of cyber attacks unfolded for weeks against Estonia's Internet infrastructure – including the websites of banks, media, and government ministries (Traynor 2007). The timing of the attacks – and the realization that most of the activity originated from computers with Russian IP addresses – left few doubts in Estonians' minds that the attacks were Russian retaliation for the relocation of the Soviet statue. Although the newly-relocated statue was quickly re-opened to the public, including a visiting delegation of Russian politicians, relations between Estonia and Russia remained tense for months afterwards. Vladimir Putin disparaged the Estonian authorities' decision to 'desecrate monuments to war heroes' by moving the site and disinterring the remains of the soldiers beneath it (Kramer 2007).

Box 1.1   Forgetting: an overview

While much attention has been paid in recent years to analyses of memory, as this volume and journals such as *Memory Studies* attest, it is characteristic of approaches within heritage studies to consider memory as ideologically opposed to forgetting. Forgetting has long been understood as an adverse process, one which carries connotations of removal, silence, and loss; but this conception has lately undergone welcome rethinking. A brief overview of revised conceptions of the nature and work of forgetting shows that rather than being polarized against memory, the two processes are dependent upon one another, reflecting more accurately 'the tenuous relationship between remembering and forgetting' (Huyssen 1999: 196)

Contemporary strains of thought on forgetting stem from Nietzsche, who argued for its necessity in fully appreciating experience in the present: 'One who cannot leave himself behind on the threshold of the moment and forget the past ... will never know what happiness is' (Nietzsche 2005: 6). His theorization of an individual incapable of forgetting was developed by William James, who argued that perfect mnemonic recall was a sign of mental illness (as Borges' fictional *Funes el Memorioso* (1999) famously illustrates). Forgetting and oblivion are no 'malady of memory,' James argued, 'but a condition of its health and life' (James 1981: 641). Forgetting in this view (also advanced by Marc Augé (2004)) is both heralded and legitimized by its selectivity: arbitrating what is required for cognitive function and discarding what is not. David Lowenthal summarizes: 'To forget is as essential to keep things in mind, for no individual or collectivity can afford to remember everything. Total recall would leave us unable to discriminate or to generalise' (Lowenthal 1999: xi).

As noted, forgetting is frequently a politically-motivated process: one regime seeking through systematic erasure to remove the memory of another. This narrative dominates contemporary heritage studies, prompting a necessary archaeology of forgotten narratives. But as Klein has noted, the process is not always centralized, but can be accidental, gradual, even contingent – arguing that the historian's writing 'should include an open-ended diagram of what information cannot be found: the document that was tossed away; the cracks in the sidewalk where the roots of trees, now gone, lifted the street' (Klein 1999: 9). Other critics theorize forgetting differently. Huyssen suggests that the abundance of monuments in postwar Germany signals a kind of overcompensation: 'The more monuments there are, the more the past becomes invisible, the easier it is to forget: redemption, thus, through forgetting' (Huyssen 1999: 192–193). Likewise, Esbenshade, considering revisionist central European history and fiction (namely Kundera's *The Book of Laughter and Forgetting* (1982)), has argued for a more subtle interpretation: 'forgetting is not the negation of memory, something necessarily false and deceptive, but 'remembering otherwise,' another revision in a stream of constant revision and evolution' (Esbenshade 1995: 87).

Finally, Forty and Kuchler (1999) have critiqued Western models of memory, noting that in non-Western societies transience and loss are paradigms in which the process of forgetting is not merely acknowledged but revered. With this context (and critique) in mind, it is possible to develop a provisional ethics of forgetting along the same lines as Margalit (2002) has developed an ethics of memory; most recently, Ricœur has laid a firm groundwork for this theorization, but subsequent directions, like the nature of the process they describe, remain to be seen.

Benjamin Morris

References

Augé, Marc (2004) *Oblivion*. Trans. Marjolijn de Jager. Minneapolis, MN: University of Minnesota Press.

Borges, Jorge Luis (1999) 'Funes, His Memory' [*Funes el Memorioso*], in *The Collected Fictions*. Trans. Andrew Hurley. London: Penguin, pp. 131–137.

Esbenshade, Richard S. (1995) 'Remembering to Forget: Memory, History, National Identity in Postwar East-Central Europe', *Representations* 49: 72–96.

Forty, Adrian and Susanne Küchler (eds) (1999) *The Art of Forgetting*. Oxford: Berg.

Huyssen, Andreas (1999) 'Monumental Seduction', in Mieke Bal, Jonathan Crewe and Leo Spitzer (eds), *Acts of Memory: Cultural Recall in the Present*. Hanover, NH: University Press of New England, pp. 191–207.

James, William (1981) *The Principles of Psychology*. Cambridge, MA: Harvard University Press (first edition, 1890).

Klein, Norman (1999) The History of Forgetting: Los Angeles and the Erasure of Memory. London: Verso.

Kundera, Milan (1982) *The Book of Laughter and Forgetting*. Trans. Michael Henry Heim. London: Faber.

Lowenthal, David (1999) 'Preface', in Adrian Forty and Susanne Küchler (eds), *The Art of Forgetting*. Oxford: Berg, pp. xi–xiii.

Margalit, Avishai (2002) *The Ethics of Memory*. Cambridge, MA: Harvard University Press.

Nietzsche, Friedrich Wilhelm (2005) *The Use and Abuse of History.* New York: Cosimo (first edition, 1873).

Ricœur, Paul (2004) *Memory, History, Forgetting*. Trans. Kathleen Blamey and David Pellauer. Chicago: University of Chicago Press.

In other cases, sites of historical violence themselves become the objects of contests between groups with different ideas about how to commemorate the past. For example, on a remote hillside near the town of Alfácar in Spain's Granada province, a grave containing the remains of four individuals has become the focus of groups with competing perspectives on how to remember the country's Franco-era past – including those who argue that this era should not be remembered at all (Abend 2008, 2009). The Asociación para la Recuperación de la Memoria Histórica or Association for the Recovery of Historical Memory (ARMH) – a non-profit organization of volunteers who have excavated dozens of mass graves and identified over 1,700 individual victims – has publicized that the site near Alfácar may contain the remains of the renowned poet Federico García Lorca, as well as three other victims of right-wing death squads (Keeley, 2009; Woolls, 2009). The news of the group's plans to potentially unearth and identify such a high-publicity persona – García Lorca's death became a powerful symbol of the Franco regime's repression – has raised objections from some Spaniards, who argue that the implicit 'Pact of Silence' surrounding the civil war has served the country well. In their view, forensic analyses and political statements that attempt to redefine the moral framework of the civil war – to incorporate Republican victims as protagonists, rather than past enemies of the state – threatens to unravel the contemporary peace (Abend 2009). The controversy between ARMH and its critics boils down to how and whether the results of the forensic investigation are to be displayed to the public, a commemorative act that each group sees as a potential disruption to dominant interpretations of the national past (see also Dacia Viejo-Rose's chapter in this volume).

Such examples of the growing demands for repatriation of patrimony and contests over the spaces, objects, and practices of commemoration reveal the heightened stakes that individuals and groups attach to key components of their heritage, tangible and intangible alike. Indeed, the stakes of commemorative practice are often intimately bound to individual and collective identity projects. How can we comprehend the nearly simultaneous emergence of policies and practices of 'world heritage' alongside new international and national laws calling for more stringent protection of the cultural patrimony of specific (typically, national) collectives (Cuno 2008; Waxman 2008)? What are the interests of different stakeholders in calling for the right to determine where and how to house specific objects? In what sense does the value of heritage objects extend beyond the strictly monetary into intimate terrains of identity?

We suggest that a fruitful method of engaging these overarching themes – heritage, memory, and identity in an era of globalization – is by turning to a focus on *remembering* as an active process. In what follows, we present a framework for understanding collective remembering as based on mediational means, particularly on narrative frameworks that mediate our understanding of the past and their effects on our present identities. We argue that this attention to cultural mediation allows for a more coherent exploration of the relationship between identity projects based on memory and globalization practices, including the perseverance of old nationalisms and the emergence of new forms.

Our framework is not intended to present an exhaustive overview of the diversity of theories of collective memory; we recognize that alternative viewpoints can be valuable for understanding these timeless issues in new ways. Instead, our purpose is to outline a framework that engages several of the key conceptual questions that often muddle discussions of collective memory, particularly in interdisciplinary dialogues between academics who subscribe to different bodies of research – and often overlapping but divergent vocabularies – to frame their arguments. A focus on the cultural tools that mediate remembering helps us conceptualize key themes as well as communicate with researchers in a broad range of disciplines, including psychology, philosophy, anthropology, and history.

Mediational means in remembering-as-process

The unit of analysis in our framework is the 'mediated action' of human agents making use of cultural tools (Wertsch 1998). This methodological strategy is based on the recognition that humans interact with their natural and social environments by drawing on a 'tool kit' that is available to them according to their position in a social structure specific to a certain time and place (Wertsch 1998). For example, contemporary Internet communications technology is both novel, growing into a popular form only in the 1990s, and relatively limited, accessible by less than one-quarter of the world's population as of 2009 (Internetworldstats.com 2009). Yet to the millions of people who use the Internet on a daily basis, this technology has become an indispensable tool. Online community relationships that influence participants' behaviors and identities would not exist without it; many practices in business, academics, and government have been revolutionized by the instant communication and data retrieval provided by the Internet. One might venture that the experience of being 'logged on' has become a central component of the subjectivity of many humans in the contemporary world, especially those from younger generations who have never known an 'un-wired' world.

Like the Internet for those of us fortunate enough to access it, the tools that play the most important roles in our experience of the world and interactions with each other are often taken for granted by users. The quotidian familiarity of the tools, their ubiquitous presence throughout our life histories, and the nearly-universal degree of their sharedness within our local communities contribute to this invisible quality. Yet every tool, from literacy in one or more languages to familiarity with specific Internet websites, offers constraints as well as opportunities. By focusing on mediated action, we are able to take into account the irreducible tension between human agents and the cultural tools that they use, recognizing that, while tools do not mechanistically determine our behavior, they do exert substantial influences (Wertsch 2002: 6).

The particular form of mediated action that we are investigating in this chapter may be called collective memory (after Halbwachs 1980), though we share Frederic Bartlett's preference for focusing on remember*ing*, which reminds us of the active nature of the phenomenon (Bartlett 1932). Our account of collective remembering emphasizes four basic points. First, we discuss differences between individual and collective remembering, and emphasize that rich psychological research into individual memory can be fruitfully applied to help us understand collective remembering, but only with caution, as there is a need to avoid drawing simple, unsupportable analogies between the two domains. Second, we critique 'strong accounts' of collective remembering that imply the existence of a disembodied collective mind. Rather than searching for an essentialist memory '*of* the group', we propose that remembering is distributed and shared among individuals '*in* the group' (Bartlett 1932). Third, we suggest that memory can be distinguished from history as a useful analytical strategy. These represent two distinct ways of relating to the past. At the same time, however, we argue that a more developed concept of collective remembering will reveal that these two ways of relating to the past are not as neatly and easily separated as some writers have assumed. Fourth, we propose that a crucial form of mediation in collective remembering, namely narratives, can be usefully examined by invoking two levels of analysis: specific narratives that describe concrete people, places, and events; and 'schematic narrative templates' that provide the abstract frameworks that underlie any range of meaningful specific narratives in a given group (Wertsch 2002). We argue that this distinction points the way toward understanding the lasting and pervasive influence of nationalist identity on people's interpretations of the past, as well as the enormous energy that people are willing to invest in order to control objects and spaces that they see as representations of their cultural heritage.

Individual versus collective remembering

One of the most robust findings from decades of psychological research on memory is that individuals are not particularly good at retaining details. Instead of producing photographic images of the past with details intact, remembering often yields only general outlines of what happened. Daniel Schacter and his colleagues discuss this in terms of experiments that measure 'specificity', which is 'the extent to which … an individual's memory is based on retention of specific features of past experience' (Schacter et al. 2009: 83). Although there are instances in which 'memory is highly specific, and may include the precise details of a previous experience' (Schacter et al. 2009: 83), the general research finding is that memory is 'more

generic, including retention of only the general sense or gist of what happened' (2009: 83).

Psychologists point out that this general lack of specificity in memory does not indicate that memory operates in a random or unstructured way. To the contrary, they have long emphasized its proclivity for organization. The combination of losing specificity, but doing so in an organized way, was outlined nearly a century ago by Frederic Bartlett, one of the founders of modern memory studies. Bartlett asked research subjects to read or listen to stories – drawn from unfamiliar folktales of North American Indians – and then try to recall them. He found that subjects tended to recall the stories in a modified form that better fit the context of their own social environment, a process he labeled *conventionalization*: 'a process by which cultural materials coming into a group from outside are gradually worked into a pattern of a relatively stable kind distinctive of that group. The new material is assimilated to the persistent past of the group to which it comes' (Bartlett 1932: 280). This finding led Bartlett to recognize that remembering is fundamentally affected by *social* processes as well as psychological ones: subjects' memories of the stories were shaped in part by the stories themselves, but also by 'the influence of social conventions and beliefs current in the group to which the individual subject belonged' (1932: 118). Unfamiliar details tended to be replaced by more conventional ones – recalling acorns instead of the relatively unknown peanut, for example – and the narrative structures of stories were revised to omit details deemed irrelevant, 'modernize' the style of the writing, or infer motivations for characters' behaviors without any basis provided in the original story (Brewer 2000).

Bartlett's explanation for these behaviors was that remembering is an 'effort after meaning', an active process in which experiences are both stored and recalled in dialogue with one's present condition, previous experiences, and orientation toward the future. This insight allows us to bridge a methodological and conceptual gap between research on individual memory – typically the domain of psychologists – and research on collective memory by anthropologists, sociologists, and historians. Psychologists have used controlled experimental settings to focus on the capacity for individual remembering of the past, leading to important breakthroughs in our understanding of memory's accuracy and distortions (Schacter 1996;

Roediger and McDermott 2000). This tendency in psychological research to rely on an 'accuracy criterion' (Wertsch 2002) contrasts with studies of remembering at the collective level, in which memory practices are typically examined in relation to broader social processes. Studies of collective remembering thus tend to rely on historical, sociological, and textual methods to examine how groups negotiate memories to construct a 'usable past' that serves their present needs (Bodnar 1992; Hacking 1996; Wertsch 2009). From this perspective, claims about accuracy take a backseat to a narrative's authority and effectiveness.

Strong versus distributed accounts of collective memory

Once we recognize the differing methods and criteria for studying individual and collective forms of remembering, it begins to become clear why incautious borrowing of research findings across disciplinary boundaries can lead to unwieldy and misguided propositions. Although many psychologists of memory are increasingly aware of the social dimensions of individual remembering, their models remain based on the functional properties of *individual minds*. Thus, 'strong version' accounts of collective memory that refer to psychological phenomena of memory at the group level present the problematic argument, usually implicit and unrecognized, that a sort of *group mind* lies at the base of collective remembering processes (Wertsch 2002). Statements such as 'America's memory of Vietnam makes it sensitive to charges that Iraq is a quagmire' may offer an enticing and pithy image to summarize one's argument, but they are vulnerable to probing questions about the manner in which the presumed process plays out: *Where* is America's memory? *How* do Iraq-related stimuli evoke recall of Vietnam? *Who* is the agent in this formulation? And how do we explain alternative and conflicting memories within the group, if collective memory is represented as the monolithic memory '*of* the group'?

A more productive and empirically-grounded approach to collective memory relies on investigating the ways that remembering becomes shared by individual members of a community: in other words, how memory comes to be distributed '*in* the group'. The simplest illustration of distributed memory would be a hypothetical case in which every member of a group shares identical experiences, such that everyone retains a homogeneous stock of memories – a scenario that Jeffrey Olick (1999) describes as 'collected', rather than collective memory (Wertsch 2002: 25). In real social groups, of course, different individuals are prone to possessing widely divergent memories – often even of the same events. Recent research by Brian Schiff and colleagues explores the ways that each partner in 'mixed' couples may interpret past events differently, with significant impacts on their relationship and the construction of a shared 'couple identity' (Schiff et al. in this volume). Further complicating the issue, group members may share 'memories' of events that affected their group before their own birth. How can we simultaneously explain the relatively high occurrence of shared memories within groups as well as the important differences and idiosyncrasies in members' memories?

The focus on remembering as a mediated action, as described above, provides an answer to this question. Rather than assuming that memory exists only in individual minds – or 'out there' in a mysterious group mind – we argue that remembering occurs with the help of various cultural tools. These 'mnemonic tools' may include texts and hypertexts, for literate societies, as well as landscapes and place names (Basso 1996), rituals (Domínguez 1989), monuments (Doss 2008), music and dance (Coe 2005), and language itself (Cimet 2002). Among the most fundamental and influential sets of mnemonic tools are narratives, which long predate literacy and may be universally primary among human forms of cognitive organization. Discussions of narratives as 'cognitive instruments' can be found in the philosophy of history (Mink 1978; White 1980), in folklore and literary studies (Scholes and Kellogg 1966; Propp 1968), and in psychology, where 'schemas' (Bartlett 1932) and 'scripts' (Schank and Abelson 1977) are used to describe the underlying cognitive structures that humans use to make sense of the world (see also MacIntyre 1984; Bruner 1986).

In particular, narratives provide a highly influential means of distributing knowledge and memory in literate societies, exemplified most classically in the emergence of nationalist identities alongside print capitalism (Anderson 2006), in 'textual communities' that organize around religious texts (Stock 1990: 23), and in the promulgation of citizenship values through compulsory universal education in modern nation-states (Wertsch 2002). Focusing on textual mediation allows us to investigate collective remembering via the concrete connections between individuals in a social group and the cultural tools they employ, without resorting to accounts of a group mind. Focusing on texts and how they are used also illuminates one of the crucial advantages that nation-states retain in shaping collective identities. Perhaps no other institutional forces in history have employed as many resources, on such a massive scale, to influence the mnemonic tools that shape group members during their upbringing. As Ernest Gellner noted, 'The monopoly of legitimate education is now more important, more central than the monopoly of legitimate violence' (1983: 34). The most important power of nation-states no longer lies in coercive forces but in the control of citizens' subjectivities.

The immense efforts of national governments to control historical narratives and collective remembering must be understood in a critical perspective. Nations are not, after all, natural or spontaneous formations; they are not even particularly old inventions (Hobsbawm and Ranger 1983). Yet the architects of nation-states activated a form of political organization and subjectivity – nationalism – that has had enormous consequences for the natural and social world. The constructed, always emergent nation-state depends on nationalism for a legitimate basis, a mythic-historical promise of primordial belonging. This tension sets the context for anxieties over education reform as well as other changes to a society's commemorative practices, such as those illustrated in the examples that began this chapter. Whether the protests are rationalized in explicit terms – such as Lynne Cheney's calls to rewrite US historical curriculum after September 11 in order to avoid moral ambiguities and boost patriotism (Wertsch 2009) – or simply express feelings of discomfort with proposed changes, the motivation may be traced to anxieties over the very fate of the social collective. Challenges to the national narrative, or to commemorative practices or important objects and sites of heritage, are threats to the roots of the nation.

Memory versus history

The controversy that arose around Lynn Cheney's proposal, as well as with many other examples of 'textbook wars' around the world (Pingel 2008;

Schneider 2008), can be more clearly understood if we make an analytical distinction between memory and history. Some scholars have articulated substantial differences between the two forms of representing the past. Peter Novick (2000: 3) sees the two in an opposition where memory is 'in crucial senses ahistorical, even anti-historical' (1999). Whereas memory resists the impression of change (though it *does* change over time), history is deeply invested in documenting changes over time, as well as adapting the narrative to fit new information about the past (Nora 1989). This historical consciousness is based in certain literacy practices wherein successive accounts of the past are compiled in textual form and the role of the historian emerges through practices of comparing, evaluating, and synthesizing these accounts, ideally to arrive at a more accurate and objective depiction of the past. The actual techniques of professional historiography (de Certeau 1992; Trouillot 1995) serve as a limit point for the production of legitimate historical narratives in most Western societies; however, it may be reasonably assumed that every society recognizes different levels of truth-claiming through different forms of narratives about the past. Arjun Appadurai (1981) reminds us that rules about 'the debatability of the past' exist for all human groups, though these rules vary widely by context and by period.

Though the rules that distinguish them may vary, both memory and history share similarities in terms of how they are organized and how they function. Namely, both history and memory draw upon narrative forms to make sense of the information they present. Scholars such as Louis Mink (1978) and Hayden White (1980) have raised key questions about the possibility for *any* narrative-based claim to truth to be truly objective. As Mink explains, the practice of writing history involves combining various details about events into a narrative structure which *explains* the events and their interrelationships. While it may be possible to judge the accuracy of any given detail, the question of the accuracy of a narrative as a whole, or 'narrative truth', cannot be resolved through empirical evidence. It always involves an act of judgement (Mink 1978: 198–199). The complexities arise, according to White, because the use of narrative impels historians to impart an order and a moral significance to the events of the past, a project of which he is skeptical: 'Does the world really present itself to perception in the form of well-made stories, with central subjects, proper beginnings, middles, and ends, and a coherence that permits us to see "the end" in every beginning?' (White 1980: 27). The inevitability of resorting to narrative structures to make sense of the world – and to communicate this significance to others – thus points to essential similarities between history and memory.

Nevertheless, there *are* critical distinctions between representations of the past that claim authority as history, and others that appeal to different forms of authority for group members' loyalties. As Trouillot put it, one who mimics the narrative forms and practices that define historical text, while fabricating their sources and inventing details, has broken the rules: they 'have not written fiction, [they] have produced a fake' (Trouillot 1995: 6–7). We might say that the inverse of Peter Novick's argument is also true: history is anti-memorial, defined in opposition to memory according to historians' desires to provide more objective, comprehensive, and analytically complex representations of the past. Whereas collective remembering is most effective at reinforcing group identity when its representations are simple, unambiguous, and able to elicit strong emotional responses, historical accounts are judged by their critical distance from the objects of description.

The upshot is that we take memory and history as two points on a continuum for representing the past. Any given text, object, or other mnemonic tool might be evaluated to recognize ways in which it serves multiple functions and draws upon different forms of authority. Take, for example, the official national narratives that are enshrined in school textbooks and disseminated to the youth of any given nation: although they are used in what we call history instruction, to what extent are they better recognized as tools for collective memory? Though there are differences of degree, textbooks typically present the past through a perspective that casts the reader's national identity group as the protagonist and central actor (Wertsch 2002). Consequently, textbooks offer an excellent opportunity to study states' official mnemonic-historical accounts – their national narratives – in a textual form.

Specific narratives versus schematic narrative templates

An underlying assumption of our analysis is that humans are story-telling animals; that is, they draw upon narrative structures to make sense of their experiences. And from this perspective there are at least two levels of narrative analysis that can help characterize the tensions between agents and narratives in 'mnemonic communities' (Zerubavel 2003). First, there is a level concerned with 'specific narratives', which include information about concrete places, actors, and actions. Specific narratives exist, for example, about the American Civil War from 1861 to 1865 and about particular events like the Battle of Gettysburg in 1863. A hallmark of narratives at this level of analysis is that they include concrete dates, actors, and places.

Standing in contrast to specific narratives are 'narrative templates', which are general, schematic forms of representation that lack the specificity found at the first level of analysis. From this perspective narrative tools act as underlying codes that differ from one mnemonic community to another. The notion of a template implies that a storyline is used by members of a community to emplot multiple specific events. In some cases, this is reflected in events' very appellation. Consider, for example, the ways in which the colossal conflict of 1941–1945 is referred to in the Russian mnemonic community. Much of what is known as World War II in the USA is called the Great Fatherland War (Великая Отечественная война) in Russia, an expression that echoes 'Fatherland War' (Отечественная война), or what in the West is known as the Napoleonic War of 1812. In contrast to the Russian terminology, which suggests that the two events are instantiations of the same underlying plot line, there is no such suggestion in Western terms for these events. The parallels between the two events are further evidenced in other ways as well. Consider, for example, the fact that the expression 'Hitler as a second Napoleon' has long enjoyed widespread usage in the Russian mnemonic community. While members of other collectives may be able to understand what it means to call Hitler a second Napoleon, the fact that this is not a standard expression for them supports the existence of different underlying codes for remembering the past.

The underlying code in this case for Russia can be outlined as the 'Expulsion-of-Foreign-Enemies' narrative template (Wertsch 2009a), which includes the following elements:

1 An initial setting in which Russia is peaceful and not interfering with others.

2 A foreign enemy attacks Russia without provocation.
3 Russia nearly loses everything in total defeat as it suffers from the enemy's attempts to destroy it as a civilization.
4 Through heroism and exceptionalism, against all odds, and acting alone, Russia triumphs and succeeds in expelling the foreign enemy.

This narrative template contains the basic story line of the Fatherland War and the Great Fatherland War, but its application extends far beyond these two events for the Russian mnemonic community. Russians often speak of a litany of alien invaders, including Tatars, Germans, Swedes, Poles, Turks, and Germans again. In short, this is a pattern of telling the same story with different characters, of employing the same underlying code to speak about multiple specific events. From the perspective of outsiders, this may lead to over-generalization, if not paranoia. For example, what appears to Estonians as a normal quest for freedom and a desire to pursue their future in Western Europe has been perceived in Russia as part of a NATO effort to encroach on its sphere of influence and fundamentally threaten its security (Wertsch 2009a).

A striking fact about narrative templates is the very generic form of representation that they employ. Indeed, a given narrative template may be so abstract and generic that it would appear to be usable by other national mnemonic communities. What grounds narrative templates in the national, however, is that along with their abstracting tendency they encourage a tendency toward what Jan Assmann (2005) calls 'ethnocentric narcissism'. In the Expulsion-of-Foreign-Enemies narrative template, this is reflected in the mention of Russia throughout. Even though the plot line might be generic, it is taken by the Russian mnemonic community as a story about *them*, not some other group. Hence national narrative templates and the mental habits associated with them constrain people to see the world from a particular bounded perspective, one that often precludes the recognition of alternatives. By taking possession of a single group-based perspective on past events – one that for most contemporary people is rooted in the structure of a nation-state – individuals tend to close themselves off from other viewpoints, often without ever consciously realizing it.

The idea of narrative templates may be traced to several sources, including the Russian folklorist Vladimir Propp, who focused on the recurring 'functions' found in many folktales rather than on particular characters and events (1968: 21). A cognitive analog of these templates may be found in Bartlett's concept of 'schemata', generalized patterns of thought and behavior that may go unnoticed, yet provide a means of orientation and self-understanding for people in their day-to-day lives (Bartlett 1932). And in more contemporary psychological research one encounters concepts of 'cultural life scripts' that illustrate repertoires of meaningful life choices recognized by many individuals within a group, though the sets of scripts vary from one group to another (Berntsen and Bohn 2009). Similar ideas are expressed in anthropological concepts of 'doxa' (Bourdieu 1977: 168) or 'cultural logics' (Fischer 2001), the latter proposed as an 'anti-anti-essentialist' (Gilroy 1993) stance that recognizes continuity and commonality in groups despite significant individual variations among members.

A potential pitfall of this line of reasoning is that it might seem to suggest a naturalization of the differences we encounter between national communities, a tendency to view them as matters of static essence. The key to avoiding this pitfall is to recognize the complexity of mediated action as the unit of analysis. From this perspective, the relationship between humans and cultural tools – including especially the narratives that help organize our representations of, and relationships to, the past – is not one of mechanistic determinism. While a focus on the enormous resources devoted by nation-states to educating their citizens is necessary, we must also consider the ways that individuals *consume* such textual resources (Wertsch 2002: 117). While citizen-subjects may play along with the rules set by top-down power structures – e.g., by mastering official national narratives in order to pass examinations and gain social mobility – it is not difficult to find instances where these same individuals are deeply distrustful of the government and media. This may be reflected in what de Certeau (1984) termed 'strategies of consumption', but they often take on more subtle and interesting forms of 'tactics of consumption'. In the latter case, individuals operate as 'guerrillas' on the textual territory of powerful authorities, but do so in an intentionally or even unintentionally subversive way.

In sum, the underlying codes of national narrative templates reflect the operation of two seemingly opposing tendencies: one toward nonspecific, generic representation that would seem to apply to several mnemonic communities and the other toward the unique perspective of ethnocentric narcissism. The latter property of the cultural tools that mediate collective identity projects often makes it difficult for group members to appreciate the perspectives of others. In extreme cases this can take the form of the 'sealed narratives' that Thomas de Waal (2003) identified as encouraging the bloody standoff between Azerbaijanis and Armenians in Nagorny Karabakh. Such tendencies are aided by the absence of specific information in narrative templates, which makes them largely unfalsifiable and hence impervious to objections by others grounded in empirical evidence. As Rogers Smith (2003) has noted in his analysis of 'stories of peoplehood', only extreme, traumatic events seem to be capable of shaking a collective's account of the past.

National narratives *vis-à-vis* globalization

Our discussion has focused on conflicts and processes at the national level for several reasons. As noted above, nation-states are historically unparalleled in their commitment to subject formation, and the production of national narratives has played a defining role in these efforts. Additionally, national communities are exemplary of the concept of 'imagined community', a circumstance that permits us to examine how practices of collective remembering extend beyond the level of individuals who directly experience events, to consider how group identities are constructed around shared narratives about the past (Anderson 2006). Beyond these methodological concerns, however, we identify other key reasons for focusing on national memory projects. While globalization has been described by some as a process of de-nationalization, the persistent role of national narratives suggests that national identity projects are still very much in force. Even in the face of increasing globalization – or more specifically, new technologies of communication, media, and transportation that allow for rapid, low-cost flows of people and information – and the proliferation of collective identity projects outside the normal bounds of nation-states, these projects still often take the shape of nationalisms. The reasons for this pattern are to be found, in part, by examining the influential role of international political and

economic organizations such as the European Union and United Nations, and the powerful spatializing efforts of nation-states the world over to naturalize their claims to territory.

Transcending negative and often dangerous national perspectives and the collective memories that underlie them will require discussions in the public sphere that begin by recognizing alternative viewpoints. As suggested by de Waal's analysis of the sealed narratives that isolate the protagonists in Nagorny Karabakh, as well as many other 'mnemonic standoffs' (Wertsch 2008), it can be extremely difficult to engage in such discussions. To begin this engagement, parties require a sense of self-reflection and humility, along with a recognition of the irony that may accompany national narratives (Niebuhr 1952). They also need to recognize and resist the temptation to conflate solid historical analysis and collective remembering. When the latter masquerades as the former, opposing parties all too often are reduced to trading charges of being brainwashed or of lying. While being realistic about the forces at work in such cases, courageous and thoughtful counter-examples can be found, and these can provide the inspiration for new efforts elsewhere.

For example, consider recent cultural and linguistic revitalization efforts among Maya communities of Guatemala. In the past three decades, the rise of a Maya intellectual class has permitted the creation of literature that features indigenous perspectives on local, national, and global events. Among the genres and themes that characterize Maya literature and knowledge production, the development of indigenous perspectives on 'historical memory' has been one of the most fraught with controversy. The Guatemalan past is filled with traumatic violence, typically following a pattern of the elite-dominated state committing atrocities against the indigenous majority – during the Spanish invasion, during the liberal reforms of the nineteenth century, and most recently in the horrific civil war, known locally as 'the Violence'. The dominant narrative explanations of these events typically gloss over the Maya or acknowledge them only as passive victims of inevitable historical forces like the birth of the Guatemalan nation or the Cold War (Montejo 2005).

Consequently, many Maya intellectuals and their allies consider it crucial that the national history be revised to incorporate the majority of citizens who have traditionally been excluded. They have pursued a variety of strategies to encourage the emergence of a more inclusive, intercultural national consciousness, including highly qualified scholarship that fleshes out the details of the past and contributes information about alternative explanations and perspectives – in other words, history. However, the more pressing need identified by Maya leaders is for the emergence of a pan-Maya identity that could lead to mobilization for political reforms. In order to understand this project *vis-à-vis* the political *status quo* in Guatemala, it is helpful to draw on the framework of national narratives, as described above. On the one hand, new historical research that complicates the dominant, monolithic portrayal of the past *may* force a wider public acknowledgement of the roles and rights of Maya citizens. In this sense, the Maya intellectual project represents a challenge to the Guatemalan national narrative to become more inclusive. This battle over the past is played out in many forms on a daily basis, including commemorative practices such as public exhumations of victims' graves, funerary marches and rituals, and the building of peace parks and monuments to victims of the Violence.

Simultaneously, the Maya project may be understood as an attempt to create an altogether alternative narrative that puts the experiences and perspectives of the Maya at its center. Kay Warren found that Maya intellectuals pursued a 'Benedict Anderson strategy' to try to promote a pan-Maya consciousness (1998), a strategy that does not insist on complete loyalty to one or another existing sealed narrative. These processes have led to subtle yet significant shifts in identity. Whereas 'Maya' as a category of self-description was rarely used a few decades ago, this term has become nearly ubiquitous today. Individuals are more likely to self-identify as Maya or indigenous, or as a member of a specific Mayan language community such as Mam or K'iche'. From this perspective, Maya efforts are constrained by the difficulty of challenging a pre-existing Guatemalan national narrative that informs the worldview of the Spanish-speaking *ladino* population, as well as lingering distrust of government among many Maya communities that were affected by the Violence. Despite this disengagement from the dominant forces in Guatemala, there is little evidence of political will toward seceding from the Guatemalan state. Even the more radical and explicit articulations of a pan-Maya political agenda retain a focus on the Guatemalan state as the object and context for reform, such as calls for revising departmental political boundaries to reflect the territories of Guatemala's twenty-two Mayan linguistic communities.

REFERENCES

Abend, Lisa (2008) 'At Last, Spain Faces Up to Franco's Guilt.' Time.com, 17 October 2008. Online: www.time.com/time/world/article/0,8599,1851334,00.html. Accessed 11 November 2009.

—— (2009) 'Exhuming Lorca's Remains – and Franco's Ghosts.' Time.com, 29 October 2009. Online: www.time.com/time/world/article/0,8599,1932879,00.html?xid=rss-topstories. Accessed 11 November 2009.

Anderson, Benedict (2006) *Imagined Communities: Reflections on the Origin and Spread of Nationalism*. Revised edition. New York: Verso.

Appadurai, Arjun (1981) 'The past as a scarce resource.' *Man* 6(2): 201–219.

Assmann, Jan (2005) 'Cultural Memories and National Narratives: with Some Relation to the Case Of Georgia', *Caucasus Context* 3(1): 40–43.

Bartlett, Frederic C. (1932) *Remembering: A Study in Experimental and Social Psychology*. Cambridge: Cambridge University Press.

Basso, Keith (1996) *Wisdom Sits in Places: Landscape and Language among the Western Apache*. Albuquerque, NM: University of New Mexico Press.

Berntsen, Dorthe and Annette Bohn (2009) 'Cultural Life Scripts and Individual Life Stories,' in Pascal Boyer and James V. Wertsch (eds), *Memory in Mind and Culture*. New York: Cambridge University Press, pp. 62–82.

Bodnar, J. (1992) *Remarking America: Public Memory, Commemoration, and Patriotism in the Twentieth Century*. Princeton, NJ: Princeton University Press.

Bourdieu, Pierre (1977) *Outline of a Theory of Practice*. Cambridge: Cambridge University Press.

Brewer, William F. (2000) 'Bartlett's Concept of the Schema and Its Impact on Theories of Knowledge Representation in Contemporary Cognitive Psychology,' in Akiko Saito (ed.), *Bartlett, Culture and Cognition*. London: Psychology Press.

Bruner, J. (1986) *Actual Minds, Possible Worlds*. Cambridge, MA: Harvard University Press.

Cimet, Adina (2002) 'Symbolic Violence and Language: Mexico and Its Uses of Symbols,' in Jacob J. Climo and Maria G. Cattell (eds), *Social Memory and History: Anthropological Perspectives*. Lanham, MA: AltaMira Press, pp.143–160.

Coe, Cati (2005) *Dilemmas of Culture in African Schools: Youth, Nationalism, and the Transformation of Knowledge*. Chicago: University of Chicago Press.

Cuno, James (2008) *Who Owns Antiquity? Museums and the Battle over our Ancient Heritage*. Princeton, NJ: Princeton University Press.

de Certeau, Michel (1984) *The Practice of Everyday Life*. Trans. Steven Rendall. Berkeley, CA: University of California Press.

—— (1992) *The Writing of History*. New York: Columbia University Press.

de Waal, Thomas (2003) *Black Garden: Armenia and Azerbaijan through Peace and War*. New York: New York University Press.

Domínguez, Virginia R. (1989) *People as Subject, People as Object: Selfhood and Peoplehood in Contemporary Israel*. Madison, WI: University of Wisconsin Press.

Doss, Erika (2008) 'War, Memory, and the Public Mediation of Affect: The National World War II Memorial and American Imperialism.' *Memory Studies* 1: 227–250.

Ellis, Joseph (1997) 'Right Time, Wrong Place.' *New York Times*, 24 March, p. A-21.

Fischer, Edward F. (2001) *Cultural Logics and Global Economies: Maya Identity in Thought and Practice*. Austin, TX: University of Texas Press.

Gellner, Ernst (1983) *Nations and Nationalism*. Ithaca, NY: Cornell University Press.

Gilroy, Paul (1993) *The Black Atlantic: Modernity and Double Consciousness*. Cambridge, MA: Harvard University Press.

Hacking, I. (1996) 'Memory Sciences, Memory Politics,' in P. Antze and M. Lambek (eds), *Tense Past: Cultural Essays in Trauma and Memory*. New York: Routledge, pp. 67–87.

Halbwachs, Maurice (1980) *The Collective Memory*. Trans. Francis J. Didder, Jr. and Vida Yazdi Ditter. New York: Harper & Row.

Hawass, Zahi (2009) 'Dr. Hawass Calls for Return of Stolen Artifact.' Press release. Online: www.drhawass.com/blog/press-release-dr-hawass-calls-return-stolen-artifact. Accessed 28 October 2009.

Hobsbawm, Eric and Terence Ranger (1983) *The Invention of Tradition*. New York: Cambridge University Press.

Internetworldstats.com (2009) 'Internet Usages Statistics: The Internet Big Picture: World Internet Users and Population Stats.' Miniwatts Marketing Group. Online: www.internetworldstats.com/stats.htm. Accessed 11 November 2009.

Keeley, Graham (2009) 'Archaeologists Dig for Remains of Spain's Federico Garcia Lorca.' Times Online, 26 October 2009. Online: www.timesonline.co.uk/tol/news/world/europe/article6889652.ece. Accessed 11 November 2009.

Kimmelman, Michael (2009) 'When Ancient Artifacts Become Political Pawns.' *New York Times*, 23 October 2009. Online: www.nytimes.com/2009/10/24/arts/design/24abroad.html?_r=1&partner=rss&emc=rss. Accessed 1 November 2009.

Kramer, Andrew E. (2007) 'Putin Likens U.S. Foreign Policy to That of Third Reich.' *International Herald Tribune*, 9 May 2007. Online: www.nytimes.com/2007/05/09/world/europe/09iht-russia.4.5642323.html?_r=1. Accessed 11 November 2009.

MacIntyre, A. (1984) *After Virtue: A Study in Moral Theory*. Notre Dame, IN: University of Notre Dame Press.

Mink, Louis O. (1978) 'Narrative Form as a Cognitive Instrument,' in Robert H. Canary and Henry Kozicki (eds), *The Writing of History: Literary Form and Historical Understanding*. Madison, WI: University of Wisconsin Press, pp.129–149.

Montejo, Victor (2005) *Maya Intellectual Renaissance: Identity, Representation, and Leadership*. Austin, TX: University of Texas Press.

Niebuhr, Reinhold (2008) *The Irony of American History*. Chicago: University of Chicago Press.

Nora, Pierre (1989) 'Between Memory and History: Les Lieux de Memoire.' *Representations* 26(Spring): 7–25.

Novick, Peter (2000) *The Holocaust in American Life*. Boston: Houghton Mifflin.

Olick, Jeffrey (1999) 'Collective Memory: The Two Cultures.' *Sociological Theory* 17(3): 333–348.

Pingel, Falk (2008) 'Can Truth Be Negotiated? History Textbook Revision as a Means to Reconciliation.' *The ANNALS of the American Academy of Political and Social Science* 617: 181–198.

Propp, V. (1968) *Morphology of the Folktale*. Trans. Laurence Scott. Printed translation of Morfologija skazki, 1928. Austin, TX: University of Texas Press.

Roediger, H.L. and K.B. McDermott (2000) 'Distortions of Memory,' in E. Tulving and F.I.M. Craik (eds), *The Oxford Handbook of Memory*. Oxford: Oxford University Press, pp. 149–162.

Romey, Kristin M. (2004) 'Flashpoint Ayodhya.' *Archaeology* 57(4).

—— (2006) 'Flashpoint Ayodhya,' in Karen D. Vitelli and Chip Colwell-Chanthaphonh (eds), *Archaeological Ethics*. Second edition. Lanham, MD: AltaMira Press.

Schacter, Daniel L. (ed.) (1996) *Searching for Memory: The Brain, the Mind, and the Past*. New York: Basic Books.

—— Angela H. Gutchess, and Elizabeth A. Kensinger (2009) 'Specificity of Memory: Implications for Individual and Collective Remembering,' in Pascal Boyer and James V. Wertsch (eds), *Memory in Mind and Culture*. New York: Cambridge University Press, pp. 83–111.

Schank, Roger and Robert P. Abelson (1977) *Scripts, Plans, Goals, and Understanding: An Inquiry into Human*

Knowledge Structures. Hillsdale, NJ: Lawrence Erlbaum Associates.

Scholes, R. and R. Kellogg (1966) *The Nature of Narrative*. Oxford: Oxford University Press.

Schneider, Claudia (2008) 'The Japanese History Textbook Controversy in East Asian Perspective.' *The ANNALS of the American Academy of Political and Social Science* 617: 107–122.

Smith, Rogers M. (2003) *Stories of Peoplehood: The Politics and Morals of Political Membership*. New York: Cambridge University Press.

Stock, Brian (1990) *Listening for the Text: On the Uses of the Past*. Philadelphia, PA: University of Pennsylvania Press.

Traynor, Ian (2007) 'Russia Accused of Unleashing Cyberwar to Disable Estonia.' *The Guardian*, 17 May 2007. Online: www.guardian.co.uk/world/2007/may/17/topstories3. russia. Accessed 11 November 2009.

Trouillot, Michel Rolph (1995) *Silencing the Past: Power and the Production of History*. Boston, MA: Beacon Press.

Warren, Kay (1998) *Indigenous Movements and Their Critics: Pan-Maya Activism in Guatemala*. Princeton, NJ: Princeton University Press.

Waxman, Sharon (2008) *Loot: The Battle over Stolen Treasures of the Ancient World*. New York: Times Books.

Wertsch, James V. (1998) *Mind as Action*. New York: Oxford University Press.

—— (2002) *Voices of Collective Remembering*. New York: Cambridge University Press.

—— (2008) 'A Clash of Deep Memories.' *Profession*. 48, pp. 46–53.

—— (2009) 'Collective Memory,' in Pascal Boyer and James V. Wertsch (eds), *Memory in Mind and Culture*. New York: Cambridge University Press, pp.117–137.

White, Hayden (1980) 'The Value of Narrativity in the Representation of Reality.' *Critical Inquiry* 7(1), pp. 5–27.

Woolls, Daniel (2009) 'Spain: Garcia Lorca Grave to be Opened in Weeks'. *Associated Press*, 5 October 2009.

Zerubavel, Eviatar (2003) *Time Maps: Collective Memory and the Social Shape of the Past*. Chicago: University of Chicago Press.

CHAPTER 2

UNESCO AND HERITAGE: GLOBAL DOCTRINE, GLOBAL PRACTICE

Yudhishthir Raj Isar

This chapter explores the ways in which the global scripts of 'World Heritage' and 'Intangible Heritage' have been propagated by the United Nations Educational, Scientific and Cultural Organization (UNESCO) and associated international bodies. It discusses how certain ideas and principles in the now globalized heritage discourse, originally elaborated in the Euro-American cultural space, have been extended and/or challenged elsewhere. The analysis also examines the ways in which stakes of power and prestige in the global intergovernmental arena have influenced the global unfolding of these questions. A set of ideas about heritage, supposedly universal, were the expression of a Western particularism still powerful enough to universalize itself. But in a changed and rapidly changing world, some of these formerly 'central' prescriptions have been challenged and new ones have been articulated in the erstwhile 'periphery'.

Heritage preservation has become a global cult, with all that this cult status entails in terms of doctrine and forms of practice. Like the notions of 'memory' and 'identity', the notion of 'heritage' has become a global script, indeed a discursive formation, in the sense discussed in the Introduction to this volume, and raises conjoined issues of practice, policy and politics. This cult of 'The Heritage' (Hall, 2005) – is served by a community of believers consisting of thousands of men and women working professionally across the world, individually or in institutions, as well as by large numbers of supporters and well-wishers, not to mention visitors, spectators and patrons who pay for the workings of the worldwide heritage industry.

The theory and practice of 'The Heritage' have been moulded internationally by the standard-setting efforts of the United Nations Educational, Scientific and Cultural Organization (UNESCO), alongside which several international non-governmental organizations have also worked, notably for our purposes the International Council on Monuments and Sites (ICOMOS).[1] These NGOs are global networks of specialists, epistemic communities in the true sense of the word, i.e. knowledge-based communities politically empowered through their command of authoritative knowledge and motivated by shared causal and principled beliefs (Haas, 1992).[2] Yet their operations, although independent, have also been strongly influenced by the imperatives of nation-state prestige and representation, which I shall explore below. This UNESCO-led alliance of bodies and groups has advanced the cause of heritage as a global public good, the notion of 'World Heritage', the shared legacy of all humanity, being its highest expression. Yet the public good has also been an eminently private one as well, as it has become the core asset of a tourism-led 'heritage industry'. Thus, as Tim Winter will argue in this volume, there are also global economies of heritage. My main emphasis here, however, will be on the *discursive practice*, on the ways in which a global belief system and ethos elaborated originally in Europe and North America in the 1960s has been globalized.[3] I shall therefore examine the ways in which the Eurocentric or exclusionary features of this heritage ethos have been addressed in other continents, how some of these have been contested, and the manner in which the scope of 'The Heritage' has been expanded to encompass the memories and identities of a plural world.

We attempt throughout this volume to explore three terms together: heritage, memory, identity. My treatment here of UNESCO's normative activity (see Box 2.1 below), emphasizes *heritage*, however, for in the discursive world of UNESCO and its allies, the term 'memory' has been little used – no doubt because it is a bit too abstract for the the world of international cultural diplomacy – and when present it has been a rhetorical figure.[4] 'Identity', on the other hand, has been a central trope and a frequent discursive companion to 'heritage'. Yet the word does not figure in the 1972

Convention Concerning the Protection of the World Cultural and Natural Heritage (commonly called the World Heritage Convention). On the other hand, the 2003 *Convention for the Safeguarding of the Intangible Cultural Heritage,* in defining what is meant by 'intangible cultural heritage', states that the latter is 'transmitted from generation to generation, is constantly recreated by communities and groups in response to their environment, their interaction with nature and their history, and provides them with a sense of *identity* and continuity...' Despite this, the process by which the scope of heritage has been considerably broadened and also divided into the binary of material/immaterial (or tangible and intangible in the current UNESCO usage) has taken its own independent course.

Box 2.1　The intergovernmental elaboration of global norms

Although today the United Nations Organization and all its Specialized Agencies, such as UNESCO, would readily describe themselves as 'global' institutions, the UN system came into being before our contemporary awareness of globality. The UN was a quintessentially modernist project, designed to realize the Kantian vision of peace and security among nation-states. UNESCO's core purpose was to build peace through the educational, scientific and cultural relations of the 'peoples of the world'. This meant governments. But as the vocabulary of the 'global' took hold in the late 1980s, international intergovernmental organizations were quick to join the bandwagon. Indeed, many of the standard accounts of globalization cite the worldwide propagation of legal and ethical norms by international organization as one of its key non-economic characteristics. By the early 1990s, then, UNESCO would be claiming global reach for the key functions it performs, and could legitimately be recognized as doing so, e.g. by acting not only as a standard-setter but also as a capacity-builder, or as a forum for international public debate, or a bridge-builder (during the Cold War, between ideological blocs, subsequently mainly along the North–South axis). However, with respect to all of these roles, leading agency has always been vested 'in Member States' – in other words, governments.

Yet UNESCO has always sought to act and represent itself as a sort of 'brains trust' at the service of humankind as a whole. Public opinion has shared this perception, even making it an expectation: in 1956 Jawaharlal Nehru famously but hyperbolically characterized UNESCO as 'the conscience of the world'. In this capacity, it has been a 'laboratory of ideas' or 'clearing house' on a range of global issues and its normative production has become global doctrine. Many see the organization as principally a 'standard-setting' institution. This dimension was mentioned in the Organization's Constitution, but restricted therein to the 'free flow of ideas by word and image' (indeed, the first instrument adopted was the 1948 Agreement for Facilitating the International Circulation of Visual and Auditory Materials of an Educational, Scientific and Cultural Character). But very quickly, the standard-setting role came to be deployed far more broadly, primarily through *Agreements* and *Conventions* (35 adopted), which are fully-fledged international treaties that create inter-state obligations. Less binding than Conventions are *Recommendations* (31 adopted), setting out principles and norms for the international regulation of procedure and practice related to a particular issue.

Finally, *Declarations* articulate seminal principles and ideas (13 adopted). Culture, understood as the arts and heritage, is the domain in which UNESCO's most significant standard-setting work has been done, beginning with the *Convention for the Protection of Cultural Property in the Event of Armed Conflict*, adopted in 1954 at The Hague, and followed by a total of 25 instruments in all the three categories cited above. The most notable are the two international treaties referred to already in the chapter, which are commonly referred to as the 'World Heritage Convention' and the 'Cultural Diversity Convention'.

The global propagation of these norms of belief and practice has been an uneven and sometimes uneasy process. Many points of doctrine and methodology have been globalized quite smoothly, others less so. Some have even been contested in the non-Western world. But far more than just ideas have been at stake, for heritage preservation has been incorporated into a worldwide political economy in which notions of the right, the good and the true have jostled with national interests, power relationships and prestige. As both the standard-setting and the acquisition of prestige have played out internationally, there have been diverging interpretations of *what* constitutes heritage and *how* it should best be safeguarded and handed down. Key lines of divergence have emerged at UNESCO. Before exploring these, however, I shall discuss some key features of the functioning of that organization as a locus of intergovernmental cultural politics.[5]

Box 2.2 Return or restitution of cultural property

Another heritage cause has been wholly contentious right from the start: the 'return of cultural property to its countries of origin or its restitution in case of illicit appropriation' (the cumbersome UNESCO term). Unlike World Heritage and cognate notions, which derive from an inherent 'good', this set of issues stems from the global 'bad' targeted by UNESCO's 1970 *Convention on the Means of Prohibiting and Preventing the Illicit Import, Export and Transfer of Ownership of Cultural Property*. The heritage concerned here consists of movable objects, and the issue revolves around the conditions and causes of their mobility. Both museums and archaeological sites, mainly in countries of the global South, have long been and still are robbed or looted for the benefit of buyers who are mainly in the global North. Global culturalist doctrine holds that governments are entitled to prevent the export of movable objects from their territories; indeed, that they have a duty to maintain the national stock of 'cultural property'. Most states have enacted legislation for this purpose, yet many are ill-equipped to implement it and the illicit trade in cultural artefacts is fuelled by high demand, principally in the industrially developed world. Although some specialists decry the futility, if not the perverse effects, of limiting trade in cultural objects, a consensus has emerged among governments and in the public at large that trafficking is a global bad. But this consensus does not apply to the movement of objects that occurred in the past, during the colonial period. The notion that countries holding such objects today should return them to their countries of origin is not only a North–South bone of contention in international cultural politics, but also in certain national settings, e.g. Native American claims for the repatriation of objects from museum collections to their communities (see the chapter by Wertsch and Billingsley earlier in this volume). Does such repatriation of cultural objects truly contribute to the cosmopolitan enterprise of cross-cultural understanding? Does it ensure the best possible transmission of heritage to future generations of global citizens (Appiah, 2006)? Is what seems to be a 'good' on the global canvas actually a 'bad'? The debate is ongoing (Isar, 2009).

The global economy of prestige

Any locus of international cultural politics is also an arena for the confrontation of ideas, interests and power with respect to symbolic meanings. Yet UNESCO's discourse privileges a kind of ideal Kantian internationalism. Phrases in its Constitution, such as the following, could also be construed as a sort of post-war international cultural diplomacy *urtext*: 'States Parties ... are agreed and determined to develop and to increase the means of communication between their peoples and to employ these means for the purposes of mutual understanding and a truer and more perfect knowledge of each other's lives.' As the organization's core mission was to construct 'the defences of peace in the minds of men', the assumption was that culture was a beneficent higher attribute that should be deployed for this purpose. Culture and cultural cooperation would help attain the overarching peace-building objective. Yet they were not limited to this instrumental role. It was not simply a question of what culture could do for UNESCO, but also about what UNESCO could do for culture – hence by extension, for the cultures of its Member States. The services thus rendered to national cultures were to become both technical and representational.

To be sure, nation-states have always also championed issues and causes for reasons of principle determined by their respective national value systems and traditions. Yet for nation-states operating in the UN organizations, adopting positions of principle has also been a way of marking territory and control in ideological and discursive terms. In other words, nations use these organizations – they are, after all, 'their' organizations – to try to make their own meanings both dominant and authoritative (Isar, 2010). The anthropologist Susan Wright, who sat in on the work of a Drafting Committee at the Intergovernmental Conference on Cultural Policies for Development held in Stockholm in 1998, remarked on how 'the delegates of the member states were asserting their power to limit definitions of "culture" for development to those compatible with various "national cultures"' (Wright, 1998: 177). Wright also identified the different 'ways that "culture" was being linked in a new semantic cluster with "creativity," "diversity," "development," "participation" and "freedom"' and the ways in which 'differently positioned actors draw on, stretch or challenge an accumulation of meanings of

"culture" (and) try to make their meaning "stick"' (1998: 175).

Earlier, in 1982, a graphic illustration of such positioning was provided by the US Delegation to the World Conference on Cultural Policies in Mexico City. This was in the second year of the first Reagan administration, during which the influence of the neo-conservative right, led by the Heritage Foundation (no terminological coincidence was intended), was to lead the US to leave UNESCO. In Mexico as well, a conference drafting group produced the 'Mexico City Declaration', containing, *inter alia*, the very broad definition of culture that has since become canonical in UNESCO's world. This definition follows (note the phrase I have emphasised).

> culture may now be said to be the whole complex of distinctive spiritual, material, intellectual and emotional features that characterize a society or social group. It includes not only the arts and letters, but also modes of life, the fundamental rights of the human being, *values systems, traditions and beliefs...*

The words 'the fundamental rights of the human being' may appear somewhat incongruous in this setting; in fact they were added at the adamant insistence of the US delegation. All American diplomats were mindful of the coded significance, in Cold War ideological warfare, of the notion of individual human rights, as opposed to collective rights and peace, which were the code words used by the *other* side and used to justify, say, support to the Palestinian Liberation Movement or opposition to South African Apartheid, or deployed against 'cultural imperialism'. Without those words, the United States would not have agreed to be a party to the Declaration.

These two conference-related anecdotes illustrate the image-building or 'branding' motivations of nation-states in forums such as UNESCO. Some national postures may well be motivated by internationalist ideals, but the imperatives of what Raymond Williams called 'cultural policy as display' tend to trump the latter. 'The public pomp of a particular social order' was Williams' gloss on the ceremonials of the British Royal Family and the like, which constituted the ritual symbolization of nationhood (Williams, cited in McGuigan, 2004: 61). In our day, the deployment of cultural assets for economic gain, would be the other face of 'display'. In UNESCO, the idea of heritage as an income earner and employment generator goes back to the late 1970s and has become even more prominent under the influence of the currently reigning 'cultural economy' discourse (cf. Anheier and Isar, 2008). So cultural policy as display drives nations as actors in UNESCO, whether they engage with their governmental counterparts or operate with broader 'civil society' interlocutors in mind. In both cases, the ideals of global conviviality are often trumped by the imperatives of national representation, recognition – and income generation. Together, these objectives constitute a larger political economy of cultural prestige, i.e. 'the various interests at stake for the institutional and individual agents of culture, the games and mechanisms and stratagems by means of which these interests assert themselves, and the ultimate role such cultural assertions of interest play in maintaining or altering the social distribution of power...' (English, 2005: 8–9). In this perspective, UNESCO is a field, in Bourdieu's sense, with its own rules of negotiation and transaction. It possesses its own forms of symbolic capital that its Member States deploy. Heritage has been foremost among those forms. Indeed, it is significant that heritage sites are termed *properties*, just as collectivities see their entire cultures as possessions and cultural economists now talk seriously, as does Throsby (2001), of 'cultural capital' (see also Henrietta Moore's chapter in this volume).

In this perspective, then, cultural property recognized as 'The Heritage' functions as *symbolic capital* for nation-states as well as smaller sub-national entities, particularly as 'local markets and local scales of value are bound into ever tighter relations of interdependence' (English, 2005: 259). Heritage has become integral to the cultural policy of display for nations, cities and regions alike. The sub-national players carry out complex processes of economic and/or political negotiation and transaction with their respective national or federal governments (in general they cannot access UNESCO processes directly) in order to obtain international recognition for local cultural goods – a classic procedure of the glocalization process. An oxymoronic aspect of this has been the way nation-states today lay claim to heritage as a national possession, yet also want the same to be shared by all humanity. In many cases, the heritage in question was created long before these nations even came into being and/or by members of societies that no longer exist. Instead of existing as a true global public good, heritage in this way becomes the 'property' of a national (or sub-national) unit. Governments – again at multiple levels within nation-states – are increasingly 'sensitive to the value of publicly asserting the value of their [distinctive] cultures in various forums that bestow and reflect international prestige' (Kurin, 2004: 68). The search for such prestige has been one of the contributors to staking out the paths along which the heritage concept has been diversified and expanded internationally. But there are others, and it is to these that I shall now turn.

The expanding notion of heritage

Many people still use the notion of heritage in the broad sense authorized by the *Oxford English Dictionary* as 'that which has been or may be inherited', or 'a condition or state transmitted from ancestors'. But till well into the 1970s, UNESCO and ICOMOS understood the notion far more narrowly, restricting it to *material* forms of expression. More narrowly still, it was the stand-alone historical monument that was the focus of attention. This restricted usage was adopted, deployed and propagated by the Euro-American architectural conservation community, communicated to the two organizations and naturalized in their terminology. This usage appears strangely limited today, when there is so much talk in the air of the 'intangible heritage'. Indeed, it was difficult for me to understand when I joined UNESCO in 1973. Entering the organization as a postgraduate student of anthropology, I was astonished to find the remit of the then 'Division of Cultural Heritage' limited to the architectural heritage and managed by a 'Monuments and Sites Section' – note the limited scope – and to museum collections, managed by a 'Museums Section'. What of 'oral traditions', I wondered, or 'popular culture', or 'endangered languages', or 'folklore', or 'folklife', etc.? After all, these too were inherited cultural forms long recognized by the humanities disciplines as being full-fledged components of heritage. One knew also of the work of the Smithsonian Institution's Center for Folklife and Cultural Heritage (it had a different name then) as well as of many other 'rescue anthropology' initiatives of scholars and institutions throughout the world that consisted of analyzing and documenting a myriad of traditional cultural forms that were in danger of disappearing. One had heard of the 'living treasures' programmes adopted in Japan and Korea, which appeared precisely to engage with the 'livingness' of these embodied forms in a way that mere documentation could not. In UNESCO, however, there were only a few scattered activities on traditional music and dance or African languages, all located in the 'Division of Cultural Studies': their object was considered ontologically distinct from the kind of 'heritage' that UNESCO envisioned when it went about its business.

This usage reflected the thinking of those Euro-American architectural conservators and museum directors who dominated UNESCO's councils in those early and formative years (1946–60). They were all marked by the depredations of the Second World War (as well as those of the First, still remembered). In France, for example, whose taxonomies directly influenced the semantics of UNESCO and still do, governmental responsibility for *patrimoine* long covered the tangible alone. Only in 1980 was a sub-division created within the French Ministry of Culture called the Mission du patrimoine ethnologique. This was done in order to compensate for the lack of attention paid to the numerous immaterial phenomena recognizable as dimensions of the 'collective memory' – a term used widely by the French and in the French language, particularly since Pierre Nora's influential work of the mid-1980s. Small compensation it was, however – and remains – compared with the massive scale on which the 'tangible' is catered for by the monuments and museum services of the French state.

World Heritage

The Euro-American experts, for whom 'heritage' was mainly monuments and sites, were the principal drafters of the *1972 Convention concerning the Protection of the World Cultural and Natural Heritage* that established the 'World Heritage' mechanisms. Two processes converged to bring this text into being. First, the International Campaign for the Safeguard of the Monuments of Nubia crystallized the idea that there are places of 'outstanding universal value' which are the heritage of *all* humankind and that their protection is therefore a shared responsibility. Archaeologists, engineers, architectural conservators and many others came together from many different countries, under the aegis of their respective governments, to save the magnificent Abu Simbel temples from the flooding that would follow the construction of the Aswan High Dam. In 1959, UNESCO launched an international safeguarding campaign to pay for the dismantling, removal and re-assembling of the Abu Simbel (and Philae) temples. This vast and complex operation ended up costing about US$80 million, half of which was donated by governments in some 50 countries, driven both by the imperatives of the economy of prestige and the emerging notions of 'international solidarity' and 'shared responsibility' in conserving outstanding cultural heritage sites as global public goods. On its heels there followed other UNESCO International Safeguard Campaigns, e.g. to save Venice and its Lagoon (Italy), to restore the Borobodur Temple (Indonesia) or the archaeological ruins at Moenjodaro (Pakistan).

A second contributing process was the idea propagated by the American historic preservation community, first within the USA and then internationally, that cultural and natural sites should be preserved together under a single integrated vision and justificatory rationale. As heritage preservationists organized themselves in the wake of the passage of the US National Historic Preservation Act that had been adopted in 1966, they saw how effectively and quickly the environmental movement had made itself a popular and politically mobilizing cause. Consequently, they lobbied for the incorporation of *historic preservation* into the environmental impact review process and by 1969 had succeeded in persuading the President's Advisory Panel on Environmental Quality to accept this. At world level, the International Union for the Conservation of Nature (IUCN) was working out similar proposals for *its* subject-matter, i.e. for some kind of international treaty on nature conservation, and wanted to present these to the United Nations Conference on Human Environment in Stockholm. Eventually, all the parties concerned agreed on a single text that would become a UNESCO Convention defining world heritage as both cultural and natural.[6] Now ratified by 186 countries, the *Convention concerning the Protection of the World Cultural and Natural Heritage* has established a sort of global honour roll, by recognizing cultural and natural sites of

Figure 2.1 Number of World Heritage properties (both cultural and natural) inscribed each year by region

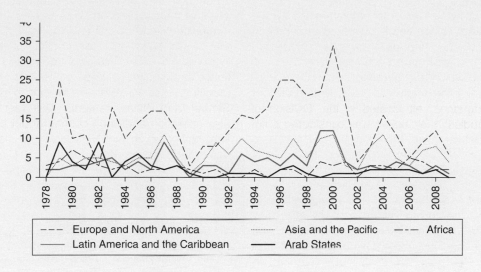

--- Europe and North America	········· Asia and the Pacific — · — Africa
—— Latin America and the Caribbean	—— Arab States

'outstanding universal value'. It sets out a global geography of the superlative in heritage terms, embodied in the *World Heritage list*, which in March 2010 numbers 890 properties. Figure 2.1 above shows the absolute numbers as well as the progression. Were the composition of the List to be carefully analyzed according to purely scientific criteria, the spurious nature of many claims to 'outstanding universal value' would become patent. Clearly, there are – many – properties present on the List simply because the World Heritage has long been used as an instrument in the operations of a global economy of cultural prestige, as outlined above.

Towards other World Heritage criteria

An intergovernmental committee (the 'World Heritage Committee') has over the years further elaborated the criteria of recognition adumbrated in the Convention itself, with a view to attributing 'outstanding universal value'. Without discussing either the functioning of the Committee or the complex conceptual apparatus underpinning these criteria (they are listed on the World Heritage Centre website: whc.unesco.org/; see also Labadi, 2007), the point to be stressed here is that after the process of listing got under way in 1978, it soon became obvious that 'outstanding universal value' was going to be interpreted in terms that reflected Western cultural history. The World Heritage List would inevitably

be skewed towards those countries richly endowed with buildings (mainly monumental) and places that satisfied criteria elaborated by experts whose value judgements reflected their own cultural moorings. Many countries – mostly in the global South – would not find adequate representation on it. Here, for example, is the distribution of sites in both the 'cultural' as well as 'mixed' category (this means sites that are significant both culturally and naturally), according to UNESCO regional categories: Africa, 45; Arab States, 61; Asia and the Pacific, 138; Europe and North America, 384; Latin American and the Caribbean, 83 (see Figure 2.2).

There have been two sets of responses to these imbalances. The first is an essentially regionalist process of seeking to enrich or stretch the inscription criteria or take them as far as they could be taken. When they work in counterpoise to global forces and flows, transnational groupings at the regional level can often exert strong leverage. In the case of the World Heritage process, such transnational cooperation could also build on regional commonalities. A good example was *Africa 2009*, a ten-year capacity-building programme launched in 1999 by the World Heritage Centre of UNESCO, together with the International Centre for the Study of the Preservation and Restoration of Cultural Property (ICCROM), and the International Centre for Earth Construction, a research centre of the School of Architecture at

Figure 2.2 Number of World Heritage properties (cultural and mixed) by region

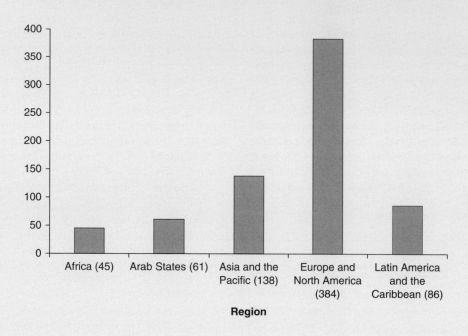

Grenoble, France (Saouma-Forero, 2006). *Africa 2009* was developed in the wake of ICCROM's Programme for Prevention in Museums in Africa 1990–2000 (PREMA), devoted to building the skills needed for preventive conservation in Africa's museums. As regards World Heritage, the need for such a programme emerged from concerns that began to be expressed in 1992 by the World Heritage Committee over the imbalanced composition of the List. The Committee adopted a 'Global Strategy' designed to achieve a more balanced regional and typological representation of cultural heritage properties. Sub-Saharan Africa did not have the 'right' kind of heritage. Furthermore, the preservationist ethos was weak among its peoples and conserving less spectacular kinds of 'old things' was a luxury for impoverished and weak states facing daunting needs in rural development, education, public health, etc. Moreover, the increasingly strict World Heritage guidelines required trained people, adequate funds and robust management plans. So ways were needed to enable the region's conservators to imagine solutions together.

A series of regional and sub-regional workshops was therefore organized, so as to tease out locally meaningful perspectives on built heritage. The workshops identified regional specificities, foregrounding, for example, the place of sacred sites. Although many of these had been inscribed or perceived – by non-Africans – as natural properties, they are profoundly cultural. The notion of *cultural landscape* was advocated, for it could help recognize, for example, the extraordinary cliffs of Bandiagara in the Dogon country of Mali. It could encapsulate the relation between nature and culture, between the already enshrined tangible heritage and the soon to be celebrated intangible heritage. So too could *cultural routes and itineraries* such as the Slave Routes; *associative sites* that evoke legend or myth, or *commemorative sites*, which mark a dramatic moment in human history such as Robben Island (or the first such site inscribed, the Auschwitz concentration camp). The role of local communities and traditional leaders as stakeholders and active agents in conservation was also emphasized: value would need to be determined not just by architects, historians, anthropologists and archaeologists; the views and aspirations of local communities would also need to be taken on board.

The findings of these workshops were disseminated across the Sub-Saharan region, opening up new vistas. The experts built up a robust corpus of evidence to show that African heritage includes cultural landscapes, sacred sites and traditional architecture which is not necessarily monumental, and that conservation had to be looked at afresh, by taking into account local knowledge and know-how, and addressing management issues with stakeholders who had conserved these properties so far. It became evident that the development of site-management practice designed solely by experts in conservation would not be appropriate. Analogous concerns emerged in other regions too, notably in Asia. Here, however, they were preceded chronologically by a questioning of architectural conservation doctrine – rules on the 'how' – that had been elaborated before the World Heritage process got under way. I shall return to this process later.

Towards the Intangible Heritage

I turn now to the second set of responses to the inbuilt limits of the original World Heritage concept and criteria of value. As the inscription process took on even more rapid momentum in the last decade of the twentieth century – 371 sites (both cultural and natural) were added between 1990 and 2000 – and as people even in the global North began to articulate broader notions of heritage, governments, particularly in the global South, became increasingly receptive to the idea of creating a system of recognition that could embrace 'their' kinds of heritage.[7] In other words, an apparatus of protection similar to World Heritage should be established in order to cater to '…the practices, representations, expressions, knowledge, skills – as well as the instruments, objects, artefacts and cultural spaces associated therewith – that communities, groups and, in some cases, individuals, recognise as part of their cultural heritage' (UNESCO, 2003: Article 2). This need for a parallel mechanism had been expressed at various earlier moments, renewed and pursued fitfully, but not always effectively.

By the late 1990s, much more than national pride or cultural diplomacy was at stake, for questions of cultural preservation had become globally salient, as a result of growing disquiet over the impacts of globalization and the widespread belief that cultures were now being corroded far more strongly than they ever had been in the past. Could traditional values, practices and forms of knowledge survive the onslaught of a global mass culture? These anxieties developed a certain momentum

and a tide of opinion began to grow in favour of a new system of protection/recognition for heritage in its immaterial forms. The election of a senior Japanese diplomat to the post of UNESCO Director-General in 1999 made that momentum unstoppable, for he brought with him Japan's own strong awareness and practices of the intangible as well as his government's determination to invest in globalizing that sensibility – as a Japanese contribution to international culture. The turn of the century also saw the emergence of a new cause in international cultural politics, the combat for 'cultural diversity', a revamping of France's 'cultural exception' claims that sought to exempt all cultural goods and services from international free trade rules (Isar, 2008). For this new militancy, the alliance with the 'intangible heritage' camp is both natural and advantageous. These factors combined to drive forward the process by which a powerful global movement was created in the UNESCO framework, leading to the elaboration in 2003 of the *Convention for the Safeguarding of the Intangible Cultural Heritage* (Aikawa, 2009). While this treaty was being negotiated internationally, UNESCO had in fact already initiated the process of selecting 'Masterpieces of the Oral and Intangible Heritage of Humanity'. For Director-General Matsuura it was essential during those years to impel the process forcefully, to press home the idea and make it 'stick', using the new recognition mechanism to building loyalty among those nations whose cultures were being honoured thereby. Three rounds of selection took place in 2001, 2003 and 2005, resulting in the listing of 90 such 'Masterpieces', all of which were subsequently folded into 'The Representative List of the Intangible Cultural Heritage of Humanity' when the Convention entered into force in April 2006.

At time of writing (February 2010), 181 properties have been inscribed on the Representative List and the regional breakdown as follows: Africa, 10.5 per cent; Arab States, 4.42 per cent, Asia and the Pacific, 49.17 per cent (China alone has 29 properties); Europe and North America, 22.65 per cent; Latin America and the Caribbean, 13.26 per cent. Clearly, right from the start, the geo-cultural distribution is perceptibly different from that of World Heritage. The share of Europe and North America is still substantial, but 25 of the 41 inscriptions are from Russia and other ex-Communist countries of Central and Eastern Europe. The inscription process has also been rather more complex than for World Heritage, reflecting both lessons learned from the latter as well as the different nature of the 'heritage' at stake. The details need not be rehearsed here, but suffice it to stress that the key criterion of inscription for Intangible Cultural Heritage (or ICH) is the notion of 'representativeness'. As the UNESCO Secretariat explains it:

> "Representative" might mean, at the same time, representative for the creativity of humanity, for the cultural heritage of States, as well as for the cultural heritage of communities who are the bearers of the traditions in question.' The Convention refers to communities and groups of tradition bearers, without specifying exactly who they might be. The Secretariat also stresses 'that such communities have an open character, that they can be dominant or non dominant, that they are not necessarily linked to specific territories and that one person can very well belong to different communities and switch communities.' (www.unesco.org/culture/ich/index.php?pg=00002, accessed 22 February 2010)

A key trope associated with the ICH is that it is 'living heritage'. Yet there is something aporetic about this vitalism, for the act of safeguarding the ICH is, after all, a sort of materialization of the immaterial. Monuments can be conserved in their materiality, but most of the time intangibles cannot. Instead, they are recorded and documented. In the case of oral history, for example, a real safeguard would be to keep such traditional forms alive by adding items to the repertoire today and ensuring the survival of existing histories; in the case of traditional music, it would ensure the continuation of these forms and their use. But real practice does not, and indeed cannot, keep all these forms 'alive'. Instead, what is involved are identifying and inventorying. Indeed, as Kirshenblatt-Gimblett tartly observes (2004: 56), referring to the notion of vitality, 'if it is truly vital, it does not need safeguarding; if it is almost dead, safeguarding will not help'. When compared with the objects typically displayed in the museum showcase – or in other 'heritage' settings – intangible cultural forms can be less easily detached from the persons who embody them. To be sure, the champions of the ICH, within as well as beyond the corridors of UNESCO, are well aware of this paradox. Indeed, they see a positive potential in it. For the necessary embodiment of ICH in living in individuals or groups has imparted a quality of demotic and communitarian energy to the cause in ways that World Heritage has never enjoyed. The latter is still perceived in many countries as a matter of either 'high culture', which is instrumentalized for the purposes of national – or local – glorification by political elites or as the preferred handmaiden of the tourism industry. Community appropriation has afforded ICH a more inclusive appeal, and not just in the non-West, giving it the potential of becoming a truly popular and global mobilizing cause. Yet governments lag behind that burgeoning societal demand. The institutional infrastructure for the safeguard of intangible heritage is very weak and the cross-sectoral interconnections needed to give coherence to this task are yet to be made. Nor is ICH likely to escape the hegemony of market forces. Indeed, since long before the term was adopted, intangible heritage manifestations of many kinds have been celebrated – and instrumentalized – in the form of public ceremonial, or enacted in arts festivals, or adopted for new rituals of state and as new material for tourist consumption (Isar, 2005).

Tweaking the canons of architectural conservation practice

The expansion of the 'what' as regards heritage to be selected for preservation has been accompanied by several sets of heterodox ideas on the 'how' of preserving it. One such line of thinking seeks to 'join up' the tangible and the intangible in architectural conservation practice. This was the cause taken up in the late 1990s by the Indian National Trust for Art and Cultural Heritage (INTACH). The 2005 *INTACH Charter for the Conservation of Unprotected Architectural Heritage and Sites in India* developed the notion of 'living heritage' constituted by both tangible material and the intangible 'extant culture of traditional building skills and knowledge, rites and rituals, social life and lifestyles of the inhabitants'. The *Charter* observed that 'while the Western ideology of conservation advocates minimal intervention, India's indigenous traditions idealize the opposite'. Indeed, the 2003 UNESCO Convention had already advocated 'an all-encompassing approach to cultural heritage … which takes into account the dynamic link between the tangible and intangible heritage and their deep interdependence' (www.intach.org/about-charter.asp?links=about3, accessed 15 February 2010).

This Indian effort was an attempt to make that link effectively 'dynamic' rather than simply 'take it into account' and to forge meaningful practice out of the 'interdependence'. To be sure, all monuments, sites and artefacts embody intangible components such as spiritual values, symbols, and meanings, together with the knowledge and the know-how of craftsmanship and construction. Without these intangibles they would not have been made in the first place, nor would they have become 'heritage' today. Without the embodied knowledge and skills identical to or at least approximating those that went into their making they could not be properly restored. While this is no doubt true everywhere, the scale of social and economic transformation in the West has relegated these intangibles to a past that is truly 'a foreign country', a 'world we have lost'. South Asian societies have not previously experienced the same ruptures and discontinuities (but today this may be changing). Their pasts are not over in quite the same way. Emblematic here is the often cited Ise Jingu shrine in Japan that is rebuilt every twenty years in the *shikinen sangu* tradition. Knowledge and skills embodied in people are the important thing here, rather than to the material products of those knowledges and skills. Thus the INTACH *Charter,* in its Preamble, refers to 'the unique resource of the "living" heritage of Master Builders ... who continue to build and are for buildings following traditions of their ancestors'. At stake is informed understanding, which can draw upon belief systems, social values and ritual practices that are still alive – in and around every temple and every mosque, for example. Yet these potential keys to deeper and broader empathy with the values and meanings embodied in architectural form are still largely under-exploited. Addressing the cultural setting and historicity of built form could be easily minimized or occulted in the good old days, when attention focused exclusively on the discrete object, be it a stand-alone historical monument or a lone artistic treasure. But as conservation has moved away from a narrow, self-referential compass, the span of attention must also be broadened. The intangible is embedded within the tangible but can only be 'got at' by tapping into value as it is articulated and/or generated by the groups in whose name the tangible

is preserved, as both their inheritance and marker of their collective identity.

A last global development I wish to explore is the contestation of the canon of good architectural conservation practice as laid down by the *International Charter for the Conservation and Restoration of Monuments and Sites*. Commonly known as the Venice Charter, this text was drafted and adopted by the Second Congress of Architects and Specialists of Historic Buildings held in Venice in 1964. At the instigation of UNESCO, the Congress also adopted a resolution creating the International Council of Monuments and Sites (ICOMOS), which since then has functioned as the principal custodian of the charter (and also serves as the technical agency that advises the World Heritage Committee on the suitability of World Heritage nominations). The group of experts who drafted the Venice Charter was overwhelmingly European in its composition and so naturally it reaffirmed and upheld a notion of 'authenticity' that has emerged directly from the European experience. At stake in particular was the radical rejection of the nineteenth-century conservation philosophy epitomized by the French civil servant Eugène Viollet-le-Duc, whose 'restorations' of historic monuments in France were marked by fully-fledged reconstructions, as well as modifications, creative additions, etc. The Venice Charter saw such practices as anathema. Restoration, the text insisted, 'must stop at the point where conjecture begins, and in this case moreover any extra work which is indispensable must be distinct from the architectural composition and must bear a contemporary stamp.' Various other principles were enunciated in the Charter, adopted as orthodoxy by ICOMOS, representing the conservation clerisy, and then endorsed by UNESCO. Within Europe itself, however, some of the dogma has over the years been sidelined, but covertly. Elsewhere, the contestation has been overt.

In Asia especially, the relationship to architectural remains and decayed buildings as the icons of pastness is a quite different one from in the West, whose conservation ethos, as Lowenthal (1985) was the first to point out, has been forged over almost half a millennium of technological change and its attendant destruction and loss, demographic changes, and social transformations. The difference in perceptions and sentiments results not just in a far more limited societal commitment to heritage conservation *tout court* (and, as just discussed, a different vision of the intangible in the tangible), but in attitudes towards the 'authenticity' enshrined in the state of an old building as it has come down to us, warts and all (Weerasinghe's chapter in this volume explores this question in greater detail). A number of different documents adopted at the regional level attest to this. Particularly significant have been the 1994 *Nara Document on Authenticity* and the 1999 *Burra Charter* (The Australia ICOMOS charter for the conservation of places of cultural significance).

The *Nara Document* was adopted at a 1994 conference sponsored by the Japanese government and organized in cooperation with ICOMOS, in response to questions that surfaced in the World Heritage Committee as to the degree of 'universality' notions of authenticity and integrity, such as those contained in the Venice Charter, could realistically attain. Conservations professionals in both ICOMOS and ICCROM had by then recognized the need to revisit some of the Venice Charter's doctrine, in particular with respect to its focus on the original material substance surviving. For many conservators, it was as important or more so to retain the original form rather than the original substance. Early in 1994, the Canadian (because they needed to spend allocated funds before the end of the fiscal year) and Norwegian governments (because Norwegian architectural conservators were interested in reviewing standards in the light of a largely timber-built heritage) sponsored a 'preparatory workshop' in the Norwegian World Heritage city of Bergen.[8] For both governments, in addition to the professional considerations, prestige-building was also involved. While reaffirming the core principles of the Venice Charter, the *Nara Document* stressed that 'judgements about values attributed to cultural properties as well as the credibility of related information sources may differ from culture to culture'. It held that the criteria of authenticity cannot be fixed but 'considered and judged within the cultural contexts to which they belong'. The Australian document, based on a pooling of Asia-Pacific sensibilities, went through several earlier iterations (1979, 1981, 1988) and the 1999 final version affirmed that cultural significance 'may change as the result of the continuing history of the place', that all acts of preservation, restoration or reconstruction must respect that significance and that adaptations in particular may be allowed but

only if they have 'minimal impact on the *cultural significance* of the place' (www.icomos.org/australia/burra.html, accessed 15 February 2010 italics in original).

This point of view has most recently been taken up by the International Network for Traditional Architecture, Building and Urbanism (INTBAU). A gathering organized by INTBAU in 2007, aptly enough in Venice, adopted a *Declaration on the Conservation of Monuments and Sites in the 21st Century.* This group, on which all regions were represented, explicitly recognized that the Venice Charter did not 'sufficiently address challenges beyond Europe and the United States, and overlooked the vital role that traditional building crafts continue to play'. Their *Declaration* states that:

> *any act of conservation or restoration is inevitably an act of alteration based upon historically partial knowledge. Hence the goal of authenticity must not be interpreted to require an absolute state of preservation of pre-categorized moments in time. Rather it must reflect the complex pattern of change and recurrence across the ages, including the present. It is to be established as much in interpretive materials as it is in the techniques of accurate conservation.*

Conclusion

The foregoing analysis has focused first on how stakes of power and prestige have played out globally in the UNESCO-led discourse on heritage. I have argued that the 'properties' inscribed as either 'World' or 'Intangible' heritage have been pawns in processes of 'capital intraconversion' practised by both nation-states and smaller collectivities. In this process, the symbolic charge these heritage properties contain has been mobilized in negotiated transactions between cultural and economic, or cultural and political, capital in the global arena (English, 2005). Concomitantly, I have looked at the global career of certain 'modern' doctrines of heritage conservation set out by UNESCO and associated bodies that emerged from the European project of modernity. The 'multiple modernities' that have played out internationally (see H.L. Moore's chapter in this volume) have challenged these hitherto 'central' prescriptions and new ones have emerged from the erstwhile 'periphery'. These developments have accompanied other, truly global, shifts in sensibility and styles of governance that have marked recent decades: a shift from a paradigm of aesthetics to a paradigm of representation (which deeply transforms the valuation as well as the valorization of the heritage); from cure to prevention; from centralized decision-making and funding to local support; from top-down to bottom-up; from the undervaluing of local distinctiveness to its vigorous affirmation. Acting together, these forces have taken architectural conservation from being just about things, to being about people as well as things, and about the ways in which people use those things in the present as mnemonics of what they call their cultural memories and to construct visions of what they see as their collective identities.

Acknowledgements

Both Mark Hayward at The American University of Paris and David Lowenthal provided comments that have greatly improved this text (the remaining imperfections are my own). Tijana Maneva produced the two diagrams.

Notes

1 The International Council of Museums (ICOM) has also been a player in the evolving mix of theory and practice, and has addressed many aspects of cultural globalization other than the specific domains of heritage theory and practice explored here. Mention should also be made of an intergovernmental training organization created at the instigation of UNESCO, the International Centre for the Study of the Conservation and Restoration of Cultural Property (ICCROM).

2 ICOMOS describes itself as 'an international non-governmental organization of professionals, dedicated to the conservation of the world's historic monuments and sites'. Its members include architects, historians, archaeologists, art historians, geographers, anthropologists, engineers and town planners.

3 For an enlightening review of national discourses, constructions and representations of heritage made by governments when nominating cultural properties to the World Heritage List, see Labadi, 2007.

4 As for example in a speech by Director-General Matsuura, in which he stated that 'intangible cultural heritage is not just the memory of past cultures, but is also a laboratory for inventing the future'. UNESCO recently launched a 'Memory of the World' programme for the preservation and dissemination of valuable archive holdings and library collections worldwide, but the archival discourse and institutional players are quite different from those of 'heritage'.

5 The World Intellectual Property Organization (WIPO) addresses community rights over intangible heritage in the context of intellectual property rights. Here too lies a lively trans-regional debate, but the issue deserves in-depth treatment; see Deacon et al., 2004.

6 Further details on this process can be found in Batisse and Bolla, 2003.

7 For a succinct and useful review of the process in English (despite some confusion about procedural aspects), see Deacon et al., 2004; for an account in French, see Aikawa, 2009.

8 Personal communication from David Lowenthal, who attended both meetings.

REFERENCES

Aikawa, N. (2009) 'Le patrimoine culturel immatériel: naissance d'une Convention', in *Le patrimoine à l'UNESCO: le défi de la sauvegarde*. Cahiers du Club Histoire, 5. Association des anciens fonctionnaires de l'UNESCO (AAFU). Paris: AAFU.

Anheier, H.K. and Isar, Y.R. (eds) (2008) 'Introduction', in *The Cultural Economy: The Cultures and Globalization Series, 2*. London: Sage.

Appiah, K.A. (2006) "Whose Culture Is It Anyway?', in *Cosmopolitanism: Ethics in a World of Strangers*. New York: W.W. Norton and Co.

Batisse, M. and Bolla, G. (2003) *L'invention du Patrimoine Mondial*. Cahiers du Club Histoire, 2. Association des aniens fonctionnaires de l'UNESCO (AAFU). Paris: AAFU.

Deacon, H., Dondolo, L., Mrubata, M. and Prosalendis, S. (2004) *The Subtle Power of Intangible Heritage: Legal and Financial Instruments for Safeguarding Intangible Heritage*. Capetown, South Africa: HSRC Publishers.

English, J. (2005) *The Economy of Prestige: Prizes, Awards and the Circulation of Cultural Value*. Cambridge, MA: Harvard University Press.

Haas, P. (1992) 'Introduction: Epistemic Communities and International Policy Coordination', in *Knowledge, Power and International Policy Coordination*, special issue of *International Organization*, 46 (Winter 1992), pp. 1–36.

Hall, S. (2005) 'Whose Heritage', in J. Littler and R. Naidoo (eds), *The Politics of Heritage: The Legacies of 'Race'*. London: Routledge.

Isar, Y.R. (2005) 'Tangible and Intangible Heritage: Are They Really Castor and Pollux?,' in *INTACH Vision 2020* (Proceedings of the conference INTACH 2020, organized by the Indian Trust for Art and Cultural Heritage, INTACH, November 2004). New Delhi: INTACH.

—— (2008) 'The Intergovernmental Policy Actors', in *The Cultural Economy: The Cultures and Globalization Series, 2*. London: Sage.

—— (2009) 'Le retour des biens culturels à leurs pays d'origine', in *Le patrimoine à l'UNESCO: le défi de la sauvegarde*. Cahiers du Club Histoire, 5. Association des aniens fonctionnaires de l'UNESCO (AAFU). Paris: AAFU.

—— (2010) 'Cultural Diplomacy: An Overplayed Hand?', *Public Diplomacy* (magazine of the Association of Public Diplomacy Scholars at the University of Southern California), No. 3, Winter 2010.

Kirshenblatt-Gimblett, B. (2004) 'Intangible Heritage as Metacultural Production', *Museum International*, Nos 221–222 (May). Paris: UNESCO/Blackwell Publishing.

Kurin, R. (2004) 'Intangible Cultural Heritage in the 2003 UNESCO Convention', *Museum International*, Nos 221–222 (May). Paris: UNESCO/Blackwell Publishing.

Labadi, S. (2007) 'Representations of the Nation and Cultural Diversity in Discourses on World Heritage', *Journal of Social Archaeology*, 7(2). London and Thousand Oaks, CA: Sage.

Lowenthal, D. (1985) *The Past is a Foreign Country*. Cambridge: Cambridge University Press.

McGuigan, J. (2004) *Rethinking Cultural Policy*. Maidenhead, UK: Open University Press.

Saouma-Forero, G. (2006) 'Africa 2009: A Story of African Empowerment', *Museum International*, Nos 229–230, pp. 83–94. Paris: UNESCO/Blackwell Publishing.

Throsby, D. (2001) *Economics and Culture*. Cambridge: Cambridge University Press.

UNESCO (2003) *Convention for the Safeguarding of the Intangible Heritage*.

Wright, S. (1998) 'Encaging the Wind', *International Journal of Cultural Policy*, 5(1):173–182.

CHAPTER 3

DESTRUCTION AND RECONSTRUCTION OF HERITAGE: IMPACTS ON MEMORY AND IDENTITY

Dacia Viejo-Rose

The destruction of cultural heritage during wartime and its subsequent reconstruction or neglect both have long-term and wide-ranging consequences for notions of memory and identity. This essay discusses the more salient of these consequences, including those that we are only now beginning to appreciate. It explores the global repercussions of certain destructive acts and the symbolic dimensions that they can come to acquire. Part of this impact is visible in ways the 'international community' has responded through reconstruction programmes and policies. The author highlights some of the dimensions of this issue that such initiatives should consider.

On 9 June 2009, a ceremony was held at the Spanish Embassy in London. The Ambassador, a man in his mid-fifties, bent reverentially towards an elderly gentleman sitting in a wheelchair in the front row of a crowded room and handed him a Spanish passport. The Ambassador repeated this gesture to a woman sitting next to him and then again, and again, six times. Being honoured were a handful of men and women from the several thousand British and Irish who had joined the International Brigades and fought on the side of the Spanish Republic against a military rebellion: over seventy years ago. Interviewed after the ceremony, Jack Edwards said: 'It has made my life worth living to be able to say now: I am Spanish'. He wore a shirt with the colours of the Spanish Republic – red, yellow and purple – and on which could be read 'International Brigade Volunteers. Spain 1938' and the names of the battles in which they fought: Belchite, Teruel, Brunete, Jarama.

Two years earlier in Poland a very different scene was played out by the Polish President Lech Aleksander Kaczyński – with Jarosław Kaczyński, his identical twin brother, as Prime Minister – and the Institute for National Memory (IPN). That conservative Polish government sought to adopt measures to have those Poles who had fought with the International Brigades classified as 'traitors and criminals', suppress their pensions and change the names of streets and schools named after them. Since 1990 the *dombrosiacos*[1] have also witnessed the removal of the columns from the Warsaw memorial to the Unknown Soldier with the names of the battles in which they had fought: Ebro, Brunete, Jarama (Ruiz Lardizábal, 2007).

These two ceremonial moments show how civil war, that ultimate uncivil destroyer of cultural heritage, can have a long-lasting impact on memories and identities well outside the location of the conflict in space and time. They also illustrate the symbolic resonance of certain events and experiences, and the long arm of memory and discord. Hence this chapter aims to explore the web of interrelations among globalization, the triad of heritage, memory, and identity, and acts of destruction and reconstruction. The inquiry could take several directions. If the aim is to determine the impact of globalization by destroying and reconstructing heritage, memory and identity, then there are two lines of questioning. In the first, globalization can be queried as a destructive force, a tidal wave of homogenization, sweeping before it local distinctiveness and replacing it with the signs, symbols and values born of the marketing and commoditization strategies of an aggressive global economy. Writing in 1972 about literacy and the future of books in a world of globalizing information communication and entertainment industries, Aberto Moravia wrote: 'The danger is that this culture will not be assimilated, but thrown together, condensed and reduced to mere formulas and synthetic aggregations in a vast grinding operation of destruction' (Moravia, 1972: 50). The second line could look at how globalization instigates a reconstruction of heritage in precisely the sense of a merchandising giant that redefines expressions of cultural heritage, memory and identity, turning them into commodities to be branded and packaged. Seen thus, the destruction of cultural heritage would appear to be a direct consequence of globalization. If, however, one turns this linear equation on its head, then one sees globalization itself to be shaped by notions of heritage, memory and identity, especially when they are used to try to counter (destroy) or reformulate (reconstruct) it and its impact.

One could also look at how the destruction and reconstruction of cultural heritage linked to memory and identity affects relations between individuals and societies internationally. It is this approach that will be the focus here. Building on the relationships laid out in the chapter entitled 'Conflict and the deliberate destruction of cultural heritage' that I contributed to the first volume in this *Series* (Viejo-Rose, 2007), here I take the issues a step further and reflect on the global impact of that destruction. This is at once global in spread and intimately individual in how it is experienced; the ensuing reconstruction occurs both in the physical landscape and in the imagined and imaginary landscapes of minds and memories. It thus raises a broad variety of issues that reflect the diversity of reactions to any one conflict or act of destruction according to time, place and circumstance. This diversity also makes it useful to take stock of the theoretical and empirical situation. This chapter sets out to present and encompass both lines of research in progress and emerging issues. Throughout the chapter I shall use examples from Spain, the Civil War and beyond, as well as case studies within the CRIC research project (see Stig Sørensen, Box 3.2), and others outside its European remit.

Destruction of heritage and its global impacts

After attempting to develop a working typology for the different ways in which cultural heritage is destroyed, in 2007 I concluded that the ways in which heritage was mobilized in wartime discourse to sow division were at the crux of this destruction. I argued that reconstructing on the basis of this division only reinforced the violence done to heritage and identity rather than repair or reverse it. The consequences of the violent wartime heritage discourse and its underpinning through subsequent reconstruction projects on memory and identity can be seen around the world. For conflict in all of its destructiveness is also a generator of heritage, memory and identity on local, national and global scales. War adds further layers to heritage sites, whether it physically damages them or not, as, for instance, the memory of a siege becomes part of the fabric of a city, its inhabitants, its memorials, and its ruins.

The destruction of cultural heritage is a global phenomenon in several ways: it occurs throughout the world; it is a form of destruction that can be read as a consequence of globalization; and because even a single act of destruction can come to be known and have repercussions throughout the world. Here the focus is on the latter. Part of the response to recent destructive acts in Bosnia, Afghanistan and Iraq has been an interest in subsequent reconstruction programmes developed with the collaboration of the international community. Although these programmes do not generally give heritage a high priority, the very nature of the destruction suffered and of the response has nonetheless placed cultural heritage explicitly in the arena of international politics. Central to this position is its relevance for medium and long-term socio-economic regeneration, identity formation and the re-creation of physical and psychological landscapes.

Heritage itself contains contradictions and has to manage conflicting needs. Heritage sites represent a conglomerate of symbols and narratives composed of an accumulation of all their past, and continually evolving, meanings. One-dimensional interpretations of heritage are exclusive and excluding, rendering sites more apt to be mobilized in supporting radical, likewise one-dimensional narratives of group identity. A consequence of this approach to heritage is that it makes it more vulnerable to targeting either by those with alternative interpretations or by those wishing to attack the originators of a particular one-dimensional account.

The destructive blows that war deals to heritage in the form of propaganda, through simplifications and radical representations of the heroic, self-sacrificing martyrs defending 'us' versus the murderous hordes comprising 'them' have destructive consequences for heterogeneous identities. Not only are any manifestations of culture and identity of 'them' targeted, and this targeting justified through anything from revenge to military necessity, in addition, comparable manifestations of 'us' become sacralized, exalted, imbued with almost mystical qualities. All the nuances on either side of the 'us' and 'them' get lost in the ever-widening divide between the two blocks that war rhetoric creates, drowned out by the military machinery and calls to battle. This does violence to the confronted groups but also causes other communities who fall outside the bipolar confrontation to be neglected.

A revealing example of this is currently being investigated by PRIO-Cyprus as part of research on the CRIC project. One discovery made early in the research was that in constructing the conflict in Cyprus exclusively along the lines of Greek versus Turkish interests, the cultural heritage of other, minority, populations was overlooked and neglected (Constantinou and Haray, 2009). This research has focused on the case of the Maronites of Cyprus. As a Christian community that speaks Arabic as well as Maronite, both sides in the conflict exclude them. In consequence, their cultural heritage, consisting of physical sites and, more significantly, of a unique language, is in danger of disappearing.[2] In contrast, some acts of destruction come to have global resonance; they stand out from others as iconic events and join a repertoire of 'world events'. What makes these acts stand out from others? What gets overshadowed and overlooked as a result? Can an act of destruction become heritage?

Global icons of destruction

The pairing of entertainment and news industries has created global celebrities, people and faces. This celebrity culture has to some degree even extended to catastrophes – natural disasters, wars, famines, and droughts – that become *cause célèbres*, the object of concerts, charity events, telethons, documentaries, books and movies. As for deliberate destruction of cultural heritage in the last twenty years, the best known instances have been Dubrovnik, Mostar Bridge and the Bamiyan Buddhas. One of the important dangers of this dynamic is that certain instances of destruction become global reference points while others are forgotten. For example, the *Maison des Esclaves* on Gorée Island off the coast of Dakar, Senegal, has become, at least in the public imagination created by tourism, the epitomic site in the incarceration and shipment of slaves throughout the eighteenth and nineteenth centuries. As a result, attention and resources are detracted from studying and preserving equally significant sites, such as Gambia's Jufureh, the slave forts of Ghana (Rév, 2008), slave houses and holding areas in Zanzibar, and recently discovered sites in Cape Verde.

A group of mines called *Sar-e-sand* (the Place of the Stone) in the Badkhshan district of Afghanistan produce the stone lapis lazuli with which ultramarine paint is made. For centuries, these mines were the source for all the ultramarine paint in Western and Eastern art, making appearances in Titian's skies and the robes of the Virgin Mary throughout Renaissance Italy, in illuminated manuscripts and in the topknots of the Buddha (Finlay, 2002: 313). One of the earliest recorded uses of ultramarine was in the frescoes painted around the heads of the two giant Buddhas of Bamiyan. These internationally renowned sculptures became victims of the Taliban and of their own fame: they were destroyed in part *because* they were recognized as important heritage sites by an international community with which their destroyers were violently confronted. Proof of this is the fact that to mark the occasion of their destruction, the Taliban made an exception in their general ban of photography, and so images of the niches empty of their Buddha sculptures were deliberately circulated to the international media. Not only were the sculptures destroyed but so were the frescoes, those first examples of the use of lapis lazuli from the mines that had been such an important point along the silk route, which crossed the Bamiyan Valley. Yet because of the international celebrity status of the statues, countless other sites of significance – their destruction, damage or neglect – have been overlooked.

The international celebrity status of the Buddhas of Bamiyan was a major ingredient in motivating their destruction, but this type of fame can have yet another consequence, that of creating a schism between the local and international significance of sites. Gernika (town) and *Guernica* (painting) are a prime example. On an international level, the painting trumped the event, becoming *the* image that came to mind in response to the sign that is the word: Guernica or Gernika. In 2007, Gernika existed both as a physical and intangible *lieu de mémoire* (Nora, 1997), a town that could be walked through and 'read', but also as a symbol in an international repertoire. It is in this latter aspect that Picasso's painting had its greatest impact, its name being associated with an image of the horrors of war. This association meant that it gradually became a peace banner, waved literally in demonstrations and rhetorically in speeches. Yet in Spain, the association was not with peace so much as with the dictatorship's repression and the false history it promulgated, and in the Basque Country it had further readings. In the town itself, all these meanings combine with the local ones, waxing and waning in their use and relevance in concordance with political and social circumstances; the peace symbolism is only one of many which often overshadow it. Even on an international plane, references to Gernika/*Guernica* are used to call for peace or for armed intervention, a dynamic that came to the fore in 2003 in the preliminaries to the invasion of Iraq (Viejo-Rose, 2009).

In order to understand the symbolic capital that lies in a 'sign' (Barthes, 1973) such as Gernika, its constantly evolving and shifting meanings and uses needs to be looked at.[3] As Nora (1996: xix) has written: 'It was no longer enough simply to select objects; instead those objects would have to be constructed: In each case one would have to look beyond the historical reality to discover the symbolic reality and recover the memory that sustained it.' This introduces two further topics, the mediated transmutation of symbols through their reproduction, repetition and reuse in different contexts and war as generator of heritage.

Mediated acts of destruction

An act of destruction cannot become globally known without some form of mediation. The construction of a collective sense, or memory, of events 'experienced' in a mediated way thus seems to rely on trace and the visual image. Photography has played a key role in imaging the aftermath, the remnants and ruins caused by war and violence. It shows that, in the words of Susan Sontag: 'War tears, rends. War rips open, eviscerates. War scorches. War dismembers. War *ruins*' (Sontag, 2003: 7). Since Sontag's influential essay, *Regarding the Pain of Others* (2003), a field of critical analysis has emerged called 'late photography' (Campany, 2003), which focuses on those images that depict the aftermath of destruction, be it through natural disasters, war, or other forms of violence. Revealingly, the identification and analysis of late photography as a particular field within the study of photography developed in the aftermath of the attacks on 11 September 2001 against Manhattan and Washington and the Tsunami of December 2004.

In a sense, the destruction of the Bamiyan Buddhas was performed for the international media, for a global audience. Their destruction, to borrow from novelist García Márquez, was a chronicle of a death foretold. This is not to lay the responsibility for the destruction on journalists or even their editors, but it would be irresponsible not to recognize the part they play as an eager audience. In the case of Gernika/*Guernica*, the evocative and symbolic success of Picasso's painting in the international sphere came to seriously contest and at times seemed to overshadow the local, deeply contextual and personally experienced event and its aftermath. Here we see a locally experienced and memorized act of destruction converted to an international icon of catastrophe, a collective experience and international property to be imagined by all.

The dichotomy between global symbolism, local realities and the impact both have on the evolution of the meanings associated with heritage can be seen in the case of the Iraq National Library and Archive (INLA). From November 2006 until July 2007, the Director of INLA wrote a diary that was posted as a blog on the websites of the British Library, Britain's Society of Archivists and the Spanish newspaper *El País*. It is a poignant account of the ravages that dictatorship, war, occupation, and the political instability and social frailty that follow can wreak on such an institution. The INLA also has its own website, and even a *Facebook* group, so the evolution of the institution can be followed by anyone around the world with internet access. Undoubtedly, this global presence and access to information on INLA's situation have helped in the advocacy work done by its Director to raise funds, awareness and recover documents that were looted internationally.[4] Yet, the problems faced by the library and archive today have more to do with the national political situation, with a local sense of ownership over the collections, and with the diverging interests of Kurds, Shi'is and Sunnis in preserving the archive (Eskander, 2009). One of the principal goals of INLA is thus to raise the awareness of Baghdad's population about protecting records of the city's history. One project developed by the institution to this end in 2007 is the Baghdad Memory Project, a series of television programmes produced in collaboration with al-Rafdain TV.

Paradoxically, while we draw on symbols to communicate because of a presumed agreement on their meaning, with each new use of the symbol its meaning is added to and altered. To reference 'Gernika' when discussing alternatively Madrid, Dresden, Hiroshima, Belfast, Sarajevo, Faluja or Ramallah is to selectively draw on a different aspect of Gernika's symbolism and to add to it. The symbolic capital of a site does not remain static: with each use it evolves, gathers new meaning and relevance. This is what keeps the symbol pertinent but also means that it cannot be understood to carry a singular, clearly defined meaning to be communicated. Every time that one of these symbols of destruction is contemplated, referenced, or reproduced – *Guernica*, the Bamiyan Buddhas, the Mostar Bridge – it acquires a new identity in the mind of every new viewer, neither guilty nor innocent, and is subject to the ever-changing landscape and context within which it exists.

War and the creation of heritage

War not only destroys heritage, it transforms, adds new meaning, and even engenders new heritage. There is no doubt that the consequences that war has on the valorizing and valuing (see the Introduction to this volume) of heritage, on the shaping of memory, and on the crystallization of identity are long-lasting. The various narratives of belonging abound with stories of wars, battles, sieges and catastrophes of various kinds (famines, epidemics and natural disasters). This repertoire and its protagonists are called on time and again to give a sense of gravitas, continuity, or legitimacy to situations in the present. The material remains of past conflicts often become heritage sites or memorials.

The coasts of Britain are dotted with the remnants of a violent and embattled past: Liverpool's buildings and streets are still marked by the names and representations of the slavers and their trade;[5] Martello towers still stand awaiting Napoleon's advance; listening devices created to detect U-boats during the First World War; gun batteries built to defend against German aviation during the Second World War; tunnels and mines dug by prison labour on the Channel Islands. Inland the country is replete with battlefields that today host re-enactments and memorial services, attracting tourists and the media.

In the present volume, Morris discusses how natural disasters become an important source of memory, spurring heritage sites and local identities. This is also the case with war. There is the phenomenon of war tourism (visitors being taken to inactive battle sites while the war they formed a part of is still raging), and tourism of war sites (after the war is over). There are war museums, museums about a particular war, event or protagonist in a war, and other museums intimately related to war (such as the museum of the International Red Cross and Red Crescent in Geneva and Auschwitz concentration camp which receives a million tourists a year), and the list goes on. War creates ruins that in turn can become heritage sites or monuments: not to mention a great variety of memorials in all their forms. Heritage sites related to war invariably involve dimensions of both history and memory, their becoming sites of memory can be 'intentional' or 'unintentional' (Riegl, 1982: 21), 'dominant' or 'dominated' (Nora, 1996), imposed or 'grassroots' (Sánchez-Carretero and Ortiz, in this volume). A triumphal arch is an example of a deliberate form of memorializing war in monumental terms whereas the beaches of Normandy becoming sites of memorial pilgrimage is more an example of a circumstantial form of memorial which emerges through affective and narrative (historical and memoristic) relations to a place. Examples of a third, emergent, category of memorials being termed spontaneous or grassroots are the offerings left at the sites of the train bombings that were perpetrated on Madrid on 11 March 2004.

Monuments and memorials, particularly of the imposed and dominant variety, can in turn become sites of conflict and contestation. Moments of political transition are replete with instances of gestures reminiscent of the *damnatio memoriae* of Ancient Rome, by which all effigies and references to rulers fallen from grace were destroyed and literally erased from public places, sentencing them to oblivion, to be eternally forgotten. Over the past thirty years effigies of General Franco have been gradually disappearing from Spain's public spaces, the fall of the Berlin Wall saw colossal statues of Lenin and Stalin similarly being removed from prominent places and, more recently, effigies of Saddam Hussein were toppled and destroyed in Iraq. Such gestures raise questions about how societies choose to remember and forget and about the consequences of these decisions. Removing them from the public domain entirely, rejecting and forgetting part of history will not necessarily be conducive to better dealing with its consequences. The policy of 'recovering historic memory' of the civil war and dictatorship in Spain is one of many examples of how silencing or relegating to oblivion the traumatic periods is not effective in the long term. In order to disarticulate the time bomb that historical injustices can represent they have to be openly discussed and negotiated, witness the increasing number of Truth and Reconciliation Commissions (TRCs) around the world.

The long arm of memory

Recordar: To remember; from the Latin re-cordis, to pass back through the heart. (Galeano, 1991: Epitaph)

Acts of destruction not only shape memory, they are also shaped by memory of past destructions. The experience of the Franco-Prussian War (1870–71) determined the attitudes of the German military when invading France in 1914. Then, in turn, the fierce resistance that they met from the civilian population subsequently influenced the tactics and degree of aggression they applied to civilians when invading again in 1940. The important point is the centrality of emotions, affectivity, to the study of heritage, memory or identity, and all the more so when they relate to conflict and its aftermath. The affective relationships that people develop with landscapes, places, and objects in the wake of conflicts will determine their relationships towards the other groups in the conflict (Navaro-Yashin, 2002 and 2010). Acts of public remembering – the French Armistice and the British Remembrance Day on the 11 of November to mark the end of the First World War – remind citizens to remember particular parts of a narrative of shared past. They are not remembering personal experiences but what they have been taught, through education and the media, and this act of remembering is intended to evoke emotions of group identity that bind a group and underline boundaries of 'insider' and 'outsider': pride, mourning, outrage at an historical injustice or sacrifice.

The long arm of memory applies not only to war but to other forms of violence against heritage as well, looting being a prime example. In 1924 Harvard University sponsored the explorer-archaeologist Langdon Warner to uncover ancient trade routes and collect pigment samples from the sacred caves of Dunhuang in the Gansu province of China. Along with the paint samples, he also removed and took back with him complete murals and a kneeling Bodhisattva from the Mogao Caves. Today a plaque explains that China's 'heart was broken' with the looting of this figure (Finlay, 2002: 132). This was only one of many instances in which the caves were looted since the eleventh century. In another case, this time in Africa, in 2005, sixty-eight years after taking it to Rome, Italy returned the Aksum obelisk to Ethiopia. This return was accompanied by an information campaign entitled 'Home Coming and Re-erection of the Aksum Obelisk, Celebrating Ethiopia's Cultural Heritage and Cultural Diversity', and was further enhanced with capacity-building activities coordinated by UNESCO, including the training of Ethiopian restorers, a workshop on the management of the Aksum World Heritage site, and the preparation of tourist guides. The symbolic significance of the return – the rhetoric of identity and memory that it naturally spurred – was thus capitalized on to create an impetus for practical initiatives in developing awareness and professional training for the safe-guarding of heritage.

Yet there are still many unresolved cases that continue to spark friction between countries, as in the case of the ivory mask of Queen Idia which Nigeria has been asking for from the British Museum for years.

Reconstructing memory and identity through time and space

Time and space are two critical factors in determining the long-term and broad geographical impact of conflict and its destruction of cultural heritage. There is a spiral-like quality to the way that past conflicts are alternately disregarded and then recalled. In November 2005 when confrontations between immigrant youth and police broke out in the Parisian *banlieue*, followed by riots in many of France's major cities, terms dating from the Algerian War of Independence (1954–62) returned: words such as the racist term *bougnoule* or *bavure* – acts of excessive police violence (Hussey, 2008: 42–44). In 2006, the year that marked the 70th anniversary of the outbreak of the Spanish Civil War in 1936, the language of the war returned with obituaries marking anniversaries of people killed 70 years earlier accused, on the one hand, the *hordas rojas* and, on the other, the *bandas fasciosas* of the killings. In effect, heritage time moves in non-linear ways. The memory and heritage of conflicts seems to be particularly resilient to the passage of time although it waxes and wanes, acquiring varying significance and interpretations with time.

Violence suffered, when accompanied by a strong sense of injustice and of crimes committed with impunity, seems to incur a particularly long memory, one that outlives those that suffered from these events first hand. In Cambodia, the trials of five senior Khmer Rouge officials commenced in Phnom Penh in 2009, thirty years after the fact. In Argentina, groups are still trying to find the names and fates of those 'disappeared' by the dictatorship of the 1970s. Aside from the initiatives that seek some form of truth or justice concerning past crimes, there are other important elements in maintaining a 'memory' of traumatic historical events that are more explicitly linked to heritage: ritualized commemorative events and anniversaries, monuments, museum collections, archives, cemeteries, and re-enactments.

The memory of destruction, traumatic events and loss is no longer contained within the boundaries of the physical, emotional and mnemonic spheres in which they occur. The movement of people – reporters, refugees, mediators, NGO and IGO personnel, soldiers, aid workers – and the communication of information, images, and eye-witness accounts mean that the memory of destruction moves and that 'vicarious memories'[6] are formed by people who never experienced the event. Spatial and temporal disruptions – war, conflict or crisis – have an impact on a collective's sense of continuity, and are remembered differently by different groups, who might uphold divergent accounts of the 'historical truth' or 'authentic memory' of an event. This is particularly evident in the diverging accounts of history, memory and identity that are constructed by communities of exiles and by those who remain in the post-war country. Conflict disperses populations and the movement of memories can result in diasporic 'communities of memory'.[7] This memory can be transmitted explicitly through the recounting and commemoration of events or through a silence that can be just as eloquent.

The affective relationships that emerge among those who remain in a country after conflict and those who flee it or go into exile to escape its results, is inevitably different. Narratives of the war that shape memories, create a sense of identity or give meaning to heritage also evolve differently. For those who leave, memories and events in the homeland are viewed through the kaleidoscopic lens of nostalgia, longing, homesickness, a sense of loss. Communities of exiles can thus come to 'reconstruct' the homeland in the imagination. For those who remain in the country, memories of the war are supplanted by more pressing interpretations of how those memories of events and the resulting identities come to bear on everyday life of post-war realities. Tensions can arise when the imagined-scape constructed abroad does not match the reality of the place left behind and which has continuously changed. The different memories, or interpretation of those memories, can divide societies long after a conflict is officially over (cf. Hashimoto, in this volume).

Acts of destruction shape memory in several ways: by adding new memories, by adding new meanings, creating new associations with the perpetrators, discourses, contexts, and sites of the destruction, and by consigning to the realm of memory those sites that are destroyed. Memories of destruction are resilient, be they on a significant physical and symbolic scale, such as with the bombing of a town, or on the personal and intimate scale, such as the theft of a family heirloom from the ruins of the family home.

Memorials: space markers and space makers

If a truth is to be settled in the memory of a group it needs to be presented in the concrete form of an event, of a personality or a locality.
(Halbwachs, 1992: 200)

War can be remembered through a wide array of material culture, expressions and performances: cemeteries, sermons, visual art, popular songs, folklore, memorial days, public sculpture, memoirs, diaries, autobiographies and correspondence, films, advertising, tourist trinkets and souvenirs, re-enactments, the physical landscapes of battles and trenches, even through legislation. How wars are remembered contributes to creating a sense of group belonging and war memorials are highly selective in terms of what and how they portray what and who is to be remembered or not (Rowlands, in Forty and Küchler, 2001). As such, memorials can be interpreted in such a way that they carry violence of a conflict long into the future, acting as signs in the landscape that efface time by equating past events with present generations: 'remember how we suffered', 'remember what we sacrificed', 'remember what you owe us for your present prosperity', 'remember what they did to us'. Yet, even when these are the messages that these structures were built to communicate, thus contributing to fixing a state's grand narrative of a shared past and collective duty, memorial sites have proven to be far more complex, their meanings changing with time and with use.

The memorial-scape of Bosnia and Herzegovina reveals another way in which memorials can act in more ways than as mere mnemonic devices in the landscape and how they can keep conflicts alive. In 2003, the Srebrenica-Potočari Memorial and Cemetery to Genocide Victims was inaugurated by Bill Clinton on the site of the massacre of Bosnian

men eight years earlier. At the inaugural ceremony of the memorial, which cost over 5 million US dollars, the Bosnian Serb government agreed to contribute 1 million euros to the Foundation charged with maintaining the memorial and cemetery. Yet, in the summer of 2005, days before the tenth anniversary of the massacre, Serbian police discovered bombs at the memorial site. This act of contention, of protest, by a local group against the memorial is echoed in the parallel memorials that have sprung up in the villages around Srebrenica, an area that is now predominantly Serbian, commemorating the deaths of Bosnian-Serbs during the war. A question also arises concerning the intended 'audience' of this memorial and whether it was built for the surviving family members of those killed – no longer living in the area – or for the international community and its sense of collective guilt at not having been able to prevent the tragedy.

The intention is not to argue that a significant memorial should not have been built, but rather that the messages communicated by memorials and the impact they have are not easily controllable. Writing about the Yarnton Declaration of Jewish Intellectuals on the Future of Auschwitz (May 1990), James E. Young notes: 'no memorial is ever-lasting: each is shaped and understood in the context of its time and place, its meaning contingent on evolving political realities' (Young, 1993: 154). Imbedded in memorial activities – plaques, prayers, anniversaries, and ceremonies – is a revealing story about who, ultimately, has the right to mourn and be mourned. With every public act of remembering the dead, a message is also conveyed about who is not to be remembered. Associated with traumatic events, memorial practices can become rallying social events used to make demands of politicians by demanding actions or explanations (Sánchez-Carretero and Ortiz, in this volume). However, the need to gather around meaning can also be seen in peacetime, as is witnessed by the gradual transformation of cultural heritage sites into places of pilgrimage, as if a search for an 'authentic' past might offer reassurance in a world of rapid change. This way of regarding heritage sites has the effect of ascribing to them an almost sacred quality which is all the more so in the case of memorials, battlefields, or the sites of mass deaths or other traumatic events.

Present-day Iranian policies towards the remains of unknown martyrs also demonstrate the sacralization of space through memorial practice. These are being dug up from the front lines of the Iran–Iraq War (1980–88) and reburied in spots that thereby become sacred. Since memorials are owned by the army and the remains of martyrs create sacred space, by creating these sites in places such as universities or museums they become accessible to the military and religious authorities as well as visitors (Khosronejad, 2009). Here we see how the remnants of one conflict are used in the present to delineate and mark territory.

The destruction of heritage is thus motivated in part by efforts to shape identity and re-inscribe memory to be deployed as a mark of group identity, as 'proof' of an historic presence in a territory. Another factor is its intimate association with power, be it political, economic or religious. According to Warnier (in this volume) autochthony is bound to a narrative and a graveyard. It is not surprising, then, that so much importance is given to cemeteries and memorials to martyrs and fallen soldiers – both named and unknown. Targeting cemeteries, destroying graves and sprinkling a territory with memorials are all examples of attempts at imposing narratives on a landscape.

The garbage of memory

Fear dries the mouth, moistens the hands and mutilates. Fear of knowing condemns to ignorance, fear of doing reduces us to impotence. Military dictatorship, fear of speaking, made us deaf and dumb. Now democracy, with its fear of remembering, infects us with amnesia, but you don't have to be Sigmund Freud to know that no carpet can hide the garbage of memory. (Galeano, 1991: 112)

In the wake of war, one way of driving society down the path of reconciliation has been an injunction to forget. This approach can be traced back to 403 BC Athens and the interdiction, in the name of reconciliation, to remember any crimes committed during the preceding period of civil strife (Connerton, 2008: 61–62). Yet even when there is a desire to forget the immediate past, remembering to forget is hardly a recipe for success when the reconstruction

process has to be built on the ruins and power structures left by the conflict.

A reverse approach that has been gaining ground since the Nuremberg trials that followed the Second World War has been a process of shedding light on events, a refusal to sweep an uncomfortable past under a rug of oblivion but rather to face it in all of its horror. This process has taken the form of War Crimes Tribunals, Truth Commissions, Truth and Justice Commissions, or Truth and Reconciliation Commissions (TRCs) (see Table 3.1 on page 62). Even when the lapse of time between the period of violence and the process of 'truth telling' is half a century or more, investigations and commissions are being set up (i.e. Spain and Cambodia) – it has taken some thirty years for Khmer Rouge leaders to stand trial for crimes of war.

In Spain there are examples of both approaches: the injunction to forget and the civic demand, after a few decades, for a form of truth and reconciliation. In 2004, nearly seventy years after the end of the Civil War, José Luis Rodríguez Zapatero's government initiated a move to unearth what had been buried during the construction of Franco's New Spain. The year 2006 was declared the *Year for the Recovery of the Historic Memory*, marking an important shift in how Spain deals with the history of the Civil War and the Franco period. The government also insisted on legislating this process through creating the law popularly known as the Law of Historic Memory. The law recognizes victims on both sides of the Civil War, as well as the victims of the Franco Regime, and creates an administrative framework for supporting the excavation of unmarked and mass graves. The law also deals with symbols, and legislates the removal of all material remnants of the Franco regime from public places (statues, commemorative plaques, inscriptions, street names). These aspects of the law and the initiatives that it has facilitated have caused the opposition party, *Partido Popular*, to protest vociferously, leading some commentators to remark that the battle lines of the Civil War seem not to have disappeared.

Notions of shared or collective memory have been contested by scholars who dispute their utility and emphasize the intimately personal quality of memory. In Spain, the term that emerged from

Table 3.1   Truth and Reconciliation Commissions (TRCs)

Since 1974 an estimated 32 commissions have been established in 28 countries in order to establish the facts about crimes committed during periods of armed conflict and dictatorships (Amnesty International, 2007).

Commission	Country	Year established
National Commission on the Disappearance of Persons	Argentina	1983
National Commission of Inquiry into Disappearances	Bolivia	1982
Extraordinary Chambers in the Courts of Cambodia for the Prosecution of Crimes Committed During the Period of Democratic Kampuchea	Cambodia	2004
Commission of Inquiry on the Crimes and Misappropriations Committed by the ex-President Habré his Accomplices and/or Accessories	Chad	1991
National Commission for Truth and Reconciliation	Chile	1990
National Commission on Political Imprisonment and Torture	Chile	2003
Truth and Reconciliation Commission	Democratic Republic of Congo	2003
Truth and Justice Commission	Ecuador	1996
Truth Commission	Ecuador	2007
Commission of Truth	El Salvador	1992
Commission of Inquiry for the Assessment of History and Consequences of the SED Dictatorship in Germany	German	1992
National Reconciliation Commission	Ghana	2002
Truth and Reconciliation Commission	Grenada	2001
Commission for the Historical Clarification of Human Rights Violations and Acts of Violence which Caused Suffering to the Guatemalan People	Guatemala	1997
National Commission for Truth and Justice	Haiti	1995
Truth and Reconciliation Commission	Indonesia	2004
Truth and Reconciliation Commission	Liberia	2005
Equity and Reconciliation Commission	Morocco	2004
Commission of Inquiry to Locate the Persons Disappeared during the Panchayat Period	Nepal	1990
Human Rights Violations Investigation Commission	Nigeria	1999
Truth Commission	Panama	2001
Truth and Justice Commission	Paraguay	2003
Truth and Reconciliation Commission	Peru	2000
Truth and Reconciliation Commission	Sierra Leone	2002
Truth and Reconciliation Commission	South Africa	1995
Presidential Truth Commission on Suspicious Deaths	South Korea	2000
Presidential Commission of Inquiry into Involuntary Removal and Disappearances of Persons in Western Southern and Sabaragamuwa Provinces	Sri Lanka	1994
Presidential Commission of Inquiry into Involuntary Removal and Disappearances of Persons in the Central, North Western, North Central and Uva Provinces	Sri Lanka	1994
Presidential Commission of Inquiry into Involuntary Removal and Disappearances of Persons in the Northern & Eastern Provinces	Sri Lanka	1994
Commission for Reception Truth and Reconciliation	Timor-Leste	2002
Commission of Inquiry into the Disappearance of People in Uganda	Uganda	1974
Commission of Inquiry into Violations of Human Rights	Uganda	1986
Investigative Commission on the Situation of Disappeared People and its Causes	Uruguay	1985
Peace Commission	Uruguay	2000
Truth and Reconciliation Commission	Federal Republic of Yugoslavia	2001

2006 was that of 'historic memory' and this too was criticized by observers who argue that the two terms should not be conflated. Yet, by what other name should a film like Florian Henckel von Donnersmarck's *The Life of Others* be called if not 'recovery of historic memory'; or the individuals and associations throughout Spain currently trying to locate the physical remains of their parents, grandparents, aunts, and uncles. 'Historic memory' can also be seen as applying an historical approach to studying the past that takes into account the diversity, and occasional divergence, of different versions, accounts, perspectives, memories, and interpretations of events. Thus it is a means by which to break away from the grand narratives of history constructed by those in positions of power and encompassing the multiplicity of ways of experiencing, understanding, and remembering an event without succumbing entirely to the minutiae of individual, unique, deeply context-dependant and incomparable experiences and memories.

While displays of public mourning for traumatic events and deaths that are experienced, and expressed, collectively have taken on new dimensions of performativity in Spain with multitudinous demonstrations in response to terrorist attacks (Sánchez-Carretero and Ortiz, in this volume), mourning for the dead of the Civil War and Franco dictatorship still frequently takes on a furtive tone.

Are some forms of mourning or some memories used to cover, replace, or exonerate others? 'Remembrance', writes Connerton (2008: 61), 'is an overt action while acts of editing out and erasure are covert.' That which is edited out in the reconstruction process as a new master narrative can nonetheless be constructed through acts of memorial remembrance. The many initiatives that have gradually developed and multiplied over the past fifty years to gather and record oral histories of wartime experiences are a memorial exercise that defies silence and forgetting, as do TRCs.

Silence, omission and amnesia

Silence is a critical issue to consider when examining the consequences of war's impact on heritage, memory, and identity. This silence manifests itself in many ways: in the voices, narratives, memories, and understandings that go unheard, un-uttered, and also in the absence of people and buildings: the spectres and the ruins of war. In his exploration of forgetting, Connerton writes: 'Newly shared memories are constructed because a new set of memories are frequently accompanied by a set of tacitly shared silences. Many small acts of forgetting that silences enable over time are not random but patterned...' (2008: 63).

Box 3.1 Armistice Day in France

In Paris on 11 November 2009, Armistice Day, the Champs-Élysées were closed off to traffic. Under the Arc de Triomphe and in front of France's Tomb of the Unknown Soldier, where they jointly laid a wreath and lit an 'eternal flame', the President of France, Nicolas Sarkozy, and the Chancellor of Germany, Angela Merkel, stood side by side. While the speeches of the two leaders were somewhat predictable and tame, symbolically the event was forceful and eloquent. German and French flags lined the Champs-Élysées, German and French military personnel in their respective uniforms stood beneath the Arc de Triomphe, the French and German anthems were played, and a German and a French child accompanied the two Heads of State, thereby symbolizing a future of friendship. All of this took place in the presence of French veterans form the Second World War. To conclude the ceremony the European anthem (Beethoven's *Ode to Joy*) was played, repeatedly, and blue and yellow balloons were released: the colours of the European Union flag, but likewise a colour from each of the national flags of France (blue) and Germany (yellow).

While the gesture of a joint commemoration between two once warring parties was important, it was also a persuasive (and impressive) display of selective memory at work. Though each speech ended in 'long live France, long live Germany, long live Franco-German friendship', it is notable that both leaders seemed to jump effortlessly from a representation of common suffering during the First World War to one of shared jubilation at the fall of the Berlin Wall with little mention of the Second World War, the last time that German flags, uniforms and anthems were displayed on the Champs-Élysées on such a scale. Furthermore, Sarkozy began his speech by admitting that this joint ceremony could only take place in 2009 after the last *poilu*, French veteran of the First World War, had died. Moreover, the speeches avoided references to any sense of responsibility for the wars and the destruction they caused.

These speechs show how memories can be represented in a new light, given new significance, and used in order to overshadow, or silence, other memories. The unspoken and the silenced can become the elephant in the room and have more or less detrimental effects – creating distance, misunderstandings and resentment among family members. This is not a unique process but common to all forms of memory that become part of a public – and political – domain. The use, reinterpretation, acquiring of meaning is part of the symbolic capital that is the basis for all heritage. How long before a similar commemoration can take place about the Second World War and with a choice between possibilities such as Coventry, Stalingrad, Berlin, and Hiroshima, where would it take place?

Dacia Viejo-Rose

Paradoxes and policy implications

In 1986, the geological formation on the coast of Northern Ireland known as the Giant's Causeway was added to UNESCO World Heritage List. Until then this site and its immediate landscape had been well preserved despite attracting many visitors from the region. In 1995 after the IRA cease fire, the number of visitors to the site nearly tripled and with a predicted million visitors per year a new conflict has sprung up, this time between geologists and developers. The latter say that they will invest in a visitor's centre and facilities if they can add hotels, restaurants and golf courses (BBC, 2005), leaving the former horrified at the impact that this will have on the unique site and with the World Heritage Committee warning that they can withdraw the prestigious status if they feel that development in anyway compromises the site's integrity. Where the Troubles somehow preserved the site, peace and the promise of prosperity are threatening it. Other cases in which war has served, counter-intuitively, to preserve heritage can be found in no-man's lands around the world. Along the border that once divided Germany, between Finland and Russia, and that still today separates North and South Koreas, 'green belts' have developed, areas where nature and the environment

were preserved because they were no-go areas for people and for development. As a result, species that disappeared elsewhere in these countries were able to survive in these border areas.

There are seemingly remarkable contradictions even in some of the most iconic memorial sites. In Gernika, following Franco's death in 1975, buildings that had survived the bombing and the dictatorship's heavy-handed reconstruction were surprisingly pulled down to make way for modern houses at a time when the historiography of Gernika's destruction and the town's symbolic role in the Basque country was beginning to be publicly recovered. Clearly this reflects a dichotomy and open conflict between economic and symbolic interests. In Dresden, despite the fact that the trajectories of parades commemorating the bombing vary, they all, regardless of their politics or claims, try to go along the river at some point in order to pass by that reconstructed façade of Dresden, a precious reminder of what the city had once looked like. Yet, in 2009 Dresden became the second site to actually lose its World Heritage status because of the city's plans to build a bridge that the World Heritage Committee believed would seriously compromise the integrity of the site and its value as heritage. Have these two cities become such potent symbols that their meaning has become divorced from their material, architectural integrity? Undoubtedly, a significant part of their heritage lies in their symbolism, a symbolism that has been built up and built on for over fifty years through a rhetoric of words and images that has coupled them with an array of causes and meanings.

Box 3.2   Cultural Heritage and the Re-construction of Identities after Conflict

Throughout recorded history, cultural heritage has suffered damage and destruction in times of conflict. Whereas this has been noted for a long time, it is only recently that such destruction has been explicitly linked to the centrality of heritage and history in providing people with a sense of *identity*, of belonging somewhere and of being a part of something. Substantial issues for the welfare of societies are involved when cultural heritage is destroyed and subsequently reconstructed. 'Cultural heritage' refers to a wide range of features, and can take tangible as well as intangible forms, but the Cultural Heritage and the Re-construction of Identities after Conflict (CRIC) project focuses on the physical heritage, i.e. monuments, architecture, land- and townscapes. Using the physical, tangible heritage as a basic reference point also allows the project to pursue less tangible aspects and responses as these are expressed in, for instance, memorials, symbols, and anniversary ceremonies.

The CRIC project uses five case studies to empirically document the relationships between cultural heritage and conflict, and on this basis it engages in comparative analyses centred on core themes. Four themes have become concretized as the research has progressed. One is memorialization practices and their changing forms. Despite the sense of permanence and repetition that these convey, they are actually changing continually in more and less explicit ways. Another theme is the sense of the sites themselves, how they get selected a particular moments, the reasons behind this selection and the status with which they are imbued. A third theme that has become significant is the role of media in the construction of non-local understandings; for instance, the role of television, photography, literature, the visual arts, and also the internet, in the creation of 'shared memories'. The final theme is the effect of time, and in particular changing and transmitted memories, as the areas between personal, private, public and shared memories are revealing themselves as important transformative factors.

To create a robust and viable theory concerning identity, conflict and cultural heritage requires that the project draws on disparate yet interrelated examples from which larger generalizations can arise. The case studies were selected with this aim in mind. Their disparity stems in part from their varied geographic region, linguistic background and demographic makeup, but far more importantly, the differences and comparative measures also arise from these being examples of different historical contexts. The case studies include civil wars, wars between countries, and the two world wars; they are situated in France, Germany, Spain, Cyprus and Bosnia. Each case study takes a long historical view that runs from the time of the conflict being examined through to the present in order to trace the evolution of sites and memorial practices. Apart from academic outputs, in-depth analyses of these relationships will be useful to policymakers, practitioners and regional actors, and guide crucial discussions regarding why and how cultural heritage can be reconstructed. The CRIC project has been funded by the European Union under its Seventh Framework Programme as a Collaborative Project under the action line: 'Histories and Identities: Articulating National and European Identities'. The project began in 2008 and will run until 2012. The following website provides regular up-dates the progress of the research: www.cric.arch.cam.ac.uk

Marie Louise Stig Sørensen

What lessons can be drawn for individuals and organizations designing policies and projects that require a sense of the heritage, identity and memory? In 2007, I criticized international involvement in reconstruction projects that reinforced the divides created by the war. As outlined above, this can have long-term consequences on societies, structuring their sense of belonging and memory on a discourse of antagonistic difference and discrete identities. This danger should be recognized in policy and project design. For example, InterSOS is an Italian NGO that restores damaged Ottoman heritage and Orthodox churches in Kosovo and also, in an effort to straddle the ethnic divide, organizes cultural heritage tours of these sites for people from all groups.

Three key issues are identity, reconstruction and essentialization. Identity is to a large degree rooted in the notions of heritage and history, of knowing where one comes from as an individual and a society and of belonging somewhere. When heritage is deliberately targeted and destroyed, these actions resonate within communities and their experience of identity, enhancing the sense of 'insiders' and 'outsiders', and relationships with place and history. Reconstruction demands a series of choices in determining what sites of cultural heritage are to be preserved, restored, rebuilt or not. The narrative that binds these decisions together affects the future development of meaning, symbols that are central to the construction of social memories and identities. By influencing how communities perceive themselves and 'others', actions impinging on heritage will have consequences on how societies perceive and interact with one another. An appreciation of the essentializing effect of conflicts on identity should be present in developing reconstruction policies and projects, and in determining the priorities and the values that they seek to embed.

Furthermore, it would seem that Truth and Reconciliation Commissions (TRCs) are emerging as an organized form of bearing witness, coordinating and networking the efforts of civil society to make itself felt in the long wakes of wars. At their best, TRCs represent an attempt to make claims on the narration of conflicts to facilitate a multitude of voices, experiences and interpretations of events to be heard. They are emerging as a new form of civil society organization and could come to play a similar role to that of NGOs today. They would, however, have to show the wisdom to avoid a tiger-trap signalled by Hobsbawm (2009: 50): 'The most underrated danger to culture is the tendency to establish historical truth, not by evidence and argument, but by law.'

In light of the above, it would seem that careful attention and planning of interventions that address culture and cultural heritage issues in the aftermath of war is no luxury. Attitudes towards the past, decisions about what historic moments to celebrate and how to memorialize conflicts will all shape post-conflict society. They can be a revealing marker of the nation-building process, in planning third-party interventions, and could potentially be a valuable indicator of dysfunctional and failing states.

Box 3.3 Memory and its absence in two Lebanese museums

How have questions of national identity and collective memory come to the fore in the National Museum of Beirut (NMB) and the Al-Khiyam Prison Museum (APM)? This question is related to the absence in Lebanon of a collective memory of the Lebanese civil war (1975–90) and the thirty-three day July 2006 war. This memory gap has had serious consequences on the construction of national identity. This is a serious issue in the context of a nation that is unstable politically, economically and socially, and in which archaeological and historical sites and museums seem to have been left behind. For the Lebanese government, there are much more important responsibilities, such as regenerating the economy and reconstructing the country after all the years of war and turmoil. The Lebanese public has come to associate the past with export commodities. Hence, few Lebanese have interiorized the belief that heritage belongs to all and that it has to be preserved in order to promote cultural identity. On the other hand, heritage in Lebanon today is very political. Perhaps it needs to be depoliticized before it can be appreciated by the public.

In this context, if it is true that museums are the mirrors of a nation, then the history and evolution of Lebanese museums could help us understand the socio-political transformations that have taken place. For 'political museumizing' (Anderson, 1991) indeed plays a major role in the process of nation-building and in the promotion of patrimony by the nation-state by the very selection and valuation of a certain collection of artefacts or archaeological sites. The early 1990s were a 'recovery period' during which the Lebanese wanted to forget the civil war. It is only now that we witness some change – the forgetfulness and the silence that marked the early years of recovery are being broken. But this has not taken place in the National Museum. In the second, established by Hezbollah after the liberation of Southern Lebanon from Israel in May 2000, which was actually destroyed by the Israeli invasion in 2006, war atrocities were, on the other hand, clearly exposed. The absence of the civil war in the first (apart from a single showcase depicting some melted glass artefacts) is an example of severing time from space and contradicts the function of the museum as a carrier of time. The collective memory of the civil war has been ignored by the curators. Rather than being 'sites of memory', as Pierre Nora has termed them, they became places of amnesia and the war has been forgotten and erased from the discourse of history. The establishment of the APM was somewhat controversial and it was never considered by the Lebanese local authorities as a museum. The APM was a memorial to the liberation struggle and a symbol of the victory over Israel claimed by Hezbollah. It became a valuable asset for propaganda and revived the struggle of Hezbollah against Israel. The question is why the NMB erased the civil war discourse from its edifice whereas the APM did not. Different political agendas in Lebanon have given rise to a clash of memories – the construction of social memory is not monolithic but rather is influenced by identity and religion. In the APM, memory and trauma are linked to a space of resistance in an erstwhile prison; whereas in the NMB, memory and forgetfulness are juxtaposed and the space becomes a physical landmark and emerges clean, hollow and serene.

The interpretation of the Lebanese past is made out of selections of that past, and what people want to remember and what they want to forget in order to recreate meanings of both the past and the present. Therefore, memory becomes a key issue in interpreting the past in the museum space. It is true that we must distinguish between history and memory: 'memory is a perpetually actual phenomenon, a bond tying us to the eternal present; history is a representation of the past' (Nora, 1989: 8). Yet history is the only means to make sense of our past in the present and memory is an emotional expression that should bind us together and be linked to a place or *lieu* and in our case the museum. I would like to argue that Lebanese museums should become 'barometers' of urban culture. They should not only be 'containers' of artefacts, but also offer a spatial experience that is shared with others. This is considered more important than the individual stake. The museum should become a resource, a 'lively space' that enlightens the public on certain themes and encourages social debate. The choice of objectives and themes depends on the evaluation of public demand (this must be the starting point of any educational activity) and the existing educational potential that is found within the museum. Social, cultural, political, economic and religious diversity summarize the characteristics of a post-civil war Lebanese population beset by all sorts of quotidian problems. The common denominator is the absence of a collective memory that might contribute to forming a sense of community. If a 'culture of contact' and reconciliation is to emerge, more attention has to be paid to how the recent past is represented. For, Lebanese museums do have the potential to be places for 'reconciliation' work to be done, drawing on the rich cultural heritage of the country as part of a broader peace-building process.

Lina G. Tahan

References

Andersen, B. (1991) *Imagined Communities: Reflections on the Origin and Spread of Nationalism*. London: Verso (Revised edition).
Nora, P. (1989) 'Between Memory and History: Les Lieux de Mémoire', *Representations* 26: 7–25.

The final scene of Truffaut's (1966) film version of Ray Bradbury's *Fahrenheit 451* (1953) has refugees from a future in which firemen burn books walking through the foggy landscape of their exile, each reciting a book that they have committed to memory. In order for the books to exist independent of their materiality they have to be memorized, but since this takes such a considerable effort, each person is only able to memorize one, thereby becoming the heritage incarnate: living heritage. If the books are not physically endangered but readily stored and available in public and private libraries, then there is no need to memorize them, but that does not mean that they are forgotten. Their content, the stories they tell, the morals and information that they communicate, exist, however fragmentarily, in the minds of those who have read them. Each reader takes with them the most relevant parts, for them, through their intimate experience of reading. Similarly with other forms of heritage, their contribution to the construction of identity and memory depends on how they are individually experienced but ultimately affects the collective.

Notes

1 The Polish International Brigaders in Spain were called *dombrosiacos*.
2 This realization has been emerging through the CRIC research project as a particularly significant and previously understudied area.
3 This work on Gernika is being carried out by the CRIC research project.
4 While some international NGOs, professional institutions and governments offered their support, notably an important amount of archival material was illegally taken out of Iraq by other foreign military, journalists and NGOs (Eskander, 2009).
5 For instance, Penny Lane, made famous in a song by The Beatles, was named after a slave trader.
6 By 'vicarious memories' I mean those that are told, retold, communicated and transmitted by those with first-hand experience of events to others who in turn internalize these memories, making them part of their personal understanding of 'what happened'.
7 These communities of memory are to be understood as distinct from religious, cultural or ethnic characteristics that might otherwise tie such groups. For instance, the Russian diaspora formed in cities such as London and Paris after the Russian Revolution have a different memory-heritage from communities of Russians formed during the Second World War or those that have been emerging since 1989.

REFERENCES

Amnesty International (2007) www.amnesty.org/en/international-justice/issues/truth-commissions, last viewed: 26 October 2009.

Barthes, R. (1973) *Mythologies*. Translated by A. Lavers (original 1957). London: Paladin.

BBC (2005) 'Northern Ireland', in *Coast*, Series 3, Episode 6. London: BBC with the Open University.

Bradbury, R. (2004) *Fahrenheit 451*. London: Voyager. [Originally published: London: Rupert Hart-Davis Ltd, 1953.]

Campany, D. (2003) 'Safety in Numbness: Some Remarks on Problems of 'Late Photography', in D. Green (ed.), *Where is the Photograph?* Kent: Photoworks.

Connerton, P. (2008) 'Seven Types of Forgetting', *Memory Studies*, 1 (1): 59–71. London: Sage.

Constantinou, C. and M. Haray (2009) 'Identity, Ethnic Conflict and Conflicted Heritage in Cyprus', paper presented at the ECPR conference, Potsdam, 9 September.

Eskander, S. (2009) 'Iraq National Library and Archives in Transition: Old Tasks and New Responsibilities', paper presented at the Centre for Research in the Arts, Social Sciences and Humanities at the University of Cambridge, 30 October 2009.

Finlay, V. (2002) *Colour: Travels through the Paintbox*. London: Hodder and Stoughton.

Forty, A. and S. Küchler (eds) (2001) *The Art of Forgetting*. Oxford: Berg.

Galeano, E. (1991) *The Book of Embraces*. Translated by Cedric Belfrage. London and New York: W.W. Norton & Company.

Halbwachs, M. (1992) *The Legendary Topography of the Gospels in the Holy Land*. Translated by Lewis A. Coser. Chicago: University of Chicago Press.

Hobsbawm, E. (2009) 'How Should We Rate 2009?', *Prospect*, 166: 50.

Hussey, A. (2008) 'The Paris Intifada: The Long War in the *banlieue*', *Granta*, 101: 41–60. London: Granta Publications.

Khosronejad, P. (2009) 'To Whom It May Concern: War Memorials and Constructing the Past in Postwar Iran.

Khorramshar Sacred Defence Museum', paper presented at the Centre for Research in the Arts, Social Sciences and Humanities at the University of Cambridge.

Moravia, A. (1972) 'The Image and the Word', reprinted in The UNESCO *Courrier*, March 1996, dedicated to The Roots of Racism. Paris: UNESCO.

Navaro-Yashin, Y. (2002) *Faces of the State: Secularism and Public Life in Turkey*. Princeton, NJ: Princeton University Press.

Navaro-Yashin, Y. (2010) *The Make-Believe Space: Affect, Law, and Governance in an Abjected Territory*. Durham, NC: Duke University Press.

Nora, P. (1996) 'Between Memory and History', in *Realms of Memory: Rethinking the French Past*. Vol. 1: *Conflicts and Divisions*. English-language edition edited and with a foreward by Lawrence D. Kritzman, translated by Arthur Goldhammer. New York: Columbia University Press.

Nora, P. (1997) *Realms of Memory: Rethinking the French Past*. Vol. 3: *Symbols*. English-language edition edited and with a foreword by Lawrence D. Kritzman, translated by Arthur Goldhammer. New York: Columbia University Press.

Rév, I. (2008) 'The House of Terror', in R. Ostow (ed.), *(Re) visualizing National History: Museums and National Identities in Europe in the New Millennium*. Toronto: University of Toronto Press.

Riegl, Alois. (1903) *Der moderne Denkmalkultus, sein Wesen, seine Entstehung* (Vienna). Translated by K.W. Forster and D. Ghirardo as 'The Modern Cult of Monuments: Its Character and Its Origin' in *Oppositions* 25 (Fall 1982), pp. 21–51.

Ruiz Lardizábal, J. (2007) 'Polonia repudia las Brigadas Internacionales', *El País*, 9 March 2007.

Sontag, S. (2003) *Regarding the Pain of Others*. New York: Picador.

Viejo-Rose, D. (2007) 'Conflict and the Deliberate Destruction of Cultural Heritage', in H. Anheier and Y.R. Isar (eds), *Conflicts and Tensions: The Cultures and Globalization Series*, Vol. 1. London: SAGE Publications.

Viejo-Rose, D. (2009) 'Reconstructing Cultural Heritage after Civil War: Making Meaning and Memory'. PhD dissertation, University of Cambridge, Cambridge.

Young, J.E. (1993) *The Texture of Memory*. New Haven, CT, and London: Yale University Press.

CHAPTER 4

THE POLITICAL ECONOMIES OF HERITAGE
Tim Winter

In recent years much attention has been paid to how heritage, memory and identity are socially actualised in both material and non-material ways, for example to the relationship between heritage and capital, particularly in light of apparent processes of globalisation. Though the focus has been rather narrowly conceived and pejorative in tone, bemoaning the 'commodification' of culture and supposed loss of 'authenticity', the casual use of that term as a generic way of understanding the cultural-economic dyad masks the real complexities of this relationship. This chapter seeks to illustrate why more nuanced, multi-vector understandings are required. It will consider how heritage and memory are being produced and shaped in particular contexts through a series of political and economic processes that have now become global and will also highlight how such processes involve the privileging of certain forms of expertise and cultural knowledge

The globalisation of heritage funding

As we embark upon the second decade of the twenty-first century, there is little doubt that more organisations, more resources and more effort are being put into the preservation and restoration of cultural heritage than ever before. As the notion of conservation continued to grow and geographically expand over the course of the twentieth century, so too did the links between culture and capital at the local, national, regional and global levels. As we shall see over the course of this chapter, the predominant sources of heritage funding can be very different across different contexts, but invariably the meshing of these multi-scalar sources of funding is a feature of heritage preservation within contemporary globalisation.

Indeed, one of the defining features of today's interconnected world is the proliferation of globally roaming organisations operating in the field of cultural conservation. Notable and familiar examples here include the various intergovernmental organisations and associated bodies known primarily around the world through their acronyms: UNESCO, ICCROM, ICOM, and ICOMOS (see Isar's chapter in this volume).[1] There are also private foundations and charitable entities in this field, such as the J.P. Getty Trust, the Aga Khan Trust for Culture, the World Monuments Fund, the Global Heritage Fund, etc. But in recent decades we have also seen a major expansion in the number of non-governmental organisations and foundations that have looked towards the conservation of heritage as an effective tool for advancing their core goals, many of which may not be directly related to the cultural sector; examples here include The Henry Luce Foundation, The Rockefeller Foundation, Fondazione Zegna, and The Lee Foundation. Scattered among these various organisations we also see examples of philanthropy and the role this has played in the heritage sector. Perhaps most notably, the United States has a well established tradition of private, philanthropic aid supporting the cultural sector. With tax incentives greatly assisting the flow of funds into heritage-related initiatives, financing in this sector has been characterised by the causes and interests of individual donors. Interestingly, this has also meant that some of the most impoverished communities and fragile locations in the developing world have benefited significantly as those with abundant wealth have travelled internationally.

One of the most interesting developments in the internationalisation of heritage conservation has been the 'cultural turn' in the 'development' sector. Since the early 1990s organisations like the the United Nations Development Programme (UNDP), the World Bank, the Inter-American Development Bank, the Asian Development Bank, the African Development Bank and the European Commission, all of which can be loosely grouped together through the nature of their transnational, multi-sector and multilateral initiatives, have undertaken various heritage-related programmes. The Millennium Development Goals have also proved significant in strengthening the links between these organisations and the ties between cultural preservation and socio-economic development. However, the ongoing rise of multilateral aid in developing countries since the end of the Second World War has not meant a decline of the nation-state in such affairs (Drainville 2003). Bilateral aid continues to be a defining feature of today's global heritage–development nexus, an area I will return to shortly.

Box 4.1 Saturated by souvenirs: art and identity in Zanzibar's Stone Town

The architectural legacy of an East African trade in spices, slaves, and ivory situates Zanzibar's Stone Town as a mosaic of identities and histories. Valorised through its World Heritage listing in 2000, Stone Town has been declared by UNESCO as significant for 'outstanding material manifestation of cultural fusion and harmonization'. This listing has acted as a magnet to draw in travellers, many already venturing to Tanzania's natural World Heritage Sites (Ngorongoro Conservation Area, Selous Game Reserve, Kilimanjaro National Park and Serengeti National Park). As a result of booming tourism the urban landscape is being shaped by an industry which caters to 125,000 foreign visitors each year. Interwoven through the streets and alleys of the 2.5 square kilometre listed town boundary is a souvenir art market, dominated by objects and stereotyped images of Masai warriors, safari animals, and 'African' masks. Created to satisfy the foreign consumer, a cacophony of around 200 shops display competing notions of what 'authentic' Zanzibari heritage is and should be.

Zanzibar-born carvers, artist cooperatives, and women's groups produce carved chests, textiles, and paintings which are dedicated to expressing 'their' heritage and simultaneously capitalise on the tourist presence. However, souvenir representations that mirror Stone Town's architectural landscape and local cultural traditions are overshadowed by an abundance of objects imported from the Mainland. Methods used to mass manufacture, buy, market, and sell souvenirs are mobilised through ethnic solidarities, notably Meru and Masai who draw on their existing experiences from the tourist gateway Arusha. When asked if there is a style of 'Zanzibar art', local artists and shopkeepers frequently refer to an intangible form, such as the Muezzin's call to prayer, Taarab music, culinary traditions, and particular styles of wearing Kanga, Kikoy and Kofia. In contrast, the very tangible Tingatinga paintings from Dar es Salaam and masks from various interior nations can be found in trinket stalls throughout East Africa. Spurred by an economically rooted struggle to exploit the urban heritage as a resource, shops have become symbols of power in the town's streetscape. Objects in the souvenir marketplace thus serve as 'instruments for territorial self-fashioning' (Isar, Viejo-Rose, and Anheier, in this volume), a process that results in a tension between super-local Zanzibari and pan-East African identities.

The production and sale of more generic images blurs concepts of what is 'authentically Zanzibari'. Souvenirs saturate the streetscape to an extent that both tourists and locals are culturally transported between the historic landscape and a homogenised representation of East Africa based on the concentration or lack of imported imagery. Zanzibari painter Mussa expresses a local understanding of Stone Town's cultural heritage:

We want to show, for example there, there, that corner [*pointing outside*], it is for one to see, to meet this way of life. It's not like Samora Street, Dar es Salaam. Not like Kisutu. That would not be suitable. There are many hotels of Stone Town. Eh they are Stone. Particularly, they are the history from the years of 1800 and 1700. This is history. Buildings are like memories. Indeed, the meaning of many homes mark the building places as records, that is, they are of the long ago. They are of rocks/stones. I have come from stones. I am born of stones. To take care of them is to remember. (Mussa, 4 April 2008)[1]

Mussa is referring to what he thinks Zanzibaris should present to the visiting public and defines the space as 'authentic' in terms of its ability to transmit memory. Enhanced by the contemporary tourist trade, custodial responsibility to 'their' stones and respective memories is a juxtaposition of the local self to place and 'other'. These bodily links to the physical space are challenged by non-local images and customs, which become an obstacle for local artists' in their ability to connect with or profit from 'their' heritage.

For some, the very presence of incongruent objects degrades and blemishes territorial attachments.

It ruins the heritage here. It ruins things, like this home; it trashes these things, [*pointing*] chests, and doors. … It's ruining the appearance/expression of the city. … Its just litter, they are littering doing this [*business*]. (Abeid, 20 March 2008)

'They' is in reference to the groups of vendors who come mostly from Arusha and who are responsible for approximately 120 of the shops in Stone Town. Notions of authenticity segregate the populations who are capitalising on Stone Town as a heritage site. This is exacerbated by the economic strength of Mainland themed shops, which propagate, promote, and profit from the imported images.

For others, the act of selling carvings is misrepresenting Zanzibari culture and, more importantly, disrespects ideological customs. Hammid likens carvings to beer in an attempt to illuminate an overt opposition to Islamic principles.

All the carvings are from the Mainland. There are so many shops that sell those vinyago/carvings. Carvings have been brought here like beer. They have brought beer. Beer is from the Mainland. (Hammid, 16 April 2008)

Cultural heritage becomes a tool with political leverage, confronting different visions of local and regional identity, which through its commodification fuels tensions. These tensions are not simply a question of who has the right to use the World Heritage resource; rather they are about valuing 'authentic' representations. Some Zanzibari souvenir artists articulate it as a binary of whether or not to adopt the successful outside models and conform to aspects of foreign identities, or maintain cultural integrity and bypass tangible economic gains. In fact, the experience of those quoted above is not articulated in terms of passive acceptance; rather it is in terms of assimilatory lament. Objects are viewed as allegorical tools employed by the 'other' to trash the landscape, to impose a 'foreign' set of moral, aesthetic and cultural references on it, thus exploiting and misrepresenting Zanzibar heritage and lifestyle.

Within the souvenir art market, supply-side negotiation for spatial and visual representation has marginalised Zanzibari artists and created a super-local sense of self and 'other'. As mass tourism integrates local communities into a larger regional network of souvenir icons, economic profitability underlines the issue of how an urban World Heritage Site can be used and contested. In the case of Stone Town, competition to cash in has destabilised many local inhabitants' connections to the place; hardly the harmonisation that UNESCO has suggested.

Kara A. Blackmore

---

[1]Interviews conducted in March and April 2008, translated from Kiswahili.

In addition to these international developments, there is ample evidence around the world of the many ways in which governments have responded to, and shaped, cultural globalisation by pushing more and more resources into their domestic heritage sectors. A number of key factors have been driving this, many of which can be seen in the major international Expo held in Shanghai in 2010. Thematically subtitled 'Better City, Better Life', the Expo involved the transformation of what was largely an industrial landscape alongside the Huangpu river. Rather than erasing the memories of the site's history, the Expo celebrated and adaptively re-used the 'industrial heritage' architecture of Shanghai. From this base, one of the key themes of the six-month Expo was the twinning of cultural conservation with urban development. Of course Shanghai is not alone in identifying such a relationship, as countless local and central government authorities have looked to appropriate the past for the socio-economic regeneration of urban environments. But what is particularly interesting in this case is the accelerated transitions from industrial to post-industrial economies now occurring in so-called 'developing countries', like China. Clearly, in fast-changing regions such as Asia the long time frames, which have characterised such transitions in the West previously, are now being collapsed into a number of simultaneous presents. And as we know, the trajectory of Shanghai's development and the staging of the Expo there also exemplify how cities have an ever greater reliance upon tertiary sector economies like tourism and leisure consumption. But as with other mega-events like the Olympics, such spectacles are heavily bound up in the identity theatrics of nation-building as governments seek to construct specific identities both at home and on the international stage. As Beijing and Shanghai vie for the world's attention, we see a vivid example of how heritage becomes enmeshed in the political economies of subnational, regionalised identities as a country projects itself onto the international stage.

Capital flows and Geo-politics

If we are to reflect more closely upon how this landscape of heritage has evolved at the international level, it is also necessary to consider how the directional flows of capital are shaped politically. As we shall see, the heritage sector is now very much part of the global geo-political landscape. An appreciation of such processes also reveals the limitations of accounts that suggest that globalisation, as manifest in the agencies like UNESCO, has led to a geographically seamless, homogenising form of cultural governance.

If we consider more closely the operations of organisations like the Aga Khan Trust for Culture, the World Monuments Fund or the Getty Conservation Institute, it is apparent that there are distinct cultural/geographical weightings or imbalances in the distribution of their projects (as regards UNESCO, see the chapter by Isar in this volume). While a number of these organisations claim to be 'global' in nature, in reality various historical and political factors are at play that mean their geographical coverage is rarely even. Even the archetype and architect of today's global heritage movement, UNESCO, remains deeply imbalanced in its coverage, as their map of the World Heritage Sites by region illustrates.[2] The overwhelming concentration of World Heritage properties in Europe speaks as much about the political standing of the region in the second half of the twentieth century, combined with UNESCO's institutional history in Paris, as it does about the histories of population settlement or distribution of 'natural wonders' across the globe. Although UNESCO is working hard to address its eurocentric leanings, the inherent complexities of reforming such a large organisation mean this will take considerable time to work its way through.

In the case of the Aga Khan Trust for Culture, this sense of cultural and geographic concentration is explicitly expressed, with the organisation openly declaring its focus primarily as communities of the Muslim faith. Although actively engaged in a number of Western European countries, including the UK, Portugal and Switzerland, as well as in Canada and the USA, many of their long-running heritage projects have been housed within a larger organisational remit of social, cultural and economic empowerment across the most impoverished countries of Asia and Africa where Islam is a prevalent faith. As the umbrella institution, the Aga Khan Development Network – the Trust for Culture being one of its member organisations – is made up of agencies dedicated to health, education, economic development, and the advancement of civil society. Today, the vast majority of the organisation's activities are financed through a highly advanced set of partnerships with national governments, private donors and a variety of non-governmental bodies. As of 2010, the AKDN conducts operations through collaborations with thirty-five governments and their aid agencies and around twenty organisations that might be best categorised as multilateral. Examples of this latter group include the African and Asian Development Banks, the UN High Commissioner for Refugees, World Health Organisation and International Atomic Energy Agency. A number of projects have also been co-sponsored by universities around the world, cultural sector institutions like the Smithsonian and through grants from the Ford, Gates, and Shell Foundations. In this respect, the AKDN is typical of the global infrastructure and financing of cultural heritage which has come into being. Indeed, what is clear is that cultural heritage has become part of that amorphous entity known as 'global civil society', what Keane (2003: 8) describes as a 'new cosmology', and defines as:

> a dynamic non-governmental system of interconnected socio-economic institutions that straddle the whole earth ... an unfinished project that consists of sometimes thick, sometimes thinly stretched networks, pyramids and hub-and-spoke clusters of institutions and actors who organise themselves across borders, with the deliberate aim of drawing the world together in new ways.

Indeed, the Aga Khan Trust's links into this institutional arena of social and economic development has many parallels across the world today. The early 1990s saw a significant shift away from post-Second World War ideas of culture as an obstacle to socio-economic development and modernisation. Through a language of 'sustainability', notions of 'human capital' have come to the fore, with culture increasingly seen as a resource for 'sustainable development' and wealth generation. In various contexts, both cultural and natural heritage have come to be seen as mechanisms for leveraging localised communities, improving incomes and improving environmental awareness. Not surprisingly, much of the critical literature documenting such shifts has addressed the multilateral aid sector, with studies by Hawkins and Mann (2007), Hirsch and Warren (2002) and Radcliffe (2006) being among those that have considered the 'evolution'

in policies of the World Bank, and the regional banks of Africa, Asia and Latin America. While such accounts have been highly productive, it is also important to recognise the parallel role played by government-affiliated agencies providing bilateral aid. In recent years, organisations like DfID (UK), USAID (USA), AFD (France) SIDA (Sweden), GTZ (Germany), AusAID (Australia) have all expanded their interest in heritage as a viable component of humanitarian aid.[3] In Yemen, for example, the German development agency GTZ has established an award-winning programme in the historic city of Shibam – and more recently extended it to Zabid – whereby the restoration of traditional architectural structures has been employed as the catalyst for a wider social and economic revival of a fast-decaying urban environment.[4]

But as heritage becomes increasingly integral to the bilateral aid sector, interesting questions arise regarding the cultural politics of international and post-colonial relations. As numerous authors have highlighted, the provision of financial assistance through aid is inherently political and shaped by past and present world orders. While it might be tempting to regard the provision of assistance in the 'revival' or 'preservation' of a country's cultural heritage as a benign, politically inert activity, closer inspection reveals how donor states have effectively engaged in this sector as a mechanism of 'soft power' (Khanna 2008). Even if heritage bodies are not state funded, when operating overseas their operations become part of a country's 'cultural export' and as such they are, in many cases, absorbed into the bureaucratic structures of diplomacy and international relations. In the case of the USA, the John Paul Getty Trust and the Rockefeller and Luce Foundations are among those that contributed to favourable diplomatic relations and the country's popular appeal as it increased its global influence during the second half of the twentieth century. The cultural–political dynamics of heritage funding can also be clearly seen in the context of today's post-colonial relations. For the former European powers of Britain, France, Portugal and Spain, for example, the export of heritage projects and assistance often aligns with governmental priorities for maintaining ties with former territories. The heritage sector provides the ideal forum through which linguistic and cultural links can be celebrated, promoted and reaffirmed. Moreover, although this might be a more established sector in the industrialised West, countries such as Brazil, China, India, Mexico and Thailand are among those in the developing world now actively exporting their expertise and cultural knowledge via cultural heritage. In many cases, such activities are an effective means of securing influence at the regional level. If we take India as an example, overseas heritage conservation and museum-related projects have been pursued in regions like Southeast Asia in order to maintain and, in some cases, re-establish long-lost cultural, political and economic ties.

Post-conflict and disaster contexts provide arguably the most vivid and sensitive settings within which heritage, memory and identity have become enmeshed in the cultural politics of aid and international relations. Recent years have seen an increasingly rigorous analysis of the complex ways in which today's global aid networks merge development and security in loose, supranational spaces of governance (Chandler 2006; Duffield 2001 and 2007). Much attention here has been given to the application of neo-liberal models of development and reconstruction (Ferguson 1994; Klein 2007). However, with the bulk of these studies being conducted within the analytical frames of political science, development studies or economics, they often give less attention to the activities of cultural sector institutions in disaster or conflict recovery. Nonetheless, projects conducted in Afghanistan, across the Balkans and in Sri Lanka together illustrate some of the ways in which cultural heritage has become a vital part of the wider humanitarian goals of today's global civil society (Kalisa 2006; Thompson 2007; Viejo-Rose 2007).

One of the most remarkable examples of the complex geo-politics of cultural heritage funding in post-conflict contexts is Angkor in Cambodia. As Cambodia re-opened its borders and restored diplomatic relations with various countries in the early 1990s, the political space required for international interventions in the country's cultural recovery sector opened up accordingly. After a period of more than two decades of violent conflict and profound social turmoil Cambodia needed at once to restore its cultural, economic and political infrastructures. The speed at which the country embraced modernity and globalisation during this period grossly accentuated the paradoxes inherent to these two transformative processes. A real energy to develop, to move forward, modernise and depart from the revolutionary, socialist politics of the recent past, was partnered by an intense desire to look back, to reclaim, and to retrieve what was lost. It was widely recognised that a key focal point for these interweaving agendas would be the World Heritage Site of Angkor in the north-west of the country.

The addition of Angkor to the World Heritage List in 1992 stemmed from a need to protect, restore and manage one of Southeast Asia's most important cultural landscapes. In the nomination process, however, the discourse of 'value' centred on the site's monumental and archaeological remains. The turmoil of previous decades had left Cambodia with wholly inadequate governmental, administrative and legal structures. The country also lacked expertise in monumental conservation, archaeology, community development, tourism, urban planning or forestry. Given Angkor's immense historical importance, along with its global prestige, it was not surprising that an unprecedented influx of international assistance quickly formed around the site. Indeed, since the early 1990s more than twenty countries – including France, Japan, China, India, America, Germany, Italy and Australia – have together donated millions of dollars to help safeguard the temples.

However, as I have written elsewhere, this international arena of conservation needs to be understood through the double lens of post-colonialism and Asian regional politics (Winter 2007). In essence, the assistance provided for Angkor formed part of the 'cultural arm' of aid and assistance provided by countries like France, Japan, India and China, each one seeking influence in the strategically important region of Southeast Asia. In the case of France, providing funds and unparalleled expertise for the conservation and rejuvenation of architectural structures enables the narrative of a benign, indeed benevolent, former colonial power to be maintained. For the likes of India, China, Korea, Taiwan, Thailand and even Australia and New Zealand, countries like Cambodia have emerged as strategically pivotal in a region of rapid economical growth and potential political volatility. In effect, Angkor's architectural antiquities have entered the arena of interstate cultural politics, an area which, as Yúdice (2003) has illustrated, has become an essential constituent of contemporary globalisation, and its transnational geographies of capital flows.

Heritage tourism

Sites like Angkor also offer a signpost to the future with regard to the long-term growth of tourism. Today it is well recognised that tourism, rather than merely being a force of cultural destruction or homogenisation, actively contributes to the production of heritage and memory (Timothy & Nyaupane 2009). As we know, regardless of context, tourism is an industry that straddles multiple industries and creates complex public-private sector relationships. In the heritage sector, even the most cautious institutions, previously fearful and resistant to the tourism industry have learnt to see it as a source of potential, if not vital, income. English Heritage is one such entity that now actively engages with the tourism sector through collaborative agreements with tour operators, regional and national tourism boards as well as mainstream media channels. With countless cities around the world seeking to maintain growth through post-industrial, tertiary sectors of the economy, as noted earlier, substantial funding has fed into the rejuvenation of historic properties or quarters (Drainville 2003). In many cases, though, conservation bodies have been somewhat late to the table in such discussions. With deep-rooted fears of 'commodification' and modernity within the heritage sector, architects, urban planners, and service industry entrepreneurs have been among those driving the transformation of heritage into a 'resource' for tourism-related development. Operating at the international level, the World Heritage Alliance initiative represents an interesting case of a collaboration driven in large part by the tourism industry itself. Set up in 2005, the scheme is supported by more than sixty partner organisations spanning numerous countries, with the aim of promoting forms of 'responsible tourism' that help facilitate the conservation of the host world heritage sites.

Similarly, throughout the world, it has become commonplace for tour operators and hospitality companies to assist with community-based conservation projects through the promotion of 'cultural', 'eco' or 'adventure' tourism products. In the case of the Silk Road, for example, the network of tour operators running tours along the route are extensively embedded in a range of cultural heritage projects. In addition to the direct funding that comes from the agencies themselves, these tours are a well-established source for the types of private philanthropy highlighted earlier.[5] Heritage tourism along the Silk Road also provides a good example of the links that have emerged between the public and private sectors. In Gansu, China, the World Bank has conceived a five-year project spanning 2008–13 that directs substantial funds into the region's cultural and natural heritage. In addition to enhancing capacities for environmental conservation, a programme of 'sustainable heritage tourism' provides the vehicle for advancing their broader socio-developmental aims, including improved sanitation, health and social services and the upgrading of physical infrastructures.[6]

Of course, the benefits of creating public-private partnerships in the field of heritage tourism have long been recognised by non-governmental agencies working within a paradigm of community-based development. In many developing countries, projects that focus on the production of handicrafts in order to make heritage an economically viable part of everyday life, and at the same time maintain continuities between cultural pasts and the present, have now become commonplace. By examining such processes in the context of Mexico, Valerie Magar considers the role of material culture for both rural communities as well as the visiting tourist. Focusing on the post-conflict recovery of the southern region of Chiapas, Magar indicates how handicrafts create the material and semiotic connections between tourists, local residents and the region's Mayan archaeological ruins, a process which is vital to the long-term viability of the region's tourism economy (Magar 2007).

Science and capital

Finally, in order to fully appreciate the cultural economies of heritage today, it is necessary to consider how the predominance of particular discourses or forms of knowledge expertise within the heritage sector occurs precisely because they are both privileged by capital *and* at the same time enable the production of capital, a process, which, by implication, allows certain forms of heritage, memory and identity to prevail. In its diversity, the cultural heritage sector draws upon and integrates a wide array of expert knowledge forms, ranging from archaeology, architectural conservation, anthropology, engineering, sociology, art history, and more. However, as we shall see, certain ways of understanding and conserving a heritage resource come to be privileged in particular contexts, in large part because of the relation that knowledge form has with capital. Countless studies have been conducted regarding the difficult and often tense situations that arise when archaeological remains are discovered or buildings are deemed worthy of preservation at sites undergoing development and construction. In essence, what such studies document is the ways in which a language of cultural heritage stands in resistance to, or as an obstacle to those seeking capital gain from a site. At the same time, however, and as we have seen, it has also become increasingly apparent that the heritage sector has become deeply embedded in the economies of cities, communities and nations.[7] What remains less well understood, are the complex and subtle ways in which certain heritage discourses directly enable capital accumulation, and are simultaneously enabled themselves by the political and economic processes through which a site, building, object or community is prescribed 'value'.

Box 4.2   The margin of a centre: heritage, space and memory in Salvador

The city of Salvador, capital of the state of Bahia, is today one of Brazil's most treasured tourist destinations. A UNESCO World Heritage site since 1985, the city is well known both for its rich colonial architecture and as Brazil's most *African* city, a status that is due to its past as capital of the colony and first slave port in the continent. Since its inscription on the World Heritage List, Salvador has become 'the proper place for defining tradition and locating blackness in "racial democracy"' (Collins, 2008: 279). On Brazil's Ministry of Tourism website, the city is described as a mythical foundational site, a place of singular beauty, uniquely heterogeneous, harmonious and authentic – the country's *true* 'cultural capital' or the '*black* Rome of the Americas' (Agier, 2000). The government of Bahia, as the city is metonymically known, has played no small part in fostering this image and, since 1985, has spared no effort to transform the city's old colonial district of Pelourinho into its main tourist attraction. Yet the slow reconstruction of Salvador's historic centre has become the object of intense dispute, laying bare the tensions and challenges that underlie heritage conservation in urban settings marked by profound social exclusion.

Located in Bahia's *cidade alta* (higher city), overlooking the bay, the city's port and commercial district, Pelourinho and its surrounding quarters, once home to the colony's administrative apparatus as well as to its rich landowning elite, possess a remarkably high density of colonial style mansions, churches and squares. Abandoned by Bahia's middle and upper classes from the early twentieth century onwards, in 1985 the area was described as a crumbling red light district, a place of disrepute, inhabited by a population of impoverished, mostly black Bahians, who had moved in, parcelled out and occupied the old mansions, in successive waves, since the turn of the century. Few of them possessed either title deeds or tenancy contracts. In some cases, small rents were paid to people claiming responsibility for the buildings (Zanirato, 2007), while in others abandoned property was illegally occupied. In general, though, maintenance was left entirely to the care of the district's severely impoverished residents and, as a consequence, it slowly deteriorated (Neto, cited in Zanirato, 2007).

With the city's recognition by UNESCO, however, Pelourinho became an absolute priority of Bahia's authorities. By 1992, the IPAC (Institute for Artistic and Cultural Patrimony) announced the newly approved project for the restoration of Pelourinho, to take place in stages. According to IPAC's own directives, the restoration would turn the area into a tourist attraction, endowed with commercial infrastructure to meet tourist needs and purged of some of its worst problems. The area was generally deemed inadequate for residential use and, consequently, its inhabitants themselves became a major problem, to which a swift and effective solution must be found. Following a series of studies, these inhabitants were offered indemnities to leave the area – these were generally insufficient, given the conditions previously defined by the authorities for the allocation of resources, whereby duration of residence, age, marital status, not to mention contractual entitlement, were all factored in. Compliance was obligatory, as the government had technically followed procedural rules and could thus order removal by force.

In the early stages of restoration, contestation of the project was low-key. Most of the people who had been offered indemnification were acutely poor: the insignificant sums offered were initially viewed as a welcome start to a new life (Zanirato, 2007: 42). Soon, it became apparent that most could not meet the cost of relocation even to the most remote peripheral neighbourhoods of the city. So a large number simply moved to one of the adjacent zones, which had yet to be renewed (Rodrigues, 1995: 89). The apparent silence on the part of the inhabitants was all the more unusual since among them were some of the most vociferous elements in Bahia's Black movement. Some of these groups were extremely proactive in mobilising resources and acquiring property in the centre, soon becoming a staple of what the city's authorities proclaimed to be Bahia's *unique* cultural landscape. Yet contradictory forces were at play in this complex scenario. For if, on the one hand, the centre's architectural value was evidently important to Bahia's main institutional and economic actors, on the other, it was deemed secondary to the city's true source of singularity: its population of African descent. The Bahian authorities acknowledged as much in their institutional relation with the Black movement. Yet, in its rush to 'clean' the historic centre of an undesirable population, Bahia's authorities 'failed' to notice that many of those forcefully moved out were Bahians of African descent, long established in the historic centre, often involved in the kind of informal commerce that would soon become an important tourist attraction – food vending and cultural performance.

By the late 1990s, the population that had seemed initially unable to mobilise against its forceful removal was still central to the historic centre's economic life. A group of inhabitants of the adjacent zone had also come together and sought legal aid to fight their own imminent removal from the area. Because of their success, by 2006, governmental policy had changed: the seventh stage emphasised the need to attend to Pelourinho's residents' rights. In spite of this, the problems that faced the project from its inception remain. When I first conducted fieldwork in Bahia, I lived in the so-called no-go perimeter around the centre and interacted daily with its *marginal* population. I was constantly told stories about Pelourinho of before, of a Pelourinho that was no longer in existence, a Pelourinho where being black and poor was not a spectacle carefully managed for the tourist gaze, but a *real* place inhabited mostly by Bahians of African descent who struggled to survive. These were *not* stories about *being* heritage or memory. They were stories about identity, broadly defined. But, to end with the cynical remark of one of my interlocutors: 'Now, I will speak of being a slave, of being heritage, of being like the items in the new Afro museum (*Museu Afro*) and I will feel all the more like one for it.'

Marta de Magalhães

References

Agier, Michel (2000) *Anthropologie du Carnaval: la Ville, la Fête et l'Áfrique à Bahia*. Marseille and Paris: Parenthéses, IRD.

Collins, John (2008) '"But What if I Should Need to Defecate in Your Neighbourhood, Madame?": Empire, Redemption and the "Tradition of the Oppressed" in a Brazilian World Heritage Site', *Cultural Anthropology* 23(2): 279–328.

Rodrigues, João Jorge (1995) 'O Olodum e o Pelourinho', in M.A. Filgueiras (ed.), *Pelo Pelô: História, Cultura e Cidade*. Salvador BA: EDUFBA.

Zanirato, Sílvia Helena (2007) 'A Restauração do Pelourinho no Centro Histórico de Salvador, Bahia: Potencialidades, Limites e Dilemas da Conservação de Área Degradadas (História, Cultura, Cidade)', *História Actual (Online)* 14: 35–47.

www.emtursa.ba.gov.br

whc.unesco.org/en/list/309

In her account of the 'Uses of Heritage', Laurajane Smith discusses such themes via the framework of *authorised heritage discourse* (AHD). As she rightfully points out, an AHD 'defines who the legitimate spokespersons for the past are' (Smith 2006: 29). She also indicates how 'the authority of expertise' takes on its form through close reference to the materiality of heritage, whereby the custodians to discrete buildings, places, sites or objects are typically archaeologists, architects or historians. In primarily focusing on such institutional and discursive relations as the key productive agents of AHDs, Smith's account, while instructive, inadequately recognises the role capital plays in such processes.[8] As Smith and others have highlighted, much of the activity in today's heritage profession continues to revolve around specific sites or locales. While the desire to reduce complexity and the preference for de-politicised, techno-managerial approaches have been cited as explanatory reasons for this, it is also vital that we recognise the all too common convergence between the value regimes of conservation and landed property (Hamilakis & Duke 2008). Those forms of heritage associated with or bound to land are, or have the potential to become, capital intensive for a variety of reasons. Regeneration, redevelopment, speculation, or the growth of new economies are the familiar expressions of wealth accumulation. In such contexts, those discourses of heritage that feed directly into such agendas tend to prevail. In the case of the built environment, for example, despite the fact that claims of valuing community memories, preserving intangible culture and so forth are commonly asserted, fields like anthropology or social history rarely receive the same attention as the techno-scientific discourses of architecture and architectural conservation.

Given the skills sets required to tie heritage into the construction sector and structures of spatial governance and planning, this situation is hardly surprising, but it is worth noting for it points towards some of the ways in which capital shapes how spaces, places, and their buildings are valued and preserved as sites of memory and collective identity (see the chapter by Aksoy and Robins in this volume). Nowhere is this more apparent than in the context of cities, where the price of real estate ensures those expert knowledges that serve the ends of capital investors remain dominant. Even a cursory look at the staff profiles of any urban conservation agency illustrates the skills sets and forms of professional training that prevail.

Similarly, in the case of archaeological sites, certain strands of research and knowledge production are more likely to prevail when they connect with existing or possible forms of capital investment from other sectors. In numerous countries, as archaeology has morphed into a body of high value, professional expertise, approaches more akin to traditions of positivism and empirical rationalism have remained stubbornly dominant. The discourse of 'Cultural Resource Management' (CRM) popular within the North American heritage profession is an example. Despite long-standing critiques of positivist and post-positivist paradigms by post-processionalist archaeologists, such approaches endure in large part because they provide the type of unequivocal, predictive knowledge base that drives capital accumulation. For those with financial interests in an historic site, including government bureaucrats, private investors, planners or tourism entrepreneurs, such forms of archaeological expertise are now commonly brought in to create or uphold a narrative that serves their economic ends. Programmes of 'urban renewal', 'sustainable development' or 'cultural tourism' provide the arenas through which such connections are made. Not surprisingly, then, in many instances heritage-based research or conservation projects are thematically or intellectually oriented in ways that maximise their potential for multi-sector connectivity. To return to the context of developmental aid, for example, it is now commonplace for heritage projects operating in these environments to be conceived in terms of 'capacity building', 'gender equality', 'democracy', 'economic empowerment' and so forth in order to obtain support from embassies, sponsors or host governments.

Of course while the mantra of sustainability appears to be all-conquering as we embark upon the complex challenges of the twenty-first century, in certain cases the heritage sector continues to unwittingly advance the very ties between culture and capital that it is trying to resist by deploying techno-managerial approaches. The case of cultural heritage preservation in Tibet, as taken up by Robert Shepherd, provides us with an illustration of this (Shepherd 2006, 2009; see also Winter 2007). Shepherd examines the interplays between heritage policies and the narratives of tourism in the ongoing construction of Tibetan culture as the geographically remote, backward 'other' of modernity. The long-held notion of Tibet as the real-life Shangri-La, the quintessential exotic, mountainous culture, neatly fits into Chinese government programmes for tourism development which align minority groups with backwardness and as communities in need of modernisation (Shepherd 2006: 250). Crucially, the Chinese state uses this vision of Tibet and its people to advance a model of tourism that depoliticises the region. Stripped of their political and social values, Tibetan cultural practices are transformed into cultural motifs in readiness for consumption by both international and domestic tourists. Aesthetically rendered, traditional Tibetan culture thus emerges as a celebration of the nation's cultural diversity. At the same time, a language of sustainable tourism development enables the state to modernise the region in a way that draws it 'closer' to Beijing. As an illustration of this process, Shepherd describes how parts of Lhasa have been demolished to make way for a museum and a large square modelled on Tiananmen Square (2006: 250). Perhaps the most assertive move in this direction, however, has been the construction of a rail-link into the region, connecting Lhasa up to a host of other cities in China, including Chengdu, Shanghai, Guangzhou, Shanghai and of course Beijing.

For Shepherd, a complicit partner in this process has been UNESCO. The organisation's approach to conservation in Tibet has been underpinned by their twin-pronged worldview concerning the promotion of cultural diversity/cultural pluralism and the safeguarding of culture from the destructive forces of modernisation, including those delivered by tourism. Once again, however, it is a concern that results in an intervention principally focused on the scientific, technical aspects of material conservation. Shepherd's critique thus focuses on UNESCO's reluctance, or perhaps negligence, to acknowledge the cultural politics of heritage in the region, citing the nomination of the Potala Palace in Lhasa as evidence of this. Rather being nominated because of its importance within a Tibetan national history, the palace supposedly represents the 'outstanding skills of the Tibetan, Han, Mongol, Man and other nationalities' (UNESCO 1993, cited in Shepherd 2009: 258). Reduced to questions of aesthetics and the technicalities of material conservation, and thus stripped of all its political impetus, an iconic structure of Tibetan nationalism is absorbed into a wider narrative of Chinese modernisation and national progress. Crucially here, and as Shepherd points out, it is a paradigm of heritage conservation that feeds directly into the cultural tourism–development nexus created by the state.

Conclusion

Seen together, then, the various examples offered here begin to illustrate some of the ways in which today's global capitalism, described by Hardt and Negri as an encompassing, geographically seamless 'Empire', comes to value the traditional, the exotic, the primitive and the local (Hardt & Negri 2000). As Castro-Gómez puts it, this 'Empire' is a totalising system that continues to depend on the dualities of the traditional and the modern, the universal and the particular. Indeed, as he states, today's capitalism is 'a machine of segmentary inclusions, not of exclusions. Non-occidental knowledge is welcomed by the global agendas of Empire because it is useful' (Castro-Gómez 2007: 441).

Having sought here to illustrate some of the ways in which today's global heritage movement directly feeds into such processes, and actively reinforces its dynamics, I would also suggest this is an analytical position that runs contrary to mainstream thinking in the heritage profession. The majority position holds that the traditional is seen as something that is ontologically disconnected from the modern (Hamilakis & Duke 2008). Indeed, heritage conservation frameworks and models often continue to be oriented around the idea of globalisation as a convergence between the bipolarised 'global' and 'local'. It is a language which tends to present the local as either pristine nature or the culturally authentic, endangered by the homogenising and modernising (read universalising) forces of the global. The analysis offered here, however, points towards the need to move away from the polarised binaries of the local/global, traditional/modern, cultural/economic and instead see such pairings as mutually constitutive. It also demands a recognition of how the coming together of the traditional and modern contributes to the ordering of today's global capital relations. In departing from the conventional position that sees these two as chronologically ordered, the examples cited here demonstrate why they need to be read as synchronous. They also highlight how the privileging of certain forms of expertise and cultural knowledge in the conservation sector today intimately ties cultural heritage into a variety of wider political economic processes. The realisation, then, is that, in all these cases, that which is inherited from the past is no longer in the past, but is instead thoroughly constituted and reconstituted in, and by, the political economies of the modern.

Notes

1 UNESCO (United Nations Educational, Scientific and Cultural Organization), ICCROM (International Centre for the Study of the Preservation and Restoration of Cultural Property), ICOM (International Council of Museums), and ICOMOS (International Council on Monuments and Sites).
2 whc.unesco.org/en/wallmap
3 DfID: Department for International Development, USAID: United States Agency for International Development, AFD: Agence Française de Développement, SIDA: Swedish International Development Cooperation Agency, GTZ: Deutsche Gesellschaft für Technische Zusammenarbeit, AusAID: Australian Agency for International Development.
4 For further details see: www.shibam-udp.org.
5 Notable examples here include Sairam Tours, Oriental Travel and Audley Travel.
6 For further details see: web.worldbank.org/WBSITE/EXTERNAL/TOPICS/EXTURBANDEVELOPMENT/EXTCHD/0,,contentMDK:21782457~menuPK:430436~pagePK:64020865~piPK:149114~theSitePK:430430,00.html
7 See, for example, Timothy & Nyaupane (2009) and Zukin (1991).
8 For more insights of this kind, see the work of scholars in the discipline of cultural geography.

REFERENCES

Castro-Gómez, S., 2007, The Missing Chapter of Empire: Postmodern reorganization of coloniality and post-Fordist capitalism, *Cultural Studies*, 21(2–3), pp. 428–48.

Chandler, D., 2006, *Empire in Denial: the politics of state-building*, London: Pluto Press.

Drainville, A., 2003, *Contesting Globalization: space and place in the world economy*, London: Routledge.

Duffield, M., 2001, *Global Governance and the New Wars*, London: Zed Press.

Duffield, M., 2007, *Development, Security and the Unending War*, Cambridge: Polity Press.

Ferguson, J., 1994, *The Anti-Politics Machine: development, depoliticization and bureaucratic power in Lesotho*, Minnesota, MN.: University of Minnesota Press.

Hamilakis, Y. & Duke, P., 2008, *Archaeology and Capitalism: from ethics to politics*, walnut creek, CA: Left Coast Press.

Hardt, M. & Negri, A., 2000, *Empire*, Harvard University Press, Cambridge, MA.

Hawkins, D.E. & Mann, S., 2007, The World Bank's role in Tourism Development, *Annals of Tourism Research*, 34(2), pp. 348–63.

Hirsch, P. & Warren, C., 2002, *The Politics of Environment in Southeast Asia Resources and Resistance*, London: Routledge.

Kalisa, C., 2006, Theatre and the Rwandan Genocide, *Peace Review*, 18(4), pp. 515–21.

Keane, J., 2003, *Global Civil Society?* Cambridge: Cambridge University Press.

Khanna, P., 2008, *The Second World: empires and influence in the new global order*, London: Allen Lane.

Klein, N., 2007, *The Shock Doctrine: the rise of disaster capitalism*, New York: Metropolitan Books.

Magar, V., 2007, Cultural Heritage in Postwar Recovery, in N. Stanley-Price (ed.), *Armed Conflict and Culture Change in Chiapas, Mexico*, Rome: ICCROM, pp. 75–86.

Radcliffe, S. (ed.), 2006, *Culture and Development in a Globalizing World Geographies, actors, and paradigms*, London: Routledge.

Shepherd, R., 2006, UNESCO and the Politics of Cultural Heritage in Tibet, *Journal of Contemporary Asia*, 36(2), pp. 243–56.

Shepherd, R., 2009, Asia on Tour: exploring the rise of Asian tourism, in T. Winter, P. Teo & T.C. Chang (eds), *Cultural Preservation, Tourism and 'Donkey Travel'*, London: Routledge. pp. 253–63.

Smith, L., 2006, *Uses of Heritage*, London: Routledge.

Thompson, J., 2007, Conflicts and Tensions, in H. Anheier & Y.R. Isar (eds), *Performance, Globalization and Conflict Promotion/Resolution: experiences from Sri Lanka*, Los Angeles, CA: Sage, pp. 102–18.

Timothy, D.J. & Nyaupane, G.P., 2009, *Cultural Heritage and Tourism in the Developing World: a regional perspective*, London: Routledge.

Viejo-Rose, D., 2007, Conflicts and Tensions, in H. Anheier & Y.R. Isar (eds), *Conflict and the Deliberate Destruction of Cultural Heritage*, Los Angeles, CA: Sage, pp. 102–18.

Winter, T., 2007, *Post-Conflict Heritage, Postcolonial Tourism: culture, politics and development at Angkor*, London: Routledge.

Yúdice, G., 2003, *The Expediency of Culture: uses of culture in the global era*, Durham, NC.: Duke University Press.

Zukin, S., 1991, *Landscapes of Power: from Detroit to Disney World*, London: University of California Press.

CHAPTER 5

UNSETTLING THE NATIONAL: HERITAGE AND DIASPORA

Ien Ang

This chapter discusses the complex and problematic relationships between heritage and diaspora. Bringing these two concepts together opens up a range of tensions which trouble the intimate interrelationship that presumably exists among (national) identity, memory and heritage. A diasporic perspective cracks open the nationalist narrative of seamless national unity, highlighting the fact that nations today inevitably harbour populations with multiple pasts, bringing memories and identities into circulation that often transcend or undercut the homogenising image of nationhood and national heritage. At the same time, applying a heritage lens on the diasporic experience reveals some of the internal tensions and contradictions in the very idea of diaspora, which exemplify the multifaceted complexities of identity formation in the contemporary globalised world, which cannot be contained within the cultural and geographical confines of the nation-state.

Introduction

The ideology of the nation-state generally presumes the relationship between identity, memory and heritage to be one of smooth equivalence. National identity, national memory and national heritage (should ideally) mirror one another, fastened by a perfect mutual correspondence and a unitary homogeneity. A nation, in this regard, is a territorially bounded entity comprising one people, one culture, and one history. Globalisation has disrupted this comfortable nationalist presumption, as nation-states are increasingly subjected to the effects of border-crossing transnational flows, not least that of people. As people from elsewhere come to reside inside the nation and retain connections with other parts of the world, what constitutes the national culture – and who has the right to define it – becomes unsettled and contestable. This is the challenge posed by 'diaspora', just like 'heritage' a key concept of our time.

The heightened salience of invocations of diaspora is a direct correlate of the intensification of transnational flows and migrations of people across regions, countries and continents in this era of accelerating globalisation. Indeed, the prominence of diaspora today can be seen as a key index of our contemporary globalised world. As Kachig Tölölyan stated in 1991, 'diasporas are the exemplary communities of the transnational moment' (p. 3). In other words, the current popularity of diaspora – both as a cultural discourse and as a social practice – is a key expression of the unsettling dislocations associated with contemporary globalisation.

In this chapter, I will focus on the complex and problematic relationship between heritage and diaspora. Specifically, I will discuss how bringing these two terms together opens up a range of tensions which trouble the intimate interrelationship that presumably exists between (national) identity, memory and heritage. A diasporic perspective cracks open the nationalist narrative of seamless national unity, highlighting the fact that nations today inevitably harbour populations with multiple pasts, bringing memories and identities into circulation that often transcend or undercut the homogenising image of nationhood and national heritage.

As a focal concern of public policy, heritage can be thought of as a 'socially sanctioned, institutionally supported process of producing memories that make certain versions of the past public and render other versions invisible' (Hamilton & Shopes 2008: 3). The memories produced and made public by heritage are overwhelmingly those that suit the needs and interests of the nation-state: this reflects heritage's role, as David Lowenthal (1998: xv) puts it, 'in husbanding community, identity, continuity, indeed history itself'. In this regard, what counts as national heritage serves the purpose of projecting a selectively favourable image of a nation's history and identity, one that is capable of instilling a sense of pride, loyalty and common fate among its citizens. Towards the close of the twentieth century the heritage endeavour has gained increasing salience as a key plank of national cultural policy throughout the world. Ironically, this is precisely the time when the unifying power of the nation-state has begun to be eroded by the transnationalising forces unleashed by rapid globalisation. Diaspora is an important conduit of these transnationalising forces.

In short, what I argue in this chapter is that thinking about heritage and diaspora together leads us to a productive mutual problematisation of both concepts, with interesting critical and policy implications. On the one hand, a diasporic perspective necessarily triggers a contestation of the meaning of heritage because it brings into view aspects of human history and social experience that are not easily captured within dominant nationalist modes of heritage designation. On the other hand, applying a heritage lens on the diasporic experience will reveal some of the internal tensions and contradictions in the very idea of diaspora. These tensions and contradictions exemplify the multifaceted complexities of identity formation in the contemporary globalised world, which cannot be contained within the cultural and geographical confines of the nation-state.

Diaspora: nation, migration, displacement

Literally meaning 'the scattering of seeds', the most long-standing and distinct use of the term 'diaspora' occurs with reference to the history of forced dispersion of the Jewish people since the sixth century BC. The long and complex history of the Jews as a people without a homeland found enduring expression in the image of 'the wandering Jew' in Christian mythology. In association with this archetypical Jewish case, the diasporic experience is classically described in terms of exile, isolation and loss, of displacement from the ancestral homeland as a traumatic experience, where some catastrophic event – often but not always of a political nature – is collectively remembered as the starting point of the original dispersion. Concomitantly, a longing for a *return* to the homeland is classically assumed to be integral to diasporic consciousness (Safran 1991). In the Jewish case, this longing for return was expressed politically in the Zionist struggle and search for a new Jewish homeland, which culminated in the creation of the modern nation-state of Israel in 1947. This development highlighted the assumption that all peoples must have a distinct territorial homeland and that living away from it – as is the case for diasporic subjects – is an unnatural and undesirable condition. In the modern era, this meaning of diaspora as a state of exception is strongly associated with the dominant idea of nation-states as sovereign and clearly bounded entities with a perfect overlap of nation, people, territory and culture.

Since the late twentieth century, however, the term 'diaspora' is increasingly used in a more generalised sense to refer to all kinds of people who have a history of dispersion or migration. Groups variously referred to as immigrants, expatriates, refugees, guest workers, exiles, and so on – that is, potentially all groups living outside their putative homeland – are now regularly referred to as diasporas (Tölölyan 1991). Diasporas are implicitly and explicitly presumed to suffer from a double estrangement, reinforced not only by their separation from their putative original homeland, whether forced or voluntary, but also by the experiences of marginalisation or discrimination in their country of settlement: of not being fully accepted by, and partly alienated from the 'host society', where one does not feel (fully) at home.

This means that the traumatic aspect of the diasporic experience is not only related to the past, associated with the moment of exile or departure. The sense of hurt is timed as much in the present, expressed in a nostalgia for the distant 'homeland' and a lack of (full) belonging in the nation-state where one finds oneself. From this angle, the diasporic condition is articulated as the experience of living away from one's ancestral homeland on a more permanent basis. The (real or perceived) impossibility of return is more or less naturalised in this context, feeding an enduring (if sometimes merely residual) sense of dislocation and displacement. This has been the experience of many migrants who, by virtue of their ethnic, racial or cultural difference from the mainstream population, find themselves minoritised and, often, made invisible within dominant representations of the hegemonic national culture and history of the 'host' society.

At the same time, the increased volume and intensity of people flows and mobility in the era of globalisation has weakened the hold of the modern nation-state on the identities and identifications of the populations who have come to live within their borders. Diasporic subjects can now affirm their collective identities through transnational connections not only with those 'back home', but also with co-diasporans beyond the boundaries of the nation-state, interconnected, for example, through trade networks or the Internet. For example, although they have dispersed themselves to all corners of the world for several centuries (but especially since the late nineteenth century), migrants of Chinese ancestry may continue to maintain links with their co-ethnics elsewhere and with the homeland itself through countless overseas Chinese community organisations and diasporic networks spanning continents, creating transnational Chinese identities and communities in the process. This is a common process for virtually all diasporic groups. Thus, while Chinese living outside China are one of the largest and most longstanding global diasporas, smaller and more vulnerable groups of displaced peoples, such as Hmong, Somali or Iraqi refugees, evince similar tendencies to form cross-border diasporic connections, often driven by the need for practical, cultural and affective sustenance as they establish new lives in foreign lands.

In short, diasporas are a key phenomenon of cultural globalisation (Cohen 1997; Esman 2006). Signifying the increasing importance of people on the move around the globe in the twenty-first century, they evoke a vocabulary of flow and mobility, travel and border-crossings, cultural translation and transnationalism. Diasporic identities are not rooted in a singular place, but are forged in and through movement between places. Moreover, diasporic identities present themselves not only as peripheral to national cultures, but also as fundamentally ambivalent to it. What does all this mean for heritage?

Box 5.1 Transnational initiatives

The African Diaspora Heritage Trail (ADHT) is part of the UNESCO Slave Route project. Initiated by the Department of Tourism and Transport of Bermuda in 2002, the ADHT is explicitly presented as a multinational heritage tourism initiative to promote sustainable development in African Diaspora countries. In October 2009, when the annual ADHT conference was held for the first time in Africa, in Tanzania, the Premier of Bermuda and key architect of the project, Ewart Brown, stated that 'the African Diaspora Heritage Trail movement is going back to its roots', calling it an 'Africa homecoming'. Bringing together professionals from tourism ministries, education, conservation, museum archives, and cultural and scientific organisations, the ADHT is now a charitable organisation which aims to help 'to establish heritage trails linking Diaspora traditions in Africa, South and Central America, Bermuda, the Caribbean, Europe, the United States and Canada by developing a network of collaborators who identify, build, finance, promote and market memorable heritage destinations' (www.adht.net). The intention is to promote the production of 'quality cultural products that expose visitors to authentic African Diaspora history and culture, and motivate local populations to become active participants in the preservation and dissemination of their history and culture'. A stated aim is to 'allow African descendants of different origins to engage one another and discover cultural affinities created through their shared histories of enslavement' (portal. unesco.org/culture/en/ev.php-URL_ID=31680&URL_DO=DO_PRINTPAGE&URL_SECTION=201.html).

Here heritage and diaspora are brought together in a genuinely transnational undertaking to benefit from the rise of cultural and heritage tourism in a range of developing countries, with the additional stated benefits of intercultural dialogue and sustainable development. It is no surprise that the history of slavery provides the anchor point for the identification of the African diasporic experience here; it is part of a well-known global narrative and what millions of descendants, especially in the Americas, recognise themselves in, providing the opportunity for the tourism venture. But it is important to note that slavery is not the only significant strand in the history of African migration, which comprises much more multifaceted and heterogeneous movements in and out of diverse parts of the continent. In Olabily Joseph Yai's pointed words: 'Given the many countries of Africa, we are wrong to concentrate attention only on the Atlantic diaspora that followed the "curse of Christopher Columbus".' (Yai in *Museum International* 2004: 190). Seen this way, capitalising on transatlantic slavery is again a particular mode of reductionist territorialisation which the process of authorised heritage valuation necessarily entails.

A similar comment can be made about the Museum of the African Diaspora (MoAD) in San Francisco, the first museum, in the world dedicated to this subject, which opened in 2005. In a discussion of this museum, Brandi Wilkins Catanese (2007: 91) points out that containing a diaspora in a museum is inherently 'ironic': 'How does the museum with its traditional emphasis on acquiring the imposing order upon objects, accommodate the logic of diaspora, with its emphasis on dynamic forces of belonging and mobility?' Here the enduring tension between heritage (as an essentially territorialising process) and diaspora (as a formation that always encompasses a deterritorialisation of identities and memories) is clearly illuminated. As Jacqueline Brown (quoted in Campt 2002: 97) has argued, the African diaspora itself is less a concrete geographical trajectory than a set of relations: 'There is no actual space that one could call "the African diaspora", despite how commonly it is mapped onto particular locales.' The heritage designation of particular objects, traditions or sites as items or places of significance for the African diaspora fixates this more abstract, intangible notion of diasporic experience. Indeed, the interpretative fluidity of what the African diaspora might contain is evidenced by the MoAD's curatorial choice to universalise their ambit by reminding us 'that Africa is the birthplace of humankind'. In this way, all of humanity is invited to see themselves as a part of the African diaspora, even though the museum dedicates its space mostly to the very particular historical experience of transatlantic slavery and the US civil rights movement.

There are other museums and heritage centres around the world with a transnational diaspora focus. The large Chinese Heritage Centre in Singapore was founded in 1995 to promote 'awareness and understanding of Chinese culture and tradition among people in Singapore and the world through the collection, preservation and display of artworks and other objects of Chinese culture' (www. chineseheritagecentre.org). Singapore is an apt location for such cultural centre because, with about 75% of the population of Chinese descent, it is one of the most culturally Chinese nation-states in the world outside mainland China. The Centre's main attraction, a permanent exhibition entitled 'Chinese More or Less', invites visitors to ask questions such as: How Chinese am I? In what sense am I Chinese? What does it mean to be Chinese? Interestingly, the last section of the exhibition addresses the complex ambiguity of these questions by stressing the cultural significance of hybridity: 'The visitor will discover that the world is more plural, that it changes faster and that there are now a variety of reference points that are other than Chinese.' This is showcased, for example, in the work of Paris-based painter Zao Wou-ki, who wrote his first name in Chinese characters and his last in Western orthography. Does this symbolise a double heritage: 'Chinese' and 'other-than-Chinese', as the exhibition suggests? Or does it illuminate the very displacement – and partial dissolution – of (Chinese) identity in the diasporic context?

Ben Hatefuthsoth, the Museum of the Jewish Diaspora in Tel-Aviv, Israel, 'tells the unique and ongoing story of the Jewish People .... The museum presents thousands of years of a flourishing, multifaceted culture, bringing to life the unity that underlies the diversity of the Jewish civilization' (www.bh. org.il/about-us.aspx). Not surprisingly, the museum's aspiration is to 'enhance the bonds between Jews in Israel and around the world' and to 'nurture a sense of pride in Jewish heritage, Jewish achievements, and Jewish contributions to the world'. Notwithstanding the scattered, traumatic and conflicting trajectories of Jewish diasporic experience, Israel is presented here as the surefire focal point for an unbroken diasporic community, held together by a consecrated sense of 'Jewishness'.

Ien Ang

Diaspora contra heritage

The most far-reaching aspect of the idea of diaspora is its transcendence of territorialism, founded in a history and experience of displacement. Displacement 'refers to the separation of people from their native culture' (Bammer 1994: xi), not just in a physical sense, but also in a deeper, existential sense. In spatial terms, diaspora is always fundamentally in tension with the quintessential territorialism of the nation-state: diasporas are manifestations of being dis-placed. At the same time – and this refers to the cultural dimension of diaspora – diasporic subjects do not and cannot live outside particular, nationally-framed spaces and places: they are uprooted but cannot remain completely rootless, they are dis-placed but always face the task of re-placing themselves. As James Clifford (1997: 255) put it, diasporas are 'not-here to stay.' Diaspora cultures thus embody the 'lived tension … of separation and entanglement, of living here and remembering/desiring there'. If they exist 'in-between' two (or more) places, they always tend to be subjected to the conflicting pulls of 'where they're from' and 'where they're at'. Paul Gilroy (1993) has described this abiding experience of cultural displacement in terms of a 'double consciousness', but the diasporic state of mind is more profoundly rendered as a fragmented, shifting and mixed-up consciousness. That is, diasporic identities are always simultaneously and ambiguously deterritorialised and reterritorialised, they always hover in a movement between 'home and away', attachment and detachment, identification and disidentification.

Heritage, meanwhile, is essentially a territorialising concept, not just in practical terms (i.e. the predominance of locating heritage value in 'tangible' objects and places), but also in a broader, symbolic sense (i.e. heritage as the more or less exclusive 'possession' of a particular group). More specifically, heritage tends to operate as an overwhelmingly nationalising cultural process. As Ashworth et al. (2007: 57) observe, '[t]his supremacy of the national compromises and constrains the effectiveness of all forms of representing heritage, place and identity'. As a consequence, as I will elaborate below, applying heritage knowledge and procedures to diaspora tends to result in a reductionist understanding of the diasporic experience by highlighting its territorial attachments (to either homeland or hostland), at the expense of its unsettled and unsettling dimensions.

As socio-cultural formations diasporas are not only complex, but inherently contradictory. On the one hand, they can be described as what Sudesh Mishra (2006) 16) calls 'scenes of dual territoriality', where home and host territories function as the stable and determinate coordinates of a tensional split of identity and belonging. But they are also 'scenes of situational laterality', where diasporic identities are 'linked to situation-specific *becoming*, or the middle passage (milieu) in the active sense, rather than the tensional pressures exercised by bipolar nation-states' (2006: 17). In Clifford's (1997: 246, 248) words, 'multi-locale diasporas are not necessarily defined by a specific geopolitical boundary' and they betray a 'principled *ambivalence* about physical return and attachment to land'. The idea of 'return' may only be a mythical constituent of the diasporic experience, and diasporic agency tends actually to be oriented not so much to holding on to the memory of the distant homeland but on continuing efforts to re-establish one's cultural identities in diverse new locations, where the old homeland remains effective as a mere but persistent trace of genealogical influence and virtual attachment. From this perspective, diasporas are dispersed, fluid, hybrid transnational formations with shifting, and constitutively ambivalent (dis)identifications to many places around the world, shaped by the contradictory experience of 'dwelling-in-displacement'.

This more peripatetic aspect of the diasporic experience is much harder to capture in heritage (although, as discussed in Box 5.1, attempts have been made, for example in relation to the African diaspora). It is also where the limits of heritage as a way of knowing and valuing the complex trajectories of human life are revealed. As a consequence, the relationship between diaspora and heritage will never be one of coextensive harmony. On the contrary, what this chapter will highlight is the ultimate impossibility of 'heritagising' the experience of (physical and cultural) displacement as such: the ambivalent condition of (non)belonging, of the fragility of diasporic identity as it is fractured by the push and pull of competing nationalising pressures, is difficult to objectify as distinctive heritage.

The fact that dominant, officially sanctioned definitions of heritage – as a public discourse and a metacultural form – are overwhelmingly nationalist and territorially based is in line with the predominance of nation-states as units of governance in the modern world system. National heritage policies are predicated upon the need and value of preserving and commemoralising items of the past that are deemed important for the nation-building process. In this sense, the meaning of heritage lies in its contribution to the construction of an authoritative national narrative, what Laurajane Smith (2006) calls an authorised heritage discourse, which seals the nation's understanding of itself as a distinct cultural unity and affirms the continuity between the national past and its present.

Diaspora poses a problem for this authorised national heritage because it is by definition a denationalising, transnationalising force. The incursion of a diasporic perspective unsettles the seamless equivalence between heritage, identity and nationhood that has guided prevailing policies and practices of heritage designation. It also unsettles the tendency to locate heritage value in the longstanding ties and attachments to place. In this sense, the cultural processes associated with heritage and diaspora are in inherent tension with one another.

But there is one dimension where diaspora bears an intimate relationship, if not conceptual complicity with heritage. This is the temporal dimension. Diaspora shares with heritage an orientation towards the past in that both involve practices of remembrance. After all, diasporas are founded on a story about the past, on looking back to some point of origin, just as heritage involves an act of preserving an aspect of the past for the present. The diasporic imagination is fundamentally informed by the – more or less distant – memory of a place left behind, and a history of displacement. Diasporic memory is about dislocation, exile, separation from a place, loss of (and nostalgia for) home. The question is: can this kind of memory be publicly asserted and officially acknowledged *as* heritage in the contemporary world? If so, in which ways and with what implications?

Diaspora in national heritage

The presence of diasporic groups within nation-states generally results in the *de facto* pluralisation of culture and society as such groups bring elements of their traditions, customs, languages, and so on with them from the places they have left behind. Dominant ideologies of national unity and homogeneity tended to suppress this cultural diversification through the imposition of policies of assimilation and integration. In such a context, the heritage practices of diasporic groups – that is, their attempts to keep the memory of their past homelands alive – tends to remain hidden from public view. Much memory-work of migrants occurs not in the public sphere (from which they are often excluded or marginalised), but in the private sphere, for example through the display of valued photographs and objects of the homeland in the home (Buciek & Juul 2008).

Assimilationism ran out of favour since the 1960s, partly because political and ideological resistance to the ideal of assimilation grew as the recognition of human diversity became a more prominent part of global governance after the Second World War and in the wake of decolonisation, but more pragmatically also because that very ideal of ethnic purity and cultural homogeneity proved to be increasingly unrealistic. While newly independent post-colonial nations often had to grapple with their internal ethnic diversity from the start, for most European nation-states the inevitability of diversity was realised as a consequence of increased immigration in the latter part of the twentieth century, when large waves of people from the 'Rest', who have very different cultural and ethnic backgrounds from the majority population, came to settle in the West.

The – sometimes grudging – admission of the irreducibility of cultural difference and diversity has led to the adoption of more self-consciously pluralist understandings of society. This involves a pluralising of the past (Ashworth et al. 2007): an undertaking to broaden the scope of national history to make space for the role of migrants and other minority groups. Often this involves a revisionist rewriting of the authorised heritage discourse to incorporate a more multicultural national narrative. An example is the evolution of the heritage significance conferred on the Snowy Mountains Hydro-Electricity Scheme in arid south-eastern Australia. The scheme, the largest engineering project ever undertaken in Australia, commenced in 1949 and was completed in 1974. Comprising 16 dams, 80 kilometres of aqueduct pipelines, 13 major tunnels, three service towns, seven power stations and eight switching stations, the scheme was built by a workforce of more than 100,000 people from over 30 countries, more than two-thirds of whom were post-war migrants and displaced persons recruited from Europe. During the 1950s, at the height of the assimilation era, the Snowy scheme was described by then Prime Minister Ben Chifley as 'one of the greatest milestones on the march of Australia to full national development' (Ashton 2009: 384). While the migrant origins of the workers did not go unnoticed, they were incorporated into the scheme's official significance as an icon of national progress and efficiency. By the time of the fiftieth anniversary of the Snowy Mountains scheme in the 1990s, however, it came to represent a rather different national narrative. The Australian Heritage Commission placed the scheme on the Register of the National Estate, describing its cultural significance in terms of 'the history of Australia's post-World War II migration' and, therefore, as 'a major basis of Australian multicultural society'. In this way, the scheme was retrospectively made to mean 'the birthplace of Australian multiculturalism' (quoted in Ashton 2009: 386). This evolution of cultural meaning clearly illustrates how heritage, as Paul Ashton observes, can be 'enlisted by the State to accommodate social and cultural change – the relatively rapid transition of Australia from a mono- to a multicultural society – and minimise social conflict' (2009: 387). What is designated as the national heritage, in other words, now needed to incorporate the migrant story, and the historical legacy of migration more broadly.

The policy imperative to open representations of national culture and history up to the perspectives of migrants is an international trend that gained momentum in the late twentieth century, precisely when large-scale transnational migration had reached unprecedented levels in the post-war era and globalisation had begun to undermine the cultural sovereignty of all nation-states. International cultural agencies such as UNESCO have played a proactive role in this, initiating major shifts in the ideological orientations of national cultural institutions. For example, at the nineteenth meeting of its General Assembly in 1998 the UNESCO-officiated International Council of Museums (ICOM) passed a resolution concerning museums and cultural diversity, advocating 'the development of museums as sites for the promotion of heritage values of significance to all peoples through cross-cultural dialog' (Silverman & Fairchild Ruggles 2007: 6). In this regard, museums are asked to play a brokering role in reconciling national societies with the diversity in their midst, a social and political issue perceived as urgent in today's irrevocably interconnected world and rising threat of intercultural conflict and disharmony.

While in many countries the theme of migration is now taken up within the ambit of more general national history museums, one especially remarkable development has been the proliferation of museums dedicated specifically to migration history and heritage in the past two decades. Migration can be treated in different ways in museums: focus may be either on immigration or on emigration. Understandably, in countries with large migrant populations the emphasis is on museums of immigration.

Of these, the Ellis Island Immigration Museum in New York is obviously the most well known and longstanding: it was refurbished in the 1980s to re-open in 1990 to exhibit the story of America as the quintessential nation of immigrants. Most other museums dedicated to immigration have been established only from the late 1990s onwards. It is no surprise that immigration museums in new world settler societies such as Australia, Brazil and Canada were some of the first to be established worldwide. In Western Europe, the only truly national immigration museum to date is the Cité Nationale de l'Histoire de l'Immigration in Paris, which opened in 2007 (see Julie Thomas's chapter for a detailed analysis). In several other European countries efforts have been stepped up to establish immigration museums (Hermansen & Møller: 2007; see also special issue on migration museums of Museum International (2004); Stevens 2009).

In Germany, the Documentation Centre and Museum of Migration in Germany (DOMiD) was set up in 2007 out of a merger between a grassroots organisation of Turkish immigrants in Germany in 1990, which aimed to preserve and make visible the history and heritage of Turkish migrants, and a Cologne-based network of researchers and activists to create a national museum which will focus on the immigration history of a wide variety of migrant groups. One of the most recent projects of DOMiD was a virtual exhibition of lieux de memoire relevant to the history of immigration throughout Germany (www.migrationsroute.nrw.de/). The Museo de Historia de la Inmigración de Cataluña (Catalonian Museum for the History of Immigration), established in Barcelona in 2004, is the first museum dedicated to immigration in Spain. Interestingly, the main focus of the MHIC is not contemporary immigration but historical immigration to Catalonia from other Spanish regions, reflecting the nationalist ideology pervading Catalonia today (Carrera Suárez & Viñuela Suárez 2007). This illustrates the fact that the impulse behind the establishment of immigration museums is generally driven by concerns for immigration's role within a strictly nationally defined field of heritage.

Whatever their differences in emphasis and style, immigration museums tend to share similar objectives: to acknowledge the contributions of immigrants to their host societies, to deconstruct stereotypes about migrants, and to raise public awareness and understanding about migration. An International Network of Migration Institutions has been set up by UNESCO and the International Organisation for Migration (IOM) to promote the development of such museums. As the Network's website points out: 'This kind of museum would, in particular, help collect, safeguard, highlight and make accessible to the general public certain elements relating to the history and culture of immigration, and to the process of integration of migrant communities' (www.migrationmuseums.org).

This recent propagation of the immigration museum as a disseminator of migration heritage has clearly been motivated by a cultural and political problematic which is felt particularly strongly in Western European nations: it coincides with the need for these countries to stem the twin tide of anti-immigrant sentiment and migrant discontent which has grown more manifest, especially after the events of September 11, 2001. These nations are being forced to recognise that they are no longer homogeneous imagined communities but are now irrevocably multicultural societies, which needed to be reflected in the national heritage. The attention now paid to the heritages of migrants and ethnic minorities, for which such museums act as 'authorities of recognition' (Stevens 2007), is thus a form of heritage pluralisation that can be seen to be driven by a politics of inclusion designed to insert notions of difference and diversity into the cultural self-understanding of the nation-state (Ashworth et al., 2007). But if this involves a positive pluralising of the past, this more inclusive past is still framed within a *national* history – the history of the nation of residence (the 'host' nation). In this context, what constitutes migration heritage needs to fit within the preferred national narrative of the 'host' society.

As Lowenthal (1998) has argued, heritage involves the domestication of the past to serve present purposes, and this necessarily entails selective memory. Thus, the memory of migration, from the point of view of national history, tends to be framed as the story of migrant incorporation and integration within the nation-state, downplaying more disruptive memories of separation, exclusion or alienation. As Ashton (2009: 387) remarks with regard to the commemoration of Australia's Snowy Mountains Scheme, this officially-branded memorial for multicultural Australia is not remembered 'as a site of racial tension and partial segregation, as a place of hard and dangerous labour undertaken by foreigners recruited specifically to undertake work most Australians did not want to do, or one of binge drinking, fighting and prostitution'.

In immigration museums, too, the story of migration tends to be told in a selectively positive, if not celebratory, fashion: as an enriching contribution to the receiving country, and as an ultimately gratifying experience, despite possible episodes of pain and suffering, for the migrants themselves. Negative historical realities which often inform migration – such as persecution, poverty or racism – are generally recollected as barriers or problems which migrants have managed to overcome through courage and the welcome handed out by the receiving society. The experience of the diasporic migrant is here framed as a teleological, largely redemptive narrative of leaving, journey and, finally, arrival. The so-called 'suitcase narrative' (Witcomb 2009) is an exemplary strategy of story-telling here: migrants are asked to remember what they had with them in their suitcases when they arrived in the country they now live in. Immigration museums typically exhibit objects which migrants had in their suitcases, and sometimes the suitcases themselves, as tangible exemplars of migration heritage.

Such heritage strategies are generally seen as a welcome validation of migrant identities, not least by migrants themselves, and as having a cosmopolitanising impact on society at large. And indeed, the value of this kind of migration heritage as instances of what Charles Taylor (1992) has called 'the politics of recognition' should not be underestimated. They do, however, represent only a very partial and limited grasp of diaspora. In particular, they tend to simplify the complex instabilities of the diasporic experience by reducing the diasporic subject to the frozen, one-dimensional identity of the 'immigrant'. By giving meaning to this identity only in terms of its relationship to the country of settlement, the discourse of immigration territorialises the diasporic experience, excluding or overlooking its more unsettling, deterritorialising elements. Those aspects of migrant history that do not fit within the national narrative tend not to be memorialised, and disappear from view.

Diaspora and the myth of return?

If diasporas are conceived to be 'scenes of dual territoriality', then the migrant's identity is shaped not only by where she ends up residing, but also by where she's 'from'. The lost homeland, remembered as the place left behind, may also become the site of heritage value and preservation. For Charles Orser (2007: 93), this raises the following question: 'Should members of diasporas have rights when it comes to decisions about the management and use of sites and properties in their (or their ancestors') original homeland?' Orser discusses the example of a group of descendants of residents of the Irish townland of Ballykilcline (now a major archaeological site), who were forced to leave their home after being evicted in the wake of a rent strike in the nineteenth century. Now living in the United States, these descendants established a society for 'the lost children of Ballykilcline' after the memory of the townland was rekindled following the publication of a book detailing the history of the eviction, emigration and resettlement in 1995. Since then the society has organised annual reunions at the site of the townland, the first of which took place in 1999.

It is interesting to note that this diasporic history did not seem to exist within the descendants' individual and collective memories before the publication of this book. The fact that the community of descendants could establish and sustain itself so quickly and fervently after so many decades of forgetting is itself a revealing instance of 'rediasporisation' precisely at a time of intensifying globalisation. No longer satisfied with being 'just' Americans, these people found new meaning in identifying themselves as members of the Ballykilcline diaspora. As Orser (2007: 100) observes:

Viewed through the lens of Ballykilcline, we must acknowledge that the once-contiguous townland has become a series of tiny, disconnected territories located throughout the United States. Though not contiguous, the people living in those places are cognitively linked, both within the United States and across the Atlantic to county Roscommon, Ireland.

The problem, Orser argues, is that because the descendants are not citizens of the Republic of Ireland and do not own land in Ballykilcline, they do not have any legal standing, even though their heritage claims might outweigh those of the current landowners. Instead, as US citizens, their heritage rights 'are spatially limited by the national boundaries of the territory of the United States'. For Orser (2007: 102) this is unsatisfactory, and he suggests that we should consider whether the heritage of displaced persons should be located 'in the land and history that they have left behind, or in the new one where they now reside'.

This highlights a diaspora heritage issue that is potentially surrounded by difficult political sensitivities to do with contestations over property and ownership, for example in cases of returning exiles or refugees, or indigenous people asserting their right to reclaim land previously taken away from them in the process of colonisation (Jones & Birdsall-Jones 2008). This is a political hot potato I will not go into here. Instead, what I wish to highlight is the existential dimension of the diasporic experience at stake. In this regard, Orser's formulation of the issue is too narrow because it is too territorially bound and nation-centred. From his perspective, the problem seems to be limited to the need to reconcile the dual territoriality of the diasporic experience, with a focus on reconnection with the old homeland – no matter how many generations ago the ancestors departed – being the key heritage challenge. But how can we explain the very need and desire of these descendants of Ballykilcline to identify themselves as a diaspora in the twenty-first century? How can their shuttling *between* the old and the new country be addressed?

If in the example of Ballykilcline the initiative for reconnection was initiated by the diasporic subjects themselves, the heritage push can also be instigated from above, by the homeland nation-states who, for economic, political or other reasons, wish to tie the diasporas who had moved away back to the old country. What comes into central focus here is not immigration, but emigration. For example, in 2007 a number of villages in Kaiping county in southern China were given UNESCO World Heritage status for being a significant site that gave rise to the dispersal of Chinese peasants to North America and Australasia during the goldrush era from the mid-1800s onwards. The villages, which have many striking buildings built by returning *émigrés* in a distinct style fusing Chinese, Victorian and Baroque architectural elements, are described as 'embodying the roots of the Chinese diaspora' (*China Daily*, 2007). The motivation of Kaiping officials to acquire World Heritage designation was primarily economic: enlistment would bring in much needed funds for the restoration of the buildings through diaspora return tourism – a common motive for 'origin' countries to embark on diaspora heritage projects.

This local Chinese initiative reflects a broader effort on the part of the government of the People's Republic of China to strengthen its embrace of diasporic Chinese peoples, all in the name of love and loyalty for the ancestral homeland (Garnaut 2009). In India, too, there have been initiatives to step up its embrace of its far-flung diaspora. In 2007 the Indira Gandhi National Centre for the Arts established a Diaspora Program, designed to promote 'a cross-cultural interdisciplinary dialogue among Indians in India and the world' (www.ignca. nic.in/id_concept.htm). One of the principal objectives of the Diaspora Program is to set up a Diaspora Ethnographic Museum which 'reflects history of migration, artistic nuances of migrants at the time of their departure in India, the artistic and cultural traditions the migrants carried with them, the changes in their ideas and traditions, values, beliefs and customs in the new lands, emergence of a composite Indian culture, conflict and cooperation with the host society'. Both China and India, then, the two emerging superpowers of the twenty-first century, are clearly working towards an expansion of their global cultural influence by laying claim on their diasporic subjects through an emphasis on their persistent Chineseness or Indianness despite being far removed, in time and space, from the homeland.

This kind of state-driven outreach towards global diasporas is part of a broader international trend in international cultural diplomacy to pursue the national interest in today's increasingly entangled globalised world: an attempt to capitalise on the history of mobility of populations across national borders for national purposes. In the European context, this has been expressed in a recent boom in emigration museums, most of which were established in response to the growth of 'genealogy tourism', especially from the United States. Examples are the German Emigration Centre in Bremerhaven, Germany, which opened in 2005, the Museum of Emigration and the Communities, Portugal, the (online) Scottish Emigration Museum and the National Emigration Museum (Museo dell'Emigrazione Italiana) in Rome, Italy (*opened in 2009*).

Such museums may handle the subject of emigration in more or less sophisticated fashion, illuminating the complexities and varieties of diasporic experience. For example, the German Bremerhaven museum, which received the 'European Museum of the Year' award in 2007, has as its centrepiece the recreation of the experience of the transatlantic crossing, but temporary exhibitions have also covered subjects such as the experience of those forced into exile during the rule of the Nazis. The creation of such narratives is obviously very valuable, as they contribute to a broadening of the national imagination beyond its territorial borders.

The bottom line, however, is that here again a reductionist understanding of diaspora is at work. The paradigm of emigration, the venturing outward, involves a re-rooting of diasporic memory back to the site of the original homeland, which represents a territorialisation based on a geo-physical definition of heritage. Importantly, this kind of heritage practice constructs the diasporic experience as a linear history between two stable sites of origin and destination, with the diasporic subject suspended in-between, always able to be pulled back into the symbolic fold of the original homeland, the unquestioned source of his of her identity. Assumed here is a quintessentially essentialist, fixed and static notion of identity – of Chineseness, Indianness, Germanness, Portugueseness or whatever – which, however far you have gone and however long ago you left, remains the unerasable, immutable core to which the diasporic stands inevitably in a peripheral, derivative relationship.

Diaspora and transnational heritage

The bifurcation of migration into immigration and emigration, and their divergent treatment as separate heritage categories, illuminates the way in which diaspora tends to be conceived predominantly as a 'scene of dual territoriality', with the nation-states of origin and destination competing for the diaspora's attention and affection. Once diasporas are more complexly conceived as 'scenes of situated laterality', however, the emphasis will move beyond the to-and-fro logic of dual territoriality towards a more transgressive, transnational, multi-local diasporic imagination where the experience of displacement as such – the movement across different places – becomes more central. Stable notions of identity rooted in place or forged by attachment to place give way to more fluid and hybrid notions of identity shaped by mobility and flux. The formative experience here is that of 'routes' rather than 'roots', as Gilroy cleverly punned in his influential book *The Black Atlantic* (1993). In this book Gilroy proposed a new paradigm for understanding the African diasporic experience, one which 'transcends both the structures of the nation-state and the constraints of ethnicity and national particularity' (1993: 19). Instead he suggested an approach that takes the 'black Atlantic' as an interconnected, transnational and intercultural space where the formation of African diasporic experience can be captured in the image of the (slave) ship, the mobile means of transport that stands for 'the shifting spaces in between the fixed places' joined by it (1993: 16).

In this model, diasporic trajectories are more likely conceived as non-linear, perhaps endlessly circular: notwithstanding the physicality of actual displacement, the diasporic subject may never really leave nor never really arrive, but also never really return. Any 'return' to the ancestral homeland, whether physical or virtual, is never quite so: for example, the 'Africa' of the African diasporic imagination is not the real, geographical Africa. Identity here is not to be understood in terms of roots and rootedness, but as a process of movement and mediation, of diasporic routes. This dynamic, transient and elusive aspect of the diasporic experience is difficult to capture in official heritage categories. Yet this resolutely transnational dimension of diaspora is sometimes being addressed in heritage projects which explicitly aim to transcend nation-centric framings (see Box 5.1). Perhaps not surprisingly, the African diaspora has been a particular focus, highlighting the influence of Gilroy's idea of 'the black Atlantic'.

These diaspora-linked initiatives are all focused on inspiring a sense of transnational belonging which is ultimately confined by their resolutely ethno-specific point of identification: a symbolic (re)territorialisation of identity, memory and heritage which roots itself in the closure of what I would call a transnational nationalism (Ang 2001), a diasporic identity which, despite its decentring, remains enveloped in its imagined originary beginnings.

Beyond heritage, beyond diaspora

Moving from 'roots' to 'routes' in our understanding of diaspora implies that the diasporic experience is not just about the nostalgic remembering of the past, the place left behind, but also about life in the present and the process of reinvention towards a new future. This process of reinvention under conditions of displacement and in new sites of settlement (temporary or permanent) may also require a rupture with the past, rather than its virtual continuation through preservation of heritage. In this sense, heritage may act as a constraining factor for diasporic migrants, because its focus on preservation tends to de-emphasise and devalue the importance of change, transformation and hybridity. Recognising migrant groups through heritage, either in the land of settlement or in the country of origin, may in fact freeze them in an image of the past, and hence may reinforce their cultural marginalisation, rather than their empowerment. Thus, being locked into the identity of 'immigrant' forever reminds the diasporic subject that he or she comes from 'elsewhere' and doesn't really belong 'here'. At the same time, being cast as one who got 'away' from 'home' may only strengthen a sense of cultural dependency and inferiority *vis-à-vis* the putative 'homeland', where the diasporic subject will always tend to be positioned as having 'lost' their 'authentic' cultural identity.

Against this abject scenario, it is understandable that many people with histories of migration may actually choose to discard their diasporic attachments in favour of new, hybrid identities that are not chained to the gravitational pull of ancestral origin. Active disinheritance is at play here, substituted by a determination for reinvention, making oneself anew. Here we arrive at the limits of the usefulness of 'heritage', but also at the conceptual limits of the discourse of 'diaspora' itself: both are complicit in the validation of a conservative notion of culture and identity. In reality, however, neither heritage nor diaspora will soon dissipate as strong forces of passionate identification, forced or voluntary: the pull of the past, however imagined, will remain an undeniable aspect of the present, if only because it suits the nation-state. What bringing 'heritage' and 'diaspora' together highlights, then, is the enduring tension between freedom and belonging, embrace of the new and fidelity to the old. This gets us to the heart of the experience of displacement, and the ambivalence that shoots through it. If we *must* turn diaspora into heritage, then, as we have seen in this chapter, the biggest challenge for policy and best practice is to allow the careful, creative and intelligent articulation of that ambivalence, the unsettling of the national (whichever nation it may be).

Acknowledgement

I would like to thank Dr Nayantara Pothen for research assistance during the preparation of this chapter.

REFERENCES

Ang, Ien (2001) *On Not Speaking Chinese: Living Between Asia and the West*. London: Routledge.

Ashton, Paul (2009) '"The Birthplace of Australian Multiculturalism?" Retrospective Commemoration, Participatory Memoralisation and Official Heritage', *International Journal of Heritage Studies*, 15 (5): 381–398.

Ashworth, G.J., Brian Graham & J.E. Tunbridge (2007) *Pluralising Pasts: Heritage, Identity and Place in Multicultural Societies*. London: Pluto Press.

Bammer, Angelika (1994) *Displacements: Cultural Identities in Question*. Bloomington, IN: Indiana University Press.

Buciek, Keld & Kristine Juul (2008) '"We Are Here, Yet We Are Not Here": The Heritage of Excluded Groups', in Brian Graham & Peter Howard (eds), *The Ashgate Research Companion to Heritage and Identity*. Aldershot: Ashgate, pp. 105–123.

Campt, Tina (2002) 'The Crowded Space of Diaspora: Intercultural Address and the Tensions of Diasporic Relation', *Radical History Review*, 83 (Spring): 94–113.

Carrera Suárez, Isabel & Laura Viñuela Suárez (2007) 'The Use of Archives for Research in Migration and Gender Studies'. Discussion Paper, Changing Knowledge and Disciplinary Boundaries Through Integrative Research Methods in the Social Sciences and Humanities Project, York University, available at: www.york.ac.uk/res/research integration/Integrative_Research_Methods/Carrera%20 Suarez%20Archives%20April%202007.pdf.

Catanese, Brandi Wilkins (2007) '"When Did You Discover You Are African?' MoAD and the Universal, Diasporic Subject', *Performance Research*, 12(3): 91–102.

China Daily (2007) 'Chinese Diaspora Villages Made World Heritage Site', *China Daily*, 28 June 2007 (accessed online 15 February 2009).

Clifford, James (1997) *Routes: Travel and Translation in the Late Twentieth Century*. Cambridge, Mass: Harvard University Press.

Cohen, Robin (1997) *Global Diasporas*. IDEM Current Debate: Authenticity and Diaspora, with Sidney Littlefield Kasfir and Olabiyi Babbalola Joseph Yai. *Museum International* (2004) no 221–222 (56, 1–2), 190–97.

Esman, Milton J. (2009) *Diasporas in the Contemporary World*. Cambridge: Polity Press.

Garnaut, John (2009) 'Rally Around flag, China Tells Diaspora', available at: chinadigitaltimes.net/2009/07/rally-around-flag-china-tells-diaspora/

Gilroy, Paul (1993) *The Black Atlantic: Modernity and Double Consciousness*. Cambridge, MA: Harvard University Press.

Graham, Brian & Peter Howard (eds) (2008) *The Ashgate Research Companion to Heritage and Identity*. Aldershot: Ashgate.

Hamilton, Paula & Linda Shopes (eds) (2008) *Oral Histories and Public Memories*. Philadelphia, PA: University of Pennsylvania Press.

Hermansen, Cathrine Kyø & Thomas Abel Møller (2004). 'The Danish Immigration Museum of Furesø: The History of Immigration and the Collecting of Memories', *Museum International*, (2007) 59(1) 137–44.

Jones, Roy & Christina Birdsall-Jones (2008) 'The Contestation of Heritage: The Colonizer and the Colonized in Australia', in Brian Graham & Peter Howard (eds), *The Ashgate Research Companion to Heritage and Identity*. Aldershot: Ashgate, pp. 365–380.

Hermansen, Cathrine Kyø & Thomas Abel Møller (2007) 'The Danish Immigration Museum of Furesø: the history of immigration and the collecting of memories', *Museum International* 59 (1), pp. 137–44.

Lowenthal, David (1998) *The Heritage Crusade and the Spoils of History*. Cambridge: Cambridge University Press.

Mishra, Sudesh (2006) *Diaspora Criticism*. Edinburgh: University of Edinburgh Press.

Museum International (2004a) Special issue on migration museums, No 221–222 (56, 1–2).

Museum International (2004) 'Current Debate: Authenticity and Diaspora', with Sidney Littlefield Kasfir and Olabiyi Babbalola Joseph Yai, 56 (1–2): 190–97.

Museum International (2007), special issue on migration museums, 59(1): 4–160.

Orser Jr., Charles (2007) 'Transnational Diaspora and Rights of Heritage', in H. Silverman & D. Fairfield Ruggles (eds), *Cultural Heritage and Human Rights*. New York: Springer Verlag, pp. 92–105.

Silverman, Helaine & D. Fairchild Ruggles (2007) 'Cultural Heritage and Human Rights', in H. Silverman & D. Fairchild Ruggles (eds), *Cultural Heritage and Human Rights*. New York: Springer Verlag, pp. 3–22.

Safran, William (1991) 'Diasporas in Modern Societies: Myths of Homeland and Return', *Diaspora*, 1(1): 83–99.

Smith, Laurajane (2006) *Uses of Heritage*. London & New York: Routledge.

Stevens, Mary (2007), 'Museums, Minorities and Recognition: Memories of North Africa in Contemporary France', *Museum and Society*, 5(1): 29–43.

—— (2009) *Stories Old and New: Migration and Identity in the UK Heritage Sector*. A Report for the Migration Museum Working Group. London: Institute for Public Policy Research.

Taylor, Charles (1992) *Multiculturalism and the Politics of Recognition*. Princeton, NJ: Princeton University Press.

Tölölyan, Kahchig (1991) 'The Nation-State and Its Others: In Lieu of a Preface', *Diaspora*, 1 (1): 3–7.

Witcomb, Andrea (2009) 'Migration, Social Cohesion and Cultural Diversity: Can Museums Move Beyond Pluralism?', *Humanities Research*, 14(2), online.

CHAPTER 6

TERRITORIALIZATION AND THE POLITICS OF AUTOCHTHONY

Jean-Pierre Warnier

In September 2007, the United Nations adopted a 'Declaration on the Rights of Indigenous Peoples' (IPs). This text was the result of half a century of activism on the part of NGOs and Indigenous movements and was designed to protect inter alia their heritage, memory and identity. IPs justify their activism on the grounds of their autochthony. They claim fundamental and special rights to territories. Yet a closer examination of Indigenous movements around the world shows that they have quite different and sometimes conflicting agendas. This has not prevented them from converging on a global scale and confronting the top-down policies of states with a stake in territorializing their populations and controlling migratory flows. As a result, Indigenous People's politics of heritage, memory and identity are intertwined with complex global issues.

Introduction

In September 2007, the General Assembly of the United Nations adopted a 'Declaration on the Rights of Indigenous Peoples'.[1] This text was the result of half a century of activism on the part of NGOs and Indigenous movements such as the Indigenous Peoples Caucus[2] with the UN Human Rights Council. For the purposes of this chapter, I will read the term 'Indigenous' as 'autochthonous', which is indeed the word used in the French version of the Declaration.[3] In English, the relevance of the term to the present discussion derives from its reference to people who claim to be born on a territory occupied by their ancestors from time immemorial and with which they maintain a specific economic and spiritual relationship. The Declaration is meant to protect Indigenous Peoples (henceforth 'IPs') from state policies threatening to deprive them of their cultural values and ethnic identities (art. 7); their land (art. 7 and 10); their archaeological, historical, and sacred sites, together with their sacred objects (art. 11 and 12); their language, oral traditions, names and literature (art. 13); their own system of education (art. 14); their cultural heritage and memory (art. 31). As the last clause indicates, the cause of protection is intimately bound up with the issues discussed in this volume.

The Declaration does not devote any *ad hoc* article to defining the notion of 'Indigenous People'. However, many articles contribute to giving the notion semantic content. An IP enjoys an 'ethnic identity' of its own (art. 8, 2, a); it forms a distinct self-identified 'community' or 'nation'; it relates to a distinct territory, with its land (art. 8, 2, 4; and 10) with which the group maintains specific spiritual links (art. 25); it claims an intangible and tangible heritage. The entire Declaration makes it clear, especially articles 14 to 46, that the state is responsible for protecting IPs, and for attributing 'IP' status to a given community. This state responsibility opens up a broad space for the politics of recognition and representation. If a given group intends to claim such a status, it has to give evidence of its special ethnic *identity*, *heritage*, and *memory* attached to certain '*lieux de mémoire*', such as archaeological and historical sites, as well as to sacred objects and places, together with the narratives attached to them and to the group's past. Consequently, any 'nation' or 'group' claiming IP status has a vested interest in 'reviving' its identity, heritage and memory – an interest which in fact amounts to a right (art. 11, 1).

One of the major complaints voiced by IPs during the second half of the twentieth century concerned the dispossession of their lands they suffered under the pressure of colonization or violent seizure by states, dominant elites and multinational companies in search of resources and agricultural land. Consequently, the Declaration mentions the rights of IPs on their lands, territories and associated resources (art. 8, 2, 4; 10; 25, etc.). This amounts to linking the politics of autochthony to an identifiable territory. Accordingly, the politics of autochthony are part and parcel of a process of territorialization by or against states. These politics became global in the 1980s. Why global? First, because two successive globalizations – the first, brought about by western imperialism at the end of the nineteenth century and the second, more encompassing, wave of accelerated contemporary globalization that began in the 1970s – by triggering a ruthless scramble for land and resources, have displaced, marginalized, or even destroyed many IPs. Second, in order to counteract the effects mentioned above of the time/space compression which impacted on them, IPs have organized on a global scale, putting to use all the resources offered by the globalization process, for example global media, modern means of transportation, the Internet, international NGOs, etc.

Today, several million people have obtained recognition as IPs. But potentially *hundreds* of millions could in fact claim this status. In UN documents, Indigenous Peoples are said to comprise some 300–370 million people belonging to between 5,000 and 6,000 distinct groups living in more than 70 countries. They are the 'first' peoples and those maintaining a 'traditional' lifestyle (typically, the Indians of the Amazon basin, African Pygmies, the Andaman Islanders, etc.) as against the other, more mixed, peoples whose way of life could be said to be more 'modern'. However, the divide between Indigenous and non-Indigenous cannot be reduced to a dichotomy between tradition and modernity. For example, North American Indian activists are mostly middle-class urban professionals, not to speak of the casinos they operate. With such elastic criteria, perhaps as much as a third of the world population could qualify for the status of Indigenous People, including the Basque and Breton in France, or the Tamils in Sri Lanka.

In a nutshell: identity, heritage and memory have become key issues wherever and whenever autochthony is at stake, and autochthony is a key issue in matters of citizenship, access to land, forests, fishing and hunting rights, mineral resources and water, that is, to a territory. Face to face with peoples' politics of autochthony, we find nation-state policies of territorialization/deterritorialization of people. International migrations, border controls, the exploitation of natural resources, local and regional conflicts, all lead to the containment, control, or displacement of millions of people cut off from the land they claim to be theirs, and no longer in a position to substantiate their claims. Autochthony has become an argument to resist such policies. Conversely, it has also become a tool in the hands of states, used increasingly to expel people considered to be strangers or to deny them the kinds of rights they could claim under the Universal Declaration of Human Rights of 1948. Consequently, the politics of autochthony emerge at the point of juncture between bottom-up movements on the one hand and the top-down state policies of territorialization of people and resources.

Africa, the American continent, and Russia provide different settings in which the politics of autochthony have been played out. A rapid survey of these different histories will support my argument that the Declaration would never have been brought to existence if Indigenous activist movements all over the world had not joined forces in a globalized endeavour, and with quite different agendas. In this sense, the politics of autochthony are very much a product of the second contemporary wave of globalization. [4]

Africa

At the time of independence, in the 1960s, most African countries insisted on nation-building and unity within national borders inherited from the colonial powers as the condition for political and economic development and to counteract the fissiparous forces of ethnicity. Local policies of heritage, memory and identity were downplayed. Intra- or interstate migrations induced by urban, industrial and agricultural dynamics were often encouraged.

For example, under President Houphouet-Boigny, Côte d'Ivoire actively attracted many northerners to its southern towns and plantations, and millions of foreign immigrants, especially from Burkina-Faso. By contrast, from the early 1990s, Côte d'Ivoire, Cameroon, the two Congos, Senegal, Zambia and Malawi began actively promoting various policies of autochthony within their borders which seem to be the exact opposite of the nation-building practised during the first thirty years of independence. For example, in 1991, Zaire conducted an *'opération d'identification des nationaux'* according to their ethnic origins. In 2002, Laurent Gbagbo, the President of Côte d'Ivoire, followed suit and conducted an *'Opération Nationale d'Identification'* (National operation of identification) along the same lines. Each resident was asked to register in his 'village of origin' and to vote there. This operation has been described and analysed by Marshall (2006: 28) and Geschiere (2009: 3–4). In Côte d'Ivoire, it provided the rationale for the expulsion of millions of migrants, ending in a civil war.

Peter Geschiere (2009), following several scholars (e.g. Bayart, Geschiere, and Nyamnjoh, 2001; Comaroff and Comaroff, 2001), claims that it is a response to the 'neoliberal turn' of the late 1980s, and especially to the processes of democratization and decentralization that swept the African continent in the early 1990s. Thus, in Africa, the politics of belonging and autochthony are recent developments. As from the so-called 'Washington consensus' summarized by Ferguson (2006: 39), the centralizing corrupt African state was less and less seen as the most essential tool for development and more and more as a major barrier. Quite logically, the alternative to state-sponsored pilfering and underdevelopment was a policy that aimed to bypass the centralizing state, deflate the 'corrupt' and inefficient civil service, redirect development funds towards 'civil society', and foster political democratization *cum* decentralization. As part of this policy, the World Bank developed a 'Global Fund for Indigenous Peoples'[5] with the funds going straight to IP organizations. Thus in the early 1990s, in several African countries (Cameroon, Côte d'Ivoire and Zaire, now Republic of Congo), members of the elite, especially the civil servants, were encouraged to become cultural entrepreneurs and to found local associations based on specific languages and identities and through which the resources of extraversion (state, development and NGOs funds) could be channelled. They were also expected to negotiate these resources against political support for the regime. This response to democratization and decentralization was all the more successful in that it coincided with a growing international concern with the rights of IPs.

At the local level, its impact was spectacular. It is illustrated by the 'return of the kings' at the forefront of the African political landscape (see Perrot and Fauvelle-Aymar, 2003). This process started in the 1980s when the kings were able to negotiate the revival of their kingdoms by offering in return the extra legitimacy needed by widely discredited political regimes at state level. Palaces were rehabilitated, while furniture and *regalia* were renovated and enriched as valuable heritage. The rituals were dutifully performed. In the 1990s, the politics of autochthony considerably reinforced this trend. In the Western Highlands of Cameroon, for example, many of the local kingdoms (there are some 150 of them) founded local NGOs. Their acronyms were often terminated by CUDA which stands for 'Cultural Development Association'. Thus, the kingdom of Mankon created MACUDA ('Mankon Cultural Development Association').[6] It has subsidiaries in all major towns of West-central Africa in which there are Mankon diasporic groups, and even in Great Britain and the United States. They keep in touch with the palace of the king, largely through the Internet, and maintain the memory and identity of the kingdom (see Warnier, 2009).

This move quickly translated into active policies of *heritage*. In the early 2000s, like three other kingdoms of the Western Highlands of Cameroon, the kingdom of Mankon built a local museum with the help of two Italian NGOs. The aim of the museum, stated by the King in the Preface to the luxurious catalogue produced by Notué and Triaca (2005), is to help maintain the identity, memory and heritage of the kingdom. The king's autobiography (Fo Angwafo III, 2009) states how this cultural policy is directed towards maintaining the claims of the Mankon people to political representation at state level and to their land in a context of land shortage. This kind of museumization process in Africa may be perceived as a (Western) technology of heritage potentially at odds with African ways of preserving heritage, an issue discussed by De Jong and Rowlands (2007). For example, along quite a different line of cultivating memory, the neighbouring kingdom of Bali-Nyonga founded an NGO, the

'Bali-Nyonga Development and Cultural Association', the first undertaking of which, analysed by Page (2007), was to build a mortuary to help with repatriating the corpses of its citizens (normally members of the elite) who had died far away from home. The case of this kingdom illustrates two major aspects of the definition of autochthony mentioned by Detienne (2003), a historian of Ancient Greece, in the case of Athens, that is, a narrative concerning origins and a *graveyard* (my emphasis). Ancestral graves on indigenous land are among the best arguments to claim ancient rights of occupation.

The unrelenting support of the politics of autochthony by the Cameroon state in the 1990s fostered severe local conflicts. In major cities all over the country, people who had sold their land to migrants coming from other parts of Cameroon several decades ago started challenging the rights of ownership of the non-native tenants (Socpa, 2006; Geschiere, 2009). The politics of autochthony, in that sense, was a success for the regime of President Paul Biya, as a 'divide and rule' response to the democratization exercise of the early 1990s.

America

In North America, by contrast with Africa, the politics of autochthony has a long history, documented by Rostkowski (2001), as regards the Indians in the United States. This history explains the leading role played by 'Native Americans' in the take-off in the 1970s of various IP movements and their subsequent globalization, as well as the differences in the politics of citizenship in America as compared with other continents such as Africa – three points to which we shall return later. Let us start at the end of the nineteenth century, when most Native Americans were living in reservations created following the displacement of an estimated 25–30 million people. In 1868, the Grant administration launched a campaign to convert the 'Indians' to Christianity and to give them US citizenship in conformity with the 'melting-pot' ideology. Those who were willing to abandon their status were required to go through a ceremony during which they shot a last arrow and received agricultural implements and a new (Euro-American) name. The women were given a purse and a work bag. The performance of this ceremony came to an end in 1924. In the 1930s, with the improvement of communications

between the various tribes, a pan-Indian consciousness began to crystallize against the melting-pot ideology. Representations were made to the League of Nations. The involvement of Native Americans in World War II called for more integration in mainstream American society, which induced the Federal Administration to abolish the system of reservations in 1953. This was one more step in the politics of 'de-indianization' practised by the Federal Bureau of Indian Affairs. Native Americans responded by creating the American Rights Association. *Corporate* rights regarding *land*, forests, water, dams, etc., were at the heart of the conflict. From 1900 to 1950, American Indians had lost 60 per cent of their territories.

The misconstrued initiative of the Federal government caused a shock which boosted Native American activism. Many natives joined the National Congress of American Indians (NCAI) which had been created in the early 1940s (with a clear reference to Mahatma Gandhi and the Indian National Congress). They started seeking international recognition. In 1961, the National Indian Youth Council was created, on a more radical agenda than that of the NCAI. The Federal administration had to back down and the reservations were saved. The year 1962 saw the creation of the Institute for American Indian Arts and of the Native American Caucus.

At the end of the 1960s, the powerful American Indian Movement (AIM)[7] was created. This body innovated on two accounts. First, it emphasized the spiritual dimension of the Indian endeavour, illustrated by their special relationship to the cosmos, the earth and the natural environment. Second, it relied on spectacular actions that could attract media coverage. The quarterly magazine *The Sentinel* and the journal *ABC* (*America Before Columbus*) expressed its views. But it also called on non-native media, including international ones, by staging spectacular events. In November 1969, the abandoned prison of Alcatraz built on a rock in the Bay of San Francisco was occupied for 18 months. This action helped publicize a manifesto signed by IAT (the Indians of All Tribes). In 1972, activists of the AIM occupied the Bureau of Indian Affairs in Washington DC, and appealed for the implementation of the treaties once passed between the USA and the Indian Nations. They launched the campaign 'Trail of Broken Treaties'. One year later, thousands of Native Americans occupied the village of Wounded Knee to which is attached the memory of the massacre of Lahota Sioux, including women and children, at the end of the nineteenth century. These innovations propelled the American IPs to prominence on the global stage.

At about the same time (1970), the Native American Rights Funds (NARF) was created. The AIM and the NARF were staffed by educated urban-dwelling Native Americans who assumed the role of cultural entrepreneurs. In 1977, the AIM sent a delegation in full Indian outfit to speak at the United Nations in Geneva. This spectacular gambit was emblematic of a nascent globalized solidarity between IPs all over the world. Much emphasis was put on spiritual values and on the preservation of cultural heritage and memory. The 1980s and 1990 were years of lively creativity in domains such as literature, arts, cinema, language, newspapers, teaching, religious cults (the observance of which had been prohibited until as late as 1934), cultural festivals and spectacular pan-Indian gatherings known as 'Pow Wows'. In 1999, the Native American Graves Protection and Repatriation Act was passed in Congress: autochthony, as we saw, is bound to a narrative and a *graveyard*.

At this juncture, I wish to stress two points. First, the agenda of the 'North American Indians', when claiming 'IP' status was radically different from the issues motivating African movements since the early 1990s. The former began at least a century earlier. It was the result of many local conflicts, aggregating very slowly to produce a pan-Indian consciousness in the 1930s. From the 1940s onwards, this awareness grew and became articulated in the 1950s around the question of how to accede to full US citizenship while preserving an Indian *identity*? How could American Indians preserve the *memory* of past events, and above all of what they had lost at the hands of the dominant society, most members of which wanted to suppress the said memory? What could be done to collect and illustrate their tangible and intangible *heritage*? The answers were complex, but they all converged on *corporate rights on land*, on material resources, on sacred sites and other '*lieux de mémoire*', that is, on the territorialization of the people in the reservations. This is why the decision of the Federal government to abolish the reservation system in 1953 triggered such an upsurge. In the USA, the autochthony movement was not a response to the 'liberal turn' of the 1980s; rather, it

largely preceded that movement. Yet the ethos of the 1980s provided a ready-made ideological kit when the IP movements became globalized at the end of the twentieth century.

The second aspect worth highlighting is the violence, often extreme and unwarranted, experienced by Native Americans in their relationship to mainstream American society. As late as 1973, the occupation of Wounded Knee, which kept alive the memory of a massacre (in the context of the Vietnam War and the My Lai Massacre trial), was the pretext of a damaging repression against the AIM. It triggered a severe counter-attack by anti-Indian movements (the motto 'a good Injun is a dead Injun' was still in everyone's mind). This violence should be remembered when reading the very sketchy narrative I have given above.

Canada's 'First Nations' followed a parallel course, while on the other side of the Rio Grande, in Mexico, Indigenous movements followed quite a different one, resulting from the Spanish, Catholic, and colonial framework, starting with the conquest in 1521. Lopez Caballero (2009) provides an illustration of this sharp difference from the US and Canadian contexts by discussing two foundation narratives written by the same Nahuatl village named Milpa Alta, near Mexico City, in order to support a land claim against another village. The first one, dated 1690, narrates how the village had been elected by the Virgin Mary of the Assumption. She had defined its limits and indicated where the people could find spring water for their use. As a counter gift, the villagers built a church and worshipped their Saint patron. No mention was made of any pre-Columbian past. The memory was linked to the land and to a Christian cult and sanctuary. By contrast, the 1934 narrative was elaborated after the 1910–1917 Zapatist peasant revolution against the excessive power and wealth of the Church. After the murder of Emilio Zapata in 1919, the new political regime adopted a strong nationalist and 'indigenist' discourse conducive to the enhancement of Indian identity and to the pre-Columbian heritage and memory repressed under colonization. However, the political elites denied any continuity between the pre-Columbian highly 'civilized' Aztecs and the present-day 'lazy and degenerate' Indians. The connection was established by professional anthropologists and archaeologists under the leadership of Manuel Gamio, who had been trained by Franz Boas. Gamio became a key actor in providing the new regime with a nationalistic ideology. Accordingly, the 1934 narrative of the Milpa Alta foundation linked the establishment of the village not to the Virgin Mary but to the guidance of a tutelary Aztec god who directed the first inhabitants to their land by following a cosmic sign. In this context, the memory of the colonial, Catholic, past was suppressed as spurious, just as the pre-Columbian memory had been suppressed between 1521 and 1910. Once again, the villagers were deprived of their living memory by an educated elite which took upon itself the task of redefining and reshaping the memory and identity of the Other. However, 'Official indigenism' as a state doctrine was conducive to the mushrooming Indigenous NGOs, who joined with other, international, ones when the movement became globalized in the 1980s.

In South America, Indigenous movements have progressed since the 1970s under the influence of a complex mix of Zapatism, Guevarism, Liberation Theology, the churches, the programme 'Man and Biosphere', development NGOs and the environmental movement, especially in Amazonia. Even more importantly, the activism of Native American movements in the USA seeking allies in their attempt at globalizing their protest and at drawing new recruits to the 'Indigenous Peoples Caucus' has played a role. But the South American movement is more tightly connected to the globalization process of the 1980s than the much older activism in the USA and Canada.

Russia

According to Donahoe et al. (2008), Russia has a long experience of state-instigated construction of ethnicity going back to the encounter between representatives of the Empire and inhabitants of Siberia in the late sixteenth century. Very early on, small size, insignificance, social backwardness and a need for protection were seen as characteristics of the Russian minorities. In the mid-1920s, this categorization was given a statutory content (Donahoe et al., 2008: 995). The peoples concerned (located mostly in Siberia and along the southern border of the Federation in central Asia, such as the Aleut, Dolgan, Kamchadal, Oroch, Taz, Udege, etc.) enjoyed a number of privileges (tax exemptions, exclusive hunting and fishing rights, compensations for mining and other activities by the state or private companies, etc.).

In the last years of the Soviet regime, the rise in political visibility of the globalized Indigenous movements reached the Russian minorities. The Soviet approach to ethnic minorities under the 1926 statute and its evolutionary matrix were perceived as demeaning and patronizing. Indigenous leaders reacted by creating the 'Russian Association of Indigenous Peoples of the North' (RAIPON), accompanied by a change in terminology. The word *malye* ('small' people) was replaced by a newly coined word – *karennye* – which derives from the Russian word for 'root' and conveys the idea of rootedness – in other words, autochthony. It is this term that most closely approximates, and is most often translated into English as, 'indigenous' (Donahoe et al., 2008: 997).

The new statutes drawn up by the Russian Federation recycle most of the content of the Soviet era legislation, especially the demographic threshold of a maximum of 50,000 persons to qualify as an IP and enjoy the associated legal rights. Many ethnic groups have applied, and the number of those who were granted the status grew from 26 to 45 between 1993 and 2000. It should be kept in mind, however, that the 50,000 persons benchmark is just a proxy for the more qualitative and numerous criteria of autochthony. As Donahoe et al. (2008: 994) put it, Indigenous Peoples are defined by the Russian law as 'people living in the territories of traditional settlement of their ancestors, preserving a traditional way of life and a traditional economic system and economic activities, numbering within the Russian Federation fewer than 50,000 persons, and recognizing themselves as independent ethnic communities'. By 'traditional' is meant roughly the way of life that obtained in the late nineteenth century. This legal definition opens up a vast arena for the deployment by IPs of the politics of identity, memory and heritage linked to a given territory. In that respect, Russia is no exception to what is taking place elsewhere in the world. Yet the 50,000 threshold seriously limits the number of peoples who may be entitled to benefit from their recognition as 'indigenous'. Russia has nearly 200 nationalities. Of these, writes Donahoe et al. (2008: 995), 'approximately 130 (with 20 million people or 14 per cent of the population of the Russian Federation) could, according to the definition … lay claim to 'indigenous' status', which would prove very costly for the Russian Federation.

Our tour round the indigenous globe should be extended to the Asia-Pacific region, whose two giants (India and China) would provide relevant data for the present discussion. To be sure, the situation of minorities in China and India raises specific and difficult issues, as might be expected in such different political settings. Unfortunately, for lack of space it is not possible to address them. Let us nevertheless mention that their minorities actively participate in the globalized Indigenous movement.

The politics of autochthony 'at large'

The world's Indigenous Peoples movements converged in the last decades of the twentieth century. The chronology of events spells out the globalization of the issues:

- 1977 – Delegation of US Indians to the UN in Geneva;
- 1981 – World Conference of NGOs on IPs;
- 1982 – creation of a Permanent Working Group on Indigenous issues by the UN Human Rights Council;
- 1989 – the International Labour Organization passes Convention 169 under the title 'Indigenous and Tribal Peoples Convention';
- 1993 – International Year of Indigenous Peoples.

From the early 1990s onwards, the globalized Indigenous movement has fixed its specific vocabulary and key words (Indigenous, land, territory, resources, heritage, identity, memory, spiritual) and their official equivalents in all major languages. It has its own world capital (Geneva) and its specialized NGOs (the Indigenous Peoples Caucus, Survival International, etc.). It is producing globalized information and legal instruments.

Yet, I have argued that, at the local, national, regional and continental levels, the Indigenous movements display a great diversity of trajectories and of conflicting agendas. Probably the oldest players in the game were the United States and Russia, with two, quite different, endogenous histories concerning their minorities, which took shape in the nineteenth century. The record leads us to think that native Americans played a leading role in the emergence of world Indigenous activism after World War II. In the USA, they found occasional synergies with Afro-American, Civil Rights, and counter-culture activists, and succeeded in organizing at a national level. Their agenda was quite clear: they aimed at becoming full US citizens without having to abandon their corporate lands and to suppress their Indian identity, memory and specific heritage. Theirs was a logic of inclusion and territorialization.

The case of Africa is strikingly different from that of North America. African Indigenous movements were largely induced from the outside, either as a response of a number of African states to the neoliberal turn in the early 1990s, or as a result of the alliance between local minorities (such as the Pygmies or the San) and international NGOs active in the defence of the environment and/or IPs. There is much disagreement among African countries regarding the agenda. In some countries (Côte-d'Ivoire, Cameroon, the two Congos, Zambia, Malawi and to some extent South Africa) autochthony is an instrument of *exclusion* of other Africans considered as undesirable, and of inclusion of nationals mediated by their territorialization predicated on reified identities. Most other African countries try to stick to the post-independence agenda of nation- and state-building. This is reflected in the updates provided by the UN Permanent Forum on Indigenous Issues[8] which shows that only three African states (Zambia, Cameroon and South Africa) consistently supported the successive drafts of the Declaration. Ghana, Nigeria and Senegal were reluctant to support the Declaration. In 2006, Namibia called for further consultations with the African Group of States (altogether 53 countries).

The claim by Native Americans to be the 'First Peoples' and to have inalienable corporate rights on their sacred sites could be clearly established since the white Americans and the Afro-Americans were latecomers whose migrations were historically documented and dated. In America, the Indigenous movements opposed the 'First Peoples' to the latecomers in a quest for full citizenship. In Africa, by contrast, the politics of autochthony opposed some groups/categories of Africans to others, and, as noted by Geschiere (2009: 26–30), historical claims to being 'autochthonous' or to being the 'first' are rather difficult to establish. The reasons for this include the constant intermingling of populations before colonization, the lack of reliable historical evidence, and a colonial situation which differed markedly from the North American one. No doubt, taking into account Asia and the

Pacific would bring out a number of cases without any colonial presence, or with the experience of a colonial situation more akin to that of Africa than to the North American one. The vote of the Declaration at the General Assembly of the UN in October 2007 is a testimony to the globalization of the movement *despite* extremely diverse and sometimes conflicting agendas. It was the result, as it were, of a working misunderstanding. Eleven countries abstained (including Russia), 143 voted for, and the four that were against (Canada, New Zealand, Australia, the USA) are the countries that tend to represent themselves as having the most progressive Indigenous policies. In less than three decades, Indigenous issues, standards, terminology, agendas and administrative practices have been globalized and are now recycled all over the world. They impact on the politics of heritage, memory and identity with diversified and sometimes dramatic effects at the local and national levels.

The territorialization of the state, memory, identity, heritage

In this final section, I wish to tackle the issue of territorialization which is at the heart of the relationship between IPs and the state. Since the nineteenth century, there has been a scramble for land and natural resources all over the world. In the evolutionary common sense of the time, most IPs were defined as 'lacking' in law, land tenure systems, writing, economic potential, political organization, in other words in 'civilization'. This provided a rationale for displacing them, pushing them to the margins, and depriving them of their lands and resources. IPs have succeeded in reversing the ideological trend. Instead of being perceived as lacking, they are seen as being endowed with identity, memory, heritage, with an authenticity and an autochthony that has been lost by the rest of the world population. Yet, with 7 billion people at the beginning of the twenty-first century, humanity is putting increasing pressure on land and natural resources. China and Middle Eastern countries are purchasing millions of hectares of arable land elsewhere in the world. Land-and-people is the issue. That is, it is becoming obvious that people who are unmoored from a given space are at risk of being the outcasts of a globalized world. Such a moorage can be achieved by establishing one's corporate

rights on a given territory as an autochthon, or on a national space as a citizen, or both.

If we take globalization as meaning the time/space compression achieved by the acceleration of cultural, commodity, financial and other flows, the demographic flows present a special case. They disrupt the links between people and space. Displaced people and migrants are more at risk of becoming unmoored. Land, indeed, is static, and does not move with them. More and more states channel and control migration flows more tightly. This does not concern only western industrial countries, as recent cases at the southern border of Morocco, and in Ivory Coast and Congo demonstrate. The scramble for land, space and resources impacts directly on people who relate to them. There is a premium on territorialization. Everywhere in the world, nation-states are directly involved in the process of closure *cum* territorialization.

This issue requires a short discussion as it seems to challenge the theory of the 'weakening' or 'decline' of the state put forward, among others, by Strange (1996). Bayart (2004) remarks, following Appadurai (1996), that the 'decline' thesis rests on the assumption that states have emerged in various parts of the world following local dynamics, and then as in a kind of afterthought, have come into contact with each other, and have created a globalized space of interaction 'at large' which undermines their strength. From a historical standpoint, this view is flawed. Interactions came first, and they raised local problems as regards goods and persons circulating, as it were, 'unmoored' from the local. The processes of closure and territorialization, which is what the state is all about, have been responses to those interactions and that unmooring.

This is particularly obvious when it comes to people-and-land. The globalization of financial and commodity flows would have normally called for a globalization of demographic flows, which is what happened with the first globalization in the nineteenth century. In a sense, this is also what could have happened in the second part of the twentieth century with labour and tourist migrations, except that, in various parts of the world, especially in Europe, the USA, the Middle East, and some parts of Asia, states have reacted more and more strongly, even violently, to prevent, control, check, channel, vet, or cause, outgoing or incoming migrations. Migration policies have become key issues and have *reinforced* state power and control on land-and-people. Land, in fact, is immobile and cannot be fed into globalized flows, except by purchase.

The issue of the 'decline' of the state may be clarified if one distinguishes between different processes. State 'shrinking', as analysed by Crawford (2007), concerns the process of state withdrawal from a number of fields such as social security, health and education. Does this process mean that the state is becoming 'weaker'? There is much evidence to the contrary. In Africa, for example, the Washington consensus was expected to weaken and bypass the failed African states by shifting power and resources to civil society, including IPs. Yet, the grip of the states on their populations tends to be reinforced at the very time some of them withdraw from the protection of the said populations.

In a nutshell, IPs and states join hands in the global politics of territorialization which could be defined as a drive at partitioning space, achieving its closure and control, attaching particular groups and categories of people to particular spaces and pushing others to the margins. Bottom-up drives join together with top-down policies. Consequently, there is a continuum of statuses between, on the one hand, IPs whose essential corporate rights to a given land are recognized, and, on the other hand, the refugee who has lost any clearly recognized bond to a given territory, is undesirable wherever he goes, and ends up in an enclosed camp in which the memory of what has been lost in terms of heritage shapes his identity, especially at the second and following generations. In between, there are different kinds of statuses, including the status of citizen with his freedom of movement and land tenure within a national or regional space.

As an emblematic case of territorialization, refugee camps (and, to some extent, reservations) deserve a special mention since they exemplify the negative image to that of the IPs. Camps are shaped by the implementation of two sets of technologies. Both directly address the body of the refugee. The first concerns the containment and control of space and the mobility of people; it includes walls, fences, camps, patrols along borders and coasts, specialized scouts, armed forces and intelligence services, CCTV cameras, eye scans and DNA tests more or less regulated by national and international laws and institutions. All these mechanisms are implemented mostly by the military or by

other armed groups. The other set of technologies addresses the vital survival of the refugee. They are the humanitarian technologies which, according to Agier (2008), amount to a fully-fledged 'humanitarian government' (with 575 NGOs operating in the camps in 2007), in which the most emblematic action consists of 'screening' the incomers in order to assign them to a given category according to their age, sex, origin, condition, and degree of 'vulnerability'.

The IP, the citizen and the refugee thus embody three emblematic regimes in the politics of autochthony in their relationship to the territorialization/deterritorialization process. Those three regimes impact on the capacity of each of these ideal types to manage their identity, memory and heritage. As regards IPs, the politics of autochthony open up an arena in which leaders such as 'traditional' authorities, NGO representatives, and political activists can promote the invention or revival of cultural traditions, enhance the specific identity of their people, build museums and memorials. African kings are a case in point. Such leaders may be considered as cultural entrepreneurs. Indigenous cultural entrepreneurship introduces some amount of *social inequality*. African kings engage in business and politics. Another case in point is provided by the Southern Pacific nationalist elites use of the 'Pacific Way' and of '*Kastom*', as described by Hau'ofa (1987) and Babadzan (2009). These elites come from the same social background, churches and academia; they all enhance traditional values, and are happy with the fact that these are embodied not by themselves, but by the poor indigenous villager who is trapped in a state of underdevelopment with no alternative but to live a so-called 'traditional' way of life and material culture, with little access to education and medical care.

Cultural entrepreneurs engage in the *invention of tradition* and the *reification* of essentialist identities in a globalized world (see Meyer and Geschiere, 1999). In many cases, they may reap *economic benefits* depending on the capacity of given Indigenous People to occupy certain niches (such as the casinos in the USA) or to attract certain forms of tourism (such as 'ecotourism' supported by NGOs), employment, or development funds. They usually work hand in hand with national and world organizations for technical, legal and financial support. They are at the interface between the local and the *globalized* politics of autochthony.

Towards more research and development in law

In the short space of this chapter, my aim has been to sketch the bottom-up and top-down politics of autochthony. As regards the policy implications of such a sketch, one may wonder if the politics of autochthony are not a solution, albeit a second-rate one, in cases when the IPs are forced to chose between full citizenship rights and particular *corporate* rights, or the alternative of being second-rate citizens parked in reservations. If this were the case, the Indigenous movements could be considered as limited, provisional, responses to a postcolonial situation, pending a shift in national and international law away from the definition of human rights in purely *individual* terms. The UN Declaration of 2007 could be seen as symptomatic of a general trend towards the recognition of a more corporate, collective definition of citizenship, which would complement the 1948 Universal Declaration which accords primacy to the individual.

This line of reasoning deserves more investigation than is possible here. Yet it does suggest two broad recommendations. The first is that UN organizations and Councils (Human Rights, UNESCO, ILO, WTO, etc.), and NGOs should support the corporate rights of IPs at the local, state and continental levels. However, knowing the ambiguities of the globalized Indigenous movements (especially inequalities, the ambiguous role of cultural entrepreneurs, and the predicament of refugees), the kind of support that is needed should guarantee equal access of all individual members of a given IP to corporate rights. Such a balance between corporate and individual rights is certainly quite difficult to achieve and needs much innovative research. The second would be to deepen our understanding of collective rights in their relationship with citizenship, so as to broaden their scope beyond the case of the IPs, which seems to be an exceptional and perhaps provisional one. In other words, is it possible to conceive of a more corporate citizenship, that is, a citizenship that would not be exclusively defined at the level of the individual, but also, to some extent that remains to be determined, at the level of a given organized social group?

Towards resolving tensions and contradictions

This chapter has underlined the 'working misunderstanding', tensions and contradictions that pervade the politics of memory, heritage and identity linked to the globalized claims to autochthony by IP movements. The local agendas of the IPs, for example in Africa as against the Americas, often contradict each other. More sharing of information and experiences might be useful to reduce the contradictions and promote a sustainable Indigenous movement, for example by:

- discovery trips to other countries/continents by senior and junior members of IPs;
- IP internships to participate in local programmes in different countries/continents;
- exchanging information on local experiences and policies;
- translations in different languages of key books and documents on memory, heritage and identity;
- the use of documentary films, exhibits and other media produced by IPs themselves to promote the sharing of knowledge and experiences;
- promoting social science and legal scholarship on the articulation between corporate rights on given territories with the memory, heritage and identity attached to them on the one hand, and individual rights and citizenship on the other hand.

So far, Indigenous movements have been very successful on a world scale by putting together their common concerns. However, they did it at the cost of playing down their local contradictions. It is doubtful that this situation could carry on without damage to whatever has been achieved in matters of memory, heritage and identity. This remark calls for new developments in the politics of autochthony. The 'Declaration on the Rights of Indigenous Peoples' passed in October 2007 should not mark the end of a long struggle, but the beginning of a new dynamics in matters of memory, heritage, identity and corporate rights.

Notes

1   www.un.org/esa/socdev/unpfii/en/declaration.html.
2   www.ipcaucus.net.

3 '*Déclaration des Nations Unies sur les droits des peuples autochtones*'
4 I am most grateful to the editors of this volume and to Michaela Pelican for invaluable suggestions and critical comments.

5 www.worldbank.org/indigenous.
6 MACUDA in the USA has a web page: www.macuda america.com.
7 www.aimovement.org.
8 www.un.org/esa/socdev/unpfii.

REFERENCES

Agier, M. (2008) *Gérer les indésirables: des camps de réfugiés au gouvernement humanitaire,* Paris: Flammarion.

Appadurai, A. (1996) *Modernity at Large: Cultural Dimensions of Globalization.* Minneapolis and London: University of Minnesota Press.

Babadzan, A. (2009) *Le spectacle de la culture: Globalisation et traditionalismes en Océanie,* Paris: L'Harmattan.

Bayart, J.-F., Geschiere, P., Nyamnjoh, F. (2001) Autochtonie, démocratie et citoyenneté en Afrique, *Critique internationale,* n° 10, 2001, p. 177–194.

Bayart, J.-F. (2004) *Le gouvernement du monde: Une critique politique de la globalisation,* Paris: Fayard.

Comaroff, J. and Comaroff, J.L. (2001) 'Naturing the nation: aliens, apocalypse and the Postcolonial State', *Journal of Southern African Studies,* 27(3): 627–651.

Crawford, B. (2007) 'Globalization and cultural conflict: an institutional approach', in H. Anheier and Y.R. Isar (eds), *The Culture and Globalization. Series 1, Conflicts and Tensions,* London: Sage, pp. 31–50.

De Jong, F. and Rowlands, M.J. (eds) (2007) *Reclaiming Heritage: Alternative Imaginaries of Memory in West Africa,* Walnut Creek, CA: Left Coast Press.

Detienne, M. (2003) *Comment être autochtone? Du pur Athénien au Français raciné,* Paris: Seuil.

Donahoe, B., Habeck, J.O., Halemba, A. and Santha, I. (2008) 'Size and place in the construction of indigeneity in the Russian Federation', *Current Anthropology,* 49 (6): 993–1020.

Ferguson, J. (2006) *Global Shadows: Africa in the Neoliberal World Order,* Durham, NC: Duke University Press.

Fo Angwafo III S.A.N. of Mankon (2009) *Royalty and Politics: The Story of My Life,* Bamenda: Langaa RPCIG.

Geschiere, P. (2009) *The Perils of Belonging: Autochtony, Citizenship and Exclusion in Africa and Europe,* Chicago and London: The University of Chicago Press.

Hau'ofa, E. (1987) 'The New South Pacific Society: integration and independence', in A. Hooper et al. (eds), *Class and Culture in the South Pacific,* Suva (Fiji): University of the South Pacific, pp. 1–12.

Lopez Caballero, P. (2009) 'Quel héritage pour quels héritiers? Passé précolombien et héritage colonial dans l'histoire nationale du Mexique', in www.fasopo.org/reasopo. htm#revue, 15 (May).

Marshall, R. (2006) 'The war of "who is who?": autochtony, nationalism, and citizenship in the Ivorian crisis', in 'Autochtony and the Crisis of Citizenship', P. Geschiere and Stephen Jackson (eds), spécial issue, *African Studies Review,* 49(2): 9–43.

Meyer, B. and Geschiere, P. (eds) (1999) *Globalization and Identity: Dialectic of Flow and Closure,* Oxford: Blackwell.

Notué, J.-P. and Triaca, B. (2005) *Manko: Arts, Heritage and Culture from the Mankon Kingdom,* Milan: 5 Continents Editions.

Page, B. (2007) 'Slow going: the mortuary, modernity and the hometown association in Bali-Nyonga, Cameroon', *Africa,* 77 (3): 419–441.

Perrot, C.-H., and Fauvelle-Aymar, F.-X. (eds) (2003) *Le Retour des rois: Les autorités traditionnelles et l'Etat en Afrique contemporaine,* Paris: Karthala.

Rostkowski, J. (2001) *Le Renouveau indien aux Etats-Unis: Un siècle de reconquêtes,* Paris: Albin Michel.

Socpa, A. (2006) 'Bailleurs autochtones et locataires allogènes: enjeu foncier et participation politique au Cameroun', *African Studies Review,* 49 (2): 45–67.

Strange, S. (1996) *The Retreat of the State: The Diffusion of Power in the World Economy,* Cambridge: Cambridge University Press.

Warnier, J.-P. (2009) *Régner au Cameroun: Le Roi-pot,* Paris: CERI-Karthala.

CHAPTER 7

GRASSROOTS MEMORIALS AS SITES OF HERITAGE CREATION

Cristina Sánchez-Carretero and Carmen Ortiz

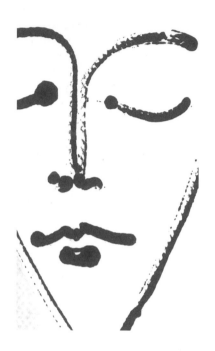

Various ritual forms of memorialization, mourning and protest in public spaces have emerged in recent years; a fixed pattern of memorials located at the places where particular deaths are considered 'unjust' and traumatic, either because a famous person has been killed or because anonymous citizens have been the victims of a massacre. These improvised memorials have been dubbed 'grassroots memorials' by Margry and Sánchez-Carretero (2011) in order to highlight both their political dimension and their non-institutionalized character. This chapter explores such memorials, with particular reference to the Archivo del Duelo *(Archive of Mourning) – a research project established in response to the terrorist attacks of 11 March 2004 in Madrid.*

Grassroots memorials: a global and mediatized phenomenon

The appearance, as an international phenomenon, of grassroots memorials in public spaces, usually on the site of the events that have caused the tragic and violent death of a famous person or, as in the case of the Madrid bombings of 2004, a group of ordinary people, has caught the attention of anthropologists in recent years. Several have explored how these deaths are coped with collectively (Santino 1992, 2006a, 2006b; Haney et al. 1997; Grider 2000, 2001; Fraenkel 2002; Chulilla et al. 2005; Doss 2006, 2008; Margry and Sánchez-Carretero 2007, 2011; Sánchez-Carretero, 2011). Comparative studies on the construction of memory in response to deaths that society considers traumatic are particularly significant in this regard.[1] The performative dimension is one of the characteristics that grassroots memorials have in common. We use the adjective 'performative' in the Austinian sense (Austin 1962) in relation to the acts involved in the process. Grassroots memorials are more than a public expression of mourning: they are actions that can trigger other actions. Citizens not only place their offerings in memory of the dead, but also demand other actions: explanations of what has occurred, that guilty parties be found, or that someone take responsibility (Margry and Sánchez-Carretero 2007: 2). The dual performative and commemorative nature of these altars in public spaces is therefore one of their essential properties: they bring the element of individual remembrance and commemoration together with the component of social intervention, for example by drawing attention to the social and political conditions that led to the deaths, and by consequently mobilizing the population.

There is no consensus about how to name this type of memorial. The term 'spontaneous shrines' was coined in 1992 by Jack Santino in a study of the places created to memorialize political deaths in Northern Ireland (Santino 1992). The use of the word 'spontaneous' indicates the unofficial nature of the display; no institution – nation, state or church – issues an invitation to take part in this ritual; it is a popular activity, in the sense that people are its active subject. The word 'shrine' is used because they are places of communion between the living and the dead. They are also places of pilgrimage, where people go to commemorate and memorialize, but they are open to the public at large (Santino 2006b: 11–12), unlike monumental memorials, which include limited or no participation of the general public in the rationale behind them, whose objectives are controlled by some type of political or religious authority, and which are also distant in time from the events they commemorate (Young 1993).

A subsequent debate regarding the religious sense of using the term 'shrine' as well as the questionable spontaneity of the memorials has led other researchers to employ the term 'improvised' or 'ephemeral' memorials (Stengs 2003). In the media, however, the most common term is 'makeshift memorial', although in academia, 'makeshift' is not commonly used because of its negative connotations.[2] To avoid the focus on the 'temporality' aspects, and the problems regarding the 'spontaneity' of the memorials, in a recent study Margry and Sánchez-Carretero coined the term 'grassroots memorials' in order to highlight the fact that what unifies these ritualized patterns for the expression of mourning is their component of political action, in the widest sense of the term, and their non-institutional nature (Margry and Sánchez-Carretero 2011). That is to say, there are other types of ephemeral memorial, which are not necessarily grassroots memorials, such as flowers, letters or other offerings that are placed on the tombs of loved ones or on a monument, but what connects the pattern of contemporary grassroots memorials is not their temporality, but instead the connection that they make between commemoration and protest, on the one hand, and on the other, the fact that at group level, the death is considered as something traumatic. Not only are objects deposited in memory of the victims or the deceased, but there is also an implicit message that 'this should not have happened', or that 'something has to be done'.

With regard to the type of death that characterizes these memorials, in his paper 'The New Public Mourning', Tony Walter (2008) establishes two categories of the deceased, commemorated through what the author refers to as 'new public mourning': media personalities and victims. The second group includes the victims of acts of terrorism, and the victims of catastrophes and accidents.

While conventional memorials are erected as permanent monuments with a future audience in mind, grassroots memorials are intended for an immediate audience. The first are passive, while the second are extraordinarily dynamic (Grider 2001: 3). Grassroots memorials also have a firmly political nature, as silent witnesses to violence and pain. Although, depending on the deaths intended to be commemorated, the rituals may tend more towards a commemorative function rather than a political denouncement, in all of the cases the aim is to achieve a specific commemoration of the victims, individualizing them. This became apparent in the rituals of public mourning that occurred after the attacks of 11 March 2004, when the messages, photos, personal letters, dedications and offerings were all made for and aimed at individual victims, often addressing them by name. Photographs of the dead appear frequently, in an attempt to resist their becoming statistics; and special focus is placed on presenting them as real people. In that sense, grassroots memorials are political declarations to prevent individual voices from being silenced (Santino 2006b: 13). The memorials insist on the presence of those people now absent, a position that was reiterated after the attacks in Madrid with the frequently-repeated cry of 'we were all traveling in that carriage', 'we were all in that train'.

The same words of condolence, of mourning, of sharing in the grief of the family that can be found in private mourning rituals were also found in the stations, written in a wide variety of formats, supports, types of writing and forms of expression. Through these expressions, the participants in these rituals of mourning establish personal relationships with the deceased; relationships which, while imaginary, are nonetheless very real (Santino 2006b). The large number of photographs of the victims that appeared on the memorials in the stations, and also the reports on practically every one of the victims that appeared in the media, are reminders of this ritual function.

Contextual information about grassroots memorialization in Madrid

From the very day of the bombings in Madrid, people began to visit the epicentres of the explosions, leaving behind poems, flowers, letters, messages, candles, cuddly toys and religious images in memory of the victims. Our focus is on the material culture of the grassroots memorials placed in Atocha, El Pozo and Santa Eugenia, the three stations along the 'Corridor of the river Henares' where the four bombs killed 192 people and injured a further 1,857 – according to the official figures included in the judicial process. Similar memorials also appeared in other parts of the city, in the workplaces of people who had died in the explosions, and on emblematic monuments, shops windows and the façades of private homes in Madrid and throughout the rest of Spain. But citizens did not only take hold of public spaces in order to sacralize the places where the attacks had taken place and remember the dead; during this period of shock and horror, first information and then responsibilities were sought from the government and authorities. The shrines at the stations were one form of public response to the attacks, and they can also be considered within the context of the actions that also occurred in the political sphere after the attacks, which preceded the general elections by only three days (Sánchez-Carretero 2006: 334). The demonstrations of 12 March saw 11 million people take to the streets in cities all over Spain to express their repulsion of the attacks. On the following day, 13 March, popular political action took the form of a campaign carried out by mobile phone and SMS that called for the public to reject and oppose the version of events being upheld by the government, which insisted that the attacks had been carried out by the Basque terrorist movement ETA. The massive mobilization of the Spanish population on 12 and 13 March 2004 has to be considered in the light of previous demonstrations against the war in Iraq, which protested against government propaganda in favour of the war, and the intrumentalization of certain media to support the war (Sampedro 2005). That the grassroots memorials which appeared in the train stations were not only an expression of pain, grief and remembrance of the victims, but part of the strategy for action in the political arena becomes evident when the materials deposited at the stations are examined. Among these materials, the same banners appeared (literally the same banners used in the demonstrations of 12 March in Madrid) as offerings.

Another important contextual piece of information not directly related to the bombings, but that needs to be taken into account when conducting research about mourning and memory in Spain, is the politicization of mourning in contemporary Spain. The mourning of victims of the Spanish Civil War (1936–1939) introduced a division of mourning and its rituals as a means of political legitimization during Franco's dictatorship and afterwards (Cruz 2009: 13–17; Viejo-Rose 2009, and in this volume). To do this, the 'victorious' group, which formed the post-war Spanish State, separated 'mourning' for those who had fought and died on its side and whose memory it maintained and commemorated from 'forgetting' and de-ritualizing the deaths of those it considered to be enemies, making them disappear physically and socially. As a result, a classification system emerged whereby: 'The dead who are incumbent upon the state are included in a ritual symbolic system, which the state activates in order to create and recreate a sense of "community", and to produce citizens who are uniform and loyal in social terms' (Frigolé 2003: 31). By taking over the public space to ritualize their grief for the attacks of 11 March, the general public response, in a sense, also sought to pre-empt any type of manipulation by the political powers of the time.

The Archive of Mourning project

Within this context, the Archive of Mourning is a research project[3] imed at documenting, archiving and analyzing the displays of mourning that occurred after the terrorist attacks of 11 March 2004. The project has two objectives. The first, of an undeniably heritage-based character, consists of creating a collection of documents and materials that are expressions of mourning and which, due to their ephemeral and anonymous nature, usually disappear. This process provides a unique opportunity to preserve individual and collective displays of mourning such as drawings, letters, poems and other objects that were deposited at Atocha and the other railway stations where the explosions occurred. An agreement was signed between the Spanish railway company (RENFE) and the Spanish National Research Council (CSIC) to collect these materials. The second objective is to analyze processes of mourning experienced in the days after the attacks, based on the tenets of the anthropology of violence, and analysis of civic space, group expressions, rituals of mourning, and popular religion.

Until now, these types of collective and ephemeral display had not been considered as objects that formed a part of a 'heritage' process.[4] These expressions of mourning, which are not appreciated as formal or integral components of our historical legacy, are significant however, for they are the forms of expression chosen by citizens in times of crisis. This makes it essential to study them in order to understand the mechanisms of mourning that occurred in response to the attacks. The work of creating an ethnographic archive is central to research in that it provides the primary material for interpreting the meaning of events and discovering the value that specific popular displays can have. Yet, as has been indicated in a number of research and heritage initiatives that emerged in New York after the attacks of 11 September 2001, the archive project also forms a part of a citizens' movement through which many of the actions carried out by professionals (photographers, journalists, specialists in communication, ethnographers, etc.) had the same function and the same objective: to mobilize people in order to overcome the paralysis and shock caused by the attacks. In a sense, the need to start this project developed as a need to leave evidence of what was happening, to mark the grassroots memorials so that they could not be ignored, and to document a part of reality in order to attempt to understand it (Taylor 2003: 241).

The origins of the archival project lie in the days that followed the train bombings of 11th March,[5] when the CSIC research group called on colleagues – anthropologists, sociologists, ethnologists, and social workers – to collaborate in documenting the memorials that were springing up on a largescale in the railway stations, as well as to gather oral testimonies and collect electronic messages about the attacks and the emotions they provoked. The first materials collected consisted mainly of photographs and video footage of displays of grief recorded by colleagues, together with a series of objects and electronic messages. Eventually, the project also received material gathered through other initiatives, such as *Madrid in Memoriam*, a project whose website included thousands of photographs taken by professionals and amateurs both in Madrid and in many other European cities in the days after the attacks.[6]

Three months after the attacks, all of the offerings left in the stations were removed. Their size, especially those in Atocha, the fire hazard posed by the presence of thousands of lit candles, the extra work that they created for the cleaning and maintenance staff (i.e. to remove dry flowers and burnt out candles and to man the railings around the memorials) combined with the desire that the stations return to their normal operations, led RENFE to remove them. In their place, a 'cyber shrine' was created, known as the *Espacio de Palabras* (literally, 'Word Space')[7] which allowed people to leave electronic messages of condolence or in memory of the victims at the entrance to Atocha and El Pozo stations.[8] RENFE employees published a letter in the newssheet *Rojo y Negro* of the trade union CGT (Confederación General de Trabajadores or General Confederation of Workers) asking for the removal of the candles and other ephemeral offerings in order to be able to continue with their work, ending the letter: 'we ask for the candles in the entrance to the station to be removed, and that a permanent monument be built nearby. We ask for respect for the memory of the dead, and for the grief of the survivors. Basically, we ask that we be allowed to overcome this tragedy.'[9] On 9 June 2004, the grassroots memorials of Atocha were removed, and the Minister of Public Works, Magdalena Álvarez, inaugurated the cyber shrine. Thanks to an agreement signed between RENFE and the CSIC, the Archive of Mourning received the objects that were removed from the stations by the company, together with almost 60,000 messages received in the first few months of the Word Space initiative. The resulting inventory of the Archive of Mourning consists of 2,482 photographs, 495 objects, 6,432 messages written on paper, 76 audio and video recordings, and 58,732 electronic messages.

The structure of memorials to the attacks of 11 March

The grassroots memorials commonly took the form of objects and written messages attached to the walls and gates of the train station where the bombs were detonated. As these spaces filled up, offerings began to be placed on the ground. Flowers were often stacked vertically, as they were leant against walls, while red candles were placed on the ground, thus creating a visually striking image of vertical walls of flowers and horizontal surfaces of burning candles. People deposited their offerings with great care to avoid disturbing those that were already in place. An indication of the memorial intention behind these gestures can be evidenced in how at the different stations and locations small groupings of offerings appeared, echoing the layout of the offerings they replaced, or joining others which stood alongside them (Grider 2001: 3). Further analysis of the objects deposited also reveals a type of visual 'vocabulary' that is often found in these types of ritual despite the specific features of individual cases. The offerings most commonly found are flowers, candles, and a series of objects deemed appropriate for such occasions: teddy bears and toys (particularly if there are children among the victims), religious images, photographs, flags, T-shirts with messages, banners, drawings and paintings, and, in this case, a huge variety of messages written on paper, as if taken together they composed an immense, informal book of condolences (Grider 2001).

The grassroots memorials, and the objects of which they are composed, are revealing of the people and the community to which they are dedicated, and also tell us about the people and the community that create them. For example, in the case of other terrorist attacks, such as those of 11 September 2001 in New York, a particularly important element was the appearance of patriotic symbols, especially the American flag. Spanish flags also appeared in memorials in Madrid, although there were equally as many (or perhaps more) from other autonomous regions within Spain and from other countries, in honour of the diverse origins of the victims. Flags were also used as backdrops on which to attach messages of various kinds: insults against politicians, against terrorists, peace messages, and condolences, among many others. As one-third of the 192 people who died in the trains were immigrants, the memorials included a wide variety of offerings for people from specific communities, particularly Rumanians and Ecuadorians (cf. Chulilla et al. 2005; Sánchez-Carretero 2006).

There were noticeable differences between the displays of mourning in the different stations. For example, El Pozo and Santa Eugenia, which are tightly-knit communities with a strong neighbourhood spirit (in fact many inhabitants of El Pozo had a direct relationship with victims), the offerings and memorials were more individualized in nature: messages dedicated to the deceased left there by people who knew them personally (Sánchez-Carretero 2006: 341). Although these types of personalized offering were also to be found in Atocha,

a much larger number of people visited this central Madrid station, which attracted many visits from people not residing in the city – i.e. political figures, athletes travelling through Madrid for competitions, religious congregations, school groups, and tourists.

Among the types of message deposited there are letters (some of those in the Archive of Mourning are still sealed, remaining exactly as they were left at the sites), poems by famous authors and by members of the general public written *ex professo*, narratives of very different kinds, notes and letters of condolence addressed to specific victims, and others addressed to the terrorists responsible for the massacre. The messages are written in many languages and on a wide range of supports: some written directly on the walls themselves, others left on *Post-Its* or even documents, like in the case of a letter of condolence from a Moroccan immigrant written on the back of an official document requesting the renewal of her resident's permit. Frequently the pieces of paper stuck to the walls of the stations and deposited on the shrines came to host dialogues as different authors added to or completed messages that had been left by others (Chulilla et al. 2005: 370). There are many complex and compound texts of this kind, including messages left by groups of teenagers which include signatures from all members of the group. There are also mixed objects that combine photographs, flags, newspaper clippings, and objects as well as works of art that include a large number of drawings.

Heritage, memory and mourning

The cataloguing process of the archive project, which was completed in 2008, was based on the conviction that these manifestations of mourning are an important element in the memorialization of the 11 March bombings. Other records of the attacks, such as police records, documents from the courts and parliament, newspaper articles and official commemorative monuments are usually well documented. With this initiative, grassroots memorials are recognized as part of the long-term 'memory' of the attacks.

The methodological and theoretical problems that underlie the creation of an archive of this kind are a result of the ephemeral nature of the material of which it is comprised, and of a functionality that is exclusively aimed at the present (Gardner and

Henry 2002). A similar situation is discussed by Barbara Kirshenblatt-Gimblett (2003) in connection with the materials corresponding to the attacks on the World Trade Center in New York (Sánchez-Carretero 2006: 335). There are a number of important heritage preservation initiatives for this type of material throughout the world, something which attests to the widespread occurrence of grassroots memorials (cf. Doss 2008: 16-17; Gardner 2011). Examples include the archive created in Genoa that is dedicated to the young anti-globalization demonstrator, Carlo Giuliani, killed by the police in July 2001 (Caffarena and Stiaccini 2005), the Smithsonian collections related to September 11 (Gardner and Henry 2002; Gardner 2011), or the collection of the grassroots memorials after the assassination of politician Pim Fortuyn in Amsterdam (Margry 2003, 2011). However, the attempt to turn material that was made to be ephemeral, or to be lost, into a legacy, and thus 'formalize the informal' (Margry and Sánchez-Carretero 2011), raises ethical questions. Without doubt, this is one of the debates that grassroots memorials present to academics concerned with the process of heritage creation in a globalized world.

Many voices can be left out of the 'consensual narratives' that appear after a social trauma and one of the objectives of the research project linked to the Archive of Mourning is to participate reflexively in the construction of these consensual narratives. The mass media, politicians and legal documents will almost certainly form a part of these narratives. For this reason, the presence in time of the ephemeral is essential in order to preserve the 'voices of the others'. Heritage centres such as museums have an important symbolic and semantic power: it is understood that the items preserved in them have been recognized as heritage. In this case, researchers working with grassroots memorials are acting in the opposite direction: not rescuing the past from the present, but rather preserving material that could be considered new heritage, thus leaving space for voices that are normally silenced. Importantly, this project is occurring at a time when our attention as a public is being increasingly called on to consume external grief through the media; a time in which every effort is made to reduce individual grief to a relative minimum, even when mourning the death of loved ones; a time in which the rituals of mourning are simplified and left in the hands of professionals. As this is happening, we are also witnessing the emergence of new rituals of collective mourning, different ways of expressing grief in the face of traumatic events that are experienced collectively.

Recent research has made it clear that it is possible to refer to a type of contemporary phenomenon, which is growing at a steady rate (at least in the west) and which consists of the anonymous demonstration in public spaces of rituals of mourning in the case of certain deaths, considered as traumatic. Some of these events have led to various forms of documentation or collection initiatives that are studied and/or conserved by universities or academic institutions. In this sense, the ways in which the general public expresses mourning can form a part of a process of 'heritage creation' through which they acquire value, becoming, in the words of Novelo (2005: 86):

'something' that 'someone' considers as worthy of being evaluated, conserved, catalogued, included in an inventory, exhibited, restored, refurbished and admired, and that 'others' should share this choice, freely or through some type of imposition so that the phenomenon of identifying with this 'something' can take shape, so that it is considered as 'our own'.

Notes

1 The introduction to the *book Grassroots Memorials. The Politics of Memorializing Traumatic Death*, edited by Margry and Sánchez-Carretero (2011), provides a detailed bibliography about various types of grassroots memorial, including a broad selection of references on roadside memorials.

2 For a study of the various uses of the terms 'makeshift memorial', 'improvised memorial' and 'spontaneous shrine' see Margry and Sánchez-Carretero 2011.

3 The 'The Archive of Mourning' project was funded by the Spanish Ministry of Science and Culture (HUM2005-03490) and is part of CRIC (Cultural Heritage and the Reconstruction of Identities after Conflict) funded by the European Union 7FP (Ref. 217411). The participants of the project are members of the CSIC research group GIAP (Anthropological Research Group on Heritage and Traditionalization Processes).

4 Margry uses the term 'heritageization' to describe the process of heritage creation (Margry 2011). See also Sánchez-Carretero and Ortiz (2008).

5 For information on the stations, the attacks, the number of victims and the ritualization processes in public spaces in Madrid, see Ortiz (2011).

6 See their web at www.madridinmemoriam.org.
7 The 'cyber shrine' included a computer connected to a larger screen which showed an audiovisual were images of the grassroots memorials were displayed. The computer had a scanner were the hand of the person writing the message could be scanned. In addition, a short message could be written. The cyber shrine was linked to a web page, www.mascercanos.com (no longer available). The almost 60,000 messages of the *Espacio de*

Palabras can be consulted at the Archive of Mourning project.
8 Many other 'cyber shrines' and initiatives of this kind were set up. Apart from Madrid in Memoriam, these include: enciendeunavela.wad-net.com; www.lacabramecanica.com/musica/silencio/silencio.htm; dreamers.com/noviolencia and www.imakinarium.net/comic/11.3.4/index.htm.
9 The letter can be read at: www.rojoynegro.info/2004/article.php3?id_article=1603 (last accessed on 28 October 2009).

REFERENCES

Austin, John (1962) *How to Do Things With Words*. Oxford: Clarendon Press.

Caffarena, Fabio and Stiaccini, Carlo (eds) (2005) *Fragili, resistenti. I messaggi di Piazza Alimonda e la nascita di un luogo di identità collectiva*. Milan: Terre di Mezzo.

Chulilla, Juan Luis et al. (2005) 'Presencia de las comunidades inmigrantes en los santuarios Populares del 11-M', in J.L. Chulilla et al., *Espacios urbanos e inmigración en el Madrid del s. XXI*. Madrid: La Casa Encendida, pp. 364–403.

Cruz, Rafael (2009) 'Introducción', in Jesús Casquete and Rafael Cruz (eds), *Políticas de la muerte: usos y abusos del ritual fúnebre en la Europa del siglo XX*. Madrid: Libros de la Catarata, pp. 9–21.

Doss, Erika (2006) 'Spontaneous Memorials and Contemporary Modes of Mourning in America', *Material Religion* 2(3): 294–319.

Doss, Erika (2008) *The Emotional Life of Contemporary Public Memorials: Towards a Theory of Temporary Memorials*. Amsterdam: Amsterdam University Press.

Fraenkel, Beatrice (2002) *Les Ecrits de Septembre: New York 2001*. Paris: Textuel.

Frigolé, Joan (2003) *Cultura y genocidio*. Barcelona: Universitat de Barcelona.

Gardner, James B. (2011) 'September 11: Museums, Spontaneous Memorials, and History', in Peter Jan Margry and Cristina Sánchez-Carretero, *Grassroots Memorials: The Politics of Memorializing Traumatic Death*. New York: Berghahn.

Gardner, James B. and Henry, Sarah M. (2002) 'September 11 and the Mourning After: Reflections on the Collecting and Interpreting the History of Tragedy', *The Public Historian* 24(3): 37–52.

Grider, Sylvia (2000) 'The Archaeology of Grief: Texas A&M Bonfire Tragedy is a Sad Study in Modern Mourning', *Discovering Archaeology*, 2(3): 68–74.

Grider, Sylvia (2001) 'Spontaneous Shrines: A Modern Response to Tragedy and Disaster', *New Directions in Folklore*, 5 (www.temple.edu/isllc/newfolks/shrines.html).

Haney, C. Allen, Leimar, Christina and Lowery, Julian (1997) 'Spontaneous Memorialization: Violent Death and Emerging Mourning Rituals', *Omega* 35(2): 159–171.

Kirshenblatt-Gimblett, Barbara (2003) 'Kodak Moments. Flashbulb Memories: Reflections on 9/11', www.nyu.edu/classes/bkg/ewb.

Margry, Peter Jan (2003) 'The Murder of Pim Fortuyn and Collective Emotions: Hype, Hysteria and Holiness in the Netherlands?', *Etnofoor* 16(2): 102–127.

Margry, Peter Jan (2011) 'Memorializing a Controversial Politician: The "Heritageization" of a Materialized *Vox Populi*', in P.J. Margry and C. Sánchez-Carretero (eds), *Grassroots Memorials: The Politics of Memorializing Traumatic Death*. New York: Berghahn.

Margry, Peter Jan and Sánchez-Carretero, Cristina (2007) 'Memorializing Traumatic Death', *Anthropology Today*, 23(3): 1–2.

Margry, Peter Jan and Sánchez-Carretero, Cristina (2011) 'Rethinking Memorialization: The Concept of Grassroots Memorials', in P.J. Margry and C. Sánchez-Carretero (eds), *Grassroots Memorials: The Politics of Memorializing Traumatic Death*. New York: Berghahn.

Novelo, Victoria (2005) 'El patrimonio cultural mexicano en la disputa clasista', in Xosé Carlos Sierra Rodríguez and Xerardo Pereiro Pérez (eds), *Patrimonio cultural: politizaciones y mercantilizaciones*. Sevilla: El Monte, pp. 85–99.

Ortiz, Carmen (2011) 'Memoriales del atentado del 11 de marzo en Madrid', in Cristina Sánchez-Carretero (ed.), *El Archivo del Duelo: Análisis de la respuesta ciudadana ante los atentados del 11 de marzo en Madrid*. Madrid: CSIC.

Sampedro, Víctor F. (2005) 'La red del 13-M: A modo de prefacio', www.nodo50org/multitudesonline.

Sánchez-Carretero, Cristina (2006) 'Trains of Workers, Trains of Death: Some Reflections after the March 11th Attacks in Madrid', in Jack Santino (ed.), *Spontaneous Shrines and the Public Memorialization of Death*. New York: Palgrave Macmillan, pp. 333–347.

Sánchez-Carretero, Cristina (2011) 'The Madrid Train Bombings: Enacting the Emotional Body at the March 11

Grassroots Memorials', in P.J. Margry and C. Sánchez-Carretero (eds), *Grassroots Memorials: The Politics of Memorializing Traumatic Death*. New York: Berghahn.

Sánchez-Carretero, Cristina and Carmen Ortiz (2008) 'Rethinking Ethnology in the Spanish Context', *Ethnologia Europaea* 38(1): 23–28.

Santino, Jack (1992) '"Not an Unimportant Failure": Rituals of Death and Politics in Northern Ireland', in M. McCaughan (ed.), *Displayed in Mortal Light*. Antrim: Antrim Arts Council.

Santino, Jack (ed.) (2006a) *Spontaneous Shrines and the Public Memorialization of Death*. New York: Palgrave Macmillan.

Santino, Jack (2006b) 'Performative Commemoratives: Spontaneous Shrines and the Public Memorialization of Death', in J. Santino (ed.), *Spontaneous Shrines and the Public Memorialization of Death*. New York: Palgrave Macmillan, pp. 5–15.

Stengs, Irene (2003) 'Ephemeral Memorials against 'Senseless Violence': Materialisations of Public Outcry', *Etnofoor* 16(2): 26–40.

Taylor, Diana (2003) 'Lost in the Field of Vision', in *The Archive and the Repertoire: Performing Cultural Memory in the Americas*. Durham, NC, and London: Duke University Press, pp. 237–264.

Viejo-Rose, Dacia (2009) Reconstructing cultural heritage after civil war: making meaning and memory. PhD thesis, University of Cambridge, Cambridge.

Walter, Tony (2008) 'The New Public Mourning', in Margaret S. Stroebe, Robert O. Hansson, Henk Schut and Wolfgang Stroebe (eds), *Handbook of Bereavement Research and Practice: 21st Century Perspectives*. Washington, DC: American Psychological Association, pp. 241–262.

Young, James E. (1993) *The Texture of Memory: Holocaust, Memorials and Meaning*. New Haven, CT: Yale University Press.

CHAPTER 8

SITES OF CONSCIENCE: HERITAGE OF AND FOR HUMAN RIGHTS

Liz Ševčenko

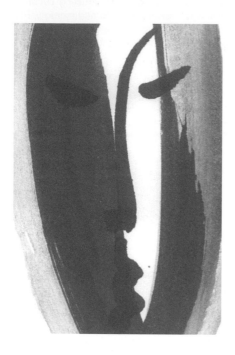

In 1999, the directors of nine historic sites in different settings came together to explore a shared question: how could heritage sites promote human rights? Together they imagined a new type of space, which they called a 'Site of Conscience'. These work at the intersection of historic preservation, human rights, citizen engagement, education, and the arts. To achieve their vision, these sites wrestle with a variety of critical issues. What does a heritage practice for human rights look like? What is required to promote a lasting culture of human rights and civic participation in a society? And what role can heritage play in that process? This chapter explores tensions and creative innovations that emerge from Sites of Conscience around the world.

Introduction

In 1999, the individuals responsible for nine historic sites in very different contexts – including the Gulag Museum in Russia, the Slave House in Senegal,

Memoria Abierta in Argentina, and the Lower East Side Tenement Museum in the USA – came together to explore a shared question: how can heritage sites promote human rights? Their museums had little in common in terms of the history or themes they interpreted, or the scope and scale of their properties, but their directors shared a commitment to placing heritage at the service of building lasting cultures of peace and democracy. They imagined a new type of space, which they called a 'Site of Conscience', defining this as museums that made three commitments: to interpret history through a site; to engage in programs that stimulate dialogue on pressing social issues today; and to share opportunities for public involvement in those issues. To achieve that vision, they decided to work as a coalition.

Sites of Conscience operate at the intersection of historic preservation, human rights, citizen engagement, education, and the arts. They wrestle with a variety of critical issues. What does a heritage practice for human rights look like? What is required to promote a lasting culture of human rights and civic participation in a society? And what role can heritage play in that process? Should Sites of Conscience advocate for particular political positions or serve as spaces for open public dialogue on a range of approaches to an issue? How can or should Sites of Conscience be integrated into larger transitional justice or democracy-building efforts, such as Truth Commissions or other post-conflict programs?

Tensions and creative innovations have emerged from these efforts in relation to three issues of particular relevance to the theme of this volume: memorializing practice; 'memory wars'; and destruction and reconstruction of heritage, memory, and identity in post-conflict contexts. This chapter will explore these issues as well as the emerging concept of 'Sites of Conscience' itself in contrast to other frameworks, such as *lieux de mémoire*, as memorializing practices that acknowledge memory as inherently dynamic and contested, and therefore try to embrace contests over memory as a fundamental process of building democratic cultures. It will analyze the diverse relationship of these practices to nation-states – in some contexts critical to the definition of new national identities, and in others building international solidarity among local, anti-state movements. This approach has implications for form, process, and policy around memorialization, and impacts policy-makers in both heritage and human rights.

Sites of conscience: developing a global framework

In retrospect, it's quite surprising that the nine museum directors who first came together in 1999 found any common ground, let alone decide to form a coalition. Some commemorated histories of the eighteenth century; others the 1980s. Some came from small, community-driven struggles against state oppression, like the District Six Museum in South Africa; others from century-old, multi-million dollar government enterprises like the US National Park Service or the British National Trust. Some were life-long human rights activists coming to the practice of heritage for the first time; others were life-long historic preservationists asking for the first time whether their work could be socially relevant. The idea that brought them all together was the possibility of developing a heritage practice *of and for human rights*. Putting this idea into action required combining the strengths and experience of the historic preservation field and movements for social justice. It also required new ways of thinking about what to remember, and how.

Critiquing 'Never Again'

Whether they came from the fields of heritage or human rights, the original founders shared a common ethic of 'Never Again' – the idea that we must remember the past in order to prevent atrocities from recurring. However, the group had also had enough experience to recognize that the connection between remembering past atrocity and fighting human rights abuse in the present was far from automatic. While 'Never Again' has been a mantra of memorials from Berlin to Buenos Aires, this group sought to develop a framework that would critically analyze the relationships between memory and action, and identify specific strategies for

sites in different political contexts to play a more intentional role in addressing current social issues. For many Sites of Conscience, the most important step in achieving 'Never Again' is to build a culture of accountability: a guarantee that people who commit human rights abuses will be punished. But who do we think needs to be held accountable? A small group of direct perpetrators, or a larger society that allowed them to act? And what role do heritage sites have to play?

A heritage site designed to inspire conscience would need to expand on definitions of heritage as a collective memory of cultural practices, moving away from any that support essentialist formulations of race, ethnicity, or national identity. Instead, Sites of Conscience would need to shape a heritage based in a collective memory of moral acts and choices – of cruelty, compassion, and courage – and offer a space for the ongoing interrogation of the nature of those choices, the reasons for them, and what they suggest for the future. In other words, Sites of Conscience would need to develop a heritage of *doing* rather than *being*. Not who we were in the past and who we are today, but what we did do in the past and what we want to do today. This requires not only remembering what we want to prevent, but also the values and ideas that we want to preserve, and everything in between. It requires the simultaneous celebration, condemnation, and critical analysis of different individual acts – not only remembering past horror.

Defining sites of conscience

Founders began by developing a vision of a new type of institution, called a Site of Conscience. They felt strongly that it was important to clearly articulate and continually debate the values and practices defining this vision. The worry was that the overall idea of using the past to shape the future, or of course the loose concept of 'conscience' itself, could be co-opted to legitimize projects that instrumentalized the past to foster violent conflict or promote repressive regimes. Defining Sites of Conscience would ensure that both states and local communities would be held accountable to international standards and values. At the same time, the Sites wanted to create a means to ensure these international standards would be continually enriched and renewed by local innovation.

Perhaps the most important feature of this vision is that it did not depend on the particular history of the sites interpreted. Instead, it depended on the commitment made by the sites' stewards to activate them in the service of 'Never Again' by:

1 Interpreting history through site;
2 Stimulating dialogue on pressing social issues and promoting democratic and humanitarian values;
3 Sharing opportunities for public involvement in the issues raised at the sites.[1]

These commitments have taken diverse forms in different contexts, and have been shaped and reshaped through vigorous debate across the Coalition as it has grown.

Interpreting history through site

Coalition members share a belief in the special power of place to promote cultures of 'Never Again'. Members stated that:

> we believe that when visitors explore the architecture and landscapes that shaped or bore witness to the development of human rights and democracy, they may better recognize where similar struggles are occurring today. Further, we believe that places of memory have special power to inspire human connection to larger issues, and therefore to move people to participate in addressing these issues.[2]

Many historic sites are interpreted for their symbolic significance because an important event took place there. Interpretation at these sites describes how the site 'bore witness' to an event, and tries to inspire visitors with the authenticity of the place – they are standing on the spot where something actually happened. In order to use the full potential of sites to inspire understanding and commitment to social justice, Coalition members sought to develop a framework that would tap into the power of place more deeply and intentionally. Its framework requires that interpretation 'uses the site – its location, structure, features, feeling – to help visitors "read" the issues the site represents' and 'explores the social or political forces that define how the site came to look as it does, and uses the physical shape of the site as a starting point for education and discussion of social or human rights

issues'[3]. For example, when 15 visitors climb the narrow staircase at the Lower East Side Tenement Museum's 1863 building at 97 Orchard Street and squeeze into a cramped apartment once home to a family of as many people, they learn that every window, lamp, and sink they see is the result of decades-long battles over working peoples' rights to air, light, and water. The head of Russia's Memorial Society said that despite the extensive collections in Memorial's archives, he was dedicated to preserving a remote Gulag camp so that his son could stand behind the layers of barbed wire, step in to dank cells and, as he put it, 'breathe unfreedom'.)

Despite a shared belief in the particular power of place for inspiring a culture of human rights, many Coalition members have been challenged by a lack of access to the sites that tell the most important and least known stories about human rights struggles and their legacies. This lack of access is often due to the very struggles that members sought to remember: the sites were hidden so people would not know what was happening there. For example, Memoria Abierta, a coordinated action of human rights groups preserving the memory of the dictatorship in Argentina, sought to raise public awareness of the hundreds of ordinary places throughout the city of Buenos Aires that were secretly used as sites of torture and detention during the dictatorship. These ranged from police stations to gas stations, peppered throughout residential neighborhoods, and along commercial thoroughfares. Indeed, the most infamous site for victims was a massive Naval Academy campus in the very center of the city. Despite being under everyone's noses, given the multiplicity of owners and ongoing uses of these sites, only in rare cases did Memoria Abierta, forensic archaeologists, or the general public have access to their interiors. In response, Memoria Abierta painstakingly mapped sites across the city and the country and created a 'Topography of Memory', which they made available online, in publications, and school curricula. Memoria Abierta and other groups also made the histories of these places visible through public art, performances, and ceremonies outside the sites. In this way they hoped to help make the mechanisms of repression visible to Argentineans in the landscape of a city they thought they knew, and question how a repressive system was allowed to operate in plain sight.

Box 8.1   Gulag Museum at Perm-36, Russia

Four hours from Perm, in a remote village in the Ural mountains, lies the barracks and barbed wire of Perm-36, part of the vast system of Gulag camps used to harness labor and control the population during the Soviet era. Perm-36 was in use from the Stalinist period through to the 1980s, holding high-profile political dissidents and ordinary citizens. A pioneering group of human rights activists and historians rescued the camp from deliberate destruction to create the Gulag Museum at Perm 36. Today, museum directors bring students through the cells and work yards and talk about the human experience of living there, and how the camp fit into the larger system of Soviet repression. The museum works with students to help them interview their own family members to learn of their experience during the Soviet period, often initiating conversations for the first time. Using the history of the camp and of their own families, students conduct workshops to define their vision of democracy and identify how they can promote it. In the 'I Have Rights' program, students are asked to write or draw their associations with the word 'freedom' on a large piece of construction paper and pin it up on a wall. Students then debate each other's concepts of the word 'freedom' and, reflecting on the stories from the camp and their own families' experiences, they debate what it takes to support and protect those visions of freedom. A facilitator frames questions such as: 'What allowed this system of repression to exist? What allowed it to be dismantled? What is your vision of democracy and freedom today? What can you do to achieve those visions? What kinds of institutions and civic actions are required to sustain democracy? How should we balance between preserving civil liberties and protecting ourselves from terrorism?'

Because of its remote location, the Gulag Museum receives about 15,000 visitors each year, but it has worked to promote the lessons of the site more broadly. It worked with the Perm regional school system to introduce histories of the Gulag and other repression into the school curricula for the first time. It built a Russian Sites of Conscience Network to support museums developing at other Gulag camps, as well as NKVD prisons and massacre sites from Western Russia to the ends of Siberia. Most recently, it founded a Museology School for municipal museums – small town cultural centers interpreting the history of their community from the dinosaur age to the present – to help them integrate their local histories of repression for the first time. It has also collaborated with other sites of detention in countries across the Coalition on how to use these sites to help young people understand and combat state repression.

In other contexts, sites were remote because they were created to isolate people from population centers. The Gulag Museum in Russia preserves a labor and political prisoners' camp that was active from the Stalinist period through to the 1980s and was located a four-hour drive from the nearest major city, Perm. Nestled among small towns in the Ural mountains, the museum serves as the public access center for artifacts from the inhospitable moonscape of Magadan in Siberia thousands of miles east, where gulag camps proliferated. Although the Museum still welcomes about 15,000 visitors per year, it also uses the place and the stories of the people detained there to develop school curricula, websites, teacher training, and other tools to develop a broader-based public awareness of Gulag history.

In all these cases, the location, structure, and feeling of sites are still used as the primary teaching tool implements, catalysts of awareness of and engagement on current human rights issues.

Stimulating dialogue on pressing social issues and promoting democratic and humanitarian values

Sites of Conscience acknowledge that a 'conscience heritage' requires paying attention not only to *what* is to be remembered, but also how it is remembered. Achieving 'Never Again' requires a citizenry and state that takes action to stop abuse before it happens. The challenge to Sites of Conscience is to identify what specific role they can play in fostering that kind of action. If we imagine Sites as microcosms of civic life, spaces where we can promote the interactions between people that we hope to see in society generally, then we need to develop a heritage practice that both helps people remember and encourages them to address the implications of the past for the present. If we want to help people implement diverse visions of democracy on a day-to-day basis – for example, to think critically, or analyze mechanisms of repression and liberation, or engage in non-violent approaches to conflict, or embrace difference – then what would they need to do at our sites? For example, if we lecture at young people and give them no chance to question the authorities or each other, even if the information we are sharing challenges repressive narratives, would we run the risk that they will remain as passive and disengaged as before? How could we develop ways of remembering and reminding that move beyond passive learning or reflection, but involve ongoing debate and action? In other words, how can these sites serve as spaces for communities to perform their diverse visions of democracy and a culture of human rights?

At the heart of this active memory framework is the idea of 'stimulating dialogue on pressing social issues'.[4] The Coalition's accreditation criteria elaborate that:

> We believe it is the obligation of historic sites to assist the public in drawing connections between the history of a site and its contemporary implications, and to inspire citizens to be more aware and involved in the most pressing issues affecting them. To that end, Sites of Conscience should provide a forum for open discussion of pressing contemporary issues among diverse publics.[5]

Guidelines further suggest that sites 'Draw explicit connections to contemporary issues, either by providing information on the shape of these issues today, or by asking visitors questions about where they see these issues manifested today'; 'Raise multiple perspectives on an issue, rather than promoting a single solution to a problem'; and 'Inspire and facilitate dialogue among diverse publics at the site – a process of sharing ideas, information, experiences, and assumptions about difficult issues for the purposes of collective learning'.[6]

Box 8.2   Corporación Parque por la Paz Villa Grimaldi, Chile

Villa Grimaldi is the former site of one of the most important clandestine centers of detention and torture in Chile, where thousands of prisoners were incarcerated, and 230 disappeared or were executed under the command of the security forces of the Pinochet regime. Inaugurated in 1997 in a poor neighborhood with a high indigenous (Mapuche) population, Parque por la Paz Villa Grimaldi provides a public space welcoming people from diverse political, cultural, and religious backgrounds that is dedicated to remembering the victims of human rights violations, to disseminating information on the history of state terrorism in Chile, and to promoting a culture of human rights.

In addition to serving as an important healing center for the immediate victims of the site and others like it, Villa Grimaldi works to communicate the lessons of the site to a new generation. This does not only mean bringing students on tours of the site with survivors so that they hear first-hand accounts of what happened there. In addition, Villa Grimaldi works with students and teachers to identify the most pressing issues young people are facing in schools today which are related to or a legacy of the dictatorship. Villa Grimaldi discovered persistent cultures of exclusion, violence, and authoritarianism that result in high rates of bullying, xenophobia, and other forms of discrimination. Because so many of the people disappeared to places like Villa Grimaldi were student activists, the most severe legacy of the dictatorship was a lack of political engagement among young people, creating a culture of apathy that allows violence in schools to go unchecked.

In response, Villa Grimaldi developed partnerships with the Ministry of Education, the Ministry of Human Rights, teachers, and school administrators to develop a youth program that uses the site and its history as the starting point for dialogue on how students can confront the issues they face in schools today. The program identifies mechanisms of discrimination, othering, and systemic violence at work at Villa Grimaldi as well as successful strategies for organizing resistance and building social movements that led to their dismantling. Each class identifies a specific issue in its school and designs a project to address it.

Villa Grimaldi is a leading site in the Coalition's Latin American Sites of Conscience Network, a space for sites across the region to exchange experiences of remembering associated with sites of state terrorism and develop a regional approach for how to deal with these legacies.

'Dialogue' is perhaps the most vigorously debated idea across the Coalition, shaped by both global exchange and local specificity. Each site is rooted in a different experience of struggles for democracy and human rights, and in different traditions of education, civic engagement, and negotiation of difference. These shape a range of visions of what forms of engagement among visitors the site is trying to promote. One of the greatest debates about the definition of dialogue is how to raise multiple perspectives without slipping into moral relativism. In some contexts, 'stimulating dialogue' simply means saying things that were never said before – exposing histories that had been suppressed in a society and publicizing them through everything from public tours of a site to media attention. In others, what has been suppressed is debate and dissent: their 'stimulating dialogue' meant facilitating face-to-face discussions across diverse perspectives about important, unresolved questions in a community. In still others, it meant facilitating exchanges between diverse people about their life experiences and sense of identity in order to promote tolerance and new understanding of difference.

Sharing opportunities for public involvement in issues raised at the sites

As the final step in building a culture of 'Never Again', members felt that Sites of Conscience had a responsibility to encourage visitors to move beyond dialogue towards action. Here again different visions of what kind of action best supported a lasting culture of human rights shaped different visions of the role that sites should play to inspire such action. Should Sites of Conscience be advocates or open forums? For some, it was quite clear that to prevent abuses from recurring, Sites should take public stands protesting any injustices they see happening in the present, and mobilize their publics to take specific action against these injustices. But others

were concerned that this could convert heritage sites into blunt political instruments rather than catalysts of broader democratic and humanitarian values.[7] Indeed, members working together to define a global framework of Sites of Conscience might easily find their specific politics at odds with each other. For example, the Gulag Museum in Russia might critique communism while the Workers' Library Museum in South Africa might embrace it; Terezín Memorial in Czech Republic might defend Israel's occupation of the West Bank while the Museum of Free Derry in Northern Ireland might denounce it. Further, if Sites were too prescriptive, telling their visitors what to do and think, then they could actually retrench the very patterns of passivity and lack of critical thinking they were trying to break.

The group ultimately focused on promoting active engagement instead of specific actions, stating that while 'the Coalition supports efforts to move visitors to Sites of Conscience from talking about an issue, to getting actively involved in shaping it in their own way', that 'to protect their effectiveness as open forums, Sites of Conscience should not prescribe a specific course of action to its visitors. To that end, Sites of Conscience should provide information on where visitors can go to learn more or become more involved in shaping the issue in a variety of ways.'[8]

Towards 'Conscience Heritage' Policies

As outlined in the previous sections, Sites of Conscience work from a few core premises:

- Simply representing something that happened in the past – for example, erecting a monument to a human rights struggle – does not ensure that it will not be repeated. In fact, in many cases, memorialization can be instrumentalized to inflame unresolved conflicts. While it is critical for families and communities to have victims publicly recognized, it is also true that some conflicts – such as in Northern Ireland or the Balkans – have been symbolized and even sustained through memorials to the victims of each side. Each context requires critical reflection on the possibilities and obstacles to preventing future abuse, as well as different possible approaches to remembering the past, and what impact each would have on the particular political and cultural dynamics. In other words, a strategic approach to memorialization is required.

- In addition to conveying knowledge about the dynamics of human rights abuses or struggles for social justice, Sites of Conscience can offer spaces in which people can model, or perform, the kind of behavior or interaction among people that would sustain a culture of human rights in their context. The Gulag Museum at Perm-36 in Russia invites students to walk the daily paths of prisoners in the cells and work yards of a former camp, while analyzing the system of repression that brought people there. But going a step further, the Museum then brings students to a classroom on the site. Working in small groups, students debate questions such as 'What made it possible for the Gulag system to develop? What could make it possible for something like this to develop today? What is your definition of democracy – what is required to sustain it? What can I do?' The program, titled 'I Have Rights Club', seeks to model one form of democratic participation for young people, and encourage them to sustain it in their schools and communities.

- Heritage sites are inherently sites of contestation. They represent terrains on which people play out conflicts in the present. Conflicts over whether or how a site should be remembered are most often rooted in deeper conflicts over identity, rights, ownership, or other social issues. The contested nature of heritage can be embraced as an opportunity to tap into, as opposed to an obstacle to overcome. Sites can offer programs that invite and facilitate ongoing public dialogue about the underlying questions or concerns the site raises. In this way, sites become a new resource, a new civic space, in which societies may grapple with new problems as they arise. The Lower East Side Tenement Museum restored a five-story apartment building, home to over 7,000 people from more than 20 different nations between 1863 and 1935, to tell the stories of immigrants to New York City. As the museum was being developed, it faced criticisms from local communities and visitors alike over which nationalities' experiences would be interpreted in the museum. Recognizing that the contests over representation in the museum were rooted in conflicts among ethnic groups over who held claim to the neighborhood and its scarce resources, the Museum invited community leaders to participate in facilitated dialogue programs to share their groups' histories, and discuss the issues that divided them today. These led to a series of dialogue programs for different groups, including new immigrants, students, and tourists, on immigration past and present. Through programs like these, heritage sites can provide new perspective on contemporary problems and new spaces for people to confront each other across difference without violence.

- This principle does not only apply to sites that commemorate recent human rights struggles. Centuries-old monuments in the Middle East, the Balkans, Northern Ireland, and elsewhere have been the subjects of violent conflict. This is not to impose contemporary readings on ancient history, for instance to claim that the Pyramids at Giza are significant only as products of labor exploitation. Instead, it is to acknowledge that no historic sites stand entirely outside their contemporary social context. It is to acknowledge debates over their meaning and ownership, and that tensions between tourism, development and conservation are all rooted in deeper economic and social relations. And it is to acknowledge that the process of preserving ancient sites can also be used to address contemporary social divisions. Perhaps the most celebrated recent example is the sixteenth-century Mostar bridge in Bosnia-Herzegovina, which was destroyed in the conflict of the 1990s and reconstructed from 2001 to 2004 through a collaboration including Muslim and Croat experts and residents. As the Project head, Rusmir Cisic, explained, 'We do not want [the bridge] only to link two sides of a river like bridges usually do. We want to link peoples in Mostar, which after the conflict remained one of the most destroyed cities in Europe.'[9]

- Heritage is not exclusively about defining nations, but about shaping and sustaining cultures of conscience everywhere, from the individual and local to the global level.

These insights suggest new directions for heritage policy:

Framing heritage as democratic process

Heritage policy is currently focused on developing static products: preserving sites and writing a narrative of what happened there, or building new museum structures. A 'conscience heritage' requires a more organic, process-oriented approach. From the earliest idea stage, heritage sites can serve as spaces for collective engagement with any conflicts around the site or contemporary social issues the site raises. For example, when the infamous former detention center at the Escuela Mecánica de la Armada in Buenos Aires had only just been declared a 'Space for Memory and Human Rights' by President Nestor Kirchner, but was still occupied by the Navy and far from any concrete memorial plan, Memoria Abeirta convened an ongoing series of workshops among victims' groups and public discussions titled 'The Museum We Want'. While the discussions were ostensibly about what different groups would like to see in a future museum about the period of state terrorism, the discussions became an important space for dealing with that period's legacy, including unresolved questions about justice, accountability, and social conflicts festering in Argentinean democracy. Without an opportunity for open and ongoing discussion, sites risk becoming divisive lightning rods that can exacerbate underlying social conflicts. Funding and planning for heritage needs to include time and space for such discussions, as a fundamental and ongoing part of heritage management. And heritage managers need new training on how to facilitate effective public dialogue on sensitive, conflictual issues.

In practical terms, this suggests a slower, phased approach to preserving sites, in which people are granted access to the site before preservation interventions are made, and invited to respond and envision what stories are most important to tell and why, and after which small portions of the site are preserved at a time, continually informed by the responses of key stakeholders. Perhaps most importantly, a 'conscience heritage' requires building the infrastructure for ongoing dialogue from the beginning – for example, including spaces for discussion in the architectural design of a museum building, or planning for education programs and the people to run them as a fundamental part of the site, not an add-on.

There are at least two major challenges to implementing a dialogue-based heritage process. The first relates to the value system underlying current public or institutional approaches to creating place-based memorials to difficult histories. The most common model for physical memorials that valorize a victimized group and reject the forces that victimized them is to build a major monument. Whether this takes the form of a memorial or a museum, the emphasis is on aesthetics and form – on creating a grand symbol that makes an unequivocal statement about the seriousness of the issue. Anything less seems to be an insult to the victims, and could imply that what happened to them was not a very serious crime. While creating a magnificent structure certainly does not prevent it from including spaces and programming to actually address the causes of the atrocity, it's the static structure that is most valued, and is what most publics hold the authorities behind them accountable for. As a result, it is often where the overwhelming proportion of resources goes.

The second challenge relates to the terms and mandates of political office. Many memorials are initiated from governments or public officials who wish to make a major public statement of conscience. Whether this comes from a self-serving interest to establish a visible legacy for themselves, or whether it is to ensure that certain values are communicated to the citizenry before a change in government occurs, these memorials face major time constraints, as they must be erected or show significant visible progress within a term of office. This mandate further supports product over process, an immediate aesthetic impact over a lasting ethical one.

These two challenges probably cannot be resolved entirely through policy prescriptions, but by shifting public perceptions of what kinds of memorial forms and activities show the society validates the experience of victims and the values they represented. For Sites of Conscience, it will be important to find ways for public dialogue processes to be made visible and valuable to public officials and their constituencies.

Imagining a flexible global exchange

Heritage policy is now primarily administered by nation-states, guided by standards set by international intergovernmental bodies. For countries rebuilding in the wake of conflict or repressive regimes, Sites of Conscience can play an important role in building a new national vision. But Sites of Conscience do not exclusively define nation states; in connecting their local experiences, they can also articulate important transnational phenomena, such as forced institutionalization of aboriginal/first nations peoples across the British colonies, or the set of dictatorships and region-wide practices of torture and detention in the Southern Cone. These connections between like experiences are critical for raising public conscience about how certain systems of repression work globally. In order to make them visible, heritage leaders can explore alternative structures for governing aspects of heritage policy, structures that are organized not around nation-states, but around multiple points of connection: from national to regional to thematic. Recent attempts to develop collaborative international approaches to managing sites in the transatlantic slave trade suggest a promising direction.

Looking back and moving forward

In 2004, Tshepo Nkosi, then marketing director for the Johannesburg Development Agency, offered a new framework for heritage management when he described his vision for Constitution Hill, a complex where South Africans could tour a prison museum remembering struggles for justice under apartheid, and then observe debates on justice today in the new Constitutional Court. 'We hope', he said,

Box 8.3   Constitution Hill, South Africa

In 1995, the Constitutional Court judges of South Africa selected the Old Fort prison in Johannesburg as the site for the new Constitutional Court building. The prison complex once symbolized the worst abuses of the old apartheid regime. Visitors to what is now Constitution Hill tour a museum in restored parts of the prison that tells the stories of prisoners and the system that criminalized them. They can then explore the Court building and learn about the latest issues the Justices are debating. An open space between the museum and the Court is used for public dialogues and events encouraging civic participation in new issues facing the South African Constitution.

The museum at Constitution Hill uses the history of the site to raise difficult questions about justice past and present. The Old Fort prison held high-profile political prisoners like Nelson Mandela and Mahatma Gandhi, as well as ordinary people arrested for acts criminalized under the apartheid regime, such as pass violations or miscegenation. But it also held people who committed acts still considered criminal in South Africa today, such as murder or robbery. An exhibit entitled 'Who is a Criminal?' profiles a range of people incarcerated in the Old Fort and asks visitors to write their responses to which of these people they believed to be rightfully convicted. In this way, they open debate about visions of justice in the new South Africa.

The museum tries to provide historical perspective on issues being debated in the Court and involve diverse publics in those debates. For instance, in the wake of the Court's decision on gay marriage, the museum featured an exhibition on the history of gays and lesbians under apartheid and in the anti-apartheid movement, together with a variety of forums for people to debate the decisions of the Court.

Finally, programs for young people raise awareness about the Constitution and try to foster active citizenship through *lekgotla* dialogues. *Lekgotla* is derived from a Sesotho word for community councils of Botswana villages, in which communities debate and decide important issues by consensus. Drawing from this practice, students sit in a circle in the outdoor plaza between the Court and the prison and discuss questions including: What are your rights as a citizen under the Constitution? Are there any other rights you think you should have? What do you think your obligations are as a citizen?

Constitution Hill will become a national lekgotla, a gathering place for ongoing debate and discussion about how we can ensure that the fundamental values enshrined in our Constitution – freedom, equality, dignity – become more than just words on paper ... just like South African society itself, [Constitution Hill] will never be completed, for every generation of visitors will add its own experiences and memories to the site.[10]

This framing suggests heritage sites as spaces for ongoing democratic engagement, explicitly integrated into civic life not as mere reflections of cultures or social dynamics, but as catalysts for civic participation. It's a framing that diverse communities and societies around the world are trying on for size. Margarita Romero, President of the Villa Grimaldi Peace Park in Chile, says she has worked hard in her context to develop programs in this former detention center that create

a space of debate and discussion about the recent past which we know does not exist inside many educational establishments in the country. The persistence of an authoritarian school culture, remnants of the old repressive regime, fear of debate, conflict and difference ... can be transformed into hope of a society more aware of human rights.[11]

Putting this vision into practice requires us to reimagine the relationship between heritage, human rights, and democracy. If heritage is to be explored and embraced as an integral part of civic life, heritage process and products need to model the values and vision of democracy in their distinct contexts. This means that the way heritage is constructed – what stories are told, who decides, whether and how people are invited to respond – need to be held to standards of transparency, inclusivity, collective decision-making, and open debate that parallel, or even exceed, those being sought in the larger society. It requires a delicate dance, a mutual exchange, between looking back and moving forward.

Notes

1 International Coalition of Sites of Conscience, 'About the Coalition', www.sitesofconscience.org/about-us/en/#section1.

2 International Coalition of Sites of Conscience, 'Annotated Accreditation Criteria', www.sitesofconscience.org/wp-content/uploads/Annotated-Accreditation-Criteria.pdf, 1.

3 Ibid.

4 International Coalition of Sites of Conscience, 'About the Coalition', www.sitesofconscience.org/about-us/en/#section1.

5 International Coalition of Sites of Conscience, 'Annotated Accreditation Criteria', www.sitesofconscience.org/wp-content/uploads/Annotated-Accreditation-Criteria.pdf, 2.

6 Ibid.

7 International Coalition of Sites of Conscience, 'About the Coalition', www.sitesofconscience.org/about-us/en/#section1.

8 International Coalition of Sites of Conscience, 'Annotated Accreditation Criteria', www.sitesofconscience.org/wp-content/uploads/Annotated-Accreditation-Criteria.pdf, 3.

9 'Historic Mostar Bridge Being Rebuilt,' *BBC News*, World Service, Europe Section, 7 June 2001.

10 Lauren Segal et al. (2006) *Number Four: The Making of Constitution Hill*. London: Penguin, p. 219.

11 Sebastian Brett et al. (2007) *Memorialization and Democracy: State Policy and Civic Action*. New York: FLACSO-Chile, International Center for Transitional Justice, and International Coalition of Historic Site Museums of Conscience, www.sitesofconscience.org/wp-content/documents/publications/memorialization-en.pdf, 15.

CHAPTER 9

'NOT JUST A PLACE': CULTURAL HERITAGE AND THE ENVIRONMENT

Benjamin Morris

This chapter examines the many diverse relationships between cultural heritage and the environment. Beginning with the premise that conventional divisions between nature and culture can no longer be maintained, it explores the multiple forms of heritage that the natural world has occasioned, such as protected spaces and conservation movements. Acknowledging the increasingly varied forms of heritage, it examines the ways in which natural events such as disasters have been memorialized into heritage, and likewise, the process by which the natural world has given rise to local and national identities. Looking to the future, the chapter takes anthropogenic global warming as a context in which natural events will simultaneously impact cultural heritage sites and traditions, and provide an opportunity to reconnect societies fragmented by the forces of globalization.

Introduction

Asking a human being to consider the nature of language, the novelist Walker Percy once noted, 'is like asking a fish to consider the nature of water' (Percy 1991: 419–20). The same might be said of the natural world: complex, dynamic, and ubiquitous, it cannot be separated from its inhabitants any more than they can be separated from it. Despite this truism, the contemporary understanding of the natural world remains in flux: directly affected in profound ways by physical processes over which humans have little control, but also shaped and reshaped by aesthetic, political, and economic forces resulting directly from human society. Even the term 'nature', like the terms heritage, memory, and identity, undergoes constant reinvention – Raymond Williams famously suggested that it is 'perhaps the most complex word in the English language' (Williams 1983: 219) – suggesting that humankind's relationship to the world 'out there' is never stable, despite the many different efforts by many different stakeholders to define it and fix it in place. These efforts arise for a variety of reasons – from conservation and protection, to development and exploitation, to enjoyment and appreciation – but one of the main premises of this chapter is that such separations rarely stand, given the necessary intertwining of the natural world with human society. In other words, considering the nature of water is a task humans must undertake, on behalf of those species which cannot.

This chapter outlines and explores issues of heritage, memory, and identity that arise in connection with the natural world, taking each of those respective themes in turn. In this way, it will complement other chapters in this volume, providing a platform to explore heritage, memory, and identity using a suite of examples drawn from across the globe – indeed, from the globe itself. It is important to stress that this frame is not constructed in opposition to urban or built contexts but in dialogue with them: illuminating latent issues and pressures that might not otherwise arise in those other contexts, and rounding out case studies and methodologies that do not always directly consider their environmental dimensions. Globalization has a particular role to bear, in that human impacts on the natural world are simultaneously local (in natural resource extraction and use) and global (responding to multinational political and economic demands, as well as impacting local environments from a distance). Correspondingly, global impacts on the environment have signaled in recent years a resurgence of interest in reconnecting diverse societies; these interlinked themes of globalization and interdependence are explored further in the conclusion.

But first, a note on terms. Rather than subscribing to the vision of the natural world as merely 'out there,' as described above, in what follows the arguments take the more nuanced notion of the natural world and the human world as mutually influencing, responding to, and co-producing one another. Though for ease of reference I use the terms 'environment,' 'natural world,' and 'landscape' as synonyms throughout this chapter, this usage foregrounds the environment, *pace* Oyama (2006), as the concatenation of agents, influences, and pressures that create a dynamic system. The term 'environment' here harbors two purposes: to refer both to the *physical* environment of biomes, climates, and ecosystems (for the purposes of investigating the idea of 'natural' heritage) and to the *developmental* environment (of which the physical environment is but one part). 'The environment here,' she argues, 'is not just a place or a supplier of materials; it is an integral part of a constructive system' (Oyama 2006: 55). The environment is not – is never – just a place. Put another way, when asked by a journalist if he painted 'from nature,' the artist Jackson Pollock once replied, 'I am nature' (Krasner 1964–68).

Heritage

In considering the relationships between heritage and the environment, the most widespread is arguably the perspective of a heritage *of* the environment. This perspective explores the ways in which national and international legislation has set portions of the natural world (often called 'the natural resource') apart for purposes such as conservation of biodiversity, protection of rare and endangered species, and development of ecotourism. Despite Pollock's riposte, contemporary policy regarding separate protected spaces still governs much of the present-day thinking about nature – by

aiming to shield natural areas from harm and safeguard them for future generations, the core aims and philosophies differ little from the conservation and management of 'cultural' heritage sites. This practice, as Child (2004) has noted, rather than being a modern-day invention, is in fact many thousands of years old. I shall therefore outline the principles and impacts of conservation areas on national and international scales before exploring the 'darker' side of viewing nature as heritage, following from Papayannis' and Howard's twofold interpretation of this process:

> On the one hand, [viewing nature as heritage] associates nature with human beings, as 'heritage' and 'inheritance', let alone 'patrimony', are highly anthropic terms (at least in this context). On the other, it implies a sense of responsibility of the natural wealth that has been received from our ancestors and the natural dividends that we shall leave to our descendents – unless we manage to 'bankrupt' the natural world. (Papayannis and Howard 2007: xi)

This sense of responsibility (stemming in Western culture partly from the biblical notion of man's 'dominion' over the earth and the corresponding injunction to be good stewards of it) is a core theme in conservation efforts, and underpins much of its legislation. As Adams observes in his history of the nature conservation movement, 'The dominant "big idea" of conservation throughout the twentieth century has been the establishment of protected areas: nature reserves, game reserves, sanctuaries and national parks – the names vary, as has the way people think protected areas should be managed, but the principle has changed very little' (Adams 2004: 3). That principle – that certain spaces in the natural world should be reserved in order to sustain and protect biophysical and ecological processes – draws on not just aesthetic or scientific, but indeed moral force. Exploitation of the environment, particularly its nonrenewable resources, is among many traditions of faith, community, and polity seen as a road to societal ruin, a historical phenomenon that Diamond (2005) has illustrated across numerous instances and cases, most memorably Easter Island.

An important part of the impulse towards conservation, however, stems from a historical affinity, and awe of, those natural spaces that are considered to be *wilderness*: places still unaffected by human impacts. Bill McKibben has argued that:

One proof of the deep-rooted desire for pristine places is the decision that Americans and others have made to legislate 'wilderness' – to set aside vast tracts of land where, in the words of the federal statute, 'the earth and its community of life are untrammeled by man, where man himself is a visitor who does not remain.' Pristine nature, we recognize, has been overwhelmed in many places, even in many of our national parks. But in these few spots it makes a stand. If we can't have places where no man has ever been, we can at least have spots where no man is at the moment. (McKibben 2003: 57)

This vein of thinking – that national and international legislation is able to aid the natural world in 'making a stand' against human encroachment – has since the nineteenth and twentieth centuries, when the majority of the legislation began to be formed, undoubtedly succeeded at preserving far more of the natural heritage of nation states and communities than otherwise would have survived. As historians such as Sellars and Sheail argue, however, the routes to such legislation are often hotly contested, given the vast range both of their stakeholders and their impacts – on scientific research, on natural resources, on business interests, and on future policy itself (Sellars 1997; Sheail 1998).

On the national level, each country has its own means of defining and measuring areas for conservation, which, like other cross-country inventories and analyses in other sectors including the built cultural heritage, renders comparison difficult (Hall and Page 2006: 313; the complexity of this practice is long-known in the creative industries, as Cunningham et al. 2008 have detailed). Moreover, those inventories in the United States, Europe, and Australia that have been undertaken have been done so largely with a view toward determining recreational use: a purpose that, as Hall and Page argue, ignores 'the significant range of other values of a wilderness area,' such as research, monitoring, biodiversity conservation, and education (Hall and Page 2006: 342). These difficulties have often prevented effective cooperation in monitoring and assessment of the natural resource, and were formally recognized by the 2008 International Union for the Conservation of Nature (IUCN) World Conservation Congress. In Barcelona, the IUCN called in Resolution 4.020 for 'a consultation process for the development, implementation, and monitoring

of a global standard for the assessment of ecosystem status, applicable at local, regional, and global levels,' (IUCN 2008) citing a lack of such standardized process as one of the major impediments to the swift and efficient disbursement of resources (in other words, prioritization – a political process, as Nicholson below has shown).

The UNESCO World Heritage List is one such form of international standardization that has attempted to promote cross-country expertise, consultation, and resource sharing. As of the 2009 inscription, UNESCO has listed 176 'natural' sites on the World Heritage List alongside 25 'mixed' sites, compared to 689 'cultural' sites (see the relevant Indicator Suites in Part 2 of this volume). According to the 2008 *Operational Guidelines for the Implementation of the World Heritage Convention*, natural sites are defined under three primary headings:

1 Natural features consisting of physical and biological formations or groups of such formation, which are of outstanding universal value from the aesthetic or scientific point of view,
2 Geological and physiographical formations and precisely delineated areas which constitute the habitat of threatened species of animals and plants of outstanding universal value from the point of view of science or conservation, and
3 Natural sites or precisely delineated natural areas of outstanding universal value from the point of view of science, conservation, or natural beauty. (UNESCO 2008: 15)

The selection criteria for natural sites for the World Heritage List follow similar guidelines; while it is beyond doubt that the designation is coveted for many reasons (publicity and prestige, but also access to those expertise and consultation processes), the direct impact itself of World Heritage listing on specific sites has been questioned. Through survey work on World Heritage site managers, Hall and Page have suggested that 'the rate of increase or decline in visitation since designation as World Heritage was little different from overall trends with respect to tourism visitation,' and that impacts where they are present are disproportionate in nature: that the World Heritage listing of a site may have more impact in developing nations due to the greater need (and opportunity) in those nations for additional infrastructure and accessibility development (Hall and Page 2006: 323).

But while conservation areas are set aside as heritage for numerous reasons, it is important to recognize the political dimension of many of these areas. As Hinchliffe argues, '...when we describe a landscape as "natural" we often mean to suggest that it is undeveloped, untouched and that the social or human-made world is largely absent. But such a view, attractive and seductive though it can be for some, is often difficult to sustain' (Hinchliffe 2007: 10). There are numerous instances of this kind of appropriation of nature and natural elements, not all of which are benign. Emily Nicholson (2009), for example, has noted the role of national identity in New Zealand in spurring conservation areas for the kiwi bird, claiming that efforts to ensure its survival have stemmed not simply from the fact that it is an 'evolutionarily distant' species – a species of special scientific interest for research into genetic history – but also because it is the national bird of New Zealand, an arbitrary designation on scientific grounds but which has rendered this species with particular symbolic importance. This symbolic importance therefore displaces species potentially more deserving of conservation, in the name of sustaining a debatable form of 'national' heritage.

Seen in this light, the conservation of nature is rarely, if ever, uncontroversial. And some conservation efforts have much wider unintended consequences: Child notes that at the beginning of their modern history, the 1933 'Convention Relative to the Preservation of Flora and Fauna in their Natural State' in London provided a framework for European colonial powers to demarcate natural spaces in their respective colonies in sub-Saharan Africa; even though its aim was to formalize biodiversity conservation and public ownership of natural spaces, the long-term effects of this colonial intervention have had problematic repercussions (Child 2004: 1–2). Many of these long-term effects take the form of top-down management structures, holdovers from prior governmental administrations that did not adequately involve local communities in natural resource management. For instance, Rogers et al. have shown how changes in the management of the Mkomazi Game Reserve in north-eastern Tanzania over the past half-century have resulted in the disenfranchisement and displacement of the local communities who use the land for grazing, hunting, and subsistence. In order to more efficiently monitor and regulate the Reserve, local

authorities forcibly relocated the communities who had lived there for generations – and who had formed complex, deep knowledge systems about it that could have aided in the management of the site (Rogers et al. 1999).

And regardless of legislation, widespread degradation of natural heritage continues: 16 of the 31 sites currently on the World Heritage List in Danger are natural sites, including the Galapagos Islands (one of the first sites inscribed in 1972), and as regular reports from the IUCN and the Nature Conservancy detail, planned agricultural development, the spread of drought and desertification, and deforestation increasingly threaten natural areas across the globe. In some cases, even the legislation itself may be cosmetic: Peleggi notes that flouting the strict National Forest Reserves Act of 1964, development and internal colonization in Thailand had shrunk the country's forest cover (home to indigenous flora, fauna, and local ethnic groups known as 'hill tribes') from 60 per cent of the country's surface area to approximately 25 per cent – an exponential rise in the rate of deforestation compared to the previous centuries (Peleggi 2007: 28–29). The example of deforestation is salient: following the influential analysis of Myers (1988), rainforests, particularly tropical rainforests, have long been understood as the world's most significant biodiversity hotspots, but also as one of the most vulnerable biomes in part because of their high economic resource value. In Thailand, the poaching of sandalwood is an illegal economic activity that threatens to undermine not just the stability of the ecosystem but which will, paradoxically, create its own end when the resource is depleted.

These examples serve as reminders of the constructed nature of natural spaces. In sites under robust state protection, the benefits have been numerous, including continued opportunities for scientific study – from conservation of endangered species of flora and fauna to discovery of new ones previously unknown to science. But as simultaneously human creations, even despite the innate tendency of natural spaces to grow and evolve independently of us (as Alan Weisman has explored in his provocative thought experiment *The World without Us* (2007)), human impacts upon nature must be seen in terms far beyond measurements of pollution, loss, or salvage: rather, the first impact is the act of *conception*. As Latour (1999), Watson

(2003), and others have argued, natural spaces are still constructed, by scientific and political regimes that then translate natural areas into classifiable schemes, systems of representation that then impact reciprocally on the communities that live in, near, and outside them. And these acts of translation condition the relationships individuals and communities have with nature, whether destructive or protective – a phenomenon it is easy to forget while hiking in a national park.

Memory

Shifting the focus from the physical spaces to the symbolic spaces of the environment, this section addresses the ways in which remembrance and memorialization occasion and are occasioned by the natural world. One immediate way, as Jones among others has noted, is the manner in which the physical environment still contains the material record of the human past – serving as a reservoir of archaeological and historical knowledge, and a space of epistemic potentiality as a result (Jones 2007). But it is equally important to highlight the way in which the natural world, through a variety of ecological phenomena, creates a mnemonic landscape all of its own: routine coastal erosion, seasonal storms and floods, and extraordinary events such as earthquakes and volcanic eruptions alike have the potential to radically reshape the communities they affect, to become flashpoints in social memory, and to give rise to museums and memorials (in the tradition of *lieux de mèmoire*, discussed by Pierre Nora (1984–92) and elsewhere in this volume).

The forms of memorialization that pertain to the natural world are as diverse and complex as any that mark heritage sites of other origins, and each deserves fuller treatment in its own right – in particular, literary memoir of encounters with nature, such as Mabey (2005) and Deakin (1999), has in recent years presented itself as a rich vein for analysis. To focus the discussion, however, I shall take events, specifically natural disasters, as a departure point for an investigation into memory. In what follows, three primary kinds of memorialization of the natural environment are charted, moving (loosely) from the more material to the least material: first, the kind in which a disaster leaves its physical imprint on a landscape; second, the kind in

which a community collectively remembers a disaster in memorial or museum format; and finally, the collective memory of disasters that bridges generations and lifespans.

First, perhaps the most immediate memorial tendencies govern those landscapes which have been ravaged, and which have remained either by neglect, accident, or deliberate non-intervention in those ravaged states. Such landscapes are often left *in situ*, as in the town of Ghibellina in Sicily, destroyed by an earthquake in 1968. Rather than rebuild the town (and entertain future risk from more earthquakes), local survivors chose to build a new town to the west, Ghibellina Nuova, and hired the sculptor Alfredo Burri to encase the remnants of the ravaged village with pure concrete in an act of commemoration, blurring the lines between memorialization, fossilization, and art. His sculpture, called *il Cretto*, or 'The Crater,' now contains the ruins of the old city. As Woodward observes,

> The shattered houses were levelled to a uniform height, boxed in by wooden planking, and the white molten concrete poured into the mould. The result is a powerful experience for the tourist. ... The fields in the valley flourish but Nature will never revive under the impervious, suffocating concrete. (Woodward 2002: 84)

In cases such as these, the destroyed environment (stabilized for health and safety reasons, or quarantined in the worst cases, as in Chernobyl) becomes the stage on which the disaster is repeatedly played out by the act of visiting, imagining, and recreating it. In this way, natural events become the subjects of public curation, the second kind of memorialization, a process visible either in temporary exhibitions or even the subjects of museums wholly dedicated to the event. The *Watersnoodmuseum*, for example, near Ouwerkerk in the Netherlands, is devoted to the 1953 floods in the North Sea which ravaged coastal and inland portions of England, France, Denmark, Belgium, and the Netherlands and claimed over 2,000 lives in total (this disaster was recently commemorated again in the 2009 film *De Storm* by Ben Sombogaart). In cases such as these, societies preserve and cultivate the memory of natural events, typically by interpreting them in various ways: as lessons about preparedness (or the lack thereof) for disaster, accounts of heroism in the face of danger, chronicles of the impact on the local communities, and assessments of organized governmental and/or nongovernmental response.

Since many of these museums receive public funding, it is comparatively rare to find as part of their curatorial message indictments against actors who did not adequately perform in the time of crisis (as in the case of the widely-criticized federal response to Hurricane Katrina in New Orleans in 2005). Rather, attempts to maintain objectivity or value-neutrality in the interpretation of the disaster are often supplanted by technical accounts of infrastructure, of the failure of warning systems, engineering works, or civic defense mechanisms. In these cases, the official public memory of a disaster is often cleansed of its racial, economic, or gendered undertones, given that natural disasters are commonly held to affect populations equally – despite the fact that, as Steinberg (2000) and others have argued, this is rarely, if ever, the case. Hence the 'official' representations of these kinds of 'natural' events can fall sway to the same selective tendencies toward elision, negation, and silence that drive the erasure of particular narratives from museums of armed conflict and war, leaving room (where data, records, and survivors exist) for subsequent scholarship to reclaim those lost narratives and reintegrate them into the history of ecological events.

But as with the natural heritage described earlier, museums of this kind are also constructed for economic development purposes. Davis has detailed the proposed plans for 'the world's first earthquake theme park in Tangshan [China],' near Beijing, where in 1976 a 7.8M earthquake devastated the city and took the lives of hundreds of thousands of residents. The proposed 'Earthquake City,' he writes, announced in 1996 by the Chinese authorities,

> ...would incorporate ruins from the 1976 catastrophe, 'most notably the preserved college whose intact four upper storeys remain perched on the rubble of the collapsed ground floor.' Simulated earthquakes would give visitors the adrenaline rush of surviving the Big One. 'The chief aim of the park is said to be education rather than tourism, but there's little doubt that the park scheme is intended to attract visitors and their money to a region that currently sees only 1,000–2,000 foreigners a year. (Davis 1999: 52)

The Earthquake City proposal was ultimately realized as a museum in Tangshan – whose methods of presentation, interpretation, and display echo that of the *Watersnoodmuseum* – but it still raises numerous questions about the right to exploit the suffering of local citizens, about how the scales of a disaster are measured (where best, for instance, should a museum of the 2004 Boxing Day tsunami be located, given that the Indian Ocean earthquake that spawned it directly impacted 20 countries?), and how the narratives of disaster are performed and enshrined. In this last respect, disaster museums are particularly problematic for how the claims to loss become a jockeying point among museums eager to claim the title of what constitutes the 'worst,' 'biggest,' 'most devastating,' 'most widespread,' or 'longest-lasting' disaster (as the Tangshan museum does, claiming in one wall panel, *sans* scholarly citation, that the earthquake 'is regarded as one of the ten biggest disasters of [the] twentieth century'), undoubtedly for tourism purposes – an entry into the growing genre of global disaster tourism ('dark tourism', as Foley and Lennon (2000) have termed it). While these practices of commemoration frequently invoke local testimonies of survival alongside loss, whether the proceeds generated by these museums necessarily reach back into those affected local communities, or contribute to a wider public discourse about risk, settlement, and the inherent complexity of the natural landscape is rarely guaranteed.

Finally, disasters also occasion memories of other disasters in the same region or of the same scale. In the United States, the entire Gulf of Mexico region harbors a collective memory of hurricanes – Hurricane Katrina in 2005 reawakened memories of Hurricane Camille in 1969 and Hurricane Betsy in 1965, which in turn echoed the Mississippi River floods of 1927. (As of this writing, Hurricane Ida was making a beeline across the Gulf towards southern Alabama and Florida.) Across the region, especially in storm-battered towns such as Galveston, Texas, now-legendary hurricane names, such as Andrew, Ivan, and Hugo, still have the power to inspire informal sessions of storytelling and recollection among local residents. Even Katrina, whose impacts on New Orleans have proven generational in scope, was briefly supplanted by Hurricane Gustav of 2008 (DeBerry 2008), demonstrating that no single event, or memory of it, can remain unique and unaltered over time in a risk-prone region. In a simple formulation with profound implications, disaster can become the heritage of a place. Part of this process is contingent upon the specific type of disaster – hurricanes are mobile, variable, and subject to atmospheric and climatic conditions that impact on their trajectory and intensity – but other disasters that do not share these properties still impact on residual memory formation, as Neisser et al. (1996) have shown with earthquake memories. Anecdotally, Chang (2008), for instance, records how the 2008 earthquake in Sichuan Province recalled the Tangshan event, just as Bolin and Stanford (1998) note how the 1994 Northridge quake in California echoed the famous 1906 combined event (earthquake and fire) in San Francisco.

Whether earthquakes, for instance, or volcanic eruptions are more prone to reawaken memories of prior disasters because of their situatedness in place is a question worth further consideration. But regardless of the mobility of the natural hazard under consideration, certain landscapes are suffused with a measure of risk that will never be resolved, only adapted to or mitigated against. These landscapes, as Anthony Oliver-Smith has argued in his analysis of a devastating landslide at Yungay, Peru, often take on special significance to their local communities, and form part of their identity as dwellers within, users of, and participants in the natural world (Oliver-Smith 1986).

Identity

The exploration of memory invites an exploration of how 'identity' takes shape, and what roles the natural world plays in this process. If what a society cares for is a marker of that society's vision of itself, then its relationship to its environment is a key indicator for an investigation of those narratives. Issues of agricultural production and land-use as a matter of historical record have increasingly been accompanied by questions of sense of place, local knowledge, and the repercussions of environmental migration. If, however, living in and with the natural world has required a constant form of adaptation, the impact of adaptation on identity requires a reassessment of the classical forms and narratives of identity: issues which today constitute legal problems for nation-states on whose doorstep refugees from natural disasters land.

Despite Bolin and Sanford's claim that earthquakes are 'a phenomenon as synonymous with the state [of California] as Disneyland, freeways, and smog,' disaster is not the only way in which communities form attachments to place, and shape and sustain identities out of those attachments (Bolin and Stanford 1998: 11). Natural spaces, such as the Great Barrier Reef in Australia, the Kruger National Park in South Africa, and the Central Amazon Conservation Basin in Brazil, share multiple roles for local, national, and international stakeholders, roles which can come into conflict with one another when divergent interests meet in and around these spaces. And local and national environments have long been recognized for creating personal associations, senses of ownership and custodianship, and the deep, inbuilt knowledges that come from dwelling – and, conversely, claims to defending those associations, custodianships, and knowledges. Those claims can quickly become collectivized, as Lowenthal has argued, and therefore become themselves terrain on which both ideological and physical battles are fought. 'Each people,' he writes,

> treasures physical features felt to be distinctively their own. Landscapes are compelling symbols of national identity. Patriotic feeling builds on talismans of space and place: hills and rivers and woods become ideological sites of shrines, battles, birthplaces. Every national anthem praises special scenic splendours and natural bounties. Rugged mountains, dense forests, deep lakes, storm-scarred coasts and cliffs equip myriad chauvinisms. Thus, the Swiss ascribe their sturdy freedom to frugal, communitarian mountain life and pure Alpine air. In contrast, the English vaunt humanized rural scenes as schools of decorum. Environment is everywhere an emblem of national identity. (Lowenthal 2000: 198)

But if the environment is an emblem of national identity, it must first be formed and nourished at the local level, a process that is most frequently a result of dwelling, and as research into indigenous lifeworlds has also brought to the fore (Ingold 1999). The act of dwelling and the refined sense of place it creates together contribute to the process of local identity formation, as Feld and Basso have charted in their investigation of what the 'sense of place' actually entails: '…the terrain covered here includes the relation of sensation to emplacement; the experiential and expressive ways places are known, imagined, yearned for, held, remembered, voiced, lived, contested, and struggled over; and the multiple ways places are metonymically and metaphorically tied to identities' (Feld and Basso 1996: 11).

The metaphorical link present here, and its reliance on an act of creation and construction, mirrors the act of demarcation detailed in the first section of this chapter: communities simultaneously establish and reveal who they are by the acts of positioning they inscribe in relationship to their natural surroundings. As Ashworth has argued, '…individuals and social groups endow their local environments with meanings that are not intrinsic to the physical forms themselves but are ascribed to them by people. … This is the sense of place which is a powerful instrument in shaping and reinforcing feelings of identification with specific areas in individuals, who in turn, by their reaction, further strengthen such identities' (Ashworth 1998: 112). Reciprocating these impacts over time requires a form of infrastructure which is itself metaphorical; the family bonds of intimacy and storytelling, as Sørensen has argued (Sørensen 2009: 172–173), play a significant role in furthering the narratives that sustain identity formation.

While certain attempts to link a sense of place with an individual or group identity are measured, deliberate, and programmatic (and in this sense, political), the process is not always so straightforward. The accidents of border creation can also give rise to processes of identity formation. In a process that may tentatively be termed geographical nationalism, or *geo-nationalism*, two cases have arisen that provoke unusual questions about the relationship between historical contingency, geographic appropriation, and the creation of national identity. The borders of both Spain and Thailand resemble the animals in which their national mythology figures most prominently, respectively, the bull and the elephant: in the case of Spain, the skinned hide of a bull is represented by the shape of the central provinces against the northern provinces of Galicia and Catalonia. Similarly, in Thailand, the shape of the country is popularly seen to resemble that of an elephant (a sacred animal in Thai culture) in profile: the head represented by the northwestern provinces, the ear by the northeastern provinces bordering Laos, and the trunk the provinces of the 'Deep South' cascading down into the Andaman Sea and bordering Malaysia. In both Spain and Thailand, ceremonies and rituals surround their national animals on holidays, festival occasions, and religious observances – practices which are simultaneously physical, metaphorical, and performative. This last aspect is one of the most salient means towards identity formation, as numerous authors have argued (e.g. Roach 1996). What inferences can be drawn from these historical accidents, or what further questions may follow from them, are outside the scope of this overview, but they do show that the performance of national identity does not require a map when the map is already internalized (or when it is blocking traffic).

Any discussion of borders, however, necessarily invokes their porosity (Appadurai 1996), a feature that the present century will see increasingly as global currents of capital, political pressure, and armed conflicts lead communities to abandon places seen as bearing too much risk for long-term sustainable dwelling. To this list of 'drivers' for migration has recently been added environmental pressures: while the mechanisms by which the environment becomes a factor in determining the likelihood of population migration are still in contention, it is clear that ecological pressures such as water shortages, shorter and less productive growing seasons, increased frequency and intensity of natural hazards such as droughts and floods, and the perception of increased opportunities in metropolitan or cosmopolitan contexts will contribute to border crossings in decades to come (Wrathall and Morris 2009). Some of these border crossings will be permanent: the low-lying island nations of the Pacific Rim such as Tuvalu, Kiribas, the Maldives, and the Carteret Islands are already in negotiation with neighboring governments such as Australia and New Zealand over the issue of national relocation, a chilling scenario of a prospective future (inter)national park.

Finally, how migrants will experience alterations to their identity – from agrarians to urban dwellers, for instance, especially in the context of contemporary megacities (Bohle and Warner 2008) – is a question that will resonate through the coming century. Moreover, how migrants will retain, refashion, or reject memories of their homeland (much less come to terms with the heritage of a novel place) is a process whose contours are still to come into sharp focus. Yet globalization has, Clark argues, reinforced the well-worn manner of dividing non-human nature from human culture. 'In the context of accelerating globalization,' he writes,

> questions of belonging and territorial identification have risen to prominence in political discourse over recent decades. Today, few critical thinkers are willing to admit that peoples spring forth from a native soil or that they belong, by any natural or absolute right, to a fixed parcel of land. In this light, politically sensitive commentators on bioinvasion have taken pains not to allow their cautionary words about the invasive species problem to slip into a condemnation of migrants, refugees, or other mobile human groups. ... Territoriality might be practised or enacted on the part of our own species, but with regards to other life-forms, it appears to be pre-existent and inviolable. (Clark 2003: 176)

Conclusion

In this sense – of recapitulating shopworn dichotomies – but also in thinking about the natural world more broadly, one would be hard-pressed to find a better motto than *plus ça change*. Throughout this overview, the lens has been trained on the natural world and natural phenomena without an overt invocation of the force that could well shape them more than any other in the decades to come: anthropogenically-induced global warming, or as it is now known, climate change. Part of the reason for this emphasis has been to outline the issues involved in heritage, memory, and identity without an overarching framework stabilizing and directing them: if anything, as Lähde (2006) and Hulme (2009) have argued, invocations of climate change can reduce the number of avenues available for analysis rather than expand them. Lähde argues:

> ...the function of simplistic accounts of climate change is to make climate change into a viable target for a straightforward policy. According to this definition, human interference has disturbed the natural state of the climate, and for nature to recuperate that interference must be curbed or removed. Thus, the idea of the State of Nature in climate is an archetypal example of how an

> immensely complex process is being reduced to an abstract division between a supposed norm and deviations from the norm. This abstraction bypasses the fact that the climate is in a state of flux, no matter what is done. (Lähde 2006: 87)

Consequently, it is crucial to understand how the relationships between heritage, memory, and identity in an environmental context take shape regardless of that essentializing narrative, given that the narrative of climate change will occasion further impacts that will, in many cases, operate on the same principles outlined above, and on nearly all kinds of heritage sites currently under protection. In the past decade, the reality has set in: major reports by governments, NGOs and IGOs (English Heritage (2005), the National Trust (UK) (2006), the Nordic World Heritage Foundation (1999), the 'Noah's Ark' EU-FP6 consortium (2004–07), ICOMOS (2006–07) and UNESCO (2007)) have highlighted the impacts of climate change on heritage sites. While these reports frequently adopt conservation-based approaches, shared among all parties are concerns that if climate change continues unchecked, known hazardous impacts will be strengthened, hastened, and frequented irrevocably. As the Fourth Report of the Intergovernmental Panel on Climate Change (founded by the United Nations Environment Programme and the World Meteorological Organization) (2007) notes, it is already too late to prevent some impacts due to current alterations in the atmosphere, oceans, and polar regions, ensuring that a new generation of heritage sites at risk will be added to watch lists maintained by UNESCO and the World Monuments Fund, which in 2008 added sites at risk from climate change for the first time.

In mapping out the issues linking culture, heritage, and globalization, then, climate change is undeniably at the forefront due to just this global nature. As is now well known, impacts on the environment in one region of the world (high-carbon emitting developed nations) can have far-reaching, and severe, impacts in distant, seemingly unconnected regions (low-emitting, developing nations). The imbalance of the burden between polluter and sufferer has served, paradoxically, to reconnect those agents. '[It] is no longer possible to think about global social processes,' argue Smith, Clark, and Yusoff, *without also considering pressing global ecological issues – most notably climate change and biodiversity loss. The coincidence of economic and cultural globalization with the maturing of global environmental change science is carrying a whole body of academic, political and media practitioners into new and unfamiliar terrain where it is necessary to grapple simultaneously with the dynamics of the earth's atmosphere, hydrosphere, lithosphere, cryosphere, and biosphere (air, water, rock, ice and life) and with ongoing transformations in a globalising economy and cultural system. (Smith, Clark, and Yusoff 2007: 347)*

Climate change is not merely a global process acting on the environment, it is also, crucially, a global process acting on the societies that govern and maintain that environment. This reciprocal impact and its attendant economic, political, and ecological implications now further leverage against the separation of nature and society. But if the climate is in a state of flux, as Lähde argues, then so are our relationships with it. Viewing the environment as heritage can lead to gestures of conservation, and in some cases, gestures of art. Responding to the challenges that climate change poses, the American artist Amy Balkin has attempted listing the global atmosphere as a UNESCO World Heritage Site – an act of protest, activism, and subversion all at once (Balkin 2009). But as with all forms of heritage, the environment can also stir reassessments of the societal values, norms, and expectations attached to it. In this sense, it fulfills the systemic role invoked earlier, constantly challenging and upending our ideas of it. As Oyama claimed, the environment is not just a biome or an ecosystem: it is never just earth, or sky, or water. Hence stemming the tide of its exploitation and degradation requires a change in the way that the heritage is not just used, but how it is *conceived*, by the purpose sought for the natural world. While international gatherings such as the yearly Conference of the Parties organized by the United Nations Framework Convention on Climate Change provide the opportunity for policy-makers to debate (and, one would hope, agree upon) the best mechanisms for the protection of the natural world, they will be ineffective without an abiding relationship to the environment that gives

force and meaning to a policy negotiation. Thus the task is not to understand climate change *per se*, but to understand environmental change over the long term.

This task, which will far outlast any Conference of Parties, is both a global task and a personal task, and the best place to begin must necessarily be at the individual level: by putting on one's boots and going for a walk. In *The Wild Places* (2007), Robert Macfarlane does just this, setting out in pursuit of the wilderness still remaining in the United Kingdom. At the end of his years and his miles on the road, he concludes – rightly – that a more nuanced understanding of 'the wild', and nature more broadly, is not to be found in any space legislatively decreed as such. Rather, wilderness worth saving is located in a different intangible space: in a dynamic repositioning of the self not *in* but *with* the landscape. For wilderness is neither fully exterior nor fully interior. Created in dialogue with the natural world, it is neither an extant fact nor a declaration by fiat, but a construction, and continual reconstruction, somewhere in between. 'It was not that places such as Hope and Rannoch, the last fastnesses, were worthless,' Macfarlane writes.

No, in their stripped-back austerity, their fierce elementality, these landscapes remained invaluable in their power to awe. But I had learned to see another type of wildness, to which I had once been blind: the wildness of natural life, the sheer force of ongoing organic existence, vigorous and chaotic. … There was as much to be learned in an acre of woodland on a city's fringe as on the shattered summit of Ben Hope. (Macfarlane 2007: 316)

Acknowledgements

Thanks are due to a number of individuals who helped in the formation of this chapter. First are the co-editors of this volume, for their insightful feedback and criticism, without whom this chapter would be much the poorer. I would also like to thank Abbie Garrington, Joe Smith, Robert Butler, Bradon Smith, Caspar Henderson, Matthew Child, Marie Louise Stig Sørensen, Rebekah Scott, and Robert Carter for their ideas, their encouragement, and in some cases, their whiskey.

REFERENCES

Adams, William M. (2004) *Against Extinction: The Story of Conservation*. London: Earthscan.

Appadurai, Arjun. (1996) 'Sovereignty without Territoriality: Notes for a Postnational Geography', in Patricia Yaeger (ed.), *The Geography of Identity*. Ann Arbor, MI: University of Michigan Press. pp. 40–58.

Ashworth, Gregory. (1998) 'Heritage, Identity, and Interpreting a European Sense of Place', in David Uzzell and Roy Ballantyne (eds), *Contemporary Issues in Heritage and Environmental Interpretation: Problems and Prospects*. London: The Stationery Office. pp. 112–132.

Balkin, Amy. (2009) 'Public Smog'. Available at: www.publicsmog.org/.

Bohle, Hans-Georg and Warner, Koko. (eds) (2008) 'Megacities: Resilience and Social Vulnerability'. United Nations University Institute for Environment and Human Security SOURCE 10. Available at: www.ehs.unu.edu/file.php?id=462.

Bolin, Robert and Stanford, Lois. (1998) *The Northridge Earthquake: Vulnerability and Disaster*. London: Routledge.

Chang, Anita. (2008) 'China Disaster Stirs Memories of 1976 Quake.' *USA Today*, 6 June 2008. Available at: www.usatoday.com/news/world/2008–06–06–411224944_x.htm.

Child, Brian. (2004) 'Introduction', in Brian Child (ed.), *Parks in Transition: Biodiversity, Rural Development, and the Bottom Line*. London: Earthscan.

Clark, Nigel. (2003) 'Feral Ecologies: Performing Life on the Colonial Periphery', in Bronislaw Szerszynski, Wallace Heim, and Claire Waterton (eds), *Nature Performed: Environment, Culture and Performance*. Oxford: Blackwell. pp: 163–182.

Cunningham, Stuart, Banks, John, and Potts, Jason. (2008) 'Cultural Economy: The Shape of the Field', in Helmut Anheier and Yudhishthir Raj Isar (eds), *Cultures and Globalization Series 2: The Cultural Economy*. Los Angeles and London: Sage. pp. 15–26.

Davis, Mike C. (1999) *Ecology of Fear: Los Angeles and the Imagination of Disaster*. London: Picador.

Deakin, Roger. (1999) *Waterlog: A Swimmer's Journey through Britain*. London: Chatto & Windus.

DeBerry, Jarvis. (2008) 'Now we know how much we have to lose'. *New Orleans Times-Picayune*, 29 August 2008. Available at: blog.nola.com/jarvisdeberry/2008/08/now_we_know_how_much_we_have_t.html.

Diamond, Jared. (2005) *Collapse: How Societies Choose to Fail or Succeed*. New York: Penguin.

English Heritage and UCL Centre for Sustainable Heritage. (2005) *Climate Change and the Historic Environment*. London: English Heritage.

Feld, Steven and Basso, Keith H. (1996) 'Introduction', in Steven Feld and Keith H. Basso (eds), *Senses of Place*. Santa Fe, NM: School of American Research Press. pp. 3–11.

Foley, Malcolm and Lennon, John. (2000) *Dark Tourism: The Attraction of Death and Disaster*. London: Continuum.

Hall, C. Michael and Page, Stephen J. (eds) (2006) *The Geography of Tourism and Recreation: Environment, Place and Space* (3rd edn). London: Routledge. (1st edn, 1999.)

Hinchliffe, Steve. (2007) *Geographies of Nature: Societies, Environments, Ecologies*. London: Sage.

Hulme, Mike. (2009) *Why We Disagree about Climate Change*. Cambridge: Cambridge University Press.

ICOMOS (2006–07) *World Report on Monuments and Sites in Danger*. Available at: www.international.icomos.org/risk/world_report/2006–2007/pdf/H@R_2006–2007_web.pdf.

Ingold, Tim. (2000) *The Perception of the Environment: Essays in Livelihood, Dwelling, and Skill*. London: Routledge.

International Union for the Conservation of Nature. (2008) Resolution 4.020. Accessed 1 November 2009. Available at: www.iucn.org/congress_08/assembly/policy/.

Jones, Andrew. (2007) *Memory and Material Culture*. Cambridge: Cambridge University Press.

Krasner, Lee. (1964–68) 'Oral History Interview with Lee Krasner, 1964 Nov. 2–1968 Apr. 11', Archives of American Art. Washington, DC: Smithsonian Institution. Available at: www.aaa.si.edu/collections/oralhistories/transcripts/krasne64.htm.

Lähde, Ville. (2006) 'Gardens, Climate Changes, and Cultures', in Yrjö Haila and Chuck Dyke (eds), *How Nature Speaks: The Dynamics of the Human Ecological Condition*. Durham, NC: Duke University Press. pp. 78–105.

Latour, Bruno (1999). *Pandora's Hope: Essays on the Reality of Science Studies*. Cambridge, MA: Harvard University Press.

Lords Select Committee of the United Kingdom. (2006) *Science and Heritage: Report with Evidence*. Available at: www.parliament.uk/parliamentary_committees/lords_s_t_select/heritage.cfm.

Lowenthal, David. (2000) 'Environment as Heritage', in Kate Flint and Howard Morphy (eds), *Culture, Landscape, and the Environment: The Linacre Lectures 1997*. Oxford: Oxford University Press. pp. 197–217.

Mabey, Richard. (2005) *Nature Cure*. London: Chatto & Windus.

Macfarlane, Rob. (2007) *The Wild Places*. London: Granta Books.

McKibben, Bill. (2003) *The End of Nature: Humanity, Climate Change and the Natural World* (2nd edn). London: Bloomsbury. (1st edn, 1989.)

Myers, Norman. (1988) 'Threatened Biotas: 'Hot Spots' in Tropical Forests'. *The Environmentalist*, 8: 1–20.

National Trust. (2006) *Forecast–Changeable? Climate Change Impacts around the National Trust*. London: The National Trust.

Neisser, Ulric, Winograd, Eugene, Bergman, Erik T., Schreiber, Charles A., Palmer, Stephen E., and Weldon, Mary Susan. (1996) 'Remembering the Earthquake: Direct Experience vs. Hearing the News'. *Memory*, 4(4): 337–357.

Nicholson, Emily. (2009) 'Decision Theory in Conservation', paper presented at the Conservation Today: 'Open Ground' conference, London, 20 June 2009.

Noah's Ark. (2004–07) *Global Climate Change Impact on Built Heritage in Historic Landscapes*. European Union Sixth Framework Programme. Available at: noahsark.isac.cnr.it/.

Nora, Pierre. (1984–92) *Les Lieux de mémoire* (vols 1–3). Paris: Gallimard.

Nordic World Heritage Foundation. (1999) *Report on Sustainable Tourism and World Heritage*. Available at: www.nwhf.no/files/File/culture_fulltext.pdf.

Oliver-Smith, Anthony. (1986) *The Martyred City*. Santa Fe, NM: University of New Mexico Press.

Oyama, Susan. (2006) 'Speaking of Nature', in Yrjö Haila and Chuck Dyke (eds), *How Nature Speaks: The Dynamics of the Human Ecological Condition*. Durham, NC: Duke University Press. pp. 49–65.

Papayannis, Thymio and Howard, Peter. (2007) 'Editorial: Nature as Heritage', in Peter Howard and Thymio Papayannis (eds), *Natural Heritage: At the Interface of Nature and Culture*. London: Routledge. pp. ix–xviii.

Peleggi, Maurizio. (2007) *Thailand: The Worldly Kingdom*. London: Reaktion Books.

Percy, Walker. (1991) 'Questions They Never Asked Me', in *Signposts in a Strange Land*. London: Bellew. pp. 397–423.

Roach, Joseph. (1996) *Cities of the Dead: Circum-Atlantic Performance*. New York: Columbia University Press.

Rogers, Peter J., Brockington, D., Kiwasila, H., and Homewood, K. (1999) 'Environmental Awareness and Conflict Genesis – People versus Parks in Mkomazi Game Reserve, Tanzania', in TiiaRiitta Granfelt (ed.), *Managing the Globalized Environment: Local Strategies to Secure Livelihoods*. London: IT Publications. pp. 26–51.

Sellars, Richard West. (1997) *Preserving Nature in the National Parks: A History*. New Haven, CT: Yale University Press.

Sheail, John. (1998) *Nature Conservation in Britain: The Formative Years*. London: The Stationery Office.

Smith, Joe, Clark, Nigel, and Yusoff, Kathryn. (2007) 'Interdependence', *Geography Compass*, 2: 340–359.

Sørensen, M.L.S. (2009) 'Between the Lines and in the Margins: Interviewing People about Attitudes to Heritage and Identity', in M.L.S. Sørensen and John Carman (eds), *Heritage Studies: Methods and Approaches*. London: Routledge. pp. 164–177.

Steinberg, Ted. (2000) *Acts of God: The Unnatural History of Natural Disaster in America*. Oxford: Oxford University Press.

UNESCO. (2007) *Case Studies on Climate Change and World Heritage*. Paris: UNESCO.

UNESCO World Heritage Centre. (2006) *Predicting and Managing the Effects of Climate Change on World Heritage*. Paris: UNESCO.

UNESCO World Heritage Committee. (2008) *Operational Guidelines for the Implementation of the World Heritage Convention*. Available at: whc.unesco.org/archive/opguide08-en.pdf.

United Nations Intergovernmental Panel on Climate Change. (2007) *Fourth Assessment Report (AR4)*. Available at: www.ipcc.ch/.

Watson, Matt. (2003) 'Performing Place in Nature Reserves', in Bronislaw Szerszynski, Wallace Heim, and Claire Waterton (eds), *Nature Performed: Environment, Culture and Performance*. Oxford: Blackwell. pp. 145–163.

Weisman, Alan (2007). *The World without Us*. New York: Thomas Dunne Books.

Williams, Raymond. (1983) *Keywords: A Vocabulary of Culture and Society*. London: Flamingo.

Woodward, Christopher. (2002) *In Ruins*. London: Vintage.

Wrathall, David and Morris, Benjamin. (2009) 'Confronting Environmental Migration: A Framework for Research, Policy, and Practice'. United Nations University Research Brief. Available at: www.ehs.unu.edu/article:712.

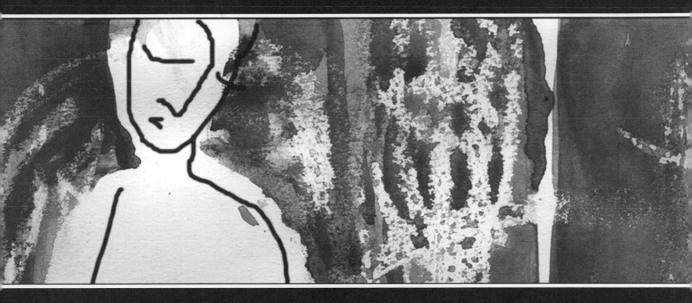

CHAPTER 10

LIVING SACRED HERITAGE AND 'AUTHENTICITY' IN SOUTH ASIA
Jagath Weerasinghe

The key concept of authenticity, argues the author of this chapter, needs to be re-examined and adjusted in the era of globalization, particularly in relation to the category of living sacred heritage. Local cultural contexts are no longer isolated islands of thought and tradition; they are in fact 'globalized contexts' inhabited by communities and individuals conscious of their rights who may well resist the interventions of heritage professionals who are solely guided by the authorized heritage discourse. The heritage can no longer be seen as a static entity belonging in the past. It is not a 'thing' but a cultural process, the author argues, and as such preservation procedures and the role of the expert need to be redefined.

Introduction

Current forms of globalization and heritage-identity politics in Sri Lanka or India are interlinked in complex ways, many of which have been marked by postcolonial conditions. Popular ideas about these linkages are often deceptive and misleading for it is often assumed that globalization and identity politics are at loggerheads. In fact, they are accomplices, as will be revealed in this chapter. Globalization is popularly perceived as just a new chapter in the history of western domination and exploitation of Asian societies, as a scheme intended to undermine and dismantle Asian cultural and religious value-systems and knowledge bases and replace them by western norms. In such popular discourse, globalization is usually aligned with the spread of American popular culture (see Holton 2000 for a lengthy treatment of the cultural consequences of globalization).

Anti-western sentiments of these kinds, which have semantic affinities with the heritage and identity politics of the local and the regional, abound among ultra nationalist and religious political groups (cf. Jaffrelot, Gayer and Maheshwari, 2008). Such truculent political parties have been able to claim and occupy a clamorous, and in some places, murderous (see Ratnagar 2004), position in the political arena of South Asian societies.[1] While such politically motivated groups and parties gain popularity among suburban and rural masses by pitting local heritage and identity against globalization, transnational companies, who are the real movers and shakers of globalization, also utilize the cultural emotions of the local and the regional to establish and expand their profit-making ventures. They have begun to exploit archaeologically and culturally important and politically powerful symbols in their promotional campaigns.[2] The international popularity of folk/vernacular music and dance forms, such as the Rajasthani folk music of India, can also be considered in this light.

While these two seemingly incompatible registers within globalization work upon and within heritage and identity politics in their own ways to gain symbolic and monetary capital, there is yet another set of players operating within the processes of globalization. These are the civil society groups – the NGOs that are funded by globally active institutions such as HIVOS (Netherlands), the European Union, or the Ford Foundation (USA), to name a few, are in fact in most cases founded upon various noble humanitarian causes with the intention of empowering the marginalized, the under-privileged, and the socially victimized groups in countries like Sri Lanka, India or Pakistan. Local and regional activities of civil society groups have contributed towards an increase in the general awareness of political, cultural and heritage rights. These efforts have given rise to a subjectivity that is intended to be self-redeeming by critically positioning individuals within their traditional value systems. In other words, the civil society groups too work within and upon the social habitus governed by heritage and identity politics of the local and the regional.

The three registers of activities that operate upon heritage and identity – the political, the corporate and the civic – described above, though they might appear to be discrete, in fact are strongly, yet subtly, interconnected. In a way, I would argue that these three registers of operations actually endorse politics of nationalism in some form or the other, by the very fact that they utilize, rephrase, and redefine heritage and identity politics to achieve their goals. Except for the register of ultra-nationalist and religious politics, the other two registers position themselves within and in relation to heritage and identity politics in an apparently milder and an indirect manner. What emerges in the final analysis is a heightened and somewhat defiant sense of collective identity, a certain cultural polarization. The defiance thus expressed finds itself inevitably caught up in the rhetoric of nationalism that performs such a major role in South Asian politics. In turn, societies also get drawn into working against another register that operates within globalization: the propagation of global norms regarding various aspects of human and societal affairs, including heritage preservation.

Hence my intention here is to look closely at the confrontation, as Isar has already done in his chapter in this volume, at the defiant nexus between the heightened sense of collective identity that globalization promotes in the local and the regional and the global standards in heritage preservation advocated by global institutions such as UNESCO (in particular its World Heritage Centre) and the International Council on Monuments and Sites (ICOMOS). I shall do so from a heritage management perspective. Obviously, a heightened sense of collective identity in relation to heritage is not an unhealthy

situation, but it can become detrimental when given effect in combative terms by local and regional groups who have been or claim to be the communities most closely associated with particular heritage sites. Such combative stances are commonly encountered in the field of heritage management and preservation in South Asia.

One very important conceptual category that occupies an authorized position in the heritage management discourse is the concept or category of 'authenticity'. This concept can exercise an enormous amount of power over heritage sites and heritage professionals across the globe when a country aspires to get World Heritage inscription for its sites, and can indeed be considered as the most crucial determinant in devising preservation approaches. The main problem, however, in using the concept or the category of authenticity in assessing the archaeological, historical or cultural values of a heritage site is that it is not sufficiently articulated. In this chapter I shall therefore first examine the history of this concept and its current position within the heritage discourse. I shall then explore the current limits of the use of this concept, taking the restoration of the bomb-damaged Sacred Tooth Relic Temple at Kandy, Sri Lanka, as a case study. I shall conclude with the thesis that authenticity as a pivotal concept needs to be considered with the understanding that heritage is not about a place or a thing but a cultural process in which people participate. My concluding section will also suggest the possible adverse scenario if the heritage profession fails to understand and theorize heritage in a manner that would acknowledge and address the local and the regional anxieties surrounding heritage in South Asia. One of the painful truths about the triad of heritage, memory, and identity is that there is an undeniable complicity between contemporary popular perceptions of this triad and the nationalist/religious political movements in South Asia. This alliance, for sure, will last for a long time into the future since the forces of globalization inevitably stoke this complicity, both directly and indirectly.

The concept of authenticity and heritage professionalism

The concept of authenticity has drawn much critical attention on the part of heritage professionals over the past couple of decades. The year 1994 marks a high point in the debate on authenticity; the year in which world authorities in heritage management gathered to discuss this issue in Bergen and Nara. The papers presented at the conferences held in these cities and the discussions that ensued clearly showed the highly complex nature of the concept of authenticity as used in the discourse of heritage. Concerns on defining authenticity and attempting at developing methods to apply this concept as a pragmatic principle in heritage preservation have always occupied a central position in the heritage profession. In short, the debate on authenticity is not a new phenomenon. In fact, it is perhaps as old as the heritage profession itself (Jokilehto 1994: 9–34; 1995: 17–45). However, it was with the inclusion of the 'test of authenticity' in the *Operational Guidelines for The Implementation of the World Heritage Convention* in the 1970s, where authenticity was considered in the four areas of design, material, workmanship and setting of the sites considered for inscription in the World Heritage List, that the term came to the forefront of debate[3]. It may have appeared that everything was said at Bergen and Nara about the concept, the history of its use, the difficulty of it and its philosophical complexities (Larson and Marstein 1994; Larson 1995). However, those discussions had not looked at the anxieties of conserving *living sacred sites* and the applicability of the standard concept of authenticity in such contexts.[4] Yet sacred heritage is perhaps the largest single category of heritage in the world (Stovel 2005: 2). Besides the fact that the Bergen and Nara meetings did not consider living sacred heritage in their discussions, there are other reasons to revisit the ideas that came up at those meetings, for those ideas opened up new ways of thinking about heritage, the beginnings of a new philosophical approach.

Yet more than a decade later, there is a need to bring more specificity to the question of how to enlarge the notion of authenticity in relation to living sacred heritage. In other words, as Stovel (1995) has also pointed out, the practical implications of the now broadened understanding of the criteria of authenticity need to be examined. This is what I am attempting to do here. Any discussion on authenticity has to take into consideration the positions and ideas expressed in the Venice Charter of 1964, the Bergen and Nara meetings on Authenticity and the *Operational Guidelines referred to above*. The papers presented at the Bergen and Nara meetings

constitute a critical body of ideas and arguments on the use and misuse of the concept of authenticity in contemporary culture and the heritage profession. The two meetings together can be considered as the most discursively critical moments in the recent history of the heritage profession. The ideas and arguments that formed the core of the Bergen and Nara meetings have to be considered seriously in our discussions. Further, such discussions will also have to take into consideration the basic ideas presented in the 1972 and 2003 UNESCO Conventions on the protection of cultural heritage.

Authenticity and the Venice Charter

When critically examining the concept of authenticity and its application to sacred heritage, one has to recognize that the notion, as affirmed in the Venice Charter, which is one of the most powerful foundational tools of the western philosophy on conservation, cannot be taken as the essential 'qualifying factor' concerning values and meanings pertaining to living sacred heritage. Article 9 of Venice Charter claims that the aim of restoration 'is to preserve and reveal the aesthetic and historic value of the monument and is based on respect for original material and authentic documents' (ICOMOS.org/charters.htm). But it does not address religious or ritual aspects or the 'community', 'living' and 'continuity' aspects of 'monuments' within the discourse it establishes, which Smith (2006) has identified as the Authorized Heritage Discourse (AHD). As shown by many writers (Ndoro and Pwiti 2001; Miura 2005; Wijesuriya 2005; Kato 2006; Ragunathan and Sinha 2006; Smith 2006; Taylor and Altenburg 2006), the AHD and the texts that peg the boundaries of this heritage discourse have no room for 'community', 'living' and 'continuity' activities of heritage in general, specifically of living sacred heritage. We should have no quarrel, however, with the drafters of the Venice Charter, whose efforts represented the outlook and the social and political anxieties of their particular historical moment. As the distinguished conservationist Raymond Lemaire, a co-signatory of the Venice Charter, mentioned during the preparatory workshop for the Nara meeting in 1994, the participants in the Venice Congress could not foresee the complexities of international preservation, and indeed there was no reason for them to speculate on the future (Larson and Marstein 1994: 131). They had only wanted to clarify issues pertaining to preservation of ancient buildings and their settings (Larsen and Marstein 1994: 131). The problem lies rather with the profession today, if and when current practitioners fail to see the social and political dynamics and anxieties of our present historical moment. The problem, as I would suggest, is the dogmatic treatment that the Venice Charter had received by the heritage establishment; it may not be an exaggeration to say that the Venice Charter has been elevated to the status of scripture.

Writing on authenticity and the World Heritage Convention, von Droste and Bertilsson opine that the time has come to reconsider the basic philosophy of the Venice Charter. They also indicate that it may never be possible to establish a single 'true meaning' of authenticity (1995: 14). As discussed below, authenticity is very much a contextual thing, since heritage itself is a contextually fashioned entity. Similar ideas and concerns were indeed put forward by many speakers at the Nara Conference; Herb Stovel, Henry Cleere, David Lowenthal, and Jukka Jokilehto all expressed concern over the ambiguous nature of the concept of authenticity, and also commented on or interrogated at varying levels the limited scope and potential of the accepted criteria on authenticity. They agreed that authenticity has to be understood in relation to the socio-cultural context and/or the historical continuity of the 'life' or 'spirit' of a monument or site (Larson and Marstein 1994; Larson 1995).

I would take this point of agreement as my own point of departure. Agreeing on something is one thing, but developing mechanisms and procedure for what is agreed is quite another. The Nara Document redefined the concept/criteria of authenticity, it underlined the need to consider the contextual nature of authenticity. While the concept itself needs no further redefinition, I argue, it is nevertheless necessary to consider or reconsider it in relation to specific aspects of the 'living' and the 'sacred' in living sacred heritage.

Authenticity and the World Heritage Convention

According to the *Operational Guidelines*, authenticity is manifested in several kinds of attributes. These are give in an hierarchical order: 'feeling' and 'spirit' are at the bottom of the ladder, while 'form' and 'design' are at the top. The *Operational Guidelines* also contain a special note on the difficulty of quantifying or objectively measuring attributes such as

'feeling' or 'spirit' of a heritage site. While I would take no major issue with this, I would suggest that it inevitably creates an uneasy feeling when dealing with heritage sites that are heavily encumbered/associated with traditional ritual practices and maintenance systems and methods. Privileging the fabric of a heritage and aspects directly pertaining to the fabric as more open for objective appraisal than intangible aspects, I would argue, possibly marginalizes the living/continuity aspects of heritage and places the appraisers of heritage on an uncomfortable footing.

Surely it is obvious that when it comes to living sacred heritage sites what matters most to the millions of devotees/worshippers who come to these places are the rituals in which they take part. These rituals in turn impart meanings both to the site and to the devotees. It is here that heritage professionals need to improve their theories and methods (Stovel 2005). The criterion of authenticity needs to be grounded in the parameters that manifest the living realities of living sacred heritage. Since the ground realities of each category of living sacred heritage are bound to differ, particularly in relation to different histories, authenticity must necessarily be processed through a discursive engagement that takes into account these dynamic living realities. Formulae on considering authenticity that are centrally concocted for universal use may not have much validity.

The dissent

Various authors have described the limitations of certain western standards of heritage management in relation to living heritage sites and cultural landscapes (Von Droste and Bertilsson 1995; Ndoro and Pwiti 2001; Baig 2003; Miura 2005; Wijesuriya 2005, 2007b; Kato 2006; Ragunathan and Sinha 2006: 490, 500–501; Taylor and Altenburg 2006: 267–282; Sully 2007). All these authors have directly or indirectly questioned or commented on the basic premises that constitute the western philosophy of conservation. The latter may be characterized by the following fundamental belief/thesis: heritage belongs in the past and the current generation is the guardian of heritage who must ensure its passage to the future in the full richness of its authenticity in terms of materials, design, and setting (see also Waterton 2005; and Smith 2006: 88–95). This thesis is at the core of the AHD. In contrast, the dissenting discourse argues that heritage does not belong in the past, but in the present.

Thus the meanings and values of heritage reside not merely in the fabric, but more in the way the heritage functions in relation to various communities that are linked with it.

It may now be pertinent to illustrate how certain dissenting voices have articulated the need for a new philosophy of conservation. For this I take Laurajane Smith and Gamini Wijesuriya, since both these scholars confront the established norms of heritage management both pragmatically and theoretically. Smith is an academic with a professional background and Wijesuriya is a professional with an academic background. For Smith (2006), heritage is a cultural process and is essentially intangible. It would be pertinent here to quote Smith's own words:

> The premise that 'heritage' is not a 'thing', it is not a 'site', building or other material object. While these things are often important, they are not in themselves heritage. While these things are often important, they are not themselves heritage. Rather, heritage is what goes on at these sites, and while this does not mean that a sense of physical place is not important for these activities or plays some role in them, the physical place or 'site' is not the full story of what heritage may be. Heritage, I want to suggest, is a cultural process that engages with acts of remembering that work to create ways to understand and engage with the present, and the sites themselves are cultural tools that can facilitate, but are not necessarily vital for this process.

What is important to note here is that Smith's thesis that heritage is a cultural process is a general one that is applicable to all types of heritage. Wijesuriya's work, on the other hand, has mainly addressed living sacred heritage directly. For Wijesuriya (2003: 42; 2005; 2007b: 96), the past does not reside out there behind us, but in the present. He has substantiated his thesis by taking the case of the restoration of the bomb-damaged Temple of the Tooth Relic at Kandy, Sri Lanka, which is a World Heritage site. The bomb explosion damaged only the 'fabric of the temple' but not the function, not the meanings, not the values.

What emerges from both Smith's and Wijesuriya's arguments is that heritage is essentially a living thing and, by implication, there is no 'dead heritage'. Heritage is the way or the manner that people think about and communicate with a place that is signified

as heritage (Lowenthal 1985; see also Dick 2000, quoted in Smith 2006: 44–45; Harvey 2001). Many others (Bouchenaki 2007; Jokilehto and King 2000; Jokilehto 1994) have also expressed their dissatisfaction or concern on the current status of thinking on.

In order to accommodate the dissenting voices that have emerged as a response to growing demands and political and social issues that surround heritage in various parts of the world, it is necessary that the current discussions in heritage management reconsider the criteria of authenticity. Since authenticity is the criterion that also holds the integrity of a heritage, this can be considered a cardinal term that guides the entire spectrum of heritage activities pertaining to a heritage site.

Reconsidering 'authenticity' in relation to living sacred heritage

The Nara Document on Authenticity marked a major turning-point in the way heritage professionals think about authenticity. It affirmed and institutionalized the importance of considering cultural diversity when interpreting authenticity. It broadened the limits of the concept of authenticity. However, it remains a 'fabric'-bound formulation. This is not because of what it mentioned, but because of what it did not mention. It is the voices that have been made silent that make the Nara Document a 'fabric'-bound thing. In the manner that the Venice Charter couldn't mention that revealing and preserving of religious or functional values of a monument as an aim of restoration, the Nara Document couldn't mention the need to consider such aspects as 'livingness', 'continuity' and 'original function' of a heritage when interpreting authenticity. The absence of these terms is of great importance in the current discussion since 'livingness', 'continuity' and 'original-function' constitute the core values of a living heritage site, in particular a sacred one. These attributes make a living sacred site an entity of the present rather than a thing belonging in the past. As such, by implication, heritage in general and living sacred sites specifically are politically charged sites that are readily invested by contending interests and become contested terrain.

It should be added that the qualifier 'living' involves values that may not be found in the case of other types of heritage. A cultural property may be termed 'living' when the original function, as perceived and planned by the original creators, is preserved. This means that the community connection to the heritage is also preserved and therefore the spatial aspects of the heritage is understood to be evolving and changing (Wijesuriya 2005: 30–31; 2007: 59–66). The other important qualifying term that we are concerned with in this study is 'sacred'. Sacred is treated here as synonymous with religious. At the risk of tautology, heritage can be considered sacred when it has a history or associations that show belief in or reverence for a deity, a religious teacher or a unique individual, and when, by implication, it is believed by the faithful to be sacrosanct and inviolable. When a property possesses both the above aspects, it can be considered living and sacred.

Nine years after the Nara Document, in 2003, the next most important discursive and self-critical meeting on heritage thinking was organized by the ICCROM, in Rome. This was the 'Forum on Living Religious Heritage: Conserving the Sacred' (Stovel, Price and Killick 2005). However, unlike at the Nara and Bergen meetings of 1994, the professionals who gathered at this meeting mostly discussed pressing pragmatic issues that one encounters in the field when one confronts traditional custodians, associated communities, and dynamic realities of living sacred heritage. The papers presented in the forum showed the limits of currently established heritage thoughts and methods when confronting these specific stakeholder and need sets. What unfolded in the papers presented was the story of our profession's inability to come into terms with the realities of a form of heritage that is predominant across the world and to address the local and regional political concerns related thereto. As Dean Whiting (2005: 180) observes in relation to Maori heritage, 'technical conservation knowledge is not enough to deal with the complexities of recognizing and maintaining the cultural and spiritual values of a site or place'. This captures the essence.

Living heritage in the era of globalization
Conserving living and sacred heritage is a very sensitive issue, in terms of both ethics and politics (Stovel, Stanley-Price and Killick 2005). Contemporary democratic politics and the power-amassing and mass-manipulating mechanisms it has generated in regions such as South Asia are closely associated with such heritage (Baig 2003). The heritage professional should not underestimate the fact that when a heritage is sacred and living, it can become a political tinderbox. The forces of globalization have thrown the political power of heritage in democratic political systems into high relief. Among the ethical values promoted by globalizing forces are individual rights, human rights and various notions of community. To be sure, these are progressive public and private values that are crucial to contemporary life. But when liberal notions of individuality and community are appropriated into extreme political movements they can become detrimental to the society at large by undermining the society's capacity for collective action in general. Such developments, as a rule, position heritage within a culturally and politically exclusive social discourse. For example, a global document like the UNESCO *Convention on the Protection and Promotion of the Diversity of Cultural Expressions* (2005), which asserts the sovereign right of states to formulate cultural policies, also authorizes the construction of the idea of 'national culture'. The diverse and ambitious objectives of the *Convention* provide sufficient grounds for extreme nationalist movements to formulate ideas about heritage that represent extremely exclusivist and chauvinist positions.

Restoration of the bomb-damaged Temple of the Tooth Relic

For the Buddhists of Sri Lanka, the Temple of the Tooth Relic is perhaps the most sacred place in the country. It also epitomizes the 'Buddhist–clergy–politics' of Sri Lanka's contemporary political culture. It is the site where presidents, prime ministers, ministers, leaders of political parties from right to left, and high government officials proclaim their allegiance to Buddhism and the *Sangha* (the Buddhist order), usually after taking their respective oaths of office. The Temple is visited daily by thousands of worshippers coming from all corners of the island, and the sacred tooth relic is considered and treated as the living Buddha. An elaborate series of daily rituals is performed to venerate the relic, according of a tradition considered to be very ancient. The Temple, which was originally built during the reign of Vimaladhramsuriya II (1687–1707) is also the key feature of the Kandy World Heritage Site, inscribed in 1988.

On 25 January 1998, the temple was bombed by Tamil LTTE guerrillas, who were fighting for a separate state in the north and east of the island. This was a catastrophic event for many Sinhalese Buddhists, who comprise 69 per cent of the population. It was one of the worst national disasters of twentieth-century Sri Lanka. Restoration of the temple was declared as a project of national importance. What is important for our discussion here is that the restoration was a story of negotiation and reconciliation of most of the accepted 'truths' as regards the restoration of built heritage. The political/social power of the Temple of the Tooth Relic as a living sacred site demanded and defined the methods that were actually used. These were far different from those advocated in the global documents we have already discussed. The concept of authenticity enshrined therein had no purchase in this case.

The traditional custodians of the Tooth Relic Temple laid out the basic principles regarding the decision-making procedures pertaining to the restoration of the Tooth Relic Temple. The country's heritage experts in the two state institutions that were involved with the restoration process, who are the authorized agents of restoration and conservation of heritage buildings, were transformed into mediators. They were not the ones who took the key decisions on what should be done, but the traditional custodians of the Tooth Relic Temple, the two high priests of the most powerful Buddhists sects, the *Malwatte* and *Asgiriya* chapters, and the lay custodian, known as the *Diyawadana Nilame*. Wijesuriya (2007) provides a full description of these procedures. Restoration was completed in 1999 with a brand new roof of copper tiles instead of the traditionally used terracotta tiles, new timber for the roof and newly-carved stone sculptures. This sounds like a major attack on the accepted notion of the concept of authenticity as enshrined within the Authorized Heritage Discourse. After restoration, the Sacred Temple of the Tooth Relic 'looks new'! It's true that the roof and the stone sculptures are not 'ancient' or 'historic' any more, but has this difference changed or made any effect on the 'authenticity' of the site? The authentic meaning or the authentic function or the authentic religious values of the site are intact. The Sacred Temple of the Tooth Relic is still sacred to the thousands of devotees who visit the place daily.

Conclusion

This case study shows that the internationally agreed and stipulated guidelines on conservation are not capable of accommodating and addressing either the anxieties or the aspirations of the local and the regional (Wijesuriya 2000). Considering the local context in managing heritage seems imperative, not simply because such an approach is 'politically correct' or because the local communities should be respected for their historical links with the site, but because the 'local cultural context' is also a 'globalized' context. People in the 'local cultural context' are fully aware of their cultural and political rights. Moreover, even more acutely, they are also aware of the power they can exert on local and regional politics: democratic or otherwise.

A reconsideration of the criteria of authenticity and the role of 'heritage experts' is needed because of the very special conservation issues that attend living sacred heritage. These issues arise partly because globalization, as indicated earlier in this chapter, is also an empowering process regarding cultural and identity (or representational) rights. How that empowerment works in a particular place is dependent on and defined by the political, social and historical dynamics of that place. Managing and manipulating these dynamics is vital also in order to achieve the profit-making intentions of corporate capitalism. Idealized notions of 'heritage', 'national culture' and 'past' play a pivotal role in fashioning these dynamics in the context of contemporary democratic politics in countries such as Sri Lanka and India. Living heritage sites, sacred or otherwise, are the emblematic venues upon which such idealized notions are enacted. These notions are thus both an expression and an idealized promise of ongoing political struggles. Living sacred heritage caught up in these political realities cannot be preserved or curated simply with the help of principles and procedures developed within a conservation philosophy that considers heritage to be a 'static' entity belonging in the 'past'. The authenticity of a living sacred site cannot be reduced to or bound merely to its material fabric, but has to be sought in the function, continuity, and livingness of the site. Any conservation procedure that does not pay respect to these aspects will be refused or rejected by the powers associated with living sacred sites.

Living sacred sites are the most vulnerable category of heritage sites. They can be obliterated or vulgarized by pious devotees, traditional custodians, and local politicians with the seemingly good intention of maintaining and developing them. Living sacred sites are politically powerful institutions and, by default, they are also wealthy. A top-down and expert-centred approach to conservation is not possible in these sites, as the associated communities and the traditional custodians are capable of wielding enormous influence. As such, not only are changed understandings of the criteria of authenticity required, but also a change in the role of the 'expert'. If, as I have argued here, authenticity lies in the function, the continuity, and the livingness of the site, then the role of the expert will have to be that of a mediator between standard conservation concepts and the aspirations and concerns of the traditional custodians and associated communities, most of which are local cultural and religious organizations. Any other role on the part of an 'expert' may not be tolerated, since living sacred sites are also informed by such redeeming and empowering global concepts as cultural rights, human rights, and sovereignty. If the heritage professionals fail to take cognizance of this reality, the above-mentioned players in the different local cultural settings will simply have their way without them.

The potential that local cultural and religious institutions have to refuse or disregard internationally-established norms and agreements is not merely a product of their own narrowly parochial natures or unthinking resistance to western norms, but is sustained by the ethos of cultural and political rights. In other words, cultural polarization in heritage and identity politics is not anti-globalization as such, but a way of interpreting and appropriating global norms in the light of local and regional aspirations and ambitions. In the realm of heritage and identity politics, such appropriation is another cultural consequence of globalization.

Notes

1   The rise of *Hindutva* politics in India, of Taliban politics in Pakistan and Afghanistan, and of *Jatika Chintana* politics in Sri Lanka are examples of the ultra-nationalist and religious political parties operating in South Asia. However, it is not my intention here to imply that these three examples are similar in their activities. There are great differences among them, while each operates on a platform of heritage and identity politics.

2   An excellent example is the use of the images of several nationally important Buddhist archaeological sites by the Hong Kong and Shanghai Bank (HSBC) in Colombo and its suburbs in 2004–05. A similar case is the adoption by the global fast-food chain McDonald's of regional or traditional food items and their names such as 'McFried-rice' or 'McChicken-tikka' in their Indian and Sri Lanka outlets.

3   Over the years, the World Heritage Committee has regularly revised these *Operational Guidelines*. I refer here to the version of 1977 but further on in this chapter to later versions, the most recent being that of 2008.

4   This is not a critique but an observation on their intended goals. As Stovel (1995) has mentioned, the focus of the Nara meeting was to achieve a set of universal standards while broadening the criteria of authenticity to accommodate heritage diversity. The Bergen and Nara meetings did achieve what they set out to grasp. The Nara Document of 1994 that resulted from the two meetings established the need to find a balance between universal values and cultural diversity in conservation. Both gatherings helped to institutionalize this idea in the *Operational Guidelines*.

REFERENCES

Baig, A. (2003) 'Managing cultural significance', *Seminar*, 530 (October): 14–17.

Bouchenaki, Mounir (2007) 'A major advance towards a holistic approach to heritage conservation: the 2003 Intangible Heritage Convention', *International Journal of Intangible Heritage*, 2: 106–109.

Dicks, B. (2000) *Heritage, Place and Community*. Cardiff: University of Wales Press.

Hazvey, D.C. (2001) Heritage pasts and heritage presents: Temporility, meaning and the score of heritage studies, *International Journal of heritage Studies*, 7(4): 319–338.

Holton, Robert (2000) 'Globalization's cultural consequences', *Annals of the American Academy of Political and Social Science*, 570: 140–152.

Jaffrelot, C., Gayer, L. and Maheshwari, M. (2008) 'Cultural policing in South Asia: an anti-globalization backlash against freedom of expression?', in Helmut Anheier and Y.R. Isar (eds), *Cultural Expression, Creativity and Innovation. The Cultures and Globalization Series*. London: Sage.

Jokilehto, J. (1994) 'Questions about "authenticity", in Knut E. Larsen and Nils Marstein (eds), *Conference on Authenticity in relation to the World Heritage Convention, Preparatory Workshop, Bergen, Norway, 31 January–2 February 1994*. Oslo: Riksantikvaren, pp. 9–24.

—— (1995) 'Authenticity and World Heritage', in K.E. Larsen (ed.), *Nara Conference on Authenticity in relation to the World Heritage Convention: Nara, Japan, 1–6 November 1994*. Trondheim: Tapir Publishers, pp. 17–34.

Jokilehto, J. and King, J. (2000) 'Authenticity and conservation: reflecting on the current state of understanding', in Galia Saouma-Forero (ed.), *Authenticity and Integrity in African Context*, Expert Meeting – Great Zimbabwe, Zimbabwe 26–29 May. Paris: UNESCO, pp. 33–39.

Kato, Kumi (2006) 'Community connection and conservation: intangible cultural values in natural heritage – the case of Shirakanai-sanchi World Heritage Area', *International Journal of Heritage Studies*, 12(5), September: 458–473.

Larson, Knut Einer (1995) 'Changing concept of authenticity in the context of Japanese conservation history', in *Nara Conference on Authenticity in relation to the World Heritage Convention: Nara, Japan, 1–6 November 1994*. Trondheim: Tapir Publishers, pp. 175–183.

Larson, Knut Einer and Marstein, Nills (eds) (1994) *Nara Conference on Authenticity in relation to the World Heritage Convention: Preparatory Workshop, Bergen, Norway, 31 January–2 February 1994*. Trondheim: Tapir Forlag.

Loventhal, David (1985) *The Past is a Foreign Country*. Cambridge: Cambridge University Press.

Miura, Keiko (2005) 'Conservation of a "living heritage site", a contradiction in terms: a case study of Angkor World Heritage Site', *Conservation and Management of Archaeological Sites*, 7: 3–18.

Ndoro, Webber and Pwiti, Gilbert (2001) 'Heritage management in Southern Africa: local, national and international discourse', *Public Archaeology*, 2: 21–34.

Ragunathan, Aparna and Sinha, Amita (2006) 'Rockfort Temple at Tiruchirapalli, India: conservation of a sacred landscape', *International Journal of Heritage Studies*, 12(6), November: 489–504.

Ratnagar, S. (2004) 'The case of Ayodhya', *Current Anthropology*, 45(2): 239–259.

Smith, L. (2006) *Uses of Heritage*. New York: Routledge.

Stovel, Herb (1995) 'Foreword: working towards the Nara document', in Knut Einer Larson (ed.), *Nara Conference on authenticity in relation to the World Heritage Convention: Nara, Japan, 1–6 November 1994*. Trondheim: Tapir Publishers, pp. xxxiii–xxxvi.

—— (2005) 'Introduction', in Herb Stovel, Nicholas Stanley-Price and Robert Killick (eds), *Conservation of Living Religious Heritage*. Rome: ICCROM, pp. 1–11.

Stovel, H., Stanley-Price, N. and Killick, R. (eds) (2005) *Conservation of Living Religious Heritage*. Rome: ICCROM.

Sully, D. (ed.) (2007) *Decolonizing Conservation*. Walnut Creek, CA: Left Coast Press.

Taylor, K. and Altenburg, K. (2006) 'Cultural landscapes in Asia-Pacific: potential for filling World Heritage gaps', *International Journal of Heritage Studies*, 12(3), May: 267–282.

UNESCO (2005) Convention in the Protection and Promotion of the Diversity of Cultural Expressions. Adapted in October 2005.

Von Droste, B. and Bertilson, U. (1995) 'Authenticity and World Heritage', in Knut Eins Larsen (ed), *Nara Conference on Authenticity in relation to the World Heritage Convention: Nara, Japan, 1–6 November 1994*. Trondheim: Tapir Publishers, pp. 3–15.

Waterton, E. (2005) 'Whose sense of place? Reconciling archaeological perspectives with community values: cultural landscapes in England', *International Journal of Heritage Studies*, 11(4): 309–325.

Whiting, D. (2005) 'Conserving built heritage in Maori communities', in H. Stovel, N. Stanley-Price and R. Killick (eds), *Conservation of Living Religious Heritage*. Rome: ICCROM, pp. 12–18.

—— (2003) 'Restoring destroyed historic sites', *Seminar*, 530 (October): 25–31.

—— (2005) 'The past is in the present, perspectives in caring for Buddhist heritage sites in Sri Lanka', in H. Stovel, N. Stanley-Price and R. Killick (eds), *Conservation of Living Religious Heritage*. Rome: ICCROM, pp. 30–43.

—— (2007a) 'Guest Editorial', *Conservation and Management of Archaeological Sites*, 8(3): 121–122.

—— (2007b) 'Conserving living Taonga: the concept of continuity', in Dean Sully (ed.), *Decolonizing Conservation*. Walnut Creek, CA: Left Coast Press, pp. 59–70.

—— (2009) 'The values of heritage in the religious and cultural traditions of Southern Asia', in A. Tomaszewski (ed.), *Values and Criteria in Heritage Conservation. Proceedings of the Conference of the ICS on Theory and Philosophy*. Florence: Edizioni Polistampa, pp. 73–78.

CHAPTER 11

A CONTESTED SITE OF MEMORY: THE PREAH VIHEAR TEMPLE[1]

Aurel Croissant and Paul W. Chambers

This chapter presents an analysis of the dispute between Cambodia and Thailand over an eleventh-century Hindu temple situated along the Thai–Cambodian border known as Preah Vihear (in Khmer) or Phra Viharn (in Thai). The authors focus on Thai perceptions of and discourses on this contested site of collective memory, with a view to capturing the historical evolution and contemporary status of perceptions as regards this inter-state heritage and memory-based conflict that has taken on special salience in the context of globalization.

Introduction

Throughout history, relations between the Southeast Asian kingdoms of Thailand (until 1939 Siam) and Cambodia have been rich in conflict. With their long contiguous boundary, Thailand and Cambodia have frequently experienced territorial disputes owing to incomplete frontier demarcation. By the end of the 1990s, however, it seemed that Thai–Cambodian border tensions had diminished considerably. In the past two years, however, the two nations have seen a recrudescence of long-dormant conflict over a disputed eleventh-century Hindu temple situated along the Thai–Cambodian border named Preah Vihear (following the Khmer language of Cambodia) and Phra Viharn (following Thai language). Since mid-2008, bilateral relations have rapidly worsened and worries are arising that the temple dispute may even trigger a full-scale war between both countries. Even though the Preah Vihear conflict is one of many unresolved border disputes in Southeast Asia, it has gained considerable international attention. What makes this conflict unique is the fact that it is not only about a tiny strip of land (4.6 square kilometers) and a ruined temple. Rather, the renewed acrimony derives from Preah Vihear temple's July 7, 2008 listing as a World Heritage site by the United Nations Educational, Scientific and Cultural Organization (UNESCO).

While the government of Thailand originally supported Cambodia's initiative in 2007 to apply for the temple's inscription as a World Heritage site, domestic political factors compelled Bangkok to withdraw from the plan and instead begin to work actively against it. Since the UNESCO decision in July 2008, various Thai governments have been under continuous and increasingly strong pressure to object to any future attempt by the Cambodian side to claim effective sovereignty over the temple or its surrounding area. Since October 2008 a number of minor armed skirmishes between Cambodian and Thai troops and other border incidents have taken place near Preah Vihear temple. In addition, other sites of territorial conflict have been drawn into the controversy, deepening the potential for armed conflict between the two nations.

Two sets of perceptions

For both Thailand and Cambodia, the temple is an important symbol of national identity and territorial sovereignty. It is also a site of contested memories about the shared history of both nations. For Cambodia, the temple is a symbol of the ancient cultural grandeur of the Khmer Empire as well as an icon of today's national independence. Thailand's claims towards sovereignty over Preah Vihear and the surrounding area of 4.6 square kilometers are perceived by many Cambodians as another episode in the centuries-long history of Thailand's attempts to 'steal' Cambodian territory and destroy Khmer identity. Further, for contemporary Khmer society, the glorious past of the Khmer Empire (for which temple sites such as Preah Vihear or the much larger Angkor Wat are symbols) and the shared Buddhist religion are the two major elements of 'Khmer-ness' (Hinton 2006). Khmer-ness, in a positive meaning, is mainly defined in terms of Khmer civilization and its 'rediscovered' temples. Therefore, as a historical site, Preah Vihear is also useful in evoking a former period of national glory in which the extent of the Khmer kingdom is imagined to be much more extensive than it is now, before it was emasculated by Siamese (and, in particular, Vietnamese) incursions.

However, 'Khao Phra Viharn' is also a site of collective memory for Thais and contains relevance for Thailand's national self-imagination. The geographic boundary of Thailand, and its representation as an impenetrable 'geo-body' (Thongchai 1994), is a core symbol of modern Thai nationalism. Beginning in the late nineteenth century, the Siamese government developed a policy of nation-building from above, which forced the transformation of the multi-ethnic society of Siam into a unified Thai nation. When the ultra-nationalist regime of Phibun Songkram came to power in 1938, it followed a policy of enforced assimilation of the various minority peoples into the mainstream Buddhist 'Thai-ness' in order to develop, in David Brown's words, 'the mono-ethnic character of the state' (Brown 1994). The propagation of a pan-Thai national identity against supposed or real separatism among Lao and Khmer-speakers in northeastern Isaan, in the Muslim-Malay-dominated southern areas of the former Sultanate of Patani and the minority areas of the Thai–Burmese borderlands allowed no government to accept territorial concessions since territory (together with religion and the monarchy) became the abstract manifestations of national identity. In combination with historical rivalries and the religious importance of the Preah Vihear temple and other contested temple sites, political disputes like the recent one are predestined to turn into armed conflict, especially because political elites in both countries time and again use border disputes for their own purpose to create social cohesion, strengthen national identity, and generate a sense of community.

It is with these concerns in mind that the following analysis is offered, in the hope that it might shed fresh light on the situation. Most of the scholarly literature analyses the Preah Vihear temple controversy with regard to the question of national reconstruction, identity politics and post-genocidal nation-building in Cambodia (Cuasay 1998; Kiernan 2001; Hilton 2006; Meyer 2009), while there are few studies available on Thai perceptions toward this or other territorial disputes along the Thai–Cambodian border. Regarding quality, most of the available literature is outdated, scarcely academic, and generally polemical. Therefore this study will analyze the conflict over the temple from the particular perspective of Thai political discourse and elite perceptions. The empirical evidence presented derives from field research conducted in Thailand in summer and fall of 2008. The aim of our intellectual enterprise is to map the contours and evolution of perceptions among Thai elite actors regarding the Preah Vihear affair given that it has only been elite actors – as opposed to powerless social groups – who have proven to be relevant in Thai foreign policy. The cardinal premise of this analysis is that boundary disputes generally derive from socially constructed images of 'nations' which, at the periphery, sometimes overlap, especially where frontier demarcation remains incomplete. In this context, the behavior of the countries' ruling elites, their foreign policy priorities and their approaches to threat recognition are shaped by perceptions inspired by national identity and ideologies embedded in cultural-religious frameworks. The need to manifest imagined notions of national identity suggests that the primary cause of the crisis of Preah Vihear is not the line of demarcation between Thailand and Cambodia. Rather, the primary cause is the dividing lines that run through contemporary Thai and Cambodian politics. However, to fully appreciate what the conflict entails, its relevance for the imaginative formation of boundaries based on collective memories of grandeur, as well as of threat and confrontation, and what hinders a more moderate stance in conflicts about the temple, it is necessary to examine the evolution and contemporary state of elite perceptions. The remainder of this chapter proceeds as follows. Section one outlines the historical dimension of the Preah Vihear temple conflict. The second section analyzes why and how the temple affair has been exploited by various political forces in Thai politics for their own political gains. The third and fourth sections form the main part of the chapter, in which we present an account of major Thai perceptions regarding 'Khao Phra Viharn' as expressed in Thai literature and the results of our extended interviews with respondents from different groups of elite actors representing alternate viewpoints.

The historical dimension of the Preah Vihear temple conflict

The roots of the current temple controversy reach far back into Thai–Cambodian history. Since the early 1900s, when Siam was forced to cede the temple complex of Preah Vihear to French colonial Cambodge in the Thai–French border treaties of 1904 and 1907, Preah Vihear has been the subject of a heated dispute between Thailand and Cambodia. In 1962, the dispute between the post-colonial Kingdom of Cambodia and the Kingdom of Thailand regarding territorial sovereignty over the temple complex went to the International Court of Justice (ICJ) in The Hague. Applying the principle of *qui tacet consentire videtur si loqui debuisset ac potuisset*[2] in its 9-to-3 verdict, the ICJ ruled that Cambodia's submitted map, devised by French surveyors in 1904, placed the temple area in Cambodia proper because Thailand failed to object after the 1907 French mapping was completed. This French-made map has thus become a core element of contention in what today is the most sensitive site of Thai–Cambodian border problems. Although Thailand did reluctantly accept the ICJ ruling on the temple complex itself, it has never recognized the map on which the ICJ based its decision. Indeed, Thais have insisted that the ICJ did not address the exact boundary line between Thailand and Cambodia at the temple area. Animosities between the two countries flared up in the late 1970s, as newly-Communist Cambodia squared off against a military-led Thai government. Following the Cold War's end in 1991 and Cambodian civil war in the mid-1990s, however, tensions diminished considerably and in 1992, the Preah Vihear temple reopened.

Although both privately- and publicly-produced Thai maps continued to show Preah Vihear in Thai territory (St John 1994), in 2004, a Thai–Khmer joint panel administering the Preah Vihear sanctuary was officially established and the temple became a permanent border-crossing.

Thai politics and 'Phra Viharn'

While border tensions between the two nations declined in the 2000s, in 2008 the Preah Vihear controversy suddenly gained prominence in Thailand. This was due primarily to an extra-parliamentary opposition movement (People's Alliance for Democracy or PAD) that was struggling to find an issue around which it could build a credible campaign against the elected government of the People's Power Party (PPP) and Prime Minister Samak (2008), who was close to former PM Thaksin Shinawatra (who was forced to step aside by a military coup in 2006).

The first phase of the controversy spanned from the administration of Prime Minister Thaksin Shinawatra (2001–2006) until January 2008. During this period, Thailand's governments first supported the Cambodian application for getting the temple listed as a UNESCO World Heritage site but later withdrew this support. Under Thaksin, Thailand established a commercially active and close relationship with Cambodia. While Thaksin had supported Cambodia's proposal, the military-backed government of PM Surayud (2006–2007) pressured UNESCO to postpone a decision on inscribing the temple until 2008.

The second phase of the temple dispute started in December 2007 when the pro-Thaksin government of Prime Minister Samak was elected to office and initiated a more conciliatory policy toward Cambodia. In 2008, Cambodia submitted a boundary map of Preah Vihear. Thailand's National Security Council approved it in June, despite much public opposition and indignation in the army. Though Thailand's judiciary blocked the agreement, UNESCO voted to inscribe the monument on July 7. Thereupon, PAD activists crossed into the 4.6 square kilometer disputed area between the two countries, pursued by the Thai military. This set the stage for the exacerbation of violent tensions between Thai and Cambodian forces during the second stage of the controversy, in which the temple issue turned into a weapon of the People's

Alliance for Democracy against Thaksin's PM Samak, allegedly a 'nominee' of Thaksin. In May 2008, the PAD and pro-PAD elements within the media and the main opposition party, the Democrat Party, alleged that there were links between progress on Preah Vihear and maritime gas/oil/casino concessions in Cambodia for Thaksin. The Democrats included as the rationale for an up-coming government censure vote that Samak had compromised national security by signing a communiqué with Cambodia over Preah Vihear. Though the governments of Thailand and Cambodia worked to reduce tensions over the border temple during the summer of 2008, PAD and Democrat opposition to these talks contributed to their breakdown. As a result, the conflict escalated. In October, following another bloody incident at the temple, the PAD demanded the PM's resignation. Ultimately, the temple's name had become an anti-government rallying cry for both the PAD and the Democrats.

The third and, for the time being, last phase in Thailand's domestic controversy over Preah Vihear evolved in December 2008, when anti-Thaksin Democrat Abhisit Vechachiwa became Prime Minister. Initially, the Abhisit government sought to improve relations with Cambodia. But following yet another bloody clash at Preah Vihear, bilateral tensions again mounted in April 2009. Talks immediately took place over diminishing troop numbers along the border. In September 2009, PAD demonstrators again attempted to storm Preah Vihear but were pushed back. Despite negotiations aimed at de-escalating tensions, Thai–Cambodian boundary clashes have become increasingly common at Preah Vihear and Thai–Cambodian relations, at the time of writing, remain at a high level of hostility.

Preah Vihear temple in Thai literature

The PAD and the Democrats manipulated the issue of Preah Vihear to boost Thai nationalism against Thaksin. The Democrats, in 2008 heading the parliamentary opposition, sought to oppose the pro-Thaksin government in any way possible. Yet once in power, the Democrats followed a policy of moderation regarding Preah Vihear. Despite the fact that the temple issue became a focus for protest as it provided a potent symbol for the opposition campaign, the current conflict is also embedded in the broader context of the social construction of images of Thai national identity. The following analysis presents a description of the way the Thai scholarly literature defines the nature of the Preah Vihear conflict. While there is little literature available either in Thai or English, what has been published allows for the conclusion that, traditionally, Thai perceptions (as expressed in writings) of Cambodian claims to territorial integrity have been fraught with a combination of mistrust, condescension, and abhorrence. Still, some recent Thai viewpoints reflect a potential transformation in traditional attitudes.

Overall, four perspectives tend to dominate the Thai literature about Thai–Cambodian relations in general and the Preah Vihear temple complex in particular. Even though the appearance of these four distinct views follows a temporal sequence, in contemporary Thai literature the four coexist; in this sense they represent contentious and contested narratives of Thai history, collective memory and identity which to some extent contradict each other.

The first and earliest Thai perspective, founded upon notions of state-centrism and sovereignty was both nationalist and irredentist. This perception, emanating from the worldview of the Thai monarchy and its attendant military, tended to place Cambodia in a negative light and it has often pervaded Bangkok's policy toward Phnom Penh, contributing to a latently sour relationship. It formed the Thai meta-historical discourse regarding the Thai–Cambodian border. Writings such as M. Sivaram's *Mekong Clash and Far East Crisis* (1941) and, more recently, Manich Jumsai's *History of Thailand and Cambodia* (1988, 2001) manifest a Thai perception emphasizing the survival and preservation of Thailand, in terms of territory, monarchy, and nation, against threats of incursions from French colonial Cambodge (within Indochine) as well as from Cambodia itself.[3]

A second perspective on the Thai–Cambodian frontier paralleled the growing Cold War of the 1950s and 1960s. The politically dominant actors at this time were Thailand's military and monarchy, who were concerned with maintaining Thailand's territorial integrity with Cambodia but also winning a Communist insurgency. Furthermore, during this period, a number of Western studies appeared (Gordon 1966; Liefer 1967; United States Department of State 1966). On the Thai side (cf. Khien 1983), the literature published in this period generally emphasized Thai national security concerns along the Thai–Cambodian border in the face of foreign-inspired Communist dangers. Such fears guaranteed the primacy of the military and monarchy as the principal pillars of the country's national security.

During the 1990s, a third perspective expressing a curious mix of suspicions toward but also hopes for accommodation with Cambodia appeared as Cambodia arose out of its civil war and Thailand's role in the Mekong basin began to grow. This perspective mirrored the growing number of actors from different segments of Thai society who held contentious views on Thai history and the Preah Vihear case. In addition to 'established' opinion leaders such as the military and the monarchy, who had previously shaped the contours and contents of Thai national identity by creating their own version of historical truth, new social actors now provided their particular narratives of national history (see, for example, Suchita Ghosh's *Thailand: Tryst with Modernity*, 1997).

A fourth Thai perspective on Thai-Cambodian territorial disputes emerged in the mid-1990s. It is represented by the writings of historian Thongchai Winichakul in his highly influential monograph *Siam Mapped: a History of the Geo-Body of a Nation* (1994). He defines geo-body as a 'man-made territorial definition which creates effects – by classifying, communicating, and enforcement – on people, things, and relationships'. It is an effect of modern geographical discourse and is crucial to a nation's identity (Thongchai 1994: 17). Further, Thongchai emphasizes that Thai perspectives toward territorial disputes correspond to the Thai geo-body's need to differentiate 'we-ness' from 'otherness.' 'Since the "Khmer" are "cowardly" and "opportunistic",' they only attack Thailand when she is most vulnerable. Ultimately, Thongchai offers a refreshingly postmodernist historical approach to explaining how Thai perceptions of 'territoriality' and 'nation' have probably contributed to continuing border disputes with Cambodia today. Among certain Thai academics, Thongchai's perspective is popular, but the majority of Thais still view Thai–Cambodian border relations through either a national security or free trade lens.

A flurry of books were published in Thai in 2008 coinciding with the growing entanglement over the sanctuary. Some of these emphasized the need for closer cooperation on border issues but most stressed Bangkok's desire to stand firm against losing any territory to Phnom Penh. An example of these works is Rom Bunnag's *Khao Preah Vihear: The Last Time Thais Lost Territory* (2008). The book states that Thailand could only watch as Cambodia used the temple as a nationalist tool during the 2008 Cambodian election. Other books included Bowornsak Uwanno's *Documents Revealed: The Last Secret—Prasat Phra Viharn, 1962–2008* (2008), Anucha Paepornworn's *Exclusive: The Politics of Khao Phra Viharn* (2008), and 'Is the Boundary Demarcation Settled?' by M.L. Wanwipa Charoonroj (2008). The works by Bowornsak (2008) and Anucha (2008) offer accommodating views toward the frontier, while Wanwipa's work (2008) reiterates a traditionalist, nationalist polemic against the Cambodian government's behavior along the Thai–Cambodian boundary.

Elites' perspectives towards Preah Vihear at the height of the temple controversy

Ultimately, the aforementioned literature reflects the tenor of the times in which they were written. The views of the 1940s to the 1980s embrace a viewpoint in which the state seemed on the brink of destruction. As such, Thai perceptions toward the frontier emphasized suspicion, fear, and national survival concerns. The third perspective represents a possible move toward seeking accommodation with the Cambodian government on lingering border issues (though in 2008 there was a smattering of anti-Cambodian Thai literature). The fourth and last view, most prominently articulated by the famous Thai historian Thongchai Winichakul, provides a less nationalistic understanding of how the Thai–Cambodian boundary evolved historically.

In order to investigate how contemporary Thai standpoints in public debates compare to the perspectives identified in the (semi-)academic literature, a series of extended interviews with Thai respondents from various streams of Thai society were conducted in 2008, that is, at the height of anti-government demonstrations by PAD activists who used the Preah Vihear issue to mobilize society against the Samak and Somchai governments. Interviews were conducted with individuals representing four categories of people, each deemed to be relevant in influencing Thai public discourse and foreign policy because of their proximity to the center of Thai political power. The goals were to gauge these actors' perceptions of Preah Vihear (and other border issues) and to see how closely the standpoints reflected those in the literature. The four groups included persons close to the traditional powers (Privy Council and military), pro-Thaksin political parties, representatives of the Democrat Party, and extra-parliamentary forces.[4]

While traditional forces appear to be divided between ultra-nationalists and pragmatists on the issue of Preah Vihear, the Thai military's stand on the temple conflict seems to have been generally guided by the need to preserve Thai national security as much as possible. In the words of one respondent, given that 'the military sees itself as the defender of Thai nationalism' – which it had helped to create – it has been supportive of a hard-line nationalist policy toward Cambodia on the issue of Preah Vihear. It is worth mentioning, however, that former senior military officers also expressed a slightly more balanced opinion in interviews, stating the need for Thailand to be 'vigilant' along its border with Cambodia, but also expressing support for continued negotiations between the governments of both countries.

Those respondents representing nationalist extra-parliamentary forces (the PAD and conservative academics) exhibited the most traditionalist opinions of all respondents. As such, their positions reflected the more reactionary views expressed in the literature. The PAD especially took a nationalistic line toward the Khmer sanctuary, with leading members consistently criticizing PM Samak's first Foreign Minister Noppodon Pattama and Samak himself as traitors out to sell the nation. One PAD leader, in an interview with the authors, stated:

Khao Phra Viharn has become a spiritual center for both Thailand and Cambodia. Naturally, Thais are nationalist about it and they should be. Yes, it is difficult to resolve the Khao Preah Vihear issue. But we support soldiers fighting to protect Thai territory. And yes, it is Thai territory.[5]

Some conservative academics close to the PAD have also taken a tough line on the Thai–Cambodian border dispute. In an interview one of them stated:

If you talk to people living in the area of Khao Phra Viharn, they will tell you that it is Thailand's lost land. ... If former Foreign Minister Noppodon Pattama is not a traitor or corrupt (for agreeing to the UNESCO inscription), what is he? ... Clearly PPP and Hun Sen's CPP have a conflict of interest – a deal regarding Khao Phra Viharn. The deal over Khao Phra Viharn would have simply

helped PPP. PPP tried to fool everyone. National security should be the most important goal. Cambodia's UNESCO listing of Khao Phra Viharn does not assist Thailand's national security.[6]

Meanwhile respondents representing the pro-Thaksin camp in Thai politics supported cooperation with the Cambodian government to resolve disputes regarding the Preah Vihear temple which would allow for a win-win situation for both Thailand and Cambodia. Generally, the argument in support of this view was that Thailand would not lose a single square centimeter of territory, given that the map created by Cambodia for proposing Preah Vihear to UNESCO as a World Heritage site claimed nothing beyond what had already been granted to Cambodia in 1962. It is worth mentioning, however, that all governing political parties (be they pro-Thaksin or anti-Thaksin) tended to present a view that encouraged cooperation with Cambodia. For instance, both the pro-Thaksin governments of PM Samak Sundaravej and PM Somchai Wongsawat pushed for greater diplomatic efforts to bilaterally resolve the frontier temples issue, although the October 2008 clashes with Cambodia near Preah Vihear as well as the related PAD-encouraged Thai nationalism compelled the government to adopt a more confrontational attitude toward the Hun Sen government in Phnom Penh. When the Democrat-led coalition under PM Abhisit's government assumed office in late December 2008, the latter eventually sought greater cooperation with Cambodia. For instance, in September 2009, now leading a ruling coalition, the Democrats, under new PM Abhisit Vechachiwa and Foreign Minister Kasit Piromya, found themselves trying to live up to the anti-Cambodian nationalist rhetoric they had earlier preached (in conjunction with the PAD), while at the same time being desirous of improving ties with the Cambodian government. As such, both Abhisit and Kasit changed their polemic stances, with Abhisit now proclaiming that Thailand had not lost any territory to Cambodia.[7] The changed positions can best be understood in terms of political interest given that the Democrats' role as leading the political opposition had shifted to leading the ruling coalition, As a result, the Democrats' view, reflecting the temper of the times, was much more hard-line when it was in the parliamentary opposition and later, when it led the government, more cooperative toward Cambodia.

The issue of Preah Vihear, the adjacent territory, and other frontier temples has caused sizeable differences within Thailand's academic community. Some conservative, royalist-oriented academics have taken a more reactionary line to Thai–Cambodian border disputes, while other Thai academics appear much more eager for cooperation with Cambodia. Academics and journalists with strong relations to progressive civil society groups especially support greater use of diplomacy and promotion of peace between Thais and Cambodians, perhaps agreeing with the postmodernist literature of Thongchai (1994). Academics, such as Charnvit Kasetsiri of Thammasat University, suggest that the overlapping Preah Vihear area be declared a 'Peace-Land' to be developed for common people, although they assume that public support for this idea might be very low: 'We, present-day Thai (not Siamese), have been planted with these ultra-nationalistic emotions since the late 1930s, repeated and reproduced in the 1960s and again, right now, this minute'.[8] Another prominent so-called 'progressive academic' at Thammasat University states that although

> Cambodia uses the border temple issues as political manipulation [in] domestic politics and that the 4.6 sq kms is a tool of Thailand's traditional forces to destroy Thaksin ..., the disputed 4.6 sq kms should be a 'peace-land' governed by both countries. There should be a management process without demarcation. This is the perfect opportunity for Thai people to understand Thai culture vis-à-vis Cambodian culture. Thailand can use Preah Vihear as a tool to make peaceful conciliation.[9]

Aside from academics, Thailand's media has also been divided over Thai–Cambodian temple problems. Thai television and radio stations, dominated by the state and government viewpoints, have tended to transmit the view of the government of the day, while some independent print media have shown a nationalist disposition and support the PAD's view. This has included the newspapers *Daily News* and *Puchagan*. Other periodicals, including *Thai Post*, *Bangkok Post*, and *The Nation*, have been more even-handed.[10] However, in general it seems that most of Thailand's media is transmitting nationalist sentiments about Preah Vihear – a paradigmatic case of agenda-setting and mobilizing nationalist sentiment.[11] In sum, when it comes to perceptions of

Thai–Cambodian border problems, interviewees tended to either have generalist feelings toward Cambodia or, in some cases, dwelt on either the sea border or frontier temples. Moreover, there seem to be two distinct Thai perceptions regarding Thai–Cambodian issues. The first, as seen in discussions with respondents representing the military, Privy Council, PAD, or conservative academics, promotes a traditionalist, hard-line security stand toward the frontier. The second, representing the ruling coalition (be it led by the PPP/PT or the Democrats), endorses international cooperation, greater diplomacy, and mutual understanding to resolve the boundary conflict. The view of Thailand's leading parties (when in the parliamentary opposition) is somewhere between these two extremes. When the Democrats were in opposition, they were aligned with Thai nationalists. But once they led a coalition, their perceptions shifted toward bilateral cooperation. As for the PPP/PT, it too sought greater cooperation with Cambodia when it led a ruling coalition. The parliamentary opposition, freed from the responsibilities of guaranteeing foreign relations, has criticized the Abhisit government, shifting over to a stance similar to that of Thai nationalists. In essence, regarding the perspectives of the two political parties, each has seemed to depend on political calculation, driven by what happens to be most popular among their constituents at the moment.

Contested memories during the age of globalization

Taken together, the literature and interviews suggest first that different actor groups in Thailand have distinct interests which shape their perspectives toward the Preah Vihear temple controversy. Perhaps one could say that the general stance of each group depends on the societal or functional role each one fills. The Privy Council and military are responsible for national and monarchical security. As such, their standpoint tends to be hard-line. On the other hand, political parties in a ruling coalition (as well as the private sector in civil society) have tended to promote economic collaboration. Foreign Ministry officials also support cooperation through diplomacy, given that such tasks are part and parcel of Foreign Ministry responsibilities. Parties in the parliamentary opposition tend to support whichever side gives them the greatest leverage *vis-à-vis* the ruling coalition. The disparity in views among academics owes to the fact that different academic groups gravitate more closely to different ideological stances.

Second, perspectives are not static. For example, the perception of the parliamentary opposition, initially hard-line during July 2008, became more pragmatic by October. Finally, some groups' views are not monolithic. Elements within extra-parliamentary forces (e.g. academia) and the military have been shown to disagree in their perceptions toward Thai–Cambodian border issues. The 2008 Thai–Cambodian border crisis has clearly aggravated Thai nationalistic perceptions when it comes to territorial disputes with Cambodia. This has been proved most clearly in the recurrent tensions over Preah Vihear. Indeed, it seems that the dispute has created a snowball effect when it comes to other potential sticky issues along the frontier – other border temples, the sea boundary, and the delineation of the Emerald Triangle. Perhaps a combination of time and mostly well-established boundaries between what were once Siam and French Cambodia will endure long enough to allow for the two nations two amicably live side by side.

Still, Thailand's perspective toward the border depends on which group one is addressing – there are a myriad of views. Thailand's currently polarized domestic political arena has drawn on the subject of Thai–Cambodian boundary relations. Some reactionary groups among the extra-parliamentary forces (the PAD) have placed a negative twist on the PPP-led government losing Thai border territory to Cambodia. However, pragmatic civilian business/politician elites are increasingly trumping the influence of nationalist Thai actors, be they military or the PAD. Thus the Democrat party, initially critical of Foreign Minister Noppadon's agreement with the Cambodian government has become much more pragmatic. This trend bodes well for a quieting down of often tense boundary disputes. Greater economic and political cooperation along the border should meanwhile contribute toward more cordial Thai perceptions of Cambodia's role along the Thai–Cambodian frontier.

As mentioned at the beginning of this chapter, Preah Vihear has been the subject of heated controversies between Thailand and Cambodia since the early 1900s. Further, it is evident that old animosities were renewed with vigor since 2008 primarily for domestic political reasons. However, the temple dispute is also linked to issues of globalization,

such as the spread of new concepts of identity, boundary, and territory, represented, for instance, by architectural heritages of cultural grandeur. For many in Thailand 'Phra Viharn' is an emblem for the 'trauma' of losing territories as a consequence of the intrusion of Western concepts of territory, state, and nation into Southeast Asia in the late nineteenth to early twentieth century. The contested temple site and the surrounding area are registered in recent Thai memory as the Thais' land that was wrested away by *farang* ('Westerners'). The areas form a significant representative of the whole 'loss of territories' ideology in Thai public discourse that emerged first in the 1930s and 1940s and was later revived after the end of the Cold War, when the anti-West ideology had become stronger among those rightist and leftist groups in Thailand who saw capitalism and globalization as 'national threats'. The PAD nationalism is within this context. For conservatives and reactionary-rightists such as the PAD, the capitalist threat to the Thai nation at the beginning of the twenty-first century, which reared its head with the Asian financial crisis in 1997 and particularly during the government of telecommunications tycoon Thaksin Shinawatra, is similar in nature to the Western colonial powers' imperialism at the beginning of the twentieth century. While obviously distinct from the leftists' Leninist/Maoist anti-capitalist discourse of the 1970s,[12] these voices employ much the same anti-neo-liberalism and anti-globalization language which 'progressive' Thai intellectuals and social activists had adopted more than three decades ago, merging with royalist notions of 'sufficiency economy'. Hence, in the perception of many of the anti-Thaksin groups and conservative-elitist elements in Thai society, the Preah Vihear dispute since 2008 is another chapter in the long history of the Thai struggle against foreign domination, which began with Western colonialism in the nineteenth century.

Notes

1 To avoid confusion, this study uses the Cambodian word 'Preah Vihear' but notes the Thai usage of 'Khao Phra Viharn.' Neither usage is meant to convey bias on the authors' part. We would like to acknowledge the financial and logistic support provided by the Friedrich-Ebert Foundation for this study. In addition, we are indebted to our colleagues Sorpong Peou, Chris Roberts, Axel Schmidt, Puangthong Rungswasdisab Pawakapan,

Chap Sotharith and Siegfried Wolf for comments on earlier drafts of the manuscript.

2 'He who keeps silent is held to consent if he must and can speak.'

3 For a detailed analysis of the elite ultra-nationalist/militaristic Thai mindset during the 1930s and 1940s, which claimed the whole of both Laos and Cambodia, see Charivat (1985).

4 Overall interviews regarding Preah Vihear and other relevant topics of Thai–Cambodian relations and Thai politics were conducted with 34 respondents. Most interviews took place between August and October 2008, although a few were conducted in early 2009. Since many of the respondents requested confidentiality, we do not provide the full list of names in this chapter.

5 Personal interview with Phipop Thongchai, President of the Campaign for Popular Democracy and a leader of the People's Alliance for Popular Democracy, August 4, 2008.

6 Personal interview with M.L. Walwipa Charoonroj of Thammasat University, August 15, 2008.

7 Bangkok Post (2009b) 'PM: No Sovereignty Loss', September 13, 2009.

8 Email interview with Dr Charnvit Kasetsiri, Thammasat University, August 24, 2008.

9 Personal interview with Akharapong Khamkoon of Thammasat University, August 18, 2008.

10 Personal interview with Thepchai Yong, (head of Thai PBS), July 31, 2008.

11 Personal interview with former Secretary General of the Thai Campaign for Popular Media Reform Supinya Klangnarong, August 14, 2008.

12 In the 1970s, the Communist Party of Thailand contained both Marxist-Leninist and Maoist wings.

REFERENCES

Anucha Paepornworn (2008) *Exclusive: The Politics of Khao Phra Viharn* (in Thai). Bangkok: Thai Watana Panich.

Bangkok Post (2008a) 'Government Approves Secret Cambodia Temple Deal', June 17, 2008, www.bangkokpost.com.

Bangkok Post (2008b) 'Noppadon Releases Map, Claims Success', June 19, 2008, bangkokpost.com.

Bangkok Post (2009a) 'PAD Makes Demands on Preah Vihear', September 20, 2009, www.bangkokpost.com.

Bangkok Post (2009b) 'PM: No Sovereignty Loss', September 13, 2009, www.bangkokpost.com.

Bowornsak Uwanno (2008) *Documents Revealed: The Last Secret – Prasat Phra Viharn, 1962–2008* (in Thai), Bangkok: Chulalongkorn University.

Brown, David (1994) *The State and Ethnic Politics in Southeast Asia*. London: Routledge.

Charivat Santaputra (1985) *Thai Foreign Policy: 1932–1946*. Bangkok: Thammasat University.

Cuasay, Peter (1998) 'Borders on the Fantastic: Mimesis, Violence, and Landscape at the Temple of Preah Vihear'. *Modern Asian Studies*, 32 (4), October: 849–890.

Ghosh, Suchita (1997) *Thailand: Tryst with Modernity*. New Delhi: Vikas Publishing House.

Gordon, Bernhard K. (1966) *The Dimensions of Conflict in Southeast Asia*. Englewood Cliffs, NJ: Prentice-Hall.

Hinton, Alexander (2006) 'Khmerness and the Thai "Other": Violence, Discourse and Symbolism in the 2003 Anti-Thai Riots in Cambodia'. *Journal of Southeast Asian Studies*, 37(3): 445–468.

Khien Theeravit (1983) 'Thai-Kampuchean Relations', *Asian Survey*, XXII, (6).

Kiernan, Ben (2001) 'Myth, Nationalism, and Genocide', *Journal of Genocide Research* 3(2): 187–206.

Leifer, Michael (1967) *Cambodia: The Search for Security*. New York: Frederick A. Praeger.

Manich Jumsai (1988) *History of Thailand and Cambodia* (1st edition). Bangkok: Chalermnit.

Manich Jumsai (2001) *History of Thailand and Cambodia* (2nd edition). Bangkok: Chalermnit.

MCOT News (2008) 'Thai, Cambodian Army Stand-off at Another Disputed Temple Ruin', Thai Ministry of Communications and Technology, enews.mcot.net/view.php?id=6250.

Meyer, Sonja (2009) 'Preah Vihear Reloaded: Der Grenzkonflikt zwischen Thailand und ... Unsicherheit in Singapur'. *Südostasien aktuell*, 27 (4): 65–74.

Rom Bunnag (2008) *Khao Preah Vihear: The Last Time Thais Lost Territory* (in Thai). Bangkok: (publisher unknown).

Sivaram Madhvan (1941) *Mekong Clash and Far East Crisis: A Survey of the Thailand–Indochina Conflict and the Japanese Mediation*. Bangkok: Thai Commercial Press.

St John, Ronald Bruce (1994) Preah Vihear and the Cambodia–Thailand Borderland. *IBRU Boundary and Security Bulletin*, January.

Thongchai Winichakul (1994) *Siam Mapped: A History of the Geo-Body of a Nation*. Honolulu: University of Hawaii Press.

United States Department of State (1966) 'Cambodia Thailand Boundary' (*The Geographer*, International Boundary Study, No. 40 [Revised]-November 23, 1966). Washington, DC: Bureau of Intelligence and Research.

Wanwipa Charoonroj (2008) 'Is the Boundary Demarcation Settled?' (In Thai) Unpublished Manuscript.

CHAPTER 12

MEMORY AND IDENTITY AS ELEMENTS OF HERITAGE TOURISM IN SOUTHERN AFRICA

Susan Keitumetse, Laura McAtackney and Gobopaone Senata

The development of heritage tourism for and by local communities in southern Africa has the potential to heighten the need for the people concerned to define sources of cultural identity that can be expressed through such tourism. Archaeological remains, monuments and cultural landscapes are readily available for heritage marketing and consumption. But intangible and/or invisible aspects of heritage also exist, as storehouses of memory that can provide significant resources. Formulating identities on the basis of the latter is necessarily varied and often will not conform to conventional heritage management methods. The authors explore the potential for alternative approaches in Botswana and South Africa.

Introduction

Few studies of identity in South Africa refer overtly to heritage and memory as constituent sources. This is largely due to the fact that the field of heritage management is still evolving and, as such,

nuanced, transdisciplinary studies are seldom attempted. For some time now the assumption has been that '...memory research might currently be most productively practiced within the disciplines from which media and cultural studies borrow, rather than within the trans-disciplinary space of "memory studies"' (Radstone, 2008: 35), which includes the field of cultural heritage management. As a result, the conceptual discourses linking heritage, memory and identity remain incomplete and, precisely for this reason, if we wish to link heritage and memory, we have to deploy new ideas through which memory studies might be integrated into the field of cultural heritage management. This is our point of departure for a framework to establish the presence of what we term 'memorable identities' and extend their application within a tourism context. 'Memorable identities' are socio-cultural events that are remembered by living communities even though they may have occurred before the birth of individuals making up the community. The quality of being 'memorable' makes a heritage identity significant within a community. Our reference point here is communal memory, as detailed by Halbwachs (1992: 22) in his discussion of communal identity and its roots in individual, past realities. The very idea of community or communal memory implies that memory itself is only relevant if it is situated within a socio-cultural context. Hence community memory is ultimately social memory. Its potential uses as a source of heritage that can be aggregated, interpreted and presented for the consumption of others derives from an understanding that community or 'social memory is ultimately culturally conditioned' (McIntosh, 2000: 141) and therefore provides '...the arena in which metaphors, symbols, legends, and attitudes crystallize social action' (2000: 143) such as participation in heritage tourism activities.

Our analysis is also grounded in the notion of eco-tourism, understood as a form of tourism based on principles that include recognition of, and respect for, community cultures (Drumm and

Moore, 2002; Keitumetse, 2009). The principles of eco-tourism that distinguish it from the broader tourism enterprise and qualify it within a cultural heritage management model (Keitumetse, 2009) include benefits to the community, visitor education and self-determination (Zeppel, 2006). The International Ecotourism Society (TIES) defines eco-tourism as 'responsible travel to natural areas that conserves the environment and improves the well-being of local people' (Drum and Moore, 2002). The Botswana national eco-tourism strategy of 2002 adopted this definition, acknowledging that 'in Botswana eco-tourism refers to the country's cultural, as well as natural heritage, and great importance is placed on the active involvement (as opposed to mere participation) of host communities' (Republic of Botswana, 2006: 06). Although valued as a conservation tool, eco-tourism is also being used as a marketing tool for a particular market segment and has been criticized for focusing almost exclusively on satisfying the current traveller, and not on the impacts that such travel has on the cultural and ecological environments of the setting (Blamey, 1997; Fennel, 2001). This has prompted the authorities in both Botswana and South Africa to focus on the hosts or local communities as well as to explore alternative resources for enabling the practical implementation of eco-tourism (Keitumetse, 2009). Intangible heritage components have a potential to enable a profound implementation of eco-tourism, particularly in landscapes where tourism already thrives but where intangible heritage is or has been overlooked. Memorable identities in national parks and game reserves in Botswana as well as Robben Island provide relevant examples.

In recognizing the potential of memory in fields such as eco-tourism, it is also important to acknowledge its limitations. These arise from the tendency of both individuals and society at large to forget events or recall them erroneously (Basden and Basden, 1996; Connerton, 2008). These limitations require research approaches that invoke memory while carrying out community research that will later feed interpretations in eco-tourism. For instance, some scholars have relied on material culture (tangible heritage) to invoke the ability of different communities to memorize historical identities (Chronis, 2006). In contrast, memoirs (which are written narrations of events in the past) are conceived by some memory studies scholars as

placing memory outputs on a political level because memoirs are viewed as a practice (lived experience) that is subjective to the writer. Material culture as opposed to intangible culture is viewed as being purely functional since it is the viewer who interprets it, rather than being influenced by the interpretation contained in memoirs. For this reason, material culture is represented as a neutral information tool as opposed to memoirs, which are made up of information that is selected beforehand and presented to an observer for interpretation. This is more relevant in non-literate communities where memory as practice (or lived experience), somewhat synonymous with memoirs, provides a vital source of heritage knowledge.

The challenges applicable to memory as a source of cultural knowledge include, among others, the act and types of forgetting (Connerton, 2008) that have to be identified and explored before documenting memorable events in a community. Seven types of forgetting relevant to heritage tourism documentation have been identified by Connerton (2008): 'repressive erasure', 'prescriptive forgetting', 'forgetting that is constitutive in the formation of a new identity', 'structural amnesia', 'forgetting as annulment', 'forgetting as planned obsolescence', and 'forgetting as humiliated silence', the varieties of which highlight the various opportunities and challenges that belie ethnographic collection of historical narratives for use in heritage tourism. Furthermore, while considering the various means of forced or chosen, individual or communal forgetting one must also consider the varieties of remembering. For as Ashplant (2004: 47–65) has suggested, the very act of remembering is equally political and often reflects political decisions regarding whose narrative is worthy of remembrance.

In a broader heritage management framework, an international shift that recognizes both tangible (UNESCO, 1972) and intangible (UNESCO, 2003) cultural heritage resources has enabled the development of a platform in which memory can be recognized as a repository and source of identity. Consequently, the recognition of memory at the international level has to develop simultaneously with the formulation of formal strategies at a local level to manage intangible elements for use in arenas such as tourism. In this context, where collective memories can become sources of interpretation, material culture and intangible practices are equally indispensable as they both provide the basic sources from which identities are interpreted and presented. In general, however, memory and identity form elements of intangible heritage (UNESCO, 2003; Keitumetse, 2006) that are in a readily available format for use in tourist activities. Hence a guiding framework is necessary in order to structure implementation. With a view to defining such a framework, we shall explore two case studies. The first deals with memorable traditions associated with natural resource environments in Botswana while the other, from South Africa, concerns memorable cultural experiences within a highly political environment. Both examples have a material culture base, the first being a biophysical landscape (Okavango Delta, Botswana) and the other being a built institutional environment (Robben Island, South Africa).

Memory, heritage and tourism in Botswana and South Africa

The cultural resources management policies of both Botswana and South Africa address the tangible (Republic of Botswana, 1970, 2001; SAHRA, 1999) as well as the intangible aspects of heritage (SAHRA, 1999; Republic of Botswana, 2001). These provisions are complementary to existing and dominant legislation on natural resources management (Republic of Botswana Tourism Policy, 1990; Republic of South Africa ISRDS, 2000b; Republic of Botswana CBNRM Policy, 2007). Yet eco-tourism principles, in particular those that incorporate elements such as community empowerment and self-determination (Zeppel, 2006), actually broaden the opportunity to incorporate memory and identity as a way to diversify the tourism package and enhance the tourist experience (Keitumetse, 2009).

Several factors are responsible for the delay in the efficient use of memory in Southern African heritage tourism. In the Republic of South Africa the main problem has been a historical bias towards prehistoric (hominid) heritage that has dominated heritage interpretation for decades. The approach has excluded and/or neglected opportunities to incorporate communities' memorable identities as sources of knowledge. This predominant recognition of prehistoric heritage identity began in the 1900s and continued well into the early 1990s

when the post-apartheid government took over. The post-apartheid era (1994-present), however, has provided an outlet for the expression of memorable identities (collective identities that are remembered from generation to generation through memory). It has also modified heritage legislation in a way that recognizes memory sources as forms of heritage knowledge. For example, the South African National Heritage Resources Act, No. 25 of 1999, implemented by the South African Heritage Resources Agency (SAHRA) prioritizes 'new and previously neglected research into our rich *oral traditions and customs*' (SAHRA Annual Report, 2001: 3, emphasis added). Among non-literate societies, traditional knowledge, by its nature, is dependent on memory. The development of tourism at locations such as Robben Island therefore provides opportunities to tap into memory as a source of heritage knowledge as an expression of suppressed 'identities' imbued within collective memoirs.

The case study of Botswana draws on examining taboos and totems to illustrate the types of intangible heritage that are suppressed in the interpretation of protected areas perceived to be of value solely in terms of wilderness and wildlife. Botswana tourism has for a long time neglected the memorable identities of its human inhabitants in protected areas through a biased focus on high-paying wildlife and wilderness tourism devoid of cultural context. This approach has excluded and therefore suppressed selection, interpretation and presentation of intangible heritage associated with community cultural landscapes within protected areas (Keitumetse, 2009). Yet memory, as a store of knowledge relating to past human–environment interactions, could be tapped to explore and express unrepresented interactions using a heritage eco-tourism framework and obviously has the potential to diversify the wilderness tourism experience considerably.

In both cases – Botswana and South Africa – communities are at the heart of the discussion because they are the medium through which memorable identities are expressed. It is important to note that both sets of communities interact with heritage in limitless ways that cannot be attributed to memory alone. However, non-literate communities in some parts of rural Botswana, or in situations where literacy existed but could not be exercised, as in the case of apartheid South Africa, do rely on memory as a key source of historical events.

Botswana: taboos and totems

Within the broader heritage management literature, taboos and totems are considered intangible heritage, which, according to the UNESCO Convention, is a collection of 'practices, representations, knowledge, skills … that communities, groups and in some cases, individuals recognize as part of their cultural heritage' (UNESCO, 2003: Article 2.1). Taboos and totems are largely non-documented in most parts of Africa; in rural Africa, they exist to a large extent only in communal memory, except in a few cases where a missionary or explorer may have documented them, for example Willoughby in his 'Notes on Totemism of the Becwana' (1905), which is in present-day central Botswana. Both taboos and totems have been shown to have had an indirect impact on the conservation of natural resources (Colding and Folke, 1997).

In traditional Botswana society, a totem represents a symbol of honour of a particular tribe, clan, family or, in rare cases, individual (Knappert, 1985). A totem can be an animal, a plant or any other natural object believed to be ancestrally related to a group as a tutelary spirit (Smith, 2002). A majority of totems are portrayed and expressed in poems and folk songs passed from one generation to the next (Tlou, 1985). In contemporary Botswana, totems still act as virtual indicators of ethnic identity among communities. For example, the Baphaleng are associated with *phala* in local language (impala or *Aepyceros melampus*); the BaNgwato with a duiker; and the Bakwena with a crocodile, to mention but a few. Totems therefore mark a community's collective identity as well as retain and maintain a spirit of kingship within an ethnic group.

Taboos are profound social prohibitions relating to areas of human activity or social custom that are declared as sacred and forbidden (Colding and Folke, 1997). In this way, taboos were, and to some extent still are, traditional means that contain unwritten social rules which enable people to avoid making moral mistakes relating to environmental features that include natural resources (Colding and Folke, 2001; Baidu, 2008). Taboos are also transmitted from generation to generation through memory. For instance, in the area of study, where the totem is an animal, it became apparent that it is a taboo to kill one's totem as well as to kill those animals that one's totem feeds on.

Memories of taboos and totems

The overall aim of the research was to investigate the existence of taboos and totems attached to plants and animals as they are remembered by Sankuyo community members in Northwest district, Botswana (Senata, 2009). Sankuyo village is adjacent to the Moremi Game Reserve, one of the most pristine national parks in northwest Botswana. A segment of the research is outlined here to illustrate the potential relevance of memory in establishing community identity as it might be expressed through eco-tourism activities in environments rich in wildlife. The focus is particularly on taboos and totems as recalled by individual members of the Sankuyo community.

Although most of the community members no longer interact directly with the now-protected landscape, some members still 'remember' aspects of intangible heritage (taboos and totems) associated with that landscape – illustrating how cultural memory is a source of heritage knowledge. The documented ethnographies (Tables 12.1 (a–c) and 12.2; Figures 12.1 and 12.2) outline individual community members' recalled past interactions with the totems and taboos of the Okavango Delta landscape. They illustrate the forms of intangible heritage that can exist around protected natural environments and which can be used to enhance communities' identities with wildlife and landscapes. Drawing on this resource can facilitate meaningful community participation in three ways. First, heritage eco-tourism activities become media through which communities can reconnect with the protected environment. Second, selected communal identities can be interpreted for the purposes of up-market tourism and in the process provide a platform for community cultures that are currently overshadowed by the wilderness and wildlife resource. Finally, communal identities can enhance tourists' experiences by diversifying the wilderness and wildlife experience.

Suppressed identities relating to taboos and totems

Ethnographic research was carried out with purposive sampling of 20 young people (18–29 years) and 20 elder people (40–50+) from Sankuyo village in Northwest District, Botswana. The sampling strategy was informed by an understanding that

Table 12.1a   Gender of respondents

Gender	Frequency	Percentage
Male	16	40
Female	24	60
Total	40	100

Table 12.1b   Education level of respondents

Education	Frequency	Percentage
Never	19	47.5
Primary	4	10
Secondary	16	40
Tertiary	1	2.5
Total	40	100

Table 12.1c   Age of respondents

Age	Frequency	Percentage
18–23	16	40
24–29	4	10
40–49	9	22.5
50+	11	27.5
Total	40	100

with the generation gap, age becomes the most significant variable when it comes to the ability to remember traditional belief systems. The significance of age was observed as far back as the early 1900s by explorers working among Tswana societies who noted that 'It is generally quite useless to talk with young men about any of the old customs, they know so little, even of the lore of their own people' (Willoughby, 1905: 314). Building on this approach, 40 formal interviews were conducted in addition to five informal interviews with village elders from Sankuyo settlement (see Tables 12.1a, 12.1b and 12.1c).

Only responses to those questions that are relevant to this chapter are shown here, although several other questions were asked. One of the questions, 'Do you have totems?', was asked to establish knowledge, remembrance, and allegiance to the traditional practice. A majority (85 per cent) of the respondents consider remembering their traditional totems as a form of ethnic identity, irrespective of whether or not they observed them. Figure 12.1 indicates that the most common totems in Sankuyo settlement, as in other parts of Botswana, are those associated with animals. In contrast, Table 12.2 shows that taboos are mainly associated with vegetation, although animals also feature.

It became evident from the responses that the Sankuyo community still possesses memories relating to taboos and totems associated with the biophysical landscapes of the Moremi Game Reserve. The study also investigated the perceived role of taboos and totems as environmental

Figure 12.1 Totems practised by Sankuyo people of Northwest Botswana

Existing totems in Sankuyo settlement

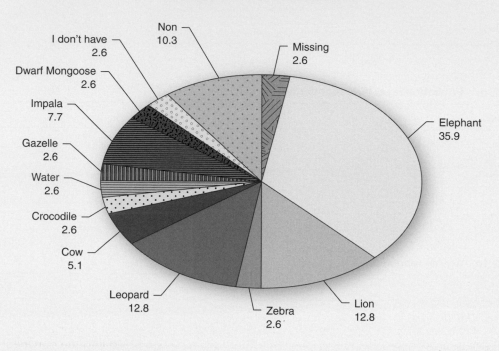

Non 10.3
I don't have 2.6
Dwarf Mongoose 2.6
Impala 7.7
Gazelle 2.6
Water 2.6
Crocodile 2.6
Cow 5.1
Leopard 12.8
Zebra 2.6
Lion 12.8
Elephant 35.9
Missing 2.6

Table 12.2 Taboos practised in Sankuyo area

Taboo feature	Frequency
Python	2
Motlopi or Shephards tree (*Boscia albitrunca*)	5
Mohata or Kalahari apple leaf (*Lonchocarpus nelsii*)	1
Mopororo or raintree/apple leaf (*Lonchocarpus capassa*)	1
Motawana (*Capparis tomentosa*)	2
Antbear	1

resources in the past. Figure 12.2 shows that although a significant number of youths (22.5 per cent) perceive the role of taboos to have been to scare people, the majority of respondents (32.5 per cent) believed that they helped protect animals and vegetation, as well as providing limits (27 per cent) as to how individuals interact with environmental features.

The most significant challenge regarding taboos and totems is fading memory as well as a profound lack of interest among young people (18–29), who are more likely to disregard traditional belief systems as a result of modern education ideals as well as the relocation from rural areas where the beliefs are practised (see Table 12.1b) to attend school and seek employment in towns.

Figure 12.2 Perceived past roles of taboos and totems in Sankuyo settlement area

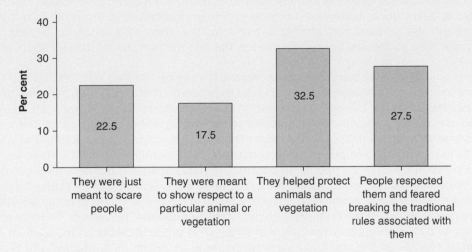

Box 12.1   The secret San

In the Kamberg Valley of the Drakensberg Mountains of KwaZulu-Natal, South Africa, there are Zulu speakers who have begun to reassert a San/Bushmen ethnicity. This was a surprising claim, as this is seen as a region where all San are supposedly extinct or fully assimilated into the dominant Zulu culture. They are recorded as a historical people who left traces of their presence in the numerous rock paintings found in rock shelters throughout these mountains (Vinnacombe 1976). They were said to have disappeared owing to colonial violence as settlers moved into the region (Wright 1971). Historians and archaeologists inadvertently perpetuate this idea on the basis of a narrow view of ethnic claims (Prins 2000; Francis 2009a).

These new claims began to arise after the ending of apartheid in 1994, but really emerged in earnest with the designation of the Drakensberg as a UNESCO World Heritage site in 2000. This community uses the ethnonym *Abatwa* to designate itself as a distinct people; their new identity is based on the notion of a primordial past of hunting and gathering and the community actively seeks out and references academic texts on heritage, especially those pertaining to the prolific rock art found here. The sites concerned have become instruments of cultural rejuvenation, but also contestation (Francis 2009b). There are other groups who affirm an indigenous status that claim the sites as well. Groups of San from the Kalahari Desert – thousands of kilometres away in an area that never had a tradition of rock art paintings – have claimed the rock art sites as their heritage too. They even filed a court interdict to stop the construction of a rock art museum to ensure they have input into the design and reap some of the benefits.

The newer flows of information and people (in the form of tourism here) that accompany globalization have created not only conditions that help make these heritage claims tangible in the form of jobs and other benefits, but also conditions for strife and conflict. The inscription of the entire region of the Drakensberg, which has literally thousands of rock art sites, on the UNESCO World Heritage List has created a national imperative to monitor and control the sites, further edifying the content in a fixed form based on a highly mythologized past that excludes the very people who live in the shadows of the mountains. The very conditions that led to their revival have now fixed the rock art as a lost culture relegated to the past and confined to a series of preset forms. Locals now manufacture copies of images for sale to tourists, and they copy directly from the rock art texts, thus forever freezing the art. Preservation is being done mainly for the gaze of foreign tourists, and the profits are by and large directed through the national and provincial parks for the state as a whole to benefit. What little income is redirected to the San is only directed to the San of the Kalahari through local and regional NGOs.

Yet it is not all negative, as the increased tourism in the region has had spin-offs for the entire community: jobs, increased economic activity and the improvement of roads and infrastructure in these previously neglected areas. The media have begun to acknowledge these changes (Mkhwanazi, 2003). The continued claims by the *Abatwa* have transformed management strategies for the rock art site, Game Pass Shelter, at the Kamberg Valley Nature Reserve that is open to the public. The *Abatwa* have been able to form a committee that is taken seriously by the management of the Reserve. They want the sites to be seen by as many people as possible, in part because it bolsters their claims, but also because it becomes part of public culture for everyone to enjoy and to gain an understanding of their past beliefs. And like the management, they have a stake in the preservation of these sites. Indigenous beliefs have been applied at the Reserve to avoid 'spiritual pollution' by visitors. Tourists are asked to rub their legs with indigenous grasses before entering. This process builds on the tourism experience and sensitizes tourists to the spiritual nature of the rock art to the local people. The history of the *Abatwa*, just as with many other previous hunter-gatherer peoples, is one of exploitation and abuse, but is also a history of creativity and survival despite the forces that have been aligned against them. So the challenge remains for the *Abatwa* to continue pressing for rights that include access to their heritage as they champion rock art conservation alongside their very claims to exist.

Michael Francis

References

Francis, Michael (2009a) 'Silencing the past: historical and archaeological colonisation of the Southern San KwaZulu-Natal, South Africa'. *Anthropology Southern Africa* 32(3 & 4).

Francis, Michael (2009b) 'The crossing: the invention of tradition among San descendents of the Drakensberg, KwaZulu-Natal, South Africa'. *African Identities.*

Mkhwanazi, Zanele (2003) 'Coming out: true stories of KwaZulu-Natal'. *The Witness*, October 10.

Prins, Frans (2000) 'Forgotten heirs: the archaeological colonisation of the Southern San'. In I. Lilly (ed.), *Native Title and the Transformation of Archaeology in the Postcolonial World.* Oceania Monograph, 50.

Vinnicombe, Patricia (1976) *People of the Eland: Rock Paintings of the Drakensberg Bushmen as a Reflection of Their Life and Thought.* Pietermaritzburg: University of Natal Press.

Wright, John (1971) *Bushman Raiders of the Drakensberg, 1840–1870: A Study of Their Conflict with Stock-keeping Peoples in Natal.* Pietermaritzburg: University of Natal Press.

Republic of South Africa

While post-apartheid South Africa's tourist strategies have continued to promote natural and prehistoric archaeological heritage, there has been a concerted attempt to incorporate many difficult elements of the recent past as part of the nation's heritage. Robben Island – specifically its Maximum Security prison and related built environment – is one example. While in some respects these approaches are holistic in their promotion of place through incorporating many aspects of the newly constituted 'Rainbow nation', including the modern and non-traditional, they largely allow interaction and understanding of a difficult past through the material remains with only piecemeal acknowledgement of intangible elements. Although the material remains of imprisonment are largely uninterpreted and left to tell their own story objectively (Sturken 2008), there is some evidence of the utilization of intangible elements. This is especially apparent in the overt use of these sites as places of understanding and reconciliation – as evidenced in numerous picture boards showing groups of ex-prisoners attending workshops at the site and onsite archives relating to political imprisonment that is continually used and added to.

The famous tourist attraction of Robben Island, 'Nelson Mandela's island prison' (Uzzell and Ballantyne, 1998: 7), is central to our exploration of the uses of memory, remembrance and the 'spirit of place', for it allows us to examine the purposes of preserving and reconstituting such sites as tourist attractions and the uses of intangible heritage in their presentation. The untapped potential of the use of memory, remembrance, the individual/communal stories and the challenges posed by the continuing role of ex-prisoners in the post-imprisonment interpretation will be explored in order to uncover how intangible memory can be used to heighten the potential of these sites as cultural, social and economic contributors. Furthermore, acknowledgement that many of these sites are in areas of outstanding natural beauty, with large rural hinterlands or areas as important for their natural ecologies as for their human stories, will be used to explore how such sites can be utilized for ecotourism through identifying the natural/cultural interactions and how they contribute to recognition of non-tangible heritage.

Prisons as heritage

Martin Carver (1996) has stated that archaeological heritage is largely assumed to comprise monumental remains whose value is self-evident and immutable. Therefore, he concludes, the conception of archaeological heritage tends to self-perpetuate as those elements that are assigned protection, and therefore are valued, often mirror existing heritage (Carver, 1996: 50). As such, it is clear that relatively recently constructed, and abandoned, prisons are not automatic choices as heritage, and it is a major statement to present them as such. Prisons as heritage are an unusual subset of heritage that is often associated with recent political upheaval or an atypical and heightened relationship between the state and imprisonment. In this respect, South Africa can be compared to states such as Northern Ireland, where prisons were not merely containers for those who were imprisoned by the state, but were places of identity creation, contestation, political power and often catalysts for change during

times of great social and political upheaval (McAtackney 2008). The significance of prisons in the breaking of apartheid and the creation of the new 'Rainbow State' is apparent not only through the sheer numbers of current and previous government ministers, including most famously Nelson Mandela, who spent much of their adult lives fighting an unjust political regime while imprisoned, but also in their treatment in the post-apartheid era.

The Truth and Reconciliation Commission (TRC) was established in 1995 as a transitory body tasked with ensuring the creation of a new Republic of South Africa (RSA) state based on the concepts of political forgiveness and reconciliation (Amstutz, 2005: 164). The decision to overtly forgive past wrongs in order to build a new more equal future ensured that whereas most states would choose to hide relics of a painful past – as is the case in Northern Ireland with the swift deconstruction of much of the security infrastructure post-Belfast Agreement (1998) – the South African state decided to not only retain these reminders of the recent painful past, but to promote them as heritage attractions. The actual physical remains of the prison sites tend not to be of great aesthetic or architectural significance; rather it is how they were used and their continued meaning that is central to their value. Therefore sites such as Robben Island not only stand as physical reminders of broader intangible experiences of injustice, prejudice and racism, they also encompass the forced hardship and inhuman conditions of individuals and communal prisoner groups. Robben Island is also unique in that its previous life, prior to apartheid, as a colonial prison, place of exile and hospitalization, confirms and reiterates later narratives of marginalization, detention and curtailed lives. In addition to these stories of human hardship are the environmental aspects of Robben Island, which are equally important.

While Robben Island has become an international symbol of hope over human suffering, the site is also recognized as a wildlife centre of great importance. It is home to the second largest penguin colony in South Africa and contains a wide variety of animals, birds, reptiles, insects and associated natural ecosystems and geology that are not only maintained, but also form part of tourist tours of the island. Robben Island is protected not only for its historic, built environment, but also as a protected nature conservation area and, as such, a balancing act between its cultural and natural resources has to be maintained. Interestingly, cultural and natural conservation are considered – as presented by the Robben Island website – as separate issues and cultural/natural interactions are not overtly considered, at least at this public presentation level (www.robben-island.org.za). A more holistic approach to the presentation of the site, which would consider how the environment shaped human activity on the island as well as how people lived in such a longstanding 'place apart', has been ignored in preference to a more piecemeal presentation. Inevitably, this leaves out the kind of environmental and historical contextualization that would add complexity and multi-vocality to this unique place.

Indeed, it is only since the end of apartheid that Robben Island was selected as a symbolically special site. Robben Island stopped holding political prisoners in 1991, it ceased to exist as a prison in 1996, and was swiftly adopted as national and international heritage site thereafter. After its closure in 1996, a museum was opened there in 1997 and the site was added to the World Heritage List in 1999. Currently, Robben Island is acknowledged as the most popular tourist attraction in South Africa. Its location, just 16 kilometres from Cape Town into the bay, is ideally placed both logistically and aesthetically for international and national tourists alike. Despite being a prison site, historic institutional landscape and wildlife reserve, it is probably the most famous example of prison heritage in the world, and is synonymous with its most famous past prisoner – Nelson Mandela. Mandela's connection to the site, despite the fact that he spent much of his imprisonment elsewhere, is such that the highlight of the visit for many tourists is his former cell, where it is possible to have one's picture taken 'behind bars', hear a recording of Mandela discussing his imprisonment experience and look at artifacts associated with him, which are housed behind glass in the cell. The cult of Mandela is such that his story, and the story of the African National Congress (ANC), can overshadow the many other narratives and intangible forms of heritage that could emerge from the site. The role of other anti-apartheid parties, with the Pan African Congress (PAC) in particular represented in effectively a private prison that housed its leader Robert Sobukwe from 1960 to 1969, is often underrepresented in this narrative. Equally forgotten are the

lives of those others who resided on Robben Island – the mentally ill, lepers, exiles, colonizers, workers – whose physical remains continue to demand attention. Furthermore, Robben Island continues to house permanent residents, with a population existing in the town both before and throughout apartheid, whose stories are not presented to tourists as they are bussed around the island.

The use of memory, identity and intangible aspects of heritage provoked by the wide range of material remains is an important means of providing multiple stories of place, especially in relation to sites like Robben Island, which have convoluted and sensitive recent histories. While maintaining and interpreting the remnants of recent conflict is a courageous policy for any government, there must be an impetus to continually revise the contemporary relevance of the site, ensuring that the interpretation evolves to be as representative and accountable as possible. Indeed, the South African government has acknowledged that the use of indigenous knowledge is 'rarely afforded any status' (Fabricus et al., 2003: 6). Whereas the use of ex-prisoners as guides is often interpreted as a means of demonstrating the authenticity of the visitor experience, a use of oral testimony and a means of enfranchising the previously silent, this approach is not without its critics. Harry Garuba (2007), whose recent studies at the University of Cape Town have focused on ex-prisoner tour guides at the site, has uncovered a difficult relationship existing between those who were previously incarcerated and the prison's new role as a place of tourism. With tour guides effectively portraying themselves as continuing to exist 'behind bars' due to their self-perceptions as being poorly treated and restricted in their freedom of interpretation, it is clear that any official interpretation of place will always be contested.

The exploration of Robben Island as more than a governmental tool for symbolizing past wrongs by incorporating the multiple tales the place has to tell would demonstrate the truly unique assets of Southern African heritage. Without such a broad approach, the interpretation of the site as either 'natural' or 'cultural' denies the integrated and interdependent relationships between the two. It also denies indigenous and local knowledge that can effectively enrich interpretations and ensure that experiences are truly rooted locally instead of being presented as generic, globalized ones. The connections to local knowledge and resources, both natural and cultural, can be made in ways that are truly sustainable and accountable.

Conclusion

Both case studies from Botswana and the Republic of South Africa have illustrated how memory can become a source of heritage knowledge that can be expressed through tourism. The example from Botswana has shown how forms of intangible heritage, such as taboos and totems, can be overlooked, although they are central to natural landscapes and

with human interactions with wildlife. Traditional knowledge systems once inventoried and interpreted according to local communities' knowledge can be juxtaposed with scientific knowledge of the environment, thus enabling a balanced narrative that reconnects communities with these protected areas now fenced off. Robben Island not only symbolizes the 'triumph of the human spirit', but is also a wildlife reserve of some importance. Hence an integrated and interdependent presentation of both its cultural and natural values could be made by incorporating its multiple, sometimes contradictory, narratives and meanings in a balanced way.

REFERENCES

Amstutz, M.R. (2005) *The Healing of Nations: The Promise and Limits of Political Forgiveness.* Oxford: Rowman and Littlefield.

Ashplant, T.G. (2004) 'War commemoration in western Europe: changing meaning, divisive loyalties, unheard voices'. In T.G. Ashplant, G. Dawson and M. Roper (eds), *The Politics of Memory: Commemorating War.* London: Routledge, pp. 263–270.

Baidu, N. (2008) 'Indigenous Beliefs and Biodiversity Conservation: The Effectiveness of Sacred Groves, in Ghana for Habitat Species Conservation', *Journal for the Study of Religion, Nature and Culture,* 2(3) 285–407.

Basden, B.H. and Basden, D.R. (1996) 'Directed forgetting: further comparisons of the item and list methods'. *Memory* 4(6): 633–653.

Belfast (Good Friday) Agreement (1998) *The Agreement.* Belfast: Northern Ireland Office.

Blamey, R.K. (1997) 'Ecotourism: the search for an operational definition'. *Journal of Sustainable Tourism* 5(2): 109–127.

Carver, M. (1996) 'On archaeological value'. *Antiquity* LXX: 45–56.

Chronis, A. (2006) 'Heritage of the senses: collective remembering as an embodied praxis'. *Tourist Studies* 6(3): 267–296.

Colding, J. and Folke, C. (1997) 'The relations among threatened species, their protection, and taboos'. *Journal of Conservation Ecology* 1(1): 6.

Colding, J. and Folke, C (2001) 'Social taboos: "invisible" systems of local resource management and biological conservation' *Journal of Ecological Applications* 11(2): 584–600.

Connerton, P. (2008) 'Seven types of forgetting'. *Memory Studies* 1(1): 59–71.

Drumm, A. and Moore, A. (2002) *Ecotourism Development: A Manual for Conservation Planner and Managers. Vol. 1: An Introduction to Ecotourism Planning.* Arlington, VA: The Nature Conservancy.

Fabricius, C., Matsiliza, B. and Sisitka, L. (2003) *Report to the Department of Environmental Affairs and Tourism and GTZ Transform: Laws, Policies, International Agreements and Departmental Guidelines that Support Community-based Natural Resource Management Type Programmes in South Africa.* Pretoria: Department of Environmental Affairs and Tourism.

Fennel, D.A. (2001) 'A content analysis of ecotourism definitions'. *Current Issues in Tourism* 4(5): 403–420.

Garuba, H. (2007) 'A Second Life: Museums, Mimesis, and the Narratives of the Tour Guides of Robben Island', in N. Murray, N. Shepherd and M. Hall (eds), *Desire Lines: Space, Memory and Identity in the post-apartheid city.* London: Routledge, pp. 129–144.

Halbwachs, M. (1992) *On Collective Memory* (edited and translated by Lewis A. Coser). London: University of Chicago Press.

Keitumetse, S. (2006) 'UNESCO 2003 Convention on Intangible Heritage: practical implications for heritage management approaches in Africa'. *South African Archaeological Bulletin* 61(184): 166–171.

Keitumetse, S. (2009) 'The Eco-tourism of Cultural Heritage Management (ECT-CHM): linking heritage and 'environment' in the Okavango Delta and Kalahari regions of Botswana'. *International Journal of Heritage Studies* 15(2–3): 223–244.

Knappert, J. (1985) *Myths and Legends of Botswana, Lesotho, and Swaziland.* Amsterdam: Brill Archive Publishers.

McAtackney, L. (2008) 'Historical Archaeology at the Maze/ Long Kesh Prison Site, Northern Island'. Unpublished PhD Thesis, Department of Archaeology, University of Bristol.

McIntosh, R.J. (2000) 'Social memory in Mande'. In R.J. McIntosh, J.A. Tainter and S.K. McIntosh (eds), *The Way the Wind Blows: Climate, History, and Human Action*. New York: Columbia University Press, pp. 141–173.

Radstone, S. (2008) 'Memory studies: for and against'. *Memory Studies* 1: 32–37.

Republic of Botswana, Ministry of Environment, Wildlife and Tourism (2002) *National Ecotourism Strategy, 2002*. Gaborone: Government Printer.

Republic of Botswana, Ministry of Environment, Wildlife and Tourism (2007) *Community Based Natural Resources Management Policy*. Gaborone: Government Printer. Republic of Botswana, Ministry of Home Affairs (2001). *Monuments and Relics Act No. 12 of 2001*. Gaborone: Government Printer.

Republic of Botswana, Ministry of Home Affairs (1970) *Monuments and Relics Act 1970*. Gaborone: Government Printer.

Republic of Botswana, Ministry of Trade, Industry, Wildlife and Tourism (1990) *Tourism Policy*. Gaborane: Government Printer.

Republic of South Africa (1999). *South African Heritage Resources Agency*. Pretoria: Government of the Republic of South Africa.

Republic of South Africa (2000) *Integrated Sustainable Rural Development Strategy (ISRDS)*. Pretoria: Government of the Republic of South Africa.

Robben Island website. www.robben-island.org.za. Accessed December 2009.

Senata, G. (2009) 'The Role of Taboos and Totems in Conservation of Animals and Vegetation: A Case Study of Sankuyo Settlement'. Unpublished undergraduate research report-GEC431-Introduction to Wetlands Research Course. University of Botswana, Harry Oppenheimer Okavango Research Centre, Maun.

Smith, E. (2002) '*Toteism under threat*'. A paper presented at the Biodiversity Reporting Award held in Accra, Ghana, from November to December 2001.

Tlou, T. (1985) *A History of Ngamiland 1790 to 1906: The Formation of an African State*. Gaborone: Macmillan Botswana.

UNESCO (1972) *Convention for the Protection of the World Cultural and Natural Heritage, adopted 1972*. The General Conference of the United Nations Educational, Scientific and Cultural Organization (UNESCO) meeting, Paris, 17 October–21 November 1972, 17th session. Paris: UNESCO.

UNESCO (2003) *Convention for the Safeguarding of the Intangible Cultural Heritage, adopted 17 October 2003*. The General Conference of the United Nations Educational, Scientific and Cultural Organization (UNESCO) meeting, Paris, 29 September–17 October 2003, 32nd session. Paris: UNESCO.

Uzzell, D. and Ballantyne, R. (1998) *Contemporary Issues in Heritage and Environmental Interpretation: Problems and Prospects*. London: The Stationery Office.

Willoughby, W.C. (1905) 'Notes on the totemism of the Becwana'. *Journal of the Anthropological Institute of Great Britain and Ireland* 35(2): 295–314.

Zeppel, H. (2006) *Indigenous Ecotourism: Sustainable Development and Management*. Wallingford: Cabi.

CHAPTER 13

MULTIPLE HERITAGES, MULTIPLE IDENTITIES: THE SOUTHWEST INDIAN OCEAN

Rosabelle Boswell

The southwest Indian Ocean is a complex space of multiple heritages and shifting identities. This chapter focuses on the people of three island nations: Mauritius, Zanzibar and Madagascar. It is argued that in these nation-states heritage, memory and identity are categories of practice. However, the deployment of heritage for the purposes of tourism, nation-building and ethnic memorialization is turning heritage into a category of analysis. Moreover, the formalizing of heritage risks homogenizing identity and recasting heritage and memory as uncomplicated reflections on the past. The current phase of globalization is complicating the process of abstraction: identity and memory are becoming more deterritorialized, ordinary people are actively engaged in the casting of their own identities and new spaces are challenging the continued salience to identity of heritage and memory-making.

On multiple identities

Heritage, memory and identity are closely intertwined in Mauritius and the southwest Indian Ocean region. They are also categories of practice as Mauritians actively create and experience heritage and memory-making. Increasingly, however, and as UNESCO and/or other policy-making entities promote heritage management in the region, heritage, memory and identity are becoming categories of analysis. This process is not uncomplicated because in Mauritius and in the southwest Indian Ocean region in general, identities are creolized and experience the impact of globalization. In this chapter, I discuss the intersection of these diverse factors and their implications for identity. It is argued that Creoles, historically identified as people of mixed descent and defined today as the descendants of slaves, actively experience heritage and memory-making. However, this is mostly a hybridized heritage reinforced by multiply-situated memories. The present political reconstruction of Creole identity encourages the disaggregation of this heritage and the reallocation of memory. The necessity of this disaggregation to nation-building and transnational heritage discourse is becoming more evident and complicates things further. Furthermore, Creoles are modern subject citizens, they also actively engage with globalization, participating in the capitalist economy and contributing to global cultural flows. For instance, the Creole Sega (traditional music), is now available online and Sega musicians relate their processes of production via podcasts. Creoles and Mauritians in general also participate in global cultural events designed to elevate and commemorate Creole cultural production. The latter produces a different kind of Creoleness, one that supersedes local political interventions and is anchored in a globalized rhetoric of hybridity.

Before exploring these issues more fully, I shall offer a brief historical overview of Mauritius and the southwest Indian Ocean, followed by a suggested theoretical frame, before engaging with the dynamic of heritage, memory and identity itself.

History

Mauritius is a Creole island (Vaughan 2005). Although successive waves of European immigrants arrived from the seventeenth century, these populations did not successfully segregate the population. The Dutch, French and the English intermixed with people from neighbouring Madagascar and Africans from the Swahili 'corridor', producing a mixed biological progeny and creolized society. As a result of slavery and colonization similar situations evolved elsewhere in the southwest Indian Ocean region. By the mid-1800s, islands such as Zanzibar and Madagascar became integrated into the social and political economy of the southwest Indian Ocean, producing vibrant, creolized social worlds.

The slaves arriving in Mauritius contributed to the establishment of a Creole group on the island. Fifty-five per cent of slaves arriving in Mauritius were captured off the east African coast and consisted of Makua, Ngindo, Yao and Ngoni peoples (Teelock 1998). The remaining 45 per cent were captured in Madagascar, as the Malagasy royals there sought to expand their power and influence by selling slaves to the French in exchange for weaponry. In the French territories (i.e. Mauritius and Reunion) slaves were subject to the *Code Noir* or 'Black Code' of 1723, which forbade marriage or sexual relationships between whites and blacks and severely impacted on slave dignity and independence. However, this did not prevent creolization or cultural cross-fertilization. Furthermore, when the British imported Indian indentured labourers to replace the loss of slave labour after 1835, Creoles (the ex-slaves and people of mixed descent), intermarried with and socialized with the Indians. They also participated in Hindu rituals such as those of the Kalimai cult and had experience of the Baharia Puja and the Muslim Ghoon rituals. These early experiences encouraged multicultural and hybridized perspectives and practices.

In the period leading up to and after political independence in 1968, an era of identity construction ensued. Creoles were publicly cast as Christians and people of mixed heritage. In public discourse, they became a people without culture or identifiable roots. Politically, they became members of a residual category. They were portrayed as distinct from descendants of Asians (Hindus, Muslims and Chinese), who were 'identifiable' as 'bounded' ethnic groups. Socially, they endured a range of discriminations and were kept at the bottom of the

socio-economic hierarchy (Boswell 2006a). In the early 1990s, this state of affairs was questioned by revisionist historians, anthropologists and Creole activists. Creole identity was re-anchored in slave history and Creole heritage was recast in the mould of slavery. Newspapers, television programmes, workshops and conferences reinforced this narrative and contributed to public memory-making. Part of this reconstruction of Creole identity had already begun in the Seychelles, mainly because the socialist government there had, since 1979, made Kreol (the French/Swahili mixed dialect spoken by African descendants) a national language. In the late 1990s, exchanges with African diaspora groups across the Atlantic (Guadeloupe, Nevis, and St Kitts) and with Africans (Mozambique and Senegal) encouraged the globalization of Creole identity and the reinstatement of its slave heritage. The present form of heritage preservation has also become more appealing, because heritage has become a source of therapy mediated by public officials.

Elsewhere in the southwest Indian Ocean, the reconstruction of slave descendant identities is not happening so smoothly. In Zanzibar, a place from which thousands of slaves had been exported to the Indian Ocean islands, the Afro-Zanzibari identity remained firmly anchored in its creolized history. In the aftermath of the Revolution of 1964, a distance developed between islanders and mainlanders. The socialist regime of Tanzania recruited Zanzibari for its army and rendered life difficult for the islanders. Increasing foreign direct investment in Zanzibar's tourism sector in the 1990s reinforced the distance between islanders and mainlanders, as the former accused the latter of stealing their profits. Moreover, nostalgic references to the era of the sultanates in Zanzibar and visits by the wealthy to Oman are currently challenging the localization of identity and memory.

In Madagascar, a country of great biological and cultural diversity, memory-making plays an important role in the maintenance of history. Past ethnic conflicts are actively remembered and stories of past conflicts are used to reinforce historical and ethnic divisions. However, there are many spaces for inter-ethnic interaction. And, in spite of successive oppressive political regimes, the Malagasy have managed to produce and maintain a dynamic (evolving) cultural heritage. Part of the reason for this is because even at the highest levels of government (as was shown in the January 2009 crisis), important references to memory, culture and identity are still made. State officials do not use these references to remind people of past conflicts. They are using such references to encourage dialogue and creativity.

Theorizing heritage, memory and identity in the southwest Indian Ocean

Given the multiple processes, levels and densities of identity construction in the southwest Indian Ocean, a poststructural approach to heritage, memory and identity offers an ideal theoretical frame. This reveals the discursive aspects of identity as it manifests itself in creolization and diasporization and allows for an understanding of the deterritorialization process. Ethnographic observation shows that while government and tourism authorities seek to homogenize, nationalize and package identity and memory, the islanders continue to creolize identity, personally manage heritage and embed these in wider a political context.

The islands under discussion in this chapter are creole societies. This necessitates an understanding of creolization as the creative combination of, and exchanges taking place between, already heterogeneous cultures (Bolland 2009: 106). Creolization is most pronounced in 'new' world societies like the ones found here (Eriksen 1999). In these, usual or dominant structural constraints may be absent, allowing for cultural hybridization. Such contexts offer 'a multifaceted, fluctuating and contested terrain' (Chavez and Zambrano 2005: 6) in which identity, memory-making and heritage management can flourish. The Creoles, a people of mixed descent living in the southwest part of the region, contributed to 'multiparty interactions of material, ideational, and discursive phenomena, among others, in complex relationships characterized more often than not by an unequal distribution of power' (Yelvington (2001: 240). Such processes involve 'forgetting [and] abandoning the illusion of authenticity' (Vergès 2005: 3), the initial acceptance of dominant cultural discourses and, later on, the conscious reconstruction of identity. To critically reflect on identity we need to consider historical impacts on creolization. Both mercantile capitalism and global capitalism encouraged agency and creativity in creolization (Cohen and Toninato 2009: 7). However, the smaller scale, slower pace, lower proliferation but more tightly controlled spread of mercantile capitalism 'localized' the

process. Today, heritage and identity are metacultural products influenced by fast transnational flows in a globally controlled environment. One thing that has not changed is that creolization (then and now) involves complex processes of 'internal restructuring, inventiveness and reflexivity' (Cohen and Toninato 2009: 13).

In the past three decades, UNESCO's elaboration and implementation of various standard-setting legal instruments (recommendations and conventions) have resulted in the salvaging and safeguarding of heritage worldwide. Critiques of UNESCO's approach suggest that the process has solidified the concept of culture, reified identities and presented heritage as a gift to be passed on from one generation to the next (Bouchenaki 2003). In this region governments might appear to have uncritically adopted this perspective on heritage. A closer look, however, reveals a more complex picture. The examples presented below show that although entangled with the broader processes of nation-building, identity expression exists beyond the control of global and national institutions. Heritage is in fact lived and memory-making exists for personal and group purposes.

Mauritius

Since their arrival on Mauritian soil, Africans and their descendants have lead difficult but culturally productive lives. They cultivated an intimate knowledge of their natural environment, developed local healing remedies, produced music, dance and contributed to oral history. These contributions were, and are, most marked in Le Morne village, situated on the southwest coast of the island. As noted previously, they intermixed with ethnically different others (Africans and Indians), producing a creolized society. However, in local discussions, Creoles were rarely defined as a creolized people but as blacks, doubly lacking in 'culture' as slave descendants and as black people. In July 1998, Mauritius and UNESCO co-hosted an international conference on slavery. This 'started' a public discussion on the situation of ex-slaves on the island and initiated the public and positive redefinition of Creoles as slave descendants. This was followed by the declaration of 1 February (the date of abolition) as a national holiday and the unveiling in 2007 of a slave *lieu de mémoire* (site of memory) outside the village of Le Morne.

Other developments included the creation of a Le Morne Trust Fund (LMTF) and the increasing involvement of the National Heritage Foundation (NHF) in the management of Creole heritage. The LMTF and NHF audited existing skills in the surrounding region and designed a management plan to harness local skills to enhance socio-economic integration. The management plan was prepared as part of the nomination process for Le Morne to be inscribed on the World Heritage List (see chapter 2), which it was, in February 2008. The village was subsequently also named as the 'Le Morne Cultural Landscape'. This obviously required residents of Le Morne (ethnically and socially diverse) to be cast as cultural subjects and to perform a version of Creole identity, as well as to draw upon publicly articulated memories to inform their identity. This has also led them to be inclined (because of their situation in a mapped landscape), to perceive the slave heritage as their only inheritance (see Boswell 2005).

International business is also reifying this view and experience of heritage. In 2008 there were plans to construct an Integrated Resorts Scheme (IRS) in the buffer zone of the Le Morne World Heritage Site (WHS). The IRS commissioned a Cultural Heritage Management Plan, partly to allay public and government concerns about tourism development near the WHS. The careful scrutiny of hundreds of interviews, audio-visual data and documentation on the region revealed the inter-ethnicity of the region and the hybrid heritages of the Creoles. Not only were Creoles involved in marine-based livelihood activities, such as fishing and the trapping of crustaceans, they also cultivated land on the hill-slopes of neighbouring villages. All of the villages were criss-crossed by pathways which were integral to the development of sociality, encouraging play among children, the collection of healing herbs, the development of stories and the creation of communities. Older generations revealed that Le Morne's neighbouring villages were populated mostly by Creoles but that some Indian families were also settled there, had ritual sites known as Kalimais and performed religious rituals such as Ganesh Chaturtee.

Creole villagers professed that they did not consider these ritual spaces to be part of 'their' heritage and Marathi (Indian) inhabitants did not consider the trails on the hills to be part of 'theirs' either. However, when questioned about more recent history – specifically the settlement of the region in the inter-war years – there was greater consensus on shared heritage. These included healing traditions, cuisine, entertainment and crafts. Interviewees also referred more readily to their membership in a working class. From these statements it could be inferred that, first, the notion of heritage is associated with specific cultural aspects (i.e. belief) and, second, that heritage is influenced by time. These two inferences impact on personal and lived heritage, memory and identity in Mauritius. They challenge the public discourse on heritage, which tends to associate heritage with geographically located, whole cultures and in so doing they also undermine the official re-allocation (or even control) of memory and identity.

Counter-impositions appear in the globalization of the Mauritian economy. Towers, residential and business complexes, the cyber city and dual carriageways remap the landscape, circumscribing 'culture' to parks, museums and other 'bounded' locales. Via performances at the Caudan Waterfront in the capital, Port Louis, Mauritians can now encounter the public presentation of their identity and heritage, particularly on Independence Day. These performances also underscore the diasporization of identity, showcasing bounded identities in a 'host' space. Global cultural flows in the form of music, dance and film also reaffirm certain diasporic links. For instance, the screening of Bollywood films at the Caudan Waterfront in Port Louis (and elsewhere on the island) helps to maintain what Rushdie calls 'imaginary homelands' for Indian descendants (1991: 10). For Creoles, diasporization is also occurring, but their diaspora has a truly imaginary homeland, one located in the Creole diaspora rather than Africa.

New spaces resulting from the current phase of globalization are also producing areas where the re-inscription of identity, memory and heritage is not attractive. These spaces are virtual (such as online communities), commercial and deterritorialized (call centres), 'inhabited' by young Mauritians of diverse ethnicities. Such spaces challenge the public articulation of heritage and identity, creating new loci for them. For instance, in the call centres, young Mauritians have to 'negate' their identity and heritage and display intimate knowledge of the current weather and other trivia in order to 'pass' as Europeans for their distant overseas interlocutors. The temporal recreation of the self in the call centre disturbs hegemonic processes of identity reconstruction and memory reallocation. In the next, brief example, I discuss identity, memory and heritage in Zanzibar.

Zanzibar

Zanzibar, an archipelago east of Tanzania, contains an ethnically diverse population (of over 1 million) and a rich cultural heritage. The archipelago consists of two main islands, Unguja and Pemba, and other smaller islets, such as Mafia Island situated in the south. Zanzibar has a history of slavery and colonization. Like Mauritius, it has an ethnically hierarchical society, a powerful minority, a Creole population, plantations and slave descendants. Zanzibar is 90 per cent Sunni Muslim, the inhabitants speak Swahili and the archipelago is about an hour by boat from the African mainland. Islam in Zanzibar is creolized and adherents draw on indigenous African beliefs to enhance their religious practices. The presence of Arabs along the Swahili coast since the arrival of Islam in Africa, the migration of Shirazi Persians to Zanzibar since the early 1800s, as well as the current phase of Arab globalization has encouraged the Afro-Shirazi to develop a creolized identity. Nostalgic references to the Arab world have not been easy for Omani descendants, mainly because Zanzibar is a semi-autonomous state (part of Tanzania) and the socialist regime compelled citizens to relinquish their ethnicity. The violent revolution of 1979 also asserted the control of Tanzania over Zanzibar and ever since, segments of the Afro-Shirazi population have sought to assert their independence. Part of this assertion is public (through party politics), but much of it is private and involves aesthetic expression (see Boswell 2006b) and references to ancestral homelands, memories and identities.

The confluence of Arab, African, European and Indian cultures led to the inscription of Stone Town on the World Heritage List in 2000. UNESCO describes Stone Town as a space which represents a harmonious blend of cultures. In the inscription, there is little mention of its violent and segregated past. The Stone Town museum, which is called the House of Wonders, appears to have obliterated the role of Arabs in the persecution and enslavement of Africans. Nostalgic and romanticized accounts of the Arab descendant princess Salme blur the

memory of slavery. The exhibition on European (particularly British) colonization of Zanzibar is relegated to a small side room, as if to diminish its significance in the memory of Zanzibar. Other spaces, such as the tourist shops in Stone Town, attempt to inscribe an alternative memory for tourists – one indicating the aesthetic contributions of Zanzibari to their society.

The Reclaiming Women's Space in Heritage project also makes use of aesthetic references in memory-making but it also highlights the contributions of women to intangible heritage via storytelling, performance and art. Participants included women living in and around Stone Town, Afro-Shirazi and those more closely identified with Omani ancestry. The digitization of the women's contributions allows for the consumption of these memories globally and the reassertion of histories locally. Specifically, women are encouraged to tell stories about their childhood in Stone Town, a main theme being 'the way it was'. International cooperation between Zanzibar and Sweden also lends this project a global dimension.

Research in Zanzibar in 2004, 2006 and 2007 revealed that in Stone Town there were both private and public efforts to revive memory and identity. In this case, however, national heritage entities did not play a major role in the recasting of identity, memory and heritage. These processes were being undertaken by the inhabitants themselves, as women, curators, shop owners and photographers. Until the end of research in 2007, institutes of heritage management in Zanzibar were mostly involved in the management of built heritage, which they saw as imperative for the maintenance of Stone Town's World Heritage status.

Madagascar

Research on memory-making and identity in Madagascar is very rich (Sharp 1993; Cole 2001; Evers 2002; Lambek 2002; Larsen 2000; and Graeber 2007). These studies investigate how the Malagasy, consisting of some 21 ethnic groups spread over a biodiverse landscape, have responded to various forms and levels of oppression from their first settlement on the island in the first century CE. Heritage and memory are categories of practice in Madagascar, as 'ordinary' people make use of their unique surroundings and rich history to craft extraordinary cultural and religious practices. This process, along with earlier phases of globalization in the region, strongly suggest that heritage is shared, creolized and is managed beyond the reach of nationally-based institutions. This example supports the argument that memory is an active engagement with the past. It feeds heritage by encouraging and allowing for a diversity of personal and social expressions. As Madagascar's history is interwoven with the history of Mauritius and Zanzibar, memory is also deterritorialized. Specifically, current discourses on slavery, encouraged by global institutions like UNESCO (in their project *La Route de L'Esclave*) revive memory and also confirm the regionalization of slavery and identity.

Unlike Mauritius, Madagascar has a large population of 19 million. The vastness of the landscape and the island's modern history of political instability mean that memory-making and identity construction is taking place in a less 'controlled' space, inscribed by multiparty interactions among unequal participants. These inequalities were initially reinforced during the nineteenth century, when the political expansion of some the islands major groups (especially the Merina) encouraged the transformation of Madagascar into a slave-exporting nation.

Today, the history of slavery is deeply inscribed in the memory and identity of the Malagasy. Lambek (2002) and Sharp (1993) indicate the influence of slavery on ancestral veneration. They suggest that the dead have a role to play in memory-making and advise the living based on their (i.e. the dead) historical experiences. What the dead offer varies and the possession of the living by the dead, manifest these memories in the present life. Graeber (2007) discusses how the memorialization of violence informs present decisions about who to vote for, who to marry, who to socialize with and on what basis. The salience of memory-making to political subjectivity in postcolonial contexts is evident (Cole 1998: 105) and, in Madagascar memory, is about 'power in the present'.

Preliminary research on heritage management in Madagascar in 2009 revealed that the Sakalava people living in the archipelago of Nossi Be off the northeast coast of Madagascar were keen to relate stories of how the dead help them to remember. Stories of their ancestors' historical encounters with the Merina not only revive memory, but also contribute to the ethnic and magico-religious demarcation of the landscape. One story concerns the pursuit of Sakalava by Merina slavers on the mainland. Rather than succumb to capture, the leader of the Sakalava compelled his co-ethnics to commit mass suicide by drowning. This they did and to this day, the river where the Sakalava drowned cannot be crossed by Merina descendants. Even the mentioning of a Merina, while crossing the river, can bring catastrophe.

However, there are also multicultural spaces which challenge boundary-making. In Dzamandzar on Nossi Be, a ritual space established by the Sakalava prince Zafinfotse, has become a space of ancestral veneration for the community's Christians and Muslims alike. Such spaces are beyond the 'reach' of heritage institutions and indicate the lived heritage of the Malagasy. Similarly, the children of mixed ethnic marriages are required to adhere to the ancestral taboos of their father. It is the duty of the ethnically different mother to ensure that these taboos are observed.

In 2009, Madagascar also experienced a political crisis. Andry Rajoelina, a former mayor of Antananarivo, ousted Marc Ravalomanana, the president of Madagascar. During the crisis Rajoelina, symbolizing the youth and 'future' identity of Madagascar as a globally competitive, modern emerging nation-state, accused Ravalomanana of using magic to obtain power and to maintain the consent of the masses. *Sampy* or talismans were apparently found on the grounds of the presidential palace. The accusation cast Ravalomanana as a traditionalist, disconnected from the current phase of modernization and globalization. It also revived the memory of Madagascar's 'cruel' Queen Ranavalona. This example shows that in the postcolonial Indian Ocean region state officials also live heritage and form part of memorialization processes. They and others of similar rank and power cannot avoid culture.

Conclusion

Beyond the realm of formal politics and institutions of heritage management, Madagascar retains a dynamic cultural heritage. Memory-making remains the preserve of Malagasy citizens and while this is not exempt from local community politics, for the moment it seems as though the Malagasy are 'free' to articulate their identities and memories. The current phase of globalization, however, is beginning to impact on identity construction and will certainly shift memory. It will be interesting see how identity and the location of memory are changing in the 'new' economic zones of the big island. On the *ylang ylang* plantations in Nossi Be, it appears that identities and memories (i.e. of the Antandroy people) are being maintained as a 'refuge' against the exploitative conditions of work, while the globalization of tourism and its potentially negative effects are leading to a questioning of historically encouraged relationships between young Malagasy girls and white men.

In Zanzibar, Omani descendants are seeking to present an authentic identity for themselves that is separate from the creolized identity of the Afro-Shirazi. Memory-making is also demarginalizing the identity of the Omani, as they assume an empowered position as producers of culture in the tourism discourse of Zanzibar. This process is assisted by an 'other' globalization, in which Islam, treated as foreign and potentially violent in the West, is reassuming its cachet as an exotic, forbidden and alternative set of cultural practices.

In Mauritius heritage, identity and memory are dominated by institutions which seek to present these as categories of analysis. There is danger here that people will not be allowed to forget particular versions of the past, that singular narratives will be forged and that memory-making will become the prerogative of the state. The globalization of tourism is hastening this process, as Mauritians seek new tourism ventures to lure high-spending tourists.

A critical reflection on heritage, memory and identity in the region strongly suggests that identity and heritage are regionalized, creolized and responsive to the current phase of globalization, whether this is seen as westernization or in the form of Fourth World politics and social movements worldwide. It also suggests that memory is revived by different means and for diverse ends. Furthermore, heritage is lived, manipulated, shared and hybridized. The analysis has also shown that each island has its particularities, forged by a specific historical trajectory and set of cultural resources. Those formulating policy regarding heritage, memory and identity need to be aware of these specific dynamics. They should make use of anthropological knowledge because it can reveal interrelations in complex social landscapes, offering an insider view as well as revealing the priorities of diverse stakeholders in heritage management. Policy-makers should reassert ethical principles by treating people as the ends and not the means of heritage management. Policy-makers should also fully recognize the fact of creolization in the islands. This will encourage a re-anchoring of identity in the region and the realization (for the benefit of humankind), of the region's rich heritage. Lastly, not all heritages and memories should be publicly managed. Doing so can rob societies of their creativity and dynamism and people of meaning and solace. Thus policy-makers need to exercise discretion in making decisions about heritage management and be prepared to listen when people speak.

REFERENCES

Alpers, E. (2002) 'Imagining the Indian Ocean World', International Conference on Cultural Exchange and Transformation in the Indian Ocean World, California: UCLA.

Bolland, O.N. (2009) 'Creolization and Creole Societies'. In Cohen, R. and Toninato, P. (eds), *The Creolization Reader: Studies in Mixed Identities and Cultures*. London and New York: Routledge.

Boswell, R. (2006a) *Le Malaise Creole: Ethnic Identity in Mauritius*. Oxford: Berghahn Books.

Boswell, R. (2006b) 'Say What You Like: Dress, Identity and Heritage in Zanzibar'. *International Journal of Heritage Studies* 12(5): 440–58.

Bouchenaki, M. (2003) 'The Interdependency of the Tangible and Intangible Cultural Heritage', The World Heritage Convention, Røros, Norway, 3–5 September.

Chavez, M. and Zambrano, M. (2005) 'From Blanquiamiento to Reindigenización: Shifting Views and Practices of Mestizaje in Contexts of Ethnic Resurgence in Contemporary

Colombia', Paper presented at the Sephis, *Mixing Races* workshop, Cape Town, August.

Cohen, R. and Toninato, P. (2009) *The Creolization Reader: Studies in Mixed Identities and Cultures*. London and New York: Routledge.

Cole, J. (1998) 'The Uses of Defeat: Memory and Political Morality in East Madagascar'. In Werbner, R. (ed.), *Memory in the Postcolony: African Anthropology and the Critique of Power*. London: Zed Books.

Cole, J. (2001) *Forget Colonialism? Sacrifice and the Art of Memory in Madagascar*. Berkeley, CA: University of California Press.

Eriksen, T.H. (1999) 'Tu dimunn pu vine Kreol'. *Revi Kiltir Kreol* (February 2002). Réduit: University of Mauritius.

Evers, S. (2002) *Constructing History, Culture and Inequality: The Betsileo in the Extreme Southern Highlands of Madagascar*. Leiden: Brill Academic Publishers.

Graeber, D. (2007) *Lost People: Magic and the Legacy of Slavery in Madagascar*. Bloomington, IN: Indiana University Press.

Lambek, M. (2002) *The Weight of the Past: Living with History in Mahajanga Madagascar*. New York: Palgrave Macmillan.

Larsen, P. (2000) *History and Memory in the Age of Enslavement: Becoming Merina in Highland Madagascar, 1770–1822* (Social History of Africa). Portsmouth: Heinemann.

Rushdie, S. (1991) *Imaginary Homelands: Essays and Criticism*. London: Granta Books.

Sharp, L. (1993) *The Possessed and the Dispossessed: Spirits, Power and Identity in a Madagascar Migrant Town*. Berkeley, CA: University of California Press.

Teelock, V. (1998) *Bitter Sugar, Sugar and Slavery in 19th Century Mauritius*. Réduit: Mahatma Gandhi Institute.

Vaughan, M. (2005) *Creating the Creole Island: Slavery in Eighteenth-century Mauritius*. Durham, NC: Duke University Press.

Vergès, F. (2005) 'Kreol Kiltirs: India-Oceanic Creolizations', Paper presented at the Sephis, *Mixing Races* workshop, August.

Yelvington, K.A. (2001) 'The Anthropology of Afro-Latin America and the Caribbean: Diasporic Dimensions'. *Annual Review of Anthropology* 30: 227–60.

CHAPTER 14

REMEMBERING AND FORGETTING COMMUNIST CULTURAL PRODUCTION

Dragan Klaic

This chapter explores the manner in which communist era cultural production in Central and Eastern Europe has been subjected to different strategies of remembrance and forgetting. Arguing that the cultural policy of that era was much more diverse and multifaceted than is commonly assumed, the author explores the ways in which various products of that policy have been appropriated by post-communist governments for the purposes of national representation and promotion or have been caught up in the processes of the globalized neo-liberal political economy. There is an ongoing tension between nationalist and neo-liberal motivations, yet there are also alternative artistic practices that raise cultural memory issues, motives and episodes in a critical perspective.

Introduction

The so-called 'transition' in Central and Eastern Europe was supposed to lead from the one-party state to a parliamentary democracy and market economy. In the twenty years that have passed, the cultural production of the discarded socialist order has met with a singular destiny. Much of this cultural production appears to have been relegated to a distant realm of embarrassing or cumbersome memory. It has become a heritage neglected, forgotten or even purposely destroyed. Not only the artifacts of the socialist culture but also its cultural policy frameworks are being written off in a discourse based on simplifications about totalitarianism and ideological monopoly. Such disqualifying epithets obscure the fact that the cultural production of socialism was far more diverse and multifaceted than is generally assumed. In different times and places, the degree of state severity oscillated considerably; formal and informal censorship was more or less intolerant and there were great variations in the output and leverage of cultural institutions.

The ideological disqualifications were understandable in the early years, but today a more considered analytical ordering is required. The systematic study of cultural policies and cultural production, distribution and consumption under communism could become a cornerstone of a new European cultural studies. Yet there are very few signs that such knowledge is being generated in the region's universities and institutes, which are all in the grip of vogue topics such as 'creative industries' (cf. Anheier and Isar 2008) or cultural tourism. The purpose of this chapter, therefore, is to address this need in the light of the present volume's specific perspectives. For this purpose, I shall examine how the cultural production of the 'socialist' period has been sidelined, dismantled or rephrased in collective memory. These strategies of effacement and/or destruction have been carried out under the aegis of today's prevailing ideological orientations and values, notably globalized notions of managerial efficiency and commodification (Katunarič et al. 1997). I shall also look at the political foregrounding of alternative cultural heritage and even newly created cultural infrastructure of a supposedly historical character. I shall identify the contrarian and even subversive artistic attempts that have been made to reveal and re-evaluate the cultural production of communism as these have emerged independently of official cultural policies and mainstream practice or from players outside the region such as cultural institutions in Western Europe. While much of the cultural production of post-socialism seeks to connect with European and global trends, serve the representational urge of the state, or provide lucrative entertainment, there are also many alternative artistic practices that deploy culture as a public good and invoke issues of cultural memory in a markedly critical perspective, one that is opposed to the official revisionist discourses. With a sense for controversy, artistic initiatives transcend black and white simplifications in the interpretation of the cultures of socialism while at the same time they criticize both the unthinking obedience to globalized trends and fads and the uncritical adjustment to market dictates.

Attitudes to cultural heritage under communism

Pre-socialist cultural heritage was chiefly preserved within a complex infrastructure of regulation, competence, institutions and public subsidy flows, but interpreted from an ideological point of view that labelled it as feudal or capitalist, peasant, proletarian or bourgeois, reactionary or progressive. Despite many restoration projects, much church property was severely neglected and many former feudal manor houses, mansions and castles deteriorated markedly after nationalization, under imposed new functions, for example as seats of agricultural cooperatives, orphanages and warehouses. Monuments to erstwhile heroes judged adversarial or reactionary by the communists were destroyed or removed. Museums were publicly owned and were expected to present the ascent of progressive forces, teach proletarian emancipation and glorify the people's struggle. Although the communist authorities financed archaeological excavations and their subsequent protection, they saw them as assets in the development of a rapidly growing tourist industry, especially as in Dubrovnik, Zadar and Split in former Yugoslavia or in Budapest, Prague and Cracow. The economic malaise of the 1980s reduced the public engagement and

ambition. All the socialist countries took part in the development of norms, standards and discourse within UNESCO and its affiliates, but except for the former Yugoslavia they remained aloof from the broad cultural remit and normative output of the Council of Europe.

Artists were frequently commissioned by the socialist authorities to deliver memorial art and architecture and thus create in virtually every city a specific topography of official remembrance. Initially, an aesthetic canon of socialist realism was imposed on such endeavours, with a predilection for massive, monumental sculptures of victorious fighters, rebelling proletarians and self-sacrificing mothers. This canon began to wane in the 1960s, gradually becoming less socialist and less realist, subverted by the encroachment of abstraction and non-illusionist symbolization, and fed more by the traditions of modernism than by the norms of this 'impossible' aesthetics, crushed under its Stalinist premises (Robin 1986). The rhetoric of memorial plaques was, however, quite heavy-handed, overloaded with political jargon, derived from the official historic interpretation of events and a nomenclature of heroes, martyrs and enemies, even in such traumatic sites as Auschwitz (Krajewski 2005). Museums of complex narratives formulated a rather rigid ideological discourse in their presentation and commentary, and even art museums were expected to foreground 'progressive' over 'decadent' bourgeois art, although by the 1980s such distinctions had become quite blurred in most of the socialist countries. Despite the Iron Curtain, mutual cultural influences on the West/East axis were considerable, albeit sporadic, irregular and sometime unpredictable and even dramatic (Caute 2005), not only in the circulation of contemporary artistic products, but in the display and safeguarding of cultural heritage and in a shared discourse about it. The Dubrovnik Summer Festival (established in 1950, www.dubrovnik-festival.hr) was clearly following the model of the Avignon Festival (established in 1947, www.festival-avignon.com) and the latter's use of architectural heritage as a spectacular setting for the performing arts and music events, a practice followed elsewhere by many other producers and presenters. Large exhibitions of national cultural heritage were organized by the governments of socialist countries abroad, even in the West, with a clearly prestige-enhancing purpose.

Cultural heritage in the post-communist transition

After the end of the communist era, cultural heritage was liberated from the previous ideological restraints, but also instrumentalized right away as a proof of the authentic and longstanding European character of the national culture, or quickly appropriated by the competitive nationalist ideologies that sought to deploy cultural heritage for self-representation and promotion. What tamed this assault was not so much the resistance of the ex-communists, transformed into socialists and social-democrats, but the prevailing neo-liberal attitudes that sought to exploit heritage primarily as a potential commodity and as a resource that could speed up integration in the European Union and its market. In fact, the vicissitudes of post-communist cultural policies in Central and Eastern Europe since 1989 could be seen as a process of ongoing tension and competition between *nationalist* and *neo-liberal forces*. The first stress a conservative and narrow view of heritage as a source and symbol of the collective identity and cultural continuity, and eagerly use it as a shield against what they perceive to be a dangerous assault by the globalized kitsch of the culture industry. The latter see heritage as a precious asset and unique selling point in the reconfiguration of the market according to European practices and standards, hoping to generate more income from tourism and reduce the dependence of the cultural sector on public subsidies.

Few significant innovations in cultural policy have taken place, apart from the elimination of official censorship mechanisms. The political rhetoric has changed and includes nowadays the mandatory discourse of European integration together with national identity affirmation as well as cultural diversity and pluralism, a verbal balancing act that avoids priority-setting and conceals many inherent contradictions. The institutional set-up and the key tools of intervention in culture as a system demonstrate a surprising degree of continuity with the habits and solutions of communist times. The preponderance of large public institutions and their practically automatic funding, regardless of the quantity and quality of output, is the key feature of this continuity, even if the subsidies have become much less generous. With so little policy innovation listed in a recent inventory (Inkei 2009), there are hardly any new approaches or strategies concerning memory, remembrance and cultural heritage. Only the positive and negative attributes have been altered and what used to be snubbed as reactionary and anti-communist is now celebrated as virtuous and enlightened, while the communist cultural heritage is seen as mere propaganda.

The articulation of a coherent cultural or economic policy of heritage was complicated by the ongoing *denationalization* process that was supposed to return to its previous owners much of the real estate appropriated by the socialist authorities' decades ago. Tracing the owners and sorting out their claims took a long time and some public cultural institutions became tenants in privately owned buildings since the authorities often did not have the means to compensate the original owners and buy them out. The return of private property especially benefited the Catholic Church, which in Slovenia, for instance, received back not only the property taken away by the Communists after 1945, but also possessions lost in the agrarian reforms of the 1920s, in the early years of the Yugoslav state, that aimed to end the dominance of the Catholic Church as a primary semi-feudal landowner (Flere 1999). With a much expanded material base, organized religion was able to become a political force, often aggressively engaged in the fabrication of clerico-nationalism (Byford 2008), and has gained political exposure and a high profile in public life and especially in the media, which in turn keeps reinforcing the wealth of religious organizations. An explosive growth of superficial religiosity in the population has brought substantial public and private means for the restoration of religious heritage, often done hastily and incompetently. It has also created a cottage industry of religious trinkets, some of domestic origin, some coming all the way from China, to appeal to the Central and Eastern European new believers, Catholic, Protestant and Orthodox.

The deployment of European Union structural funds in the ten ex-communist countries that joined the EU in 2004 and 2007 has speeded up the physical and functional upgrading of cultural heritage infrastructure, as witnessed by the rapid transformation of the urban centres of Riga, Vilnius and Tallinn, where the residua of Soviet urban planning have been eliminated or transposed. The link to tourism development strategies provides sufficient rationale to receive EU funds under a regime of complex regulations. And even if only 1.7 per cent of the structural funds available is deployed for cultural purposes (Centre for Strategy & Evaluation Services LLP 2010) the rate of return is sometimes surprising. It includes, for example, the often noisy brawls of British hen and stag parties, flown to Eastern Europe on easyJet and Ryanair for cheap binging on the old squares, and in the summer months immense crowds of tourists on Stradun, the main street of the Dubrovnik walled core, or at the Charles Bridge in Prague. Mass tourism inevitably brings with it globalized practices in hospitality, amenities and auxiliary services, thus reducing the specificity of places and the uniqueness of the cultural heritage.

In some places, the appropriation of heritage for the benefit of tourists, especially foreign tourists, has alienated local residents, and high prices in the palaces and castles converted into hotels and restaurants has taken them beyond the reach of local pockets. Museums and new heritage sites exploit their commercial potential according to prevailing European practices: extensive merchandising, café and restaurant services, subletting of premises for private parties, weddings, political and business promotion events. With such diversification of usage, the old-fashioned longstanding employees – scarcely interested in client-friendliness – find themselves embattled with a new generation of managers, marketeers and consultants. On this inner battlefield between morose die-hards and enthusiastic but callous modernizers and entrepreneurs, disgruntled ticket sellers and cloakroom attendants can easily undermine the profit-taking of a museum shop and limit the income from the former workers' canteen, turned in the evening hours into a disco (as in the Ethnographic Museum in Warsaw, www.pme.waw.pl). And taciturn, badly paid conservators have little grasp of the public-friendly themes and approaches that would in their view trivialize the mission of the museum – the entrepreneurs need their cooperation to recruit corporate sponsors for the upgrading of facilities and new exhibitions. This struggle easily escalates into an opposition of heritage specialists and marketers, old guard and new generation, even nationalists and globalists. Less scrupulous entrepreneurs usurp cultural heritage objects, devalue their cultural purpose and use them for private enrichment, chiefly through sublet manipulations, kickbacks from restoration and events subsidies and other black market flows.

Affirmation of market principles and free enterprise has meant the slow revival of the arts and antique market, the emergence of specialized stores, occasional auctions, restoration and reparation studios, such as are visible in the new antiquity row in the Falk Miksa street in Budapest. What is clearly much appreciated in these outlets are cultural goods produced before communism, objects that reaffirm continuity with the pre-World War II bourgeois culture and European modernism, items brought decades ago from Western Europe or made at home under its influence, and not artistic objects and cultural goods produced during socialism. The latter have ended up in museum storerooms and often on the flea markets and junkyards – although one must assume that there are in Central and Eastern Europe large private collections of art made under socialism and even of mass-produced communist ideological kitsch items, kept out of the public view for the time being. A revival of national arts markets and their connectivity with international arts markets has also led to a steep increase in thefts from badly guarded heritage sites and in illicit trafficking of art objects. Thousands have disappeared in the last twenty years on the globalized market and not all stolen items are duly registered and put under alert (see: www.artcrime.info). While police and customs lack resources and expertise, once much feared state agencies for the protection of historic monuments act with reduced efficiency, enjoy less authority and often go out of the way to please the newly powerful players on the real estate market.

Radical interventions

After 1989, some museums, built on ideology more than on cultural heritage value, were quickly dismantled and their premises recycled for alternative usage. Such was the fate of the Marx–Engels–Lenin museums, once abundant in the former USSR, and museums of the international workers' movement (www.russianmuseums.info/M1622). The one in Bucharest was turned into a minimalist museum of peasant life (www.muzeultaranuluiroman.ro/en), created on a minuscule budget, and awarded subsequently a Council of Europe distinction in 1996; another, in the Buda castle complex, was dismantled and the space was given to the Ludwig Museum of Modern Art, newly created by a private Swiss donor, before it moved to its newly built premises across the Danube (www.ludwigmuseum.hu).

In the wars in the former Yugoslavia, much damage was inflicted on heritage by all sides. Dubrovnik was bombarded by the Yugoslav People's Navy in the autumn of 1991, and its surroundings were plundered by 'volunteers' from Montenegro. In the ensuing months, much of the baroque architecture of Vukovar was destroyed in the military assault from Serbia into Slavonia (Zaknić 1992). In the Bosnian phase of the conflict (1992–95) confessionally marked heritage was destroyed in a systematic manner by all sides. Bosnian Serb forces levelled all the mosques of Banja Luka and poured asphalt over their foundations to create parking places, in triumphant negation of the Muslim right to even a square foot of the Bosnian soil (Riedlmayer 2002). Monuments to partisan struggle during World War II, erected by the communist authorities, were systematically destroyed in Bosnia and Croatia. This showed that the conflict contained ideological retribution at its core, behind pumped up ethnic or religious hatred. In Kosovo, after the 1999 NATO military intervention and the ensuing exodus of most of the Serbian population, along with the retreating Serbian military, Albanian villagers carried out hundreds of assaults on Serbian Orthodox churches, monasteries and cemeteries (Bjelajac 2004), despite the (not always alert) protection of international forces.

Constructed heritage sites

In the beginning, the recycling of artifacts from the past socialist era took some rather naïve forms. Discarded sculptures in the socialist realism style were collected and roughly displayed in a meadow on the outskirts of Budapest, with socialist marches blaring from the loudspeakers. This field collection of Marx, Engels, Lenin, Stalin, Rakosi statutes and sculptures of proletarian stakhanovites and other grandees of the communist pantheon are displayed without any aesthetic, cultural-historic or political framing. The Budapest Sculptures Park (www.szoborpark.hu) is in fact not so much a theme park but rather a junkyard of socialist realism production, now open for the slight amusement of ticket-paying visitors.

The Occupation Museum in Riga (www.occupationmuseum.lv) is quite another matter. It is an ambitious undertaking, replacing an exhibit on the Soviet 'liberation' of Latvia with an opposing narrative of the systematic victimization of the Latvian people and its suffering under triple occupation – Soviet in 1940, German Nazi in 1941 and Soviet re-occupation in 1945. This museum, which started as a private initiative, was quite successful in collecting from local inhabitants and the Latvian diaspora not only funds, but also photographs and documents, which it then displayed in a coherent, albeit ideologically driven, narrative. Similarly, the Terror House in Budapest (www.terrorhaza.hu), on which I wrote in the previous volume of this *Series* (Klaic 2010), seeks to construct an artificial symmetry of the fascist and communist terror and display the martyrdom of the Hungarian nation under those regimes, skipping the first nemesis rather quickly and superficially, and dwelling extensively on the latter. The creators of the Terror House made ample use of sophisticated display techniques and contemporary installation art.

Lithuanian counterparts of these revisionist edifices are of an antiquarian orientation, recalling the Romantic cult of ruins and pseudo-historic panoramas. The construction of a huge imitation of a renaissance castle in the very centre of Vilnius, next to the cathedral, is framed as a reconstruction of the residence of Lithuanian grand dukes that supposedly once stood just there (www.valdovurumai.lt). For years a large chunk of the very modest culture budget of Lithuania has been poured into this pharaonic enterprise, supplemented by volunteer contributions from Lithuania and abroad, without any plausible link between the construction plans and historic evidence, nor a clear idea of the purpose and future usage of the ambitious edifice. Apparently, this conceptual vacuum has not prevented the Lithuanian authorities from buying in Western Europe, at fairs and auctions, various medieval and Renaissance objects for the decoration of this future representative venue, a newly fabricated proof of the glorious national past. Officially 'opened' in July 2009 for the celebration of 1000 years of Vilnius and in the framework of the crumbling Vilnius Cultural Capital of Europe programme, the building is still undergoing further work and needs to be furnished and ultimately put to some meaningful use.

Recalling a more recent history, tour operators in the historic Castle district of Buda advertise a special tour of the Budavári Sziklakórház (Rock

Hospital) (www.sziklakorhaz.hu), which was built secretly underground in the 1950s by the communist authorities to provide medical assistance in the case of a nuclear war. Reopened by the theatre company Krétakör for its processional production *Nibelungen* in 2004 (www.kretakor.hu), this site remains under the administration of one of the Budapest hospitals and is stuffed with medical material from the 1950s. Such as it is, the Rock Hospital serves both as a memorial of Cold War anxieties and as an impromptu museum of historic medical provisions, but without any accompanying descriptions. Similarly, a former KGB prison at the periphery of Vilnius has been converted in a tourist attraction, a dungeon of Soviet era horrors. More elaborate is the dramaturgical rendering of a shelter that was built during the Cold War north of Vilnius in order to protect the Lithuanian nomenclature in the case of an atomic war, and now turned into a theme park on the gruesome Soviet regime (www.sovietbunker.com), to which visitors can expose themselves for a day, to be yelled at, threatened, locked up and humiliated in a supposed old Soviet style by the performers dressed as KGB officers and guards. Here militant anti-Soviet ideology adds a specific histrionic touch to the habitual trivia of the experience economy as practised in theme parks elsewhere in Europe and in the USA.

Gushing nostalgia

Nostalgia (see also Zala Volcic's chapter that follows) appears as a more docile and pleasant counterpart to these packaged horror experiences. As Svetlana Boym has demonstrated (Boym 2001), nostalgia, as an intimate and collective truncated emotion, floats well with globalization and feeds much of today's cultural industry. Parades of old-time cars in Eastern Europe include nowadays Volga, Zhiguli, Moskvich, Lada, Wartburg, Škoda and other leftovers of the ill-fated socialist car industry, well cared for by their proud owners who, in socialism, had to wait for years for the privilege of buying them. Meanwhile, the *Trabant*, that pathetic mishap of DDR car design and engineering, has become within the wave of *Ostalgia* (a nostalgic yearning for some aspects of the former DDR life – see www.visitberlin.de/english/sightseeing/e_si_berlinprogramme_ostalgie.php) a symbolic object of endearment, tenderness and much fascination,

a retro cult, comparable to the cults of the Citroen 2CV and the Mini Cooper, among other tribes of European car fanatics.

It is this silly and more awkward than oppressive image of everyday life in the former German Democratic Republic that a new museum in Berlin (www.ddr-museum.de) presents to German and foreign tourists, while outside street vendors sell Soviet military caps, decorations and insignia, and some phony Berlin Wall painted rocks as Cold War souvenirs. A bit further, Checkpoint Charlie, once a dreaded border crossing from West into East Berlin, with long waiting lines and thorough searches of people and cars, has become a docile *lieu de memoire*, reinforced by a new commercial museum (www.mauer-museum.com). The gigantic Palace of the Republic, built by the Romanian dictator Ceausescu on an artificial hill of Bucharest, is today used by a Museum of Contemporary Art (www.mnac.ro) and as the Parliament, but guided tours fail to articulate it as a *lieu de memoire*. The enormous halls and staircases fail to invoke the sacrifices made in the construction, the brutal erasure of a whole quarter of eighteenth and nineteenth-century Bucharest, and are simply both disgusting and depressing as they project instead only megalomanic kitsch. A more complex invocation of daily life under communism, inextricably enmeshed with surveillance, repression and systematic induction of fear, emerges in some recent films, such as the Romanian *4 Months, 3 Weeks & 2 Days* (*4 luni, 3 săptămâni si 2 zile*, 2007) by Cristian Mungiu, and the German *The Life of Others* (*Das Leben der Anderen*, 2006) by Florian Henckel von Donnersmarck. Their reconstruction of the minutiae of a police state is an excellent antidote to any nostalgia peddling.

And yet nostalgia is difficult to beat for its easy appeal, as Zala Volcic demonstrates below, commenting on the phenomenon of 'Yugonostalgia' as a compensatory emotion and a political stance, in opposition to the competitive nationalist discourses that became dominant in the successor states of the former Yugoslavia. There actually exists a lexicon of the Yugoslav mythology (Andrić et al. 2004), in the form of a set of pseudo-scholarly, humorous remembrances of consumer objects, social and cultural practices, ideological symbols, pop culture heroes and artifacts. More recent still is a parodistic travel guide through the Socialist Federal Republic of Yugoslavia (Novačić 2008), a country that is no longer on the map, written as a satiric, absurdist and unabashedly nostalgic recollection of disappeared Yugoslav experience. These nostalgic waves touched upon the image of Marshall Tito, once venerated, then demonized from 1990 onwards and now again re-launched as a positive icon, so that *Tito's Cookbook* (Drulović 2005), containing recipes for his allegedly favourite dishes, has also become a bestseller.

Reclaim and advocate

There is more than just nostalgia in these revisionist forays. Cultural centre Kampnagel in Hamburg (www.kampnagel.de) and the Eurokaz festival in Zagreb (www.eurokaz.hr) commissioned jointly a cluster of theatre productions inspired by Tito that are neither parodistic nor apologetic (www.ffeac. org/www.ffeac.org/423.page). That the memory of the old Marshal is in a phase of positive reconstruction and re-evaluation was visible in the 2009 exhibit 'The Tito Effect: Charisma as Political Legitimization', mounted in the Belgrade Museum of 25 May (Tito's official birthday), now re-baptized the Museum of History of Yugoslavia (www.mij.rs), once dedicated to him and keeping some 22,000 gifts he received from world statesmen, ordinary people and organizations. This exhibition went beyond mere exploitation of nostalgia and was an anthropological exploration of how 500 artistic and handcraft gifts were deployed in the service of a secular memory cult that the recent conflicts and ideological shifts could erode but not erase.

Addressing another, primarily generational myth, Radio Belgrade traced in 2008 some 80 participants of the student demonstrations that took place at Belgrade University in June 1968 and aired their reminiscences in a long documentary feature series, connecting them across the cities of the former Yugoslavia and reaching even further, to interview dispersed nineteen-sixty-eighters in Western Europe, Australia, North America and New Zealand. The end result is a global remembrance effort, which makes facile politically-inspired labelling of this complex event impossible, placing the Belgrade turmoil in the context of a global anti-authoritarian revolt and examining the first cracks in the ideological façade of Yugoslav self-management socialism (Malavrazić 2008).

'Gender Check, Gender Roles in the Arts of Eastern Europe', a large exhibition held in the Museum Moderner Kunst in Vienna MQ (www. mumok.at) in the winter of 2009–10 is a systematic effort by the curator Bojana Pejić (Pejić et al. 2009) to capture the dynamic (de)construction of gender in socialism, with its proclaimed formal equality and implicit and hidden stereotyping and inequalities. Displaying the works of over 200 artists, she shows the gap between ideology and reality, the differences in social norms and individual attitudes of women and men, the disparity between the display of the body in the officialized public space and its intimate revelations in the private sphere. With the help of a large network of curators and art critics, Pejić amassed works that reflect and also reject gender representation, subvert conventional notions of masculinity, femininity and heterosexuality, and display the growing variety of personal zones and strategies of self-definition that were possible even during socialism. In many works created after 1989, there is a reaction to the neo-conservative imposition of traditional gender roles and resistance to the commodification of the body, person and gender. In this current phase, artists subvert the gender as yet another Trojan horse of globalized iconic capitalism, as a repressive phantom produced and imposed by the advertising industry.

Tito's gifts exhibit, the book of 1968 reminiscences and 'Gender Check' all rest on a serious attempt to capture key facets of culture in socialism, reinterpret them and re-evaluate them with a sense for complexity and in ways that transcend easy ideological labels and disqualifications. These projects have been realized by non-academic researchers, curators and journalists who position themselves as activists and oppose the transition *Zeitgeist*, with its propensity for collective amnesia. Yet systematic research on culture in the socialist era still needs to be initiated. Bodies such as the Budapest Institute for the History of the 1956 Revolution (www.rev.hu/portal), the Polish archives on Solidarnosc (www.ecs.gda.pl), and the Institute of National Remembrance in Warsaw (IPW, www. ipn.gov.pl) tend to concentrate on the political rather than cultural facets of socialism. The Open Society Archive in Budapest (www.osaarchivum. org) is one of the major depositories of various materials from Central and Eastern Europe on politics, media and culture 1945–89, but the academic culture research output remains modest. Film and rock music in socialism have attracted more research attention than other cultural fields (Sarkisova and Apor 2008). The occurrences of dissident and critical theatre, often from the student and amateur circuits, are scarcely researched and whatever documentation still exists remains scattered in private archives rather than processed in the holdings of public institutions. Lifestyles, leisure activities, cultural consumption and related values and cultural policies *tout court* require much further study.

What the academic researchers fail to accomplish, however, artists achieve on their own terms, with passion and flair, confirming the thesis of Boris Groys that artists from Central and Eastern Europe have turned their experience of socialism into a lasting source of artistic material and inspiration (Groys 2008). Janos Sugar seeks to preserve the early graffiti samples from the 1980s on the walls of Budapest houses, as a new artistic project (www.sztaki.hu/providers/nightwatch/szocpol/masmunkak/sugar-m.eng.html). Barbara Klimova presents the modernist architecture of family villas, built in Brno between 1948 and 1989, as private zones of domesticity and petit-bourgeois seclusion from the mass lifestyle of socialism, but also as a symbolic affirmation of their owners' belonging to modernity. She is reconstructing an implicit value system, a dominant style, design models, technological solutions and a scarce choice of materials, characteristic of socialist architecture and urbanism (server.ffa.vutbr.cz/~barborak/?page=pd1&menu=2). In the former Lenin shipyard in Gdansk, shamelessly sold by the municipality to four real estate speculators for a few zloty, an embattled artistic collective, the Wyspa Institute of Art, seeks to offer a critical, not panegyric, rendition of the Solidarity struggle through installation art (www.wyspa.art.pl). Theatre Ulysses (www.ulysses.hr) has been transforming since 2001 the Brioni archipelago from the mythological power centre of Tito's rule to a place of imagination, in a series of site-specific productions. Michael Blom sneaks into an Ukrainian chocolate factory for a future artistic project on Marxism, hedonism and pre-capitalist consumption (www.blomology.net). In Zagreb, Bacači sjenki/Shadow Casters (shadowcasters.blogspot.com) collective has been staging a series of artistic and social projects that explore the city-dwellers' memories and induces them to recall their historic experiences. 'Vitić Dances' has been a successful campaign to mobilize the residents of a remarkable apartment house by the modernist architect Vitić to ensure its placement on the list of protected monuments and prompt its renovation after decades of neglect. Artists of the Shadow Casters revalorized a modernist architecture masterpiece as well as revitalizing its social context, patched together the urban and social history of the buildings from the scarce memory treads and revealed its utopian premises, betrayed first by self-management socialism, then by the post-1991 capitalism. Marking attractive spots of remembrance within the urban micro-topography on the basis of citizens' private documents and stories, Shadow Casters sketched and alternative history of Zagreb's public life of the past five–six decades.

Artists drawn by the remains of a culture of socialism are involved in various informal networks, engaged in multiple simultaneous cooperation projects, occasionally supported and featured by cultural institutions and thus operate in a highly mobile fashion, working in diverse places and countries. They are exposed to various cultural impacts of globalization and shaped by them in terms of prevailing trends, available opportunities, exposure and critical responses. At the same time, their focus on the specificity of a place enables them to develop an authorial strategy of resistance to the uniformizing pressures of globalization, especially if they are able to reinforce their local position in partnership with the local infrastructure of the civil society or find other ways to enhance their local acceptance and sharpen their insights and creativity. In these cases, their artistic engagement transcends the concerns about cultural heritage and collective memory and becomes almost inevitably an activist gesture to re-affirm and defend the public space from privatization, usurpation, abuse and neglect.

Ironically, it was a Dutch author, Albert Gielen, who wrote a history of communist era architecture and urban planning in Prague, and showed how Czech architects sidestepped the constraints of the socialist realist norms, reconnecting with Czech and European *interbellum* modernism and even the smuggling in of the postmodernist concepts in the late 1980s (Gielen 2010). Also from a distance, the Schweizerisches Architekturmuseum in Basel (www.sam-basel.org), produced in 2009 the exhibition 'Balkanology: New Architecture and Urban Phenomena in Southeastern Europe', shown later also in the Architekturzentrum in Vienna (www.azw.at) with an ample accompanying programme. In collaboration with architects, urban planners and critics from the region in focus, the curators present the exemplary edifices of the socialist period and major urban development projects carried out before 1989 in the former Yugoslavia, Romania, Bulgaria and Albania, followed by a display of their decay, grassroot modification and effacement under the pressures of privatization, real estate reappraisal, and the global housing and shopping-centre trends of the transition period.

Such concern with the unregulated, wild urban sprawl and private, autarchic 'do-it-yourself' mini-urbanism of the post-socialist period finds its local focus in the work of 'Pula – the Red Plan' (www.smu-research.net, postcapitalistcity.blog.hr). This group of Istrian architects strikes alarm about the decay and abuse of the public space in Pula, a Croat city of 60,000 inhabitants, where industry collapsed and where the once dominant military presence fell after 1991, and huge terrains of former military installations and barracks were abandoned. The artistic and civic interventions of 'Pula – the Red Plan' expose the inefficiency and corruption of the public authorities, their inability to manage urban transformation, and at the same time they pierce the gentrification follies of the tourism industry. 'Pula – the Red Plan' sketches red crisis zones, where fragmented private interests destroy any common sense of purpose and lead to distrust, tension and conflict. Large-scale corporate usurpation goes hand in hand with innumerable small-scale private appropriations of the public space, in a situation where all zoning and other regulations are ignored, supervision and control are non-existent, and permits are sold to the highest bidder. Pula architects are aware that what they are experiencing in their own city has been happening in many others across the world and that their strategy of resistance thus could have broader ramifications and applicability elsewhere, emerging on the ruins of a failed cultural policy concerning heritage and failed policy of urban development dominated by today's wild capitalism. Yet they still operate as a small group of local subversives and only exceptionally interact with their complementary Croat and foreign peers, who oppose similar urban practices elsewhere. An international alliance or action-driven network of critical architects and urban planners, who refuse to tacitly serve corporate and political interests, still has to emerge in the transition countries.

A policy making shift?

Post-socialist cultural policies display a puzzling stasis as regards new initiatives and instruments with respect to collective memories and the politics of remembrance. The rhetoric produced by the ministries of culture is, as a rule, not followed up by significant conceptual frameworks, programmes and funding. Cultural heritage is invoked as a source of national identity and as a resource for cultural tourism but the definitions remain vague and the approach stresses physical preservation, not critical reassessment or contemporary recycling of cultural functions. The dominance of the preservationist ideology obscures the strategic linkage of cultural heritage, collective memory and citizenship. While globalization imposes commercialization and gentrification of cultural heritage, nationalist pseudo-historic fantasies and appropriations, effacements and falsifications of the past and its remembrance and material traces appear to be mere unproductive responses of nation-states to globalization-induced anxieties. Governments are unlikely to come forward with the needed policy innovations. With accelerating competition from cities – for distinction, visibility, attractiveness, investments, jobs, talents – and the emergence of an urban hierarchy or stratification in terms of their cultural appeal and socio-economic prosperity, it is rather on the municipal level that one should expect an interlocking of cultural policy with urban development policy and a real engagement with artistic talent and research resources. Backed by such local alliances and partnerships, cultural policy would be in a stronger position to affirm cultural heritage, including the neglected cultural production of socialism, as a public good, in the public space and resist its efacement and trivialization.

REFERENCES

Andrić, I., Arsenijević, V. and Matić, D. (2004). *Leksikon jugo-slovenske mitologije*. Belgrade & Zagreb: Postscriptum.

Bjelajac, B. (2004). 'Kosovo': Nobody Charged for the Destruction of Orthodox Churches and Monasteries'. www.forum18.org/Archive.php?article_id=314.

Boym, S. (2001). *The Future of Nostalgia*. New York: Basic Books.

Byford, J. (2008). *Denial and Repression of Antisemitism*. Budapest: CEU Press.

Caute, D. (2005). *The Dancer Defects: The Struggle for Cultural Supremacy during the Cold War*. Oxford: Oxford University Press.

CSES (Centre for Strategy & Evaluation Services LLP) (2010). 'Study on the Contribution of Culture to Local and Regional Economic Development as Part of European Cohesion Policy'. Unpublished draft.

Drulović, A. (2005). *Titova kuharica*. Zaprešić: Fraktura.

Flere, S. (1999). 'Church–State Relations in Slovenia in the Ninetees'. *Facta Universitatis.* University of Niš, Philosophy and Sociology Series, 2(6): 23–26.

Gielen, A. (2010). *Het reele paradijs. Socialistische architectuur & stedenbouw in Praag 1948–1989*. Leiden: Primavera pers.

Groys, B. (2008). *Art Power*. Cambridge, MA: MIT Press.

Inkei, P. (2009). 'Culture and Development 20 years after the Fall of Communism'. Background paper for the CultureWatchEurope conference, organized by the Council of Europe and the Polish Ministry of Culture in Cracow, 4–6 June 2009. See www.coe.int/t/dg4/cultureheritage/CWE/CracowBackgroundPaper_en.pdf.

Katunarić, V. et al. (1997). *Culture in Central and Eastern Europe: Institutional and Value Changes*. Zageb: Culturelink. See www.culturelink.org/review/s97/s97cont.html.

Klaic, D. (2010). 'Creativity of Evil?' In Helmut Anheier and Yudhishthir Raj Isar (eds), *Cultural Expression, Creativity and Innovation. The Culture and Globalization Series, 3*. London: Sage.

Krajewski, S. (2005). *Poland and the Jews: Reflections of a Polish Polish Jew*. Krakow: Austeria.

Malavrazić, D. (2008). *1968: lične istorije. 80 svedočenja*. Belgrade: Radio Beograd, Službeni Glasnik & Filip Višnjić.

Novačić, D. (2008). *SFRJ za ponavljače. Turistički vodič*. Novi Sad: Stylos.

Pejić, B. et al. (2009). *Femininity and Masculinity in the Art of Eastern Europe*. Vienna: MuMoK Stift. Ludwig.

Riedlmayer, A. (2002) 'Destruction of Cultural Heritage in Bosnia-Herzegovina, 1992–1996: A Post-war Survey of Selected Municipalities'. hague.bard.edu/reports/BosHeritageReport-AR.pdf.

Robin, R. (1986). *Realisme socialiste: une esthetique impossible*. Paris: Payot.

Sarkisova, A. and Apor, P. (eds) (2008). *Past for the Eyes: East European Representations of Communism in Cinema and Museums after 1989*. Budapest: CEU Press.

Zaknić, I. (1992) 'The Pain of Ruins: Croatian Architecture under Siege'. *Journal of Architectural Education*, 46(2), November: 115–124.

CHAPTER 15

POST-SOCIALIST RECOLLECTIONS: IDENTITY AND MEMORY IN FORMER YUGOSLAVIA

Zala Volcic

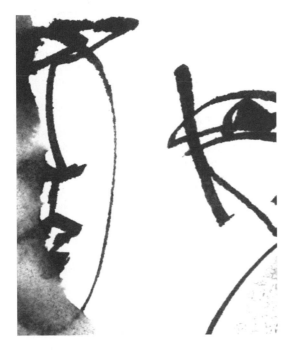

This chapter tracks several symbolic spaces and 'flows' of people, capital, and products that form the route of memorizing. Specifically, I suggest that discourses of memory and nostalgic sentiments for the former Yugoslavia circulate in a variety of texts, products and practices. This Yugo-nostalgia provides a window on to the cultural arena created by the socialist memories of the Yugoslav past and nationalist claims to an exclusionary type of national identity. At the same time, we witness the embracement of a global commercial communication order, in which culture becomes both a commodity and a source of national pride.

In the summer of 2009 I visited the Brijuni islands in Croatia, the storied summer home of Marshal Josip Broz Tito, the former Yugoslav leader. Almost thirty years after his death, the place has become an expensive tourist resort for those who want to relive the more glamorous moments of the Yugoslav past. Visitors willing to pay a premium can sleep in Tito's luxurious villa, drive his Cadillac, or eat the mandarins from trees the ruler supposedly planted himself. Tito's island paradise, where he entertained global high-profile guests from Italian screen goddess Sophia Loren to Haile Selassie of Ethiopia, Nasser of Egypt and Nehru of India in high style, has been rebranded as a high-class holiday destination.

The permanent exhibition in the island's museum, entitled *Josip Broz Tito in Brijuni* has been on display since 1984, preserved in its original form to this day. More than 200 photos depict his private and public life. Other museum exhibits include a still-living (as of this writing) cockatoo (a present to his granddaughter Sasa), and exotic animals from his zoo, including an elephant given to him by Indira Gandhi. The souvenir shop offers the usual products: T-shirts with images of Tito in Brijuni, plates with his image, caps with his signature, badges and other memorabilia. In 2007, the management of the Brijuni National Park signed an official contract with the Broz family obtaining the right to the commercial use of Tito's name, seal and image. Once the leader of a stubbornly independent socialist nation and the co-founder of the influential non-aligned movement, Tito has become one more commodity in the burgeoning tourist industry along the Istrian coast.

This iconic Tito is emblematic of Yugo-nostalgia – nostalgic feelings for the state that collapsed violently in 1991. How have different cultural practices been mobilized in former Yugoslav communities in an attempt to remember and redefine their past, and, with that, their national identities? In attempting to answer this question I have analysed journalistic discourses on memories of the socialist past, and have carried out ethnographic observation at several sites devoted to nostalgic representations of the Yugoslav past. I also conducted structured interviews with more than 60 people over the course of three years. These have included both public intellectuals as well as participants in Yugo-nostalgic activities. All the interviews were conducted face-to-face in the local languages. The interviews were semi-structured and covered different basic areas of research, such as biographical background, memories of the Yugoslav past, and arguments about the rise of national identities in the region. Overall, I wanted to show how memories of former Yugoslavia have been rebranded for the benefit of young consumers who want to wear the T-shirt with the sickle and hammer emblem, Tito's figure, or a Yugoslav flag. Ivy (1995: 56) calls this a consumer-oriented, aesthetic type of nostalgia – nostalgia of style, the packaging of 'nostalgia products' with 'no explicit appeal to return, no acute sense of loss, and no reference to embodied memory ...'. It is, however, important to point out that there are differences in experiencing *Yugo-nostalgia* – in terms of gender, generation, class, and ethnicity. Unfortunately, I do not have enough space here to go into details about these.

The rest of my account has four main parts. After a short historical overview I shall continue with the theoretical questions of how memory and, specifically, nostalgia are conceptualized. I shall then address the concept of Yugo-nostalgia and briefly present some existing views of the phenomenon. I focus on different specific Yugo-nostalgic spaces and objects of remembrance and alliances between the practices of consumerism and those of nationalism/patriotism in order to demonstrate how the commodification process glosses over uncomfortable historical truths. Finally, my conclusions will offer reflections on a 'tourist type' relationship to history that contributes to political and historical detachment and denial. I argue that Yugo-nostalgia works to restore a connection to a past that is inaccessible, but it does so using a commercial model.

Short historical context

The socialist idea of Yugoslavia promised to go beyond the contradictions of nationalism and ethnic groups, and celebrated a Yugoslav working-class identity. Thus, socialist Yugoslavia was created after the Second World War. It was a federal state within which each unit (six republics and two autonomous provinces within Serbia) had its own cultural infrastructure, institutions, platforms, and representative manifestations. Yugoslav cultural icons and events supplemented and connected

what were in fact separate, self-contained cultural realms, with their own cultural production, language and hierarchies of power, authority and influence. 'Titoism' was imagined and founded on the assumption that economic and political homogenization would lead to the creation of a pure workers' state.

Dominant accounts of the former Yugoslavia in the scholarly literature (Ramet, 1992; Sekulic, 1997) hold that it was through a combination of a socialist ideology and charisma that Tito managed to keep various nationalist interests in control during his rule (1945–1980). Under his aegis, different Yugoslav rituals were manufactured, and they were all a part of the ideological machinery introduced in order to frame the creation of Yugoslav subjects. The ritual of 'Youth Day' is one such example – it was impossible to be a Yugoslav and to be unaware of this day. Each year, on 25 May, a relay of young Yugoslavs ran through the Federation with a white baton, symbolizing the country's unity. Participation in this highly mediated ritual allowed the participants to connect themselves back to the envisioned common cultural history and across the geographical space.

As some research points out (Denitch, 1994), Yugoslavia was crucially about a specific cultural space, a civic space that was based on a common Yugoslav socialist culture. Some of the main markers of the Yugoslav identity were its unique rock'n'roll, Pan-Yugoslav media outlets and film, different Yugoslav products, sports and the Yugoslav Army. For example, music, known in the region as Yugoslav Rock, and represented by bands such as *Azra*, *Elektricni orgazam*, *Bijelo Dugme*, *Idoli*, *Sarlo Akrobata*, were seen as the cultural links between different nations. Pan-Yugoslav media, films, and TV shows were also crucial in providing and mobilizing Yugoslav identity. These media positioned and addressed the members of various nations as Yugoslavs and appeared to shape their attachment to a common, Yugoslav space. These pan-Yugoslav media outlets, such as the daily *Borba* [*Struggle*], the news agency Tanjug, the Radio Yugoslavia and the short-lived TV station Yutel attempted to hail and position the members of different nations also as Yugoslavs. Furthermore, different Yugoslav products, in their 'socialist-realist style', such as *Gorenje* (the TV sets), *Kras* (chocolates), *Zastava/Jugo* car, *Podravka Vegeta* (herbs), *Cocta* (Yugoslav Coke), *Radenska* (Mineral water), *Slovenijales* (the furniture) were popular, but in comparison with Western products (such as *Levis*), were far from glamorous and cool. However, the same products have returned in a now free-market system in a rebranded form – in a cool and trendy make-over, with the promise to possess 'a Yugoslav feel'.

Importantly, then, before the mid-1980s, the symbolic divisions of Yugoslavia into its northern and southern parts were not seen as irreconcilable. Each republic and province was seen as an integral part of Yugoslavia, and thus as a part of a cultural whole which, although internally diverse, actually strived to share a common Yugoslav identity that was something *special* (Hayden, 1991; Ramet, 1992). Both the death of Tito in 1980 and the collapse of the Yugoslav economy during the 1980s seriously challenged its identity (see Guzina, 2003). Destruction of Yugoslav identity markers came with the simultaneous escalation of competing nationalisms in the late 1980s and became a devastating hurricane only with the victory of the newly formed nationalist parties in the first multi-party elections in the republics in 1990 and the ensuing disintegration of Yugoslavia in 1991/1992.

At the end of the 1980s, the feelings of belonging slowly changed in all the former Yugoslav republics. And during the period of disintegration, so did the existing spaces of collective identifications in Yugoslavia, including collective memories and collective attachments to Yugoslav cultural spaces. As we know, all collective identities are relatively fluid constructions rather than eternal essences – they are discursively constructed, subject to rewriting. Seen thus, identities are not completely consistent, stable and fixed, but are generated differently in different contexts. Their creation is an active, dialectical process that involves the evolving construction and reconstruction of a sense of self-identity.

It was in the late 1980s that this particular image of Yugoslavia as characterized by a multicultural unity-in-diversity began to be slowly challenged. The internal diversity of Yugoslavia began to be redefined, mostly among political elites in Slovenia (and Croatia), as a barrier to its further development, and Yugoslavia itself began to be perceived as a mixture of incompatible civilizations, religions, or cultures: the Western and the Eastern, the European and the Balkan (see Ugresic, 1996). Thus it was precisely in the field of culture that the Yugoslav supra-national identity appeared first to have been questioned and contested. Mihelj (2004) suggests that different

media contributed in the overall shift from Yugoslav to national: cultural journals, the renaming of the streets, state symbols, food, theatre plays, bank notes… Each of these cultural forms played a particular role in the nationalization process. Ugresic writes how the removal of monuments and the changing of street names were among many small acts, the 'invisible losses' (Ugresic, 1996: 32) that helped to erase common cultural Yugoslav everyday life and Yugoslav belonging.

But what we witness during and after the ensuing wars among the former Yugoslav republics is precisely the process of strong remembering and (nostalgic) affirmative appropriation of Yugoslav symbols, rituals, and identities. A rising tide of former Yugoslav-themed television shows, the reinvention and rebranding of cultural products such as Yugo-films, or Yugoslav parties and compilation albums are further proof of the above. The next section introduces some theoretical frameworks in which to think about these manifestations of memory and nostalgia, and examines the ways in which mediated identity markers of Yugoslav culture have been celebrated, preserved and reappropriated in contemporary former Yugoslav public spheres. For example, one of the tourist agencies in Ljubljana, Slovenia, offers customers what it describes as 'a real Yugoslav experience'. According to one of the tourists who attended the famous 'Yugoslav tour' from Ljubljana to Belgrade (with stops in numerous iconic former Yugoslav places):

> It is great to recapture the feeling that we have lost. … I am now able to visit the country that exists no more … and at least for a week live like we all did. I feel a Yugoslav, I always did. This tour makes it possible for me to remember and not forget what a beautiful country this was…

Ethnographic attention to the variety of mediated texts will illustrate the manner in which the 'nostalgic' activities provide opportunities for a framework of thinking about Yugo-nostalgia in particular.

On memory and nostalgia

Rethinking memory

Scholars in many disciplines have focused on how a sense of the past can inform politics, religion, art and social life of different groups. The importance of memory is taken for granted, but its functioning in particular contexts is still disputed (see Kuhn, 2000). The key idea is that human memory is influenced by a variety of factors (Lowenthal, 1985: 193), one of which derives from a particular social arena in which humans are situated when they remember the past. Halbwachs (1980 [1951]) emphasized how social processes influence both people's personal memories of their own lifetime, and also their shared, collective memories of the past. Additionally, collective memories partially shape the reality that enables people to imagine the world in which they live. Margalit (2002) develops two different types of collective memory: 'shared memory' and 'common memory'. In this model, a common memory is an aggregate notion that allows individuals to remember a specific, commonly experienced event. A shared memory, however, is more than just an accumulation of individual memories, since it is about communicating and sharing it. In that way, a shared memory is an active process by which a vision is preserved. Many scholars (Kuhn, 2000; Margalit, 2002) argue that it is through 'shared memory' that any community produces and reproduces itself, and how the production and reproduction of communities depends upon a dialectics of collective remembering and forgetting.

Mapping nostalgia

In its general use the term nostalgia refers to human feelings in relation to home, or more specifically it describes the feelings one has towards home caused by some sort of separation from it (be it voluntary or involuntary, geographical or mental). Semantically, it is a compound word with its roots in the Greek words *nostos* (meaning to return home) and *algia* (meaning longing or pain). The notion was introduced into Western thought through the medical professionals of the seventeenth century, whose reports identified this peculiar condition in soldiers involved in military activities far from their home for longer periods of time (Boym, 2001; Davis, 1979). The term itself was coined in 1688 by a Swiss physician Johannes Hofer, who pedantically followed the medical tradition of naming medical conditions with Greek names. In 1731, it was classified as a disease by another Swiss physician, J.J. Scheuchzer, and for some 170 years the condition was treated exclusively as a medical problem and various treatments were recommended: from leeches and

opium, to hypnosis and pain (Boym, 2001: 3–5; Davis, 1979: 414). Indeed, Stewart (1993) characterizes nostalgia as a social disease, contending that it has been detached from any specific home and reattached to inviting objects such as souvenirs. She views it as a cultural practice that rises to the surface under the circumstances of consumer capitalism, when the self comes to experience the surrounding social world and culture itself as more fragmented, diffused, and filled with feelings of insecurity. For Stewart, at these times the self turns to nostalgia to provide the needed meaning to its feelings.

In the second half of the twentieth century the term 'nostalgia' began to cast off its medical connotations and came to be classified as an emotional space shaped by memories of the past. The elusiveness of the term is, at least partially, due to its dual nature – on one hand it is a subjectively experienced sentiment, while at the same time it is a cultural phenomenon. In other words, the effects of nostalgia are experienced in private as well as in the public sphere. Davis distinguishes between private and collective nostalgia in his book *Yearning for Yesterday: A Sociology of Nostalgia* (1979). He argues that private nostalgia is characterized by:

> the symbolic images and allusions from the past which by virtue of their resource in a particular person's biography tend to be more idiosyncratic, individuated, and particularistic in their reference; e.g., the memory of parent's smile, the garden view from a certain window of a house once lived in…. (1979: 123)

On the other hand, according to Davis, collective nostalgia describes 'the condition in which the symbolic objects are of a highly public, widely shared and familiar character, i.e., those symbolic resources from the past which can, under proper conditions, trigger off wave upon wave of nostalgic feeling in millions of persons at the same time' (1979: 122–123).

Private nostalgia rests upon particular, even intimate, personal memories that one may choose to share with a very limited number of people; collective nostalgia relies on images, symbols, and signs available to many different people within the same historical and socio-cultural context. As such, public nostalgia dwells in the content of the group's history, and exploits the group's cultural symbols, and especially its popular culture. In that respect it is not surprising that examples of public nostalgia range widely: from cultural symbols carrying historical significance, such as national anthems, flags, and royal coats of arms, to popular cultural symbols like Coca-Cola, TV shows, food items, sporting events and games. In our context, Yugo-nostalgia is not solely a public presentation; it is also a phenomenon that characterizes private spaces – numerous private homes are deliberately decorated in 'socialist' style. It is also a style of interior decoration that makes a statement in apartments and office cubicles. People decorate their personal spaces in ways that express sentiments they may not make in public or political contexts.

In her influential book *The Future of Nostalgia* (2001), Boym outlines two tendencies that shape the meaning of our nostalgic sentiments by underscoring one's relationship to the past:

> [Restorative and reflective nostalgia] do not explain the nature of longing nor its psychological makeup and unconscious undercurrents; rather they are about the ways in which we make sense of our seemingly ineffable homesickness and how we view our relationship to a collective home. (2001: 41)

For Boym, nostalgia is not limited to the domain of the personal psyche, for she insists on the links and interplay between the individual and the collective; in other words, one's frameworks of memories and one's nostalgia are to be juxtaposed with the greater framework of collective memories and collective history. This intersection of the individual and the social opens the space within which it is possible to investigate an ongoing reconstruction and the maintenance of self-identity and a sense of collective identity within the framework of nostalgia. By establishing this connection, Boym underscores that nostalgia plays an important role in relating our past experiences and memories to our present and future, thereby creating a sense of continuity in our lives.

According to Boym, restorative nostalgia occupies the domain of those concerned with reconstruction of the past in the sense of the restoration of origins and tradition. In their extreme forms, the advocates of restorative nostalgia are engaged in the 'anti-modern myth making of history', usually to be found on the right of the political continuum, and commonly are in favour of the re-establishment of ritualistic features that are held to be markers of their group identity (Boym, 2001: 41). They believe in an absolute truth and view the reconstruction process as the group's priority. At the level of everyday life the results of this view are observable in the pedantic restoration of monuments of the group's 'historical past', changing the names of streets and public spaces to reflect 'our tradition', rewriting history in public discourse etc. all in order to construct and support a single narrative of (national) origin. Instances of this type of nostalgia are easily found in the policies and acts of nationalistic parties in the post-socialist world of Eastern Europe. For example, with the rise of the Croatian nationalist movement in the late 1980s, many streets in Croatian cities were renamed after Croatian historical figures, thereby replacing names of Croats and others associated with the history of Croatia within Yugoslavia. In the Croatian capital, the main square, 'The Republic Square' became 'The Ban Jelacic Square', and in 1990 the monument to the Ban was ceremonially returned to the Square (it had been removed in 1947). These symbolic changes resulted from the restorative discourse in the Croatian public spheres aiming to reinstate a sense of 'Croatian-ness' and Croatian national history.

On the other hand, reflective nostalgia is 'more concerned with historical and individual time, with the irrevocability of the past and human finitude' (Boym, 2001: 49). Whereas restorative nostalgia is about the collective and national memory, the reflective type is about the individual and cultural memory. Importantly, Boym asserts that the two may overlap in the frame of reference, but they certainly do not endorse the same narrative of identity (2001: 49). Those engaging in the reflective type of nostalgia are not involved in any rebuilding of mythical places and are unapologetically against historical forgetting. The reflective nostalgic longing acknowledges the multiple and multi-levelled narratives of history and belonging.

Memory/nostalgia and post-socialism in Eastern Europe

'Post-socialism' refers to the period in world history (more precisely European history) that began with the fall of the Berlin Wall in 1989. At its primary level, this event signified the end of the ideologically imposed and politically exercised division of Germany that took place after World War II; it ended the forty-five years of enforced separation of the nation and opened a door for the country's reunification. On a symbolic level, the event marked the beginning of the end of a world order based on the polarity between capitalist countries advancing a liberal-democratic order (the West, i.e. the Western European countries and the USA, Canada, and Australia) and 'socialist' countries advocating a centralist model of the state (the East, i.e. Eastern European countries and the USSR). Within three years following the fall of the Berlin Wall, all of the socialist regimes of Europe collapsed: Albania, Bulgaria, Czechoslovakia, Hungary, Poland, Romania, the USSR, and the Socialist Federative Republic of Yugoslavia. More importantly, in the cases of East Germany, Czechoslovakia, the USSR, and Yugoslavia the changes in political regime were accompanied by a complete collapse and the breakdown of the state. German reunification and Czechoslovakia's division into the Czech Republic and Slovakia went peacefully; in fact, the Czechoslovakian case has become known as the 'velvet revolution'. On the other hand, the collapse of socialist regimes and the processes of the state breakdown incited different levels of violence in countries like Romania, the USSR and Yugoslavia, the most extreme case being the one of Yugoslavia, as the country spiralled into a several years of civil war and disintegrated into seven new nation states. The Yugo-nostalgia phenomenon cannot be understood apart from the concrete historical conditions. The nostalgic appeal emerges against the background of the violent Yugoslav wars that resulted in an estimated 300,000 deaths and millions of refugees.

The end of socialist regimes and the emergence of post-socialist societies has become the topic of numerous research projects in and outside academia. The collapse of the socialist system made it possible to observe and investigate first-hand the social processes, movements, and behaviour resulting from the regime and state collapse. The transition from a collectively organized and ideologically based state-socialist system to the capitalist model of liberal society with a free market economy and democratic political organization required a snowball of reforms. The main reforms were introduced in the spheres of economy

(including agriculture), politics, and government (Potrata, 2004). However, it is important to note that the processes of transition and the success rate of the reform implementation have varied among post-socialist countries. The magnitude of difference is so striking that some authors use the term 'great divide' to describe the variations (Potrata, 2004).

The realm of social relations also changed rapidly. Culture, as a set of signifying practices that provide meaning(s) in our daily life, also underwent changes, with the introduction of capitalism as a dominant discourse. The higher degree of the rationalization of time, the rapid privatization of means of production, and the significant increase in social class distinctions are just some of the elements that influenced changes in cultural and social practices. Also, as these societies become more 'Western' (i.e. capitalist) in their outlook, the pattern of consumption practices has increasingly followed the Western models.

As a result, in the post-socialist context, an already complex concept of nostalgia comes with another twist. In his writings on nostalgia in the context of East Germany (the phenomenon known as *Ostalgie*), Bach (2002: 547) suggests that 'Nostalgia is colloquially a form of longing for the past, but its modernist variant is less longing for an unredeemable past as such than a longing for the fantasies and desires that were once possible in the past'. Bach points out a peculiar property of nostalgia in relation to Eastern Europe: the radical discontinuity with the past, in other words the disintegration and disappearance of countries like East Germany, Yugoslavia and the USSR, brought about the realization that certain elements of the past have become unredeemable, not only because of the basic property of the past as a time gone, but because of the unavailability of discourses that used to exist there.

After the collapse of the socialist regimes and the disappearance of their countries, the social context of practices of socialist collectivity (rituals, festivals, ways of being...) disappeared as well. The social conditions of post-socialism and the post-war context disturbed the process of collective remembering, and not only the content of the generations' collective memory. Under these conditions, nostalgia becomes an attractive concept as a practice of preserving the collective memory. In that sense, Boym is helpful in assessing nostalgia as 'an affective yearning for a community with collective memory, a longing for continuity in a fragmented world' (Boym, 2001: xiv).

It seems necessary to suggest that some people experience nostalgia in relation to their collective memory not simply because they cannot 'turn back time' to their youth, but also because they realize that there is no prospect of their collective memory continuation. This form of nostalgia for collective memory seems to be peculiar to people experiencing the post-socialist condition. Let me briefly now turn to specific examples of Yugo-nostalgia.

Box 15.1 Dah Theatre of Belgrade

In the 1990s, Belgrade, a city of multiple 'interrupted' identities and overlapping memories, saw many expressions of nationalistic hysteria transmitted through the mainstream media and various public cultural institutions. The 'Other Serbia' developed a pacifist discourse, using art and the rare free media that existed, such as B92. As a result, there emerged at least two, if not more, parallel discourses about the past. The nationalist discourse was that of 'bourgeois nationalism', strongly laced with a sense of victimhood and anti-communism. It was also an anti-Europe discourse, based on socialist/communist traditions and pro-Russian sentiment. Both fanned a fear of minorities and tried to find permanent proofs in history that minorities were all traitors.

But the dreams of the former plural Belgrade never died. These were visions of a metropolis (from the time of the Non-aligned Movement) or at least of a regional cultural centre, a place of dialogue among southern Slavic cultures. In spite of everything – politics, the exodus of young people, the trade embargo, and sheer misery – alternative arts movements had kept Belgrade a multicultural city, in which different generations and different cultural models co-existed, albeit with different experiences. The lost aura of a cosmopolitan city was brought back by artists through public arts events produced within civil society movements, marking and constructing new memory politics. Artists knew that unless there could be open debate about issues such as genocide, massacres, or ethnic cleansing, the cosmopolitan Belgrade of yore would not reappear. Hence civil society developed a discourse based on anti-fascist memories, the memories of 'forgotten actors' such as women and ethnic minorities, nineteenth-century Europeanization and modernization processes, even socialism. Exhibitions and books like Die Deutschen unserer Stadt, or The Gypsies, Our Neighbours, could thus appear.

The performances of Dah Theatre are typical of these 'bottom-up memory politics'. Using public space theatre performance methods, this company, since its first street-art theatre based on the work of Berthold Brecht, has tried to reach out not only to a random audience, but also to groups of politically active citizens, who are willing to address critical questions for wider social debate. Using collective memories and national myths, urban legends and present media practices, the company has created works which are a major contribution towards a politics of memory from the ground up, a politics that is equally one of social responsibility and the building of trust. Courage was necessary to use public space – the main square and pedestrian street in Belgrade – and mount there a performance devoted to the victims of the Srebrenica genocide, or to introduce the voices of Bosnian women as well as those of long-disappeared minorities – Kalmiks, Armenians, Turks, Jews, but also Germans...

The strength and courage of this theatre company, led by women, has enabled different voices to be heard in Belgrade and to open Serbian public space to the voice of the 'others'. Using different 'cultural raw materials' – unfashionable or neglected writers such as Brecht or Nastasijevic, or little known artistic movements such as Zenit, Dah Theatre is exploring the past of the city seen through the lenses of its contemporary traumas. These are the traumas which public policies (educational, cultural) deliberately wish to forget, and which they therefore either ignore or neglect. Their politics of memory is based upon 'not-knowing'. This is the official policy of the State of Serbia: 'We did not participate in the war'.

Taking collective traumas, deconstructing them through individual approaches and testimonies, and returning them to contemporary life in the form of a performance, which is at the same time social critique of the city and society, Dah Theatre is again recreating public space as the locus not only of consumerist practices, or conflicts and tensions, but also of aspirations and tendencies – of opening up future horizons, by exploring painful memories of the past. The players question their own feelings and statements: How long does the sorrow imposed by historical violence last? Where are the borders of my personal responsibilities for crimes committed in my name? Their answers have all been highly personalized and emotional, confronting the audiences with the awareness, the memories and the guilt associated with ethnic violence. Performances are often based on the narratives of ordinary citizens, such as the testimonies of women in 'Women's Side of the War'. Each performance is followed by an open dialogue, in which people in the audience share their stories and memories and gives advice to others. Feelings of solidarity and togetherness emerge. The women may be Bosnian, Croatian, Albanian, Serbian, Hungarian, Roma, or German, but the same voice comes through in the end: the voice of THE European woman who screams out for peace.

The project is contributing through this new memory politics – where all of the different voices are heard simultaneously – towards an effective politics of peace-building and reconciliation ('official' projects and programmes do not really exist in this domain and war discourse is usually about 'our' victims). Performances have taken place throughout the region, as well elsewhere in Europe and the rest of the world. In December 2005, the company performed *Invisible City* in a city bus – line 26. The performances aimed to raise awareness of multicultural Belgrade, which is slowly disappearing or hiding its true face behind globalization billboards and new signs of the postmodern city of consumption. The main challenge was how to preserve the heritage of others, and especially their intangible heritage. These are the lost neighbours, ethnic groups who have disappeared or cannot keep their culture alive: the Jewish community, Gypsies, Buddhist Kalmiks, White Russians, Macedonian bakers, Gorani pastry shop owners … and Kosovo Albanians (who used to come as seasonal workers). By constantly introducing new elements and new dimensions, Dah Theatre's provocations underline the absence of any kind of consistent public cultural policy of remembrance. The city authorities began by ignoring artistic civil society, but then found it necessary to consider its claims and proposals and then finally found themselves obliged to support and integrate them in their own policies and programmes, at least partially. Yet they are never willing to be reminded of recent historical 'controversies'. For this reason, the entire independent cultural sector (Druga Srbija), which includes many bodies like the Dah Theatre, will always remain in a situation of uncertainty regarding its status and public recognition.

Milena Dragićević Šešić

Yugo-nostalgia – a commercial (re) production of Yugoslavia

Some authors argue that there is a need to differentiate between 'cultural' and 'economic' types of Yugo-nostalgia. The first type reflects the overwhelming fatigue with the nationalist rhetorics and iconology of the successor states, ruled by nationalist parties and nationalist leaders Economically, branding and marketing of Yugo symbols reflects the replacement of Yugoslav socialism with the capitalist system (Jurkovic, 2006; Slapsak, 2008). Specifically, Ugresic (1996) argues that Yugo-nostalgia is a fundamental tool in the process of the preservation of the cultural memory and history of Yugoslavia, both as a state and as an idea. In this favourable reading of Yugo-nostalgia, emphasis is placed on the positive elements of life in Yugoslavia: reasonable economic security, low crime rates, multiculturalism, freedom of movement, international recognition of the country (i.e. the politics of non-alignment), and the overall perception that life in Yugoslavia was more rewarding than it is today in the newly independent states. Understood in this manner, Yugo-nostalgia seems to be a positive and potentially productive force in the processes of reconciliation in the Balkans. However, some other authors are more critical about Yugo-nostalgia. Slapsak (2008) acknowledges the importance of 're-thinking' Yugoslavia, but contends that Yugo-nostalgia, in its primary, consumerist mode, focuses on the simplest forms and representations of Yugoslav culture. In doing so, it (re)creates stereotypes of the collapsed society and leads nowhere in terms of acquiring and clarifying historical knowledge.

My focus here, however, is on the celebratory production and consumption of Yugo-nostalgia that both appear as forms of a reappropriation of different past symbols. Importantly, there are some generational differences in producing and consuming Yugo-nostalgia. On one hand, for those who lived through Yugoslav times, Yugo-nostalgia is a way to idealize and embellish an experience that is postulated as superior to the subsequent war, suffering, exile and post-war existence in the successor Yugoslav states, a reaction to the prevailing nationalist critique of the Yugoslav communism, one-sidedness combating one-sidedness. On the other hand, for the younger generations, born at the end of the 1980s and 1990s, who don't remember/can't remember the former state, Yugo-nostalgia is an exotic construct, a mythologeme of a happy remote past, a bizarre, romanticized pocket of otherness in the overwhelming wave of globalization and its culture of commercial sameness. Based on my interviews and observations, I propose different (often overlapping) levels of Yugo-nostalgia. Of course Yugo-nostalgia takes on a variety of forms – as do all group phenomena – but for the purposes of analysis it is worth considering different aspects and examples of it.

Examples of Yugo-nostalgia

Yugo-nostalgia created various and diverse events, new spaces, identities, memories and complex media representations, such as, for example, the extremely popular Josip Broz Tito memorial webpage titoville.com in Slovenia, set up in July 1994 by two Ljubljana University students. According to one of them,

Tito seemed just a controversial figure enough to invite the visitors in cyberspace. We were building a website for a dead personality that could this

way continue his life and maintain its cult in cyberspace. We knew there was plenty of his material left – photos, books, speeches, movies, etc. We created the site as a chat-space ... where Tito directly addresses the visitor. We thought there would be some kind of feedback from browsing visitors and it really came, strong. All different kinds of offending and praising voices started to trickle in. The site really works as a reminder of lost memories, and forgotten states of mind. (personal interview)

Also, one needs to mention the creation of a 'new' proclaimed country called Yugoslavia in a suburb of the village of Subotica, Serbia. The founder of 'Yugoland' is a businessman called Blasko Gabric, from Subotica, who was so sad when Yugoslavia collapsed that he decided to recreate it in his garden. When I visited Yugoland, visitors from all the former Yugoslav states queued to buy back their Yugoslav citizenship for a couple of hundred dinars, the former Yugoslav currency. One of the informants stated that 'I am here because I miss Yugoslavia, I miss everything about that country. I don't know how to understand what happened to it, and my heart is full of sadness. Coming to this place reminds me in a way how I felt when I was happy in our common state.'

There are also Yugoslav states being introduced and created in cyberspace, such as Cyberyu.com, and RepublikaTitoslavija.com, all promising a Yugoslav cyber-citizenship, and escape into the Yugoslav past. On these websites, one can read passionate statements about the 'wonderful past'. The example below is typical:

I am here, in this virtual space, because it allows me to be together with others who feel the same: we all miss Yugoslavia, we miss brotherhood and unity, we miss the feeling of sharing a united, yet diverse country. Now, I live in a small pond only, with no multiculturalism, It's just sameness, all around me...

And then there are the annual dance festivals of socialist celebrations and the reincarnations of Tito who appear throughout the former country, either as artistic performances or political spectacles. In Skopje, Macedonia, on 25 May, the celebrations are organized on the main public square. Sellers of badges, labels and ribbons in the colours of the Yugoslav flag are seen everywhere. There have been several political calls made by political actors to reconnect and recreate 'a sort of Yugoslavia, where we have been so happy' (a Macedonian MP, in a personal interview).

It may also not be a coincidence that many popular cultural products from former Yugoslavia (films, television series, or music) expound on playful versions of Yugoslav memory. There is a rising popularity of Yugoslav-themed TV shows, pop compilation albums and films that are turning Yugo-nostalgia into mainstream entertainment.

It is difficult to provide a simple and distinctive definition of Yugo-nostalgia. Instead, I can begin to sketch out here some differences between different forms and layers of Yugo-nostalgia, and describe the most popular cotemporary Yugo-nostalgic cultural practices, as I analyse them. The goal is not to prove that Yugo-nostalgia *per se* as conceived, produced and received is a false and dangerous phenomenon. Rather, it is to show how certain ways of relating to the past became dominant and to provide an interpretation of commercial portrayals of contemporary forms of the past.

Revisiting different Yugoslav rituals. Every year on 25 May, Tito's birthday, there is a huge party of Socialist Youth in one of the main squares in the capital cities of the former Yugoslav republics. These different projects attempt to re-create a feeling of Yugoslav socialist celebrations, but at the same time they do little to challenge, negotiate, or abolish the stereotypical understanding of the Yugoslav spaces and times. Thus, if nostalgia reacquaints us with loss, it also threatens to aestheticize the banality, or the stereotypes it recalls.

Nostalgic memories of Tito. Everywhere in the former Yugoslav republics Josip Broz Tito seems to continue to impersonate the Yugoslavia that many people remember in a positive light. Accordingly, associations everywhere have been founded to honour Tito's memory: people flock to his grave in Belgrade, Serbia, and his birthplace of Kumrovec in Croatia. Across the road from Tito's house, a Tito pub draws in crowds using the memory of the former Yugoslav leader as its tourist attraction. Tito's summer cottage on the outskirts of the Kumrovec village was turned into a hotel. There are Tito's bars and restaurants in all the former Yugoslav states. They are popular among guests for serving Tito's wine, or any other type of food named after him.

When the authorities in Sarajevo, Bosnia, wanted to rename the main street after the late Bosniak leader Alija Izetbegovic, public resistance forced the municipal administration to keep its current name – Titova. The same debates around renaming Titova Street took place in Ljubljana, Slovenia, in 2009. Also, in Slovenia, an actor, Ivo Godnic, is well known for expressing emotional Yugo-nostalgic feelings: he is frequently invited to different public festivals and private parties to perform the role of comrade Tito.

In 2005, Tito's private train – called the Blue Train – was refurbished as a novelty attraction: a historic theme-park ride, as it were, for the Yugo-nostalgic. The train, complete with private compartments, fully fitted bathrooms and a conference room, was built for Tito shortly after the World War II. One can now rent it for private parties, or just purchase a ticket to travel from destination to destination. While interviewing travellers on the train, one of them claimed that 'for me, this journey is very emotional. I remember Tito on this train, and now I can travel on this train and visit our country again … see the lands, and stop in those beautiful Yugoslav town, our towns…'.

Cati, a Slovene advertising company, published a report in 2005 on the prospects and potentials of branding famous personalities. The report argued that memories of Tito are particularly strong in the region and could be appropriated and marketed. Branding Tito as a product of socialist luxurious culture does present a specific type of irony and a break from the past indeed. Like the Nike swoosh, Tito becomes an advertisement, selling cars (Slovenia), wine (Croatia), mineral water (Serbia, Macedonia) and ties (Bosnia). Yet, the tendency here is to believe that by repackaging or rebranding a specific historical character, event or a process, one can give the power back to consumers through the (commercial) consumption of history. In that way, however, a discourse of commercialization marginalizes and trivializes the unique historical events and characters.

Yugoslav music. In the arena of popular music, Yugo-nostalgic music festivals continue to draw crowds in many former Yugoslav cities. There is a move to reclaim a sense of Yugoslav identity through the spirit of Yugoslav music, and in particular the rock music that was popular in the 1970s and 1980s. In both Slovenia and Croatia, popular

Balkan parties are regularly organized, where Yugoslav music is played, and the revival of Yugo-rock has sparked the passionate appropriation of aspects of the 'Yugoslav/Balkan' lifestyle. Compilations of Yugoslav-era popular music are being released, and 1980s era rock acts have been rehabilitated to tour the former Yugoslav states. The tour of the most famous former Yugoslav band *Bijelo Dugme* (*White Button*) in the summer of 2005 attracted thousands of fans when they performed in Belgrade, Zagreb and Sarajevo. According to some reports, more than 200,000 concert-goers came to the Belgrade concert. One of the fans I interviewed said the concert-goers came to remember 'how happy we have all been, all of us, living in Yugoslavia'.

Conclusions

My research suggests that the nostalgic process of recreation involves both a descriptive recollection of past activities and the imaginative reinvention of images in memories. Despite its premise, the term 'nostalgia' is full of contradictions – posing numerous theoretical problems, but also, in the Yugoslav case, practical challenges. To oversimplify, Yugo-nostalgia works to restore a connection to a past that is inaccessible, but it does so through a commercial model. Yugo-nostalgia serves as an avoidance

mechanism that postpones indefinitely a crucial reckoning with the past and the role it played in exacerbating the tensions that erupted in the Yugoslav wars of the 1990s. The speed with which the market commodifies memory and stimulates nostalgia as a marketing strategy bolsters the forms of deferral that I associate with Yugo-nostalgia. Creating a marketable version of the past requires smoothing over its rough spots and filling in its contradictions in order to consume it rather than engaging with it.

This focus on nostalgia mainly as a form of a commodity and insincerity may dissuade us from pursuing questions about enjoyment and agency. Of course, Yugo-nostalgia *per se* is not problematic, but what I see as manipulative is precisely the manner in which it gets used, borrowed, appropriated, and exploited in the region for both nationalistic/populist and/or commercial purposes. In the former Yugoslavia, memory not only becomes a means for building individual and national identity, but also is subsumed under a moral economy of reclaiming the past. The appropriation, editing and manipulation of memory facilitate its further appropriation as a commodity. Such commodification ironically both constitutes and compromises memory as truth and justice. The politics of Yugoslav identity have not been eliminated, but have been transformed and commodified in the context of historical global dynamics and political and economic transnational forces.

REFERENCES

Bach, J. (2002) 'The Taste Remains: Consumption, (N)ostalgia, and the Production of East Germany'. *Public Culture*, 14(3): 545–556.

Boym, S. (2001) *The Future of Nostalgia*. New York: Basic Books.

Davis, F. (1979) *Yearning for Yesterday: A Sociology of Nostalgia*. New York: The Free Press.

Denitch, B. (1994) *Ethnic Nationalism: The Tragic Death of Yugoslavia*. Minneapolis, MN: University of Minnesota Press.

Guzina, D. (2003) 'Socialist Serbia's Narratives: From Yugoslavia to a Greater Serbia'. *International Journal of Politics, Culture, and Society*, 17(1): 91–111.

Halbwachs, M. (1980 [1951]) *The Collective Memory*. New York and London: Harper & Row.

Hayden, R.M. (1991) 'Yugoslavia from Civil Society to Civil War'. Paper presented at the annual meeting of the American Anthropological Association, Chicago.

Ivy, M. (1995) Discourses of the Vanishing: Modernity, Phantasm, Japan. Chicago: University of Chicago Press.

Jurkovic, J. (2006) 'Trgovanje Titom [Trading Tito]'. In K.M. Hjemdahl and N.Š. Alempijevia (eds), *O Titu kao mitu [Tito as a Myth]*. Zagreb: Filozofski fakultet, Srednja Europa, pp. 277–299.

Kuhn, A. (2000) 'A Journey through Memory'. In S. Radstone (ed.), *Memory and Methodology*. Oxford: Berg, pp. 183–186.

Lowenthal, D. (1985) *The Past is a Foreign Country*. Cambridge: Cambridge University Press.

Margalit, A. (2002) *The Ethics of Memory*. Cambridge, MA: Harvard University Press.

Mihelj, S. (2004) 'The Role of Mass Media in the (Re)constitution of Nations: The (Re)constitution of the Slovenian Nation through the Media Representations of the Plebiscite for an Independent Slovenia, Bosnian Refugees and Non-registered Migration'. Unpublished PhD thesis. Ljubljana: Institutum Studiorum Humanitatis.

Potrata, B. (2004) 'New Age, Socialism and Other Millenarianisms: Affirming and Struggling with (Post)socialism'. *Religion, State and Society*, 43(3): 366–379.

Ramet, S. (1992) Balkan Babel: Politics, Culture and Religion in Yugoslavia. Boulder, CO: Westview Press.

Sekulic, D. (1997) 'The Creation and Dissolution of the Multinational State: The Case of Yugoslavia'. *Nations and Nationalism*, 10(2): 165–179.

Slapsak, S. (2008) 'Nostalgija'. *Vecer*, 27 December, p. 52.

Stewart, S. (1993) *On Longing: Narratives of the Miniature, the Gigantic, the Souvenir, the Collection*. Durham, NC: Duke University Press.

Ugresic, D. (1996) 'The Confiscation of Memory'. *New Left Review*, 21(8): 26–39.

CHAPTER 16

CONTEMPORARY CREATIVITY AND HERITAGE IN LATIN AMERICA
Lucina Jiménez López

In Latin America, globalization has transformed understandings of the relationships between contemporary creativity and the heritage–memory–identity triad. This chapter explores this regional dynamic. It looks at the diverse expressions of creativity in different cultural fields and analyzes the ways in which these have been shaped by forces such as migratory flows, new technologies and various forms of cultural hybridity. The latter, in particular, have been generated by the collapsing of boundaries among contemporary art, traditional cultures, digital culture and the cultural industries. As a result, what new complexities and contradictions challenge the public policies of memory and heritage? What are the implications for cultural policies that hitherto have focused on the preservation of traditional cultures?

Heritage, memory and identity in Latin America

Most Latin American societies have built their nation-state under the aegis of homogenization,

while recognizing that different social groups have their own common pasts and popular culture traditions.[1] The region's early nationalisms established a strong concept of heritage that highlighted distinctive cultural values opposed to universal culture, based on a common and pre-Hispanic past. Yet each people aspired to a distinct nation, to a 'national' culture and an 'identity'. However, not all memories were included in the 'national' narrative created by the State in the early twentieth century, a narrative that emphasized integration into politically defined and accepted identities (Florescano, 1993: 10–13).

This posture profoundly influenced the way the heritage/memory/identity triad was interpreted in early Latin American modernity. The memories of the indigenous peoples or those of African descent, among others, were among those excluded. Influenced by evolutionism as well as a dose of racism, Mexico and other Latin American societies elaborated so-called improved 'integration' or indigenous 'assimilation' policies. As Manuel Gamio described this dominant discourse:

> Our cultural expressions are and have been impaired, above all in relation to the Fine Arts and the Social Sciences.[2] These deficiencies have two principal causes: the first is the ethnic heterogeneity of our populations, which has meant that there can be no truly national environment that inspires harmony and specificity in intellectual production. The second cause is feudal intellectualism, which in our countries has always paralleled the exclusivism of our governments.
>
> … To assimilate Indians we can't pretend that they suddenly become European; so let us do the opposite by bringing ourselves a little bit closer to Indian culture and presenting them with a version of their culture that has been dissolved into ours. In that way, they won't find it exotic, cruel and incomprehensible. Naturally, there is no need for us to exaggerate the proximity.

This 'intermediate culture' ... is the national culture, the culture of the future, it will become dominant when the population, being ethnically homogeneous, can feel and understand it. (1916: 93–101)

This paradigm has been eroded by many different factors. These have included globalization, the impact of the technological revolution, urban development, the emergence of social and indigenous movements, the international mobility of different sectors, claims to the recognition of difference, the mobilization of civil society organizations and the international dissemination of new notions of heritage, particularly that of the intangible heritage. Together, these factors have brought about a profound crisis of cultural definition, challenging the notions of diversity and creativity across the landscape of contemporary cultural change. Under the old conceptions, cultural policies privileged the fine arts over traditional and indigenous expressions. Only the former were legitimated as contemporary culture. Social and cultural change were admitted into State conceptions of heritage and identity, but mainly as negative influences that have promoted phenomena such as 'transculturization', 'massification' or 'loss'. Over several decades, cultural policymakers have dedicated budgets and created institutions to 'rescue' the 'authenticity' of the arts and crafts, beliefs, dances or music, masks, recipes or traditional knowledge of medicine, environment or technology. Diversity and cultural change were recognized as realities only in the last two decades of the last century. Until then, identity was yoked exclusively to the wagon of predefined and homogenizing collective memories and heritage, despite the abundance of official discourse in favor of pluralism and democracy. Hence the absolute priority accorded to the fine arts, together with libraries and reading and the preservation and promotion of material heritage (Jiménez López and Florescano, 2008).

Before the adoption of UNESCO's 2003 *Convention for the Safeguarding of the Intangible Cultural Heritage*, Latin American understandings of 'heritage' were limited to mostly material manifestations, ranging from archeological sites to museum collections (see Isar's chapter in this volume). The focus in the first half of the twentieth century was on the creation of museums, and the restoration and preservation of archeological sites and colonial heritage. These efforts were considerable. As regards traditional cultural forms, including those now viewed as 'intangible heritage', the focus was on describing and analyzing them, but as a glorious past, rather than a strong and diverse living present. Amerindian cultures were confined to museums or history books. In best-case scenarios they were treated as colorful folklore to be appropriated for the purposes of international tourism.

Thinking about contemporary art in Latin America has been totally disconnected from theorizing about heritage. Nevertheless, the fact is that contemporary art has actually already become part of the heritage and for this reason policies are needed that takes this reality into account (Arizpe, 2005). These policy frameworks must consider the economic as well as the symbolic aspects of the visual and performing arts, their connections to new media technologies as well as new audiences. The emergence of a 'creative economy' in the region also means that artistic creativity and its contributions to other sectors needs to be promoted as well (see Cunningham et al., 2008). As regards memory, the issues that arise stem from its collectively constructed nature in and for the present, as a social process that transforms or gives new meanings to common beliefs and deploy them to form visions for the future.

In 2009, the countries of Latin America together with Spain began celebrating the bicentenary of the independence struggles against the Spanish colonial empire (in Mexico it was also the Centenary of the Revolution). There might well be deep contradictions among the different versions of this history, but a question shared by all is how the collective memories of these historical events can be linked to present-day creative work in the context of sustainable human development. I read the term sustainable development broadly to include poverty elimination, the reduction of illiteracy and the school dropout phenomenon that affects millions of adolescents, environmental degradation and social exclusion. Some countries, such as Brazil, Colombia, Ecuador, El Salvador and Guatemala, have been developing policies of memory related to political processes (armed conflicts and other forms of violence, displacement, etc.). They are also beginning to heed the claims of various ethnic minorities who are pushing for the recognition of collective memories until now unrecognized in the official history or national narratives. What they find harder to achieve, however, is the reinforcement of contemporary arts practice among these groups.

There is simply not enough knowledge about contemporary creativity and innovation in traditional expressions of culture. In some cases, artistic efforts to memorialize different historical moments have actually been rejected as well. García Canclini (2004: 11) underlines the uncertainty in intellectual work and artistic creation at the beginning of the twenty-first century that is brought about by the dialectic of homogenization and pluralization inherent in globalization, as pointed out in the Introduction to Volume 2 of this Series (Anheier and Isar, 2008). These have deep implications as regards cultural policies. As Jesus Martín-Barbero has diagnosed the situation, these policies are 'held back by basically preservationist concepts of identity and disconnected from private and independent groups [and] have tended to freeze local cultural development fragment cultural consumption and create inequities' (cited in Rosas Mantecón, 2004: 14) As the Latin American State has been weakened by globalization, endemic economic crisis and the growth of poverty and inequity, all the various players in the cultural sector across the continent, including contemporary artists, are faced with inadequate support for their work and, as in Europe, have begun to articulate the need to entirely revise public policies for culture as well as the manner in which they are elaborated (Creative Europe, 2002). If globalization blurs the boundaries between the local and global, it also deepens fragmentation. Hence also the need for far more effective intercultural dialogue, not just between and within nations, but even within local communities. For cultural diversity and hybridization are now commonplace at the local level and can easily become sources of conflict and violence (see *Conflicts and Tensions*, the first volume in the *Series*), as immigrant cultures may contradict local mores and as local young people acquire increasingly 'glocalized' forms of behavior not always understood by the previous generation.

Creativity, diversity and heritage

In their Introduction to *Cultural Expression, Creativity and Innovation*, the third volume in *The Cultures and Globalization Series*, Anheier and Isar (2010) pointed out the potential, limits, and risks connected with the use of the notion of creativity in social science, in arts or in cultural expressions. Creativity, they argued, is no longer associated simply with exceptional individuals working in scientific or artistic activities; it may appear in any kind of human activity. Although Vigotsky also made this observation more than seventy years ago (2006: 7–13), we are only now beginning to heed this insight as it applies to a range of different fields, as globally shared values in any kind of professional development. Creativity has been present in different ages and cultures, but can blossom more fully 'in the intersection of cultures, where beliefs, lifestyles, and knowledges mix together in an easier way, to see new combinations of new ideas' (Csikszentmihalyi, 1997: 23).

Public educational systems in Latin America are trying to improve the curricula so as to encourage new ways of learning, of learning how to learn and of different forms of intelligence, not just rational but emotional, affective and artistic. In relation to these purposes, globalization has brought about not only homogenization, but also an increase in the social valorization of local cultures, mixed and trans-local expressions that are the products of intensified mobility, the media, digital culture and the worldwide diffusion of cultural industries. Creativity flourishes more in shared environments, in open and connected cultures, where traditional and fine arts can find themselves in a dialogue with science and technology. In many ways globalization enhances the connectivities that make identities more complex, multiple, unstable, fragmentary, or ephemeral. Traditional identities are transformed and the potential for creative expression within them is enhanced when the indigenous (i.e. Amerindian) rural or urban populations have access to arts education and cultural services as well as the media and the new information technologies, not just as consumers, but as producers who are afforded ways of creating and sharing their contemporary memories. This is particularly important in relation to the stereotypes concerning cultural minorities that are present in the media (UNESCO, 2009). New forms of horizontal communication are being created among different ethnic groups or other sodalities, such as young people, environmental activists or immigrants. In the artistic sector, fields such as design and architecture are benefiting from the availability of the new technologies and the opportunities that now exist to created different kinds of artifacts, some of which impact upon everyday life, while others serve to generate critical reflections on the future of the current scientific and technological revolution (Aldersey-Williams et al., 2008).

Yet is it possible to say that every expression of contemporary creativity is beneficial for all social groups or communities? Which of these expressions is destined to become part of the collective memory or an ingredient of the recognized heritage? How do we make the distinction between 'fashions' and abiding transformations? We need to remember that most of the ruptures and avant-gardes in the arts have usually become routine rather quickly. Is contemporary creativity relevant just as a vector for economic development? Who benefits from it? This question is particularly relevant in relation to the lack of audiences in the performing arts and the low rate of museum visitation in our countries. As Carlos Monsiváis says:

> …there is no cultural inclusion without themes and artistic experiences that are added to the known map; it is the expansion or themes and artistic genres that social demand assimilates most rapidly. The basis of the cultural inclusion is technology; its second foundation is the demographic explosion; the third is the incorporation of art and culture into daily recreation – not something outside of experience, but something that participates in different ways in experience, thereby opening up perspectives of understanding and enjoyment. The development of a civilizing influence requires a collective sensibility, and this is a way of clarifying cultural mobility.

> It is a good idea to debate the truth of whether the inclusion of the masses in the observation of museums modifies the social role of works of art, not because their viewing is cheapened, but, on the contrary, because a certain phenomenon that occurred a long time ago with La Gioconda, The Last Supper, Michelangelo's David … or Duchamp's Nude Descending a Staircase is still rooted in national and international society. (2009: 71)

I wonder how the various expressions of contemporary creativity in the arts will be retained in popular taste, memory and heritage, as there is a great distance between arts practice, audience demand and cultural policies. Here again, our educational systems have a major responsibility. International statistics show that only between 8 and 15 per cent of citizens enjoy access to the work of local artists, given the preponderance in cultural consumption of the media and the digital products of the global cultural industry (including mass concerts). Contemporary artists are looking for new kinds of relationships with society and their audiences do not necessarily respond. While at the beginning of the twentieth century theater dominated the public sphere, today theaters are empty. What, then, will the collective memories of this creative work look like in the future? Argentina, Chile, Colombia, Costa Rica, the Dominican Republic and Mexico, for example, are carrying out complex educational reforms. The question is whether these reforms will actually address the very poor coverage of issues of heritage, identity and memory in basic education curricula.

Box 16.1   Monumento al Che: participatory memorial and collective heritage

On 14 June 2008, Ernesto 'Che' Guevara returned to his roots. The first full-figure bronze statue honoring Guevara in Argentina, the *Monumento al Che*, was inaugurated in Rosario as the pinnacle event of the city's official celebrations marking the icon's 80th anniversary. The 4 metre, 1.7 ton monument was paraded through the Argentine capital before embarking up the Rio Paraná toward its destination in the birthplace of *el Che*. There, in Rosario, the statue became the centerpiece of the newly inaugurated Plaza Ernesto Che Guevara, adding the *rosarino* revolutionary to the list of historical figures whose names grace local plazas. Received by eagerly awaiting crowds, Che's 'home-coming' abounded with festivities – including circus, theater, and tango performances – and symbolic gestures, as the bronze Che was greeted by representatives of *pueblos originarios*, Cuban and Argentine government officials, Guevara's children, and the statue's sculptor, Buenos Aires-based artist, Andrés Zerneri.

Far from being the undertaking of an individual artist, the *Monumento al Che* represents a consciously collective work. Contrary to the government-endorsed or commissioned status of much contemporary public art, the monument offers an alternative vision of 'public' by emphasizing not its location in accessible city space, but rather through facilitating public participation within the statue's material construction and decision-making processes. While this collaborative initiative could be interpreted as an attempt to enact elements of Guevara's proclaimed political practices, such collective actions are also markedly reminiscent of the political and cultural productions witnessed in the wake of the country's 2001 economic and political crisis, which fomented a distinct valorization of autonomous and participatory social practices.

The collective production of this homage to Che is explicitly exemplified in the decision to accrue the massive amount of required bronze through voluntary donations of keys. Between August 2006 and the statue's final casting, over 75,000 keys and other bronze objects were donated by more than 14,500 individuals who resided not only in Argentina, but in locations around the globe. While providing a means for the general populace to participate in creating this memorial, more significantly the collection of keys allowed the project to be financially and ideologically independent of governmental, institutional or private sponsorship. Signalling its collaborative construction, impressions of individual keys were left visibly intact on the statue's base, as a reminder that larger collective goals can be achieved through the summation of small acts – a transformative potential embodied by the solitary bronze key. The monument's installation site, too, was collectively determined, being voted upon by individuals who donated bronze objects. An overwhelming majority selected Rosario – although Ernesto Guevara lived only briefly in his birth-town. Thus, upon its completion, the *Monumento* was donated to its destination city, as a gift from 'the people of Argentina'.

The performative production of a participatory public memorial was symbolically loaded. Some individuals donated material of heightened personal significance (such as the key to a house left behind when departing Argentina in exile during the 1976–1983 military dictatorship). This personalized symbolic value, latent within donated objects, contributes toward the overall social significance of the materialized public memorial, as the diverse political meanings and individual histories meld together under the communal fusion of keys to shape Guevara's final image. Similarly, the statue's physical placement facing northwest positions the Argentine monument in symbolic dialogue with the hemisphere's other Guevara statue in Santa Clara, Cuba – thus overtly situating the *Monumento al Che* in conscious solidarity with the larger Latin American region.

Furthermore, the sculpture's explicit visual reference to Alberto Korda's 1960 *Guerrillero Heroico* photograph directly inserts the monument into globalized discourses, controversies and contradictions surrounding the image and idea of Che Guevara. Commoditized and commercialized, the Korda Che has transformed into one of the most widely recognized and reproduced images in contemporary global culture – leading to convoluted legal battles over copyright and prompting the globalized (omni) presence of the Korda Che as a pop-revolutionary icon. Yet the ubiquitous distribution of a depoliticized (or rather, politically open) 'Brand Che', marketed and circulated through mechanisms of global entertainments and mass-merchandising, cohabitates with the overtly political and exceedingly divisive interpretations still evoked by the figure of Guevara. Emblematically demonstrative of the idiosyncrasies and hypocrisies formulated by contemporary global systems, *el Che* resides in a distinctly polemical position, as a signifier holding multiple and frequently contradictory meanings which can be appropriated by and adapted to vastly diverse causes and applications.

Nonetheless, the *Monumento al Che* enters into a specifically Argentine context. Privileging select events, figures and concepts within a national heritage, public monuments serve to reinforce specific visions of history within collective memory and, due to their visibility and presumed official endorsement, assume a key role in determining what aspects of this shared past should be transmitted to future generations. The performance of participatory memorial thus facilitates a popularized construction of collective heritage, allowing citizens actively to participate in the production of socio-symbolic content structuring public spaces, especially elements intended to delineate a communal identity. Consequently, the deliberate insertion of a collaboratively-produced monument to Guevara within

Argentine public space equally aims to interfere in the national public sphere. More than acknowledging Guevara's Argentine roots, the monument attempts to stimulate societal dialogue regarding collective conceptions of Argentina's history – especially contentious matters concerning leftist militancy – and how these historical tensions continue to shape the content of Argentine collective memory and national identity.

The statue's position as a vehicle for societal debate simultaneously transfigures the *Monumento al Che* into a material receptacle for displaced articulations of collective social tensions, a status made apparent in three acts of vandalism toward the monument. Fifteen days after its installation, a Nazi swastika was painted across the bronze surface; nearly one year later, the statue's hands were painted red and a large Anarchist symbol was written across Guevara's chest; and finally, in October 2009, a giant hole was gashed into the statue's leg. These defacements were criticized as being 'acts of symbolic violence' – a statement which divulges contemporary conceptions of violence as well as attitudes toward acceptable uses of public space. Yet as one observer remarked: 'And the kids writing on the statue with liquid paper, are they also attacking the monument?' While writing love notes and marking one's presence in white ink clearly are acts of socio-political purpose quite distinct from that of engraving a controversially-loaded symbol, such as a swastika, this commentary hints at the murky line delineating freedom of public expression from acts deemed as symbolically aggressive. Perhaps unintentionally, then, the *Monumento al Che* discloses the convoluted and ambiguous dimensions entrenched in negotiating the coexistence of divergent visions, values and opinions within the construction of a collective heritage.

Chandra E.F. Morrison

Globalization, artistic creativity and heritage

Globalization has broken down the borders that previously separated popular culture, crafts and artistic creation. Throughout the first half of the twentieth century, they continued to exist as different worlds, each supported by different public institutions. There was a clear distinction between artistic creation on the one hand and on the other support to crafts and/or the 'traditional cultures' of the indigenous groups, and to some extent also to people of African descent. Today, the borders between the two worlds have been dismantled and this has undermined the strategies utilized by public polices for culture. Policy-makers are confused because there are no 'pure' cultural expressions any more. These transformations have broken down the local or community perspectives in which policies used to be developed, for they bring to the fore problematic connections between tradition, memory, modernity and contemporary artistic work. Many contemporary artists incorporate histories, icons, symbols, processes, techniques and knowledge derived from the indigenous world, but not in a nostalgic way, but rather as innovations in a global perspective. Francisco Toledo, a contemporary Mexican artist with a significant presence in the international art market, whose work focuses on representations of animals from Zapotec mythology, incorporates millennia-old techniques to gradually obtain colors long used in traditional dyes and materials. He doesn't just create and recreate live elements from Zapotec memory and identity, but also promotes bonds between artists and artisans through projects and cultural institutions that he himself finances, where the blend of techniques, origins, cosmovisions and nationalities are daily occurrences. He has supported, together with the National Center for the Arts located in Mexico City[3] and the local government, the creation of the San Agustin Center for the Arts (CASA), located in the middle of the forest in a place where 40 per cent of the water for Oaxaca City is produced. The concept of CASA is to connect both visual artists and artisans working together with traditional and contemporary techniques, improving designs and using both ancient knowledge as well as digital technology. Innovation in the arts is related as well to the welfare of the regional community, and especially to the environment. San Agustin is thus considered a 'Clean Center' because of the relationship between art, the use of non-toxic techniques for engraving and photography and the cultural use of water. The idea is to get the community involved in a regional and sustainable relationship between arts education and artistic creation and natural resources. At the same time, San Agustin promotes international exchange and artistic processes not just in Mexico, or Latin America, but in the USA and Europe. Here natural heritage is considered part of human development and is linked to artistic creation: it is more than just a green landscape. Artistic creation is an engine that emphasizes community arts, biodiversity and ecological education. The goal of connecting this center to arts education in public schools has not been possible to attain yet because of political conflicts in the community (Jiménez López and López, 2008).

This center is virtually unique, for in general public cultural institutions work in isolation from the community and sometimes unintentionally to the detriment of creativity and innovation. The institutional machinery supports the arts regardless of what is going on within each artistic field, of where innovation is occurring or, even worse, of what patterns of cultural consumption and/or cultural practice are actually embraced by ordinary people. Contemporary artists, writers, videographers, and poets belonging to indigenous communities have begun to cross over into the world of the market and to function in multicultural and multilingual contexts. There are more and more indigenous rock groups that sing in their mother tongue as well as in Spanish and in English. These groups are clamoring for recognition of their compositions and want to be recorded and promoted. Their creative output and their identity are both based on hybrid and mixed expressions. Sometimes, however, they neglect or suppress their own memories not because they do not want to be recognized as indigenous, but because they want first and foremost to be recognized as contemporary musicians, rather than ethnic ones. But the cultural industries sector is insufficiently developed for this musical production to circulate properly. This affects not only indigenous groups, but also talented young musicians and musical groups producing new music. Their contribution to contemporary memories has been neglected by public and private cultural policies. Why wait until the transnational cultural industries discover them? It is good for the groups to have the opportunity to develop their

music in a global perspective, but locally the cultural system appears to be totally unable to exploit the enormous potential of artistic, professional and popular innovation and creativity. Individual artists face limited options: leaving the country to insert themselves into the transnational music market in the USA or Europe, or continue performing at the local level as part of the alternative music sector, using technology for recording and performing though informal networks or local festivals for music. Young indigenous groups increasingly demand the same working conditions as others. Some of these young musicians do not want to be identified as 'Indigenous', for example; this labeling merely underlines their unequal treatment. They prefer to be recognized simply as musicians, without the ethnic label that inevitably alters the way their music will be heard. They consider their art to be universal, hence its distinctiveness does not require ethnic legitimation. The value-added of their ethnic 'roots' must be assessed in purely musical terms rather than in anthropological ones.

In other cases, the indigenous is actually the product of hybridization that is purely contemporary and this professional identity is an integral part of the artistry on offer. Lila Downs is a prominent Mexican artist who epitomizes this duality. Daughter of an American father and a Mixtec mother, she recaptures in her music the elements of a communal musical memory, and mines the veins not only in a framework of jazz fusion, but also in traditional music and an image based on the use of modernized textiles, as she designs her own wardrobe as a mixture of old textiles and sensual modern figurative elements. She sings in several indigenous languages besides Spanish and English. She does not need support from the public sector; in fact she is seizing the opportunities offered by globalization. She is also profoundly committed to the uplifting of Mixtec communities and works on philanthropic causes in favor of women.

Most practitioners of contemporary group creativity, however, seem to be little concerned with filiations and origins, or even in appropriating or redeploying heritage forms. Likewise, there exists a strong tendency to merge what was in a given moment considered the fruit of contemporary artistic creation on the one hand and the products of popular creativity on the other. In Colombia, Mulata Library is an organization of young people of African descent working with their community on the preservation of their heritage. They have been working for a long time on the recuperation of oral traditions, recording it digitally and teaching children and young people traditional music and dance.[3] They performed at the end of a National Encounter on Arts Education, Culture and Citizenship, organized by the Ministries of Culture and Education of Colombia and the Organizacion de Estados Ibero-americanos para la Educacion, la Ciencia y la Cultura (OEI). It was obvious to me that they had been working on the mixture of traditional steps and other contemporary techniques of dance. At dinner we were seated at the same table. I asked them if they were dancing hip hop in the community. They smiled and assured me that they did, that they had a very deeply rooted hip hop movement but that they had not performed it here because of the nature of the audience. 'We wanted to show what they expected to see, but in reality we are writing lyrics talking about our history and our dreams. We enjoy dancing hip hop and break-dancing because they produce a lot of energy and we are good at improvisation.'[4]

Latin American migrations, both within the continent and beyond, have enabled the development of new manifestations of cultural heritage in a trans-local dimension. In the process, the idea that the national bases of diverse popular traditions, with the sense of identity that these elements provided, have been displaced and/or lost may be more of a myth than a reality. Identity does not depend on specific objects or products. In other cases, the development of initiatives in trans-local space mobilizes selected elements of heritage and creates not only a sense of belonging, but contributes to the prevention or resolution of border conflicts, as is the case of the work of the Coordinator of Popular Radio and Education of Ecuador, that fosters healthy cross-border coexistence between Ecuador and Colombia (most of the time). This phenomenon raises questions about the relevance of national cultural policies to expressive forms that have acquired transnational influence. The artistic communities are creating new ways of networking across national frontiers, instead of working just locally. Mexican writers or musicians may live in Europe or the USA, but are highly visible in local museum collections and exhibitions or as art critics. Official cultural policies take no account of these new strategies, however, and maintain the idea of official exhibitions, formal exchange and vertical decision-making in a sector that operates in an increasingly fast-moving horizontal way.

Memories, technology and heritage

In 2004, I took part in a panel to select projects of social or community appropriation of the immaterial heritage from different countries in Latin America. The organizing institution, the Andres Bello Convention, located in Bogotá, had designed a formal guide for the projects. Most of the participants tried to follow the instructions. Nevertheless, the description of a Brazilian project started not with its objectives, but rather by recounting its dream vision. This was related to the sounds of the birds in the jungle. They talked about how they decided to preserve their oral traditions by recording their dreams and their stories. They were using computers and technology in the middle of the Amazonian jungle. This process of systemization and preservation of historic memory has been given life thanks to innovative projects linked to digital technologies. Diverse indigenous groups make use of both audiovisual resources and digital technology, of their languages but not the written word (Guerrero 2005). This new relationship between oral memory, writing and technology raises a question: up to what point does the register of memory, even for the noble cause of transmitting it to new generations, carry with it a certain dose of something of its content in a particular moment in time that doesn't necessarily express the change and the transformation of what is considered 'recordable'.

When the contemporary Zapatista Movement was born, most of their strategies were cybernetic. They became symbolic warriors rather than military combatants. The Internet became the most powerful weapon used by them, but it is, at the same time, a strong window for voyeurism, sexual commerce and a certain cult of violence. It was a new instrument of mediation among young people with access to computers. The incorporation of scientific thinking by the visual or performing arts also brings new kinds of artistic works that greatly change the role of audiences, who become part of the event, the installation or the work, rather than simply spectators. Digital culture and visual arts have generated different kind of aesthetics and experiences, introducing new relationships between art and science. But most of the population interacts with the World Wide Web as just a commercial space. Only a minority has access to electronic and digital platforms. Another policy issue is how to preserve these contemporary technology-based creations in terms of heritage. Rapid technological progress creates several challenges for their conservation as well as in the realm of intellectual property and copyright. When a work has been created with a technological process or mechanism that has already become obsolete, how is the work to be preserved for the future. Which copy might be considered the original? In 2007, the Modern Museum Art (MOMA) in New York mounted an exhibition of the animation movies created by Pixar. They created a new collection based on animated or 3D films produced during the last ten years. The exhibition showed how characters had been created since the early drawings until the stage of computer design. Before MOMA created their new film collection, as part of the American heritage, those movies had been seen worldwide and had generated millions at the box-office. In this sense, as some analysts of the American cultural system have pointed out, there are no public policies for culture, but strategic decisions for the cultural sector are being taken by industry.

While technology is dissolving frontiers, connecting people and creating new languages and aesthetic experiences among children and young people and changing the perception of millions of them, our public cultural policies still focus almost exclusively on promoting international exhibitions based on the pre-Hispanic, colonial or twentieth-century art. Our institutions work in a very professional way, to be sure, but they are ill-equipped to promote contemporary creation. What is our international cultural image to be made of?

At the beginning of this century, a troupe of Mexican contemporary artists, invited by the National Council for the Culture and Arts, attended the Mexico Gateway of the Americas event included at the American Performing Arts Presenters annual meeting in New York. Parallel to this event is one of the largest performing arts market in the world. Most of the promoters or arts administrator participants were surprised by the mixture of the pieces and because not even one play was related to mariachi, folklore, pre-Hispanic flavor or modern art. Both Frida Kahlo and Diego Rivera, among others, were absent. The usual fare is hybrid Mexican, Colombian or Cuban music or dance, which they classify under category of 'Ethnic' or 'World Music'.

The question is whether Latin America is creating new categories for its musical movements and reorganizing markets and new types of production and international promotion for these new expressions.

I remember the speech Carlos Fuentes made at that event. He began by explaining the immigrant condition of everybody in the American Continent, and the relationship between America, Asia and Africa. He also explained the relationship between historical memory and contemporary art in Mexico. After his speech, the New York art world's mental maps were extended. You can see, appreciate or enjoy only what you are prepared for. Intercultural dialogue and communication is one of the bases of sharing cultures among countries or communities with different idioms, traditions and beliefs. Even the Mexican politicians present at the event began feeling uncomfortable about some of the performances, mainly those of the youngest dance companies. One of them was performing a very sarcastic choreography. The dancers looked provocative with their recently shaved heads, wearing short loincloths and dirty miners' boots but bare from the waist up. 'What the heck are they doing?' and 'Why didn't you get some appropriate costumes for them?', they asked, almost in secret.

Creativity, traditional identities and public policies

Two sectors that have extensive experience in the appropriation and reassigning of meanings residing in popular cultural memories and repertoires are the visual arts and design and the performing arts, especially music and dance. Latin America has advanced rapidly along the path of a market-driven commodification, in which traditional elements are reappropriated as consumer goods or as large hotels and tourist circuits have reclaimed traditional medicine for themselves. This is heritage reified and frozen for the globalized marketplace, for which museums and other cultural spaces make available recycled products and symbols. Consumption becomes conflated with or replaces the social legitimization of heritage. In Guatemala, for example, public innovation and investment in craft design are systematically tied to commercialization and the development of the tourist industry (see Winter's chapter in this volume). Local people are not necessarily the beneficiaries. A middle-class artisan sector has broadened the landscape of the art and crafts in several countries, as some art schools are developing curricula for the contemporary adaptation of traditional arts, or as one of the possible ingredients of new creation (see Friel and Santagata, 2008).

A particular kind of stratification of popular art is evident in many countries, as shown by recent changes in the popular art market. Because of migratory flows, traditional motifs are no longer confined to their places of origin. Forms such as the Satillo *zarape* from Mexico are now being produced in Guatemala; some of these have not only gone back to Mexico with migrants, but also to Colombia and El Salvador. How does this deterritorialization of symbols, textures, materials and motifs affect the collective memories of their makers? There are few *zarape* weavers left in Mexico, but in Guatemala the textile at the base of the tradition is used to make luxury bags, expensive shoes and other high-value products for the tourist industry.

In most Latin American countries, there is a strong tension between the symbolic uses of art and crafts and contemporary creativity in design, materials, commercialization and marketing on the one hand, and the tendency towards 'museumization' on the other. Contemporary artistic groups most closely tied to the market retake what was once truly an identity element but is now packaged by the international cultural industry. This is the case of the traditional dances of Veracruz, converted into a glitzy package for the national and international market that is based on the *River Dance* genre that originated in Ireland and crossed the Atlantic. The Veracruz *Son Jaroch* is a traditional Mexican dance form, a hybrid of Black and Spanish influences, performed with a string and percussion ensemble. This is the form on which the Irish rhythms and choreography have been superimposed, with great box-office success.

Pre-Hispanic and colonial dance traditions are deeply rooted in urban cultures. These have been changing. Earlier, the configurations were heritage transmitted by families. Today, it is possible to find professionals, artists, journalists, students and even foreigners practicing them. In the process, their religious meanings have been forgotten. Prayers, 'cleansings' and several rituals are part of the commercial services that some of them provide to the national and international tourist at the Zócalo, the main plaza of Mexico City. The image is almost surrealistic: dozens of 'pre-Hispanic' dancers in the historic center of the largest city in the world, sharing the same space with other urban dancers practicing hip hop, break dance, or imitating Michael Jackson. At the same time, one vendor displays a live snake. He swears that the animal provides magical medicine for almost any disease. The city government has also installed a large rink for ice skating. There is no snow in Mexico City, but skaters are wearing warm hats and gloves in the middle of the day. All are examples of hybridities of meanings, symbols and uses of public space under the impact of globalization on the traditional and urban identities. What exactly are we defending as contemporary identity or creativity?

In Lima, *mestizos* call the Indians '*cholos*', sometimes in a pejorative way. The dance of the moment is reaggeton, or 'Chuntaro Style', which is a remix of cumbia and electronic music but with remade lyrics. The music and dance are part of the contemporary identities of diverse sectors, not just in Peru, but in Mexico, Colombia or Costa Rica. Which of these rhythms will be retained as heritage? We do not know, maybe none.

What is clear at any rate is that the musical tastes of young people across Latin America are very similar and are equally ephemeral. The dance forms are influenced by the music, albeit with regional differences, and include adaptations of rap, hip hop, techno, launch, indie, neopunk, as well as cumbia, salsa or ballenato, all of which can be heard in discotheques ranging from Ibiza and Madrid to Lima or Bogotá. It was enough for the Mexican group *Los de Abajo* to team up with an ex-*Talking Head* for the resulting music to circle the globe through both live concerts and *MySpace*. It is not unusual (to quote Tom Jones) that traditional popular groups open up a 'tourist division' of their own rituals, as can be observed with the *Papantla Flyers*, a highly ritualistic dance of pre-Hispanic origin that is now exported to cities around the globe. The 2005 UNESCO Cultural Diversity Convention underlines the importance of such diversity in the field of cultural expressions, but this dimension, so widespread and complex in Latin America, is not yet adequately addressed by our cultural policies. Knowledges connected to heritage are being converted into poles of tension between the irrational exploitation of cultural resources and new forms of cultural creation linked to the social well-being and the self-affirmation of many groups. The erosion of the sources of inspiration for contemporary arts practice that reside in the intangible cultural heritage is accompanied by weak social connections and declining public relevance.

Conclusions

Contemporary arts practice in Latin America has been working in different directions, sometimes blurring the boundaries and definitions of local and global identities. It has been impacted by and at the same time influences globalization, opening up new opportunities for creativity or innovation or, on the contrary, producing massification of certain ideas of heritage and the preponderance of official memories. Accordingly, cultural change requires cultural policies that break with a purely preservationist conception of heritage and develop a contemporary concept of identity. The emerging field of intangible heritage poses challenges not only from the theoretical point of view, but also as regards the ways in which institutions are organized and the issues are considered. The local and transnational dimension of cultural expressions and the breaking down of frontiers both generate new conflicts in the definition of identities in countries where the State has adopted the paternalist idea of 'preserving' an idealized vision national 'identity'. Policies of memory are needed that recognize that diversity is not only related to ethnicity, but is inherent in many contemporary processes of identity construction. Is it the role of the State to curate the identity of its citizens? Our identities are dynamic and their malleability is tied to our human rights. However, diversity is at the same time a real challenge because of the ephemeral and unstable conditions of identity formation and because of the influence of cultural industries dominated by a few transnational enterprises, most notably in music, film and digital services. Hence the State needs to focus on the conditions of artistic creation, arts education, the distribution of cultural goods and services, and the connections that need to be built among the public authorities, civil society and the private sector. It also has a role to play in elaborating strategies of cultural financing and support for innovation and creativity. Rather than taking aesthetic decisions or making artistic judgements, the public authority needs to facilitate the exercise of cultural rights and foster interactions among artists, schools, communities, citizens, museums, theaters, public spaces and cultural industries.

The notion of cultural heritage should therefore not be used without including contemporary artistic practice unless the intention is to anchor artistic memory purely in early twentieth-century notions appropriate to a world before urbanization, the technological revolution and globalization. Cultural memories formerly linked to territories are being reconfigured: they are being delocalized by migratory flows, hybridities and new forms based on erstwhile popular art forms. Elements that were the basis of memory and identity have become part of expanded collective memories, many forms of which are also transnational. Memories embodied in artistic practice emerge in contexts of reception and social location that are totally different from those of an earlier age. This applies not only to the ways in which theaters, museums and galleries were frequented under the conditions of modernity, but also to the ways in which contemporary art forms have created totally different conditions and formats, often linked to technology, the digital environment and/or heterodox spaces beyond the 'mainstream'. The challenge is how to preserve the memory of these forms, many of which are deliberately ephemeral or doomed to obsolescence. Within globalization, contemporary creativity is creating new scenarios for cultural change and innovation, but the risk is the emergence of zones of discontinuity, making it difficult for societies to apprehend as a coherent combination of heritage, memory and identity.

Notes

1 The Spanish term *cultura popular* used in Latin America denotes a wide range of cultural practices other than so-called 'high' culture. In other disciplinary frameworks these forms might be called 'folk culture', 'mass culture', or 'working-class culture'
2 Author's translation, with the help of the editors.
3 This Center belongs to a network of decentralized arts education centers created while I was the Director-General of the National Center for the Arts. These centers are located in Guanajuato, Veracruz, Baja California and San Luis Potosí. Each has its own characteristics based on the artistic and educational interest of its community. However, all of them are connected via the Internet, a distance arts education program and their interdisciplinary academic design.
4 The Encounter took place in September 2009. I participated in the panel that selected projects that were then invited to take part in an international encounter of arts education initiatives in Mexico City planned for October 2010.

REFERENCES

Aldersey-Williams, H., Hall, P., Sargent, T., and Antonelli, P. (2008) *Design and the Elastic Mind.* New York: Museum of Modern Art.

Anheier, H.K and Isar, Y.R. (2007) 'Introduction', in H.K. Anheier and Y.R. Isar (eds), *Conflicts and Tensions. The Cultures and Globalization Series, 1.* London: Sage.

Anheier, H.K. and Isar, Y.R. (2010) 'Introduction', in H.K. Anheier and Y.R. Isar (eds), *Cultural Expression, Creativity and Innovation. The Cultures and Globalization Series, 3.* London: Sage.

Arizpe, L. (2004) 'El patrimonio cultural intangible en un mundo interactivo', in S. Singer Socher, A. Rosas Mantecón and A. Castro Muñoz (eds), *Patrimonio intangible; resonancia de nuestras tradiciones.* City México: CONACULTA-INAH, ICOM México, Fundación Televisa, ICOM, pp. 19–25.

Cliche, D., Mitchell, R., and Wiesand, A. (2002) *Creative Europe: On Governance and Management of Artistic Creativity in Europe.* Bonn: ARCult Media.

Csikszentmihaly, M. (1997) *Creativity: Flow and the Psychology of Discovery and Invention.* New York: Harper Perennial.

Cunningham, S., Potts, J., and Banks, J. (2008) 'Cultural Economy: The Shape of the Field', in H.k. Anheier and Y.R. Isar (eds), *The Cultural Economy. The Cultures and Globalization Series, 2.* London: Sage.

Florescano, E. (1993) 'El patrimonio cultural y la política de la cultura,' in E. Florescano (ed.), *El Patrimonio cultural de México.* México: Fondo de Cultura Económica.

Friel, M. and Santagata, W. (2008) 'Making Material Cultural Heritage Work: From Traditional Handicrafts to Soft Industrial Design', in H.K Anheier and Y.R. Isar (eds), *The Cultural Economy. The Cultures and Globalization Series, 2.* London: Sage.

Gamio, M. (1916) 'Nuestra cultura intelectual', in *Forjando patria.* México: Librería y Casa Editorial de Porrúa Hnos.

García Canclini, N. (2004) *Diferentes, desiguales y desconectados; mapas de la interculturalidad.* Barcelona: Gedisa.

Guerrero, A. (ed.) (2005) *Habitantes de la memoria: experiencias notables de apropiación social del patrimonio inmaterial en América Latina.* Bogotá: Convenio Andrés Bello.

Jiménez López, L. (2004) 'Patrimonio, artes escénicas y políticas públicas. La puesta en escena de vínculos no reconocidos', in S. Singer Socher, A. Rosas Mantecón, A. Castro Muñoz (eds), *Patrimonio Intangible; resonancias de nuestras tradiciones.* México City: ICOM México, CONACULTA.INAH, ICOM, pp. 53–57.

Jiménez López, L. (2005) 'América Latina: la batalla por el patrimonio cultural intangible', in A. Guerrero (ed.), *Habitantes de la memoria: experiencias notables de apropiación social del patrimonio inmaterial de América Latina.* Bogotá: Convenio Andrés Bello.

—— (2005b) 'Patrimonio, artes escénicas y políticas públicas: La puesta en escena de vínculos no reconocidos', in *Patrimonio intangible: resonancias de nuestras tradiciones.* México City: CONACULTA-INAH, ICOM Mexico, Fundación Televisa, ICOM, pp. 53–57.

—— and Florescano, E. (2008) 'Instituciones culturales: logros y desafíos', in F. Toledo, E. Florescano, and J. Woldenberg (eds), *Cultura mexicana: revisión y perspectivas.* México City: Taurus Historia.

—— and López, C. (2008) *El Centro de las Artes de San Agustín: arte, comunidad y medio ambiente en Etla, Oaxaca.* México: Taurus Historia.

Monsiváis, C. (2009) 'Museums (a rapid view of guided tours: the ruins of the future should be in shop windows)', in Salma Holo, Mari-Tere Alvarez, Elazar Barkan, and Gerardo Estrada (eds), *Beyond the Turnstile: Making the Case for Museums and Sustainable Values.* Lanham, MD: AltaMira Press.

Rosas Mantecón, A. (2004) *El patrimonio intangible y los museos en México.* in S. Singer Socher, A. Rosas Mantecón, A. Castro Muñoz (eds), *Patrimonio Intangible; resonancia de nuestras tradiciones* in *Patrimonio Intangible; resonancias de nuestras tradiciones.* México City: ICOM México, CONACULTA.INAH.

UNESCO (2009) *Investing in Cultural Diversity and Intercultural Dialogue (UNESCO World Report).* Paris: UNESCO.

Vigotsky, L.S. (2006) *La imaginación y el arte en la infancia.* Madrid: Akal Ediciones.

FIELDS AND ISSUES

CHAPTER 17

THE MANIPULATION OF MEMORY AND HERITAGE IN MUSEUMS OF MIGRATION

Julie Thomas

Based on an analysis of the permanent exhibitions of two national museums of immigration, this chapter explores the specific exhibition techniques of space and time which structure the interplay between diasporic heritage and identity and nation-state heritage and identity, identifying the ways in which, in response to the pressures of globalization, 'memory' and 'identity' have been manipulated so as to redefine 'heritage' in terms of 'process'.

Introduction

Today, having a heritage is indispensable to having a distinctive identity and cultural memory; losing a heritage is like losing a key bit of both. Heritage has come to be used as 'proof' of past, tradition, belonging, and therefore proof also of rights to place, representation and political voice. To what extent does globalization modify the interactions between heritage, memory and identity? (Isar, Viejo-Rose and Anheier, Introduction to this volume)

This chapter will investigate the interplay between diasporic heritage and identity and nation-state heritage and identity in museums of migration, and, through analysis of specific museums, attempt to identify the ways in which 'memory' and 'identity' have been manipulated so as to redefine 'heritage' in response to the pressures of globalization.

As Bennett (2005) remarks, museums are 'civic laboratories', 'machineries that are implicated in the shaping of civic capacities ... in the context of programmes of civic management which aim to order and regulate social relations in particular ways.'

Because museums 'increasingly work the borderlands between different worlds, histories, and cosmologies' (Clifford, 1999: 451), they are 'exploited by nation-states to pacify separatists or even the potential fissiparousness of all ideas of difference' (Appadurai, 1996: 39). In the context of globalization, and the perceived 'threat' to the nation-state of a globalized world of mobile populations whose transnational identities accommodate more than one specific and defined national identity, museums of migration attempt to 'pacify' multiple audiences – audiences attached to very different and perhaps conflicting definitions of heritage. As Ien Ang remarks in this volume,

> *[The] recent propagation of the immigration museum as a disseminator of migration heritage has clearly been motivated by a cultural and political problematic which is felt particularly strongly in Western European nations: it coincides with the need for these countries to stem the twin tide of anti-immigrant sentiment and migrant discontent ...*

Museums of migration also insist on the relevance of 'heritage' as associated with a particular geographical or cultural 'locality'. In a globalized world, this relevance is under constant examination, as in the recent exhibition entitled *Native Land* (the work of photographer Raymond Depardon and the commentary of Paul Virilio) at the Fondation Cartier in Paris (21 November 2008–15 March 2009). In his commentary and the portion of the exhibition curated by him, Virilio (2008) questions the continuing validity of the very concept of 'Native Land', of belonging, in a world where 'the acceleration of movement', the huge flow of migrant populations, and the globalized speed of communications and transportation nullify the relevance of geographical space – and therefore, the significance and importance of that space which, when it is redefined as 'place', becomes an integral element of 'heritage'.

Of course, when considering the forms of heritage being defined and presented in museums of migration, we are dealing not only with the representation of geographical space as 'place' of heritage, but also with another manifestation of space – the space within the museum itself, and how this space is manipulated to suggest the desired narrative of the museum. Introducing a discussion of spatiality in memorial museums, Paul Williams (2007: 77) remarks:

> The importance of space and spatial effects in the museum experience is a topic routinely neglected within museum studies. … Centrality and marginalization are related through the relative attribution of space. Accordingly, visitors create 'imaginary geographies' in which social divisions and cultural classifications are expressed using spatial metaphors or descriptive spatial divisions.

Museums of migration have not generally been included in the category of museums known as 'Memorial Museums' (although museums like the Cobh Heritage Centre in Ireland would certainly qualify as a form of memorial commemorating the Irish Famine), yet both Museums of Immigration and Emigration rely on evoking the memory of migration, the pain and uncertainty of parting and loss, and the construction of identity through these memories. Consequently, many of the techniques of spatial organization and visual display used by memorial museums are also present in museums of migration. As we shall see, the reproduction of physical experience and the creation of memory and identity through re-enactment by the visitor in the space of the museum, as well as the evoking and embodiment of the absent through the presence and visual display of material objects, are salient examples of these techniques, which make of space a 'practiced place' (de Certeau, 1988: 130). Further, as Chia-Li Chen emphasizes, 'Memories are not passively received in the museum; they are actively recalled and constructed' (2007: 187). Memory through the body – in terms of re-enactment, vicarious and/or virtual experience – addresses the sensory aspects of memory and produces a simulated memory which creates the audience not as passive witnesses but as participants in process. Spectators in the space of a museum exhibition follow not only what Lefebvre identifies as a 'logic of visualization', but also a logic of 'constant metaphorization' (1991: 98). We will attempt to examine how these 'logics' are created and employed, and to what effect, in two major, nationally-funded museums of immigration, Ellis Island in New York and the Cité Nationale de l'Immigration in Paris, both of which also draw on the previous historic and cultural associations of their sites.

Ellis Island Immigration Museum

Ellis Island can be reached only by boat, the same service that brings tourists to the Statue of Liberty, thus taking full advantage of the 'recreated experience' of immigration for the visitor. Ellis Island has been managed by the National Park System since 1965, and the museum was opened in its current form in 1990.

The website of the Ellis Island Immigration Museum (on the National Parks Service site) is careful to establish its importance, despite the fact that none of the great waves of immigrants who arrived earlier than 1892 came through Ellis Island.

A comparison with today also serves to establish a message that will be repeated in the actual exhibition and visit, which is that *plus ça change* – just as in the past, so in the present, immigration is a continuing factor in the life of the nation. However, it is worth remarking that in the contemporary United States, 'immigrants' have become 'aliens', the subtext implying that the *aliens'* status at entry is thus less straightforward than that of the welcomed immigrants of the past:

> Ellis Island was the busiest federal immigration station in America. On April 17, 1907, Ellis Island processed a record 11,747 immigrants. Today the US Customs and Border Protection processes over 700,000 aliens daily through 326 official entry points and Ports of Entry. (US National Park Service, www.nps.gov/elis)

On entering the impressive stone building that originally received landing immigrants, and now receives tourists and visitors 'just off the boat', the visitor is first greeted by a display of baggage – the hall is huge, usually crowded, and the resulting disorientation mimics the original immigrant experience. The baggage evokes the physicality of the experience – the missing bodies of the immigrants, who have 'passed on' into the reception hall, as the visitor will do. In terms of preconceptions and assumptions, what baggage does the visitor carry – what will the visitor refuse to leave behind? The text implies that bringing any baggage on this visit is foolish and unnecessary – thus the visitor will be 'freed' to participate in the process.

There is no prescribed pathway through the ground floor exhibition, which offers a striking contrast to the visit of the upper floors. (These upper floors, which are now clean and relatively empty, unlike the environment that would have greeted the original immigrant, still offer to the visitor the vicarious immigrant experience of moving in a controlled and directed manner, shuffling through the various stages of the admission process, walking the corridors to medical examination and interview rooms.) The ground floor offers a variety of maps, displays, statistics, but there is no preferred or controlled pathway. This is an important feature of the spatial technique used here. The confusion of arrival, combined with the destabilization of the lack of any recommended order – a physical and spatial lack of direction or control – not only reproduces the condition of being lost in a strange land, but also gives the audience the impression of activity – that is, of constructing from the forest of displays and statistics their own message. An exhibition text on a wall plaque, which is entitled 'The Peopling of America', informs the visitor that

Since 1600, over 60 million people from throughout the world have come to the United States, creating a multiethnic nation unparalleled in history. The exhibits in this room present a statistical portrait of this pageant of immigration ... the displays reveal patterns of growth and change in a dynamic process that continues to bring new arrivals to the United States. (Exhibition text, photographed May 2009)

Indeed, the ground floor exhibition is filled with charts, maps, graphs, and brightly coloured displays

illustrating visually and complementing the numerical and textual information offered. Immigration is analysed by race, by gender (numbers and proportions of male and female immigrants according to historical period), by countries of origin, by chronology (Immigration since 1820), compared to emigration statistics ('A Two-Way Street – Immigration vs. Emigration'), and visitors are invited to learn how to trace their immigrant ancestors. This emphasis on statistics creates a sense of historic continuity, while at the same time collapsing past and present. Huyssen remarks that:

the more memory we store ... the more the past is sucked into the orbit of the present..., [the more] a sense of historical continuity, or, for that matter, discontinuity, both of which depend on a before and an after, gives way to the simultaneity of all times and spaces readily accessible in the present. The perception of spatial and temporal distance is being erased. (1995: 253)

Emphasis on timelines (flows of time) and flows of movement (immigration/emigration) produces a narrative that can be followed backward in time (find your ancestor) or forwards (today, the future). Spatial and temporal distance having been erased by techniques of display, the visitor participates in the process of immigration and perceives all immigrants, past and present, as united in this identity of process, despite their ethnic origins, memories, or heritage of origin. Diasporic identities are acknowledged as present, but are secondary to the true heritage and identity of the immigrant: the heritage of change, movement, adaptation, and process. One of the museum texts dealing with early immigration informs the visitor:

Scholars estimate that from 1620 to 1780, over 600,000 immigrants came to the part of North America that became the United States. The majority of immigrants came as unfree labour. Almost all the blacks were brought as slaves, while an estimated 75% of the white migrants to the colonies south of New England came as indentured labour. (Museum text, photographed May 2009)

A nearby chart showing the trajectory of transported slaves is entitled: 'Forced Migration: The Atlantic Slave Trade'. Here the memory and heritage of many African Americans are manipulated to present transported slaves as immigrants whose experience is, through the text, equated with that of white indentured servants. The ethnic and racial communities evoked throughout the exhibition by graphs and charts serve to provide a subtext in which all immigrants are made equal, and no specific cultural heritage is privileged. (The impact of immigration on the heritage of the Native Americans, whose 'forced migrations' are not underlined, is not featured because they were the only group to 'people' the United States who were *not* immigrants.)

In one corner of the main exhibition hall, there is a 'language tree' showing words and expressions which have come into English courtesy of 'immigrant' cultures. Here the language, as container of multiple but equal heritages, represents the heritage of the nation-state, accommodating all. The visual expression of this narrative is a giant American flag in the centre of the hall, which is composed of the photos of hundreds of citizens of appropriately diverse ethnic and racial backgrounds. The visitor is presented with a vision of the United States where to be an immigrant is the norm, where the (English) language (not Spanish, although all the museum signage is bilingual!), like the country, owes a debt to the contributions of its multicultural, diverse citizenry. To bring the exhibition into the present, there are several video monitors presenting interviews with recent immigrants, some not in English, but subtitled in English for the hearing-impaired. These interviews testify to the capacity of the identity of the nation-state to include the varied identities, heritages and loyalties of diasporic communities – one interviewee states: 'I don't see myself as a North American – I'm proud of my heritage' (Exhibition video, photographed May 2009).

Thus, to identify with the nation-state does not necessarily mean thinking of yourself as a North American or abandoning your native heritage, whatever that might be. Here all possible identities and heritages are conflated into the desired nation-state identity, whose component citizens are all diverse, and all happy with their diversity. Indeed, the heritage of the United States is defined as diversity. If all are different, then all are the same in their difference. Problems of adaptation and the difficulties of a diasporic identity , as identified by Ien Ang in this volume, are ignored or actively denied:

… the ultimate impossibility of 'heritagising' the experience of (physical and cultural) displacement as such: the ambivalent condition of (non)belonging, of the fragility of diasporic identity as it is fractured by the push and pull of competing nationalising pressures, is difficult to objectify as distinctive heritage.

The Ellis Island Museum, by creating for all migrants a common heritage and all visitors a common memory of 'flow' and 'process', by refusing to acknowledge the 'push and pull' of competing nationalizing pressures, manages to relegate specific diasporic identities to the status of one of the 'givens' of migration. These identities are merged and subsumed in a national heritage of '*process*', of many waves of immigration through time, 'coalescing past with present': 'Collapsing the entire past into a single frame is one common heritage aim …. stressing the likeness of past and present is another … coalescing past with present creates a living heritage (Lowenthal, 1998: 139).

La Cité Nationale de l'Histoire de l'Immigration

The Cité Nationale de l'Histoire de l'Immigration is housed in the Palais de la Porte Dorée, now a national monument, which was built for the International Colonial Exposition of 1931, and which still preserves the exterior bas-reliefs of Janniot and the interior colonial murals of Ducos de la Haille celebrating France's involvement with her colonies. Since the Colonial Exhibition, the site has undergone several transformations which have coincided with changes in France's relationship to her former colonies – from the Museum of France 'Outre-Mer' to the Museum of the Arts of Africa and Oceania, which was closed in 2003 when its collections were fused with the collections of the Musée de l'Homme and for the most part transferred to the new Quai Branly ethnographic museum. The current Cité Nationale de l'Histoire de l'Immigration was founded in 2004, and opened to the public in 2007. It hosts one permanent exhibition –*Repères* – (Frames of Reference, Landmarks), and temporary themed exhibitions.

It should be noted here that the term '*Cité*' evokes not only the 'city' that is the urban destination of many immigrants, but also the 'city' which provides the very foundation of the concept of 'citizenship', a concept heavily emphasized in the discourse of the permanent exhibition. However, in contemporary French usage the term 'Cité' is often used to indicate the suburban government housing projects built for immigrants in the banlieux (suburbs) so as to preserve the pristine environments of city centres, and in this context 'Cité' conjures up an image of a 'gathering place' for immigrants, or, indeed, a ghetto. Therefore all of these associations are active in the very 'naming' of this museum of immigration: As Dias remarks:

> Like the current politics of immigration in France, debates over values such as cultural diversity in the museum world reflect, among other things, the complex and still largely unacknowledged legacy of colonialism in contemporary French society. (2008: 126)

In France, cultural policy actively envisions the role of national museums as media to preserve and propagate the 'patrimoine' – the national heritage – as cultural model. The official website of the Ministry of Culture and Communication explicitly states that this is one of their 'essential missions', and that since the 1970s policy has aimed to place culture 'at the heart of the life of people', while guaranteeing to all the right of access to 'la culture' (Official website of the Ministère de la Culture et de la Communication, www.culture.gouv.fr). The importance of the role of the Ministry of Culture is a revealing signifier of the conflation of concepts of French identity, French citizenship, and participation in French culture, as is the statement of a 'right' to 'access' an established definition of culture. Jacques Toubon, the president of the advisory board, makes clear that the notion of 'patrimoine' is at the heart of the museum, and that the museum attempts to address such questions as: 'What is the patrimony of immigrants?', 'What is the national patrimony as a result of immigration?', and 'What part does the history of immigration play in the history and culture of France?' (2007: 2). Fanny Servole (2007) identifies the envisaged goal of the museum as being to counter the idea of immigration as solely contemporary, or a 'problem.' She is careful to differentiate between the French discourse on immigration, which she sees as the dissolution of 'otherness' in the French 'melting pot', and that of the United States, where immigration is seen as 'opportunity.' Further, as Catherine Ballé

has pointed out, cultural democratization is an explicit objective of the Ministry of Culture and Communication, and most museums 'have developed strategies addressed to the entire population', with specific publics being selected as 'target groups' (2002: 142).

Diasporic and immigrant communities feature here as 'target groups' for the temporary exhibitions, which attempt to appeal to diverse immigrant communities within contemporary France. The themes of current exhibitions are, for example, addressed to the inhabitants of the banlieux (suburbs with large immigrant populations) with an exhibition of photography, or addressed to the specific immigrant community coming from the Maghreb – 'A Century of the Cultural History of the Maghrebins in France'. Also, the permanent exhibition contains work by contemporary immigrant artists in France, thus including the immigrant 'statement'. However, as we shall see, this inclusion is not necessarily transparent, as it serves to emphasize the exhibition subtext/message.

On the landing which serves as introduction to the permanent exhibition, Repères (Frames of Reference), the message is introduced by a wall text which makes a clear link between the French Revolution, the idea of citizenship, and French national identity. The French citizen is privileged, and it is implied that this is the reason why so many immigrants have chosen France as their country of destination. We are told that for two centuries, immigrants of all origins have contributed to fashion the face of France. Unlike her European neighbours, who experienced more emigration than immigration, France early became a nation of immigration, and this development is attributed to the fact that the French Revolution constructed a new definition of nationhood, and with that, a new idea of the citizen – although in law the citizen is distinguished from the 'foreigner'. Immigrants came 'in great historic rhythms' first from other European countries, then from colonies, and thus from all over the world (Exhibition text, 2009).

On the ceiling of this landing – the entire anteroom of the exhibition itself – the visitor is presented with a series of maps, timelines and statistics, as an introduction (just as on Ellis Island), but here the order of viewing is hardly random, as the order itself carries a message. The visitor, forced to look up to decipher the main maps of global flows, physically reproduces the mental act of 'looking up' to the authority of the museum.

What the visitor sees are timelines that separate migration and flows of population into clearly divided sectors: the World, France as related to the World, and then the geographical area of France itself. These maps of France, showing where immigrants have been drawn to settle depending on the demands of the period, situate the focus on French soil and the impact on France as geographical space – physical country – and nation. In this way, immigration issues are 'brought home' to the 'motherland', while at the same time visitors can see that immigration is a global issue, and not 'confined' to France. Here again, the use of maps and graphic representations of the ebb and flow of peoples over time – these flows through time and space – imply a historic continuity: immigration is a constant of history. At the same time, past and present are collapsed through this repetition of statistics and timelines.

This 'framing' of immigration prepares the visitor to enter the main exhibition hall, where brightly coloured, tall, transparent 'boxes' (separated from each other and 'scattered' through the exhibition space so that they must be 'discovered' by the visitor) 'frame' and coalesce the memories and heritages of a selection of successfully integrated immigrants from diverse ethnic backgrounds and time periods. At the beginning of the exhibition path, these 'boxes' are balanced by video 'shadow' – (black and white) projections of people packing, leaving, moving – this constant motion of 'shadows' sets the scene for the colourful 'memory' boxes which will make the immigrant experience sensual and 'real'. Thus the visitor is offered the experience of motion as preface to the reconstruction of memory through the 'embodiment' of material objects. Here the visitor may experience the diasporic memory collectively as a memory of movement and loss, but, just as the pathway past the 'boxes' to the continuation of the exhibition is 'controlled' and dictated by the space, so is the narrative message controlled. The immigrant past is here carefully reconstructed so that these heritages are 'displayed' together and 'grounded' in memory through the material culture of the immigrants' origins (the objects which they brought with them), or the objects which represent their arduous voyages to their new lives – their baggage, for example. In one such 'box', Marie Sklodowska Curie, from Poland, appears next to Baptistade Matos from Portugal, who came to France in the 1960s 'to find Liberty

and Equality for his family', and Ismael Hajji, who came from Morocco as a professional footballer in 1977. These 'witnesses' have come from different cultures and at different times, yet all have successfully gone through the 'process' of successful immigration, as further 'witnessed' by the fact that the recorded audio testimony and remembrances of these immigrants and their families may speak to the visitor, but they speak in French.

The immigrant past is here carefully reconstructed so that the *process* of individual assimilation and successful participation in French culture may be more significantly celebrated. This appeal to individual memory (and nostalgia) is important, as we will see through the narrative of the rest of the exhibition how the individual memory is 'replaced' by what Huyssen (2001) might term the 'public media memory' of the museum.

Continuing further into the exhibition, the visitor finds a repeated focus on the history of immigration. For example, anti-immigrant prejudice (the targeted ethnic groups changing with the time periods) is illustrated over the last 150 years through broadsheets, newspapers, magazine illustrations. This historical narrative is occasionally punctuated with references to the present – for example, there are contemporary photographs of protests of the 'Sans-Papiers' (immigrants who have no 'papers' and thus no legal status). This present is defused of threat or immediacy through comparison with the relentless repetition of the past, which constitutes so much of the exhibition: history will repeat itself.

One visual example which illustrates this overall 'message' is in the juxtaposition of the installation 'Climbing Down' (2004) by Barthelemy Togno (b. Cameroun, 1967) – the multi-level bunk beds of an immigrant foyer today – with photographs of the Portuguese shanty town (Bidonville) of Champigny in 1963 and the 1950s foyer of workers from the Rhine and the Danube in Lyon. This juxtaposition evokes the theme of *plus ça change* and suggests that, just as the descendants of previous generations of immigrants assimilated successfully and 'enriched French culture' (as the visitor is told by a subsequent wall text in the exhibition), so in time will contemporary problems of diasporic communities be resolved. Here the memory of past waves of immigration is called upon to construct an idealized view of 'access' to French identity, at the same time affirming the predominant value of an 'enriched French culture'. Homi Bhabha has remarked that 'the idea that history repeats itself emerges frequently within liberal discourses when consensus fails, and when the consequences of cultural incommensurability make the world a difficult place' (1996: 59). Of course, the racial difference between the Portuguese 'examples' and the perhaps Camerounian inhabitants of the bunk beds, and their consequent differences in problems of assimilation, is never alluded to, as French policy forbids racial 'classification' – on census forms, for example. However, in practice, French CVs always include a photo, so French policy often results simply in official 'avoidance' or refusal to acknowledge any problems of assimilation associated with racial issues.

There is great emphasis in the conclusion of the exhibition on the hoped-for culmination of the process of immigration, as displays emphasize various stereotypical modes of assimilation – sport and music, for example. Further displays are enhanced by an astute use of colour, where colours appear as contributing ingredients of a spectrum, as opposed to the separate and individuated colours of the 'boxed', personalized immigrant memories at the beginning of the exhibition. These final displays suggest the diversity of immigrant language, music, and food that has in the past and continues in the present to contribute to French life. Thus a diversity of memory is channelled in service to constructing the overarching national heritage, while successfully avoiding reference to a complex present except as a logical continuation of the past – the ongoing, historical process of assimilation. The wall text informs the visitor that all diasporic heritages are valuable and all diversity contributes to the constant renewal of a common and shared culture, a society in 'the colours of the world' (Exhibition Text, 2009). Through this emphasis on the 'process' of assimilation, diasporic identity is created as *collective immigrant* identity, an identity which, at the end of the process, successfully 'belongs', and the heritage of the nation-state – the *patrimoine* – is constantly being enriched and is adapting as the 'process' of history repeats itself, over and over.

Conclusion

Memory is social because every memory exists through its relation with what has been shared with others: language, symbols, events, and social and cultural contexts. ... The way we remember is determined through the supra-individual cultural construction of language, which in itself is the condition of the sharing of memory. ... Memory is also social because remembering does not take place in a social vacuum. We remember as members of social groups, and this means assuming and internalizing the common tradition and social representation shared by our collectivities. (Misztal, 2007: 381)

In the case of the immigration museums discussed here, the 'collectivity' being represented is equally and simultaneously the community of migrants and the 'collectivity' of the nation-state. Despite manipulating different narratives linked to differences of national identity and respective cultural policies, it is significant that these two museums of immigration both make use of language itself and the adoption of words or phrases from immigrant languages as a sign of this shared memory – the assimilation of 'foreignness' by the language of power being created as an ongoing and positive process, the language itself serving as a container of memory for diverse diasporic identities through their respective languages.

In the Ellis Island Museum, memory of diasporic identity qualifies as universal precedent and practically a requirement of participation in national identity. The process of immigration is literally 'naturalized'. In the Cité Nationale, memory of diasporic identity becomes transformed into the memory of assimilation, shared over time and space by all groups. France as a nation is *constructed by* the will of its diverse citizens; the United States as a nation is *composed of* diversity. But in both cases, migrants are seen to acquire status and identity through movement and process. Through re-enactment of migration, visitors acquire a 'memory' of a group identity and heritage dependent on the very movement and process which characterizes diaspora.

Like personal memory, social memory is also highly selective. ... This process of selective 'canonization' confers authority and a material and institutional facticity on the selective tradition. ... The Heritage inevitably reflects the governing assumptions of its time and context. It is always inflected by the power and authority of those who have colonized the past, whose versions of history matter. ... This is therefore an appropriate moment to ask, then, who is the Heritage for? (Hall, 2008: 221)

In the case of museums of immigration, the heritage is being constructed neither primarily for those who belong, as Hall suggests is the case with British heritage, nor for those who are experiencing the 'push–pull', as Ang has referred to it in this volume, of diasporic transnational identity, but rather for those who are being educated to belong – the school children who make up the majority of the visiting audience of such museums. Of course, many of these children are the children of diaspora, of immigration, and themselves have been born under the conflicting sign of transnational identity. But all children are quintessential 'strangers in a strange land', and teaching them to identify with the *process* of 'becoming' as heritage, rather than with specific identities or heritages, guarantees an open allegiance in the future to a heritage of the nation-state which qualifies itself as fluid, subject to change and able to encompass all forms of 'otherness', while continuing to attach itself to geographical space and cultural place.

Lip-service to individual diasporic memory manages to acknowledge the value of the contribution of diverse cultures and evokes nostalgia and cultural memory while at the same time identifying fluidity and the ability to adapt as prime virtues, virtues which remain open to interpretation when called upon in service to continued loyalty to the nation-state. As Bennett remarks with regard to the aesthetization of museum practice in museums that attempt to foster cross-cultural exchange,

there is … a risk that in the very process of fostering greater and more open cross-cultural dialogue among cosmopolitan elites, museums may do little to address racialized forms of social conflict arising from the relations between sections of the white working and lower middle classes, whose only experience of globalization is deindustrialization and unemployment, and the migrant communities who live in close proximity, usually in contexts where the housing stock, social services, and public amenities are under tremendous pressure. (Bennett, 2006: 65)

An emphasis on diasporic memory as a memory of the *process* of becoming, rather than any specific culturally-defined memory, takes this effect into account, and succeeds in normalizing and rationalizing the process of migration. The economic threat of migrant communities is defused by the narrative of *plus ça change*, and the cultural threat of transnational identities is removed as they are seen as subject contributors to the national heritage. The heritage of the nation-state is thus portrayed as a paradox – open to constant change in a globalized world, yet a model of certitude in the ability to accommodate while remaining unique. It is through this emphasis on *process* that memory, heritage, and identity are manipulated in museums of migration, and are 'interacting in response to increased mobilities, flows, and space-time compression' (Isar, Viejo–Rose and Anheier in the volume) in this current phase of globalization.

REFERENCES

Appadurai, Arjun (1996) *Modernity at Large: Cultural Dimensions of Globalisation* Minneapolis and London: University of Minnesota Press.

Ballé, Catherine (2002) 'Democratization and Institutional Change: A Challenge for Modern Museums', in D. Crane, N. Kawashima and K. Kawasaki (eds), *Global Culture: Media, Arts, Policy, and Globalisation.* London and New York: Routledge.

Bennett, Tony (2005) *Civic Laboratories: Museums, Cultural Objecthood, and the Governance of the Social.* Working Paper No. 2, CRESC Working Paper Series. Milton Keynes, UK: Centre for Research on Socio-Cultural Change, The Open University.

—— (2006) 'Exhibition, Difference, and the Logic of Culture', in I. Karp, C. Kratz, L. Szwaja and T. Ybarra Fransto (eds), *Museum Frictions.* Durham, NC and London: Duke University Press, pp. 46–69.

Bhabha, Homi (1996) 'Culture's In-between', in S. Hall and P. Du Gay (eds), *Questions of Cultural Identity.* Los Angeles and London: Sage.

Chen, Chia-Li (2007) 'Museums and the Shaping of Cultural Identities', in S. Knell, S. Macleod and S. Watson (eds), *Museum Revolutions*. London and New York: Routledge, pp.173–188.

Clifford, James (1999) 'Museums as Contact Zones', in D. Boswell and J. Evans (eds), *Representing the Nation*. London and New York: Routledge.

de Certeau, Michel (1988) *The Practice of Everyday Life*, trans. Steven Rendall. Berkeley, Los Angeles and London: University of California Press.

Dias, Nelia (2008) 'Cultural Differences and Cultural Diversity: The Case of the Musée du Quai Branly', in D. Sherman (ed.), *Museums and Difference*. Indianapolis and Bloomington, IN: Indiana University Press, pp. 124–154.

Hall, Stuart (2008) 'Whose Heritage?', in G. Fairclough, R. Harrison, J. Jameson Jr and J. Schofield (eds), *The Heritage Reader*. London and New York: Routledge, pp. 219–228.

Huyssen, Andreas (1995) *Twilight Memories*. New York and London: Routledge.

—— (2001) 'Present Pasts: Media, Politics, Amnesia', in Arjun Appadurai, (ed.), *Globalization*. Durham, NC and London: Duke University Press, pp. 57–77.

Lefebvre, Henri (1991) *The Production of Space*, trans. Donald Nicholson-Smith. Oxford and Malden, MA: Blackwell.

Lowenthal, David (1998): *The Heritage Crusade and the Spoils of History*. Cambridge: Cambridge University Press.

Misztal, Barbara (2007) 'Memory Experience: The Forms and Functions of Memory', in S. Watson (ed.), *Museums and Their Communities*. London and New York: Routledge, pp. 379–396.

Servole, Fanny (2007) 'La Cité et ses publics: images, perceptions et evolutions', *Museum International*, 233/234, Vol. 59, No. 1/2. Paris: UNESCO and Blackwell.

Toubon, Jacques (2007) 'Preface' in *Guide de l'Exposition Permanente*, *La Cité Nationale de l'Histoire de l'Immigration*. Paris: Palais de la Porte Dorée.

Virilio, Paul (2008) as cited in *Raymond Depardon – Paul Virilio 'Terre Natale, Ailleurs commence ici'*, 21 Nov. 2008–15 March 2009, Fondation Cartier pour l'art contemporain, Paris (exhibition leaflet and commentary).

Williams, Paul (2007) *Memorial Museums*. Oxford and New York: Berg.

CHAPTER 18

HERITAGE, MEMORY, DEBRIS: SULUKULE, DON'T FORGET
Asu Aksoy and Kevin Robins

In this chapter, we will consider the fate of Sulukule, a long-established Roma/Gypsy district in the historical peninsula of Istanbul. The story, it's a very simple one, is that Sulukule has been shattered and razed to the ground over the past four or five years. We will endeavour to situate the story of Sulukule in terms of the distinctive urban (but also, importantly, national) myths that have come to prevail in Istanbul – the particular system of fictions, powered-up as phantasies, shaping and structuring Istanbul's heritage narratives. How is it that a (supposedly) thousand-year old Roma settlement could come to be so rapidly demolished? What did those municipal authorities who initiated this strategic offensive against Sulukule think they were doing? And what of the better heritage – for the cleaning-away of an 'old' heritage was at the heart of the municipality's avowed 'renewal' mission – with which they are intently and, in our view, delusionally seeking to replace it?

This chapter is concerned with the recent destruction of Sulukule, a predominantly Roma district located in the historical peninsula of Istanbul. There are three principle objectives. The first is to describe the process by which the local municipality initiated a programme of radical urban 'redevelopment' in the cause of gentrification in the historic, central zone of the city. The second objective is to situate the developments in Sulukule in the context of the longer-term cultural imaginary through which the city's historical trajectory has come to be conceived (as elaborated in the literary texts of Ahmet Hamdi Tanpınar and, later, Orhan Pamuk). Third, we explore the evolving new conceptual and ideological frame that is serving as a rationale for the reinvention, in the name of development, of Istanbul's cultural heritage and identity.

Istanbul triptych

> *Palimpseste ou non, proche de l'inconscient ou non, la ville est un espace qui ruse avec la durée historique. (Mongin, 2005: 52)*

Disjunctures of mind

First, a kind of detour. We want to explore some aspects of the contradictory mentality of Istanbul, as they emerged out of the break-up of the Ottoman Empire and the formation of the Turkish Republic in the early twentieth-century. In an essay written in 1962, the Turkish writer Ahmet Hamdi Tanpınar (2008a: 145-149), no doubt the pre-eminent fictionist of twentieth-century Istanbul, presents us with the melancholic, but not at all unexpected or surprising, observation that 'We have lost the concept of the city.' 'Where did that old Istanbul go?' he asks. 'It was dilapidated, destitute and desperate. Yet, it had a life and style of its own.' 'We have lost the concept of the city long ago,' Tanpınar reiterates. It seems a straightforward rhetorical expression of regret and ornamented nostalgia for what is regarded as an irreplaceable loss for the Istanbul that he knew.

But Tanpınar was a complex figure, far more than just a conventional and commonplace nostalgist. Nostalgia was just the starting point of his trail of thinking. If he took as one of his themes this perceived disappearance of the historical, Ottoman Istanbul, Tanpınar also articulated solicitous modernising concerns about the future possible course of development of the new Republican Turkish society in which he lived. In *Istanbul: Memories of a City* (2005), Orhan Pamuk takes up and engages with this tension-filled sensibility of the early Turkish modernising elites. Tanpınar is presented as a citizen of intellectual orientation, with a strong sense of civic obligation to engage with the vast and daunting project of Turkish modernisation. Along with his good friend, the poet Yahya Kemal, he sought to evoke and promote 'an image of "Turkish Istanbul"', and to affirm 'the city's "Turkish" identity' (Tanpınar, 2008a: 226) – to evince and to advance, that is to say, a new, 'modern' *national* identity for the city. This modernising aspiration found its place, in a complex way, alongside the seemingly contrasting sensibilities of a poet of the ruined and dilapidated Istanbul of the early twentieth century, who would evoke and elaborate upon the theme of melancholic sensibility (*hüzün*) (to which Pamuk shows himself to be a regardful beneficiary; in his own knowing way, he has managed to give this well-worn motif a new, twenty-first-century lease of being and expression; Istanbul = *hüzün* is by now a familiar formula for his distant readers around the world). Thus, Tanpınar, on the *hüzün* of Istanbul's depleted ruins, states: 'Only time and the sharp shocks of history can give a neighbourhood such a face. How many conquests, how many defeats, how many miseries did its people have to suffer to create the scene before us?' (quoted in Pamuk, 2005: 224).

Orhan Pamuk introduces us into a 'tangled tale' (2005: 227) – a particular Istanbul tangle of mental perception, fabrication, and delusion. First, Tanpınar parades a rationalist-partisan (i.e. 'modern' Republican) agenda, focused on the invoked imperative for the Turkish nationalisation of Istanbul's urban space. But there is then the accompanying motif of nostalgia and reminiscence – the discursive display of melancholia for what is mourned as the 'lost' city. *Where did that old Istanbul go?* Surely the truth of every great city is that it has its own special propensities and modalities of thinking. It has its own idiom – actually, its own array of idioms – elaborated, rehearsed and put into circulation over long historical time. This is what Orhan Pamuk's *Istanbul* book is essentially about. Pamuk is inviting

us to reflect on certain idiomatic narrative tropes in this city – ones that have progressively aggregated into a distinctive Istanbul disposition and complexion of thought. We may say that it is a disposition characterised by certain *disjunctures* of mind, both intellectual and imaginative.

Focusing his attention on Tanpınar's constructed and crafted 'narratives of Old Istanbul', Pamuk is particularly interested in how a certain early-twentieth-century Turkish nationalist-modernist logic and rhetoric – with which Tanpınar and Yahya Kemal were closely associated – came to have recourse to such an 'innocent view of tradition' (2005: 236), – one that could associate urban poverty and decay with traditional and authentic identity ('soul'). What these authors delivered up, says Pamuk, was an evocative 'image in which *İstanbullu*s could see themselves'. In reality, of course, it was all just a 'dream' – a dream grounded in the 'melancholy of the ruins' (2005: 228). It was actually a delusion. '[T]hey went on walks to poor neighbourhoods in search of beautiful sights that endowed the city's dwellers with the *hüzün* of the ruined past' (2005: 227). The modern 'Turkish' city – they imagined it as emerging out of its own post-imperial dereliction. Pamuk draws our attention to what he calls (in English translation, at least) the 'lovely fiction' (2005: 232) that Tanpınar and his friend were able to etch into the public mind of Istanbul. Their observations and narratives would enter into the Istanbul way of thinking, with certain calming consequences.

Disjuncture I: Disavowal through the narrative of the city. '[W]e keep wasting this beautiful city', Tanpınar iterates (2008a: 145). In one way, this is simply a plaint of conventional memory. But, beneath the surface rhetoric, there is more to engage with. At the heart of this rhetorical articulation, there is an interesting and significant disjuncture of thought. What Pamuk signals is a certain logic of apparent reasoning – but which is at the same time a forceful trajectory of wilful imagining – according to which the modern Turkish-national future is actually to be found in, and recovered from, the old 'lost' Istanbul, by which is meant, an old 'authentic' and 'Turkish' Istanbul. In Tanpınar's fictive hold on the city, the (imagined) past and the (posited) future are strangely (impossibly) in alignment – intellectually and imaginatively requisitioned together into the ideological cause of a solicited national narrative continuity. Tanpınar, alongside his fellow wayfarer,

Yahya Kemal, would wander through the poor neighbourhoods of Istanbul 'in search of beautiful sights' (Pamuk, 2005: 227). The novelist 'preferred to look to the poor, defeated and deprived Muslim population to prove that they had not lost one bit of their identity. ... [T]o convey these neighbourhoods as traditional, unspoiled, and untouched by the West, he wrote that "they were ruined, they were poor and wretched" but had "retained their own style and their own way of life"' (2005: 227). Dreaming... on behalf of a clamant national ideological cause.

What the scholarly Republican friends beheld in the course of their purposeful wanderings, was an annexable picturesque countenance of Istanbul. It was a discursive effect that they contrived to summon out of urban degradation and the difficult conditions of existence of the urban poor. What they then produced out of this was 'a nationalist literature offering an innocent view of tradition' (2005: 236). Through the imaginative prism of their particular niche of class-cultural sensibility, and at that particular, urgent historical moment in Turkish Republican history, the picturesque city came to stand for – to stand *in* for – the city's requisite, conceived-as-imperative, new modern national identity. In their fictive domains, no inconvenient and complicating cultural complexities of the actual, complex past would be able to gain access. As Orhan Pamuk (2005: 226) properly observes, this overdrive of conventional ideological thinking very improperly 'overlooked Istanbul's multi-lingual, multi-religious heritage to support its "Turkification"'. A disavowed reality: '[T]he two were happy to forget the Greeks, the Armenians, the Jews, the Kurds and many other minorities' (2005: 225). History/lie.

What is apparent is a radical disjuncture in memorial experience between an actually far too unruly and un-recoverable multi-ethnic (N.B. including Roma! – who don't figure in Pamuk's conventional minorities list) past, on the one side, and, on the other, 'contemporary', that is to say, drastically cleaned-up, and reconstrued requirements for a more acceptably 'modern' (i.e. nationally-simplified) heritage for Istanbul. Beneath the nostalgic, comfortable-enough Istanbul surface-of-thinking, it is apparent that fundamental processes of disavowal and denial have been incorporated into the urban narrative. The superficial nostalgia is complicated and corrupted by a fundamental, and socially channelled, lie – a nationally-inspired self-deceit about the past and about the historical truth of the city.

Urban memory is subverted, and assimilated into the new discourse of Turkish nationalism and modernisation. Memory, heritage, identity – it is crucial to understand how these collective realities became so deeply invested (even through the relatively moderate disposition of such a creative one as Tanpınar) by a governing logic of deceit and self-deceit. National, everyday trajectories of phantasy and delusion.

Disjuncture II: Distanciation in the urban space. '[T]o "discover" the city's soul in its ruins,' says Orhan Pamuk, 'to see these ruins as expressing the city's "essence", you must travel down a long, labyrinthine path strewn with historical accidents' (2005: 231). And then, he continues: 'To savour Istanbul's back streets, to appreciate the vines and trees that endow its ruins with accidental grace, you must, first and foremost be a "stranger" to them' (2005: 231). Tanpınar and Yahya Kemal viewed this city 'through the eyes of an outsider' (2005: 228). Pamuk suggestively connects their perambulations back to those of the outsider-poets Nerval and Gautier, some seventy years previously. 'These two nationalist writers,' says Pamuk, 'could see the city's "beauty" only in the parts where they themselves were outsiders' (2005: 232). Pamuk is sharp in his critical engagement with this particular and familiar motif of *Istanbullu* sensibility. He draws our attention to the readily embraced accidental grace that Tanpınar and Yahya Kemal stumbled upon, which still has a certain potency to seduce us now, some seventy or more years later, in our own turn. 'Those who take pleasure in the accidental beauty of poverty and historical decay, those of us who see the picturesque in ruins – invariably, we're the people who come from the outside' (2005: 231). *We're* the people...

This modality of conspired-into distanciation and dislocation with respect to the city space represents another clear instance of social and psychic disjuncture. Tanpinar and Yahya Kemal constructed an image for the city out of ruins and remains that had nothing directly to do with them. They were outsiders to the decay and dilapidation that they would actively seek out. What this reflects is the peculiar nature of the relationship of these elites to the city – existentially positioned outside the ruins of the past, yet imaginatively embracing the idea of the ruins within their intellectual-political project. Embracing the idea of those ruins that they chose to classify, within their own cultural scheme, as 'Turkish', and as therefore having the potential to symbolise and proclaim the Turkish spirit. Committed imaginatively to the ruins that the modernity they believed in would inevitably seek to demolish – committed to old symbolic ruins that would, in the longer term, be inimical to the modern Republican re-conception of the city. They were dreaming. Again, we are in the domain of delusion. But, at that point in time, it was still possible to hold the delusion up to the light. Delusion could work and project its welcomed magical effects.

Sulukule effaced

Sulukule (finally we're there) is one of the last remaining neighbourhoods of the 'old Istanbul'. Adjacent to the city walls, between Edirnekapı and Topkapı – and crucially, therefore, within the historic peninsula of Sultanahmet – the district has been one of the main settlement areas of Roma/Gypsies in Istanbul since the eleventh century (i.e. since the Byzantine era), so it is said. But, more precisely, what we should really be saying is that Sulukule *was* one of the last remaining neighbourhoods of the commemorated old Istanbul. For this chapter is about how Sulukule has been levelled to the ground – about the violent seizure and, by now, near absolute erasure of what has been declared to be 'a thousand years of Romani cultural heritage' in Istanbul (*Sulukule UNESCO Report,* 2008: 18–20). And, in the context of the present volume, it is about how this strategically calculated and ruthlessly implemented act of brutal effacement connects in to the elaborated memory and heritage discourses of Istanbul.

The life conditions of Roma in Istanbul (as in Turkey generally – and everywhere else too) have never been easy (*We Are Here!,* 2008). But, through time, they always managed, in some way or other, to sustain their living space in the city. In the mid-1950s, however, the Roma began to suffer an onslaught, as a consequence of the accelerating concrete-belligerent transformation of the city. In 1956, the imperative 'modernisation' of Istanbul called for a vast highway (*Vatan Caddesi*) to be driven through their neighbourhood, resulting in the extensive demolition of properties, and also of part of the city wall. The end was then starting to begin. As a result of this devastation, a great many of the

residents had to move away from Sulukule proper, migrating northwards to the Neslişah and Hatice Sultan neighbourhoods, still along the city walls, but taking both the valued name and the characteristic disposition of Sulukule with them.

Sulukule proved resourceful enough to continue its existence in this new, displaced location. And it was resolute enough to sustain its style and its stance of being in the city. Much of the energy in the Sulukule disposition towards the world derived from the exuberant tradition of its 'entertainment houses' (*devriye*, as the local Roma called them) – venues, often very informal, for listening to music and eating and drinking. In the cover notes for the CD *Sulukule: Rom Music of Istanbul* (released by Traditional Crossroads in 1998), Sonia Seeman nicely describes what these places of popular congregation were like:

> *Traversed by narrow meandering streets that spill off from ancient city walls, Sulukule is a neighbourhood in Istanbul famous for its Roman (Gypsy) music and belly dancing. Here late-night private parties are provided by the local Roman residents in a space that has no other marking than an evocative name such as the 'Gazelle's Place' or the name of a person 'Sezgin', and in some cases no marking at all. The entertainment setting is a small, bare cement-floored room often outfitted with little more than rickety tables and chairs. Making arrangements for such a night out involves finding a friend who has a friend who has a phone number. Members of a Roman family organise the party and provide the necessary services, including a Roman band of up to four members to play clarinet, violin, kanun (zither-type lap harp), cümbüş (banjo-like lute) or ud (non-fretted lute), and darbuka (goblet-shaped hand drum); one or two female dancers; children or an elderly retired man to watch the car; and some appetizers and alcohol to lubricate the evening.*

Sulukule, in its translocated reappearance, remained a vibrant neighbourhood thanks to its entertainment houses (it is claimed that the entertainment business brought employment to more than 3,500 people). This relative prosperity lasted until the 1990s, when the new Chief of Security (the conservative Saadettin Tantan) ordered a clearance action against the entertainment houses on the basis of their imputed 'moral degeneracy' (Somersan and Kırca-Schroeder, 2007: 101). But more than that, more significantly in the longer term, what became apparent was that the culture of the Roma could not accord with the new urban 'vision' and the gathering city-branding drive, which was by then rapidly developing in order to fashion Istanbul as a twenty-first-century global city. The informal, unplanned, and seemingly disorderly, organisation of life in Sulukule was incomprehensible to the disdainful municipal authorities, and couldn't possibly figure in their globalising-modernising neo-liberal plans. By 1994, at which time Mr Tantan had been elevated to the mayorship of Istanbul, all of the entertainment houses had been closed down. From that point onwards, Sulukule's fortunes declined dramatically. The quality of life of its Roma inhabitants suffered immensely as a consequence of this offensive against what was a basic economic livelihood in the district. Another decisive move had been made towards the final crushing of Sulukule, towards the seeming goal of the final eradication of what Sulukule, had disconcertingly stood for in the city's cultural life.

2005 initiated the next, and the decisive, and the finally catastrophic, turning point for Sulukule. The endgame was put into play - consciously schemed and unconsciously driven by the planning and regulating authorities of the city, in close partnership with the national government. What was devised was a devastating legal-instrumental-strategic strike. In 2005, a law was passed giving extraordinary powers to local authorities to 'develop' historic areas of the city. Up until this juncture, the language of urban planning had been for the most part about modest conservation, and the scale of conception had been in terms of mere parcels of land. With this new law – the highly controversial Law No. 5366 (for the 'Preservation by Renovation and Utilisation by Revitalising of Deteriorated Immovable Historical and Cultural Properties') – so-called renewal began to be conceived on a far more ambitious scale, and according to new and commercially very serious real-estate imperatives. The fundamental objective of this law was to establish so-conceived 'renewal zones' (*yenileme alanları*) in the city, extending across whole districts, in order to open up what had become run-down historic neighbourhoods for property development. Put simply, this legal offensive 'removes districts outside the conventional planning framework and promotes intervention over a whole area' (UNESCO, 2009: 48). Over the previous decade, Istanbul had experienced very extensive development – housing, office development,

shopping malls – in its edge areas. Attention was now turning to the potential for the economic exploitation of old and poor districts in the core of the city – notably, in Sultanahmet and in Beyoğlu/Pera – of which there are a number (most notably Tarlabaşi and Süleymaniye, as well as Sulukule). What OECD observers (2008: 168) recently and rightly referred to as 'Istanbul's "semi-planning" approach' ('by which the system accommodates projects already in progress, leading to an unsustainable pattern of urban development') is, in this zone of the city, all about enforced gentrification. Semi-planning it most surely is: the 'abandonment of decision making processes to subjective evaluations' (Dinçer, 2009).

With the passing of Law No. 5366, it became, by a kind of legalistic magic, suddenly possible for municipalities and their construction partners to move very fast, towards the implementation of new, large-scale and lucrative development projects, targeting extensive unfortunate zones of the city. With the extraordinary power that this order of law gave, local authorities could categorise the building stock of newly defined-as-renewal zones as appropriate for demolition. And then they could start to make quick deals for their semi-replanned reconstruction and reinterpretation. Immediately after the law came on to the statute books, Sulukule was among the first to be categorised as an urban renewal zone – unfortunately for its Roma inhabitants. Fatih Municipality, Sulukule's local authority, with its complacent wrecking-ball mentality, passed the sentence of extinction on the district it reviled. Fatih had in its charge all the necessary right, rules and means of destruction.

According to a deal, struck in 2005, between Fatih Municipality, the Istanbul Metropolitan Municipality, and the Turkish Mass Housing Administration (TOKI), the Sulukule area was scheduled to be cleared and smashed, and then reconceived as a marketable, modern-compatible, neo-traditional neighbourhood. And in Istanbul nobody could be surprised by this gesture of combined recklessness and omnipotence – only in helpless despair. Central-city areas with historic qualities, such as this one, adjacent to the ancient city walls, had by this point become irresistibly exploitable assets, irreversibly. The Sulukule renewal project proposed the replacement of existing buildings with new housing, along with commercial and tourism facilities, including underground parking lots. Property owners, the more fortunate inhabitants of the district, were offered the chance to buy into the new housing scheme, and if they didn't want to, then they were declared free to sell their property to third parties or to the municipality. However, considering that most of the property owners were actually relatively poor, only a very small percentage could opt into the new project. All the rest ended up selling their rights very rapidly, in anguished anticipation of an impending ministerial *diktat* for emergency expropriation. And the reality, predictably, ironically, was that the placement of multiple local buildings on the real-estate market sent their value tumbling down (Foggo, 2007: 44). Those more precarious citizens of the *mahalle*, those who were only renting properties in Sulukule, were offered units in a new mass housing development in the newly-constructed, but impossibly remote Taşoluk district – a hopeless 45 kilometres away from the city (and most of the tenants who were relocated there could not afford the monthly rent, and were not able to carry on with their traditional occupations in this new location – consequently they had to move on from Taşoluk as well). From 2007 onwards, the demolitions began with an explosive vengeance. And by 2009 almost all the buildings in this once vital Roma neighbourhood, including its listed-in-vain properties, had been razed to the ground. And there was calculated symbolic violence, too – even the name was withdrawn – and what was once Sulukule, with all its symbolic-evocative-provocative spin, was designated to be known henceforth as Karagümrük.

And now a new Roma-effaced historical identity project is being compulsorily enforced upon this hitherto unsuspecting district of the historical peninsula, through the well-arranged marriage of bureaucracy and profiteering The architects designing the new neighbourhood, quite unsurprisingly, have proclaimed that their project set out to conserve the 'socio-cultural identity' and the 'inner-wall neighbourhood' character of the area. Well, of course. What else could they possibly say? We know very well how such automated and formulaic scripts come to be composed. 'In the Ottoman period,' the architects go on to advertise, 'this was a neighbourhood within the city walls,' and 'we conserved the basic values of this identity coming from the past, adding the new values that are necessary for people of today.' To continue with the traditional cultural values is not 'traditionalism', according to these architects, it is 'a contemporary attitude'

(*Mimarizm*, 2008). 'People of today', 'the basic values of this identity', a 'contemporary attitude': the routine and complacent rhetorical output of corporate scheming.

Façade device

Let us turn now to these implementers of demolition, and to their delusional relationship to the history of Sulukule, of Sultanahmet, and of Istanbul, to the wreckers and then self-declared restorers of heritage in the twenty-first-century city. Municipal agencies – both metropolitan and local – are militantly putting into circulation the discourses of urban global modernisation. For reasons of investment, tourism and image, Istanbul should conform to the norms of a world city. In this endeavour, they are able to draw upon globally-standardised templates and maquettes. But there is, at the same time, a local inflection to all of this business. For these global times are also giving rise to new conditions of heritage exploitation. In the inner-city renewal zones, the municipal authorities have decided to mobilise the distinctive heritage of 'old Istanbul' as part of the city's 'contemporary' place-marketing strategies. And, given the historical neglect of the historical areas of the city – Istanbul's modernisation 'lag' – there are most certainly lucrative central real-estate zones to be capitalised upon – places to be appropriated, commandeered, and then commercially re-envisioned. And all of this through complex manoeuvres of both evasion and instrumental negotiation with international agencies such as UNESCO, with its strict requirements of 'World Heritage values and standards' (UNESCO 2008: 3) for the historical peninsula. What we are presently seeing is the encounter of mercenary inner-city gentrification dynamics, on the one hand, and the principles of world-historic conservation, on the idealistic other.

The physical fabric of Sulukule has now been wiped out, through a ferocious decisiveness on the part of Fatih Municipality. The myths of the 'old Istanbul' will persist. Orhan Pamuk's *Istanbul* and Tanpınar's newly translated classic, *A Mind at Peace* (Tanpınar, 2008b [1949]), will no doubt gently contribute to making sure of that. Valedictory narratives for an erstwhile Istanbul identity will not prove so easy to wipe out. They still have a needed force of appeal. Thus, according to İlber Ortaylı

(2009), Ottoman historian and currently director of the Topkapı Palace Museum: 'As Turkey got rich, Istanbul was ruined. In fact, in the 1950s, which I knew, Istanbul had a distinctive poverty that gave it a certain charm.' From a charming poverty to the inescapable logic of profit-driven urban modernisation, Tanpınar lived at a time when these two dimensions of urban reality could still be somehow held-in-tension-together. Now it is far more difficult to manage this trick of attempted synthesis. The early national modernisation narrative no longer has the same illusional and idealistically compelling potency. The *hüzün* image will surely continue to have its poetic-imaginative resonance, among certain classes of concerned observers of the city at least, but it has by now broken adrift, apart and away from the old-style modernisation heroism. The getting-rich of the city has conspired to produce a contemporary mood of disenchantment and alienation. Urban development strategies are now increasingly perceived to have engineered into existence a 'self service city' (Esen and Lanz, 2005), a concomitant 'fortress Istanbul' mentality (Esen and Rieniets, 2008), and so on – that is to say, to have confrontationally devised a city vision in which public culture – and lived heritage – is systematically deleted from urban social experience. Nostalgia and modernisation both continue to exist, but they can no longer hold hands in the way they once did. A once functioning fictive ensemble is now disassembled.

That familiar narrative image of what Istanbul heritage is about has thus been operatively stretched, imaginatively weakened, and it is moving towards discursive fatigue. It is still there, but it is no longer an entirely adequate or compelling image through which to interpret the ensemble of Istanbul. Maybe we are now in a position to identify other codes coming into operation in the imaginative apprehension of the city? We should not think of them in terms of an alternative interpretative scheme, but, rather, in terms of supplementary and/or transpositional developments. New, and non-reconcilable, institutionalised forces of division and contestation have become ever more apparent in Istanbul's contemporary cultural dynamics. Fatih Municipality and the Istanbul Metropolitan Municipality are now driven for the most part by the instrumental logic of real-estate development. Which is then imperiously, and benightedly, combined with an aesthetic resolution

to (finally, authoritatively) restore the 'authentic' Ottoman heritage of the historic areas of the city. With respect to the precarious fate of the historical peninsula, UNESCO (2008: 19) recently criticised the local authorities for their 'crude workmanship', involving 'excessive replacement of original fabric and the use of inappropriate restoration techniques.' There is, they say, a 'lack of awareness' on the part of Fatih Municipality; an unawareness, that is to say, of agreed 'international standards' of heritage conservation (UNESCO, 2009: 24). Fatih's projects have 'frequently involved excessive replacement of original fabric and an approach more suited to new construction than the conservation of monuments' ('In some instances vanished monuments are reconstructed on a different site from where they originally existed') (2009: 50). What is evident is a considerable scepticism about the technical expertise of the city authorities, but also doubts about their aesthetic values, tastes and judgements, which, in the context of the present discussion, is what concerns us in particular.

What of these aesthetics? Conservative, authoritarian, pretentious, uncultivated, uncivil. To be abjured, we say, from our decidedly alienated perspective. Recently, the Istanbul Chamber of Architects (2007) declared, with great concern, that contemporary urban renewal projects were resulting in the rapid loss of heritage in Sultanahmet, and, moreover, that living spaces, like that of Sulukule, were being supplanted by 'imitations that distort history'. According to the Chamber's provocative image: 'theatre décors are being constructed according to the [stereotypical] model of the historic Turkish house.' The declaration of the Chamber of Architects was made in the wake of news that the Eminönü local municipality (now merged with Fatih Municipality) was planning a major 'renewal' programme in the nearby Süleymaniye district of the historic peninsula, involving the demolition of nearly 3,000 buildings, and their reconception and redesign in the style of 'Ottoman architecture'. 'Süleymaniye returning to its former times', as they infelicitously put it. The local authorities were intent on knocking down buildings in disrepair, but they were also after those that they judged to be inconsistent with the identity of the historic peninsula. Professor Cengiz Eruzun, potentate of the Historic Peninsula Urban Design Project, explained why they were proposing to thus reconstitute history:

'Warsaw and Leningrad were rebuilt after the Second World War. This is about cultural heritage. Istanbul's cultural heritage, in terms of civil architecture, has unfortunately been lost. We are going to construct the new buildings in this area according its heritage.' When the project is finished, said the Professor, 'the peninsula will be a synthesis of the Ottoman and the modern look. The modern will be in conformity with Turkish architecture' (*Zaman*, 2005). What can we possibly say to this? The considered response of the Chamber of Architects is that the ill-conceived Süleymaniye initiative displays nothing more than 'a stage décor mentality, in the name of Ottoman revival'. These are 'hypothetical reconstructions', as UNESCO rightly designates, and decries, them (2009: 50).

A new elucidatory metaphor for interpreting the new urban scene and cultural reality of Istanbul is surely that of the *façade*. The new historical misconstructions of the Fatih and Eminönü planners and architects are driven by a dual imperative. First, the external 'look' of the building is required to convey an impression of the 'old', and of a proposed heritage that these supposed authorities regard as correct Ottoman. What we are offered – what are up for sale – are vague architectural allusions, memorial evocations of some long-emptied historical legacy. Fatih Municipality now requires architectural projects in the area to conform to regulations concerning the façade of buildings. 'Monitoring closely the design of façades during the stage of granting building permission,' says the Municipality website, 'we can ensure that new buildings are in harmony with the texture of the historic peninsula' (Kentsel Tasarım Rehberleri, 2006). In other words, pacified neo-Ottomanism that conforms to supposedly modern taste (of certain affluent classes). And, second, the interiors of the new edifices should be entirely in the idiom of a newly-devised modern style, deploying modern materials and designs, and designed to encapsulate the lifestyle of a certain category of modern urban resident. But no good for the Roma of Sulukule! As Şükrü Pündük, head of the Sulukule Roma Culture Support Association, says:

Our houses had courtyards, this was the typical structure. The courtyard served many functions, we used to wash our dead there, have fruit trees, mulberry, cherry, plum trees. We used to have animals, chickens, birds, horses, donkeys... We live in apartments now, but living in apartments is not our way of life... we do not have this culture.

The façade provides a new way of managing the relation between heritage and modernity – through their engineered conjoinment in the physical configuration of the building structures. Exterior semblance and interior life-processes are in managed division from each other. And the façade performs the effective work of combined exhibition and concealment, at once showing off the phantasy and covering up the reality. A clever contrivance of delusion.

Contemporary renewal projects in Istanbul project and advertise their approach in terms of resuscitating the lost cultural identity of the city. And the newly-composed architectural façades are now beginning to function as the screens for projecting the recovered image of the old and the imagined Ottoman city. Municipal planning bureaux are employing their architectural workers to turn out drawing after drawing of the 'historic fabric' of historic neighbourhoods. 'We are being criticised for wanting to build houses with bay windows, for wanting to keep alive the Ottoman character', says the Historic Peninsula Professor Eruzun (2007: 11), 'we look at photographs and we apply whatever we see in them.' Images, appearances, façades – these are prevailing over any serious engagement with substance. The famous Divan Hotel, in the centre of the city, close by Taksim Square, advertises its renewal and reconstruction programme through an emphasis on the combined new-and-traditional look that its façade will take on. In this case, it is said, 'the inspiration derives from Bosphorus architecture, with terracotta panels engraved upon horizontal panel structures resembling the stone houses of old Istanbul' (Salman, 2009: 5). Some time ago, the respected architect Nezih Eldem (1992: 101) noted how the planning regulations for listed historic sites in Istanbul drew their norms from one particular period style of the imagined classic Turkish house, bringing about 'an architectural definition that suits our inclination towards façade conservation.' What is being instituted, as a consequence, is a toneless museum city – toneless, but via a perverse architectural admixture of the kitsch and the sepulchral. The neo-façades are dividing an increasingly absolutist Istanbul governance from city life as it has hitherto been experienced and valued. The Roma of Sulukule surely know this truth best of all.

REFERENCES

Dinçer, İ. (2009) 'Kentsel koruma ve yenileme sorunlarını örnekler üzerinden tartışmak: Süleymaniye ve Tarlabaşı, 26 January, Planlama.org, www.planlama.org/new/planlama.org-yazilari/kentsel-koruma-ve-yenileme-sorunlarini-ornekler-uzerinden-tartismak-suleymaniye-ve-tarlabasi.html (accessed on 21/02/2010).

Eldem, Nezih (1992) 'Tarih bilinci ve çagdas kişilik', Arradamento Dekorasyon, May: 100–101.

Eruzun, Cengiz (2007) Interview: 'stanbul nasıl yenileniyor', Yeni Mimar, June: 10–11.

Esen, Orhan and Lanz, Stephan (eds) (2005) Self Service City: Istanbul. Berlin: b_books.

Esen, Orhan and Rieniets, Tim (2008) 'Fortress Istanbul: gated communities and the socio-urban transformation', pp. 83–111 in Frank Eckardt and Kathrin Wildner (eds), Public Istanbul: Spaces and Spheres of the Urban. Bielefeld: transcript.

Foggo, Hacer (2007) 'The Sulukule Affair: Roma against expropriation', Roma Rights Quarterly. 4: 41–47.

Istanbul Chamber of Architects (2007) Tarihi Yarımada'ya çağdaş ve bilimsel bir yaklaşıla korumaya çağrı. Istanbul: Mimarlar Odası İstanbul Büyükkent Şubesi.

Kentsel Tasarım Rehberleri (2006) [Urban Design Manuals], 22 August. Available at: www.fatih.bel.tr (accessed 21/02/2010).

Mimarizm (2008) 'Aartı Planlama: "Sulukule Projesi İstanbul için bir fırsattır, çünkü bu insani ve romantik bir projedir"', mimarizm.com, 5 February. Available at: www.mimarizm.com/KentinTozu/makale.aspx?ID=341&sid=328 (accessed 19/12/2009).

Mongin, Olivier (2005) La condition urbaine: la ville à l'heure de la mondialisation. Paris: Seuil.

OECD (2008) OECD Territorial Reviews: Istanbul, Turkey. Paris: OECD.

Ortaylı, Iber (2009) 'Bizi UNESCO'ya sikayet edenleri ayıplamıyorum', Milliyet Pazar, 28 June.

Pamuk, Orhan (2005) Istanbul: Memories of a City. London: Faber & Faber.

Salman, Yıldız (2009) 'Koruma, yıkmama ve tarihselcilik üzerine', Yeni Mimar, February 2009: 5.

Somersan, Semra and Kırca-Schroeder, Süheyla (2007) 'Resisting eviction: Sulukule Roma in search of right to space and place', Anthropology of East Europe Review, 25(2): 96–107.

Sulukule UNESCO Report (2008). Istanbul: Sulukule Platform.

Tanpınar, Ahmet Hamdi (2008a [1962]) 'The city', in Osman Deniztekin (ed.), Selections from Varlık. Istanbul: Varlik Yayınları, pp. 143–150.

Tanpınar, Ahmet Hamdi (2008b [1949]) A Mind at Peace. New York: Archipelago Books.

UNESCO (2008) Report on the Joint World Heritage Centre/ICOMOS Mission to the Historic Areas of Istanbul World Heritage Site from 8 to 13 May 2008. Paris: UNESCO.

UNESCO (2009) Report of the Joint UNESCO World Heritage Centre/ICOMOS Reactive Monitoring Mission to the World Heritage Site of Historic Areas of Istanbul from 27–30 April 2009. Paris: UNESCO.

We Are Here! Discriminatory Exclusion and Struggle for Rights of Roma in Turkey (2008) Istanbul: Edirne Roman Derneği/European Roma Rights Centre/Helsinki Citizens' Assembly.

Zaman (2005) 'Süleymaniye'de ilk kazma Nisan ayında vuruluyor', Zaman, 17 October.

CHAPTER 19

KNOWING THE CITY: MIGRANTS NEGOTIATING MATERIALITIES IN ISTANBUL

Yael Navaro-Yashin

This chapter is an ethnographic examination of the ways in which migrants into two neighbourhoods of Istanbul come to know and interpret the built environment which they inhabit and which surrounds them. Weaving through migrants' ways of negotiating the materialities around them, I discover that the city is known to its contemporary inhabitants in fragmentary, partial, and bitty forms. As if collecting pieces of a puzzle or assembling units of debris, migrants attempt to understand the past and the future of the built environment significantly left behind, in these neighbourhoods, by Greek and Jewish exiles or émigrés from Istanbul.

I walk uphill along the old city walls leading on to the old Tekfur Palace in the Ayvansaray district of Istanbul. Children play ball in the playground constructed by the local municipality on the outskirts of the Palace. Looking up today, one is able to vividly notice the restoration work along the walls, as the ruined old and original stones have been topped up with geometrically straight and measured new ones to give the appearance of care for the city's heritage. Behind the Palace site is a football playing field, used by young boys from the neighbourhood, and a local coffee shop. Here, I sit and talk with elderly local men and one of them says:

> The people (halk) wouldn't know 'the old' of these places. Do you, for example, know who built these city walls? We used to think they were Byzantine. But some say that it was the Genoese who made them. I have lived in this neighbourhood for 35 years, running the football club behind the Palace ruins. Now I've retired. But if you are interested in the past of these places, we don't know. You must go to the islands. There live old Istanbuli Greeks, Armenians, and Jews. You must ask them about the history of these places. They would know best. Anyway, one must visit these places with someone who knows Greek in order to understand them well.

With these words of hesitation, this elderly man devolved knowledge about the past of the built environment which surrounded his long-lived neighbourhood to the non-Muslim minorities, claiming less or lack of inside information. He associated the ruins in the old city, as well as the past of the materialities around him, with another language (Greek) which was not his own. He deferred knowledge about 'the past' of the city on to the non-Muslim minorities, mostly gone from the old city neighbourhoods, saying 'they would know better'. He claimed 'a lack of knowledge' about the past of the surroundings where were his home and neighbourhood.

A middle-aged man named Faruk Bey, sitting in the same coffee shop, was more forceful about interpreting the built and ruined materialities which surrounded us. Wearing a badge of the ultra-nationalist National Action Party (MHP), he employed an ideological framework to politically situate the non-Muslim minorities:

Turkey is being governed by the CIA and Mossad. It is they who provoked the 6–7 September events against the Greeks;[1] and then they blamed the Turks for it. The Jews print money and live in the best parts of the city. Anyway, it's the Jews who provoked us against the Greeks. They say we are racist: did they not live under our flag for centuries? I have visited Kinali island: Armenians live there. A friend of mine who is a builder left a tape recorder in the home of an Armenian. If you heard with what hatred the Armenians speak of us. ... Well, if they act as traitors towards us, then how can we like them? And then they call us 'racist'!

This man, who said his family was originally of Arab descent from the town of Iskenderun which borders Syria, was born in the district of Edirnekapi in Istanbul, close to Ayvansaray where we were, and had lived there all his life. He came to the coffee shop beside the Tekfur Palace to play cards every day. Though his discourse was shot through with nationalist ideology, Faruk Bey interspersed his reflections on politics and the city with such comments as 'Ah, there used to be a light-faced [clean and good] Greek lady called Christina who was our neighbour' ... He walked me along the walls harbouring an old Greek cemetery behind the football field, watching the crosses which bore the framed photos of the deceased and contemplating. Then, leading me across the highway which he said had torn through old cemeteries, he brought me to a Muslim cemetery with Ottoman as well as modern gravestones. Here, he prayed silently to the deceased. Exhibiting an embodied sense of ownership over this Muslim part of the district, he walked me to an Ottoman saint's tomb whilst eagerly describing the deeds of this saint. And finally, he left to attend the noontime namaz (worship) in the mosque nearby, describing himself as "a man who is dedicated to his spirituality".'

Walking through Balat to the neighbourhood of Fener, I visited Kamil, who worked as a salesperson in a small local antiques and gifts shop. The shop was on the ground floor of an old Greek mansion and overlooked other previously Greek-owned houses leading on to the Greek Orthodox Patriarchate nearby.[2] In the gift shop, there were pillow cases made out of cloth from Turkmenistan, old wine cases which Kamil said were found in Greek houses during restoration projects and brought to the shop, a German to Modern Greek

dictionary with the owner's signature of 'Sezmazoglou' in the inside cover and the handwritten date of 1884, which Kamil said he found wrapped in a plastic bag in the basement of the Fener neighbourhood house he lived in, village-made, hand-woven dolls, and an old chandelier with nine spaces for candles (to celebrate the Jewish festival of Hanukkah), among numerous other objects. 'I asked somebody about that book,' said Kamil, 'and they told me that it was a dictionary.' 'We don't value our history. We, as Turks, don't deserve this history,' he suddenly commented, in a self-deprecating tone. He insisted in pursuing this line, however, saying, 'I am obsessed with history; I am extremely interested.' He said he was born in the Fener district. He must have been in his early 30s when I met him. Describing the contemporary inhabitants of Fener and the neighbouring Balat, he said: 'Sixty per cent are from Kastamonu [in Turkey's western Black Sea region] and thirty per cent are from Siirt [in Eastern Turkey].' He said he doesn't want to count the remaining ten per cent who are from Diyarbakir [known as the capital of Turkey's Kurdish region] 'because they are thieves or drug-sellers'. Kamil was very eager to talk to me about the UNESCO-funded restoration project which was underway in Fener and Balat at the time.[3] 'There are rumours among the people that the UNESCO is here to dig for gold in the walls and basements of old Greek houses,' he said.

You know, the municipality of Fatih [to which Fener-Balat and Ayvansaray belong] doesn't allow anyone to hammer even one nail on the wall of an old house, because these houses are considered 'old properties of value'. But the UNESCO people were able to obtain permission to completely demolish a house and rebuild it. And they found 3 kilos of gold under one house!

Kamil described to me the procedure through which UNESCO employees restored old buildings in Fener and Balat:

The UNESCO people make an agreement with the [present] owner of the house they would like to restore. They say that the owner, or his tenant, need to evacuate the house until its restoration is complete. In the contract they sign with UNESCO, the owners have to promise that they will not sell the house in the five years which follow the restoration's suit.

Kamil spoke with cynicism, unsure about the intentions of the architects and employees of the UNESCO project. He also informed me about a new project which was under planning for the district:

A planning order [ihale] for this district was granted to the son of Tayyip Erdogan [the Prime Minister]. This construction firm with the name of Calik Grubu will arrive and tell people that in return for having their homes restored, the firm will own 60 per cent of their properties. Those who accept this deal will be able to continue living in the restored homes. Those who do not will be removed from their homes and given homes elsewhere, in the outskirts of the city, as forced compensation.

Kamil said that the firm's planning order would come to local residents of Fener and Balat as an imposition, against which there would be little which they would be able to do in resistance. He then went on to describe the growing interest in this dilapidated old district on the part of prominent journalists, actors, and actresses. 'Savas Ay, Ugur Dundar and others [well-known journalists] bought houses here and then sold them for higher prices after never living in them.'

Bits and pieces

The present local inhabitants of Fener, Balat, and Ayvansaray in the old city of Istanbul tell stories about the built environment which they inhabit and which surrounds them in bits and pieces.[4] Stories emerge with hesitation or trepidation, claiming a lack or absence of knowledge, or admitting only partial knowledge. 'We were told one thing about who built these walls, and then another. We are not quite sure.' Knowledge is often deferred to the non-Muslims of Istanbul who once lived there. 'They would know better; this used to be their place.' Knowledge about the city is provided in fragmented forms, like the pieces of a puzzle which do not fit. One piece here, another there, like collections of odds and ends. Stories emerge as oddments, in the bits and shreds. Many stories are made up like pieces of cloth which form an uneven patchwork through the fragmentary rumours which circulate from mouth to mouth among these neighbourhoods' present inhabitants. 'UNESCO has come to dig for gold under old Greek houses,' says one.

The neighbour who hears this reproduces it in another form, adding another imaginative line to the story, or a speculation. One snippet of rumour feeds another and it spreads through Chinese whispers, from window to window, from ear to ear. 'If they want to restore these houses, it must be that they intend to return them to the Greeks,' says one person, standing by a neighbour's door.

And the story grows in proportion and scale as it is transmitted from mouth to mouth. 'I bet the Patriarchate is behind it. They must be conspiring with UNESCO to take back these homes.' Broken pieces of narrative develop into mythical stories which then circulate through the entire neighbourhood and its inhabitants' links beyond it. People decide to agree or refuse to have their homes restored on the basis of these bits and pieces of story. The fragments of narrative express anxiety, a sense of insecurity and instability among the poor inhabitants of this district today. 'But could the planners associated with the Prime Minister's son take our homes with title deeds from us?' says one. 'They could do anything,' says another. 'We must protest,' says a third, proposing to form a neighbourhood coalition against the 'urban renewal' project which is being imposed on the neighbourhood by the government. One person tries to fill in the gaps of the words of another, to say something between the lines with another piece of the puzzle. 'They found us poor people here; some of us are illiterate. They will come from the government with papers for us to sign. Just look at the papers: there is a blank space. They will take our signatures and then fill in these pages with whatever they wish. Just don't sign!' says one man, trying to mobilize consciousness among neighbourhood residents against the new planning projects. 'OK, we are not signing!' says an old lady who wears a black veil. 'Don't listen to them,' says another woman, wearing a headscarf and looking through her window while taking part in the spontaneous street corner conversation. 'They just blame the municipality and the government. Let the municipality clean this place. Anyway, it's full of dogs and thieves. Let it be cleansed. I can move elsewhere. I have relatives in Emirgan; I'll go there.' 'Of course, she is secure,' says her neighbour, pointing at this woman, 'She has a place where she can lean her back. What will we do?' 'The government will take over all the properties which look on to the Golden Horn and make them state properties,' says one. 'How could they do that?' says another with rage. 'They can do anything they want and those who protest will be forcefully removed.' 'The municipality will apparently demolish and rebuild all the houses on this street.' 'Look, I have a red-tile coloured home on this street, I am trying to sell it before the planners arrive. Would anyone be interested?' 'And what will us tenants do?'

The bits, the pieces, the whispers and stories, the concern, the anxiety, the insecurity and lack of trust, the bad faith, the rage, the resignations and the calls to action, spread from the corner of a street to a windowsill, from a doorstep to apartment hallway, from pavement to balcony. ... Such broken stories, like shards or rubble, are interwoven with the visibly decaying, dilapidated built environment in this neighbourhood. 'What was the past of these properties?' 'Who lives in them now?' 'What will be our future in them?' ask the residents. The past, the present, and the future of the buildings in decay throw question marks into the relations which migrants in the city form with the materialities around them.

Migrants from various parts of Anatolia, having arrived through multiple routes, live in old Greek or Jewish houses in Fener and Balat in various fashions. Some hold title deeds over their properties. 'I bought my home from a Turk who was an immigrant from the Balkans (a *muhacir*),' says Neyyire Hanim with the black veil. 'I don't know whom he bought it from before selling it to me,' she remarks. Her home of wooden outer walls looks polished and clean. 'When it's your own home, you look after it,' she says. The home of Neyyire Hanim is one of the properties which would be taken over by the government if the 'urban renewal' project with the Prime Minister's son-in-law goes ahead. 'I don't want to go,' she says. 'I have been living here for 40 years. I brought up seven girls in this house by working as a nurse.' Sukru Bey, a man in his 40s, holds a title deed over his property as well. He is trying to sell it before the government arrives to take over the properties overlooking the Golden Horn. He is trying to mobilize neighbourhood residents against the government's 'urban renewal' initiative. 'They will take our homes from us and put 100 billion liras each in compensation in our pockets. Where could I go with 100 billion? Where could Neyyire Hanim go?' he cries. An elderly lady, Hatice Hanim, living on the same street which is up for grabs because of the imminent 'urban renewal' project, stands by wondering what she will do. She eavesdrops on the conversation of her neighbours. She says she has been living in this neighbourhood since she was born, 'for 75 years'. 'This entire street was Greek,' she notes. 'That Big Fire took place and they went.' By 'the Big Fire' she refers to the 6–7 September events in 1955 when most of the Greeks who inhabited Fener departed for Greece in the immediate aftermath of attacks on their persons and properties by mobs of young men who had been mobilized after rumours of a sabotage on Ataturk's childhood home in Salonica.[5] She gave an account of how she ended up living where she did:

> A Greek lady used to live in the house I am living in now. Her son had left for Greece after the 'Big Fire' and never returned. When this woman died, it was me and Mehves Hanim who buried her in the Greek cemetery nearby. When her house was left empty, it was registered as 'state property' ('Kayyum'). I moved in there and have been paying a monthly rent to the state ever since. The rent used to be 50 million liras per month, not much, but it now is 120 million. Apparently the state is not supposed to use this money which it receives from us in rent. It needs to put it in a safe until the owner of the property returns. But the son of the Greek lady will never return. He never came back from Greece, even for a visit. Last month, I received a paper from the state saying I hadn't paid my monthly rent. I went to the public office and asked them to check their computers to see that I had paid it.

The neighbour Mehves Hanim, wearing a headscarf and known as a supporter of the government's AK party, laments the old days of the Fener district. 'It used to be clean and beautiful when the Greeks were still here,' she says. 'All of my neighbours used to be Greek.' And commenting on the living arrangements of a woman who now lives across the street, she says: 'Her home is also "ownerless".' By 'ownerless' ('sahipsiz'), Mehves Hanim implied that the owners were Greeks who departed in 1955, never to return. 'This lady across the street is paying rent to the state just like Hatice Hanim in return for living in "ownerless property". But [ironically] there are clever people in this world! This woman has rented the top two floors of the house to other people herself. She therefore only pays a fraction of the total rent of the building to the state. You see, everything can happen in Istanbul!'

The status of properties in this neighbourhood is not resolved; it is rather precarious, tentative, and in disarray. While certain properties have 'owners' who are recognized as legal title-deed holders, other properties' past and future is unknown because they are registered as 'ownerless' (and have been taken over by the state). Some migrants from Anatolia have bought properties in Fener and Balat and either live in them or rent them out. Old Greek mansions and Jewish homes have been converted to buildings with separate flats for a number of families. But most of these conversions have been done unofficially, without restoration orders or building permissions. Some of the new owners of properties have found it profitable to rent old buildings out to more than one family. Sometimes different families share one toilet or one kitchen in a building. Many rented properties are in poor condition, with floors and walls rotting from humidity, cracking and creaking floorboards, and decaying inner and outer walls. There are families of seven or eight people who share one room with a small space heater in these buildings, using the same flight of stairs to enter and exit the house as their neighbours in the other rooms of the old Greek mansions.

As the status of many properties is unknown, one property with a legal owner, the other with tenants in it, yet another registered as 'ownerless' and expropriated by the state, the relation which the present inhabitants of this district forge with their dwellings is insecure. The present is unstable, the past is little known, and the future uncertain. There is an attempt on the part of the mostly impoverished local residents of contemporary Fener and Balat to interpret and understand the built and material environment which they inhabit through puzzled odds and ends of narrative. No one story fits. No fragmentary parts of narrative come completely together. One bit of story is told here. Another there. Some scraps of narrative build up on one rumour. Others negate another. Stories are collected like the crumbs of ruined buildings. One piece from here, another from there. Myths and narratives about the past and the future of the urban dwellings are made out of miscellanea. The joined-up oddments presented by any person is a mishmash of narrative shards from here and there. Like the status of the properties and their material conditions which are precarious, bitty, and partially unknown, so are the stories about them. The odds and ends form different assortments of story. Each

person has created his or her own hodgepodge out of the snippets, to try to comprehend his or her circumstances.

Social relations in the neighbourhood are negotiated through encounters between urban dwellers who have arrived from rural parts of Anatolia, neighbours, shopkeepers, and state officials. Some who belong to political parties or distinct social movements present master narratives through which to interpret what goes on with the built environment. 'The CIA is behind this. Mossad must have a finger in the cake. The Patriarchate must have a plan,' say those who belong to the Nationalist Action Party. Ideology is used and presented to tidy up and bring together broken pieces of a puzzle. Some find this of use. How to interpret what is going on? What was the past of these buildings? What will happen to those who now live in them in the future? A sense of instability, of insecurity and lack of faith *vis-à-vis* state authorities prevails.[6] Anything that can be said is only tentative. All speak with uncertainty. A story which has been made up sounds as possibly true as another which seems to have a reliable source of information. Everyone attempts to put pieces of the puzzle together for himself or herself, and for family in one way or another to strategize for the future or to make ends meet. How to do it this way? How to understand it that way? What to do? As the rubble of old homes may be found in decay on the street corners of Fener and Balat, so can bits and pieces of story. Both materiality and narrative come in the fragments. In broken, anxious forms.

Negotiating materialities

Foregrounding recent migrants' narratives about the urban environment they inhabit in Fener and Balat, Istanbul, in this chapter I have considered the ways in which the city is known through its materialities to its present inhabitants. This knowing of the city emerges in what I have called shards of story or bits and pieces of narrative. Yet this knowing, which is sometimes devolved to the older inhabitants of the city, to the original owners of properties, and which is relayed in oddments, is not solely a discursive or semiotic relation to the world. Though the fragments of story about power struggles over the built environment's ownership have been received from various competing narratives and ideologies about the city, its past and its future, migrants also extract knowledge out of the materialities which they inhabit in themselves. In other words, it is not only human constructions that are projected on to the built environment, but the materialities themselves which 'speak back' by way of being channelled through those who now inhabit them.

Fener and Balat were neighbourhoods which used to be predominantly inhabited by Greeks and Jews until critical events like the pogrom of 6–7 September 1955. The contemporary inhabitants of these neighbourhoods, mostly poor migrants from different regions of Turkey,[7] imaginatively relate to the materialities in which they dwell.[8] They try to come up with stories about the past of the properties, of the Greeks, Jews, and Armenians who lived there. They put fragments of accounts they collect from here and there together to try to understand what the past of these properties might have been and anticipate what might be their future. The pieces of the puzzle emerge like debris gathered from the rubble without being put into any complete assembly or whole. Knowledge, as Walter Benjamin has taught us, only comes in the fragments.[9] So does migrants' knowledge of this city. But every bit of this knowledge that is articulated emerges from being negotiated with or within a materiality. Therefore, knowledge of the city must be understood as a negotiation with materialities where the tangibilities of the built environment 'speak back' through being physically dwelt in and experienced first-hand by their inhabitants.

If the twentieth century was witness to several waves of ethnic cleansing in Turkey, eventuating in the exile of entire communities out of their ancestral homes, towns, and cities, it likewise harboured the counter-migration of multiple other communities in reverse directions, and significantly from the rural to the urban areas of Turkey. The massive changes of population evidenced in the make-up of Istanbul in different decades of the twentieth century are not unique in character to this city, but might be instructively compared with similar such nationalization processes coupled with urbanization in other major cosmopolises.[10] What has occupied me in this chapter is the quality of knowledge which such transfers of population bring to material entanglements in an urban environment. The 'knowing', as I have argued, is temporally three-dimensional, referring to the city's past by reference to material remains from its former inhabitants, its present, as

dwelt in, and its future, through speculation about the fate of those who live in particular neighbourhoods which have been selected for gentrification and 'urban renewal' projects. The knowing emerges out of a two-way exchange between the migrants now inhabiting city-spaces and the material environments where they live. Here, I follow new theorists of materiality (e.g., Latour 1993; Miller 2001; Henare et al. 2007) in emphasizing the potency of objects. My own account specifically attends to the mutual implication of stories in materialities, and vice versa. City dwellers attempt to find evidence for their possible anticipated future trajectories by reference to the past and present of the materialities around them. Until now, this exchange between people and materialities has been possible through various routes of migration into the city and settlement. The new 'urban renewal' projects which are now being imposed in Istanbul, one by one in neighbourhood after neighbourhood (see the previous chapter by Aksoy and Robins), are threatening to eradicate precisely this entanglement between people and place. The 'urban renewal' decree, which was rumoured and feared, has now arrived in Fener-Balat. The neighbourhood residents who were trying to comprehend their possible futures through oddments of story, picked and assembled from here and there, have now been faced with a government order to evacuate their dwellings and move elsewhere, to the outskirts of the city, in return for compensation. The bits and pieces of story have been vertically cut through with a sovereign move, an instantiation of a major event in the life of this neighbourhood which many are already comparing with the 6–7 September events.[11] The once rural migrants will no longer be able to dwell in the inner-city districts which have been selected for 'urban renewal' projects. They will soon be forced to move to far corners of Istanbul, into modern complexes erected for their habitation. Divorced from the urban environments in the materialities of which they were entangled, stories like the ones I have here recounted will form another distant layer of memory by removal in the record of Istanbul's history.

Acknowledgements

The fieldwork for this article was funded by a grant from the Arts and Humanities Research Council

(AHRC) of the United Kingdom. I would like to thank Kristen Biehl for research assistance under this project. Helpful comments were received from participants in the authors' meeting for the present volume as well as from participants in the AHRC project conference 'Black Sea Cities: State Practices, Co-Existence and Migration', which was held in Cambridge in November 2009. Special thanks to Caroline Humphrey and Vera Skvirskaja.

Notes

1   The 6–7 September events refer to the dates in 1955 when there was an orchestrated pogrom against the Greek community of Istanbul. Other non-Muslim minorities also suffered from this pogrom. See Vryonis (2005) and Guven (2005).

2   For an account of the history of the Greek Patriarchate under the Turkish Republic, see Macar (2003).

3   For a study of the Fener-Balat initiative for urban regeneration, see Bezmez (2007). For other studies of gentrification processes in Istanbul, see Behar and Islam (2006), Coskun and Yalcin (2007), Onem and Kilicaslan (2005). For studies of Fener and Balat residents' reactions to gentrification processes, see Narli (2006) and Ilyasoglu and Soytemel (2006).

4   For an insightful account of how contemporary Istanbul residents of the Galata district negotiate dwellings left

behind by non-Muslim minorities, see Bartu (1999). For a study of narratives about the city emerging from fieldwork in Kuzguncuk, see Mills (2005).

5   For historical accounts of the 6–7 September events, see Vryonis (2005), Guven (2005), Coker (2005). For an account of the fate of Istanbul's Greeks, see Demir and Akar (1994). For an account of comparable pogroms in urban environments against those perceived as 'minorities,' see Appadurai (2000) and Humphrey (forthcoming). For accounts of the past of the Fener and Balat neighbourhoods when Greeks, Jews, and Armenians still inhabited them, see Turker (2001), Ozbilge (2005), and Deleon (1994).

6   For a study of trust and distrust *vis-à-vis* state authorities in Istanbul neighbourhoods, see Secor and O'Loughlin (2005). For a study of 'cynicism' *vis-à-vis* the state in Turkey, see Navaro-Yashin (2002).

7   See Bezmez (2007), Behar and Islam (2006).

8   For a study of peoples' affective relations with materialities and built environments they have expropriated from others, see Navaro-Yashin (2009).

9   Benjamin (1973). The motif of 'debris' by reference to knowledge is an imaginary which comes out of Benjamin's work. For a Benjamin-inspired study of 'ruination' by reference to the production of knowledge in anthropology and allied disciplines, see Navaro-Yashin (2009).

10   Compare, for example, with Berlin (see Mandel 2008) and Odessa (Humphrey forthcoming).

11   For a study of 'the materiality of sovereignty,' see Navaro-Yashin (2010).

REFERENCES

Appadurai Arjun, 2000. 'Spectral Housing and Urban Cleansing: Notes on Milenial Mumbai.' *Public Culture* 12(3): 627–51.

Bartu, Ayfer, 1999. 'Who Owns the Old Quarters?' in Caglar Keyder, ed. *Istanbul: Between the Global and the Local.* Lanham, MD: Rowman & Littlefield, pp. 31–47.

Behar, David and Islam, Tolga, eds. 2006. *Istanbul'da Soylulastirma: Eski Kentin Yeni Sahipleri.* Istanbul: Bilgi Universitesi Yayinlari.

Benjamin, Walter, 1973. 'Theses on the Philosophy of History,' in *Illuminations.* London: Fontana Press, pp. 245–55.

Bezmez, Dikmen, 2007. 'The Politics of Urban Regeneration: The Case of the Fener and Balat Initiative.' *New Perspectives on Turkey* 37: 59–86.

Coker, Fahri, 2005. *6–7 Eylul Olaylari: Fotograflar-Belgeler Fahri Coker Arsivi.* Istanbul: Tarih Vakfi Yayinlari.

Coskun, Nihal and Yalcin, Seher, 2007. 'Gentrification in a Globalising World, Case Study: Istanbul.' www.enhr-2007rotterdam.nl

Deleon, Jak, 1994. *Balat ve Cevresi: Istanbul'un Fethi ve Halic Semtleri.* Istanbul: Remzi Kitabevi.

Demir, Hulya and Akar, Ridvan, 1994. *Istanbul'un Son Surgunleri.* Istanbul: Belge Yayinlari.

Guven, Dilek, 2005. *Cumhuriyet Donemi Azinlik Politikalari ve Stratejileri Baglaminda 6–7 Eylul Olaylari.* Istanbul: Iletisim.

Henare, Amiria, Holbraad, Martin, and Wastell, Sari, 2007. *Thinking Through Things: Theorising Artefacts Ethnographically.* London: Routledge.

Humphrey, Caroline, fc. 'Odessa: Pogroms and the Built City,' in Caroline Humphrey and Vera Skvirskaja, eds. *Post-Cosmopolitanism*.

Ilyasoglu, Aynur and Ebru Soytemel, 2006. 'Balat Semtinde Yerel Degisim ve Yenilesme Sureci Icinde Balatlilar: 'Bizim Mahalle'ye Yeni Gelenler ve Farkli Stratejiler,' in David Behar and Tolga Islam, eds. *Istanbul'da Soylulastirma: Eski Kentin Yeni Sahipleri*. Istanbul: Bilgi Universitesi Yayinlari, pp. 127–42.

Latour, Bruno, 1993. *We Have Never Been Modern*. Hemel Hampstead: Harvester Wheatsheaf.

Macar, Elcin, 2003. *Cumhuriyet Doneminde Istanbul Rum Patrikhanesi*. Istanbul: Iletisim.

Mandel, Ruth, 2008. *Cosmopolitan Anxieties: Turkish Challenges to Citizenship in Germany*. Duke: Durham University Press.

Miller, Daniel, ed. 2001. *Home Possessions*. Oxford and New York: Berg.

Mills, Amy, 2005. 'Narratives in City Landscapes: Cultural Identity in Istanbul.' *Geographical Review* 95:3, 441–62.

Narli, Nilufer, 2006. 'Tecride Ugrayan Bir Bolgede Yasayan Ailelerin Soylulastirma Projesine Yaklasimi: Balat-Fener Vaka Calismasi,' In David Behar and Tolga Islam, eds. *Istanbul'da Soylulastirma: Eski Kentin Yeni Sahipleri*. Istanbul: Bilgi Universitesi Yayinlari, pp. 113–26.

Navaro-Yashin, Yael, 2002. *Faces of the State: Secularism and Public Life in Turkey*. Princeton, NJ: Princeton University Press.

Navaro-Yashin, Yael, 2009. 'Affective Spaces, Melancholic Objects: Ruination and the Production of Anthropological Knowledge.' *Journal of the Royal Anthropological Institute* 15(1): 1–18.

Navaro-Yashin, Yael, 2010. 'The Materiality of Sovereignty: Geographical Expertise and Changing Place Names in Northern Cyprus,' in P. Nikiforos Diamandouros, Thalia Dragonas, and Caglar Keyder eds. *Spatial Conceptions of the Nation: Modernizing Geographies in Greece and Turkey*. London: I.B. Tauris, pp. 127–43.

Onem, Buket A. and Kilincaslan, Ismet, 2005. 'Halic Bolgesinde Cevre Algilama ve Kentsel Kimlik.' *ITU Dergisi/a Mimarlik, Planlama ve Tasarim* 4(1): 115–25.

Ozbilge, Ahmet F., 2005. *Fener Balat Ayvansaray*. Istanbul: Baglam Yayinlari.

Secor, Anna and O'Loughlin, John, 2005. 'Social and Political Trust in Istanbul and Moscow: A Comparative Analysis of Individual and Neighbourhood Effects.' *Transactions of the Institute of British Geographers NS* 30: 66–82.

Turker, Orhan, 2001. *Fanari'den Fener'e: Bir Halic Hikayesi*. Istanbul: Sel Yayincilik.

Vryonis, Speros, Jr., 2005. *The Mechanism of Catastrophe: The Turkish Pogrom of September 6–7, 1955, and the Destruction of the Greek Community of Istanbul*. New York: Greekworks.

CHAPTER 20

DIVIDED MEMORIES, CONTESTED HISTORIES: THE SHIFTING LANDSCAPE IN JAPAN

Akiko Hashimoto

Winners and losers remember wars differently. For every victor who remembers a good, honorable war, there is a vanquished counterpart who remembers a humiliating failure. If winners accept victory as a mostly uncomplicated affair, losers, by contrast, face a predicament of living with a discredited past that stains national history. This chapter illuminates the impact of this quandary in post-World War II Japan, and its search for a renewed identity in the global world at the turn of the century. The last years of the twentieth century proved to be a critical time for Japan to revise its national goals, yet at this pivotal time of social transition, Japanese citizens remain deeply divided in their vision of the future between progressive and conservative directions.

Memory and history in a global age

In the 1980s, as shifting global politics and increasing transnational cultural flows began to impact on different parts of the world, remembering the past became vitally relevant for living the present. Such a 'culture of memory,' as Andreas Huyssen calls it, brought a renewed assessment of the past in search of an anchoring at an uncertain time (2003: 15). Oral history movements, new museum and memorial constructions, and political movements to right past wrongs are all examples of this culture of memory, in which remembering the past is a crucial experience for forging collective identity (Nora 1996 [1992]). In this world of increasing cultural flux and diverse transnational subjectivities, erstwhile approaches to collective memory that presupposed stable group memories (Halbwachs 1992) no longer seemed sufficient to grasp the dynamics of remembering and forgetting in many societies (Huyssen 2003; Misztal 2003).

This new 'culture of memory' in search of a usable past also came at a significant time in a global electronic age, with the growing awareness that historical knowledge was not absolute, irrevocable or uniform. Universal claims for truth became, for many, increasingly suspect in late modernity, posing challenges to the act of framing a national narrative. Historical representations were recognized as subjective and political, and an integral part of claim-making was framed in the dynamics of power. As multiple subjectivities and a plurality of narratives jockeyed for domination, a single narrative could no longer dominate and monopolize the imaginative construction of national identity and national interests (Bhabha 1990). This posed a particular challenge in East Asian societies such as Japan where legitimate and valid knowledge of national history had heretofore been centralized by the state (Karasawa 1955). In the post-Cold War world that required a broader reorganization of knowledge, therefore, there was an increasing contradiction between the historical relativism that necessarily emerges in the globalized arena, and the goal of official history which is to inculcate a *particular* truth (Yoneyama 2001: 338). In this context, it seemed no longer possible to produce a single and definitive public history shared commonly and objectively in a nation, and among nations.

This culture of memory also posed a particular challenge for nations burdened with tainted traumatic pasts. Japan's long-standing problem was of course the narration of the Asia-Pacific War, the discredited conflict that had wrought the trauma of brutal mass deaths and the disaster of total defeat, which is still rife with divisive questions, acrimonious debate, and unresolved emotions. As Japan looked to the national past to contemplate the nation's future, it sought to deploy usable pasts (Moeller 1996) that did not draw on a nationalistic rhetoric contaminated by the war. Forging an appropriate moral and national script for citizens in the new century meant establishing a collective identity that claimed selective continuity from the stigmatized past. In this process, past national feuds over how to narrate national history were re-energized in the public discourse and old controversies took on a renewed significance. With the post-World War II generation now two-thirds of the population, new stakeholders entered the fray to play their roles in framing the national script. The different positionality of the generations meant that people had more diverse motivations to reframe the history of the lost war. At the same time, rapidly changing geo-politics brought new uncertainties about unresolved war issues that had arisen vis-à-vis Asian neighbors, such as the spiraling lawsuits filed against Japan for compensation claims (Takahashi 2003). In times of flux such as these, it was not altogether surprising that Japan also saw a surge of neo-nationalism, especially among those who perceived global change to be threatening to their self-identity.

Narrating war history in a defeated nation

The problem of narrating contentious national history is not unique to Japan, as we know from many examples of difficulties in recounting pasts like the Vietnam War in the United States, the Cultural Revolution in China, or Stalinism in Russia (Hein and Selden 2000). In Japan's case, however, attempting to answer critical questions about the war continues to have daunting implications for many, both as citizens and as private individuals whose families participated in the discredited war effort. Was the war inevitable or could the state and

citizens have prevented it? Were our fathers and grandfathers unspeakably bad in judgement and conduct? How poorly and harmfully do these facts reflect on us as Japanese citizens today? The answers must necessarily involve painful assessments over a broad spectrum of issues ranging from state politics to individual pasts.

But controversial questions can invite as many versions of truth as there are perspectives, when people in different social positions select, organize and transmit categories of knowledge differently (Wuthnow 1987). In this vein, different stakeholders and custodians at various times have contested the 'objective' truth about Japan's war (Gluck 1993).[1] Moreover, the fickle nature of truth had already betrayed one generation profoundly: the wartime generation experienced a complete inversion of the moral order in 1945 when the US Occupation brought the new 'truth' that changed the right war to the wrong war, and the wrong war to the right war. Their children, in turn, learned that truth-building depended on who won the war, when they were ordered to ink out passages of 'false' history (Dower 1999).[2] The name of the war itself also proved immensely malleable: called 'the Greater East Asia War' and 'the Sacred War' in wartime, it was then renamed 'the Pacific War' by the US Occupation that censored imperialist militarist language and de-emphasized the significant role of China and East Asia in the conflict. The countervailing name used by Japanese progressive intellectuals to overcome such Cold War rhetoric was 'the Fifteen-Year War,' which recognized the salience of Japanese Imperial aggression in Asia for a decade preceding the war in the Pacific. Subsequent designations used to sidestep such naming politics have been 'the Asia-Pacific War,' 'the Shōwa War,' 'World War II,' and, as people became weary of the political baggage that each name carried, the war ultimately came to be called 'the last world war,' 'that war,' and even 'that unfortunate period of the past.' Seeing Japanese history so easily and frequently renamed, redefined and reinterpreted, it is not surprising that sixty-five years hence, the 'truth' is beset by a loss of credibility and revisionism. The cynicism rooted in this experience left many of the wartime generation and their offspring to interpret the war through a lens of moral relativism which has become an integral part of Japan's culture of defeat. Ultimately this experience could not help but reinforce the awareness that historical truths were elusive and mutable, like the different accounts of the same event by *Rashōmon*'s protagonists in Kurosawa's film. The 'truth,' as they learned, could not to be trusted.

Contested histories

Different perspectives like these have played out in different sites that influence the formation of national identity and heritage such as the media, museums, memorials, exhibits, and schools (Nora 1996 [1992]). Over the years, these have been sites of contentions where many voices have recounted the trauma of war and defeat in Japan. From personal accounts to commemorative speeches, and from media dramatizations to public controversies, the official and unofficial narratives of war and defeat – in their diverse and conflicting standpoints – have been inescapably present in national collective life. Contending over the master narrative of the Asia-Pacific War, social groups of different persuasions and experiences – politicians, intellectuals, teachers, bureaucrats, business leaders, media entrepreneurs, labor activists, and students, who were themselves veterans, returnees, bereaved families, orphans, atomic bomb survivors, ethnic minorities, and others – have forged diverse narratives to interpret in their own way what the war meant and what went wrong. Their narratives used different moral frames: some universalized the war and the atrocities ('All wars are bad'), while others relativized them ('We were bad, but they were bad too'), or condemned them ('We started an atrocious, reckless war'), and still others sought to triumph over the defeat ('Defeat was the harbinger of peace'). Within these frames, individuals staked out different positions: victims of a brutal war ('We all suffered and paid heavily'); victimizers in an imperial war ('We wrought so much suffering in Asia'); the repentant who vowed never to make the same mistakes again ('No more war! No more Hiroshima!'). At the same time, many also remained silent, preferring to bury their own memory, or conceal what in psychiatric terms would be called post-traumatic stress disorder.

In these diverse ways, then, a range of contending moral-political frames has shaped Japan's war memories over the past decades. Immediately after the war, and through the US Occupation (1945–1952),

the war took on a negative characterization as fervent reassessment based on the moral order of the victors inverted its meaning. Perpetrator guilt was defined explicitly in the Tokyo war crimes tribunal (1946–1948) by the Allies, according to their version of 'victors' justice' that pinned the blame for waging war on reckless and incompetent military wartime leadership. However, national reckoning with a larger scope of guilt by untold, often lesser-known perpetrators remained elusive.[3] The economic imperatives of material growth and stability took priority over punishment for past deeds, and the political imperatives of security and alliance with the United States took priority over reconciliation with communist China and the Soviet Union (Dower 1999).

After the conservative party came to dominate the Japanese government in the mid-1950s, thorny problems of the war's aftermath remained emotionally and politically volatile and defied easy resolutions. As the steward of unprecedented economic growth, the conservative regime stabilized its foothold for the long haul in a nation determined to make up for the astronomical losses of the war; this in turn gave the ruling party extensive control over the official meta-narrative of the war, which it characterized as a tragic conflict fought reluctantly for national survival. The opposition, however, skeptical and distrustful of the conservative meta-narrative, forcefully dissented and joined forces overtime with myriad countervailing social groups and movements, such as the teachers' union and various peace movements opposing the US–Japan Security Treaty, nuclear tests, and the Vietnam War. A dynamic of contentious politics ensued that entrenched a stalemate between those who wanted to remember redeeming features of the stigmatized past and those who refused to do so. While diverse stakeholders of war memory disagreed on how to remember Asian suffering inflicted by Japan during the war, they did share a measure of understanding on how to remember Japanese suffering. As such, the strong emphasis on Japanese victimhood in Hiroshima and Nagasaki, and in hundreds of air raids, developed relatively unencumbered into strong anti-military and anti-nuclear sentiments (Igarashi 2000; Orr 2001). In the 1980s and 1990s, when a global memory culture began to coalesce around an emerging human rights movement focused on redressing past wrongs, Japan's war memory was shaken out of its long stalemate.

Pressured by neighboring Asian nations and the international media, Japan's long-standing problem of reckoning with the past became an international concern that erupted on many fronts: disagreements over self-justifying history textbooks, struggles over formal apologies, compensation suits filed by former colonial subjects and victims, controversial commemorations of the war dead, disputes over museum exhibits, and others. A most significant case in point was the redress for former 'comfort women', who were mobilized or coerced as sex workers to service Japanese soldiers during wartime, and who began to break their silence and claim redress from the Japanese government. Emerging as a transnational feminist movement against sexual violence, the 'comfort women' case succeeded in bringing the world's attention to victimization of women in war, while also tarnishing the carefully crafted image of 'innocent' Japanese soldiers. Such recent shifts in the war memory were catapulted not only by global trends, but also by domestic events that contributed to changing conditions of memory-making, such as the death of Emperor Hirohito, the end of the hegemonic rule of the Liberal Democratic Party, and the shattering of the bubble economy, and regional events such as the rising political, economic, and cultural importance of East Asia. By the early 2000s, the culminating effects of change had also evoked a neo-nationalist backlash against the globalization of 'the history problem' (Dudden 2008; Gluck 2007; Krauss and Hashimoto 1996; Seraphim 2006; Takahashi 2002; Tsutsui 2006).

Divided memories

Since the 'explosion of memory productions' in the 1990s (Seraphim 2006: 262), arriving at a national consensus over the Asia-Pacific War has become even more difficult. Public opinion surveys today show that the Japanese are still deeply split in their evaluation of both the character and conduct of the war and their consequences (Makita 2000; Saaler 2005; Seaton 2007). In survey by NHK Public Television, for example, one half of respondents believed that Japan waged a war of aggression, and invaded Asian nations for material gain. About 15 per cent disagreed with this view, while one-third

claimed the 'don't know' category. Asked further about whether they thought this war was inevitable – a question that has serious implications for war responsibility – the respondents also split three ways: a third believed that the war was inevitable as nothing could have prevented it under the circumstances; another third disagreed with that view; and the remaining one-third was undecided. A 2006 survey published by *Yomiuri* newspaper reveals a comparable pattern, although using different categories: 34 per cent believed that the Asia-Pacific War was a war of aggression, while 34 per cent agreed that only the Japan–China War was a war of aggression but not the Pacific War. About 10 per cent believed that neither conflict was a war of aggression, while 21 per cent were undecided. In the 2006 survey published by the *Asahi* newspaper, using still other categories, 31 per cent of the respondents thought the war was a war of aggression, 7 per cent thought it was a war of self-defense, 45 per cent thought it had elements of both, and 15 per cent were undecided (Yomiuri Shinbun Sensō Sekinin Kenshō Iinkai 2006; Asahi Shinbun Shuzaihan 2006).*

These patterns show that the ideological divisions over war memory continue to mirror the deep dissonance in the society at large. At the same time, they also show that a sizeable proportion of Japanese citizens are willing to share the burden of war legacy today.[4] Remarkably, agreements and disagreements over taking more war responsibility show very little variation by age, suggesting that there is little generational difference in people's attitudes toward Japan's ongoing war responsibility, which have been reproduced intractably over generations (Yoshida 1995).

Reconciliation in post-conflict societies: is there a global norm?

Managing the memory of defeat in post-conflict societies is a difficult business that affects international relations, intergenerational relations, and personal and national identity. As such, Japan's experience in the aftermath of World War II resonates with those of other vanquished societies, such as the American South after the Civil War and France after the Franco-Prussian War of

---

* both are collective authorship names as used in Japan

1870–1871 (Schivelbusch 2003). Japan's current effort to deal with its war legacy, however, comes at an historical moment, when the world seems to be seeking a normative pattern for nations to come to terms with past crimes. Japan is therefore frequently compared with Germany, the other defeated nation of World War II, regarding practices to address tainted national history. Over the past decades, both Japan and Germany have struggled to reckon with what went wrong, and saw their politicians and citizens vehemently clash over how to right the wrong. In both nations, there are also those who want to universalize the atrocities and relativize history, and those who can only see themselves as victims. At the same time, in both countries there are those who want to atone, taking their guilt and shame to heart, even dedicating their lives or careers to make amends to the victims. Above all, having to rise from this devastating past motivated both nations to overcome their losses economically, politically and morally; in the latter category it was important for both to attempt to overcome the stigmatizing and humiliating memories to regain the status of respected nations in the world. However, the paths they chose to follow toward moral recovery were different: Japan sought the path of overcoming Hiroshima to become a respected pacifist nation, and Germany sought that of overcoming the Holocaust as a respected repentant nation (Hashimoto 1999).

The two nations chose their different paths of moral recovery in part because the territorial and political conditions of reconciliation were drastically different. Germany had an urgent and immediate political and economic need to reconcile with its neighbors as a land-locked nation bordering nine countries, all of which were former enemy or occupied nations. To develop stable economic and political relationships with these countries, it was imperative to start repairing those relationships as soon as possible. Germany's economic and political survival depended on showing repentance, on creating a cooperative framework with its neighbors, on integrating itself in Europe, on joining NATO, on becoming part of the European Economic Community, and finally on forging a European identity. Japan, on the other hand, does not directly border any neighbors' territories. Moreover, these neighbors across the sea – the former enemy and occupied nations – were also mostly communist nations. Japan's political and economic necessity from the very beginning of the Cold War was *not* to repent and reconcile with these former enemies and victims. Indeed, Japan found it critical to seek its pivotal economic and political relationships with the United States, not Asia. Moreover, these Asian countries were also developing countries with limited power in international politics and were economically dependent on Japan's aid.

In the shifting world of contentious memory-making, the German model of repenting the past is fast becoming something of a 'global standard', recognized as such by the subsequent and successive 'Truth and Reconciliation' commissions in different parts of the world. The Holocaust, according to Jeffrey Alexander (2004) and Bernhard Giesen (2004: 144), has now come to represent a deterritorialized and globalized cultural trauma that may serve also to represent universal moral sensibilities. Whether a 'global standard' to right past wrongs derived from a recognition of sin linked to repentance, forgiveness, and redemption can acquire profound resonance outside the Judeo-Christian civilizational orbit, i.e. in East Asia, remains, however, an unanswered question today. Whether such a model of atonement for a Holocaust that took place in Europe can also find effective political traction in Asia is also an open question. In other words, whether a 'universal model' for war memory emerges in the course of the struggle to reconcile diverse transnational memories will undoubtedly be a controversial subject for many decades to come.

Notes

1 Carol Gluck has classified the custodians of memory in four groups: conservatives, progressives, media and life stories.
2 The popular expression referring to this phenomenon is '*kateba kangun, makereba zokugun*'.
3 Several thousand B and C class war criminals, however, were prosecuted and indicted in numerous trials across East and Southeast Asia after the war.
4 Affirmative answers ranged between 27 per cent and 61 per cent of respondents. These survey results vary in part as a result of using different answering categories, such as whether respondents thought compensations or apologies were inadequate, or whether postwar generations should carry on the responsibility.

REFERENCES

Alexander, Jeffrey C. (2004). On the Social Construction of Moral Universals: The 'Holocaust' from War Crime to Trauma Drama. In J. C. Alexander, R. Eyerman, B. Giesen, N. Smelser and P. Sztompka (Eds.), *Cultural Trauma and Collective Identity* (pp. 196–263). Berkeley: University of California Press.

Asahi Shinbun Shuzaihan (2006). *Sensō sekinin to tsuitō: Rekishi to mukiau 1.* Tokyo: Asahi Shinbunsha.

Bhabha, H. (1990). *Nation and Narration.* London: Routledge.

Dower, J. W. (1999). *Embracing Defeat: Japan in the Wake of World War II.* New York: W.W. Norton.

Dudden, Alexis (2008). *Troubled Apologies among Japan, Korea, and the United States.* New York: Columbia University Press.

Gluck, C. (1993). The Past in the Present. In A. Gordon (Ed.), *Postwar Japan as History* (pp. 64–95). Berkeley: University of California Press.

—— (2007). Operations of Memory: 'Comfort Women' and the World. In S. M. Jager and R. Mitter (Eds), *Ruptured Histories: War, Memory, and the Post-Cold War in Asia* (pp. 47–77). Cambridge, MA: Harvard University Press.

Giesen, Bernhard (2004). The Trauma of Perpetrators: The Holocaust as the Traumatic Reference of German National Identity. In J. C. Alexander, R. Eyerman, B. Giesen, N. Smelser, and P. Sztompka (Eds), *Cultural Trauma and Collective Identity* (pp.112–154). Berkeley: University of California Press.

Halbwachs, M. (1992). *On Collective Memory.* Chicago: University of Chicago Press.

Hashimoto, Akiko (1999). Japanese and German Projects of Moral Recovery: Toward a New Understanding of War Memories in Defeated Nations. In *Occasional Papers in Japanese Studies 1999–01.* Cambridge, MA: Harvard University, Reischauer Institute of Japanese Studies.

Hein, L. and Selden, M. (2000). The Lessons of War, Global Power, and Social Change. In L. Hein and M. Selden (Eds), *Censoring History: Citizenship and Memory in Japan, Germany, and the United States* (pp. 3-50). Armonk, NY: M.E. Sharpe.

Huyssen, A. (2003). *Present Pasts: Urban Palimpsests and the Politics of Memory.* Stanford, CA: Stanford University Press.

Igarashi, Yoshikuni (2000). *Bodies of Memory: Narratives of War in Postwar Japanese Culture, 1945–1970.* Princeton, NJ: Princeton University Press.

Karasawa, T. (1955). *Kyōshi no rekishi: Kyōshi no seikatsu to rinri.* Tokyo: Sōbunsha.

Krauss, Ellis and Hashimoto, Akiko (1996). Memories of the War: Media's Responsibility. In NHK Broadcasting Culture Research Institute (Ed.), *World Television Coverage of the 50th Anniversary of the End of World War II* (pp. 1–19). Tokyo: NHK Broadcasting Culture Research Institute.

Makita, T. (2000). Nihonjin no sensō to heiwa kan: sono jizoku to fūka. *Hōsō Kenkyū to Chōsa*, 50: 2–19.

Misztal, Barbara A. (2003). *Theories of Social Remembering.* Buckingham: Open University Press.

Moeller, R. G. (1996). War Stories: The Search for a Usable Past in the Federal Republic of Germany. *American Historical Review*, 101: 1008–1048.

Nora, P. (1996 [1992]). Between Memory and History: Les Lieux de Memoire. In P. Nora (Ed.), *Realms of Memory: The Construction of the French Past* (pp. 1–20). New York: Columbia University Press.

Orr, James Joseph (2001). *The Victim as Hero: Ideologies of Peace and National Identity in Postwar Japan.* Honolulu: University of Hawai'i Press.

Saaler, Sven (2005). *Politics, Memory and Public Opinion: The History Textbook Controversy and Japanese Society.* Munich: Iudicium Verlag.

Schivelbusch, Wolfgang (2003). *The Culture of Defeat: On National Trauma, Mourning, and Recovery.* New York: Metropolitan Books.

Seaton, P. A. (2007). *Japan's Contested War Memories: The 'Memory Rifts' in Historical Consciousness of World War II.* London and New York: Routledge.

Seraphim, F. (2006). *War Memory and Social Politics in Japan, 1945–2005.* Cambridge, MA: Harvard University Press, Asia Center.

Takahashi, T. (2002). Kon'ichi no <rekishininshiki> ronsō o meguru jyōkyō to ronten. In Tetsuya Takahashi (Ed.) *<Rekishininshiki> ronsō* (pp. 39–50). Tokyo: Sakuhinsha.

—— (2003). *'Kokoro' to sensō.* Tokyo: Shōbunsha.

Tsutsui, K. (2006). Redressing Past Human Rights Violations: Global Dimensions of Contemporary Social Movements. *Social Forces*, 85 (1): 331–354.

Wuthnow, R. (1987). *Meaning and Moral Order: Explorations in Cultural Analysis.* Berkeley: University of California Press.

Yomiuri Shinbun Sensō Sekinin Kenshō Iinkai (2006). *Kenshō: Sensō sekinin I.* Tokyo: Chūōkōronshinsha.

Yoneyama, L. (2001). For Transformative Knowledge and Postnationalist Public Spheres: The Smithsonian *Enola Gay* Controversy. In T. Fujitani, G. M. White and L. Yoneyama (Eds), *Perilous Memories: The Asia-Pacific War(s)* (pp. 323–346). Durham, NC: Duke University Press.

Yoshida, Y. (1995). *Nihonjin no sensōkan: Sengoshi no naka no henyō.* Tokyo: Iwanami Shoten.

CHAPTER 21

MEMORIALIZATION AND THE RWANDAN GENOCIDE: THE USE OF THEATRE

Ananda Breed

This chapter explores the use of theatre to memorialize and commemorate the Rwandan genocide using as a case study Rwanda My Hope, a production written and performed by survivors of the genocide. While initially recognizing the usefulness of theatre to embody survivor testimonies and human rights discourses, the author will question its performative dimension and consider some of the ethical implications of 'genocide theatre' when presented to international audiences and donor agencies.

This chapter will interrogate the use of theatre to memorialize and commemorate the Rwandan genocide using the example of *Rwanda My Hope*, a production written and performed by survivors of the genocide.[1] *Rwanda My Hope* was originally commissioned by the UK non-governmental organization Aegis Trust for the tenth commemoration of the genocide in Kigali, Rwanda, in 2004. Subsequently, it has been performed at memorial sites, including Gisozi and Murambi in Rwanda, and as a part of UK national tours in 2006 and 2008.

While initially recognizing the usefulness of theatre to embody survivor testimonies and human rights discourses, I will question the performative dimension of *Rwanda My Hope*. Theatrical representations of the Rwandan genocide raise issues regarding the construction of master narratives for political agency, creating a trauma-aesthetic which, '[i]nstalls and smuggles into the human rights discourse a visual genealogy of witnessing and testimony-giving that sorts victim and witness into positions of hierarchical observation, compulsory visibility, and non-reciprocal appropriation of the body in pain' (Feldman, 2004: 186). How and why is the body (performed alive in theatrical productions and displayed dead through memorials) used to build master narratives? How are multiple narratives positioned into more complex understandings of the conditions through which life histories of human rights violations circulate and how do they help develop further dialogical opportunities?

In *Commemorations: The Politics of National Identity* (1994), historian John R. Gillis notes that as an inscription of memory and identity, commemoration has been used as a political device to mould collective memories and nationalism. He argues that compulsory forms of commemoration survive, but only where states are still in the process of constituting a singular national identity. What has consciously been remembered or forgotten as a national collective has changed over time, specific to events or periods in history. Gillis uses the examples of both the American and French revolutions as primary turning points in which nations were born, producing out of a violent revulsion for the past the subjectivity of the citizen of the 'new' nation state. He believes that identities and memories are 'representations or constructions of reality ... selective, inscriptive rather than descriptive, serving particular interests and ideological positions' (Gillis, 1994: 3–4).

Indeed, in Rwanda post-genocide narratives are being generated in order to rewrite history and to construct both justice and commemoration. State-selected and mandated memories of genocide are being inscribed. Commemoration in Rwanda is national and compulsory, formally taking place each year for the span of one week in early April – the time when the genocide began in 1994. During this period, newly discovered mass graves are dug up; thousands of bodies are excavated and given a burial ceremony. According to doctoral candidate Eugenia Zorbas, '[a]t the national level, each year a new site is chosen from which bodies are exhumed and given a formal burial; the President leads the ceremony, which is broadcast on state television and radio' (Zorbas, 2004: 40). Overnight vigils called *biriyo* provide a space for survivors to give testimonials in the company of fellow survivors. Shops and restaurants are forced to shut down and the people at large are mobilized to attend commemorative events such as speeches, testimonies, and theatrical performances at memorial sites. Beyond the actual commemoration week, there have been ongoing inscriptions of commemoration through the *gacaca* to try the perpetrators of the genocide: '[g]acaca means a grassy place in Kinyarwanda, a Bantu language that is the official language of Rwanda. The term actually refers to a pre-colonial form of justice in which opposed families sat on the grass as the community mediated the conflict' (Breed, 2007: 306). Citizens of Rwanda are mandated to attend the weekly trials, providing testimony and standing witness to the atrocities week after week, year after year.

This period of memory and mourning is increasingly controversial. Digging up the past can revive ethnic divisions or exclude other deaths that occurred in 1994 – including Hutu deaths perpetrated by the Rwandan Patriotic Front (RPF), which have, in some quarters, been designated as war crimes – and therefore reinforces the Tutsi narrative promulgated by the RPF-dominated government (Tiemessen, 2004: 57–76). Although the commemoration in Rwanda is linked to public acts of testimony, Human Rights Watch remarks upon the potential danger of discussing Rwandan Patriotic Army (RPA) war crimes:[2] 'Government officials have frequently said that anyone who suffered at the hands of a soldier should report him or her for prosecution. Given that discussing RPA war crimes has been and continues to be equated with holding 'genocide ideology', no Rwandan was ever likely to file a complaint.'[3]

The use of theatre for commemoration presents inherent political dilemmas. As Gillis reminds us, '[c]ommemorative activity is by definition social and political, for it involves the coordination of individual and group memories, whose results may appear consensual when they are in fact the product of processes of intense contest, struggle, and in some instances, annihilation' (Gillis, 1994: 5). Thus, the immediate struggle for power in the Great Lakes region is related to how the events of the genocide are being represented and commemorated. While international attention is focused on the horrific events of the 1994 genocide, it is more difficult to discern human rights violations conducted by the RPF in Rwanda or in the neighbouring Democratic Republic of Congo (DRC).[4] The construction of memory around the genocide fixes an epicentre from which history and culture can be written in Rwanda, but also links it to the meta-narrative of the Jewish Holocaust, which provides further political agency. Memory theorist Andreas Huyssen identifies the genocide slogan 'never again' as a social and political weapon to 'veil' ongoing atrocities:

> The universalized 'never again' command and with it the instrumentalization of memory for political purposes have become a veil covering ongoing atrocities in our present world. The Holocaust is a screen memory. We have to face the hard question: to what extent are the public memory rituals of our culture at the same time strategies of forgetting? Lest I be misunderstood, this is not a question about moral intentions. It is a question about function and politics. (2003: 19)

Although the atrocities of the genocide must be remembered, there are concerns about *how* they are being remembered and for *whom*. The horrors of the genocide and the need for the national and international community to remember the events should not be negated, but it is important to consider other political and ethical implications of contemporary politics in the Great Lakes region. Professor of African Literature and Cinema, Kenneth Harrow, notes the 'exceptionalism' of the genocide, and how the portrayal of events often represented in movies such as *Hotel Rwanda* and some theatre performances accounts for the events of 1994 in easy-to-navigate sound bites that often exclude the role of the RPF or the current crisis in the DRC.

> In crucial ways we have to think the genocide as not exceptional, as linked to the world globalized economic and political structure replicated in various places around the world. This is evinced

where conflict has been accompanied by the economic patterns of militarization, often with the trading of guns for diamonds or gold, and in ways in which these global structures are linked to the explosions of violence, with the degrading acts of child soldiers, and unspeakable violence directed against women. The concurrence of these features, exacerbated in the Congo since 1998, can not be separated from the narrativization of the genocide in Rwanda, since it is the shocking nature of the latter that serves to obscure the violence in the former. (2005: 227)

The production *Rwanda My Hope* posits an ideological and political framework from which to observe how the genocide is represented, performed, and remembered. The need for critical reflection on 'genocide theatre' in the context of political events, international audiences, and the international donor industry creates for the researcher an ambiguous (or conflicted) position where she or he is simultaneously an objective and reflective critic as well as an eyewitness, albeit a secondary one, to genocide through performance and testimony. For example, many of the original performers of *Rwanda My Hope* were genocide survivors and the theatrical enactment of the genocide through the production and memories of the actual events overlapped. As Azeda commented:

While rehearsing, it would rain. There is a scene in which the participants would have to fall flat on the ground, their bodies in the mud. The participants would complain, to which I would say that the rain and the genocide go together. That many times when bodies had been mutilated, covered with dirt to die, the rain would fall and revive people, bringing them back to life again.[5]

Performance theorist Peggy Phelan has considered that as a reflection of performativity, the outline of what has been lost might tell us about what is being performed and why.[6] The production *Rwanda My Hope* provides an emotional connection to the missing bodies – the lives lost in the genocide – through Azeda's choreography of mourning. In the case of 'genocide theatre', memory can be used for the resurrection and reconstruction of genocide for political purposes. Although I have noted the potential political and ethical dilemmas 'genocide theatre' may present, there are also personal connections to the genocide and

artistic explorations of the event that are outside my own frame of reference. For this reason, I emphatically seek not to negate the experiences and feelings attributed to the members of the cast, audience, or artistic creators of the production. The analysis of *Rwanda My Hope* strives instead to understand the outline of the bodies, as indicated by Phelan, but also to render material the bodies that are gone, in light of Huyssen's reflection on the use of narratives for 'function and politics'.

Hope Azeda – *Rwanda My Hope*

When Azeda was first approached to choreograph the production *Rwanda My Hope* in 2004, she said it had to be a dance of mourning.[7] According to Azeda, the rehearsals for the tenth commemoration consisted of over 1,000 performers – including 600 children, a 200-person choir, and 200 dancers. Following the original production for the tenth anniversary commemoration, *Rwanda My Hope* was resurrected as an instructional tool by the Aegis Trust.[8] While the goal of the performances during the UK tour was to teach schoolchildren about the genocide in Rwanda, the production that I observed in Gikongoro, Rwanda, also sought to attract funding from international donors. This section will provide an overview of the production *Rwanda My Hope* as a work by Azeda from the Tutsi Diaspora, but will also analyse the play as a representation of the genocide for international audiences and as a form of memorialization and commemoration.

Rwanda My Hope was performed in Gikongoro at a secondary school on 16 July 2005. The production was staged in a large school auditorium on a proscenium arch stage. The audience consisted of several international donors and hundreds of secondary students in a school near the Murambi memorial site. The production was purposefully planned by the Aegis Trust as a part of the memorial tour for the anonymous donors prior to their visit to Murambi memorial. At the time of the production, the Murambi memorial site was undergoing construction and the Aegis Trust was seeking additional funding. The performance of *Rwanda My Hope* was at a school; likewise, Murambi memorial is located at the site of a former school where one of the bloodiest massacres of the Rwandan genocide took place.

There was a stark contrast between the school in which the production *Rwanda My Hope* was staged for schoolchildren and the other school at the Murambi memorial, which houses the bodies of the Murambi massacre victims. I will address the performativity of the memorial site of Murambi before analysing *Rwanda My Hope*, since an aspect of the production was to commemorate the genocide and it was directly linked to fundraising for the Murambi memorial – and thereby also to contemporary political agendas to how and why theatre might be used in Rwanda post-genocide. At Murambi, the tour guide provides his testimony to memorial visitors during the tour, while the testimonies presented in *Rwanda My Hope* also come from survivors whose stories are embodied by the actors. Both the memorial tour and the theatrical production are used for the purpose of providing testimony, but through different enactments.

The Murambi memorial in Gikongoro is located at the site of a former school where over 45,000 Tutsi and Hutu moderates were massacred in April 1994. The decomposed bodies have been preserved in lime, laid out on tables for public viewing. Several of the classrooms have been divided according to the gender and age of the bodies. The children's room is piled with the bones of babies and young people, many with the remnants of clothing hanging upon the white lime skeletons. On arrival, we are given a guided tour by Emmanuel – one of four survivors of the over 45,000 who were massacred at Murambi Technical School beginning on 21 April 1994. Emmanuel is living proof of the atrocities of the genocide, embodying Diana Taylor's concept of the repertoire, often pointing to the dent in his head where he was pounded with the butt of a rifle. Taylor defines the repertoire in relation to social behaviour:

> [t]he repertoire stores and enacts 'embodied' memory – the traumatic or cathartic 'shudder,' gestures, orality movement, dance, song – in short, all those acts usually thought of as 'live,' ephemeral, nonreproducible knowledge. The embodied experience and transmission of traumatic memory – the interactions among people in the here and now – make a difference in the way that knowledge is transmitted and incorporated. The type of interaction might range from the individual (one-on-one psychoanalytic session) to the group or state level (demonstrations, human rights trials). (Taylor, 2002: 155)

Emmanuel enunciates his testimony as performative proof of the genocide, by illustrating scars and informing visitors of his tribulations. He says that he provides the guided tours of Murambi to be closer to his wife and children who were killed in the massacre, and so that people 'Never Forget'. His presence is a repertoire in Taylor's sense, an embodiment of genocide, as opposed to an archival or text-based representation.[9] Bennett and Kennedy expand upon the concept of using pain to bring memory back to life stating, '[m]oreover, memories are not stored by one group in perpetuity but are transferred through a system of exchange. Pain – or what we might refer to as trauma – is negotiated and "given away" through this system' (Bennett and Kennedy, 2003: 6). Thus, the living proof of the genocide through the performance of pain and trauma by Emmanuel transmits the memory of genocide as remembered through the curation of the memorial or commemorative event.

Although the Murambi site and *Rwanda My Hope* both memorialize the genocide, the memorial does so through openly displaying physical bodies while the production does so through the enactment of memories using survivors' testimonies and the physical embodiment of the genocide through theatrical means. Prior to being given a tour of the Murambi site, the donors were brought to a public school near the memorial site to watch a performance of *Rwanda My Hope*. The play used personal testimonies from survivors, including the following of a young boy whose birthday falls on 7 April 1994, the day the genocide began. He states, 'I was born on the 7th of April 1994. I love music and I love football, I love many things, but, BUT, I hate one thing and that is the day I was born.'[10] Images of genocide were frozen into tableau form as scenes from the 100 days of massacre were portrayed in the play – including rape, slaughter, and beating. The opening monologue referred to the connection between memory and the future, haunted by the past:

> Rwanda my home
> Rwanda my sweet home
> I have seen you smile
> I have seen you cry
> I have felt your pain.
> So deep that I cannot ignore the silence of the dead.
> Yes memory
> The future haunts the past
> Children will always ask why, why, why?

At one moment in the play, the message was no longer aimed at the audience of several hundred schoolchildren, but at the group of foreign investors in the audience. A character in the play states:

Remembering the genocide for Rwanda is important for everyone, because the whole world knew and did not do anything to stop the genocide, so everyone around the world shares a little something in our little country of Rwanda. So it is better to remember than to forget, because if you do not remember, then you do not have all of the truth.[11]

Azeda's production serves as theatre for commemoration and memory, but has also been used as a platform for the Aegis Trust. In the autumn of both 2006 and 2008, *Mashirika* was funded to tour the UK in the *Africa's Hope* tour [*Rwanda My Hope* retitled]. Thus, the personal can be co-opted by larger political forces.

Conclusion

These acts of commemoration and memorialization highlight interconnections between local and global responses to genocide. Although the Gisozi memorial has been erected in the heart of the Rwandan capital, it has been disparaged as a 'western' construct in part because it was designed and erected by the Aegis Trust.[12] A hybrid of local and international systems thus promotes reconstruction and reconciliation in post-genocide Rwanda. Here we have been most concerned with how the narratives these systems represent are constructed and maintained within the overarching paradigm of narration and performance. In effect, the construction of a genocide memorial in Rwanda by the Aegis Trust and their continued response to genocide with the creation of the Holocaust Centre in the UK, automatically links the two genocides into a master narrative regarding representation of genocide for international audiences.

The post-conflict paradigm of justice and reconciliation includes juridical, social, and commemorative acts articulating the atrocities of the genocide, but also connects those acts to other atrocities and narratives of suffering. Allen Feldman, in his study of memory theatres, virtual witnessing, and the trauma-aesthetic, claims that, '[t]o enclave the human rights violation story at a primordial scene

of violence is already to preselect the restorative powers of legal, medical, media, and textual rationalities as post-violent. There is a normative and moralizing periodization built into the post-violent depiction of violence' (Feldman, 2004: 164). He notes the complexity of post-violent witnessing and the constraints of human rights discourse by arguing that some narratives of suffering may need to stand outside the normalization of witnessing and documenting violence. He also emphasizes the need to encompass narratives outside the 'post-violent depiction of violence', questioning national juridical and commemorative practices that may ultimately frame violence into digestible and transferable representations for the mass consumption of international audiences at the exclusion of counter-narratives.

In the Rwandan context, a crucial question is how individuals have been able to respond to the violence which occurred outside the government-prescribed 'master narrative' of the genocide. Violent acts in Rwanda (as in most conflict areas) are a part of a continuing narrative of violence, and cannot be neatly contained by the period between April and July of 1994. Rather, it can be argued, the acts of violence identified as the genocide should be identified as part of a continuum of violence. With regard to the dilemma of master narratives constructed through the trauma-aesthetic often represented as commemorations and memorials, it is important to understand the conditions through which life histories of human rights violations circulate in order to develop dialogical opportunities outside those master narratives. There are life histories of human rights violations within Hutu, Tutsi, and Twa communities. These could potentially be circulated through grassroots theatre associations, which could become a venue for constructing alternative narratives regarding the roots of what has been called 'structural violence' in Rwanda – including the affects of unequal distribution of resources, poverty, and social exclusion.[13] By establishing economic reforms along with ideological campaigns for reconciliation, the grassroots associations identify poverty as one of the causes of violence and work together towards shifting contemporary Rwanda away from the structural violence that has determined the unfortunate contours of its modern history so far.

Grassroots associations allow individuals to negotiate their differences, to share stories related to conflicts, and to perform and imagine a future of tolerance. The new moral order is established through recognition of the causes of violence and an empathetic response based on shared suffering, regardless of whether individuals are categorized as perpetrators or survivors. In this way, various narratives can be explored outside the predominant national memorialization and commemoration practices. State-sponsored theatre, including *Rwanda My Hope*, is linked to officially mandated ceremonies of commemoration as exemplified through the performance at the Murambi memorial. Enactments of genocide theatre seek to embody the 'gone-ness' of those that are lost, but the memories are selective. Although President Kagame has banned the use of ethnic labels in search of unification and peace, the commemorations inherently perform the Tutsi as survivor and Hutu as perpetrator, thus encoding those two moral identities. While slogans of 'Never Again' may draw attention to the horror of mass atrocities through representations of the genocide such as *Rwanda My Hope*, it is important to also consider symbiotic approaches to representing discursive narratives outside present commemoration and memorialization practices.

Notes

1   The genocide began on 6 April 1994, when the aircraft carrying Rwandan President Habyaramana, a Hutu, and Burundian President Cyprien Ntaryamira was shot down. The war cry was to kill all Tutsi, leading to the massacre of over 1 million Tutsi and Hutu moderates from April to July 1994 and 2 million displaced persons in neighbouring countries.

2   The Rwandan Patriotic Army (RPA) consisted of primarily Tutsi refugees living in Uganda as a militarized branch of the Rwandan Patriotic Front (RPF).

3   Human Rights Watch, *Law and Reality: Progress in Judicial Reform in Rwanda*, 25 July 2008. Available at: www.hrw.org/en/reports/2008/07/24/law-and-reality [accessed 10 August 2009].

4   According to Human Rights Watch, 'free speech' has been curtailed in new administrative policies to control information in Rwanda.
    'Divisionism' is often used interchangeably with the term 'genocide ideology' – a crime that was first adopted into Rwanda's law in 2008 but that the government has used for at least five years to punish expression of any ideas that could lead to genocide. See Human Rights Watch, 'Rwanda: Restore BBC to the Air. Growing Media Restrictions Cast Doubt on Nation's Commitment to Free Speech', 27 April 2009. Available at: www.hrw.org/en/news/2009/04/27/rwanda-restore-bbc-air [accessed 6 May 2009].

5   Interview with Hope Azeda by the author. Kigali, Rwanda, 10 January 2005.

6   Phelan, P. (1997) *Mourning Sex: Performing Public Memories.* New York: Routledge.

7   Interview with Hope Azeda Interview by the author. Kigali, Rwanda, 10 January 2005.

8   Aegis Trust is a UK-based organization founded in 2000 whose mission is to campaign for the prevention of genocide. It runs a Holocaust Centre in Nottinghamshire, UK, and two genocide memorials in Rwanda, including Gisozi memorial in the capital city of Kigali and Murambi memorial located in the south of Rwanda.

9   See Taylor, D. (2003) *The Archive and the Repertoire: Performing Cultural Memory in the Americas.* London and Durham, NC: Duke University Press.

10 Quotes obtained from production *Rwanda My Hope*, transcribed by the author.

11 Ibid.

12 See Sandra Laville, 'Two years late and mired in controversy: the British memorial to Rwanda's past', *The Guardian*, 13 November 2006. Available at: www.guardian.co.uk/world/2006/nov/13/rwanda.sandralaville [accessed 4 March 2009].

13 Three hundred associations have been tracked by the National Unity and Reconciliation Commission (NURC), 60 of which have been directly assisted through the NURC in terms of training and financial support. Various initiatives include beekeeping, livestock production, craft making, and cultural troupes. Interview with Shamsi Kazimbaya by the author, 18 November 2005.

REFERENCES

Bennett, Jill and Roseanne Kennedy (2003) 'Introduction', in *World Memory: Personal Trajectories in Global Time*, (eds) Jill Bennett and Roseanne Kennedy. New York: Palgrave Macmillan.

Breed, Ananda (2007) 'Performing *Gacaca* in Rwanda: Local Culture for Justice and Reconciliation', in *The Cultures and Globalization Series: Conflicts and Tensions*, (eds) Helmut Anheier and Yudhishthir Raj Isar. London: Sage.

Feldman, Allen (2004) 'Memory Theatres, Virtual Witnessing, and the Trauma-Aesthetic'. *Biography*, 27(1): 163–202.

Gillis, John R. (1994) 'Memory and Identity: The History of a Relationship', in *Commemorations: The Politics of National Identity*, (ed.) John R. Gillis. Princeton, NJ: Princeton University Press.

Harrow, Kenneth W. (2005) 'Un train peut en cacher un autre: Narrating the Rwandan Genocide and Hotel Rwanda'. *Research in African Literatures*, 36(4): 223–232.

Huyssen, Andreas (2003) 'Trauma and Memory: A New Imaginary of Temporality' in *World Memory: Personal Trajectories in Global Time*, (eds) Jill Bennett and Rosanne Kennedy. New York: Palgrave Macmillan.

Phelan, Peggy (1997) *Mourning Sex: Performing Public Memories*. New York: Routledge.

Taylor, Diana (2002) 'You Are Here: The DNA of Performance'. *The Drama Review*, 46(1): 149–169.

Taylor, D. (2003) *The Archive and the Repertoire: Performing Cultural Memory in the Americas*. London and Durham, NC: Duke University Press.

Tiemessen, Alana E. (2004) 'After Arusha: Gacaca Justice in Post-Genocide Rwanda'. *African Studies Quarterly*, 8(1): 57–76.

Zorbas, Eugenia (2004) 'Reconciliation in Post-Genocide Rwanda'. *African Journal of Legal Studies*, 1(1): 29–52.

CHAPTER 22

NARRATING SHARED IDENTITY
Brian Schiff, Carolina Porto de Andrade and Mathilde Toulemonde

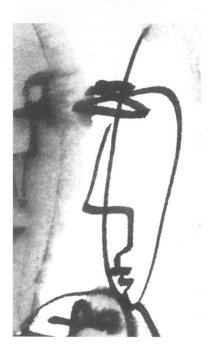

This chapter argues that collective memories can be understood as narratives that are negotiated in concrete social relationships. In the context of globalization, the task of establishing a coherent and sustaining couple identity has become more problematic. Using life-story conversations with Arab–Jewish mixed couples living in France, we describe how couples create, or fail to create, a coherent story of their identity. Our study of Olivier and Sylvie argues that finding a shared identity is fraught with difficulties. Their couple identity is shaped by relational factors internal to the couple: wishes, dreams, compromises and power contribute to the character and structure of their narrative. Their narrative is also configured by relationships external to the couple, including prejudice, and strategies for presenting their story in different contexts.

From collective memory to family memory

Although scholars have applied the idea of 'collective memory' mainly to large groups, one can equally speak about the collective memory of smaller groups. Such a move is consistent with Halbwachs' (1952/1992) theoretical formulation of collective memory. An entire chapter in his work, *Les cadres sociaux de la mémoire*, is devoted to the concept of 'the collective memory of the family.' Families, like larger social groups such as societies or generations, carry with them their own history and traditions that locate group members in distinct conceptions of selfhood, otherness, family structure, character, ideals, etc. Halbwachs (1952/1992: 59) writes, 'in most traditional societies, each family has its proper mentality, its memories which it alone commemorates, and its secrets that are revealed only to its members.' Family memories are constructed from traditions and histories that endure through time and are passed on to subsequent generations in order to serve as a useful basis for identity. Families actively guard their traditions and assimilate, or acculturate, new members into their group. Like other groups, the collective memory of the family defines the group in respect to the history re-presented in the now, but also provides a framework for understanding the very identity of the family, who 'we' are.

Couples establishing a life together confront the problem of how to create a family memory in the context of pre-existing traditions and difference. Even for couples from similar religious, ethnic, and national backgrounds, launching a new family requires orchestrating competing family identities and the invention of new stories that define the history of this particular couple. The formation of a new family memory doesn't mean that the couple must begin from scratch. The tools for writing the family's story are inherited from parents and grandparents and the terms provided by culture at large. But, the act of forming a new couple, a new family, requires partners to 'synchronize' their memories into one narrative with the same plotline. Marriage is a reality-building project that involves the creative energies of both participants (Berger & Kellner, 1964/1994). It is 'a *dramatic* act in which two strangers come together and redefine themselves'

(Berger & Kellner, 1964/1994: 5, italics in original). In the process of marriage the couple strives to build a sustaining dramatic representation that provides the structure for meaningful lives.

In the context of globalization, with increasing contact between persons from diverse religious, geographical and ethnic traditions, the task of creating a dramatic representation of the couple has become more difficult. In France, and other countries at the center of globalization, establishing a coherent and sustaining family memory is challenging. Even in 1964, when Berger and Kellner originally published, they noted 'Unlike an earlier situation in which the establishment of the new marriage simply added to the differentiation and complexity of an already existing social order, the marriage partners are now engaged in the often difficult task of constructing for themselves the little world in which they will live' (1964/1994: 24). Opposed to previous historical epochs, where the extent of contact with otherness was less radical, in the era of globalization, many couples are faced with the challenge of constructing a reality different from that of their family of origin.

From memories to narratives

In the following, we situate collective memory in the realm of narratives told in conversations. From our perspective, the lingering problem in 'collective memory' is inherent in the concept's location in the world of memory rather than storytelling or discourse. Although it is unlikely that a term with such wide interdisciplinary resonance could be renamed, it should be stressed that, in metaphorically associating the individual process of memory with social processes, Halbwachs performed an incredible disservice. Cautioning against applying models of memory derived from the study of individuals to the collective, Wertsch (2002: 37) argues that 'the conceptual baggage of such metaphors is often misleading, yet powerfully seductive.' Indeed, the concept of collective memory is as metaphorically potent as it is empirically inaccurate.

As we see it, the sole conceptual similarity between collective and individual memory is, literally, the fact that both concern the past. Following Wertsch (2002), a more radical proposition would eliminate the idea of collective memory in favor of how persons, in various social settings, create and

perform 'cultural texts' or 'collective discourses.' The process becomes descriptive rather than metaphorical. Persons tell stories about the past with the help of cultural texts. Social and cultural groups produce stories, which persons encounter and, in turn, tell. These acts of cultural and social storytelling are influential tools in our personal narrative and our personal narratives contain the seeds for cultural and social representations of the past.

The process of collective memory is not ethereal but concrete. It is enacted in situations, in which actors engage and perform cultural tools. As Wertsch (2002: 26) writes, 'instead of positing a vague mnemonic agency that is a thread running through the members of a group, the idea is that they share a representation of the past because they share textual resources.' Indeed, there is a kind of magic aura that surrounds the notion of 'collective memory.' But, unless we are going to posit a supernatural force like a universal mind or collective unconscious, collective memory must be nothing more than the day-to-day process of how persons create and appropriate stories. Remembering the past is grounded in persons and in the situations in which they enact a textual heritage. However, persons do not have direct access to cultural tools; rather, cultural tools are acquired through one's active participation in the world with others. Shared representations of the past are discovered and inscribed in social relationships before becoming a part of the individual's way of thinking (Vygotsky, 1978). Social relationships are often the means for encountering or discovering new textual resources. Despite the invention and use of a wide variety of media for directly encountering textual resources, such as television, the internet, film, books, newspapers, etc., direct face-to-face interactions continue to serve a critical role, introducing stories, ideas and identities. Even when contact with a textual resource appears more or less direct, actually watching a television show or reading a book or newspaper, the meaning of the text and its relevance to our lives is confirmed in relation to others.

Zerubavel (2004) argues that relationships can be thought of as 'lines of contact' or 'links' between persons and cultural ideas. We connect to social ideas through how we construct a mental picture of our relational world, moving closer to or distancing ourselves from ideas by how we draw up the landscape of our relationships. Although Zerubavel is concerned with the mental connections that make us feel closer to an historical event or person, the connection is not only mental but also concrete and relational. We inherit histories because we have been, literally and figuratively, 'touched by' others and because this relationship provides the means to appropriate ideas, identities and histories.

The difficult 'couple identity' of Arab–Jewish couples in France

A more satisfactory account of collective memory needs to explore persons in their relational context. Collective memories are part of a conversation that is, on the one hand, inherited from one's ancestors and, and the other hand, continues in the present moment. The conversation is continuous. The language is drawn from the past, negotiated in dialogue with others and used as an identity resource in future conversations.

The notion of a 'couple identity' is central to our understanding of this research. A couple identity can be thought of as a myth about who the couple is, their origins, traditions and what binds them together. The couple identity includes those central narratives that define the couple, including how the couple met, the pivotal choices they have made and the enduring traditions that provide their lives with sense and meaning. It is a joint construction of who 'we' are that is negotiated and performed in concert with one's partner and the exterior world and that should function as a sustaining narrative. The inability to construct a coherent, stable and meaningful sense of identity is one indicator that a couple is in danger of divorce (Carrère et al., 2000). Finding a shared sense of tradition, on religious matters, enhances stability and reduces conflict (Chinitz & Brown, 2001).

The following analysis describes the way that Arab-Jewish couples in France negotiate the meaning of who they are and their common identity. We study how these couples overcome their differences and arrive, or not, at a common story. In particular, we are interested in how persons from groups that consider themselves in conflict construct a meaningful framework for understanding their common identity and lives together. Interestingly, France's Jewish and Arab populations are made up of large portions of post-colonial immigrants from North Africa, particularly Algeria (Benbassa, 2000;

Fetzer & Soper, 2005). Many Arab immigrants first came to France as laborers, often single men without their families, but in the 1970s families followed and the migration became more permanent (Fetzer & Soper, 2005). Jews arrived in France *en masse* during and shortly after the North African colonies became independent. Benbassa (2000) writes that some 235,000 Jews from North Africa immigrated to France between 1956 and 1967. Because French laws for census-taking forbid questions of ethnicity or religion, it is very difficult to know the exact rate of intermarriage between Arabs and Jews. Data are collected by national origins and not by other indictors. However, our personal sense is that this variety of union is rare and stigmatized. And, if, as Varro (2003) argues, the French expression, *mariage mixte*, denotes a separation from the normal and carries with it the sense of otherness, marriages between French Jews and Arabs are an ideal representation of *les mariages mixtes*.

Although many thousands of kilometers from Israel and the Palestinian Territories, French Arabs and Jews identify with the participants in the Middle East conflict. But, this sense of conflict is not only global, but also local to France and Europe. In a provocative essay on anti-Semitism and Islamophobia in Europe, Bunzl (2007) argues that the formation of a unified Europe was designed to assimilate Jews into the fabric of European life as a remedy for the virulent anti-Semitism that led to the Shoah. But, at the same moment that Jews were brought into the center of Europe, Muslims became the 'other' in opposition to a reconstructed 'Judeo-Christian' European identity. Christian anti-Semitism continues to exist. But, these structural changes in European society have intensified the antipathy between the Muslim and Jewish communities, putting them on opposite sides of a divide and the object of mutual suspicion and hostility.

For couples from different traditions, there are two major challenges to creating a coherent couple identity. The first challenge is to bring their received traditions under a single narrative thread or plotline. There are several possibilities for meeting this challenge. Either one or the other person might abandon their previous heritage or the couple could build a new narrative structure that blends their traditions together into a new configuration. The second challenge is to form a couple identity that will satisfy others outside the couple – parents, extended family, friends and other members of the social world. When traditions consider themselves in conflict, the difficulty of addressing these challenges is amplified. The social distance and suspicion between Arabs and Jews in France makes this task of coming together to form a stable and coherent couple identity especially difficult.

We now proceed to a detailed analysis of how collective memory is managed in the context of long-term relationships. We use these interviews with mixed couples in order to stake out a position on memory in the context of difference. As will become evident in our analysis, when we get close to where the action is, the hegemonic notion of a collective memory is inadequate. Our vision of collective memory is much closer to how we think about the space of social life. Persons are engaged in conversations, talking about the past and their identities together, in order to write shared visions of who we are that can be used in future conversations.

Our study

In Fall 2008, we began a research project studying the stories of mixed Jewish and Arab couples in France for which we interviewed three couples. Following Chase (2003), we used a method of narrative interviewing and careful listening. Interviews were designed to gather a rich collection of specific narratives important for the person and the story of the couple. Questions were prepared in order to, as Chase puts it, 'invite stories.' An interview guide was constructed with questions on the history and identity of each person, the story of the couple's relationship, and how their family, friends and French society reacted to their relationship. Finally, we formulated questions about their interpretation of the conflict between Jews and Arabs in the Middle East. Although questions were prepared in advance, our goal was to put aside the interview guide and to have a natural conversation. Questions were asked on the basis of careful listening to the interviewee's life story in order to obtain detailed descriptions about specific experiences and their reflections on these experiences.

Interviews were interpreted using a whole life method. Our analysis endeavored to contextualize the words and experiences of each person. We attempt to remain faithful to the interview, trying to hear the voice of each interviewee and their point of view on the world. In other words, we tried to make their meanings and interpretations explicit in our analysis. How does this person tell their life story? What meaning do they give to their experience? Interviews were conducted in French and completed in a single session. Each member of the couple was first interviewed individually. After the individual interviews were completed, a group interview was conducted that included the three interviewers and both members of the couple.

Olivier and Sylvie

In the following, we describe how one of our couples, Olivier and Sylvie, tell their complex and dramatic story and the consequences of this narrative on their identity and the future of their relationship. Their stories contain numerous regrets and uncertainty about the future. The antipathy between the Arab and Jewish communities in France, and by consequence, the social stigma against Jewish–Arab marriages has played an important role in their account. However, the solutions that the couple has chosen to combat this prejudice seem to have multiplied the problem of creating a coherent and sustaining couple identity. Rather than honestly and openly presenting an account of their couple, Olivier and Sylvie have consciously chosen to conceal their identity. Their stories are punctuated by unstated facts, half-truths and, sometimes, outright lies. This plan of action has had significant costs for the stability and health of the couple. They display substantial difficulties building a stable and coherent identity that can be told in different contexts.

Beginnings

The beginning of an interview is a critical moment in establishing the positioning of each participant in the conversation (Goffman, 1959). What is this interview about? Who are the participants? How will the conversation proceed? In our interview with Olivier, impression management is monumental. As we describe, issues of self-presentation are thematic and found at various moments in the couple identity. But, it is also inscribed in the relationship between the interviewer and the interviewee. Our interview with Olivier begins with a brief conversation about the structure of the interview.

Brian: The first questions I have are about your identity.

Olivier: Do you want me to present myself, or do you have questions …

Brian: As you like. The questions I have are for you to talk a little bit about this.

Olivier: Ok, maybe I'll present myself, then, my background and all that.

And Olivier's account begins:

Olivier: Uhm, I'm the third child of a family of four children. My parents are from North Africa… They arrived in France in the 50s–60s… We are four children with varied life courses. One thing that seems important with regard to my origins is that, for example, I never learned Arabic.

Brian: But your parents speak Arabic?

Olivier: Yes, they speak Arabic. They speak it but they never taught it to us.

Brian: And what do you consider to be your identity? Your big identity?

Olivier: It's a little particular because I don't feel from [a North African country], I do feel more French. I am culturally French, but I still have an entire background that's not at all linked to my parents' country, but it's linked to the Maghreb. To Islam. I have an Oriental background, let's say, and, but I am culturally French really. I am really very very integrated. I have. My friends aren't just from the Maghreb, or, as you say in France 'beurs.' So I'm more French, but I have a whole… So, my identity, I have trouble with it in fact. I have trouble with, with, with really knowing what my identity is, as I said, I am really very French and very Western, let's say, but there are also certain things, certain values, certain ways of thinking which I think are more Eastern, and which put me a bit in a state of destabilization, because there are things in which I don't recognize myself in France, and which are quite destabilizing for me. That is to say that I'm very destabilized…

It is important to highlight that the interviewer is still confused about Olivier's identity and pursues a more direct line of questioning.

Brian: Do you think that being Jewish is something that is important for you ? Or was it something important in the …

Olivier: So, actually I was… I, I, I, so I am from Muslim origins.

Brian: Really (surprised)?

Olivier: Yes. I am from Muslim origins. That's why we are a mixed couple, it's in this way.

Brian: That's interesting, because I thought it was Sylvie.

Olivier: No, it's me.

Brian: Ah, that's interesting.

Olivier: No, so I am from Muslim origins, and I did a conversion to Judaism, and here, I have a real 'split' in terms of. Because it's very very difficult, for example, even though I converted, I continue to do Ramadan. I cannot not do it. I cannot tell myself 'that's it' and it's very, I am very, I am really divided. Because I am… I am Western in my way of living, I lived all, 80% of my life as a Muslim, and I converted to a new religion. I am divided between the three. Really. This is very difficult. So when we speak of identity, here I have an identity which is. Which is a little broken apart and which is difficult to. Which isn't easy to, not easy to deal with.

Olivier's identity is unstable. As he says, in English during the interview, 'split.' He is: an Arab who doesn't speak Arabic; a Jew who celebrates Ramadan; French and from the Maghreb; Western and Eastern; and, as he tells us later in the interview, a Muslim who doesn't know the Koran. In addition, this ambiguity is transposed into the interview situation. In fact, the interviewer is surprised to discover that it is Sylvie and not Olivier who is Jewish. There is something ambiguous in Olivier's self-presentation.

First meetings

This ambiguity is not only a product of the interview situation, but it is thematic. Olivier's identity is often misconstrued. A fact that, sometimes, he uses to his advantage. This ambiguity is part of the couple's story. It is present when the couple first meets and is found in the rest of their story. The story of how Olivier and Sylvie first met is found in both interviews. This is Sylvie's version of these events. She recounts:

At the time, when I met him actually I thought that he was Jewish. It's true, he doesn't really look like an Arab, well, Muslim, in any case. He doesn't have a Muslim name either… I came back to the office and said 'Well, that's it, I've met the man of my life'… After, I saw him again, I think mid-December, and for me actually, this whole time, for me he was a Jew… So we, we were having coffee and everything… And I said to him 'So, Hanukah, did you light your candles?' And he says, 'I don't think you've understood very well, I'm from the side of those who one kills.' (Laughs) 'Excuse me?' (Laughs) So, well, the big shock was first that we Jews kill people (laughs). 'Sorry I didn't really follow that but.' And on top of that, well to understand all of a sudden that he was Muslim. So, finally it, it just took thirty seconds, but all of a sudden I thought to myself 'yeah, wow, ok!' (Laughs). But so, after, since I had already been with Muslim guys, I wasn't closed to that sort of thing. So it wasn't, it wasn't all that serious really.

Sylvie's interest in Olivier is, in part, due to a false impression of his identity. The exchange is fascinating. Olivier's response is provocative and unsettling. He casts Jews and Muslims in the position of adversaries engaged in violent combat. Despite the fact that his assumed religious identity is one of the reasons why she is attracted to Olivier, her evaluation of the narrative mitigates the significance of religion. As she says, she isn't 'closed to that sort of thing' and 'it wasn't all that serious really.'

The marriage of her childhood

Although the first encounter was somewhat awkward and abrasive, the relationship continued past these difficulties. Olivier and Sylvie begin to live together and then decide to marry. The decision to marry is a pivotal moment in the couple's story. After meeting a local rabbi, Sylvie recounts that although she was reassured that her children would be Jewish, she realized that she wouldn't be able to have the marriage that she dreamt of since her childhood. As she says:

There are girls, for example, who, when they are little, they make a notebook and they say, 'Ah, I'm going to have this dress, there will be these flowers, there will be this orchestra and everything.' In my little girl's head, I just said to myself that I wanted it to be in the Synagogue and I wanted my grandparents to be there.

Sylvie's desire for the marriage of her dreams sets in motion a series of decisions and compromises that have profound effects on the couple's future. The most important compromise is Olivier's decision to convert to Judaism.

Olivier: It's me who decided to do it… So, for Sylvie, in her head, it was 'it's a catastrophe.' In other words, 'I will have to leave my grandparents, and everything because I won't be able to get married in a Synagogue and everything.' And so I said to myself, 'No, that's not possible, there has to be another way.' So on my own, I made the decision to make some appointments with Rabbis, and I said to myself 'I'm going to do it.' When I say 'I'm going to do it', it was for the wedding. It wasn't, it wasn't in the logic of… It was in all sincerity, but it was on a superficial level, let's say. It's actually the appointments which made me, which convinced me. And, and she didn't believe it. She would say 'You're not meant to be… You're doing this, it's kind of you, you're doing this for me and everything.' I would say to her 'I'm being sincere!' She didn't believe me… So, actually, at the beginning it came from a sense of guilt, almost. Of wanting to say to her 'we can live together, it's possible.' And after, it became natural. That's it. After it just became natural… Yeah, quite simply, at first, it was guilt, I wanted to show her that it's ok, it was possible, and, and, and quickly, well, I fell straight into the process.

Brian: The word 'guilt' is very interesting, why do you say that?

Olivier: Well, it's because, it's hard, when you love a woman, to say to yourself that she thinks that she will have to give up her family, give up the wedding of her dreams… And give up the fact of not being able to transmit, of not transmitting her religion to her children. It's unbearable for her. I was guilty. I felt guilty of making her feel that. And I was scared that it could cause our couple to fall apart, completely. I don't know if we would still be together if I hadn't converted. Not because she wouldn't have loved me or anything, but because the sacrifices would have been too difficult to make. I don't know.

It is common sense to say that a relationship is a negotiation. But, in Olivier and Sylvie's relationship, it is Olivier who is pressured to bend. He bends because he is concerned about the future of their relationship. As he tells it, Olivier's feelings are significant motivators. Olivier decides to convert because he feels guilty for asking Sylvie to abandon her childhood visions of marriage. He feels guilty for putting her family relationships at risk. Also, he bends out of fear that the relationship might not survive if he doesn't convert.

At first this decision is taken as a pragmatic step necessary for a religious wedding but it becomes more than that. As Olivier recounts, he makes the decision in all sincerity. But, this turn in the road has its effects. Acquiescing to the marriage of Sylvie's childhood is much more than a pragmatic step.

A curious decision

Complications mount as the process of conversion continues and the couple marries. Social relationships external to the couple take on increasing salience in the couple's relationship. It is here that a curious decision takes place. The decision is partly unconscious, but it is also deliberate. Rather than honestly presenting the same narrative to everyone, revealing that Olivier is a Muslim who decided to convert to Judaism, Olivier and Sylvie decide to employ a strategy of controlling and managing information. When asked about whether or not he has told his brothers and sisters about his conversation to Judaism, Olivier states:

> I prefer not to say it because… when you don't want something to be known, it's really better to hide it, because… the best way to master information is to not at all communicate it. If you start, then… you don't know how things could turn out.

The mastery of information characterizes Oliver and Sylvie's approach. The end result of this strategy is the proliferation of multiple plotlines of the couple's identity. Each version is specially suited to a particular context. With Jews, Olivier is Jewish. If you must know more, he is a convert but from a murky past. The fact that he is Arab and Muslim is concealed. In order to keep up the façade, at one point, Sylvie tells her grandparents that Olivier's family is 'pied noir.' With Arabs, Olivier conceals his conversion. He is married to a Jewish woman, but he doesn't offer the fact that he has converted to Judaism. The only persons who know the whole story are some close friends, the Rabbis involved in the conversion, Sylvie's parents and a few selected Aunts. But, if there is a danger that the lie will be exposed, those who know are enjoined to keep their insider's knowledge secret. The essential connection between all of these lies is that it is always Olivier who is asked to deny some aspect of his identity.

The secret mission

A far cry from the idealized marriage that Sylvie imagines from her childhood, their religious marriage resembles a secret CIA mission. The religious wedding in the USA, where most of Sylvie's family lives, is a delicate balance of lies and untruths designed to evade the question of Olivier's origins.

Sylvie: So, well, we organized everything. We arrived. We finished preparing our wedding, we tried to say the least possible. There were some horrible statements, and I think that… On the one hand it was useful, because, well, they were statements that were, well, really very racist. Well, it's, it's stupid but it's true. It's hard to say that about your own family. But when, well, on top of it, I was actually living these comments through him. So I thought to myself 'shit, he's going to have to deal with some pretty horrible things about Muslims, well, Arabs'… There were some moments. We did Shabbat with my grandparents. So, with the prayer and everything. Well everyone was looking to see if he was speaking. If he was saying the prayer. So, it was a little sus-, everything had become a little suspicious… Everyone wanted to know… 'So, how did it happen? What do you do? What is your name? Your parents? Your father?' So, well, it's a Jewish family, so they ask questions. And everyone asks the same question and not exactly the same way… I think that it was the most catastrophic week of his life… It's funny because … at the Synagogue, I did nothing but cry! And everything, well, it was simply the most intense moment of my life… On top of it all these lies and the fact that there were those comments. It actually confirmed to him the fact that we shouldn't say that he was Muslim… So, it was just during those few minutes. The time it took to walk. We had taken the big room, so I took a lot of steps (laughs). It was just that very moment which was just, it was the achievement of so many dreams, and I think, I really made him pay a high price. So, and it wasn't, today I still don't know if it was a good idea to have done that to him.

Because Olivier lies about his origins to Jews, he has been exposed to racist comments uttered by Sylvie's family. The comments took their toll. According to Sylvie, these racist comments have confirmed the fact that it's better for Olivier to conceal his origins. There is also a striking difference in their interpretations of the marriage. According to Sylvie, for Olivier it was a disaster, it was 'the most catastrophic week of his life.' But for her, the marriage was a fairy tale, 'the achievement of so many dreams.'

The Brit Milah
The relationship becomes even more complicated with the birth of a baby. More problematic still, the couple has a baby boy who, according to Jewish law, should be ritually circumcised at 8 days old (the Brit Milah). And, their son is ritually circumcised under the laws of Jewish tradition. But, the event is rife with conflict.

Sylvie: So after, what really scared me was what happened for the circumcision. Where really it was a battle, as if, a battle for power. So it's 'oh, I have the power over you because we did the circumcision the way I wanted', and that's just, it's just, no, it's just that I couldn't imagine it otherwise. So, it's really not good. I think that, every time, we'll find ourselves in this thing, and it's horrible for a couple that loves each other. I think that something got a little

damaged, not broken, but, a little damaged from the day when I real-, well, on top of it, I thought he had said 'yes' for the circumcision. So, a circumcision is not just that you cut, you know, it's that you cut on the eighth day with the guy who comes to cut it on the chair… So, well for me it was a done deal. So, and suddenly he tells me 'no, no, but a circumcision is just that you cut it, and maybe in a year'… 'Woah' (Laughs)… 'Uhm, no. No.' So I just can't let go of a certain number of things.

Olivier's mother wanted the couple to wait at least one year in order to be closer to the Muslim tradition. But, Sylvie couldn't, as she says, 'let go of a certain number of things.' Sylvie says that she was under the impression that Olivier agreed to the circumcision before the birth of their son. It does appear that he agreed to have his son circumcised but not necessarily under Jewish law.

The notion of power, which Sylvie raises in the above quote, is important in order to understand what happened. Once more, it is Sylvie's religion that is given priority and it is Oliver that must bend and compromise his family and identity. In addition, a circumcision is very different from a marriage. One can get married several times and make compromises. But, in principle, only one circumcision is possible. The Brit Milah is a breaking point in the couple's story, leading to, what Olivier considers to be, a decisive rupture with his family.

With their marriage, the external world comes to play an important role in the couple's identity. But, as each person affirms, this role becomes more substantial after the birth of their son. After the birth, it is almost impossible to continue to lie to everyone and the contradictions of their couple identity become more visible. As Sylvie says:

So actually, we never had, well, we lied to everybody, and we created our own little truth of our own, where we were happy. Because. We weren't bothered by anyone either, since we are lucky that people are at a distance. So it's really easy to, to lie by phone, but, when there's a baby, well… There you go.

Consequences
As we have shown, Olivier and Sylvie's couple identity is very complex. They have never arrived at

a couple identity that coherently integrates their diverse traditions and that can be faithfully and openly shared in multiple contexts. Rather, their couple identity remains complicated and secretive. Certainly, Olivier's identity has evolved during the eight years of his relationship with Sylvie. He now considers himself Jewish. It is still an identity with wide gaps and contradictions. He is Jewish-Muslim-French-Arab from the Maghreb. But, it does represent a development in his thinking, a real change. In contrast, the identity of Sylvie has stayed more constant. It is Olivier who has converted. It is Olivier who has become more distant from his family. In a sense, it is the religion, family and tradition of Sylvie that is most central to the couple's identity.

It is also important to emphasize that in both accounts there is an enormous amount of uncertainty about the future. As Sylvie recounts:

I was really naïve to think that it would be enriching And in fact, I feel like I was a real kid of 19 years old, having married a guy just out of love and not asking myself all these questions. Of having being naïve to think that it would be ok because. It won't be ok, well, at least not, not in France So the story of mixed couples, in particular, I think that there isn't a pro-, not too many problems between the Jewish religion and the Christian religion, or Catholic. With Islam, there are some things. I don't know, more, too much, bad, which make it that, that it can't really work. I don't have the impression that it can work really. It's more an observation of failure to say that we really were a little ridiculous to think that everything would be fine in the best of all possible worlds. But I don't want to finish on a sad note! (Laughs)

Sylvie asks herself if she and Olivier will be divorced in 10 years. Olivier doesn't say the word 'divorce' but he also wonders if the couple has a future. Both question if Arabs and Jews will accept their son or if everyone will hate him.

Conclusion

The process of arriving at a shared version of the past, an enduring tradition, takes place on multiple levels of analysis. Certainly, there is a macro-level of analysis in which one can envision collective memory as the construction of cultural texts that are written and revised by political and cultural actors who possess prestige and authority and who impact the realm of ideas above and persons down below. From this perspective, collective memory is a top-down process that diffuses hegemonic visions of the past for public consumption.

However, meanings are not ethereal but embodied in persons who fashion and refashion ideas in concert with one another. A second, and legitimate, way to understand collective memory is as the construction and use of cultural texts on the micro-level of analysis. From this perspective, collective memory is nothing more than how tradition and knowledge about the past, identity and world are negotiated between persons in social interactions. Here, collective memory is bottom up. It is potentially creative and potentially infectious to others who encounter new and exciting interpretations of the past, identity and world.

The case of Olivier and Sylvie helps to clarify this second, micro-level, of collective memory. Their negotiation of a couple identity may be considered, in some respects, unsuccessful. In comparison to the other couples that we interviewed, their couple identity is incomplete and incoherent. But, it is mostly unstable. These internal contradictions persist, and even flourish, until the external world intrudes into their couple life. With the presentation of the couple to the public realm, through marriage and the birth of their son, these contradictions become uncomfortably difficult to manage. The couple identity that they would like to project, fragile and ambiguous, is not powerful enough to withstand the force.

Before their marriage and the birth of their son, the couple's internal strategy of concealment was, more or less, successful. Olivier could maintain multiple identities and maneuver between them. As Sylvie states, lying is much easier at a distance. The couple maintained a complicated form of Judaism but one that was open to the disruptions that Olivier's identity presented. Internally, this was a story that both members of the couple could endorse. A consensus on Judaism is formed through Olivier's efforts. However, other identity resources that could, potentially, be part of the main plotline (Muslim, Arab, North African, Eastern, etc.) are regulated to a peripheral position in the couple's identity. Sylvie's position appears more secure. As she notes during the interview, her sense of being Jewish is very strong and deep while Olivier's sense of being Muslim is tangential. This gives her position some rhetorical force. Thus, she reasons, her Jewish card trumps his Muslim card. And, in their life together, it does.

In retrospect, we have caught Olivier and Sylvie at a difficult moment in their relationship. The prejudice and racism of their respective communities has played a critical role in their story. But, couples also have the opportunity to protect themselves and become stronger even when the social context is less than favorably disposed to their relationship.

We wonder how their strategy of concealment has impacted their couple.

Building a shared story of the past is a process negotiated between persons that involves moves and countermoves, statements and restatements. These positions find their place in an ongoing conversation that is real and situated in social interactions. This is what collective memory is, nothing more and nothing less. This is the process of drawing together a shared heritage. If, in the end, the couple identity that Olivier and Sylvie construct is damaged, tangled and porous, one should note that it is not the only path but their construction that they have arrived at together.

REFERENCES

Benbassa, E. (2000). *Histoire des Juifs en France: De l'antiquité a nos jours* (3rd edn). Editions du Seuil.

Berger, P. & Kellner, H. (1964/1994). Marriage and the construction of reality: An exercise in the microsociology of knowledge. In G. Handel & G. G. Whitchurch (Eds.) *The Psychosocial Interior of the Family* (4th edn) (pp. 19–36). Hawthorne, NY: Aldine de Gruyter.

Bunzl, M. (2007). *Anti-Semitism and Islamophobia: Hatreds Old and New in Europe*. Chicago, IL: Prickly Paradigm Press.

Carrère, S., Buehlmann, K. T., Gottman, J. M., Coan, J. A. & Ruckstuhl, L. (2000). Predicting marital stability and divorce in newlywed couples. *Journal of Family Psychology*, 14(1): 42–58.

Chase, S. E. (2003). Learning to listen: Narrative principles in a qualitative research methods course. In R. Josselson, A. Lieblich & D. P. McAdams (Eds.) *Up Close and Personal: The Teaching and Learning of Narrative Research* (pp. 79–100). Washington, DC: American Psychological Association Press.

Chinitz, J. G. & Brown, R. A. (2001). Religious homogamy, marital conflict, and stability in same-faith and interfaith Jewish marriages. *Journal for the Scientific Study of Religion*, 40(4): 723–733.

Fetzer, J. S. & Soper, J. C. (2005). *Muslims and the State in Britain, France and Germany*. New York: Cambridge University Press.

Goffman, E. (1959). *The Presentation of Self in Everyday Life*. New York: Doubleday.

Halbwachs, M. (1952/1992). *On Collective Memory*. Translated and edited by L. A. Coser. Chicago: The University of Chicago Press.

Varro, G. (2003). *Sociologie de la mixité: De la mixité amoureuse aux mixités sociales et culturelles*. Paris: Belin.

Vygotsky, L. S. (1978). *Mind in Society: The Development of Higher Mental Processes*. Cambridge, MA: Harvard University Press.

Wertsch, J. V. (2002). *Voices of Collective Remembering*. New York: Cambridge University Press.

Zerubavel, E. (2004). *Time Maps: Collective Memory and the Social Shape of the Past*. Chicago: The University of Chicago Press.

CHAPTER 23

LISTENING VOICES: ON ACTUALIZING MEMORIES
Esther Shalev-Gerz

This chapter examines, within the auspices of the author's artistic practice and via three projects within which she operates as an artist, modalities of the voice. The notion of voicing requires becoming vocal, which consequently suggests a demand or need for the contrapuntal – being listened to. In these case studies the author considers the modes of voicing and listening which have provided her with the means to ask broader questions regarding the relationship of the artist to formations of community and society and to investigate the question of belonging from the perspective of the artist as 'nomad'.

Globalization brings together people who have very different modes of both conceiving and communicating what memory, identity and heritage mean for them. Some of these modes are not even thinkable for others. This chapter is about the deflection of the larger field of language/s as an element of identification and translation, and its interaction through voice and listening (the person's body and image). In my artistic practice, I have explored the spatialization of meaning that sometimes remains wordless.

How can art create a place that does not depend only on concepts and words, but acts as a platform that opens up new encounters and thus unlocks a new access to those questions?

In my artistic practice and experience, I have worked with and through the participation of people on and in between those subjects in order to make the human figure appear. Here I shall explore this practice by describing three of my projects: *White Out* (2002), where language is silenced, *The Place of Art* (2006), where language appears as a barrier that is traversed by *experience*, and *D'eux* (*On two*) (2009), where language is a genuine access to understandings of other cultures. Two of these projects were realized in Sweden where I am a professor in an art school. Having moved from Lithuania (where I spoke Russian, Yiddish and Lithuanian) to Israel (where I learned Hebrew, then English), I moved to Paris with my second husband who was German, and where I have been living for 25 years now. In my everyday life, a lot of languages coexist, and through them I understand and conceive the world and my work. The Swedish language seemed familiar to me, as it has some similarities with German and English. Everybody in Sweden speaks English, so it was no problem to propose my teaching in English. Without understanding the native language, I approached and interacted with this country and its people and developed my projects that are *concerned* with identity, social and personal constructions of being in the world.

White out: between listening and telling

When the Historiska Museet in Stockholm invited me to do a project, I discovered that in the Saami language (the language of Lapland's population that lives in the North of Sweden), there doesn't exist a word for *war*. I decided to learn more about Swedish history, and was intrigued by the fact that Sweden has not engaged in war for 200 years. Could this have been an inspiration for the two populations that partly share the same land, I asked myself. I engaged a Swedish researcher to find out more about this by exploring media archives and to collect quotations from different kinds of speeches. One of the things that bothered me was that the Saami were constantly presented as a minority instead of being considered as indigenous, as possessing their own culture, language etc. At the same time, I was exploring the writings by voyagers to the Nordic countries in French and English.

In the research, we located the first identifiable instances of references in both Swedish and Saami culture to specified, common topics: nature, war, love, desire, gender politics, and the role and conditions of women and children. From the research findings, I produced a text component for the project, a compilation of textual excerpts that were translated into English. Within this text, two seemingly disparate histories and cultures intersect and echo each other in a new way. The text's dialogic form embodies two peoples that have coexisted for centuries in the same place, on the same land. The text component of the project draws from numerous sources, such as historical, archival, fictional and travel literatures, as well as from popular newspapers and magazines, from both Saami and Swedish sources. I selected short quotations such as:

> Sweden is not a fatherland but a 'motherland' in terms of what she engenders and teaches. The word 'fosterland' comes from 'foster', 'foetus', and 'att fostra' means to engender and to teach. (Dominik Birmann, Suède, 1968)

> And it cannot be denied, that there is a degree of truth in what a prominent Swedish politician once said, that the culture of the Lapps, to a certain degree, stands higher than the predominant European culture, which as its fruit produces the World War. (Torkel Tomasson, 'The Cultural Movement and the Organization of the Lapp People', in Samefolkets Egen Tidning, No. 1, November 1918)

> The concept of the party wall or the boundary does not exist. (François-Régis Bastide and Guy de Faramond, Suède, Petite Planète (on the Swedish concept of legal right of access to private land), 1954)

> Men as well as women wear trousers. The sexes are not differentiated more than that women wear longer coats over their other clothes and that they have certain red decorations on their heads and belts decorated with tin. (Johan Ferdinand

> Körningh, The Story of a Missionary Trip to Lappland 1659–60)

> Swedish women put on Lappish costume to go skating. (Marc Hélys, A travers le féminisme suédois, 1906)

The texts are organized like a conversational dialogue between two voices, using both fiction and non-fiction sources, and intentionally blurring these categories or modes, by reactualizing both histories and memories. It discloses how two peoples have influenced and inspired each other. It suggests the possibility of an unending discussion, a continual discourse, an infinite circle of telling and listening.

Then I met Asa Simma, a woman of Saami origin who now lives in Stockholm, and she agreed to participate in the project. I filmed Asa in her apartment in Stockholm. The video documents her reaction to the project's text component, which I read to her in a loud voice. She decided to contribute her own experiences of simultaneously living in different cultural spaces in English – she was married to a North American Indian man and discovered her own culture while living with him in Canada.

> When I was brought up, Saami people were not respected. Our language and traditions were made fun of. So for me it doubled the disappointment I had to carry. When I was brought up, our traditional singing was not heard, our Yoiks were not heard because that was a time of oppression. Everything Saami was 'blaah'. It didn't sound like anything. It sounded like something boring and monotonous.
> My mother taught me the songs in secrecy and she told me not to tell anybody I was learning these songs, because it would put me into trouble. And then, while I was brought up the sort of Saami culture 'Renaissance' was just starting in the seventies. When I was nine years old, a Saami artist, who had meant very much for me, heard that I was singing the traditional songs. So he took me on a tour, when I was nine years old, among them to inspire the Saami people not to forget the songs. We were many children and lots of old people. We travelled together one summer.

Later we flew together to the village in Lapland where she grew up, at the frontier in the North of Sweden. I asked her to choose a place for the filming, and she decided to be filmed outside, surrounded

Photo 23.1 *White Out – Between Telling and Listening*, Installation view, Historiska Museet, Stockholm, Sweden 2002, Christer Ahlin

by trees and wind. I let her listen to her own words that I recorded in Stockholm and filmed her doing this. The outcome is an unedited, 40-minute video.

In the installation at the Museum of History in Stockholm, the two videos were presented as rear-projections facing each other, one showing Asa Simma talking on one side, and listening to herself on the other. The visitor could choose where he or she wanted to stand in the installation: either behind one of the screens and thus able to see only the one, or between the two, between Asa talking and Asa listening. The text component to which she responds is presented on one side of the installation. Facing the text panels, one can see images of the collection of the Museum itself, photographs I commissioned from the Museum's photographer. I asked him to go to the repository of the Museum (where about 23 million objects are stocked in huge hangars outside the city). I didn't have permission to go there, as I am not affiliated with the Museum, so I drew the perspectives I wanted captured in the pictures. Then I reworked the images by giving them an appearance as if they were seen through foggy glass. This project's title is *White Out*, which is the word for a situation where one loses his or her

sense of orientation in a snowstorm while flying. The quotations appeared as a simultaneous mixture of Saami–Swedish preoccupations, but to the visitor, they were presented as a homogeneous, 'equal' kind of history, that also gave a special consideration to the position as a listener of far-away voices.

The place of art

Different kinds of translation are a very central part of all my works. As an artist, I sometimes translate what I perceive into images, the shy and imperfect words I hear into what I believe to be their more precise meaning. For my project *The Place of Art*, I also translated answers into visual propositions.

I developed this artwork with the participation of 38 artists who had come from different countries but who now all live in Bergsjön, a suburb of Gothenburg. I asked the local group of artists called BOB to find artists willing to participate. I asked every participant separately the two questions: 'How would you define art? Where do you locate the place where it happens?' I deliberately left it open how to respond, and the result was a very heterogeneous, engaged catalogue of answers, a miscellany not only of answers to the questions, but also of different ways of understanding and conceiving them, of thinkable proposals and political implications. Some people defined art as a creative and social practice, others approached it in a theoretical or intellectual way, while others talked about their personal implications. Some artists situated art in an exhibition space where it could be shown, while others referred to their actual working conditions and dreamed of better situations that reflect the real circumstances they live with. Some of them did not think that art has a special place.

I think art must have a big place, a fantastic place. It's important for painters. We need space I understand in Gothenburg, I can't get the place [big apartment] I need. Expensive. An apartment with a room for me. I can't be free in my home. But in the kitchen I'm free, when I sit here with my material. My kingdom. All persons here [family], they don't want to be in the kitchen. I'm a bit free here. My art friends want to make a kitchen group. We all work in the kitchen. Here in the kitchen there are possibilities to see the nature. I think I need places with air. A dream – once to have a bigger space with windows, glass, light. Meet others. Artists need light… A dream. Bigger dreams in Sweden.

(Karim Ali Sadoon)

If I had a place, a small place it would be really important for me. Where I would disturb no one. Where I could create. In the flat or outside as well. For a person to have a small room for art at home or close to the flat. It could be shared and we could all have lockers for our things; chairs, table and paints.

(Dobi)

When you have an exhibition it is often in nice galleries. But it should be in public spaces. In the streets, so that everybody can see it.

(Julia Hedsved)

I once had the dream of this very big wave coming and there's a bit of foam sparkling and there we are, mankind. It is amazing we had all this evolution and yet we are sitting there all the small water drops, and where are we going now? To me, really, there is the place of art.

(Obilot Zeuschel)

Those statements were made in Swedish. While some of the respondents speak the language perfectly, others do have difficulties in expressing themselves in this foreign tongue. We translated all the answers into English, so I could understand and work with them. For the question: 'How would you define art?' I chose sentences that worked as declarations, and rewrote them in a slogan-like style.

Photo 23.2 *The Place of Art*, Video installation view, Gothenburg Konsthall, Sweden, 2007, Dorota Lukianska

Photo 23.3 *The Place of Art*, Video installation view, Gothenburg Konsthall, Sweden, 2007, Courtesy Esther Shalev-Gerz

A silent video showed the artists in their personal homes and the participants are filmed while listening to their own answers. The atmosphere is intimate, solitary: they are shown all by themselves with their thoughts. Into these very still images, I integrated the sentences of their answers I chose by inserting them visually in the environment: they come out of the walls, appear in the shadows or in the furniture, are readable through the windows. In between the scenes, I edited a statement of an artist presented in the catalogue of *Magiciens de la terre*, an exhibition that took place in Paris in 1989, and which was the first major exhibition that showed equally artists from everywhere in the world through a post-colonial approach.

I want to make the invisible people visible.
Nasrin Pakkho (Bergsjön)

If we were able to define art, we wouldn't need artists any more.

Jiechang Yang (China)

Art is in every person. Everybody has the right to art.

Fatima Svensson (Bergsjön)

Art is less interesting than life but it helps to understand it.

John Baldessari

We can live without creation but we can't create without living.

Katarzyna Kasia Michnik (Bergsjön)

Everybody owns the song that affects him.

Luis Naranio (Bergsjön)

This part of the exhibition was projected on one of the walls of the Bergsjön Centrum, the shopping-centre that is the only meeting point in the suburb. The other part of the exhibition took place in Gothenburg's Konsthall, 5 kilometres away in the middle of the city. This displacement from the institutional art space to another place that reflected a social reality and everyday life, created another kind of translation, a dialectical confrontation that triggered new linkages between people, places and their different languages and engaged the spectator to connect to them through his passage in an active way. In the Konsthall, the exhibition consisted of four video screens. Every visitor got radio headphones that allowed movement through the installation in order to listen to the voices of the artists. Each headphone transmitted one group of the statements of the artists responding to the question about possible placements of art. On the video screens, one could follow my personal imagination of what they say: each video projection showed 3-D generated visual propositions for those imaginary spaces and places that are in a continual flux of transformation, remaining possibilities and not realities.

The extension into two venues of display for *The Place of Art* deflects institutional authority in the definition of what is included in the official art context, allowing instead the linking of different spatial constructions and cultural domains, as well as offering a platform for a continuous investigation. By being confronted only with a voice or only with the body of the participants, the visitor also reflects the questions that appear from another aspect when seen through those multicultural perspectives: the space of listening and of looking is challenged. A very important part of the exhibition was the collaboration with and participation of very different people and institutions. For a part of it I involved local culture workers and art institutions, as well as housing companies and municipal departments in the organization and in the financing. A monitoring board was thus formed. The participants in the board have different backgrounds, experiences and expectations for their involvement. But they all share the responsibilities for the work and for a sustainable development, which actually, to my surprise, continued after the end of the project and led to the process of construction of a real cultural centre in Bergsjön.

D'eux (On two)

My latest project stresses another kind of dialogue and deals with translation in several ways. The starting point of this artwork was the idea of revisiting my former works and opening up new accesses to them by a dialogic actualization for my exhibition in the *Jeu de Paume*, Paris, in February–June 2010. In this exhibition, I included ten of my former projects in Paris, the city where I have lived for the past 25 years. I first reviewed these previous projects and extracted the subjects that seemed central to me. Then I invited a 25-year-old Lebanese philosopher, Rola Younes, to participate in the project.

Photo 23.4 *The Place of Art*, **Video installation view, Gothenburg Konsthall, Sweden, 2007, Courtesy Esther Shalev-Gerz**

I met her recently in a particular way: she came up to me because she knew that I spoke Yiddish. This is a language that reminds me my childhood and the older people that were around at the time. When I listen to it, it sounds very familiar to me, but in an instinctive, unconscious way. Rola says:

> I like very much diasporic languages, like Yiddish for instance. Yiddish is not the official language of any country, not even in Israel. In Israel, Arabic is an official language, but not Yiddish. I was told that it was recognized as a minority language in Sweden…

Rola has engaged passionately in learning this 'language without land' since she came to Paris

seven years ago. She has appropriated its structure and Jewish culture in a fascinating way. In addition to Yiddish, she also speaks Hebrew and Persian, and of course the three languages she grew up with in Lebanon: Arabic, French and English. Being in Europe allows her to distance herself from the country she left. Our meeting was only possible because we both quit our homeland to live in France, even though the countries we left are neighbours and share a lot of cultural goods (such as food, habits, etc.). When we talk, we often switch languages in mid-sentence, going from French to Hebrew to English to Yiddish.

For *On two*, I asked her to answer my questions, she did by invoking her own life and experiences. She talks about the way she explores her own being through the study of different languages in a both sensitive and intellectual mode. For her, languages are doors to the Other, to possible understandings. The other person who intervenes in the installation is the French philosopher Jacques Rancière. He is filmed reading a passage from his book, *The Emancipated Spectator*, in which he describes how his thinking changed due to a reading of letters between two workers at the end of the nineteenth century. This imaginary encounter was an important moment in his thinking that led him to 'reformulate the established relations between seeing, doing and talking'. In the same passage, he comments on the function of contemporary art. For me it was very important to include a commentary on art in my work and thus to create an auto-reflexive dialogue through different levels. As Jacques Rancière puts it in his book *The Emancipated Spectator*, 'an emancipated community is in fact a community of storytellers and translators'. He also tells us that emancipation is 'the blurring of the opposition between they who look and they who act, they who are individuals and they who are members of a collective body'.

The two are filmed separately in front of green screens, which allowed me to insert different backgrounds behind them. The two landscapes I used as backgrounds come from two very different islands (*L'Île Seguin* in the west of Paris and an island in the west coast of Canada), both of which are undergoing a process of destruction and reconstruction. Here, the unstable moment of transformation constitutes a non-linear visual device. *L'Ile Séguin* has a long history: on the one hand, as a site of industrial production and, on the other, as an

Photo 23.5 *D'eux* (On two), Video projection detail, Jeu de Paume, Paris, France, 2010, Courtesy Esther Shalev-Gerz

Photo 23.6 *D'eux* (On two), Video projection detail, Jeu de Paume, Paris, France, 2010, Courtesy Esther Shalev-Gerz

artist's place. Now it is a dim, brown field under construction. The other background shows the virgin wild forest of the island in Canada. Both of them, like all islands, are limited territories that have always fired the imagination and that are conducive to heterogeneous potentialities. Sometimes I simply left the screen green instead of inserting the image of another reality. There is no obvious connection between the four protagonists of this work – the two individuals and the two islands – but each one evokes a particular displacement of boundaries so that the assemblage can suddenly be reoriented by opening out to the idea of something elsewhere.

On two presents a country inhabited by two people I met in Paris, but who do not know each other, and two landscapes that are neither in the same time nor the same space. The work is constructed around a back-and-forth movement, like a swing, in a rhythm reminiscent of the abrupt changes in a slide show. The resulting gaps encourage spectators to actively construct their own links. The two individuals thus dialogue in an imaginary space, without talking to each other.

Coming from the walls, one can hear songs in different languages (Hebrew, Yiddish, Arabic, Persian, French, English) sung by Rola. This was another important point for me: the sensory experience of listening to the lyrics of a song creates a very intimate access to a language. In the installation, it also reflects Rola's personal way of floating inside other words and of transmitting her personal awareness of how languages affect being together in different ways. The installation is about presenting forms of agency brought into play by two people in order to renew their relationship to the world.

Conclusion

In this writing I have identified the complexities of perceiving language as a universal. As an artistic practitioner, to whom discourses regarding voicing and listening are significant, I must also discover, on a project-by-project basis, how these problematics may be examined, represented and be capable of being traversed into an art historic context that reveals how the problematics of language may problematize cultural relativism and defy identitarianism through pluralistic modes of translation. In my consideration of each case study I have identified specific representations of place but, significantly, I have consistently revealed that each project may also be considered as a catalyst of encounters. The encounters catalyzed in my works are responsive to the possibilities of meaningful dialogues that represent the potential, not of the universal, but of difference. I have demonstrated in this writing, and the projects discussed, that heritages and linguistic heritages as forms of identity may be considered as significant in how their mutability may becomes transformative. In these three case studies of my artworks I suggest that the notion of translation should focus on the carefully considered endeavour of translatability – not only in terms of voicing and listening, but in the aesthetic possibilities through which the lived experience of one enters the consciousness of another. In conclusion, this writing suggests that through acts of dialogue, punctuated by the effort towards translatability, we may share in the voicing and reception of difference and that in its passing to the framework of art translation may become transformative.

COMMENTARIES

CHAPTER 24

INTANGIBLES: CULTURE, HERITAGE AND IDENTITY
Henrietta L. Moore

A rapid perusal of the usual sources provides definitions of 'intangible' as 'incapable of being perceived by the sense of touch'; 'incorporeal or immaterial'; 'vague, elusive, fleeting'; 'not definite to the mind'. Perhaps more arresting is the idea that intangibility applies to assets, as in the good will of a business. Amusingly, if you search for the term 'intangible' on Dictionnary.com, it offers you the option to 'see images of intangible'. A quick click on that link gives you images relating to intangible cultural heritage in Estonia, Fiji and Vietnam, among other places. A series of further clicks on randomly chosen images from among the same set inevitably results in the response 'website could not be found'! The intangible appears and disappears, but what remains is a series of questions worth exploring about the links between intangibility, culture, and assets.

UNESCO's own position underscores the significance of these links: '...research undertaken by UNESCO on the functions and values of cultural expressions and practices have opened the door to new approaches to ... the cultural heritage of humanity. This living heritage, known as intangible, provides each bearer of such expressions a sense of identity and continuity, insofar as he or she takes ownership of them and constantly recreates them.'[1] Culture is here a resource, an asset, ownership of which guarantees the validity of identity claims (see Isar's chapter in this volume). UNESCO's *Universal Declaration on Cultural Diversity* of 2001 identified its object, cultural diversity, as 'the common heritage of humanity' (Article 1), hence aimed fundamentally at heritage preservation, and this is congruent with a widely-held view that the forces of globalisation and modernity are eroding cultural traditions. In fact, as a number of contributors to this volume point out, cultural diversity is both eroded and recreated by processes of globalisation, and information technologies are playing a significant role in preserving and disseminating cultural heritage and traditions. Official and popular pronouncements on cultural diversity draw consistent analogies with biological diversity, and figure both as the 'heritage of human kind', as foundational 'to our common humanity'. Cultural diversity is constructed as a public good and as that understanding enters international agreements and conventions, and passes into national forms of governance, an easy elision is made between human rights and cultural rights, between the right to culture and the right to distinctive identities and life ways.

The recognition of culture as a right provides the basis for making further claims, especially those over resources. The issue is not so much the commodification of culture as the underlying assumption that everyone's culture has a value and the concomitant demand that such values must be recognised (Moore, 2007). The move to understanding culture as both an index of diversity and as a resource means that culture is consistently refigured as value, and it is a short step from there to its construction as an intangible asset. This volatile mix of rights and proprietary assets has the inevitable result of tying cultural claims ever more closely to conflict, violence, exclusion and even war (see Isar et al., this volume). More worrying still, the impossibility of fully defining or settling cultural values and proprietary rights to them means that appeals to traditionalisms can only ever end in perpetually emerging ethnicities and nationalisms. The logical conclusion of the argument that people should have their group identities recognised, and enjoy their own sub-cultural/sub-national expressions and life ways is that lines must be drawn, and identities ever more firmly based on exclusions, rather than similarities. This is why even such potentially recuperative moves as the demand that heritage sites should promote human rights (see Ševčenko, this volume) will always be haunted not only by the memories of past violence, but also by the potential for future eruptions. Distressingly, the increasing encompassment of cultural heritage within the wider humanitarian goals of contemporary global civil society only serves to underscore this point further (see Isar, this volume). As international bodies, national states and civil society actors and communities seek to leverage cultural assets, conflicts over values and resource allocation necessarily multiply. In this process, cultural distinctiveness/cultural diversity is accorded a primary value, and one that attracts capital and investment, as well as becoming complicit with national and international regimes of governance and regulation, as Winter (this volume) demonstrates. Far from encouraging homogenisation, contemporary forms of capitalism are engaged in long-run circuits of value production involving cultural diversity, constantly seeking an exotic or different other. Modernity requires not only the consumption of cultural value and tradition, but its constant production and recreation. This is what Winter means when he says that 'the coming together of the traditional and the modern contributes to the ordering of today's global capital relations'.

However, while we might agree that the traditional and the modern are synchronous rather than chronologically ordered we need to go further and recognise that it is not enough to characterise them as mutually constitutive, we need to explore historical shifts in that process of mutual constitution in order to be able to push the analysis further. In addition, we need to recognise that our analysis of culture and of the impact of globalisation on culture is constrained and/or restricted by the reigning notion of culture as difference, and as a form of asset over which one can have proprietary rights. As a first step in such a process, it might be helpful to turn our attention away from heritage and tradition towards the equally problematic notion of modernity. What modernity is, when it happened and who was involved is part of a very long-running debate in the academy, and one of immense importance right across the social sciences and the humanities. But, the very scale of the debate and the detail it has involved mean that as an analytic term 'modernity', as Fred Cooper suggests, has very little purchase. From his perspective, it has been characterised as everything from an historical epoch to a state of mind, and has become little more than a cover word for 'everything that has happened in the last five hundred years' (Cooper, 2005: 127).

Anthropology has characteristically tried to deal with this problem of definition by making the term plural, and the discipline's embrace of the notion of multiple modernities does have the advantage of avoiding the hubris of retelling everyone else's history in terms of that of Europe, as well as recognising that other cultures/societies/nations have forward-moving plans for social transformation that are distinct, but possessed of varying degrees of interconnection with and differentiation from the European project of modernity. The juggernaut of modernisation as an inevitable process has rightly been criticised for promulgating a theory of change that leaves everyone not defined as the 'west' in a permanent condition of catch-up, but the recognition of alternatives or plural modernities has not done away with the binary dynamics inherent in the term itself because the modern as something self-evidently new must always be haunted by its constitutive outside, the past, tradition (Cooper, 2005: 115–116).

If the ordinary and accepted definition of modernity is the new, then modernity, like the poor, will always be with us. In 20 years, what is modern will be new, but it will not necessarily be what we think of as modern now. Modernity as a package that involves industrialisation, commercialisation, individualism, secularism, rationalism and capitalism is a poor fit for the histories of Africa and Asia, but also as it happens for Europe and America too (Cooper, 2005: 121). One of the difficulties here is with the definition of the modern, the way it is so frequently portrayed as a break with the past, as an epoch defined by a here and now that is the opposite of there and them, a form of space-time distanciation which supports a distinction between a past where cultures are authentic and a present where they are under threat. A situation which is further confused by having to deal with the multiple meanings of modernity itself: modernity as progress, advancement in science and the arts, and modernity as social breakdown, erosion of values and the destruction of meaningful life. These antinomies are not very helpful, but they are immensely powerful and they keep appearing and reappearing as pre-theoretical assumptions even as we try to expunge them from our analyses.

Cultural entanglements: Japan and the West

The larger failure, as Cooper suggests, is the difficulty we encounter in trying to frame the social changes we seek to analyse in terms of modernity versus tradition, or 'our modernity' versus 'their modernity'. One way to explore what Cooper means is to look at the case of Japan. Let's begin with a well-known representation of encounter. The quintessential oaf, Pinkerton hoves into view waving the American flag, acquires a temporary wife, gets her pregnant and leaves. He returns to carry away his son to the bright future of America, and Butterfly, realising that the boy's future will be better secured, takes the honourable route of suicide. Puccini's *Madame Butterfly* was first performed in 1904, and dramatises for us the illusions of fantasy, desire and projection that exist between cultures, as well as the realities of power differentials and miscomprehension. But, this is only a very small part of the story to be told about the relations between Japan and the West in that extraordinary 50-year period between 1860 and 1910.

For example, in 1876, Monet exhibited a picture of his wife dressed in a Kimono. The context for this extraordinary image was an immense craze for all things Japanese that was to have a significant impact on the way modern life was depicted and experienced in Europe and America. As Susan Napier has shown, Monet, and many of his contemporaries, were fans of the great woodblock print artist Hokusai and his *manga* (sketchbooks). The

depiction in Japanese woodblock prints of nature and human life, and especially their use of colour, light and motion, as well as their exoticism and eroticism, had a major impact on the impressionists, encouraging them to move away from the gloomy conventions of the salon and the melodrama of the Romantics to depict the natural world and late nineteenth-century urban social life in all its movement and intensity. Their innovations in perspective, brushstrokes, lines and light were inspired by Japanese art, and their subject matter influenced by the enormous range of human, animal, and natural life depicted in the *manga*s (Napier, 2007: 21–22).

Japanese art was not the only influence on the impressionists, and not everyone liked it, but many of the major artists, intellectuals, entrepreneurs and journalists of the time had large collections of Japanese works, and their love of the art extended to other aspects of the culture, including poetry, gardens, Zen Buddhism and *sake*. By the 1870s, 'women paraded on the streets of Paris in kimono-esque designs'. French and English women entertained at home in 'tea-gowns'. The Japanese tea ceremony spawned tea shops throughout Europe, and Japanese gardens influenced garden design. Japanese departments opened in the newly created department stores, like Liberty in London. Operas, plays and novels flourished. The middle classes collected fans, parasols and dolls, and the wealthy bought woodblock prints, religious art, screens and swords (Napier, 2007: 30). A gallery of Japanese art opened in Paris in 1880, and the fans of Japan, *les Japonisants*, visited the Japanese village in Knightsbridge, met for Japanese dinner parties in Paris, and took part in full costume in *tableaux vivants* (Napier, 2007: 30–35).

Susan Napier argues that part of the turn to Japanese art at this period, with its exquisite colours and delicacy, and to Japanese religion and other cultural forms, was inspired by what the Europeans perceived to be a turn to nature, away from the ugliness of industrial production and technological invention. The nineteenth- and early twentieth-century fans of Japan did not necessarily visit the country, and most saw no need to do so. This moment of artistic and cultural innovation was partly enabled through the West's imaginative definition and redefinition of itself in relation to the East, where ways of thinking, feeling and producing were animated both by difference and through projective identification. The technologies of Japan – like mass-produced woodblock prints – were used to offer new possibilities for depicting and experiencing the dynamism and urbanism of Euro-America, while simultaneously representing those aspects of the natural, human and, mythological worlds that had been erased by the rise of mechanisation and modern consumption (Napier, 2007: 38–48). But, this was not an encounter between the traditional and the modern, but between two trajectories of modernity and their concomitant forms of projective identification, representation and distributions of power.

Simon Harrison has recently advanced a provocative theory that cultural differences are in many instances simply a form of denied resemblance. He argues that resemblance and imitation are ontologically primary, and differences are actually secondary effects produced by the regulation, suppression or denial of similarities (Harrison, 2006). His larger thesis is that cultures have a common visual language for expressing differences – clothing, flags, etc. – and that because certain kinds of identity symbols are vulnerable to appropriation and loss, imitation is a threat to identity. In this thesis, violence, when it occurs, is the result of the fact that it is the perceived similarities of the other that are threatening, and not their differences. Harrison's theory would not explain the West's love affair with Japan (one that was reciprocated) in the late nineteenth century, but it is refreshing because it calls attention to processes and mechanisms of mimesis, interdependence and desire. There are many ways in which cultural differences are seductive – tourism, travel, the collecting of artefacts, the reading of ancient texts and the learning of other languages are only some of the obvious examples. These seductions are very ancient – they are not in any way new or merely a product of modernity – but the processes of mimesis and identification that underpin them are perhaps not well captured by current theories in the humanities and social sciences which speak of hybridities, metissage, and the encroachment of modernity on tradition (Moore, 2011). To explore this point further, it might be helpful to what is happening now in the long love affair between Japan and the West.

We see a strange kind of parallel between the end of the nineteenth century and the beginning of the twenty-first because there is once again a great craze for Japan. Japanese technologies and cultural products are together creating and developing spaces, mechanisms and opportunities for consumers/

individuals to enhance their cultural capacities to explore complex worlds. In the last ten years, the global value of sales of Japanese animation and character goods has exceeded US$80 billion. Many of the most successful children's series worldwide, such as Pokemon (Tobin, 2004), and their associated products come from Japanese production houses, as does almost all of the animated content for the most popular computer games and films. This has not just been as a result of concerted marketing by Japanese media companies and their global partners, but has been fuelled to a very large extent by *anime* and *manga* fans who have used newly available technologies – most of them made in Japan – to build and expand their communities based on desire for these materials, and who have simultaneously developed, through their active engagement and participation, new possibilities for the production and consumption of *anime* and *manga* (Jenkins, 2006: 160–161).

There is currently a great debate, inside and outside the academy, as to whether Japanese animation is actually Japanese in content and character. Critics point out that the characters do not look Japanese – they are, at the very least, 'white' by default – and that most of the viewers who enjoy *anime* and *manga* have no sense that it is Japanese. Koichi Iwabuchi suggests that the popularity of these products is probably dependent both on a pleasure to be found in Japanese culture itself and in things Japanese, and on the fact they are racially, ethnically and culturally disembedded to a certain extent (Iwabuchi, 2002). Anne Allison has argued that the attractiveness of Japanese products is that they engage the consumer in a world that is both imaginary (imaginary places, creatures and adventures) and real (activities, exchanges, purchases, social relations, quests). The imaginary aspects involve and provoke strong emotional attachments, and invoke a Japanese 'tendency to see the world as animated by a variety of beings, both worldly and unworldly, that are complex, (interchangeable), and not graspable by so-called rational (or visible) means' (Allison, 2006: 12). Susan Napier emphasises that the traditional arts of Japan, like Hokusai's woodblock prints and *manga*, but also theatre and dance, have always produced wonderful images of other worldly characters, including ghosts, ogres, goblins and demons, that are at once grotesque and uncannily beautiful (Napier, 2007: 160). Allison maintains that while this animist sensibility draws on aspects of Shintoism and Buddhism, it must not be understood as timeless component of a stable and homogeneous Japanese culture, but as an evolving aesthetic, investing objects – including consumer items – with human, non-human and spiritual life in a way that re-enchants the lived world (Allison, 2006: 12–13). What appeals is the way in which familiar forms break down and recombine using human, machine and organic parts, and can thus be reassembled into new hybridities and possibilities. As Allison says, the attraction is a world of polymorphous perversity or more prosaically a set of tensions and possibilities between the fantastic and the real, the foreign and the familiar, the strange and the everyday. It is a fantasy world, but one that people also want to inhabit and to be at home in (Allison, 2006: 275–277)!

What, if anything, does this have to do with Japan or with Japanese culture in the ordinarily understood sense of the term? Susan Napier points out that many of the American fans of *anime* and *manga* she worked with had a strong interest in Japanese culture, were knowledgeable about many aspects of Japanese culture and history, and spoke the language (Napier, 2007: chapters 6 and 7). Anne Allison argues that 'Japan' signifies something important, but the signifier is shifting; it is a marker of fantasy and difference, albeit one that is anchored in an existing place (Allison, 2006: 275). Many *anime* not only reference, but pay homage to diverse sources, such as American television cop shows of the 1970s, European Glamrock fashions of the 1980s and French New Wave cinema from the 1960s (Pointon, 1997: 44, cited in Napier 2005 [2001]: 22). The young artists who produce these works think of themselves as Japanese, but do not necessarily see contemporary Japanese culture as exclusively Japanese in origin or future orientation. Napier suggests that while the world of *anime* is Japanese, it is not necessarily coincident with the space of Japanese culture. Rather than necessarily reinforcing Japanese cultural identity, *anime* narratives problematise the nature of Japanese identity. *Anime* reflects Japan to the West, but also gives Japanese viewers 'a distinctive vision of non-Japanese worlds' (Napier 2005 [2001]: 24-25). Contemporary *anime* is best understood, I suggest, not as an example of cultural hybridity – a mixing of cultures – but of a rather more powerful process of 'cross-pollination' (Napier 2005 [2001]: 22) or imaginative entanglement.

Technology is what makes this world possible because it gives access to information, to immediate visual images, to others with whom one has shared interests, to worlds that are distant but absolutely proximate. As Henry Jenkins suggests, more and more individuals are enjoying participating in online knowledge cultures and discovering what it is like to expand one's knowledge, cultural capacities, social connections, and emotional experiences by linking in to the combined expertise of technological, mediated (and periodically physically co-present) grassroots communities. Popular culture is no longer just about reading, viewing or accessing, but it involves doing, exploring, comparing, creating, archiving, commenting, and much more. These activities are the most human of cultural capacities. They are not in any way new, but they are freshly imagined and enhanced by contemporary information technologies. Culture has always involved the management of symbols, the play of signs, and the delineation of values, meanings, and lifeways at the intersection of world and signs. From one perspective, culture is about the selection or constraint of meaning, the arresting of difference, the presentation of a certain perspective on the world, the enactment of a series of embodied practices. The struggle for representation takes different forms and has different purposes across cultures and through historical time. Classical realism, for example, is not something that art forms in other cultures have sought to achieve. Aesthetics have no universal standing. However, the engagement of human technologies with representation, and the effort to bring forms closer to movement and action in life, to resonate and interfere with the work of affect, is one explanation for the productivity of cross-cultural exchange, for why mixing, mimesis and identification enhance cultural capacities and are productive of new cultural forms and new cultural ontologies.

What is significant is how engaged fans are in creating worlds of meaning. Participation in a wide range of cross-media platforms is now becoming ubiquitous for those who are connected, and an increasing part of everyday life, work and leisure. It is important to be precise here because while there are many millions of people in the world who are not on the internet, not close to a cinema showing international films, and have never seen a computer game in their lives, it is also the case that because the speed and quality of information transfer is not proportional to its costs, and because multinational media companies work to exploit global markets, the spread and reach of these technologies is impressive and significant. However, their reach is not just a function of their distributed, interconnected, global nature – for which the internet is iconic – but of the fact that the character and nature of these technologies means that they are able to create and develop spaces and opportunities for emergent forms of sociality, and for groups and individuals to develop and enhance their cultural knowledge(s). Modern information technologies enhance these capacities and opportunities because the sharing, reusing and co-production of digital assets – knowledge, graphics, animation – combined with the ability of the online world to create strong emotional attachments and affective states through its repetitions and ramifications across space and time, allows for constant crossover between virtual worlds and the world of the everyday (Moore, 2011).

Places of identity

A focus on new forms of sociality and enhanced cultural capacities potentially frames debates on intangibility and culture understood as a resource or a set of proprietary assets in new ways. The heritage and culture of many communities around the globe is intangible in a double sense as such things as oral performance, language, rituals and dance are transformed into digital assets to be recorded, archived and stored. These 'stores' of knowledge are not like the museums or archives of the past, as a number of contributors to this volume have pointed put, but are open to sharing, supplementation and modification by communities of individuals who may be widely spread in space and time.

Timothy Webmoor has discussed how a site like Teotihuacan in Mexico is the locus for a variety of engagements at a multitude of scales. The spiritually oriented rituals that take place on the site may be performed by Mexico City Aztec dance troops, Toltec shamans from Los Angeles and Gaia worshippers from Europe (2008: 183–184). The understandings of the site and its context with regard to local communities have to be placed alongside the understandings and interests of anthropologists, archaeologists, cultural heritage managers and corporations. The very fact that intangible cultural heritage is a living heritage, not something of the past, but of the present, forces attention, as Weerasinghe (this volume) demonstrates, to the importance of rituals and performance in imparting meaning both to sacred sites and to the devotes who make them part of their lifeways. It is not just that professionals no longer control – if they ever properly did – the interpretations that can be inscribed in and ascribed to rituals and sites, but that the co-production of new meanings is ongoing, dynamic and collective. The notion of hybridities or of the impact of modernity on tradition is a limp concept/set of tools with which to analyse the material and emotional politics of intersection and co-production evident in such examples.

Webmoor's discussion is informative because he indicates not only the shift in meaning transmission and interpretation that such a 'democratisation of participation signals' (see also Jenkins, 2007), but he emphasises how the shift to Web 2.0 provides a platform that operates via non-hierarchical networks of individuals and technologies that determine both the form and the content of what is online. The open source software that powers Web 2.0 works through the right to distribute rather than the right to exclude, and as such it puts 'cultural activity back at the center of what drives high-tech development' (Webmoor, 2008: 190). Digital information – text, image, sound – combined with the convergence of media platforms means that media of all kinds are mutable, and can be combined and recombined, customised and retooled (Webmoor, 2008: 191–192). Information technologies and new media are enhancing very ancient cultural capacities. Culture as the interpretation of meanings and symbols, the use of language, and participation in constructed life worlds is the oldest form of hypertext.

Clearly in such situations, there are many discussions to be had about the preservation and management of digital data, and about how local, national and international politics and distributions of power and resource are involved in access to data, and their interpretation and distribution. Sharing and co-production are not processes that are devoid of conflict and contestation, and sharing is not always something that proceeds from the basis of equality. For every instance of cultural mimesis, co-production and sharing around the global there are as many, if not more, exclusionary, divisive, violent moves and boundary settings. However, situations such as Webmoor describes for Teotihuacan do raise important questions about how we might envisage the relationship between living heritage and emplacement, and they in their turn invite us to rethink the reigning view of culture as something over which we can have proprietary rights, or at least to reconfigure the oscillation between culture as difference and culture as shared/co-produced.

These two aspects of culture are clearly, and properly, in a relation of dynamic tension, and they are co-dependent. However, as Lucina Jiménez López (this volume) suggests, any focus on heritage and identity, despite the well-recognised importance of the notion of living heritage, has a tendency to concentrate attention on history and the past. This inevitably creates a kind of disconnect between heritage and contemporary artistic creativity. The connections between the visual and the performing arts and technology, new media and audiences, raises questions about cultural change and technological innovation, and how they are to be connected to ideas about cultural diversity, emplacement and living heritage. Contemporary art is part of a global market, and one which has become increasingly dependent on large international exhibitions in which cultural diversity is not always celebrated, but is certainly referenced. Bill Anthes has discussed the complex role of native artists in this configuration of global markets and nationalist expression, and wondered whether 'local identities and sovereignty movements' can be commensurate with the logic of global nomadism (Anthes, 2009: 109–110). In other words, what happens to the identity of authentic cultural emplacement when artists produce work that seeks to transcend identity politics? We might broaden Anthes concerns to indigenous artists more broadly and ask why they should have to be the guardians of cultural diversity? Indigenous artists are particularly located in these debates because earlier incarnations of the global market and indeed of activist and sovereign movements linked the aesthetic authority of such artists to their emplacement within a specific culture or landscape.

Much new work by indigenous artists moves away from the binary opposition of tradition/local versus the global towards an emphasis on travelling, interconnection, and displacement (Mercer, 2008). The desire to place indigenous artists within the 'local' has been debated and criticised since the 1980s, but its renewed relevance comes from the way that culture as 'asset' is tied to identities in contemporary contexts. Many artists, such as Yinka Shonibare – with his juxtapositions of African textiles, Victorian drawing-rooms and late nineteenth century oils – use their work to explore the stabilities and uncertainties of cultures and identities, and the larger geo-political contexts in which they are situated. These sustained critiques of the relations between culture and identity take old debates in novel directions, but not necessarily in ways that are well captured by current languages of analysis in the social sciences and cultural studies. Terms such as hybridity, translocality and transnationalism presuppose a moment or time when cultures could be securely placed and linked to identities, when difference reigned, when cultural expressions were grounded in single or bounded communities.

Jiménez López has discussed how problematic the assumed links between emplacement, culture and identity are with regard to popular Latin American musical forms, but she still retains the terminology of hybrid/mixed/translocal identities to try to capture the complexity of new musical expressions and engagements. However, ultimately, these terminologies, and the pre-theoretical assumptions that underpin them, are inappropriate, I suggest, for processes of cultural creativity and expression that are not concerned with the authenticity or origins of the forms they employ, but with contemporary processes of identity construction – Latin American, Japanese, Kenyan – that depend on cultural diversity and cultural change, on borrowing, mimesis, identification and projection. Culture has many uses and many ways in which it can be deployed, many definitions and interpretations that are both congruent with and resistant to forms of power and exclusion. In the contemporary world, we see these various means and methods at work across the globe, as the chapters in this volume demonstrate, but we should keep in mind that there is no single way in which culture is tied to or presupposes identities, and that this relationship is itself undergoing rapid change.

Note

1   portal.unesco.org/culture/en/ev.php-URL_ID=34325&URL_DO=DO_TOPIC&URL_SECTION=201.html.

REFERENCES

Allison, A. (2006) *Millennial Monsters: Japanese Toys and the Global Imagination*. Berkeley: University of California Press.

Anthes, B. (2009) 'Contemporary Native artists and international biennial culture', *Visual Anthropology Review*, 25(2): 109–127.

Cooper, F. (2005) *Colonialism in Question: Theory, Knowledge, History*. Berkeley: University of California Press.

Harrison, S. (2006) *Fracturing Resemblances: Identity and Mimetic Conflict in Melanesia and the West*. New York: Berghahn Books.

Iwabuchi, K. (2002) *Recentering Globalization: Popular Culture and Japanese Transnationalism*. Durham, NC: Duke University Press.

Jenkins, H. (2006) *Convergence Culture: Where Old and New Media Collide*. New York: New York University Press

Kramer, L. (2002) *Musical Meaning: Towards a Critical History*. Berkeley: University of California Press.

Mercer, K. (2008) *Exiles, Diasporas, and Strangers*. Cambridge, MA: MIT Press.

Moore, H.L. (2007) 'The problem of culture', in D. Held and H.L. Moore (eds), *Cultural Politics in a Global Age*. Oxford: One World.

—— (2011) *Still Life: Some Thoughts on Hopes, Desires and Satisfactions*. Cambridge: Polity Press.

Napier, S. (2005) [2001] *Anime: From Akira to Howl's Moving Castle*. New York: Palgrave Macmillan.

——(2007) *From Impressionism to Anime: Japan as Fantasy and Fan Cult in the Mind of the West*. New York: Palgrave Macmillan.

Pointon, S. (1997) 'Transcultural orgasm as apocalypse: Urotsukidoji – The Legend of the Overfiend', *Wide Angle*, 19(3): 41–63.

Tobin, J. (ed.) (2004) *Pikachu's Global Adventure: The Rise and Fall of Pokemon*. Durham, NC: Duke University Press.

Webmoor, T. (2008) 'From silicon valley to the valley of Teotihuacan: the "Yahoo!s" of new media and digital heritage', *Visual Anthropology Review*, 24(2): 183–200.

CHAPTER 25

FROM THE TOWER OF BABEL TO THE IVORY TOWER
David Lowenthal

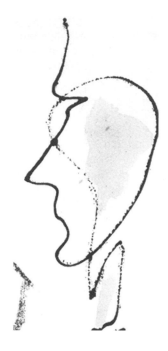

All the earth had the same language and the same words. Each said to his neighbors, 'let us build a city and make a name for ourselves.' YHWH said, 'Look, it is one people, and one language for all of them. Let us go down and confuse their speech there, so that each will not understand the language of his neighbor.'

– Babel Recension[1]

Globalization is an enduring utopian ideal. But it is in immemorial conflict with heritage and identity. Hence global hopes are perennially dashed. We long to return to the God-given Edenic unity of the earliest days, when 'the whole earth was of one language, and of one tongue.' What shattered this unity after the Flood was, in essence, a hunger for heritage, the desire to forge an identity that would immortalize the memory of human accomplishments. The Tower of Babel elevated human pride to heaven itself, 'to make a name for ourselves, otherwise we shall be scattered abroad upon the face of the whole earth' (Genesis 11.1, 4), incommunicado and forgotten.

Babylon's memorialist counterparts today are the potentates and plutocrats whose names and deeds are inscribed on countless public edifices and sites of remembrance. But like the impious Babylonians who vied with divine creation, moderns' quest for immortality founders against their mere transient renown. 'The iniquity of oblivion,' warned Sir Thomas Browne in *Urn-Burial* (1658), 'deals with the memory of men without distinction to merit of perpetuity.' Far from being eternal, fame is closely calibrated, as donor Leon Levy learned when promised that New York's Metropolitan Museum of Art would preserve his name on the new Greek and Roman Court 'in perpetuity.' 'How long is that?' he asked director Philippe de Montebello. 'For you, fifty years.' Levy's $20 million upped the eternal ante to seventy-five.[2]

'Pride goeth before destruction, and an haughty spirit before a fall' (Proverbs 16.18). Just as an angry God scattered men abroad and left them incommunicable, so time effaces the most perdurable memorial identities. Shelley's *Ozymandias* limned the sorry remnants of Rameses' imperial hubris:

Two vast and trunkless legs of stone
Stand in the desert. Near them, on the sand,
Half sunk, a shattered visage lies, whose frown,
And wrinkled lip, and sneer of cold command
Tell that the sculptor well those passions read
Which yet survive, stamped on these lifeless things,
The hand that mocked them and the heart that fed.
And on the pedestal these words appear:
'My name is Ozymandias, King of Kings:
Look on my works, ye mighty, and despair!'
Nothing beside remains. Round the decay
Of that colossal wreck, boundless and bare,
The lone and level sands stretch far away.

The ruins of the Tower of Babel similarly attested the dispersal that sundered tribe from tribe, spatially and linguistically. Mankind was condemned to a babbling confusion that bred lasting internecine misunderstanding and strife. Each tongue's speakers spawned distinct identities out of remembered legends. And these separate identities then hardened and reified in factional and divisive heritages.

The Genesis story reflects certain prehistoric realities. Periodic Paleolithic and Neolithic migratory waves out of Africa to the ends of the habitable globe sundered any original Ur-linguistic unity. Communication among far-flung hunter-gatherer bands diverged more and more over time. Reinforced by physical segregation, the confusion of tongues gave rise to manifold incommensurate and often hostile local, tribal, and national cultures. To ensure cohesion and solidarity, each group crafted its own exceptionalist narrative of origins, history, and destiny – a heritage, like their language, necessarily opaque to outsiders. When men on the move came into contact, ruthless competition for land, for goods, and for women exacerbated differences between 'us' and 'them.' Insider identity, defined by opposition to alien others, was certified by collective tribal and national memories, first through oral tradition and then through the written record.

In short, heritage, bolstered by memory and validating identity, became humanity's defense against our inherent 'great blooming, buzzing confusion.'[3] Heritage provided insular havens of like-minded certitude in stormy seas of outlandish ways. We confront one another armoured in identities whose likenesses we ignore or disown and whose differences we distort or invent to stress our own superior worth. Most heritage is about personal or communal self-interest. Things are valued as *my* heritage or *our* heritage. Even a shameful past may earn self-admiration for facing up to it. In celebrating symbols of their histories, societies in fact worship themselves. Exclusive to us, *our* past is unlike anyone else's. Its uniqueness vaunts our superiority. Heritage *distinguishes* us from others; it gets passed on only to descendants, to our own flesh and blood; newcomers, outsiders, foreigners erode or debase it. Each group's heritage is, by definition, incomparable. The past we prize is domestic.

Lauding our own legacies and excluding or discrediting those of others, we commit ourselves to endemic rivalry and conflict. Some assert their heritage's moral or military, mental or material prowess; others claim exclusive rights to traits and emblems crucial to their identity. Both types of claim mirror stereotypes that arrogate virtue to us and deny it to others: *we* are civilized and steadfast;

they are barbarian and fanatical, or primitive and blind. Obsessive emphasis on exclusive, unique, and fiercely acquisitive identities suffuses heritage debate with tension and conflict. Boasts of precedence and pre-eminence deny and clash with others'; so do rival claims to the same valued heritage icons.

Pious modern affirmations of global unities based on mutual respect for 'the heritage of all mankind' founder on the shoals of this or that ethnic, religious, linguistic, or national claim of privileged entitlement. The 'self-congratulatory swamp of collective memory' embracing heritage and identity, of which I wrote fifteen years ago, now also inundates the terrain of contrition – the accusatory lineaments of museums of conscience and monumental commemorative apologia. But it is still a fearsome quagmire. Whether recalled with glory or with grief, the past is increasingly occluded in a miasma of moral self-righteousness.[4]

Heritage remains stubbornly parochial in essence. Beyond a few starry-eyed dreamers, 'one world' is a remote pipe-dream. Invented no less than inherited tradition is jealously particularist. The globalization of professional heritage in UNESCO and other international protocols, the worldwide deployment of similar techniques of recording, depicting, conserving and restoring the past, aggravate rather than alleviate animus among claimants of art and antiquities, natural resources and cultural icons. No all-embracing global narrative even begins to match the evocative power of tribal myths and national legends. For humanity's few thousands to feel and act in concert at the time of Babylon was hard enough. For their ten million-fold far-flung descendants today it seems inconceivable.

In heritage's recurrent discords, lip-service to collaboration incites new conflicts. The drumbeat of dispute pervades the chapters in this book. Hence injunctions forbidding heritage destruction and despoliation in time of war are regularly flouted by adversaries who aim thereby to break the enemy's spirit. Hence art and antiquities appreciation (and an avid global market) reinforce legal insistence on the exclusive sanctity of national origins, spurring rather than stemming tomb-robbing. Hence Euromed heritage 'partnership' programs intended to benefit the poorer south end up in Brussels-mandated northern hands. Hence consensual non-partisan histories are jettisoned for self-justifying divisive nationalist and tribalist tracts. Hence the scanty yield of meaningful contrition in countless reparations and truth and reconciliation commissions.

Apt to be overlooked even by devoted preservationists is heritage's overriding commitment to future generations. Utterly indebted to our inherited past, we are bound above all to ensure its transmission to the future. We cannot know what our heirs may value. But we owe them at least an equitable share of the accumulated legacies, both material and intangible, of our ancestors' creative contrivances and, now most urgently, of our ancestral environments.

The environmental heritage is alike local *and* global. Every local and national community owes its identity and collective well-being to familiarity with place, attachments to inhabited and domesticated landscapes. Even the most restlessly mobile of peoples, even those widely detached by diaspora, retain memories that spell 'home' and are powerfully conducive to cohesion. And even the most insular and self-reliant peoples are increasingly dependent on the global heritage of land, water, and air, of minerals and soils and forests, flora and fauna, of an intermeshed terrestrial ecology. 'No man is an island', said John Donne four centuries ago; today no island is an island, all locales bound together in a web of mutual support. Globalization is implacably inescapable in the ecological constraints of our island earth. 'Global interdependence makes heritage universal', I wrote fifteen years ago. 'The legacy of nature – ecosystems and gene pools, fresh water and fossil fuels – is common to all, and requires the care of all. Exploitative technology diminishes and noxious residues despoil a natural legacy whose stewardship requires worldwide action.' The need to husband that imperilled legacy is much more urgent today.

The necessity of treating environmental heritage as global, of stewarding it for the sake of all humanity if not of all life, has become apparent only in the last century and a half. Until quite recently few took that need seriously, because the long-term consequences of gutting resources were beyond temporal comprehension and concerns. Palaeolithic hunter-gatherer heritage hardwired ancestral brains to ignore futures more than two generations ahead.[5] Civilized humanity found it difficult to sustain societies even a few centuries ahead. No millennial scheme lasts a tenth of its intent.

But the two-thirds of a century since the Second World War have radically transformed environmental circumstances and awareness. The bomb and nuclear fall-out unleashed awareness of risks more horrendous and more imminent than any before. And the ecological consequences of runaway population growth, resource depletion, environmental degradation, and species and habitat loss became ominously clear. Just as science lengthens memory backward into cosmic antiquity, so technology's innovations force us to focus not just on generational but geological future timescales. Long-term precautionary thinking is already apparent in the millennial Svalbard seed bank and in the requirement, by a federal appeals court, that the US Environmental Protection Agency guard against nuclear waste leakage at Yucca Mountain *300,000 years ahead* (subsequently lengthened to a million years).[6] Future generations, should any survive, may bless us for such foresight.

Imminent climate change, notably global warming and sea-level rise, now threatens both local and global environmental heritages within a few centuries or even decades. The speed of predictable change may leave us estranged in unrecognizably transformed homelands, forcibly exiled migrants to sub-polar habitats, hungry competitors for diminished and dwindling global resources. Along with this global-warming deprivation goes much of the world's architectural heritage. The great majority of our urban fabric will be abandoned to rising seas or, with portable legacies, degraded by salinization, wind-driven rain, ice-to-water and salt-to-brine transitions, mould, and a host of other corrosive agents.

The distressing effects of conflicting heritage claims detailed in this book pale into insignificance beside imperative needs to reconceive identity on a global level. We must learn to dwell less on memories of unjust pasts than on preparations for salvageable futures. Stewards of tradition must give up narrow and exclusive sectarianism. Increasingly, our only affordable heritage is the one we share with all.

To convert national, tribal, and religious sectarians into world citizens will be no easy task. Precious identity is at stake in mystiques of uniqueness, in emphases on difference. But the confusion of tongues, our lamentable legacy from the Tower of Babel, should no longer be an impediment. We now know that all languages and all systems of writing and reading derive from universal features common to all at birth. Neuronal plasticity can enable near-universal intercommunicability. Growing up Chinese or Finnish, Italian or English alters brain functions concerned with memory and privileges different patterns of thinking, but no language need be impenetrable even to adult outsiders. Information science is rapidly reducing the complexity and cost of translation, which Jacques Derrida in 1985 termed both 'necessary and impossible.'[7] Google Translate already offers instant conversion among 52 languages, from Afrikaans and Albanian to Welsh and Yiddish.

Synchronic automatic translation systems (SATS) promise almost instantaneously available voice-to-voice, voice-to-text, and text-to-voice messaging. Foreign language environments will then become monolingual for all users. This will vastly increase mutual comprehension, stimulating migration, tourism, and manifold intercultural contacts. On balance, it should reduce social tension, political friction, and armed conflict, all far less prevalent among peoples able to communicate easily and accurately with one another.

Far from reducing linguistic and cultural diversity, however, SATS is likely to help preserve it. The ease of machine translation will make it unnecessary for most people to learn foreign languages at all. Continuing to speak, read, and write in their own tongues will sustain their distinctive cultural legacies. Translation will never completely bridge, let alone efface, different mental worlds. But it may lessen divergences of norms and values and help disarm lethal differences of ideology. Paradoxically, 'the power of babble' may succeed the tower of Babel.[8]

A truly cosmopolitan heritage should replace Babel with a later Old Testament edifice, Solomon's ivory tower, despite its current negative image. 'To say of a man that he lives in an ivory tower has come to be one of the most insulting remarks that can be passed without leading to an action for slander or libel', noted the art historian Erwin Panofsky of 'deep-seated antipathy' to egg-head aloofness and refinement. 'What makes the practical man so indignant is not only that the [scholar] shuts himself away in a tower; [but] that his tower is of so costly, so aristocratic, and at the same time so brittle a material as ivory. ... It combines the stigma of egocentric self-isolation (on account of the tower) with that of snobbery (on account of the ivory) and dreamy inefficiency (on account of both).'[9]

Those who disparage ivory cloisters as unworldly forget their protective function. The *Song of Songs* likens the ivory neck of the lady beloved to 'the tower of David, builded for an armoury, whereon there hang a thousand ... shields of mighty men.' The mighty men use the shields in battle. It is up to the tower watchman to sound the alarm. Similarly, sharp-eyed Lynceus, the Greek hero in Goethe's *Faust* confined to a tower and thus prevented from hunting, fighting, and dying with his comrades in combat, is able from above to espy danger below. It is his high calling to warn of the perils ahead.

The ivory tower exemplifies trust in heritage stewardship. It is a metaphor for curbing the reckless present with the elevated lessons of the past.

Notes

1 Hermann Gunkel, *Genesis* [1910], transl. Mark E. Biddle (Macon, GA: Mercer University Press, 1997).
2 Leon Levy with Eugene Linden, *The Mind of Wall Street* (New York: Public Affairs, 2002), 190.
3 William James, *The Principles of Psychology* [1890], 2 vols. (New York: Cosimo Inc., 2007), 1: 488.
4 David Lowenthal, 'On Arraigning Ancestors: A Critique of Historical Contrition', *North Carolina Law Review*, 87 (2009): 90–166.
5 Edward O. Wilson, *The Future of Life* (New York: Knopf, 2002), 40–41.
6 Matthew M. Wald, 'Court Deals Blow to Effort to Bury Nuclear Waste in Nevada', *New York Times*, 8 July 2004; Neil J. Nusbaum, 'Radiation Risk to Future Generations from Long-Lived Radioactive Waste', *Journal of Community Health*, 31 (2006): 363–367.
7 Jacques Derrida, 'Des tours de Babel' [1985], in *A Derrida Reader* (New York: Columbia University Press, 1991), 249.
8 Sam Lehman-Wilzig, 'The Tower of Babel vs the Power of Babble: Future Political, Economic and Cultural Consequences of Synchronous, Automated Translation Systems (SATS)', *New Media & Society*, 2 (2000): 467–494.
9 Erwin Panofsky, 'In Defense of the Ivory Tower' [1953], expanded in *Harvard Alumni Magazine*, 6 July 1957; reprint *Centennial Review of Arts & Science*, 1 (1957): 111–122.

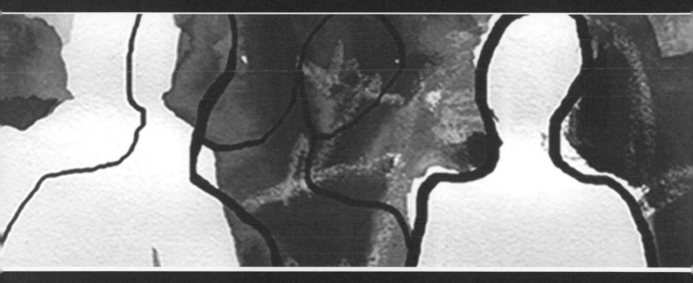

Indicator Suites for Heritage, Memory, Identity

Michael Hoelscher

INTRODUCTION

The indicator suites, introduced in detail by Anheier (2007), are an integral part of each volume of the Cultures and Globalization Series. Their purpose is to offer an empirical portrait of key dimensions of the relationships between cultural change and globalization, while also presenting empirical evidence about the specific topic of the volume in question, in the present case heritage, memory, and identity.

OVERVIEW OF THE INDICATOR SUITES IN THIS VOLUME

This volume contains 20 indicator suites. Although many of them span the three topics of heritage, memory, and identity, each of them can be broadly assigned to one of the three. Thus, seven are in the field of heritage, seven in memory, and six in identity. The titles of the suites are shown in Table 1.

Each indicator suite is accompanied by a digest that summarizes the results of the indicators presented, provides additional background information, and highlights main issues surrounding the topic. Without being able to give a comprehensive overview of all findings, the next paragraphs will introduce the indicator suites in more detail.

Table 1: Overview of the Indicator Suites

HERITAGE	MEMORY	IDENTITY
World Heritage Sites	Memorialization	Geographical Identities
Legal + Political Frameworks	Contested Memories	Internet Identities
Museums	Global Collective Memories	Multiple Citizenship
Intangible Heritage	Places	Popular Culture
Tourism	Media	Identities in the Economy
Sustainability	Migration and Diaspora	Religion
International Organizations + Heritage	Education	

For the purpose of assigning indicator suites to the main topics, the guiding principle was that heritage is something relatively independent of the people, but nevertheless shared by them; memory is what people make of this heritage in their minds; and identity is what results from the interplay of people's memories and their everyday lives.[1]

HERITAGE

One of the main global initiatives on heritage is certainly UNESCO's initiative on **World Heritage Sites** to assemble natural and cultural places and spaces around the world. Because they are deemed worthy of being remembered by the whole of humankind, they are one of the most visible expressions of a truly global heritage. In most instances, countries and sites benefit from this status, either through increased tourism or through direct access to additional resources, especially for the poorer countries.

However, the resources of international and intergovernmental organizations are often limited. An important mechanism through which they nevertheless can have an impact is the development of **legal and political frameworks** for protecting heritage and harmonizing procedures on a more or less global scale. Such initiatives seem to be especially successful in the cultural field.

Another way of securing heritage is its safekeeping in **museums** (e.g., Kirshenblatt-Gimblett, 1998). However, museums not only keep heritage safe, but they (re-)interpret and (re-)present it to their audiences, thereby shaping our heritage and memories. Questions of how to present their collections, posed for example by the new museology, are as important as the content of the collections. Globalization processes can be found on both levels.

Especially difficult to preserve is **intangible heritage**. Although in recent years the importance of intangible forms of heritage such as languages, customs, and indigenous knowledge has been increasingly recognized, adequate modes of preservation are still being discussed. The popular strategy of storage via digitalization is quite different from keeping traditions alive! Intangible heritage also is a field in which the general question of benefits and costs of global distribution becomes highly visible and relevant: Does worldwide distribution save local heritage from oblivion, or do massification and decontextualization accelerate its disappearance?

The same ambivalence echoes in the field of **tourism**. Tourism is an increasingly important and global phenomenon, and this refers not only to the amount of actual movement between places: Even though we cannot see the whole world, "the touristic gaze and imaginary shape and mediate our knowledge of and desires about the rest of the planet" (Franklin & Crang, 2001: 10). But only to the extent that tourists are open to integrate experiences of foreign cultures into their own worldview may tourism contribute to increased creativity and understanding across cultures. Otherwise there is a danger of homogenization and dominance, with tourists destroying local cultures as well as natural sites.

This leads one to questions of **sustainability**. This indicator suite comprises quite different aspects. Sustainability is mainly used to denote a healthy handling of nature, but the concept can equally be applied to the healthy handling of our cultural environment. One of the classic books about globalization, Ulrich Beck's *Risk Society* (1986), claimed that globalization was coming about, inter alia, because of the perception of global risks, like pollution, transgressing national borders. Turning this argument around, one could also claim that globalization nowadays is involved in producing such risks itself. But assessing sustainability is tricky: For instance, many traditions or customs stay alive and influential by permanently adapting to changing circumstances, as, for example, Ong (2002) and Goody (1986) have shown for oral traditions. Many other "traditions" with a purported long history are just more or less new inventions (Hobsbawm, 1988). The Scottish kilt is but one example.

Important actors in heritage politics are different kinds of **civil society** organizations. They are especially influential when it comes to non-national, that is, local or transnational, topics of heritage. One important example is indigenous interest groups that claim respect for their traditional knowledge and customs. Another example are globally acting foundations, often having more resources at their disposal than many developing countries. Therefore, civil society challenges national claims regarding heritage and its definition on both the global and sub-national or regional levels. This opens up still unsolved questions of legitimacy.

MEMORY

Memory is one of the buzzwords in current social sciences and humanities (for a critical encounter, see Berliner, 2005). While the heritage indicator suites already contain some data on what psychologists call semantic and procedural memory stores (Boyer, 2009: 4), the memory suites add information on episodic memories as well. However, although data on individual memories are presented, the suites focus on their collective aspect. How are individual memories shaped by globalization in a collective way? How do societies reassure themselves about their shared past? And is a global "imagined community" (Anderson, 1991) evolving, maybe based on something like "world events" (Nacke, Unkelbach & Werron, 2008)? These are the questions the suites seek to address.

There is a long-standing debate about whether collective memories are shaped functionally on purpose to contribute to groups' identity or some kind of dominant ideology (Abercrombie & Turner, 1978). One way of gaining influence on people's memories are different means of **memorializing** certain events and people. Monuments, street names, and even the figures on coins, selected consciously by a certain group of people, contribute to collective remembrance. An interesting stream of research tries to pin down global collective memories by asking people to name, from their perspectives, the most important figures and events in world history (e.g., Liu et al., 2005). While there definitely is a national bias (people tend to name events that took place in their country or affected its particular history disproportionately often), a remarkable share of people in quite different countries, such as China, Turkey or Spain, select only from a limited set of events and figures, thereby exhibiting a great deal of global concordance in memories.

However, memories are not only shared, but often **contested** (e.g., Tunbridge & Ashworth, 1996). It seems even "that the 'contested past' matters precisely because it is contested. Shared narratives of the historical past are all the better when they are such that others, and especially identified others, could not possibly endorse them" (Boyer, 2009: 13). To be contested, they have to be shared, however, and looking into events and figures that are considered to have global importance cross-nationally, the results are strikingly similar. Although some events from the individual's own national and regional past are often added, there seem to be some commonly shared parts of a global history.

Memories are often connected to certain **places**, as is well documented by Pierre Nora (1984-1992). What happens to these places and the associated memories when they are occupied by ever more people from diverse backgrounds? Especially cities are often such places where creolization (Hannerz, 1992) leads to increased creativity (the topic of the previous volume of the C&G series; cities will be the focus of the next volume). This touches on the question of the relationship between creativity and heritage/memory. Does, for example, cultural policy put too much emphasis on heritage preservation and too little on contemporary creativity and innovation, as a worldwide sample of experts suggests (Anheier & Hoelscher, 2010)?

Cities are also crystal nuclei for **migration and diaspora** processes. Experiences of migration and the search for an identity that combines old and new cultural contexts, that is, acculturation, are affecting ever more people.[2] Diasporas often combine the provision of local support to immigrants with the establishment of networks keeping in touch with their former home regions, an important part of "transnationalism" (Vertovec, 2010). This breaks up old notions of nationally bound heritage, memory, and identity.

Media play an important role in these processes. They are an important means to store our memories and transmit them to others. However, in modern societies media are more than storage devices, as many of our experiences are media-based. Think, for example, of September 11: We all "experienced" the attack on the World Trade Center in New York, but for most of us only filtered through television and other media. In this respect, new media developments will have an important impact on our memories and identities.

Education is the last indicator suite placed under the memory rubric, although it relates also significantly to heritage and identity. As Gellner (1983) showed, nation-building often was the result of the need to create, besides other things, an educational system and administration. He claimed that the educational system's task was to provide the people with a common set of skills and a sense of a shared context and identity so that the economy could prosper. One important characteristic of educational systems is that they could be influenced by governments through curricula and the selection of appropriate teachers. However, even education is increasingly influenced by globalization processes (for higher education, see e.g., Hoelscher, forthcoming). Although the rise in the number of internationally mobile students has not kept pace with the growth of students overall, an increasing absolute number of students have international experiences. Additionally, curricula are internationalized, putting national history in a global context, and a rising number of learned foreign languages allows those who speak them to access foreign cultures more easily. All this contributes to a less ethnocentric view of the world.

IDENTITY

The relationship between identity and globalization is not easy to grasp (e.g., Castells, 2004). There are different approaches one may use to tackle this question. In sociology, one of the most popular perspectives on identity is that of national identity. However, national identity is not the only, and maybe not the main, level of a **geographically bound identity**. There is a growing interest in regional and also transnational identities as well (e.g., Mühler & Opp, 2006). Globalization in this respect could mean a shift from local or national identification processes to transnational units of identification, sometimes called "cosmopolitanism" (Norris & Inglehart, 2009),[3] but it could also mean a decrease in the geographical boundedness of identity in general, called "deterritorialization" by García Canclini (1995). This "means that the significance of the geographical location of a culture – not only the physical, environmental and climatic location, but all the self-definitions, ethnic boundaries and delimiting practices that have accrued around this – is eroding" (Tomlinson, 2007: 360). In a survey of more than 200 cultural experts, 75 per cent of them expect this to happen, as shown in Table 2 (Anheier & Hoelscher, 2010). With respect to their own identity they show a rather mixed picture, which could be called "patchwork identities" (Keupp et al., 1999).

Table 2: Geographical Identities of Experts

I SEE MYSELF AS ...	AGREE (STRONGLY)	MOST IMPORTANT IDENTIFICATION
... a world citizen	92.1%	8.9%
... a citizen of the continent I live in	74.9%	3 %
... a citizen of my country	82.8%	3.9%
... a member of my local community	77.3%	3.9%
... an autonomous individual	81.8%	12.8%
No single most important identification		67.5%

Beyond physical places, there is a new global "location" where identities may be formed: cyberspace. Online social networks, such as Facebook, MySpace, or YouTube, gain ever more popularity, despite their risks (e.g., Gross, Acquisti & Heinz, 2005). The **Internet** may help to stabilize identities by allowing individuals to keep in contact with like-minded people from all over the world. On the other hand, though, many people feel threatened by the overwhelming amount of most heterogeneous information that is presented to them through the Internet. As Internet identities cannot easily be aligned with their real-world "creator," they also allow for play with different identity aspects, most visible maybe in the avatars in different sorts of virtual worlds. Again, there is a negative side to this, as identity fraud is a big problem on the Internet (e.g., FIDIS Project; Javelin Strategy & Research, 2009).

However, the Internet as a medium is primarily a technology, which has to be filled with content. There is a whole industry concerned with producing such content by offering identification opportunities. **Popular culture** is not only part of an important economic branch, the "cultural economy" (Anheier & Isar, 2008), but is also important for many peoples' identities: Fans identify with their fan-objects, and many subculture scenes are grouped around certain musical styles. Compared cross-nationally, it becomes apparent that large parts of popular culture are nowadays globally distributed and consumed.

National identity, it was argued above, is still very important. But what happens when people hold **multiple citizenships** due to migration and so forth (Pitkänen & Kalekin-Fishman, 2007)? While the topic of migration and diaspora was dealt with already under the Heritage section, this indicator suite touches mainly on more or less formal aspects, presenting data on legislation allowing for dual citizenship or on citizenship tests, as well as on attitudes toward naturalization.

Economy and religion are the topics of the last two indicator suites. One of the dominant assumptions in globalization theory is that the **economic** sphere "is the crucial element, the sine qua non of global connectivity" (Tomlinson, 2007: 353). With regard to identity, there are at least two aspects: How are transnational identities, for example for expatriates, shaped through work as one of the most important spheres of life? And how does a globalized economy with transnational brands and flows of goods and services influence our identities? (Non-) consumption, as an important part of the economy, is based in certain lifestyles as the expression of certain identities. This refers back to the popular culture theme, as there are always many cross-references possible between different suites.

For many people, their **religious** affiliation is much more important than their nationality (see datapoints 4a and 4b in the suite on "Geographical Identities"), questioning secularization theory (Jagodzinski & Dobbelaere, 1995). Religions are also used to construct Huntington's transnational civilizations, which are supposed to clash in the future (Huntington, 1997). For some, international terrorism by religious fundamentalists (and the fight against it) is already a sign of this. However, research also shows that, at least in the industrialized world, there is a shift from church-based traditional religious beliefs to much more personalized and hybrid engagement with questions about the meaning of life and transcendentality (Norris & Inglehart, 2004). As a result, for example, pilgrimages are often not only seen as a religious duty any more, but are part of broader cultural experiences.

Many other datapoints and approaches to the topics of heritage, memory, and identity can be imagined, some of which are mentioned in the accompanying digests. However, the indicator suites described here comprise a wide variety of data addressing the most important economic, political, and social aspects on the individual, the national, and the transnational level. We feel confident that these data give a rich overview and introduction to the empirical treatment of questions of these three fluid, though highly important topics, thereby providing a good starting point for further research in the field.

OUTLOOK

Heritage and memory are important bases for our identities. However, current trends, such as the increase in travel (tourism, migration), or developments in the technological realm, such as Twitter or the Internet with its blogs and social networking sites,[4] put heritage and memory in a globalizing context. A set of more than 200 cultural experts from all over the world predict the emergence of a hybrid world culture, however, in the form of a multi-polarity of competing centers of creativity and innovation (Anheier & Hoelscher, 2010).[5] For some people, this opens up new possibilities for identity construction. Others just feel scared and are anxious with regard to their traditional identities. This ambiguity can be found in all the topics addressed. Globalization can promote, but also put pressure on, traditional heritage, memories, and identities. In this context it is an open, though pressing question which heritage and memories should be preserved and protected against pressures from globalization. Resources play a crucial role here, but they cannot be the normative guideline for this decision.

However, the relationship between globalization and culture is not unidirectional. Heritage, memory, and identity are not mere passive entities that are subjected to globalization processes. They are themselves active processes, shaped intentionally or unconsciously by the people, influencing globalization in positive or negative manners.

More generally, one important lesson learned throughout this book, and also from the previous volume on creativity and innovation (Anheier & Isar, 2010), is that people are dependent on heritage, memory, and identity, but that these three are much less stable than they sometimes appear. The dynamic of culture is one of its most important characteristics, and, while globalization probably has increased the pace of cultural change, this dynamic has probably been one of culture's most stable features over time. A thorough empirical description of this dynamic and its consequences in global perspective is still missing, but the Cultures and Globalization Series contributes to this undertaking.

REFERENCES

— Abercrombie, N., & Turner, B. S. (1978). The dominant ideology thesis. *British Journal of Sociology*, *29*(2), 149-170.

— Anderson, B. (1991). *Imagined communities: Reflections on the origin and spread of nationalism.* London: Verso.

— Anheier, H. K. (2007). Introducing "cultural indicator" suites. In H. K. Anheier & Y. R. Isar (Eds.), *Conflicts and tensions.* London: Sage.

— Anheier, H. K., & Isar, R. (Eds.). (2010). *Cultural expression, creativity and innovation.* London: Sage.

— Anheier, H. K., & Hoelscher, M. (2010). Creativity, innovation, globalization: What international experts think. In H. K. Anheier & R. Y. Isar (Eds.), *Cultural expression, creativity and innovation* (pp. 421-433). London: Sage.

— Anheier, H. K., & Isar, Y. R. (Eds.). (2008). *The cultural economy.* London: Sage.

— Beck, U. (1986). *Risikogesellschaft. Auf dem Weg in eine andere Moderne*. Frankfurt am Main: Suhrkamp.

— Berliner, D. (2005). Social thought & commentary: The abuses of memory: Reflections on the memory boom in anthropology. *Anthropological Quarterly, 78*(1), 197-211.

— Berry, J. W., Phinney, J. S., Sam, D. L., & Vedder, P. (Eds.). (2006). *Immigrant youth in cultural transition: Acculturation, identity, and adaptation across national contexts*. London: Erlbaum.

— Boyer, P. (2009). What are memories for? Functions of recall in cognition and culture. In P. Boyer & J. V. Wertsch (Eds.), *Memory in mind and culture* (pp. 3-28). Cambridge, England: Cambridge University Press.

— Brecht, B. (1982[1932/33]). Der Rundfunk als Kommunikationsapparat. In B. Brecht, *Gesammelte Werke* [in 20 volumes], Vol. 18 (pp. 127-134). Frankfurt a. M.: Suhrkamp.

— Castells, M. (2004). *The power of identity* (2nd ed.). Maiden, England: Blackwell.

— Eliot, T. S. (1948). Notes towards a definition of culture. London: Faber & Faber.

—*FIDIS Project: The Future of IDentity in the Information Society (Home)*. Retrieved May 5, 2010, from http://www.fidis.net/

— Franklin, A., & Crang, M. (2001). The trouble with tourism and travel theory? *Tourist Studies, 1* (1), 5-22.

— García Canclini, N. (1995). *Hybrid cultures: Strategies for entering and leaving modernity*. Minneapolis: University of Minnesota Press.

— Gellner, E. (1983). *Nations and nationalism*. Ithaca, NY: Cornell University Press.

— Goody, J. (1986). *The logic of writing and the organisation of society*. Cambridge, England: Cambridge Unversity Press.

— Graham, B., & Howard, P. (Eds.). (2008). *The ashgate research companion to heritage and identity*. Aldershot and Burlington, England: Ashgate.

— Gross, R., Acquisti, A., & Heinz, H. J. I. (2005). *Information revelation and privacy in online social networks*. Paper presented at the 2005 ACM workshop on Privacy in the Electronic Society. Retrieved March 25, 2010, from http://portal.acm.org/citation.cfm?id=1102199.1102214#

— Hannerz, U. (1992). *Cultural complexity*. New York and Chichester, England: Columbia University Press.

— Hobsbawm, E. J., & Ranger, T. (Eds.). (1988). *The invention of tradition* (Repr. ed.). Cambridge: Cambridge University Press.

— Hoelscher, M. (forthcoming). Universities and higher learning. In H. K. Anheier & M. Juergensmeyer (Eds.), *Encyclopedia of Global Studies*. London: Sage.

— Huntington, S. P. (1996). *The Clash of Civilizations and the Remaking of World Order*. New York: Simon & Schuster.

— Jagodzinski, W., & Dobbelaere, K. (1995). Secularization and church religiosity. In J. W. v. Deth & E. Scarbrough (Eds.), *The impact of values* (pp. 76-119). Oxford, England: Oxford University Press.

— Javelin Strategy & Research. (2009). *2009 Identity Fraud Survey Report: Consumer version*. Pleasanton , CA: Author.

— Keupp, H., Kraus, W., et al. (1999). *Identitätskonstruktionen. Das Patchwork der Identität in der Spätmoderne*. Reinbek, Germany: Rowohlt.

— Kirshenblatt-Gimblett, B. (1998). *Destination culture: tourism, museums, and heritage*. Berkeley: University of California Press.

— Liu, J. H., Goldstein-Hawes, R., Hilton, D., Huang, L.-L., Gastardo-Conaco, C., Dresler-Hawke, E., et al. (2005). Social Representations of Events and People in World History Across 12 Cultures. *Journal of Cross-Cultural Psychology*, 36(2), 171-191.

— Mühler, K., & Opp, K.-D. (2006). *Region - Nation - Europa. Die Dynamik regionaler und überregionaler Identifikation*. Wiesbaden: VS Verlag.

— Nacke, S., Unkelbach, R., & Werron, T. (Eds.). (2008). *Weltereignisse. Theoretische und empirische Perspektiven*. Wiesbaden: VS Verlag.

— Nora, P. (Ed.). (1984-1992). *Les Lieux de Mémoire*. Paris: Gallimard.

— Norris, P., & Inglehart, R. (2004). *Sacred and Secular: Religion and Politics Worldwide*. Cambridge, England: Cambridge University Press.

— Norris, P., & Inglehart, R. (2009). *Cosmopolitan communications: Cultural diversity in a globalized world*. Cambridge, England: Cambridge University Press.

— Ong, W. J. (2002). *Orality and literacy. The technologizing of the word* (2nd ed.). New York: Routledge.

— Pichler, F. (2009). "Down-to-earth" cosmopolitanism. Subjective and objective measurements of cosmopolitanism in survey research. *Current Sociology, 57*(5), 704-732.

— Pitkänen, P., & Kalekin-Fishman, D. (Eds.). (2007). *Multiple state membership and citizenship in the era of transnational migration*. Rotterdam and Taipei: Sense.

— Roudometof, V. (2005). Transnationalism, cosmopolitanism and glocalization. *Current Sociology, 53*(1), 113-135.

— Smith, L. (Ed.). (2006-2007). *Cultural heritage*. London: Routledge.

— Tomlinson, J. (2007). Cultural globalization. In G. Ritzer (Ed.), *The Blackwell companion to globalization* (pp. 352-366). Oxford, England: Blackwell.

— Tunbridge, J. E., & Ashworth, G.J. (1996). *Dissonant heritage: The management of the past as a resource in conflict.* Chichester: John Wiley.

— Vertovec, S. (2010). *Transnationalism* (Repr. ed.). London: Routledge.

NOTES

[1] This is much too easy, as there exist interrelations between all three terms. For example, heritage is "chosen" on the grounds of one's identity. The relationship between heritage, memory, and identity is laid out in more detail in the introduction to this volume (see chapter 1). See also the very informative book edited by Graham and Howard (2008) as well as the book series by Smith (2006-2007).

[2] An important contribution on how to measure acculturation is Berry et al. (2006).

[3] See for a theoretical debate on the term Roudometof (2005), for an empirical one Pichler (2009).

[4] At least some people are hopeful that this points in the direction of a fullfilment of the old call, formulated already by Bertold Brecht in 1932: "The radio has to be transformed from an apparatus of distribution into an apparatus of communication" (Brecht, 1989). However, when thinking in progressive terms, it becomes apparent, as Brecht also already observed, that it is not merely a question of technology, but mainly of content that opens up emancipatory potential.

[5] This very much reflects T. S. Eliot's ambivalence, when he wrote already in 1948: "A world culture which was simply a uniform culture would be no culture at all. (...) But on the other hand, we cannot resign the idea of a world-culture altogether. (...) We can only conceive it as the logical term of relations between cultures. (...) We must aspire to a common world culture, which will yet not diminish the particularity of the constituent parts." (Eliot, 1948: 62 f.).

Heritage

WORLD HERITAGE SITES

LEGAL + POLITICAL FRAMEWORKS

MUSEUMS

INTANGIBLE HERITAGE

TOURISM

SUSTAINABILITY

INTERNATIONAL ORGANIZATIONS + HERITAGE

World Heritage Sites

1A Number of Cultural Properties Inscribed By Region (1978 – 2008)

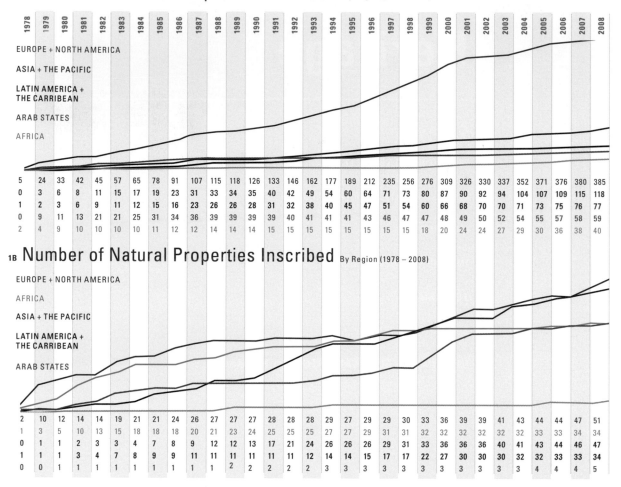

EUROPE + NORTH AMERICA
ASIA + THE PACIFIC
LATIN AMERICA + THE CARRIBEAN
ARAB STATES
AFRICA

	1978	1979	1980	1981	1982	1983	1984	1985	1986	1987	1988	1989	1990	1991	1992	1993	1994	1995	1996	1997	1998	1999	2000	2001	2002	2003	2004	2005	2006	2007	2008
	5	24	33	42	45	57	65	78	91	107	115	118	126	133	146	162	177	189	212	235	256	276	309	326	330	337	352	371	376	380	385
	0	3	6	8	11	15	17	19	23	31	33	34	35	40	42	49	54	60	64	71	73	80	87	90	92	94	104	107	109	115	118
	1	2	3	6	9	11	12	15	16	23	26	26	28	31	32	38	40	45	47	51	54	60	66	68	70	70	71	73	75	76	77
	0	9	11	13	21	21	25	31	34	36	39	39	39	39	40	41	41	41	43	46	47	47	48	49	50	52	54	55	57	58	59
	2	4	9	10	10	10	10	11	12	12	14	14	14	15	15	15	15	15	15	15	18	20	24	24	27	29	30	36	38	40	

1B Number of Natural Properties Inscribed By Region (1978 – 2008)

EUROPE + NORTH AMERICA
AFRICA
ASIA + THE PACIFIC
LATIN AMERICA + THE CARRIBEAN
ARAB STATES

	1978	1979	1980	1981	1982	1983	1984	1985	1986	1987	1988	1989	1990	1991	1992	1993	1994	1995	1996	1997	1998	1999	2000	2001	2002	2003	2004	2005	2006	2007	2008
	2	10	12	14	14	19	21	21	24	26	27	27	27	28	28	28	29	27	29	29	30	33	36	39	39	41	43	44	44	47	51
	1	3	5	10	13	15	18	18	18	20	21	23	24	25	25	25	27	27	29	31	31	32	32	32	32	32	33	33	34	34	34
	0	1	1	2	3	3	4	7	8	9	12	12	13	17	21	24	26	26	29	31	33	36	36	36	40	41	43	44	46	47	
	1	1	1	3	4	7	8	9	9	11	11	11	11	11	12	14	14	15	17	17	22	27	30	30	30	32	32	33	33	34	
	0	0	1	1	1	1	1	1	1	1	2	2	2	3	3	3	3	3	3	3	3	3	4	4	4	5					

2 Approved Budget for World Heritage Convention in thousands US$ (2008/09)

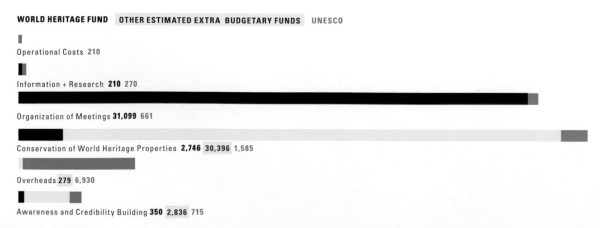

WORLD HERITAGE FUND   OTHER ESTIMATED EXTRA BUDGETARY FUNDS   UNESCO

Operational Costs 210

Information + Research 210 270

Organization of Meetings 31,099 661

Conservation of World Heritage Properties 2,746 30,396 1,585

Overheads 279 6,930

Awareness and Credibility Building 350 2,836 715

3 Sources of Funding for World Heritage Sites in Europe

by Region (% of countries mentioning that source for their WH Sites) (2006)

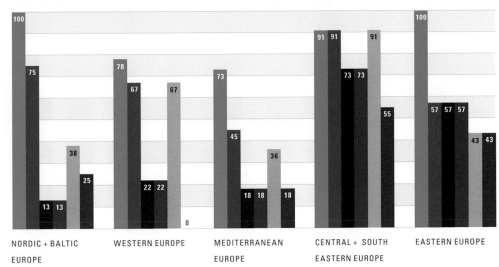

Legend:
- STATE PARTY BUDGET ALLOWANCE
- LOCAL / REGIONAL AUTHORITY BUDGET ALLOWANCE
- FUNDRAISING
- NON-GOVERNMENTAL ORGANIZATION
- PRIVATE SECTOR
- INTERNATIONAL ASSISTANCE FROM THE WORLD HERITAGE FUND

NORDIC + BALTIC EUROPE — 100, 75, 13, 13, 38, 25
WESTERN EUROPE — 78, 67, 22, 22, 67, 0
MEDITERRANEAN EUROPE — 73, 45, 18, 18, 36, 18
CENTRAL + SOUTH EASTERN EUROPE — 91, 91, 73, 73, 91, 55
EASTERN EUROPE — 100, 57, 57, 57, 43, 43

4 Overview Reported Issues Threatening World Heritage Sites by Region, in % (1986–2004)

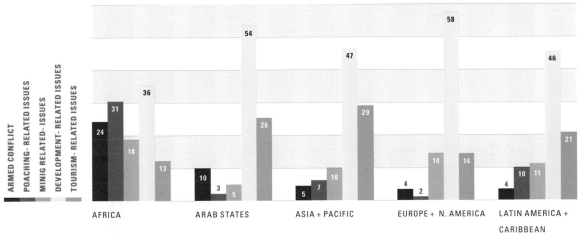

Legend:
- ARMED CONFLICT
- POACHING-RELATED ISSUES
- MINIG-RELATED-ISSUES
- DEVELOPMENT-RELATED ISSUES
- TOURISM-RELATED ISSUES

AFRICA — 24, 31, 18, 36, 13
ARAB STATES — 10, 3, 5, 54, 26
ASIA + PACIFIC — 5, 7, 10, 47, 29
EUROPE + N. AMERICA — 4, 2, 14, 58, 14
LATIN AMERICA + CARIBBEAN — 4, 10, 11, 46, 21

5 Use of World Heritage Sites in Europe by Subregion, in % (multiple categories possible)(2006)

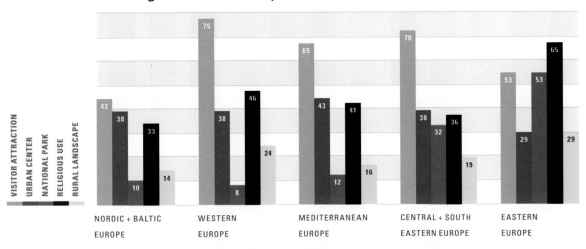

Legend:
- VISITOR ATTRACTION
- URBAN CENTER
- NATIONAL PARK
- RELIGIOUS USE
- RURAL LANDSCAPE

NORDIC + BALTIC EUROPE — 43, 38, 10, 33, 14
WESTERN EUROPE — 75, 38, 8, 46, 24
MEDITERRANEAN EUROPE — 65, 43, 12, 41, 16
CENTRAL + SOUTH EASTERN EUROPE — 70, 38, 32, 36, 19
EASTERN EUROPE — 53, 29, 53, 65, 29

DESIGN: RYAN WEAFER

World Heritage List *by Category and Region, in %*

LATIN AMERICA + CARIBBEAN (10%)   **EUROPE + NORTH AMERICA** (57%)   **ASIA + PACFIC** (20%   ARAB STATES (6%)   **AFRICA** (6%)

Category				
ARCHAEOLOGICAL PROPERTIES	5%	17%	26%	36%	17%
ROCK ART SITES	8%	12%	38%	35%	8%
HOMINID SITES	21%	14%	64%		
HISTORIC TOWNS/URBAN ENSEMBLES	5%	14%	13%	50%	18%
RELIGIOUS PROPERTIES	3%	6%	26%	56%	9%
TECHNOLOGICAL + AGRICULTURAL LANDSCAPES	4%	78%		16%	
MILITARY PROPERTIES	5%	10%	13%	64%	8%
ARCHITECTURAL + ARTISTIC MONUMENTS	2%	7%	20%	58%	13%
MODERN HERITAGE	80%	20%			
VERNACULAR ARCHITECTURE + SETTLEMENTS	14%	11%	9%	56%	11%
SYMBOLIC SITES	19%	33%	43%	5%	
CULTURAL LANDSCAPES	5%	2%	23%	65%	5%
CULTURAL ROUTES	13%	88%			
BURIAL SITES	3%	13%	33%	48%	5%
MIXED SITES	5%	5%	38%	43%	10%

World Heritage Sites

Heritage is our legacy from the past, what we live with today, and what we pass on to future generations. Our cultural and natural heritages are both irreplaceable sources of life and inspiration. Places as unique and diverse as the wilds of East Africa's Serengeti, the pyramids of Egypt, the Great Barrier Reef in Australia, and the baroque cathedrals of Latin America make up our world's heritage. (UNESCO World Heritage Centre, 2010)

This indicator suite presents certain aspects of the distribution, funding, and threats to sites listed on the World Heritage List created by virtue of the 1972 Convention Concerning the Protection of World Cultural and Natural Heritage. Complex realities lie behind the institutional rhetoric highlighted above, and many details need to be further quantified and interpreted. As discussed by Isar in this volume, the 1972 Convention provided the rationale for a global geography of the superlative, whose central defining idea is that among the myriad material traces of past human achievement (or among the many natural wonders found in the territory of different nations) a select few can be deemed to be of "outstanding universal value". Such World Heritage "properties" would thus become the shared legacy of all humankind, and indeed a large number of such cultural and natural sites are to be found across the entire world. Before examining some characteristics of this distribution, as revealed by the data, it may be recalled that for the Convention, world cultural heritage would be chosen from among the following:

Monuments: architectural works, works of monumental sculpture and painting, elements or structures of an archaeological nature, inscriptions, cave dwellings, and combinations of features that are of outstanding universal value from the point of view of history, art, or science;

Groups of buildings: groups of separate or connected buildings that because of their architecture, their homogeneity, or their place in the landscape, are of outstanding universal value from the point of view of history, art, or science;

Sites: works of man or the combined works of nature and man and areas including archaeological sites that are of outstanding universal value from the historical, aesthetic, ethnological, or anthropological point of view.

WHAT DO WE KNOW?

Some comparative data have already been provided by Isar. In addition, data point 1 shows that while the majority of cultural heritage sites listed are located in Europe and North America, natural sites are distributed relatively more equally across regions. Data point 6 reveals a more fine-grained categorization of site types. While Europe and North America show a rather balanced distribution across different groups, in Africa sites are concentrated in only two groups: hominid and symbolic.

The touristic exploitation of World Heritage sites that is part of the global "economy of prestige" is thought to have an important economic impact. Data from Europe show that most sites are used to attract visitors in all sub-regions, except Eastern Europe (see data point 5). While globalization eases access to World Heritage Sites, this kind of commodification may threaten their integrity, as for example when too many tourists strain the "carrying capacity" of monuments, archaeological sites, and nature reserves (data point 4).

The maintenance of heritage sites is very costly, and in poor countries both natural and cultural sites are threatened by the lack of financial resources. While most of the money for their protection and enhancement comes from national sources, funding from international organizations and private foundations such as the World Monuments Fund can make an important difference. The World Heritage Convention's approved budget for the conservation of World Heritage Sites in 2008/09 was limited, merely some $35 million US (see data point 2); these funds were disbursed mainly in the global south. While no Western European country received international assistance from the World Heritage Fund, 55 per cent of the countries in Central and South Eastern Europe did (data point 3).

WHAT ARE THE ISSUES?

Globalization has accentuated competition among nation-states for the recognition of "their" World Heritage Sites. Governmental representatives continue to strive to correct the over-representation of European and Northern American heritage resulting from the domination of specialists and officials from those regions in the definition and early implementation of the World Heritage mechanisms. The growing flow of visitors to World Heritage Sites calls for more effective and sustainable tourism management (UNESCO, 2002, and see also Tourism suite). Sustainability is also important to protect World Heritage Sites against the negative effects of climate change (Der Spiegel, 2009). The sad reality, however, is that many countries simply do not have the financial resources to rise to these challenges and both human resources and technical know-how are often lacking as well.

Legal + Political Frameworks

₁ Total Number of Countries Signing per UNESCO Treaty

■ OTHER
■ HERITAGE
■ INTELLECTUAL PROPERTY
■ EDUCATION

125	ICD (2005)	International Convention Against Doping in Sport. 2005
34	CDP (1974)	Convention Relating to the Distribution of Programme-Carrying Signals Transmitted by Satellite. 1974
51	EPD (1958)	Convention Concerning the Exchange of Official Publications and Government Documents Between States. 1958
99	IES (1950)	Agreement on the Importation of Educational, Scientific and Cultural Materials. 1950
38	ICM (1948)	Agreement for Facilitating the International Circulation of Visual and Auditory Materials of an Educational, Scientific and Cultural Character With Protocol of Signature and Model Form of Certificate provided for in Article IV of the Above-Mentioned Agreement. 1948
99	CPPD (2005)	Convention on the Protection and Promotion of the Diversity of Cultural Expressions. 2005
116	CSI (2003)	Convention for the Safeguarding of the Intangible Cultural Heritage. 2003
186	CPW (1972)	Convention Concerning the Protection of the World Cultural and Natural Heritage. 1972
159	WII (1971)	Convention on Wetlands of International Importance Especially as Waterfowl Habitat. 1971
118	PIC (1970)	Convention on the Means of Prohibiting and Preventing the Illicit Import, Export and Transfer of Ownership of Cultural Property. 1970
123	PCP (1954)	Convention for the Protection of Cultural Property in the Event of Armed Conflict With Regulations for the Execution of the Convention. 1954
26	CPU (2003)	Convention on the Protection of the Underwater Cultural Heritage. Paris, November 2 2001
8	MCA (1979)	Multilateral Convention for the Avoidance of Double Taxation of Copyright Royalties, With Model Bilateral Agreement and Additional Protocol. 1979
77	CPP (1971)	Convention for the Protection of Producers of Phonograms Against Unauthorized Duplication of their Phonograms. 1971
65	UCC (1971)	Universal Copyright Convention as Revised at Paris July 24 1971
91	PPP (1961)	International Convention for the Protection of Performers, Producers of Phonograms and Broadcasting Organizations. 1961
47	IEP (1958)	Convention Concerning the International Exchange of Publications. 1958
100	UCCA (1952)	Universal Copyright Convention, With Appendix Declaration Relating to Articles XVII and Resolution Concerning Article XI. 1952
48	CRQ (1997)	Convention on the Recognition of Qualifications Concerning Higher Education in the European Region. 1997
17	CTV (1989)	Convention on Technical and Vocational Education. 1989
21	CRSAP (1983)	Regional Convention on the Recognition of Studies, Diplomas and Degrees in Higher Education in Asia and the Pacific. 1983
22	CRSA (1981)	Regional Convention on the Recognition of Studies, Certificates, Diplomas, Degrees and Other Academic Qualifications in Higher Education in the African States. 1981
46	CRSE (1979)	Convention on the Recognition of Studies, Diplomas and Degrees Concerning Higher Education in the States Belonging to the Europe Region. 1979
14	CRSAS (1978)	Convention on the Recognition of Studies, Diplomas and Degrees in Higher Education in the Arab States. 1978
12	CRSASE (1976)	Convention on the Recognition of Studies, Diplomas and Degrees in Higher Education in the Arab and European States Bordering on the Mediterranean. 1976
19	CRSLAC (1974)	Regional Convention on the Recognition of Studies, Diplomas and Degrees in Higher Education in Latin America and the Caribbean. 1974
34	CDE (1962)	Protocol Instituting a Conciliation and Good Offices Commission to Be Responsible for Seeking the Settlement of Any Disputes which May Arise Between States Parties to the Convention against Discrimination in Education. 1962
96	CDIE (1960)	Convention Against Discrimination in Education. 1960

Europe / North America

1973	1974	1975	1976	1977	1978	1979	1980	1981	1982	1983	1984	1985	1986	1987	1988	1989	1990	1991	1992	1993	1994	1995	1996	1997	1998	1999	2000	2001	2002	2003	2004	2005	2006	2007	2008	2009
1	3	6	9	10	13	14	16	17	19	21	22	24	24	25	28	29	30	32	38	44	46	50	51	53	53	54	54	55	56	56	56	56	56	57	57	57

Asia / the Pacific

| 0 | 1 | 1 | 2 | 3 | 4 | 5 | 8 | 8 | 8 | 9 | 10 | 12 | 13 | 16 | 18 | 19 | 21 | 22 | 25 | 25 | 26 | 27 | 27 | 28 | 29 | 29 | 30 | 32 | 36 | 36 | 36 | 36 | 36 | 36 | 36 | 37 |

Latin America / Carribean

| 0 | 1 | 1 | 2 | 5 | 7 | 10 | 12 | 13 | 14 | 17 | 18 | 19 | 20 | 20 | 21 | 22 | 24 | 26 | 26 | 26 | 26 | 27 | 27 | 28 | 29 | 29 | 29 | 29 | 30 | 31 | 31 | 32 | 32 | 32 | 32 | 32 |

Africa

| 0 | 9 | 8 | 9 | 12 | 12 | 13 | 12 | 15 | 21 | 22 | 24 | 24 | 25 | 29 | 30 | 30 | 30 | 32 | 32 | 32 | 32 | 32 | 32 | 33 | 35 | 36 | 39 | 41 | 42 | 43 | 44 | 46 | 48 | 49 | 49 | 49 |

Arab States

| 0 | 1 | 4 | 4 | 4 | 6 | 7 | 7 | 7 | 7 | 8 | 8 | 8 | 8 | 8 | 8 | 8 | 8 | 9 | 9 | 9 | 9 | 9 | 9 | 9 | 9 | 9 | 10 | 11 | 11 | 11 | 11 | 11 | 11 | 11 | 11 | 11 |

₃ Use of Operational Guidelines for World Heritage Sites

14% **CRITERION I:** Represents a masterpiece of human creative genius

21% **CRITERION II:** Exhibits an important interchange of human values, over a span of time or within a cultural area of the world, on developments in architecture or technology, monumental arts, town planning, or landscape design

20% **CRITERION III:** Bears a unique or at least exceptional testimony to a cultural tradition or to a civilization that is living or that has disappeared

28% **CRITERION IV:** Is an outstanding example of a type of building or architectural or technological ensemble or landscape that illustrates (a) significant stage(s) in human history

6% **CRITERION V:** Outstanding example of a traditional human settlement, land, or sea- use representative of a culture/cultures, or human interaction with the environment especially when it has become vulnerable under the impact of irreversible change

11% **CRITERION VI:** Is directly or tangibly associated with events or living traditions, with ideas, with beliefs, or with artistic and literary works of outstanding universal significance

₄ Agreement of Dealers in Art, Antiques, and Antiquities to Object-ID Standards †(1997)

MEASUREMENTS	98%
MATERIALS & TECHNIQUES	97%
INSCRIPTIONS & MARKINGS	97%
DATE OR PERIOD	96%
TYPE OF OBJECT	95%
MARKER	95%
OBJECT NAME	94%
PHOTOGRAPHS	93%
TITLE	90%
DISTINGUISHING FEATURES	88%
SUBJECT	85%
RELATED WRITTEN MATERIAL	82%
DESCRIPTION	79%
DATE DOCUMENTED	79%
CONDITION OF OBJECT	74%
PLACE OF ORIGIN/DISCOVERY	73%
CROSS- REFERENCE TO RELATED OBJECTS	73%
OBJECT ID NUMBER	72%
NORMAL LOCATION OF OBJECT	64%
RECORDER'S NAME	64%
CUSTODIAN OF OBJECT	62%
ESTIMATED VALUE	56%
LEGAL STATUS OF OBJECT	52%
ACQUISITION	48%

† Responses to this survey were received from 181 dealers' associations and individual dealers in 13 countries.

Object ID is an international standard for describing cultural objects. It has been developed through the collaboration of the museum community, police and customs agencies, the art trade, insurance industry, and valuers of art and antiques.

It is being promoted by major law enforcement agencies, including the FBI, Scotland Yard and Interpol; museum, cultural heritage, art trade and art appraisal organisations; and insurance companies.

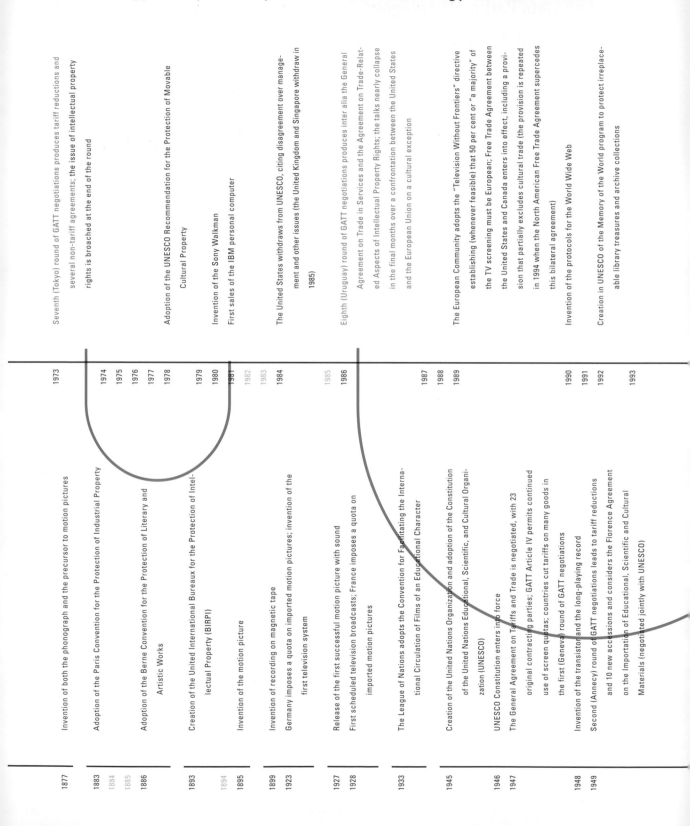

Top of timeline (1973–1993):

- 1973 — Seventh (Tokyo) round of GATT negotiations produces tariff reductions and several non-tariff agreements; the issue of intellectual property rights is broached at the end of the round
- 1978 — Adoption of the UNESCO Recommendation for the Protection of Movable Cultural Property
- 1979 — Invention of the Sony Walkman
- 1981 — First sales of the IBM personal computer
- 1984 — The United States withdraws from UNESCO, citing disagreement over management and other issues (the United Kingdom and Singapore withdraw in 1985)
- 1986 — Eighth (Uruguay) round of GATT negotiations produces inter alia the General Agreement on Trade in Services and the Agreement on Trade-Related Aspects of Intellectual Property Rights; the talks nearly collapse in the final months over a confrontation between the United States and the European Union on a cultural exception
- 1989 — The European Community adopts the "Television Without Frontiers" directive establishing (whenever feasible) that 50 per cent or "a majority" of the TV screening must be European; Free Trade Agreement between the United States and Canada enters into effect, including a provision that partially excludes cultural trade (the provision is repeated in 1994 when the North American Free Trade Agreement supercedes this bilateral agreement)
- 1990 — Invention of the protocols for the World Wide Web
- 1992 — Creation in UNESCO of the Memory of the World program to protect irreplaceable library treasures and archive collections

Years (top axis): 1973, 1974, 1975, 1976, 1977, 1978, 1979, 1980, 1981, 1982, 1983, 1984, 1985, 1986, 1987, 1988, 1989, 1990, 1991, 1992, 1993

Years (bottom axis): 1877, 1883, 1884, 1885, 1886, 1893, 1894, 1895, 1899, 1923, 1927, 1928, 1933, 1945, 1946, 1947, 1948, 1949

Bottom of timeline (1877–1949):

- 1877 — Invention of both the phonograph and the precursor to motion pictures
- 1883 — Adoption of the Paris Convention for the Protection of Industrial Property
- 1886 — Adoption of the Berne Convention for the Protection of Literary and Artistic Works
- 1893 — Creation of the United International Bureaux for the Protection of Intellectual Property (BIRPI)
- 1895 — Invention of the motion picture
- 1899 — Invention of recording on magnetic tape
- 1923 — Germany imposes a quota on imported motion pictures; invention of the first television system
- 1927 — Release of the first successful motion picture with sound
- 1928 — First scheduled television broadcasts; France imposes a quota on imported motion pictures
- 1933 — The League of Nations adopts the Convention for Facilitating the International Circulation of Films of an Educational Character
- 1945 — Creation of the United Nations Organization and adoption of the Constitution of the United Nations Educational, Scientific, and Cultural Organization (UNESCO)
- 1946 — UNESCO Constitution enters into force
- 1947 — The General Agreement on Tariffs and Trade is negotiated, with 23 original contracting parties; GATT Article IV permits continued use of screen quotas; countries cut tariffs on many goods in the first (Geneva) round of GATT negotiations
- 1948 — Invention of the transistor and the long-playing record
- 1949 — Second (Annecy) round of GATT negotiations leads to tariff reductions and 10 new accessions and considers the Florence Agreement on the Importation of Educational, Scientific and Cultural Materials (negotiated jointly with UNESCO)

1994 — Conclusion of the Uruguay Round of GATT negotiations; the U.S. government releases control of the Internet, thus privatizing the World Wide Web

1995 — Negotiations for a Multilateral Agreement on Investment in the Organization for Economic Cooperation and Development fail due to conflicts over (among other issues) a cultural exception; the World Trade Organization comes into effect, replacing (and incorporating) GATT; invention of the digital video disk (DVD)

1996 — The Information Technology Agreement is negotiated, eliminating tariffs on many electronic items for countries representing about 80 per cent of global trade; adoption of the WIPO Copyright Treaty

1997 — The United Kingdom rejoins UNESCO

1998

1999

2000 — The Committee of Ministers, Council of Europe, adopts the Declaration on Cultural Diversity

2001 — The Doha Round of WTO negotiations (also known as the Doha Development Agenda) is launched; the UNESCO Universal Declaration on Cultural Diversity is adopted by the General Conference

2002

2003 — The Doha Round stalls at the failed WTO ministerial meeting in Cancún; the United States rejoins UNESCO; UNESCO General Conference adopts by consensus a resolution inviting the Director-General to submit at the 33rd session (2005) a preliminary draft convention on the protection of the diversity of cultural contents and artistic expressions

2004 — The scope of the Doha Round is narrowed in the "July Package," with some issues laid aside (e.g., competition policy and investment), but market access for goods and services is still on the table; UNESCO holds the first Intergovernmental Meeting on the preliminary draft International Convention on the Protection of the Diversity of Cultural Contents and Artistic Expressions

---

1950 — Third (Torquay) round of GATT negotiations leads to tariff reductions and four new accessions

1951 — First commercial sales of computers; invention of the videotape recorder

1952 — Entry into force of the GATT/UNESCO Florence Agreement on the Importation of Educational, Scientific and Cultural Materials; a UNESCO intergovernmental conference adopts the Universal Copyright Convention

1953 — Invention of the transistor radio

1954

1955

1956 — Fourth (Geneva) round of GATT negotiations leads to tariff reductions

1957

1958 — Invention of the photocopier, the integrated circuit, and the computer modem

1959

1960 — Fifth (Dillon) round of GATT negotiations focuses primarily on issues related to the founding of the European Economic Community and its Common External Tariff

1961

1962 — Invention of the audio cassette

1963

1964 — Sixth (Kennedy) round of GATT negotiations produces both tariff reductions and some non-tariff agreements; the United States proposes that the GATT Article IV provisions regarding screen quotas not be applied to television programming, leading to examination of the issue but no decisions

1965 — Invention of the compact disk

1966 — UNESCO adopts the Declaration of the Principles of International Cultural Co-operation

1967

1968

1969 — Establishment of ARPANET, the precursor to the Internet

1970 — The World Intellectual Property Organization replaces BIRPI; adoption of the Patent Cooperation Treaty; adoption of the UNESCO Convention on the Means of Prohibiting and Preventing the Illicit Import, Export, and Transfer of Ownership of Cultural Property

1971 — Invention of the videocassette recorder

1972 — Adoption of the UNESCO Convention concerning the Protection of the World Cultural and Natural Heritage; invention of the word processor; pay television on cable is introduced

DESIGN: GEORGE BROWER

Legal + Political Frameworks

Global flows of media content, migrants, and tourists question traditional national understandings of heritage, memory, and identity. UNESCO's World Heritage List (see the corresponding indicator suite) exemplifies an intergovernmental discourse and practice relating to a certain category of heritage (Isar, 2008, and in this volume). The September 11, 2001, attacks on the United States, and the generation of '68 are certainly part of a global collective memory (Hoelscher, 2011, and suite on Memories of the Century), and migrants as well as top managers may develop transnational identities. Although such developments transcend the nation-state–based remit of the international standard-setting institutions, these new or emerging patterns of culture are also being addressed (see data point 1).

WHAT DO WE KNOW?

The principal international cultural standard-setting body is the United Nations Educational, Scientific and Cultural Organization (UNESCO), but others such as the World Intellectual Property Organization (WIPO) or the International Labour Organization (ILO) are also relevant. Heritage-related conventions are the most signed and salient of the many normative instruments in the field of culture elaborated by UNESCO. The International Centre for the Study of the Preservation and Restoration of Cultural Property (ICCROM), primarily a training body, also develops norms of professional practice, as do international NGOs such as the International Council on Monuments and Sites (ICOMOS) and the International Council of Museums (ICOM).

The key heritage-related legal framework is UNESCO's *Convention Concerning the Protection of World Cultural and Natural Heritage* from 1972 (see data point 2). The World Heritage Committee that manages the inscription of properties on the World Heritage List has developed specific criteria for their designation as World Heritage Sites (ICOMOS, 2008). The number of cultural criteria used for each property varies greatly, but the most-used criterion is that of "an outstanding example of a type of building or architectural or technological ensemble or landscape which illustrates (a) significant stage(s) in human history." This criterion has justified the designation of an estimated 70 per cent of Heritage Sites (see data point 3). The *Convention for the Safeguarding of the Intangible Cultural Heritage* adopted in 2003 is gradually acquiring an impact that could make it possible to gather numerically significant data in a similar manner. As regards the entanglements between the notion of national "identity" and that of "cultural diversity" as understood by the 2005 *Convention on the Protection and Promotion of the Diversity of Cultural Expressions,* interesting data may also become available once implementation of the Convention has advanced further.

The *Convention on the Means of Prohibiting and Preventing the Illicit Import, Export and Transfer of Ownership of Cultural Property* (1970) was adopted to combat the global "bad" resulting from the robbing or looting of museums and archaeological sites, mainly in countries of the global south, for the benefit of buyers who are mainly in the global north. An "Object ID-Standard" has been developed by the museums community in cooperation with the police and customs agencies, the art trade, and the insurance industry (see data point 4) for the description and recognition of cultural objects to fight the steadily growing illicit traffic (UNESCO, 2009b).

Data point 5 shows the relation of key developments in technology and law of cultural trade. These developments ease a global flow of intangible heritage and affect identities and memory.

WHAT ARE THE ISSUES?

A number of questions can be raised. First, that of enforceability, since intergovernmental organizations that adopt normative instruments also have to respect the primacy of state sovereignty. Do national governments have the capacities to adequately enforce the commitments they subscribe to? Can their compliance be monitored? What about affirmations of heritage, memory, and identity at the sub-national level? Finally, there are various perverse motivations and/or outcomes; as Boswell observes in this volume, the international legal framework "has solidified the concept of culture, reified identities and presented heritage as a gift to be passed on from one generation to the next."

Museums

1 Bodyworlds 1: The Original Exhibition of Real Human Bodies
OF VISITORS

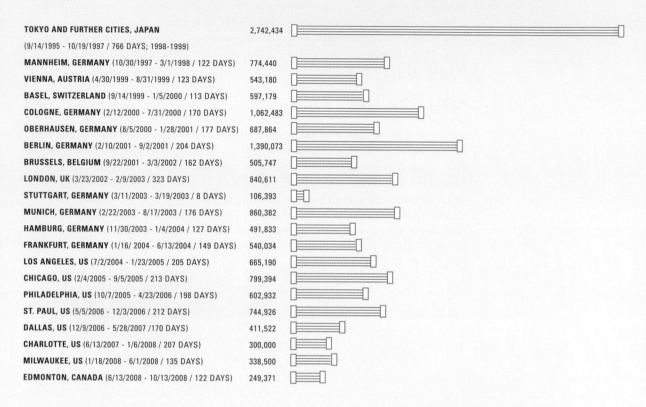

TOKYO AND FURTHER CITIES, JAPAN (9/14/1995 - 10/19/1997 / 766 DAYS; 1998-1999)	2,742,434
MANNHEIM, GERMANY (10/30/1997 - 3/1/1998 / 122 DAYS)	774,440
VIENNA, AUSTRIA (4/30/1999 - 8/31/1999 / 123 DAYS)	543,180
BASEL, SWITZERLAND (9/14/1999 - 1/5/2000 / 113 DAYS)	597,179
COLOGNE, GERMANY (2/12/2000 - 7/31/2000 / 170 DAYS)	1,062,483
OBERHAUSEN, GERMANY (8/5/2000 - 1/28/2001 / 177 DAYS)	687,864
BERLIN, GERMANY (2/10/2001 - 9/2/2001 / 204 DAYS)	1,390,073
BRUSSELS, BELGIUM (9/22/2001 - 3/3/2002 / 162 DAYS)	505,747
LONDON, UK (3/23/2002 - 2/9/2003 / 323 DAYS)	840,611
STUTTGART, GERMANY (3/11/2003 - 3/19/2003 / 8 DAYS)	106,393
MUNICH, GERMANY (2/22/2003 - 8/17/2003 / 176 DAYS)	860,382
HAMBURG, GERMANY (11/30/2003 - 1/4/2004 / 127 DAYS)	491,833
FRANKFURT, GERMANY (1/16/ 2004 - 6/13/2004 / 149 DAYS)	540,034
LOS ANGELES, US (7/2/2004 - 1/23/2005 / 205 DAYS)	665,190
CHICAGO, US (2/4/2005 - 9/5/2005 / 213 DAYS)	799,394
PHILADELPHIA, US (10/7/2005 - 4/23/2006 / 198 DAYS)	602,932
ST. PAUL, US (5/5/2006 - 12/3/2006 / 212 DAYS)	744,926
DALLAS, US (12/9/2006 - 5/28/2007 /170 DAYS)	411,522
CHARLOTTE, US (6/13/2007 - 1/6/2008 / 207 DAYS)	300,000
MILWAUKEE, US (1/18/2008 - 6/1/2008 / 135 DAYS)	338,500
EDMONTON, CANADA (6/13/2008 - 10/13/2008 / 122 DAYS)	249,371

2 Top 15 Most Visited Museums 2008
TOTAL VISITORS

#	Museum	Total Visitors
1	LOUVRE, PARIS	8,500,000
2	BRITISH MUSEUM, LONDON	5,930,000
3	NATIONAL GALLERY OF ART, WASHINGTON	4,964,061
4	TATE MODERN, LONDON	4,950,003
5	METROPOLITAN MUSEUM OF ART, NEW YORK	4,821,079
6	VATICAN MUSEUMS, ROME	4,441,734
7	NATIONAL GALLERY, LONDON	4,382,614
8	MUSÉE D'ORSAY, PARIS	3,025,141
9	MUSÉE D'ART MODERNE DE LA VILLE, PARIS	2,981,000
10	MUSEUM OF MODERN ART, NEW YORK	2,900,157
11	MUSEO NACIONAL DEL PRADO, MADRID	2,759,029
12	CENTRE POMPIDOU, PARIS	2,750,000
13	NATIONAL ART CENTER TOKYO, TOKYO	2,475,323
14	STATE HERMITAGE MUSEUM, ST. PETERSBURG	2,359,600
15	NATIONAL PALACE MUSEUM, TAIPEI	2,244,284

3 Top 10 Exhibitions by Type
REAGGREGATED ON CITY LEVEL; INCLUDES CITIES WITH MORE THAN ONE
EXHIBITION UNDER SIX TOP 10 EXHIBITIONS 2008 BY CATEGORY

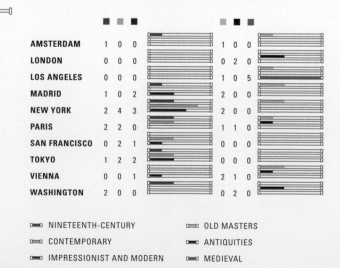

City						
AMSTERDAM	1	0	0	1	0	0
LONDON	0	0	0	0	2	0
LOS ANGELES	0	0	0	1	0	5
MADRID	1	0	2	2	0	0
NEW YORK	2	4	3	2	0	0
PARIS	2	2	0	1	1	0
SAN FRANCISCO	0	2	1	0	0	0
TOKYO	1	2	2	0	0	0
VIENNA	0	0	1	2	1	0
WASHINGTON	2	0	0	0	2	0

NINETEENTH-CENTURY — OLD MASTERS
CONTEMPORARY — ANTIQUITIES
IMPRESSIONIST AND MODERN — MEDIEVAL

Museums in Europe

Country	Total	Art, Arch. & History	Science & Tech, Ethnology	Other	Participation (%)
AUSTRIA, 2006	399	79	53	267	39
BELARUS, 2008	145	126	11	8	
BELGIUM, 2004	162	192	58	56	22.7
CROATIA, 2007	222	64	25	133	
CZECH REPUBLIC, 2007	449	64	2	383	46.4
DENMARK, 2004	258	242	10	6	19.5
ESTONIA, 2007	210	50	107	53	37.5
FINLAND, 2006	322	131	43	148	23.5
FRANCE, 2003	1,173	780	400	90	
GERMANY, 2006	6,175	2,235	3,840	100	
GREECE, 2007	176	176			33
HUNGARY, 2002	661	197	155	309	24.5
IRELAND, 2005	258				
ITALY, 2007	430	430			
LATVIA, 2007	128				32.1
LUXEMBOURG, 2006	39	13	15	11	
MACEDONIA, 2006	22	21	1		
NORWAY, 2007	173	121	28	24	21
POLAND, 2005	690	211	170	309	
PORTUGAL, 2007	557	222	137	198	10
ROMANIA, 2007	748	446	125	177	26
SLOVAK REPUBLIC, 2003	85	36	11	38	27
SLOVENIA, 2006	177	126	33	7	31.2
SPAIN, 2006	1,343	636	316	391	54
SWEDEN, 2007	207	159	34	14	
SWITZERLAND, 2005	948	288	593	167	38
THE NETHERLANDS, 2005	775	498	265	12	42
UNITED KINGDOM, 1999	1,850				

- TOTAL MUSEUMS
- ART, ARCHAEOLOGY AND HISTORY MUSEUMS
- SCIENCE AND TECHNOLOGY MUSEUMS, ETHNOLOGY MUSEUMS
- OTHER MUSEUMS
- MUSEUM PARTICIPATION (IN % OF POPULATION)

5 Ecomuseums

Country	# Operating	# In the making		Country	# Operating	# In the making
ARGENTINA	4			THE NETHERLANDS	1	
AUSTRALIA	2			NORWAY	2	
BELGIUM	4			POLAND	15	7
BRAZIL	12	4		PORTUGAL	9	4
CANADA	11	2		SENEGAL	1	
CHINA	9	1		SLOVAKIA	1	
COSTA RICA	3	1		SPAIN	36	5
CZECH REPUBLIC	3	1		SWEDEN	12	
DENMARK	4			SWITZERLAND	4	
FINLAND	1			TURKEY	1	
FRANCE	87			UNITED KINGDOM	1	2
GERMANY	2			UNITED STATES	1	
GREECE	1			VENEZUELA	1	
INDIA	1			VIETNAM	1	1
ITALY	69	15				
JAPAN	9					
MEXICO	1					

- # OPERATING
- # IN THE MAKING

6 Top 10 Most Visited Museums 2007

LANGUAGE SERVICES AVAILABLE TO INTERNATIONAL VISITORS

#	Museum	Homepages	Audio/Multimedia	Guided Tours
1	LOUVRE, PARIS	4	7	
2	CENTRE POMPIDOU, PARIS	3		7
3	TATE MODERN, LONDON	12	5	2*
4	BRITISH MUSEUM, LONDON	8	9	1**
5	METROPOLITAN MUSEUM OF ART, NEW YORK	10	9	7
6	NATIONAL GALLERY OF ART, WASHINGTON	5	6	
7	VATICAN MUSEUMS, ROME	2	7	7
8	NATIONAL GALLERY, LONDON	8	6	
9	MUSÉE D'ORSAY, PARIS	5	9	5
10	MUSEO NACIONAL DEL PRADO, MADRID	10	5	

- # OF LANGUAGES ON THE HOMEPAGES
- # OF LANGUAGES FOR AUDIO / MULTIMEDIA GUIDES
- # OF LANGUAGES FOR GUIDED TOURS
- * PRIVATE TOURS ARE AVAILABLE IN OTHER LANGUAGES ON REQUEST
- ** GROUP TOURS ARE AVAILABLE IN OTHER LANGUAGES

DESIGN: CAMILE ORILLANEDA

Museums

Museums by nature tend to evoke debates about the valuing and valorization of cultural heritage. For example, Becker asks in his book *Art Worlds* how museums and other storage institutions would "decide what goes into their collections and what does not merit such care." Museums try to conserve the cultural heritage "of the country or of all humanity" (Becker, 1982: 220). But what museums possess and decide to exhibit depends on decisions of a network of curators, museum trustees, patrons, dealers, critics, and aestheticians. Museums therefore show "work that meets the aesthetic standards of some or all of those people, and those standards develop in response to the requirements of such institutions as museums" (Becker, 1982: 220). The choice about what to exhibit is also "a choice about how to represent 'other cultures'" – which has "consequences both for what meanings are produced and for how meaning is produced" (Hall, 1997: 8).

WHAT ARE MUSEUMS?

The International Council of Museums (ICOM) defines a museum as "a non-profit, permanent institution in the service of society and its development, open to the public, which acquires, conserves, researches, communicates and exhibits the tangible and intangible heritage of humanity and its environment for the purposes of education, study and enjoyment." Museums are seen as "institutions of modernity": Because of their conservation ambitions, they reflect "the modern esprit of control and appropriation through classification and taxonomy" (Pieterse, 2005: 169f.).

WHAT DO WE KNOW ABOUT MUSEUMS?

- Paris held four positions within the world's 15 most visited museums in 2008, attracting nearly 17.5 million visitors, followed by London, where three top museums attracted more than 15 million people (see data point 2).
- In the context of the top 10 exhibitions by type in 2008 (ranked by daily visitors), six categories were selected and leading cities were determined. New York has the most exhibitions within this group (see data point 3). With 24 exhibitions, it also dominates the ranking of the top 100 exhibitions, followed by London and Paris (each with seven exhibitions), Washington (five) and Tokyo (two).
- Data point 4 shows the number of museums by type of collection and the number of European attendees. The Czech Republic achieved the highest museum participation: 46.4 per cent of Czech respondents said that they had visited a museum or gallery at least once in the past 12 months. Germany attained the highest number of museums.
- Data point 5 provides some figures about a new form of museum that emerged in France in the 1970s: ecomuseums. Currently, most ecomuseums are located in Europe, with the front-runners France (87 operating ecomuseums), Italy (69), and Spain (36).
- The formidable success of museums like the Louvre in Paris or the Metropolitan Museum of Modern Art in New York is probably highly correlated with their

internationality. Sixty-seven per cent of the Louvre's visitors in 2008 were foreigners, and only a third of the visitors were French (Le Louvre). The number of languages on the museums' homepages is highest for Tate Modern (which is located in London and the third most visited museum in 2007): People can select from 12 different languages (English, French, German, Italian, Portuguese, Spanish, Japanese, Greek, Russian, Polish, Arabic, and Chinese) (see data point 6).

•   Finally, as a curiosity, the venues of what is perhaps the world's most popular travelling exhibition "Body Worlds 1" (called "Körperwelten" in Germany, where the method of plastination was invented in Heidelberg by exhibition curator Gunther von Hagens) are shown in data point 1. The Berlin "Body Worlds" attracted more visitors (around 1.4 million) than the most successful art exhibition in 2008 ("Tutankhamun and the Golden Age of the Pharaohs," exhibited at the 02 Millennium Dome in London, attracted "just" 1.1 million people).

WHAT ARE THE ISSUES OR TRENDS?

Debates about the tasks of museums in the 21st century abound. Many views focus, as they long have, on the educational role of museums in developing better understanding of history and culture. Different positions are also expressed as to why people visit museums, about visitor expectations and how audiences can be built and the new global audience can be better served (cf. Waltl, 2006: 4 [see the scheme below]). Indeed, additional insights into the context of globalization could be gained from case studies that aim to document the percentage of international visitors (e.g., Le Louvre). Beyond that, few data are available about the "transnationalization" of museum stocks and museum collaborations – the weighting and exchange of national and international artists and art works.

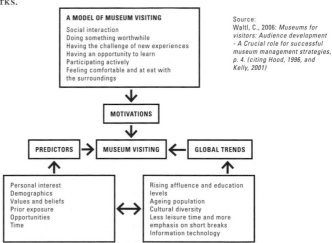

A MODEL OF MUSEUM VISITING

Social interaction
Doing something worthwhile
Having the challenge of new experiences
Having an opportunity to learn
Participating actively
Feeling comfortable and at eat with the surroundings

Source:
Waltl, C., 2006: *Museums for visitors: Audience development - A Crucial role for successful museum management strategies*, p. 4. (citing Hood, 1996, and Kelly, 2001)

MOTIVATIONS

PREDICTORS → MUSEUM VISITING ← GLOBAL TRENDS

Personal interest
Demographics
Values and beliefs
Prior exposure
Opportunities
Time

Rising affluence and education levels
Ageing population
Cultural diversity
Less leisure time and more emphasis on short breaks
Information technology

There is also much professional and critical debate about "new" practices of museology that break with traditional models. The new museology – one of whose initial manifestations was the ecomuseum – specifically questions traditional museums approaches to issues of value, meaning, control, interpretation, authority, and authenticity' (Stam, 2005: 54; see also the chapter by Thomas in this volume).

INTANGIBLE HERITAGE

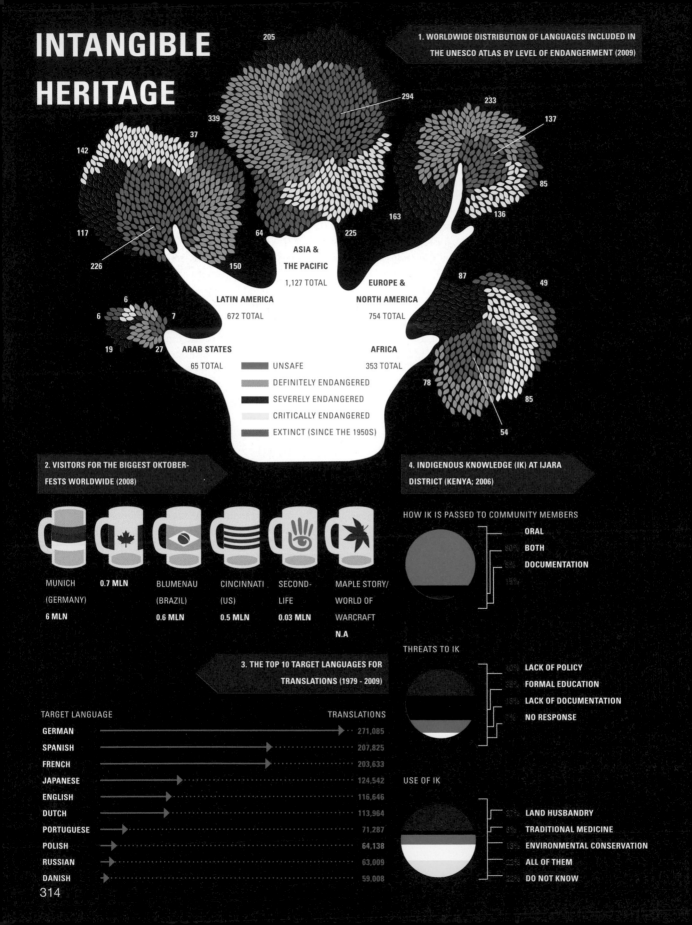

205
294
339
233
137
37
142
85
117
64
225
163
136
226
150
87
49
6
7
6
19
27
78
85
54

ASIA & THE PACIFIC 1,127 TOTAL

LATIN AMERICA 672 TOTAL

EUROPE & NORTH AMERICA 754 TOTAL

ARAB STATES 65 TOTAL

AFRICA 353 TOTAL

- UNSAFE
- DEFINITELY ENDANGERED
- SEVERELY ENDANGERED
- CRITICALLY ENDANGERED
- EXTINCT (SINCE THE 1950S)

2. VISITORS FOR THE BIGGEST OKTOBER-FESTS WORLDWIDE (2008)

MUNICH (GERMANY) 6 MLN

0.7 MLN

BLUMENAU (BRAZIL) 0.6 MLN

CINCINNATI (US) 0.5 MLN

SECOND-LIFE 0.03 MLN

MAPLE STORY/ WORLD OF WARCRAFT N.A

4. INDIGENOUS KNOWLEDGE (IK) AT IJARA DISTRICT (KENYA; 2006)

HOW IK IS PASSED TO COMMUNITY MEMBERS

- ORAL 80%
- BOTH 5%
- DOCUMENTATION 15%

THREATS TO IK

- LACK OF POLICY 40%
- FORMAL EDUCATION 35%
- LACK OF DOCUMENTATION 18%
- NO RESPONSE 7%

USE OF IK

- LAND HUSBANDRY 37%
- TRADITIONAL MEDICINE 6%
- ENVIRONMENTAL CONSERVATION 13%
- ALL OF THEM 22%
- DO NOT KNOW 22%

3. THE TOP 10 TARGET LANGUAGES FOR TRANSLATIONS (1979 - 2009)

TARGET LANGUAGE	TRANSLATIONS
GERMAN	271,085
SPANISH	207,825
FRENCH	203,633
JAPANESE	124,542
ENGLISH	116,646
DUTCH	113,964
PORTUGUESE	71,287
POLISH	64,138
RUSSIAN	63,009
DANISH	59,008

561,161   833,124   1,084,996   1,426,541   1,553,269   1,028,362   ,868,926   3,064,609   4,051,186   4,332,486   4,689,40'   ,548,178

5. PATENT APPLICATIONS (1883 - 2005)

OF PATENT APPLICATIONS

1883-1890   1886-1900   1906-1910   1916-1920   1926-1930   1936-1940   1946-1950   1956-1960   1966-1970   1976-1980   1986-1990   1996-2000

YEARS

6. MASTERPIECES OF THE ORAL AND INTANGIBLE HERITAGE OF HUMANITY (UNESCO PROCLAMATIONS)

THE MASTERPIECES REPRESENT
INTANGIBLE HERITAGE FROM DIFFERENT
REGIONS. THE MASTERPIECES FIT IN
THE FOLLOWING CATEGORIES:

-ORAL TRADITIONS AND EXPRESSIONS
INCLUDING LANGUAGE AS A VEHICLE OF
THE INTANGIBLE CULTURAL HERITAGE;

-PERFORMING ARTS (SUCH AS TRADI-
TIONAL MUSIC, DANCE, AND THEATER);

-SOCIAL PRACTICES, RITUALS, AND
FESTIVE EVENTS;

-KNOWLEDGE AND PRACTICES CON-
CERNING NATURE AND THE UNIVERSE;

YEARS

2009   20   50   7   1   2

2008   25   24   16   9   4

2005   11   13   7   11   2

2003   6   10   5   5   1

2001   6   5   4   4

MASTERPIECES

EUROPE/NORTH AMERICA

ASIA/PACIFIC

Intangible Heritage

The notion of "intangible heritage" has in the past decade broadened and deepened the idea of "heritage" in international cultural relations, notably in intergovernmental organizations, and appeals strongly to local, national, and global imaginaries (see Isar's chapter in this volume). According to UNESCO's 2003 *Convention for the Safeguarding of Intangible Cultural Heritage* (ICH), this type of heritage is the driving force of cultural diversity and provides a guarantee for sustainable creativity (UNESCO, 2003). In Article 2, the *ICH Convention* states that

1. Intangible cultural heritage means the practices, representations, expressions, knowledge, skills – as well as the instruments, objects, artifacts and cultural spaces associated therewith – that communities, groups and, in some cases, individuals recognize as part of their cultural heritage. (...)

2. Intangible cultural heritage, as defined above, is manifested inter alia in the following domains:

(a) oral traditions and expressions, including language as a vehicle of the intangible cultural heritage;

(b) performing arts;

(c) social practices, rituals and festive events;

(d) knowledge and practices concerning nature and the universe; and

(e) traditional craftsmanship.

One of the key mechanisms of the *Convention* is the "Representative List of the Intangible Cultural Heritage of Humanity," discussed in chapter 2 (data point 6).

WHAT DO WE KNOW?

Data in this area are still scarce; the items selected for presentation and comment are based on what is available and hence do not necessarily represent the most significant aspects.

A shared international concern is that globalization endangers indigenous knowledge – an important part of intangible heritage (Centre for International Research and Advisory Networks, 2001). International policies might be a means to protect indigenous knowledge, as the lack of supportive policies is often seen as a major threat, as an example from a Kenyan region, the Ijara district, shows (see data point 4). However, nearly as many people see formal education as the most important threat. This view points to the contested nature of preservation initiatives for intangible heritage: In which ways can modernization processes contribute to its safeguarding instead of being harmful? While globalization in some instances might lead to the disappearance of some forms of intangible heritage, it might also contribute to the global distribution of traditions across cultures for some other forms. Data point 2 shows a range of the most popular *Oktoberfests*, traditionally a German beer festival, worldwide. Notably, the *Oktoberfest* takes place even in the virtual world (e.g., Second Life, World of Warcraft, and MapleStory). However, the question remains whether such distribution is supportive or destructive of the traditions' original meaning.

Knowledge, such as Einstein's theory of relativity or the teachings of Confucius, is a specific part of intangible heritage. Ways to prevent dilution, but also to limit the usage of knowledge, are intellectual property rights. While the granting of patents demands the production of "new" knowledge and the number of patent applications is rising, only time will prove how many of these inventions will become part of our cultural heritage (data point 5).

Likewise, languages are a key component of intangible heritage, just as they are integral in preserving and distributing it. Some 241 languages have become extinct since the 1950s, 718 languages are unsafe, and about 2,500 languages are endangered (data point 1). Scientists estimate that, while around 1000 B.C. some 20,000 languages existed, only about 6,500-7,000 languages are spoken today, of which only 4,500 will survive until 2050 (Haspelmath, 2009; Summer Institute of Linguistics, 2010). Yet languages not understood are barriers to the distribution and sharing of human knowledge. The numbers of books translated – in order to circumvent those barriers – are an indicator of the distribution of knowledge and culture across borders (data point 3). Over the last past 30 years, while the English language was the main source for translated books, German was the top target language. Japanese is the only Asian language in the top 10 target languages.

WHAT ARE THE ISSUES?

A key global North-South bone of contention revolves around intellectual property in traditional knowledge (American Association for the Advancement of Science, 2008). The patenting of knowledge is contentious in relation to its prior existence as intangible heritage. For example, the sale of drugs based on traditional plant-based medicines alone amounts to over US \$32 billion a year (World Bank, 2004), while none of the revenue flows back to the indigenous people that were the depositories of the knowledge of the source plants and how to exploit them. Even indigenous words and names get trademarked and are used commercially (WIPO, 2009).

TOURISM

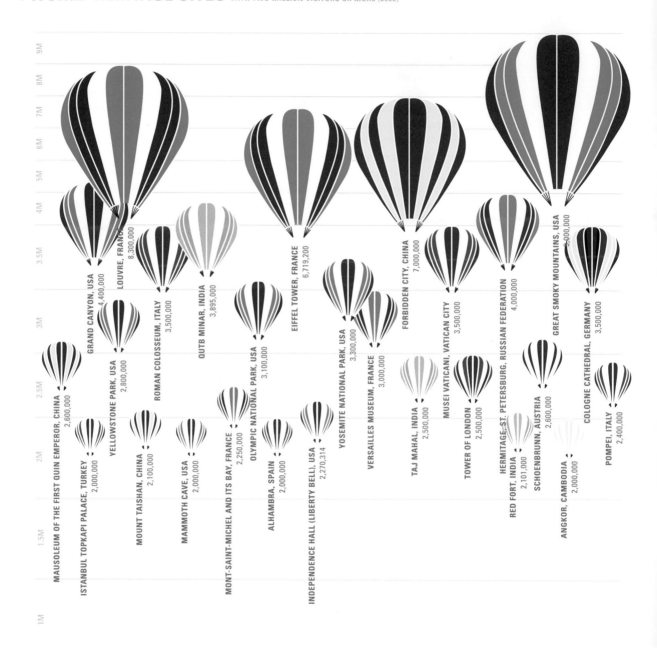

9M
8M
7M
6M
5M
4M
3.5M
3M
2.5M
2M
1.5M
1M

MAUSOLEUM OF THE FIRST QUIN EMPEROR, CHINA
2,600,000

ISTANBUL TOPKAPI PALACE, TURKEY
2,000,000

GRAND CANYON, USA
4,400,000

YELLOWSTONE PARK, USA
2,800,000

MOUNT TAISHAN, CHINA
2,100,000

LOUVRE, FRANCE
8,300,000

ROMAN COLOSSEUM, ITALY
3,500,000

MAMMOTH CAVE, USA
2,000,000

QUTB MINAR, INDIA
3,895,000

MONT-SAINT-MICHEL AND ITS BAY, FRANCE
2,250,000

OLYMPIC NATIONAL PARK, USA
3,100,000

ALHAMBRA, SPAIN
2,000,000

INDEPENDENCE HALL (LIBERTY BELL), USA
2,270,314

EIFFEL TOWER, FRANCE
6,719,200

YOSEMITE NATIONAL PARK, USA
3,300,000

VERSAILLES MUSEUM, FRANCE
3,000,000

FORBIDDEN CITY, CHINA
7,000,000

TAJ MAHAL, INDIA
2,500,000

MUSEI VATICANI, VATICAN CITY
3,500,000

TOWER OF LONDON
2,500,000

HERMITAGE-ST. PETERSBURG, RUSSIAN FEDERATION
4,000,000

RED FORT, INDIA
2,101,000

SCHOENBRUNN, AUSTRIA
2,600,000

ANGKOR, CAMBODIA
2,000,000

GREAT SMOKY MOUNTAINS, USA
9,000,000

COLOGNE CATHEDRAL, GERMANY
3,500,000

POMPEI, ITALY
2,400,000

2 THE **MAJOR MOTIVATION** FOR EU CITIZENS, MAIN HOLIDAY TRIP (2008)

DON'T KNOW 1%
WELLNESS 3%
SPORTS 3%
NATURE 6%
RELIGION 7%
CULTURE / CITY TRIPS 7%
VISITING FRIENDS / RELATIVES 16%
SUN / BEACH 20%
REST / RELAXATION 36%

318

3 REAL TRAVEL & TOURISM (1989-2009)

ACTIVITY GROWTH: PERSONAL & BUSINESS TRAVEL, %

PERSONAL

BUSINESS

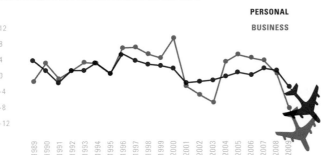

12
8
4
0
-4
-8
-12

1989 1990 1991 1992 1993 1994 1995 1996 1997 1998 1999 2000 2001 2002 2003 2004 2005 2006 2007 2008 2009

4 INTERNATIONAL TOURIST ARRIVALS BY SUB-REGION (1990-2008)

1990	1995	2000	2005	2006	2007	2008	
438	534	684	804	853	904	922	WORLD
265.0	309.5	392.6	441.8	468.4	487.9	489.4	EUROPE
55.8	82.0	110.1	153.6	166	182	184.1	ASIA AND THE PACIFIC
92.8	109	128.2	133.3	135.8	142.9	147	AMERICAS
15.1	20.0	27.9	37.3	41.5	45	46.7	AFRICA
9.6	13.7	24.9	37.9	40.9	46.6	55.1	MIDDLE EAST

5 DESTINATIONS OF EU CITIZENS' MAIN HOLIDAY TRIP IN 2008 (TOP THREE DESTINATIONS)

100%

50%

0%

HOME COUNTRY: DESTINATION 1, 2, & 3

BELGIUM: FRANCE (27), IN COUNTRY (10), SPAIN (9)
BULGARIA: IN COUNTRY (76), GREECE (4), TURKEY (3)
CZECH REP.: IN COUNTRY (26), CROATIA (18), ITALY (10)
DENMARK: IN COUNTRY (16), SPAIN (10), FRANCE (8)
GERMANY: IN COUNTRY (25), SPAIN (11), ITALY (9)
ESTONIA: IN COUNTRY (26), FINLAND (11), SWEDEN (8)
GREECE: IN COUNTRY (86), ITALY (1), FRANCE (1)
SPAIN: IN COUNTRY (76), ITALY (4), PORTUGAL (3)
FRANCE: IN COUNTRY (56), SPAIN (8), MOROCCO(4)
IRELAND: SPAIN (21), IN COUNTRY (15), US (10)
ITALY: IN COUNTRY (63), SPAIN (5), FRANCE (3)
CYPRUS: GREECE (46), IN COUNTRY (17), UK (6)
LATVIA: IN COUNTRY (14), RUSSIA (7), TURKEY (7)
LITHUANIA: IN COUNTRY (43), TURKEY (8), LATVIA (5)
LUXEMBOURG: FRANCE (16), SPAIN (9), ITALY (9)
HUNGARY: IN COUNTRY (62), CROATIA (5), GREECE (5)
MALTA: ITALY (20), IN COUNTRY (16), UK (16)
NETHERLANDS: IN COUNTRY (18), FRANCE (13), SPAIN (8)
AUSTRIA: IN COUNTRY (23), ITALY (16), CROATIA (8)
POLAND: IN COUNTRY (67), ITALY (3), GREECE (2)
PORTUGAL: IN COUNTRY (59), SPAIN (11), FRANCE (4)
ROMANIA: IN COUNTRY (37), ITALY (7), GREECE (3)
SLOVENIA: CROATIA (41), IN COUNTRY (14), GREECE (5)
SLOVAKIA: IN COUNTRY (30), CROATIA (20), GREECE (6)
FINLAND: IN COUNTRY (39), SPAIN (8), THAILAND (5)
SWEDEN: IN COUNTRY (38), SPAIN (10), THAILAND (5)
UK: IN COUNTRY (23), SPAIN (14), FRANCE (8)

6 ATTRACTIONS INFLUENCING THE CHOICE OF DESTINATIONS

OF EU CITIZENS' HOLIDAY (2009)

DON'T KNOW 6%
OTHERS 8%
FESTIVALS/OTHER EVENTS 5%
ART 5%
GASTRONOMY 7%
ENTERTAINMENT 15%
CULTURAL HERITAGE 24%
THE ENVIRONMENT 31%

Tourism

Tourism is an ever-growing global phenomenon with significant economic, social, and cultural dimensions. "In both developed and developing countries, tourism is one of the fastest growing sectors of the economy and a major source of employment and investment" (Wearing et al., 2010: 2). Data point 4 reveals the global trend: more than twice the number of tourist arrivals within 20 years.

The United Nations World Tourist Organization defines tourism as "the activities of persons traveling to and staying in places outside their usual environment for not more than one consecutive year for leisure, business or other purposes" (UNWTO, 1995: 10). However, the phenomenon we now call tourism has a long history. Human beings have long traveled for religious (pilgrimage) or occupational reasons. Until recently, however, only the rich could afford recreational travel. This has changed with the exponential growth of mass tourism in the past few decades.

Academic study of tourism combines examination of (a) the sites visited with (b) the activities engaged in and (c) the subjective experience itself (Wearing & Wearing, 2001: 151). There are several systems of classification depending on the criteria: origin (inland or external tourism), number of travelers (mass or individual tourism), age (youth or senior), duration (short trip or long-term tourism), or season (summer or winter tourism) (see, e.g., Zins, 2004). However, one of the most common classifications is the distinction between leisure, that is, personal, and work, that is, business, tourism (see data point 3). Additionally, several niches have developed that are referred to as "adjectival tourism." This comprises the better known tourism purposes, such as medical, ecological, religious, or cultural tourism, as well as newer specialties, such as "dark tourism," which means traveling to places and sites affiliated with pain, suffering, and death (see Richter, 2005: 266).

WHAT DO WE KNOW?

In a comparative perspective it became apparent that the premises for leisure tourism vary significantly. According to a new study (Mercer, 2009), workers' holiday entitlement in Finland, Brazil, and France is highest with 30 days, whereas in Canada and China workers are entitled to only 10 days of holiday.

As with the differences in holiday entitlement, there are differences in tourism activities and the choice of destinations. Data point 5 provides information on the top three destinations for the main holiday trip of EU citizens in 2008; this also reflects a noticeable preference for more domestic destinations. This may well be connected to the current economic recession experienced in most parts of the world.

The main motivations for tourism are still recreation and rest (see data point 2), whereas cultural reasons play a tangential role. But when it comes to choosing a destination, cultural surroundings and heritage are important considerations (see data point 6). Nevertheless, cultural heritage on its own is a prominent tourist attraction as data point 1 reveals. The listed World Heritage Sites, visited by two million people or more, are both an expression of this appeal and represent the huge number of people traveling. Cultural heritage is undoubtedly a vital element of the global tourism phenomenon, playing a significant economic role. Table 1 compares the turnover of the

European cultural heritage sector with financial measures of other economic sectors/companies (Nypan, 2003):

Table 1. Turnover of Cultural Heritage Sector in Comparison (in Billion Euro, Estimated for 2001-2002)

R&D spending of major US companies	183
Turnover of VW Group (2001)	89
Turnover of BMW Group (2001)	39
Revenue of US computer peripheral industry	17
Turnover of cultural heritage sector for tourism Europe	338

WHAT ARE THE ISSUES AND TRENDS?

"The scale of contemporary tourism, including the relative accessibility of destinations, and the ease (…) of the travel experience [...can be] markers of the democratization of travel and reasons to be optimistic about the consequences and possibilities of globalization" (Wearing et al., 2010: 128). But there are also reasons to be critical as regards the impact of tourism and globalization on identity or heritage. A synopsis by Guttentag reports some counterexamples to the seemingly idealistic image of a specific kind of tourism, that is, volunteer tourism, combining an interest in traveling with an interest in helping others: Possible negative impacts can include "a neglect for locals' desires, a hindering of work progress and completion of unsatisfactory work, a disruption of local economies, a reinforcement of conceptualizations of the 'other' and rationalizations of poverty, and an instigation of cultural changes" (Guttentag, 2009: 537). International terrorism additionally has an important impact on tourism. Further research should explore what kind of effects cultural commodification via tourism will have: On the one hand it can lead "to a recognizable 'ethnic group' identity" (Cole, 2007: 955); on the other hand tourism and cultural commodification "are taking our culture away" (Kirtsoglou & Theodossopoulos, 2004).

Sustainability

1 # of officially protected agricultural products EU countries (2009)

Natural Products   Processed Products   Drinks

2 Preservation of Cultural Heritage:

UNESCO Memory of the World Project

Number of objects in selected countries (2009)

3 % of Estimated Threatened Species by groups of organisms, IUCN Redlist (2004 – 2009)

Vertebrates   Invertebrates   Plants   Fungi & Protists

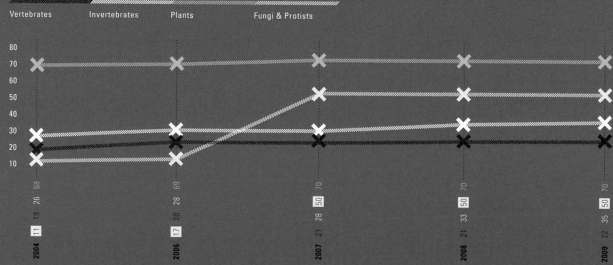

4 Attitudes Toward the Coexistence of Nature and Human Beings

in selected countries, by % (1995/96 – 2000/01)

Legend:
- Should Master Nature
- Should Coexist
- Other

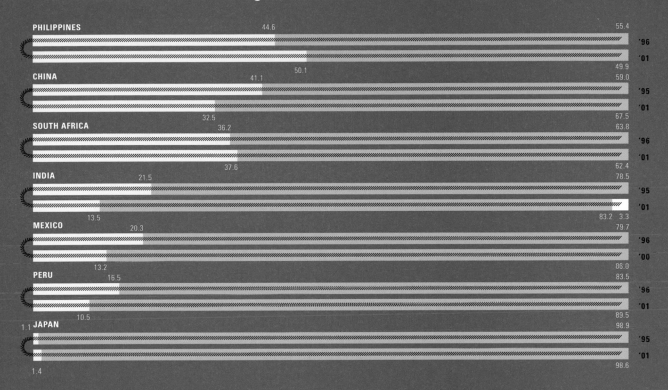

PHILIPPINES
- 44.6 / 55.4 — '96
- 50.1 / 49.9 — '01

CHINA
- 41.1 / 59.0 — '95
- 32.5 / 67.5 — '01

SOUTH AFRICA
- 36.2 / 63.8 — '96
- 37.6 / 62.4 — '01

INDIA
- 21.5 / 78.5 — '95
- 13.5 / 83.2 3.3 — '01

MEXICO
- 20.3 / 79.7 — '96
- 13.2 / 86.0 — '00

PERU
- 16.5 / 83.5 — '96
- 10.5 / 89.5 — '01

JAPAN
- 1.1 / 98.9 — '95
- 1.4 / 98.6 — '01

5 Happy Planet Index: Life Satisfaction, Health, and Ecological Behavior

by region (2009)

Higher score indicates high life expectancy, high life satisfaction, and low ecological footprint

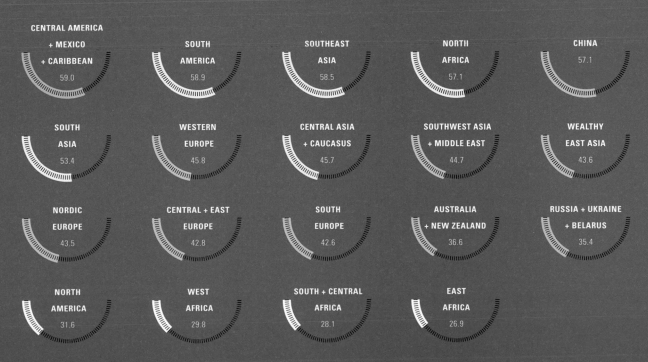

- CENTRAL AMERICA + MEXICO + CARIBBEAN — 59.0
- SOUTH AMERICA — 58.9
- SOUTHEAST ASIA — 58.5
- NORTH AFRICA — 57.1
- CHINA — 57.1

- SOUTH ASIA — 53.4
- WESTERN EUROPE — 45.8
- CENTRAL ASIA + CAUCASUS — 45.7
- SOUTHWEST ASIA + MIDDLE EAST — 44.7
- WEALTHY EAST ASIA — 43.6

- NORDIC EUROPE — 43.5
- CENTRAL + EAST EUROPE — 42.8
- SOUTH EUROPE — 42.6
- AUSTRALIA + NEW ZEALAND — 36.6
- RUSSIA + UKRAINE + BELARUS — 35.4

- NORTH AMERICA — 31.6
- WEST AFRICA — 29.8
- SOUTH + CENTRAL AFRICA — 28.1
- EAST AFRICA — 26.9

DESIGN: RYAN WEAFER

Sustainability

WHAT IS SUSTAINABILITY OF HERITAGE?

The sustainability data suite attempts to capture the diverse meanings of heritage, as it encompasses cultural traditions, collective pasts, and identities in relation to the natural world (Lowenthal, 1994). As Benjamin Morris observed in chapter 9, the natural world and the human world simultaneously mutually influence, respond to, and co-produce one another. Sustainability of heritage in this perspective refers to how the conservation of its physical, natural, and intangible components determines which items are of value for future generations. Key questions in the context of globalization include: What is the role of the natural heritage in relation to the mechanisms used to preserve biodiversity? How do culture and identity relate to environments, both natural and constructed? Do conservation mechanisms actually lead to sustainability of both cultural and natural resources?

WHAT DO WE KNOW ABOUT THE SUSTAINABILITY OF HERITAGE?

Global bio-cultural diversity is clearly threatened by our current consumption patterns. For example, according to data from the International Union for the Conservation of Nature (IUCN), the number of threatened species is increasing. The attempt to measure global biocultural diversity is as much a product as a part of globalization, stemming from the global network of institutions and scientists who work together to provide relevant data. In terms of biological diversity alone, there are still large gaps in the data, demonstrated by the large proportion of species that have not yet been documented. Of the fungi and protists as well as the invertebrates, less than 1 per cent of the estimated species have yet to be evaluated (IUCN Standards and Petitions Working Group, 2008) (see data point 3).

Neoliberal capitalist hegemony has led to unchecked consumption of natural resources in many parts of the world, with Europe and North America leading the way. The destruction of nature and the exploitation of its resources impact the biological environment and culture, memory, and heritage that are inextricably bound to it. The Happy Planet Index (HPI) with its dimensions high life expectancy, high life satisfaction, and low ecological footprint seeks to demonstrate that a high quality of life is possible without exorbitant costs to the Earth (Abdallah et al., 2009). High-scoring countries in the HPI are thus less wealthy countries with significantly smaller ecological footprints per head combined with high levels of life expectancy and life satisfaction. Regions like Central and South America top the index, whereas highly- developed regions like Western Europe and North America are located toward the middle and the end of the ranking (data point 5).

The needed shift toward valuing natural and cultural resources more deeply than economic goods cannot be brought about by institutions alone. It has to be based on complementary values and awareness of the need for environmental protection. Attitudes concerning the coexistence of nature and humankind show huge differences between different countries. In Japan, 98.9 per cent of the population in 1995-1996 and 98.6 per cent in 2000-2001 endorse the coexistence of nature and humankind, whereas in the Philippines, the will to master nature is high and increasing (1995-1996: 44.6 per cent; 2000-2001: 50.1 per cent) (data point 4).

The agricultural product quality policy of the European Union (EU) offers another understanding of the sustainability of heritage. The program's goal is to protect agricultural products produced, processed, and prepared in a given geographical area, using recognized know-how or products. The differences in dispersion and composition of products are considerable and show specific country profiles: Among the 182 protected products of Italy, 110 are processed products. France has a total of 166 protected products with 103 of them belonging to the natural products category, and in Germany 36 of 66 protected products are drinks (data point 1).

For the preservation of cultural heritage, the Internet and digitalization techniques offer new mechanisms of achievement. UNESCO's "Memory of the World" project is one example of a significant number of digitalization projects, the aim of which is to protect the archival heritage and make it accessible to the public. Other projects are the ECHO project, the Europeana project, Google Books, or the World Digital Library (data point 2).

WHAT ARE THE TRENDS?

Possibilities for the preservation of heritage have reached a new level. New techniques like digitalization may foster attempts to protect cultural heritage. Regarding natural heritage, humankind's responsibility for the preservation of natural wealth is connected to climate change and global warming. The debate about global warming may also increase the consciousness for the preservation of natural heritage on Earth (see Morris's chapter in this volume).

Heritage, cultural as well as natural, and its meanings are constructed by society (cf. the chapters by Croissant and Chambers and Winter in this volume). Thus, the role and form of these constructions are not static and stable but built discursively, differing over time (e.g., Marquardt, 2005). Similar questions may arise when considering the definition and construction of sustainability. In each epoch a new definition of what should be preserved needs to be found (see chapter by Aksoy and Robins in this volume). The preservation of heritage and traditions may also cause some dangers for societies by disincentivizing creativity and innovation.

International Organizations + Heritage

1 Heritage Issues
INTERNATIONAL ORGANIZATIONS WORKING EXPLICITLY ON HERITAGE ISSUES (1992-2006)

* 2001 – 2002 INCREASE DUE TO CHANGE IN CATEGORIES

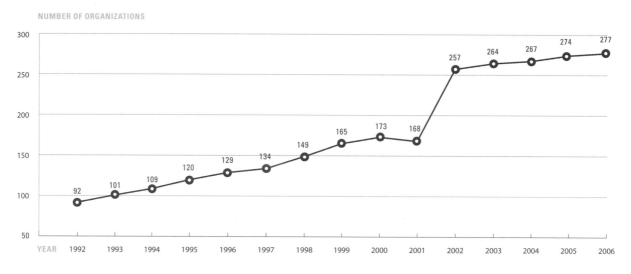

NUMBER OF ORGANIZATIONS

YEAR	1992	1993	1994	1995	1996	1997	1998	1999	2000	2001	2002	2003	2004	2005	2006
	92	101	109	120	129	134	149	165	173	168	257	264	267	274	277

2 Concern of Leading People

AREAS OF CONCERN OF LEADING PEOPLE IN
INTERNATIONAL ORGANIZATIONS (2007)

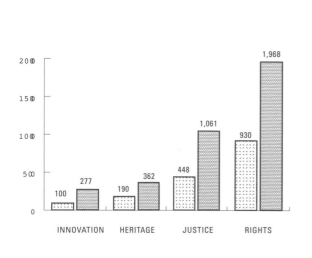

NUMBER OF LEADING PEOPLE NAMING THE AREA

NUMBER OF INTERNATIONAL ORGANIZATIONS
ACTIVE IN THE AREA

3 The World Heritage Fund

REGIONAL EXPENSES IN CONSERVATION PROJECTS
BY THE WORLD HERITAGE FUND IN MLN US$ (2006–2008)

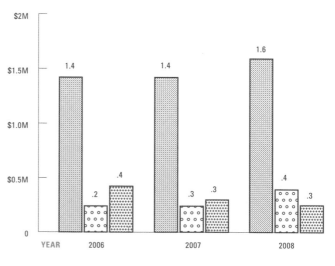

AMERICA

ASIA AND PACIFIC

EUROPE, MIDDLE EAST, AND AFRICA

Combination of Languages
MOST FREQUENT COMBINATIONS OF LANGUAGES IN INTERNATIONAL ORGANIZATIONS

This table gives totals for combinations of the most commonly used languages in international organizations, as represented in biographies of leading people. For example, 1 biography includes Arabic and Dutch in the list of languages in which he or she is proficient, 1,175 biographies include English and French, 285 include French and Italian, and 163 include Italian and Spanish.

	ARABIC	DUTCH	ENGLISH	FRENCH	GERMAN	ITALIAN	PORTUGUESE	RUSSIAN	SPANISH
DUTCH	1	—	—	—	—	—	—	—	—
ENGLISH	86	260	—	—	—	—	—	—	—
FRENCH	56	244	1175	—	—	—	—	—	—
GERMAN	17	198	664	541	—	—	—	—	—
ITALIAN	13	57	296	285	167	—	—	—	—
PORTUGUESE	2	14	108	94	37	47	—	—	—
RUSSIAN	5	8	100	71	59	26	4	—	—
SPANISH	13	59	480	407	183	163	98	29	—
SWEDISH	2	4	89	50	61	8	5	9	23

5 # of UN Registered Indigenous Peoples Organizations BY CONTINENT (2009)

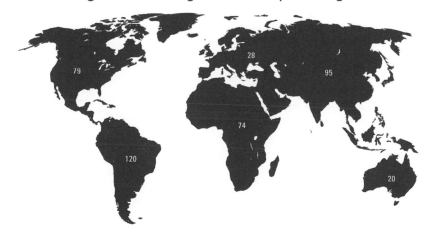

AFRICA	74
ASIA	95
EUROPE	28
NORTH AMERICA	79
OCEANIA	20
LATIN AMERICA AND CARIBBEAN	120
NOT SPECIFIED	729
TOTAL	1,145

6 NGOs and UNESCO NGOs' HEADQUARTER LOCATION AND MAINTENANCE OF OFFICIAL RELATIONS WITH UNESCO (2005)

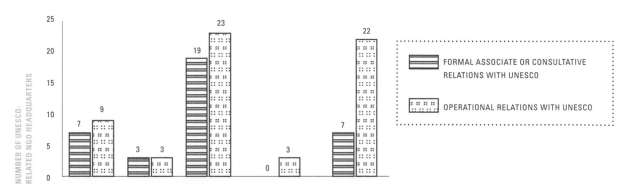

NUMBER OF UNESCO-RELATED NGO HEADQUARTERS

LONDON: 7, 9
NEW YORK: 3, 3
PARIS: 19, 23
WASHINGTON, DC: 0, 3
BRUSSELS: 7, 22

FORMAL ASSOCIATE OR CONSULTATIVE RELATIONS WITH UNESCO

OPERATIONAL RELATIONS WITH UNESCO

DESIGN: DONNIE LUU

327

International Organizations + Heritage

This indicator suite focuses on the relationship between cultural heritage and activities undertaken by international organizations, both governmental and non-governmental. Like unsustainable levels of tourism and various states of armed conflict, the insufficiency of resources is a significant and concrete, man made menace to the safeguard of cultural heritage (Anheier & Isar, 2008: 365). For that reason financial resources and the organizational degree of associative activities in the field of cultural heritage are the focus of this data suite.

WHAT DO WE KNOW?

Over the past decade the number of inter-governmental organizations, international non-governmental organizations, and multinational enterprises working explicitly on heritage issues has increased (see data point 1). A major part of this growth can be explained by the significant increase in the number of NGOs with an international or trans-national remit (Anheier & Themudo, 2002: 194).

International organizations and especially NGOs represent very heterogeneous areas of concern. Some subjects appear higher on the agenda, as the four selected areas of data point 2 indicate. Rights and justice generally are of more concern than innovation and heritage. This holds true for the organizations and their leaders alike. The most frequent combination of languages spoken by people in leading positions is English and French (data point 4).

Cultural heritage relates not only to historic buildings, monuments, and sites, but also to intangible cultural practices such as languages, expressions, and culturally embedded knowledge (see corresponding Indicator Suite). The notion has special resonance with the Indigenous Peoples as recognized by the UN (United Nations Permanent Forum on Indigenous Issues, 2010; see also Jean-Pierre Warnier's chapter in this volume) in relation to

- Self-identification as an indigenous individual and acceptance by the community as their member;
- Historical continuity with pre-colonial and/or pre-settler societies;
- Strong link to territories and surrounding natural resources;
- Distinct social, economic, or political systems;
- Distinct language, culture, and beliefs;
- Forming a non-dominant group of society;
- Resolving to maintain and reproduce their ancestral environments and systems as distinctive peoples and communities.

Some of these criteria are difficult to pinpoint, such as linking indigenous peoples to territories and respecting migration at the same time (see Ien Ang's critique in this book). On the empirical level, although the UN's ICSO system (http://esango.un.org/civilsociety) has made ground-breaking contributions, the data available are still sketchy. Data point 5 shows that for most indigenous peoples' organizations, geographical placement is not documented by the UN statistics database. However, according to UN experts, the most fruitful approach is to identify – rather than define – indigenous people based on the fundamental criterion of self-identification as underlined in human rights documents such as the UN Declaration on the Rights of Indigenous Peoples adopted by the General Assembly in 2007.

Strong financial support for cultural heritage preservation comes from individual non-profit organizations. Two powerful examples are the World Monuments Fund (WMF), headquartered in New York, and the Global Heritage Fund (GHF), based in California (see data point 3; for other examples see Tim Winter's contribution in this book). Most of GHF's resources are spent in the Americas, while the WMF truly invests all over the globe, as it works in more than 90 countries to safeguard important heritage sites. One indicator of the organization's importance is the capacity of financial resource provision. WMF's investment in the fiscal year 2009 was $14.1 million. Of more than $16 million of revenues in 2009, the fund received 73 percent from individual donors and 22 percent from foundations. Only 5 percent were contributed by investment income and grants from corporations (WMF, 2009: 30)

For NGOs active in the field of cultural heritage interactions with the United Nations Educational, Scientific and Cultural Organization (UNESCO) are decisive (see Isar's chapter in this volume). An interesting finding is that out of the 332 NGOs having official relations with UNESCO, 28.9 per cent have their headquarters in five leading world cities as defined by Taylor (2005) (data point 6). Besides the cities mentioned here, Geneva, Nairobi, and Manila are also to be considered as important cities for NGO activities in relation to UNESCO (Taylor, 2005: 1602).

WHAT ARE THE ISSUES?

A problem in analyzing the relationship between civil society and cultural heritage is the scant availability of systematic data. Besides the UN bodies and the efforts of the Union of International Associations, little transnational data on heritage and civil society organizations is to be found.

Regarding interpretation of the relationship between heritage and the transnational civil society sector, diversity of approaches to heritage will benefit from multiple income sources and hence from a diversity in funding. The field explored is composed of heterogeneous values and political views, but still the power-related perspective asks whose heritage is supported (Tunbridge, 1984).

International non-profit organizations like NGOs and international foundations finance a variety of projects but are not obliged to guarantee financial transparency in all legal systems, which makes it harder to publicly access data on financial support to cultural heritage from organizations other than those based in the United States and Europe. Furthermore, already accessible annual reports must allow the reader to see which organizations or subject fields are financed to ensure transparency.

Memory

MEMORIALIZATION

CONTESTED MEMORIES

GLOBAL COLLECTIVE MEMORIES

PLACES

MEDIA

MIGRATION AND DIASPORA

EDUCATION

Memorialization

₁ Public Holidays   % OF PUBLIC HOLIDAYS BY TYPE: IN SELECT COUNTRIES (ABSOLUTE # OF PUBLIC HOLIDAYS IN BRACKETS)

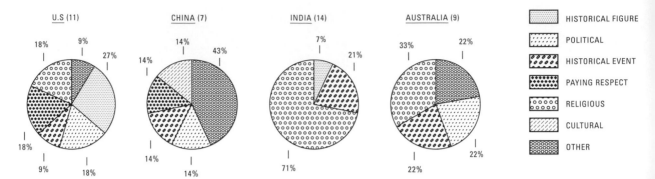

U.S (11) CHINA (7) INDIA (14) AUSTRALIA (9)

Legend:
- HISTORICAL FIGURE
- POLITICAL
- HISTORICAL EVENT
- PAYING RESPECT
- RELIGIOUS
- CULTURAL
- OTHER

₂ Airport Names   SELECT LIST OF AIRPORTS NAMED AFTER FAMOUS PEOPLE BY REGION

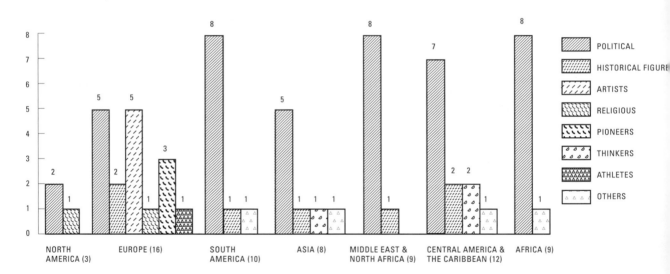

NORTH AMERICA (3), EUROPE (16), SOUTH AMERICA (10), ASIA (8), MIDDLE EAST & NORTH AFRICA (9), CENTRAL AMERICA & THE CARIBBEAN (12), AFRICA (9)

Legend:
- POLITICAL
- HISTORICAL FIGURE
- ARTISTS
- RELIGIOUS
- PIONEERS
- THINKERS
- ATHLETES
- OTHERS

₃ Euro Coins   EURO COINS CLASSIFICATION BY SOCIETAL REALM: EU COUNTRIES

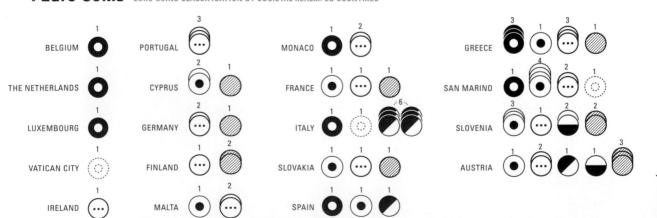

4 Street Renaming

in Bucharest (1990 – 1997)

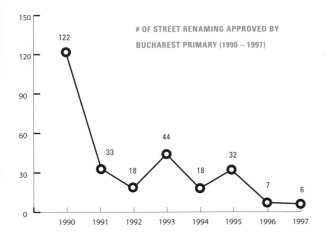

OF STREET RENAMING APPROVED BY
BUCHAREST PRIMARY (1990 – 1997)

150
122
120
90
60
44
33
32
30
18   18
18
7   6
0
1990 1991 1992 1993 1994 1995 1996 1997

BUCHAREST,
ROMANIA

● ● ●

COIN CATEGORIES

POLITICAL FIGURE	HISTORICAL FIGURE	SYMBOL
RELIGIOUS FIGURE	ARTS / ARTIST	THINKERS / WRITERS
NATURE		

5 Countries and Territories

Name Change Over Time

LIST OF COUNTRIES AND TERRITORIES THAT CHANGED THEIR NAMES

OLD NAME	YEAR	NEW NAME
NEW GRANADA	1820	COLOMBIA
NEW SPAIN	1822	MEXICO
PERSIA	1935	IRAN
IRISH FREE STATE	1937	IRELAND
NETHERLANDS EAST INDIES	1946	INDONESIA
TRANSJORDAN	1946	JORDAN
BRITISH MANDATE OF PALESTINE	1949	ISRAEL
SIAM	1950	THAILAND
GOLD COAST	1958	GHANA
FRENCH SUDAN	1961	MALI
MALAYA	1964	MALAYSIA
NORTHERN RHODESIA	1965	ZAMBIA
NYASALAND	1965	MALAWI
BASUTOLAND	1966	LESOTHO
BECHUANALAND	1966	BOTSWANA
BRITISH GUIANA	1967	GUYANA
SPANISH GUINEA	1968	EQUATORIAL GUINEA
CEYLON	1972	SRI LANKA
EAST PAKISTAN	1972	BANGLADESH
BRITISH HONDURAS	1974	BELIZE
ABYSSINIA	1974	ETHIOPIA
PORTUGUESE GUINEA	1975	GUINEA BISSAU
DUTCH GUIANA	1975	SURINAME
DAHOMEY	1976	BENIN
SPANISH SAHARA	1976	WESTERN SAHARA
AFARS AND ISSAS	1978	DJIBOUTI
ELLICE ISLANDS	1978	TUVALU
CENTRAL AFRICAN EMPIRE	1979	CENTRAL AFRICAN REPUBLIC
GILBERT ISLANDS	1979	KIRIBATI
ZIMBABWE-RHODESIA	1980	ZIMBABWE
NEW HEBRIDES	1980	VANUATU
UPPER VOLTA	1984	BURKINA FASO
BURMA	1988	MYANMAR
SOUTH WEST AFRICA	1990	NAMIBIA
UZBEK SOVIET SOCIALIST REPUBLIC	1991	REPUBLIC OF UZBEKISTAN
TAJIK SOVIET SOCIALIST REPUBLIC	1991	TAJIKISTAN
BYELORUSSIA	1992	BELARUS
KAMPUCHEA	1992	CAMBODIA
MOLDAVIA	1992	MOLDOVA
WESTERN SAMOA	1997	SAMOA
DEMOCRATIC REPUBLIC OF CONGO	1998	ZAIRE
PORTUGUESE TIMOR	2002	EAST TIMOR
FEDERAL REPUBLIC OF YUGOSLAVIA	2003	SERBIA, MONTENEGRO, KOSOVO

Memorialization

Memorialization on the individual level is the practice of bestowing something to individual memory for future rendering. However, on the collective level, memorialization refers to the social commemoration of people, experiences, and events transmitted from the past to the present. Such social memorialization tends to focus on what is seen by a society as its most important icons and these may include politicians, scientists, artists, historians, battles, war victories, colonial independence, or anything of special value shared by members of the society through oral or written approaches. These collective memories are key building blocks of the construction of the nation as "imagined community" (Anderson, 1991).

WHAT DO WE KNOW?

- National holidays, that is, occasions for remembering certain events or people, are celebrated differently in different countries. In India and Australia, for instance, 71 per cent and 33 per cent of public holidays, respectively, are celebrated for religious purposes. In the U.S., 27 per cent of holidays commemorate historical figures, such as Martin Luther King Jr., Christopher Columbus, and George Washington (see data point 1).

- Airports, which serve as entry points for international travelers, are often named after famous people from the political sphere: after politicians, including presidents, kings/queens, ministers, senators and the like. However, in Europe, several airports are named after artists, including actors, comedians, composers, singers, and directors (see data point 2).

- A nation's currency and coins commemorate key events or historical personalities and symbolic significant markers of national identity. Even after the economic integration and currency unification of most EU member countries, these nations were each determined to choose their own designs on Euro coins. In Luxembourg, Belgium, and the Netherlands, one motif, representing a significant political figure in the nation's past, appears on all of its coins. The Vatican City is represented by a picture of Pope Benedict the 16th on all of its coins, thus identifying itself as a religious country. Italy identifies itself as the country of ancient art using six different art figures on its coins (see data point 3).

- A change in a country's political order often goes hand- in- hand with redefining or rebranding national history, which involves simultaneous processes of de-commemoration and new commemoration. When a new regime in Romania, called the National Salvation Front (NSF) and led by Ion Iliescu (a former Commmunist party leader), took power in the ambiguous circumstances of December 1989, renaming streets was an integral part of the process of creating a new iconographic landscape— a sign for the beginning of a new political era. In 1990, Bucharest City Hall approved 122 street name changes. This number declined steadily over the following years to 30-40 street name changes annually (see data point 4).

- Data point 5 represents a list of all the countries and territories that changed their names for a variety of reasons. Most of the countries on the list are former colonies of nations such as France, Great Britain, and others. Upon attaining independence, these countries changed their names and attested to their emancipation by purposefully seeking to de-commemorate the past existence of their occupiers and by purposefully asserting their distinctive cultural heritage, memory, and identity.

WHAT ARE THE ISSUES?

The United States is said to have created a culture of cosmopolitanization of memory and to have defined it as a worldwide event commemorated by all humankind.members of the universe. According to Levy and Sznaider (2002), cosmopolitanization of memory refers to a process in which local memories become global experiences. The authors tried to rationalize the transition from local memory to global memory by providing an account of the Holocaust and the way it is remembered in Israel, Germany, and the United States (see also the suite about collective memories of the century.) The challenging question is how a society can memorialize events that do not have a direct link to its culture or ancestors and how the memory of this event is changed thereby (see chapter by Breed in this volume).

Another issue is why certain events are globally memorialized while others are ignored. One may argue that the magnitude of the event is the determining factor, but could the media and interest groups that stress the importance of certain events at the expense of others have a say in this as well? (See chapter by Breed in this volume). Global migration and communication lead to incremental shifts of memorialization from the national to the global level, generating benefits but also creating challenges. The global nature of memorialization does not mean the death of national landscapes (Levy & Sznaider, 2002). Instead, it means the transformation of national perspectives into more complex structures shared by different cultures.

Contested Memories

1 Religion AMERICAS' PERCEPTIONS OF ISLAM (2002-2009)

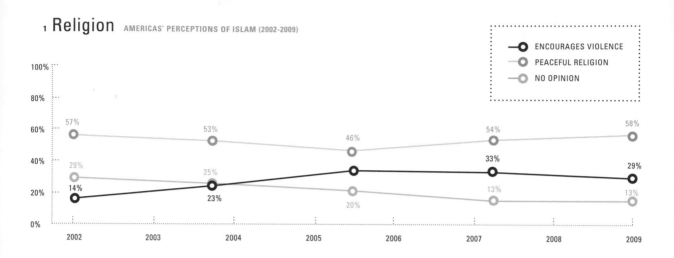

Legend:
- ENCOURAGES VIOLENCE
- PEACEFUL RELIGION
- NO OPINION

PEACEFUL RELIGION: 57%, 53%, 46%, 54%, 58%
ENCOURAGES VIOLENCE: 14%, 23%, 33%, 33%, 29%
NO OPINION: 29%, 25%, 20%, 13%, 13%

Years: 2002, 2003, 2004, 2005, 2006, 2007, 2008, 2009

2 US and UK Leaders, Opinions on Weapons of Mass Destruction in Iraq

PERCENTAGE OF PEOPLE BY COUNTRY WHO BELIEVE US & UK LEADERS LIED ABOUT WEAPONS OF MASS DESTRUCTION IN IRAQ (AS OF 2004)

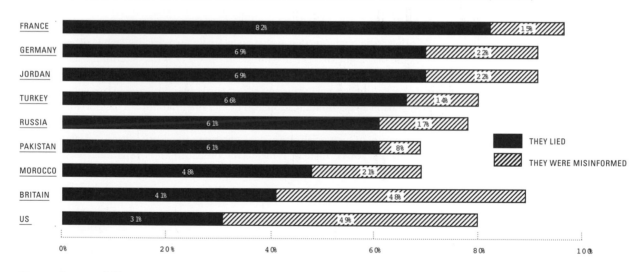

Country	They Lied	They Were Misinformed
FRANCE	82%	15%
GERMANY	69%	22%
JORDAN	69%	22%
TURKEY	66%	14%
RUSSIA	61%	17%
PAKISTAN	61%	8%
MOROCCO	48%	21%
BRITAIN	41%	48%
US	31%	49%

Legend:
- THEY LIED
- THEY WERE MISINFORMED

3 Freedom of Press PERCENTAGE OF COUNTRIES BY REGION

NOT FREE PARTLY FREE FREE

Region	Not Free	Partly Free	Free
AMERICAS	6%	46%	49%
ASIA-PACIFIC	35%	28%	38%
CENTRAL & EASTERN EUROPE	36%	36%	29%
MIDDLE EAST & NORTH AFRICA	79%	—	21%
SUB-SAHARAN AFRICA	48%	38%	15%
WESTERN EUROPE	8%	—	92%

₄ Democides LARGEST DEMOCIDES BY REGIME IN THOUSANDS (1900-1987)

Democide is defined as "the killing of people by a government because of their indelible group membership" (R.J. Rummel)

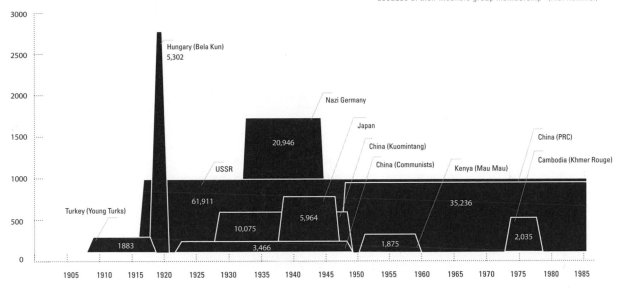

Hungary (Bela Kun)
5,302

Nazi Germany
20,946

Japan

China (Kuomintang)

China (Communists)

USSR
61,911

Kenya (Mau Mau)
35,236

China (PRC)

Cambodia (Khmer Rouge)

Turkey (Young Turks)
1883

10,075

3,466

5,964

1,875

2,035

₅ Evolution US PERCEPTIONS OF EVOLUTION BY POLITICAL AFFILIATION (2007)

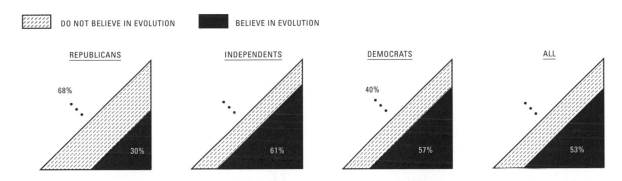

DO NOT BELIEVE IN EVOLUTION   BELIEVE IN EVOLUTION

REPUBLICANS — 68% / 30%
INDEPENDENTS — 61%
DEMOCRATS — 40% / 57%
ALL — 53%

₆ Cultural Conflicts COUNTRIES WITH STRONGEST NATIONAL CULTURAL CONFLICTS (1945–2007)

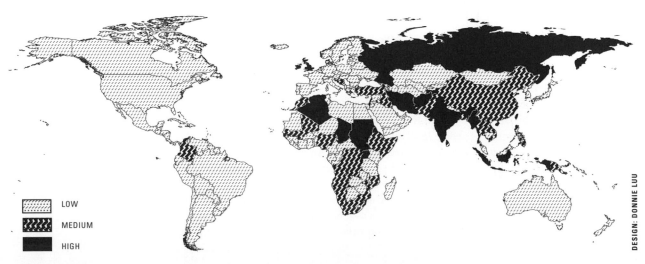

LOW

MEDIUM

HIGH

DESIGN: DONNIE LUU

Contested Memories

"One may say that the individual remembers by placing himself in the perspective of a group, but [it is also true that] the memory of the group realizes and manifests itself in individual memories." (Halbwachs, 1992: 40)

Psychologists have known for decades that individual memory depends on group membership. In fact, it is often due to inquiry and stimulus from our peers that we remember. Thus, our culture and our values actively influence what and how we remember events. Therefore, it is not surprising that the same event may be remembered in different ways by different groups or individuals (see chapter by Croissant and Chambers in this volume). Contested memory refers to events or places that, in some way or another, are disputed by one or more party either involved in the event or as outsiders. This can include both memories that are denied because they are inconvenient as well as events that are genuinely believed to have occurred in a different way. The most infamous current act of deliberate contestation of events taken for granted in the collective memory of the West is the denial of the Holocaust by Iranian President Mahmoud Ahmadinejad in 2005. Other forms of contested memories involve contested sites or places that result from armed historical or political conflicts between countries that aim at strengthening their national identities or establishing a sense of community cohesion (the chapters by Hashimoto and Volcic discuss questions such as these; Viejo-Rose discusses how destruction and reconstruction of heritage may affect contested memories.)

Contested memory exists not only on a collective but also on an individual level. Neurological research suggests that individuals tend to forget or alter memories that are hurtful, a process called dissociation (Brown, Scheflin & Hammond, 1998).

However, data in these fields are scarce. Therefore, this suite mainly presents only indirect indicators of contested memories and identities or on aspects related to the latter; it does not amount to a comprehensive review of the topic.

WHAT DO WE KNOW?

Social identity theory (Tajfel & Turner, 1986) tells us that people try to establish positive images of their ingroups and that information is often interpreted in a way supporting this image. Data point 2 illustrates this on the basis of perceptions on the weapons of mass destruction (WMD) justifications for the Iraq War, delivered by US Secretary of State Colin Powell in 2003. While the majority of people in the US and Britain believe the fact that no WMDs were found constituted a serious misjudgment of evidence, the majority of people in all other surveyed countries believe US and British leaders deliberately lied to justify military action. An interesting question for memory scholars in the future will be whether this understanding will become lodged in the collective memories of these societies or not.

Likewise, a clear point of contention across cultures is religion and hence of religious memories. For example, after 9/11, discussions sprang up among Muslims as to whether the Qur'an can be interpreted as approving violence or not. In this context and that of the ensuing invasion of Iraq, a growing number of Americans perceived Islam as a religion that encourages violence. Since then, the trend has been reversed slightly (data point 1).

If public information is successfully altered, (wrong) collective memories may be contested and even changed (see Ševčenko on the role of museums for the promotion of human rights through appropriate education). Accuracy of collective memory is supported, though not guaranteed, in a major way by the free flow of information. Data point 3 shows a measure of freedom of the press by region. As can be seen, most countries in Western Europe are considered free in terms of media reporting while the majority of Middle Eastern and North African countries are not blessed by free press systems.

Events that are often contested involve genocides and democides (see chapter by Breed in this volume). The term *democide* was coined by R. J. Rummel (1994), a political scientist. Democides are not limited to government killings due to ethnicity or group membership (genocides), but include all mass killings, direct and indirect, due to government policies. According to Rummel, the largest democide by any one government was committed by Communist China, in large part due to famines caused by agricultural policies (see data point 4).

Data point 5 deals with beliefs about the origin of the human species, which could be construed as a form of collective memory, showing how people with different political affiliations can have different convictions, in this case, how evolution is perceived by members of the various political persuasions in the United States.

WHAT ARE THE ISSUES?

People see individual and collective memories as providing a basis for identities. On a political level, they can be used for self-serving purposes (see chapter by Croissant and Chambers in this volume). Contested memories may contribute to national and international cultural conflicts (data point 6), but they may also be the result of a legitimate fight for recognition of minority groups against dominant ideologies. Contested memories are often bound to certain historical places (an example is given by Croissant and Chambers; see also Ortiz García and Sánchez-Carretero on grassroots memorials) or objects passed down from ancestors (see Thomas on the manipulation of memories by museums), as these places and objects have no meaning in themselves, but only become part of one's heritage through assigning (different) meaning to them. Changing these places and objects is therefore also often connected to conflict (see chapter by Viejo-Rose).

Global Collective Memories

1 Most Important World Figures in the Past 100 Years in 12 Countries (2003 – 2006)

	CHINA	INDIA	EAST TIMOR	INDONESIA	RUSSIA	UKRAINE	POLAND	TURKEY	HUNGARY	BRAZIL	PORTUGAL	SPAIN
HITLER	58% -1	61% -0.4		58% -1.2	57% -2	62% -1.7	86% -2.7	60% -1	94% -2.5	43% -2	77% -2.8	64% -2.8
GEORGE W. BUSH		11% -2	51% +0.6	30% -2.1				24% -2.8		35% -2.5	16% -1	30% -2.9
EINSTEIN	42% +1.5	16% +1.8		23% +1.4			14% +2.2	25% +1.8			23% +2.2	11% +2.6
GANDHI		75% +0.9		18% +1.8		38% +1.3			7% +1.2	16% +2.5		31% +2.5
MOTHER TERESA		22% +1.6		20% +2			11% +2.6			11% +2.8	18% +2.7	25% +2
POPE JOHN PAUL II			17% +2.9			15% +1.4	48% +2.7				26% +2.5	11% +0.8
STALIN					56% -0.4	33% -2.6	38% -2.7		45% -2.1		10% -2.5	

2 Distribution of Memorable Events Over the Past 50 Years Among Chinese Countryside Villagers and Cadres (1996)

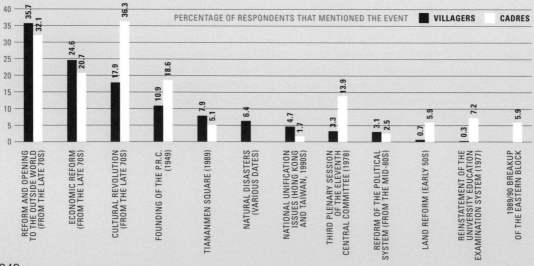

PERCENTAGE OF RESPONDENTS THAT MENTIONED THE EVENT ■ VILLAGERS □ CADRES

Event	VILLAGERS	CADRES
REFORM AND OPENING TO THE OUTSIDE WORLD (FROM THE LATE 70S)	35.7	32.1
ECONOMIC REFORM (FROM THE LATE 70S)	24.6	20.7
CULTURAL REVOLUTION (FROM THE LATE 70S)	17.9	36.3
FOUNDING OF THE P.R.C. (1949)	10.9	18.6
TIANANMEN SQUARE (1989)	7.9	5.1
NATURAL DISASTERS (VARIOUS DATES)	6.4	
NATIONAL UNIFICATION ISSUES (HONG KONG AND TAIWAN, 1990S)	4.7	1.7
THIRD PLENARY SESSION OF THE ELEVENTH CENTRAL COMMITTEE (1978)	3.3	13.9
REFORM OF THE POLITICAL SYSTEM (FROM THE MID-80S)	3.1	2.5
LAND REFORM (EARLY 50S)	0.7	5.9
REINSTATEMENT OF THE UNIVERSITY EDUCATION EXAMINATION SYSTEM (1977)	0.3	7.2
1989/90 BREAKUP OF THE EASTERN BLOCK		5.9

3 Most Important Events in World History in 12 Countries (2003 – 2006)

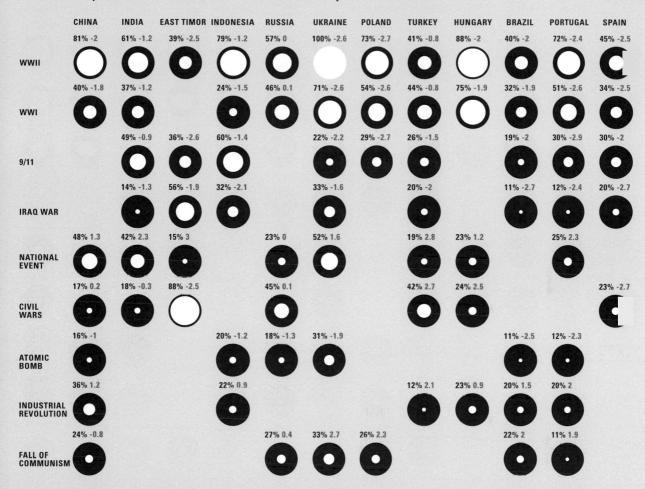

	CHINA	INDIA	EAST TIMOR	INDONESIA	RUSSIA	UKRAINE	POLAND	TURKEY	HUNGARY	BRAZIL	PORTUGAL	SPAIN
WWII	81% -2	61% -1.2	39% -2.5	79% -1.2	57% 0	100% -2.6	73% -2.7	41% -0.8	88% -2	40% -2	72% -2.4	45% -2.5
WWI	40% -1.8	37% -1.2		24% -1.5	46% 0.1	71% -2.6	54% -2.6	44% -0.8	75% -1.9	32% -1.9	51% -2.6	34% -2.5
9/11		49% -0.9	36% -2.6	60% -1.4		22% -2.2	29% -2.7	26% -1.5		19% -2	30% -2.9	30% -2
IRAQ WAR		14% -1.3	56% -1.9	32% -2.1		33% -1.6		20% -2		11% -2.7	12% -2.4	20% -2.7
NATIONAL EVENT	48% 1.3	42% 2.3	15% 3		23% 0	52% 1.6		19% 2.8	23% 1.2		25% 2.3	
CIVIL WARS	17% 0.2	18% -0.3	88% -2.5		45% 0.1			42% 2.7	24% 2.5			23% -2.7
ATOMIC BOMB	16% -1			20% -1.2	18% -1.3	31% -1.9				11% -2.5	12% -2.3	
INDUSTRIAL REVOLUTION	36% 1.2			22% 0.9				12% 2.1	23% 0.9	20% 1.5	20% 2	
FALL OF COMMUNISM	24% -0.8				27% 0.4	33% 2.7	26% 2.3			22% 2	11% 1.9	

4 National and World Events Since 1930 Most Often Mentioned by US Respondents (1985, 2000, and 2002)

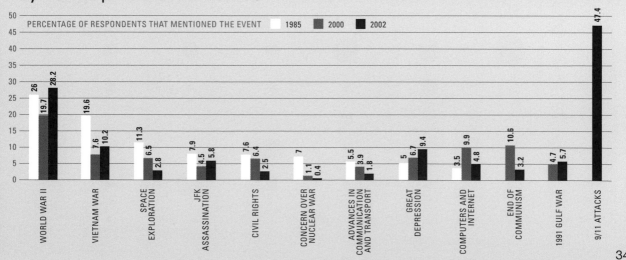

PERCENTAGE OF RESPONDENTS THAT MENTIONED THE EVENT ☐ 1985 ▨ 2000 ■ 2002

Event	1985	2000	2002
WORLD WAR II	26	19.7	28.2
VIETNAM WAR	19.6	7.6	10.2
SPACE EXPLORATION	11.3	6.5	2.8
JFK ASSASSINATION	7.9	4.5	5.8
CIVIL RIGHTS	7.6	6.4	2.5
CONCERN OVER NUCLEAR WAR	7	1.1	0.4
ADVANCES IN COMMUNICATION AND TRANSPORT	5.5	3.9	1.8
GREAT DEPRESSION	5	6.7	9.4
COMPUTERS AND INTERNET	3.5	9.9	4.8
END OF COMMUNISM	10.6	3.2	
1991 GULF WAR	4.7	5.7	
9/11 ATTACKS			47.4

DESIGN: ROXANE ZARGHAM

341

5 Most Important Events in World History in 12 Other Countries (1996 – 2002)

	JAPAN	TAIWAN	HONG KONG	SINGAPORE	AUSTRALIA	NEW ZEALAND	PHILIP-PINES	MALAYSIA	US	UK	FRANCE	GERMANY
WWII	52%	69%	81%	94%	68%	73%	68%	60%	86%	77%	64%	68%
WWI	29%	60%	52%	84%	60%	64%	54%	60%	50%	64%	30%	60%
FRENCH REVOLUTION	23%	10%	14%	9%		15%	16%		14%		54%	49%
INDUSTRIAL REVOLUTION	17%	23%		19%	19%	20%	15%	28%		18%		
DISCOVERY OF AMERICAS	9%	22%	14%			16%			38%	18%	28%	32%
FALL OF COMMUNISM		15%	23%	10%		16%			12%		19%	23%
MAN ON MOON		25%			24%	37%	11%			26%	16%	
ATOMIC BOMB	9%				21%		13%	17%		15%	20%	
VIETNAM WAR	17%			11%	18%				20%	28%		20%

6 Intercontinental Perception of Regional Political Events of the Past 100 Years

		RESPONDENTS FROM:					
		EUROPE	N. AMERICA	LATIN AMERICA	AFRICA	ASIA	OCEANIA
REMEMBER EVENTS THAT TOOK PLACE (IN %):	EUROPE	79.3%	55.2%	67.9%	38.3%	44.2%	41.7%
	N. AMERICA	11.2%	44.8%	25.5%	18.5%	20.3%	30.5%
	LATIN AMERICA	1.7%	2.3%	30.7%	0%	1.1%	2.1%
	AFRICA	3%	6.4%	2.9%	60.5%	2.1%	8.6%
	ASIA	11.9%	25.8%	21.2%	29.6%	69.2%	28.3%
	OCEANIA	0%	0%	0%	0%	0%	16.0%

342

Global Collective Memories

"Like the present, the past is to some extent also part of a social reality that, while far from being absolutely objective, nonetheless transcends our own subjectivity and is shared by others around us." (Zerubavel, 1997: 81)

Which events and experiences occupy the collective memories of societies, as opposed to individual memories? How are these collective memories mediated through cultural tools and artifacts? Both the Introduction and the Wertsch and Billingsley chapter in Part I explore such questions. The present suite is based on data from global surveys of what people consider to be the most important events or figures of the past 50 to 100 years or even in human history. The answers to the surveys were aggregated on the country level, showing which of these memories are shared by larger groups. Aggregation at the national level allows for a glimpse into the nation-state as a highly influential mnemonic tool to influence group memory (chapter by Wertsch and Billingsley).

WHAT DO WE KNOW?

The data suggest that, across countries, certain events are commonly engraved in collective memories. Globally, respondents mention the two World Wars and the September 11, 2001, attacks on the World Trade Center, the Pentagon, and Flight 93 as part of this trans-national memory. Other frequently cited events include nuclear bombings, the fall of communism (and related events), and the Industrial Revolution. Also mentioned are the first man on the moon, the Vietnam War, the French Revolution, and the European discovery of the Americas (see data points 3 and 5).

While this shows an astonishingly high level of trans-national collective memory, there are also significant points of divergence, both with regard to selection of events and their evaluation. In general, when asked about world history or global events, people tend to have biases toward the impact of their own national historical heritage and often focus on negative events, mainly political or war-related. Within these national specifics one can detect again regional and cultural similarities, for example, when Australia and New Zealand have women's suffrage and the birth of Christ within their national top 10 events. The latter appears also in the United States, Great Britain, and Poland (where the election of a Polish pope and the death of the latter are also part of the top 10) and is a sign of the importance of the religious sphere for heritage, memory, and identity.

Some of these events are connected to memories about certain people, as with Hitler and World War II (datapoint 1). However, some figures are popular on a global level due to other reasons, such as scientific achievements (A. Einstein) or social engagement (Mother Teresa).

The data also depict memories over time within a country (datapoint 4). Predictably, the 9/11 attacks had an immense impact on the collective memory of US citizens. Another level of disaggregation is the social status of respondents. Data point 2 compares the memories of Chinese peasants with that of communist party cadres. Although there are some interesting differences (e.g., concerning natural disasters or the breakup of the Eastern bloc), both groups have the same top four: reform and opening to the outside world, economic reform, cultural revolution, and the founding of the People's Republic of China.

WHAT ARE THE ISSUES?

It is difficult to determine whether our memories are becoming increasingly global. The only available comparison over time presents mixed results (data point 4). The end of communism emerged as a new non-US topic, but the most important new event is the 9/11 attack. Whether this is perceived in its global relevance, or as a nationally relevant event, cannot be specified, showing one of the shortcomings of the surveys. Comparisons of age groups within countries regularly show that memories of the two World Wars, still the most important global events overall, are decreasing among younger cohorts (e.g. Schuman, Akiyama & Knäuper, 1998).

While these studies are some of the few addressing collective memory in a comparative perspective, there are methodological drawbacks. For example, more qualitative approaches would be needed to explain why the memories are seen as important. A second problem is whether or not national samples are representative— sometimes they are rather small and from a selective background (e.g., students in higher education). A third issue is the influence of other factors on responses. Especially the age of respondents has an important impact on chosen events. Most studies therefore split up their samples by age groups, but due to space constraints, this could not be done in this suite. Other factors are ethnic or social background (see data point 2), while gender does not seem to make a major difference.

Places

₁ Foreign Born Population in Major US Cities

2000

KEY

Foreign born persons
%

Langage other than English spoken at home
%

CITY

NEW YORK	LOS ANGELES	CHICAGO	HOUSTON	PHOENIX	TOTAL US
36% 48%	41% 58%	22% 36%	26% 41%	20% 32%	11% 18%

₂ Berlin Internationalization

Net Migration Into Berlin (1992-2004)

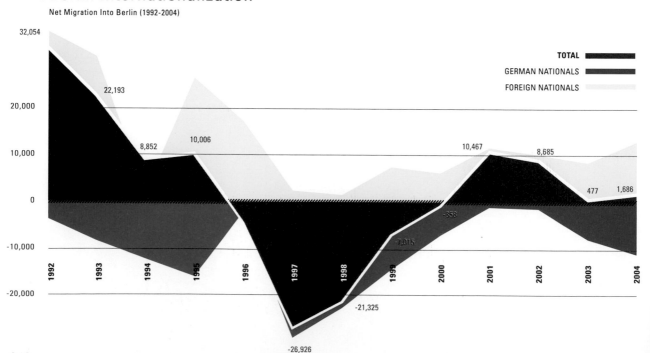

TOTAL
GERMAN NATIONALS
FOREIGN NATIONALS

32,054
22,193
8,852
10,006
20,000
10,467
8,685
10,000
477   1,686
0
-858
-7,015
-10,000
-21,325
-20,000
-26,926

1992 1993 1994 1995 1996 1997 1998 1999 2000 2001 2002 2003 2004

346

Global Top 10 Cities
(2008)

Rank	Business Activity	Human Capital	Information Exchange	Cultural Experience	Political Engagement	Total Score	
1	1	1	4	3	2	289	NEW YORK
2	4	2	3	1	5	285	LONDON
3	3	11	1	2	4	279	PARIS
4	2	6	7	7	6	272	TOKYO
5	15	4	11	5	17	248	LOS ANGELES
6	7	35	5	10	19	224	SEOUL
7	12	3	24	20	20	221	CHICAGO
8	6	7	15	37	16	219	SINGAPORE
9	5	5	6	26	40	218	HONG KONG
10	26	10	18	4	24	218	TORONTO

Architecture Degrees in the U.S.
Awarded to Minorities (1991 vs. 2008)

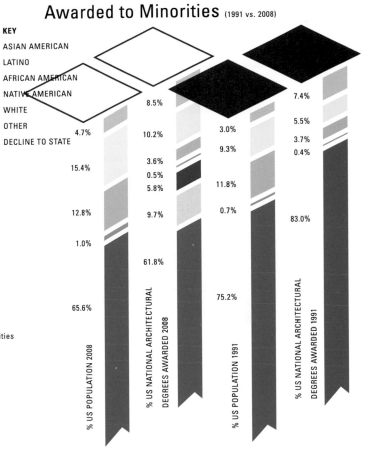

KEY
- ASIAN AMERICAN
- LATINO
- AFRICAN AMERICAN
- NATIVE AMERICAN
- WHITE
- OTHER
- DECLINE TO STATE

% US POPULATION 2008: 4.7%, 15.4%, 12.8%, 1.0%, 65.6%

% US NATIONAL ARCHITECTURAL DEGREES AWARDED 2008: 8.5%, 10.2%, 3.6%, 0.5%, 5.8%, 9.7%, 61.8%

% US POPULATION 1991: 3.0%, 9.3%, 11.8%, 0.7%, 75.2%

% US NATIONAL ARCHITECTURAL DEGREES AWARDED 1991: 7.4%, 5.5%, 3.7%, 0.4%, 83.0%

5

City Cultural Employment

Cultural Employment as % of National Cultural Employment in Select Cities

City Population
(% of National Population)

City Culture Employment
(% of National Culture Employment)

LONDON — 7371 (12%) — 525 (24%)

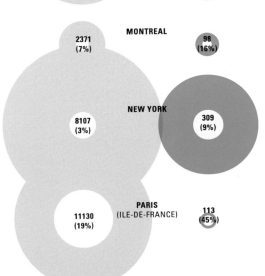

MONTREAL — 2371 (7%) — 98 (16%)

NEW YORK — 8107 (3%) — 309 (9%)

PARIS (ILE-DE-FRANCE) — 11130 (19%) — 113 (45%)

6

Honeymoon Sites Japan

Preferred Honeymoon Destinations of Japanese Women 2008

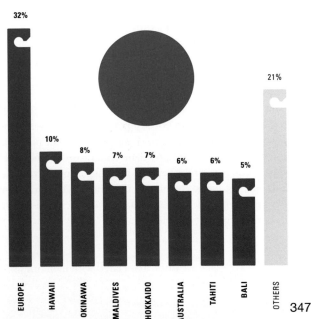

EUROPE	HAWAII	OKINAWA	MALDIVES	HOKKAIDO	AUSTRALIA	TAHITI	BALI	OTHERS
32%	10%	8%	7%	7%	6%	6%	5%	21%

DESIGN: GEORGE BROWER

Places

Heritage, memory, and identity are frequently linked to particular places or spaces. These locations are used and shaped by people of various backgrounds. Often, these places— modern and busy— provide the foundation for creativity and new cultural development. Chinatowns everywhere, for example, have become centers of cultural activity. Hip-hop, now a broad and mainstream musical phenomenon generating billions of dollars worth of revenue annually, started in small clusters of multi-ethnic urban communities (see Indicator Suite in volume 3 of this series). Furthermore, as we saw from volume 3 of the present series globalization is transforming the creative landscape in many different ways. Together with the traditional fine arts, the cultural or creative industries such as graphic design now loom large. Los Angeles, among many cities, has seen a decline in employment in art galleries and an increase in product design between 2002 and 2007 (Otis College of Art and Design, 2008). Conversely, places can be sites of major cultural and heritage-related conflict and tension such as the Preah Vihear Temple discussed by Croissant and Chambers in chapter 11.

WHAT DO WE KNOW?

The most marked effects of globalization on urban areas are generated by migration and the cultural diversification of the population. Data point 1 shows that the share of households in which non-English languages are spoken is significantly higher in large US cities than the national average. Immigrants tend to settle in cities, which then become the locational recipients of diverse cultural contributions. For instance, with a large population of Chinese descent, Bangkok boasts some of the finest Chinese cuisine as well as hybrid dishes that have evolved out of the mixed Chinese and Thai heritages. Data point 2 outlines this trend over time (from 1992 to 2004) using Berlin, Germany, as a case study. In recent years, the city has experienced net emigration by German nationals, while there clearly was net immigration by people of foreign birth. The result is a cultural melting pot that leads to new hybrid cultures and innovations as well as to tensions and a shifting or disparate collective concept of national identity and heritage.

Architecture is considered to be part of the heritage and hence of the identity of different groups; it also influences the way we perceive the world. Different ethnic groups and cultures display different patterns in terms of local cultural production. Data point 4 shows how different ethnicities have the potential to shape architecture in the United States. In both 1991 and 2008, Asian- Americans, for instance, received a share of architectural degrees far greater than the percentage of the American population that they represent. African- Americans, on the other hand, are underrepresented when it comes to architecture. The consulting firm AT Kearney looked at large cities and sought to gauge the impact that they have internationally (data point 3). Part of this analysis included an examination of which cities worldwide have the most to offer in terms of cultural experience.

Memories of place are often associated with memories of events. The obvious example is September 11, 2001, in Manhattan (see also Carretero and Ortíz in this volume). On a far more benign plane, one of the most memorable events in many people's lifetime is their wedding/honeymoon. Data point 6 shows the honeymoon destination preferences of Japanese women in 2008. Globalization is having an effect on honeymooners everywhere, making exotic and far away locations top the list. International and diverse regions, colorful and culture-rich as they are, attract young couples who then become active participants in the cultural experience and connect their personal memories to the location of choice.

WHAT ARE THE ISSUES?

Place has become increasingly important to cultural production and in some new ways. Data point 5 shows the nexus between cities and culture. Researchers in the field of culture believe that, in addition to individual creativity, there is a significant network component to innovation. "... [A]lthough some creative solutions can be seen as the products of individual insight, many others are the products of momentary collective processes." (Cattani and Ferriani, 2008; see also volume 3 of the series). Heterogeneity and a connection to both the cultural core as well as the periphery are conducive to cultural creation, which implies that innovation may take place in the city, or not too far from it. However, in terms of production, cultural goods enjoy significant agglomeration effects, which explain their strong urban presence (Power, 2002). Obviously, also, cultural globalization also has a conflictual dimension. Many researchers, including David Throsby (2008), have observed how access to the cultural expressions of many others broadens horizons and supports artistic creations, yet also often provokes strong and sometimes violent local resistance.

Media

1 Wikipedia: Top 10 Multilingual Ranking (OCTOBER 2008)

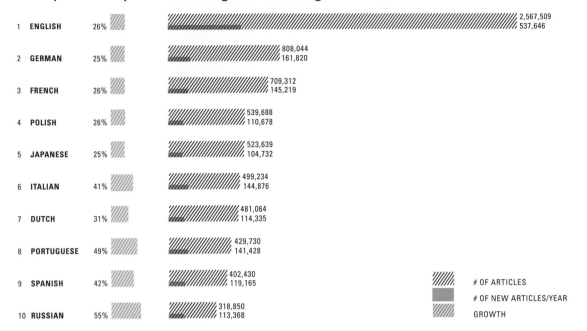

#	Language	Growth	# of Articles	# of New Articles/Year
1	ENGLISH	26%	2,567,509	537,646
2	GERMAN	25%	808,044	161,820
3	FRENCH	26%	709,312	145,219
4	POLISH	26%	539,688	110,678
5	JAPANESE	25%	523,639	104,732
6	ITALIAN	41%	499,234	144,876
7	DUTCH	31%	481,064	114,335
8	PORTUGUESE	49%	429,730	141,428
9	SPANISH	42%	402,430	119,165
10	RUSSIAN	55%	318,850	113,368

OF ARTICLES
OF NEW ARTICLES/YEAR
GROWTH

2 Top Rated History Movies of All Time Worldwide (1961-2004)

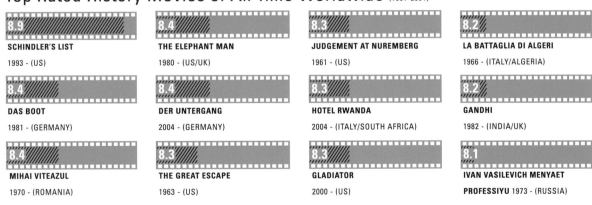

8.9 SCHINDLER'S LIST
1993 - (US)

8.4 THE ELEPHANT MAN
1980 - (US/UK)

8.3 JUDGEMENT AT NUREMBERG
1961 - (US)

8.2 LA BATTAGLIA DI ALGERI
1966 - (ITALY/ALGERIA)

8.4 DAS BOOT
1981 - (GERMANY)

8.4 DER UNTERGANG
2004 - (GERMANY)

8.3 HOTEL RWANDA
2004 - (ITALY/SOUTH AFRICA)

8.2 GANDHI
1982 - (INDIA/UK)

8.4 MIHAI VITEAZUL
1970 - (ROMANIA)

8.3 THE GREAT ESCAPE
1963 - (US)

8.3 GLADIATOR
2000 - (US)

8.1 IVAN VASILEVICH MENYAET
PROFESSIYU 1973 - (RUSSIA)

3 Stock Size of the Top 10 Largest Libraries of the World IN MLN OBJECTS

#	Library	Stock (mln objects)
1	LIBRARY OF CONGRESS (US)	32
2	THE NATIONAL LIBRARY OF CHINA (CHINA)	27
3	DEUTSCHE BIBLOTHEK (GERMANY)	24.7
4	LIBRARY OF THE RUSSIAN ACADEMY OF SCIENCES (RUSSIA)	20
5	NATIONAL LIBRARY OF CANADA (CANADA)	18.8
6	BRITISH LIBRARY (UK)	18
7	HARVARD UNIVERSITY LIBRARY (US)	16.1
8	INSTITUTE FOR SCIENTIFIC INFORMATION ON SOCIAL SCIENCES OF THE RUSSIAN ACADEMY OF SCIENCES (RUSSIA)	13.5
9	VERNADSKY NATIONAL SCIENTIFIC LIBRARY OF UKRAINE (UKRAINE)	13
10	NEW YORK PUBLIC LIBRARY (US)	11

4 Evolution of Information/Media Storage Timeline: Prehistory to Present

LIFE EXPECTANCY IN YEARS

		Life Expectancy (bar)	Information Density
CLAY TABLET	10,000		74
PAPYRUS	5,000		85
ILLUMINATED MANUSCRIPTS	1,000		141
GUTENBERG	1,000		25
MOBY DICK	100		100
NEWSPAPER	50		124
MICROFILM	300		12,000
MICROFICHE	100		36,400
TAPE	30		10,000
DISK	15		108,250
OPTICAL DISK	5		50,000,000
CD-ROM	5		786,432,000
DVD	30		5,046,586,572

Legend:
- ▬ LIFE EXPECTANCY (IN YEARS)
- ▨ INFORMATION DENSITY (CHARACTERS/SQ INCH)

5 *Europeana* Collection by Type and Language (2009)

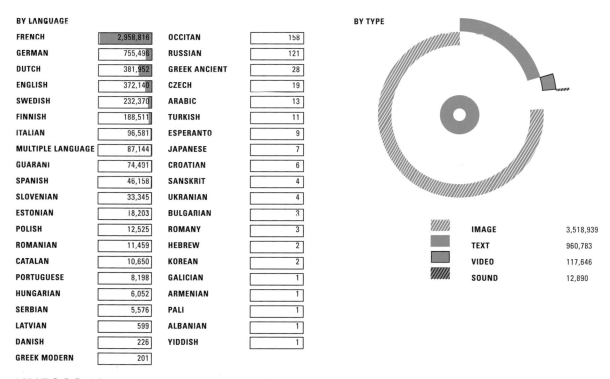

BY LANGUAGE

FRENCH	2,958,816	OCCITAN	158
GERMAN	755,496	RUSSIAN	121
DUTCH	381,952	GREEK ANCIENT	28
ENGLISH	372,140	CZECH	19
SWEDISH	232,370	ARABIC	13
FINNISH	188,511	TURKISH	11
ITALIAN	96,581	ESPERANTO	9
MULTIPLE LANGUAGE	87,144	JAPANESE	7
GUARANI	74,491	CROATIAN	6
SPANISH	46,158	SANSKRIT	4
SLOVENIAN	33,345	UKRANIAN	4
ESTONIAN	18,203	BULGARIAN	3
POLISH	12,525	ROMANY	3
ROMANIAN	11,459	HEBREW	2
CATALAN	10,650	KOREAN	2
PORTUGUESE	8,198	GALICIAN	1
HUNGARIAN	6,052	ARMENIAN	1
SERBIAN	5,576	PALI	1
LATVIAN	599	ALBANIAN	1
DANISH	226	YIDDISH	1
GREEK MODERN	201		

BY TYPE

IMAGE	3,518,939
TEXT	960,783
VIDEO	117,646
SOUND	12,890

6 UNESCO Memory of the World Program

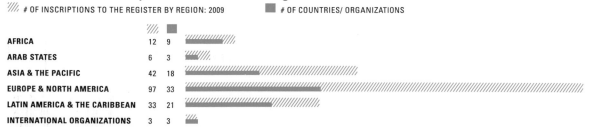

▨ # OF INSCRIPTIONS TO THE REGISTER BY REGION: 2009   ▬ # OF COUNTRIES/ ORGANIZATIONS

	# OF INSCRIPTIONS	# OF COUNTRIES
AFRICA	12	9
ARAB STATES	6	3
ASIA & THE PACIFIC	42	18
EUROPE & NORTH AMERICA	97	33
LATIN AMERICA & THE CARIBBEAN	33	21
INTERNATIONAL ORGANIZATIONS	3	3

DESIGN: CAMILE ORILLANEDA

Media

The notion of media is understood in many different ways; for our purposes we may understand media to be any means of communication that influences formations of heritage, identity, and memory (see chapters by Volcic and Moore in this volume). Newspapers, radio, and television and other traditional forms of media are often referred to today as *old media*. The term *new media* has been used since the 1960s, and its usage has grown since the emergence of the Internet in the 1990s. According to Hartley (2002), new media technologies have diversified the material basis for society, thus enabling globalization and tremendous cultural shifts. Yet, the terms *old* and *new* have to be put into historical context. The introduction of a technology is considered new until an alternative technology arises. For instance, television was a new media technology to baby boomers, but to the Internet generation it is perceived as old. New media, however, do not replace old media, but are the continuation of their predecessors (see the discussion of the term *new* in Chun & Keenan, 2006).

WHAT DO WE KNOW?

Key findings of this indicator suite relate to the transition from old to new media and their influence on our memories in an era of globalization:

- English topped the list of languages in the Wikipedia multilingual ranking, with more than 2.5 million articles and an annual growth rate of 26 percent. Russian comes in 10th but has the strongest growth rate at 55 per cent (see data point 1).
- Movies can transmit historical knowledge and may shape people's memories and emotions toward certain events. According to a survey by the Internet Movie Database (IMDB), the top-rated historical movie of all time is an American movie called *Schindler's List*, which was released in 1993 and tells the story of a German businessman who saved the lives of thousands of Polish Jewish refugees by hiring them in his factories (see data point 2).
- National libraries archive memory in the form of books. Although many of these books and manuscripts are now in the process of being digitized, libraries still play a major role in preserving collective heritage and memory. The Library of Congress in the United States is the largest library worldwide with more than 32 million items, followed by the National Library of China and the *Deutsche Bibliothek* in Germany with 27 and 24.7 million items, respectively (see data point 3).
- While older media storage forms have lower information capacity, their life expectancy is much higher than that of newer forms. Papyrus rolls, for instance, date back to 4000 BC and have a life expectancy of 5,000 years but can only carry 85 characters per square inch. Newer forms of media storage such as CDs and DVDs only have 5 to 30 years of life expectancy but can carry billions of characters per square inch (see data point 4). This might lead to potential digital archiving problems when it comes to storing enormous quantities of data and information and is one of the major reasons why libraries are expected to remain very important archiving resources.
- There are significant efforts under way internationally to digitalize data on heri-

tage. The EU- project *Europeana* was launched only in 2008 but already provides access to more than 4.6 million digital items including images, texts, videos, and sounds. That number is projected to increase by about 100 per cent in 2010 (see data point 5).

- The Memory of the World Program was initiated by the UNESCO in 1992 as a means of preserving heritage through archives of documents, oral traditions, and anything of universal value. Europe and North America accounted for almost half of the items inscribed in the register in 2009 (see data point 6 and the sustainability suite of this volume).

WHAT ARE THE ISSUES?

Mere information has to be actively processed by people and incorporated into their cultural contexts to become part of their heritage and memory. New media, though, are often seen as taking information out of context and producing a global information overflow, challenging people's limited capabilities to process media content (Southwell & Mira, 2004). Related to this issue is the lack of filters that prohibit users from finding good and accountable content. Another problem is posed by the rapid changes in content, resulting in a low overall stability. A Wikipedia page, for instance, may be edited hundreds of times by any registered contributor.

Perhaps one of the most important issues is the so-called "digital divide." Even though the digital revolution has increased access exponentially in many countries, most of the world's population is still excluded. The gap is being reduced fast, yet everywhere there are also certain groups of the population, for example, the elderly or the less educated, who find the new media difficult to use (Charness & Holley, 2004, and chapter by Moore in this volume). What this means for global heritage is yet to be seen, but some argue that it leaves less competent individuals and countries behind, at least for the time being.

MIGRATION AND DIASPORA

1 FOREIGN-BORN POPULATION (1986–2005)

BY REGION AND COUNTRY (DIFFERENT YEARS)

SOUTH AMERICA / OCEANIA / NORTH AMERICA / EUROPE / ASIA / AFRICA

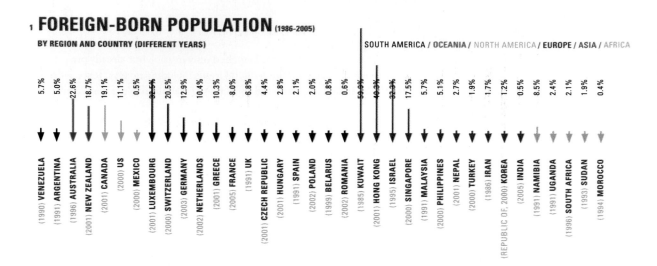

Country	%
(1990) VENEZUELA	5.7%
(1991) ARGENTINA	5.0%
(1996) AUSTRALIA	22.6%
(2001) NEW ZEALAND	18.7%
(2001) CANADA	19.1%
(2000) US	11.1%
(2000) MEXICO	0.5%
(2001) LUXEMBOURG	32.6%
(2000) SWITZERLAND	20.5%
(2003) GERMANY	12.9%
(2002) NETHERLANDS	10.4%
(2001) GREECE	10.3%
(2005) FRANCE	8.0%
(1991) UK	6.8%
(2001) CZECH REPUBLIC	4.4%
(2001) HUNGARY	2.8%
(1991) SPAIN	2.1%
(2002) POLAND	2.0%
(1999) BELARUS	0.8%
(2002) ROMANIA	0.6%
(1985) KUWAIT	59.9%
(2001) HONG KONG	40.9%
(1995) ISRAEL	32.3%
(2000) SINGAPORE	17.5%
(1991) MALAYSIA	5.7%
(2000) PHILIPPINES	5.1%
(2001) NEPAL	2.7%
(2000) TURKEY	1.9%
(1986) IRAN	1.7%
(REPUBLIC OF, 2000) KOREA	1.2%
(2005) INDIA	0.5%
(1991) NAMIBIA	8.5%
(1991) UGANDA	2.4%
(1996) SOUTH AFRICA	2.1%
(1993) SUDAN	1.9%
(1994) MOROCCO	0.4%

2 REFUGEES AS A PERCENTAGE OF INTERNATIONAL MIGRANTS (1990–2010)

1990 / 1995 / 2000 / 2005 / 2010 (ESTIMATED)

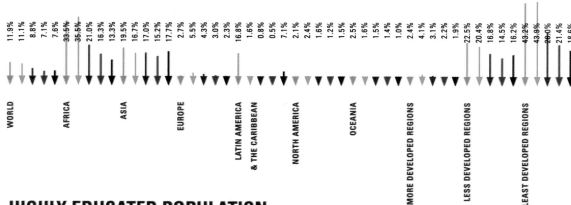

Region	1990	1995	2000	2005	2010
WORLD	11.9%	11.1%	8.8%	7.1%	7.6%
AFRICA	33.5%	35.5%	21.0%	16.3%	13.3%
ASIA	19.5%	16.7%	17.0%	15.2%	17.7%
EUROPE	2.7%	5.5%	4.3%	3.0%	2.3%
LATIN AMERICA & THE CARIBBEAN	16.8%	1.6%	0.8%	0.5%	7.1%
NORTH AMERICA	2.1%	2.4%	1.6%	1.2%	1.5%
OCEANIA	2.5%	1.6%	1.5%	1.4%	1.0%
MORE DEVELOPED REGIONS	2.4%	4.1%	3.1%	2.2%	1.9%
LESS DEVELOPED REGIONS	22.5%	20.4%	16.8%	14.5%	16.2%
LEAST DEVELOPED REGIONS	43.2%	43.9%	26.0%	21.4%	18.6%

3 HIGHLY EDUCATED POPULATION (2005)

BY PLACE OF BIRTH IN SELECTED OECD COUNTRIES

POPULATION AGE 15+ WITH TERTIARY EDUCATION (IN %)

NATIVE-BORN / FOREIGN-BORN / EXPATRIATES

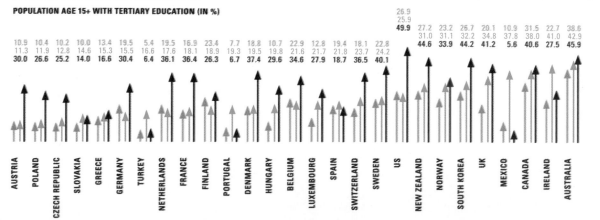

Country	NATIVE-BORN	FOREIGN-BORN	EXPATRIATES
AUSTRIA	10.9	11.3	30.0
POLAND	10.4	11.9	26.6
CZECH REPUBLIC	10.2	12.8	25.2
SLOVAKIA	10.0	14.6	14.0
GREECE	13.4	15.3	16.6
GERMANY	19.5	15.5	30.4
TURKEY	5.4	16.6	6.4
NETHERLANDS	19.5	17.6	36.1
FRANCE	16.9	18.1	36.4
FINLAND	23.4	18.9	26.3
PORTUGAL	7.7	19.3	6.7
DENMARK	18.8	19.5	37.4
HUNGARY	10.7	19.8	29.6
BELGIUM	22.9	21.6	34.6
LUXEMBOURG	12.8	21.7	27.9
SPAIN	19.4	21.8	18.7
SWITZERLAND	18.1	23.7	36.5
SWEDEN	22.8	24.2	40.1
US	26.9 / 25.9 / 49.9		
NEW ZEALAND	27.2	31.0	44.6
NORWAY	23.2	31.1	33.9
SOUTH KOREA	25.7	32.2	44.2
UK	20.1	34.8	41.2
MEXICO	10.9	37.8	5.6
CANADA	31.5	38.0	40.6
IRELAND	22.7	41.0	27.5
AUSTRALIA	38.6	42.9	45.9

4 TOP 20 COUNTRIES BY MIGRANT REMITTANCE OUTFLOW IN MLN US$ (2008)

KAZAKHSTAN 3,559.1
BELGIUM 3,688.8
KUWAIT 3,824.2
CZECH REPUBLIC 3,825.9
FRANCE 4,541.1
JAPAN 4,743
NORWAY 4,775.6
UK 5,048.2
OMAN 5,180.8
CHINA 5,736.7
MALAYSIA 6,384.5

NETHERLANDS 8,431.4
LUXEMBOURG 10,922.4
ITALY 12,718
SPAIN 14,656.3
GERMANY 14,975.8
SAUDI ARABIA 16,067.5
SWITZERLAND 18,954.4

RUSSIAN FED. 26,145.2
US 47,181.9

TONGA 39.4% (99.5)
MOLDOVA 34.1% (1,498.2)
LESOTHO 27.7% (443,3)
GUYANA 25.8% (278.5)
LEBANON 23.7% (5,769.2)
TAJIKISTAN 45.5% (1,690.8)

SAMOA 22.8% (119.8)
JORDAN 21.7% (3,434.1)
HONDURAS 21.5% (2,624.7)
KYRGYZ REP. 19.1% (714.8)
JAMAICA 18.8% (2,143.6)
EL SALVADOR 18.2% (3,711.3)

HAITI 18.2% (1,222.1)
BOSNIA & HERZEGOVINA 17.8% (1,222.1)
NEPAL 16.8% (1,733.9)
SERBIA 13.9% (739.6)
ALBANIA 13.6% (1,488.0)
NICARAGUA 12.9% (739.6)
GUATEMALA 12.6% (4,253.9)

PHILIPPINES 11.3% 16,302

5 TOP 20 COUNTRIES BY MIGRANT REMITTANCE INFLOW

AS SHARE OF GDP (2007) RANKING OF THOSE COUNTRIES ONLY, FOR WHICH REMITTANCES INFLOW DATA WERE AVAILABLE.
TOTAL MIGRANT REMITTANCE INFLOW GIVEN IN BRACKETS (IN MLN US$).

6 INTERRACIAL MARRIAGES US %

OF MARRIED PEOPLE WHO HAVE DIFFERENT RACE SPOUSES (1900-2005)

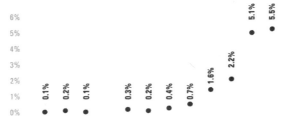

6%
5% — 5.1% — 5.5%
4%
3%
2% — 2.2%
1% — 0.1% 0.2% 0.1% 0.3% 0.2% 0.4% 0.7% 1.6%
0%

1900 1910 1920 1930 1940 1950 1960 1970 1980 1990 2000 2005

7 TOP 15 H1B-VISAS & GREEN CARD

US SPONSORING COMPANIES (2000-2009)

1. MICROSOFT 28,800
2. SATYAM COMPUTER SERVICES 24,779
3. ENTERPRISE BUSINESS SOLUTIONS 12,931
4. IBM 12,738
5. ORACLE 10,821
6. PATNI COMPUTER SYSTEMS 9,528
7. INTEL 9,087
8. ERNST & YOUNG 7,772

9. INFOSYS TECHNOLOGIES 7,712
10. XCELTECH 7,116
11. RAPIDIGM 6,783
12. CITIGROUP 6,649
13. LARSEN TOUBRO INFOTECH 6,304
14. MOTOROLA 6,253
15. CISCO SYSTEMS 6,251

Migration + Diaspora

Migration flows, both for the receiving community and the immigrant and his or her community, have a profound effect on individual and group collective memory. It is these memories that are used to construct a sense of shared cultural identity heritage (on the role museums play in this process, see chapter by Thomas in this volume). Diasporic memory lies in the liminal space between two cultures and geographies, often morphing into a fusion of the two and creating a new cultural heritage altogether, thereby challenging the often-assumed congruence of identity, memory, heritage, and the nation state (see chapter by Ang in this volume). This is exemplified in the inherent tension between preservation of traditional ties to the homeland and the process of acculturation, which leads to varied changes in both the immigrant and the receiving community that transform concepts of identity (Berry, 2001). This suite explores the interaction of migration with cultural heritage, collective memory and the question of identity. How do recent increases in global population movements destabilize and transform cultural identity and associated memories?

WHAT DO WE KNOW?

Key findings of this data suite highlight multiple themes including current geographic characteristics of migration patterns, financial flows stemming from population movement, and patterns of forced migration. Selected results include

- Data point 1 shows that the proportion of foreign-born persons within the population of Asia and the Middle East far exceeds that of other regions. Kuwait contains the highest proportion with 60 per cent of the population foreign-born, followed by Hong Kong with 40 per cent and Israel with more than 32 per cent. In Europe, Luxembourg and Switzerland have the highest percentages of foreign-borns. Africa, Eastern Europe, and Mexico have notably low levels of foreign-born residents. These areas tend to be senders of migrants rather than receivers.
- Trends in forced migration are shown in data point 2, which examines refugees as a percentage of the total immigrant population by region. Generally speaking, the proportion of refugees has declined since 1990. The most substantial declines occurred in Latin America, the Caribbean, and Africa. Asia has made little progress in this regard and refugees represent close to 18 per cent of all immigrants. However, these data do not reflect within-country forced migration trends. The number of internally displaced persons has been rising over the past several years, particularly in Africa (IMDC, 2008).
- Moving to the educational characteristics of foreign-born compared with native-born residents, data point 3 illustrates differences across selected OECD countries. In the majority, a higher proportion of expatriates have undertaken some form of tertiary education. Differences in the prevalence of tertiary education levels are less clear between foreign-born and native-born residents. Turkey, Portugal, Mexico, and Ireland have significantly larger proportions of educated foreign-born residents compared with native-born. The converse is true, although to a lesser magnitude in Germany, Netherlands, and Finland. These differences are likely attributable to labor demands and immigration policies.

- Financial flows from immigrants play a large role in the global economy through remittances sent and received. The patterns and relative importance of these flows to national economies vary greatly. Data points 4 and 5 exhibit inflows and outflows of remittances by country. Overall, inflows are evident mainly for developing countries and outflows for middle- or high-income countries. However, Russia exhibits the second largest outflow of remittances (the United States is first, Switzerland third, and Saudi Arabia fourth). Also surprising is that Tajikistan, Tonga, and Moldova are the top three receivers of remittances as a share of GDP. Kuwait, although it hosts the largest proportion of foreign-born residents, falls behind in terms of outflows of remittances.

WHAT ARE THE ISSUES?

Stuart Hall has identified two contradictory approaches to defining cultural identity: "first, identity understood as a collective, shared history among individuals affiliated by race or ethnicity that is considered to be fixed or stable; and second, identity understood as unstable, metamorphic, and even contradictory" (Hall, 2003: 233). This framework clearly articulates the contradictions inherent in any examination of cultural identity in relation to diaspora communities. While mass population migration has gone on for thousands of years and is clearly not a new phenomenon, today's global Diaspora communities have access to air transportation, the Internet and mobile phones. While advances in technology increasingly allow migrants to remain connected to home country "cultural identity," they also open a cultural portal from the receiving country back to the home country. Not only are people moving more rapidly, so too are cultural products; many consider that they still flow primarily from the West to the Rest, although there has been much diversification in recent years. Conditions conducive to patterns of fusion and morphing have been expanded through migration (see chapter by Navaro-Yashin for an example) as well as through technology. Creolization of culture and identity is but one important result, where the "diaspora has a truly imaginary homeland, one located in the Creole diaspora" (see chapter by Boswell in this volume) rather than in any particular nation-state.

EDUCATION   ₁ DECADAL CHANGE IN NUMBER OF TERTIARY VS

1975 - 1985

71.4%

1985 - 1995

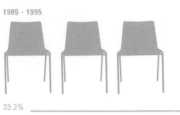

33.3%

1975 - 1985

37.5%

1985 - 1995

54.5%

₂ HOLOCAUST TEACHING BY COUNTRY

COUNTRY	ARGENTINA	AUSTRIA	CROATIA	DENMARK
OFFICIAL DIRECTIVE FOR COMPULSORY EDUCATION	Basic Common Contents for General Elementary Education	"Civics Education in Schools"	"International: Declaration of the Washington Conference on the Holocaust, Dec 1998, National: "The Day Of Remembrance of the Holocaust and the Prevention Of Crimes Against Humanity' Adopted 30 October 2003"	None
% OF SCHOOLS TEACHING HOLOCAUST	100%	100%	100%	No Data
INDEPENDENT SUBJECT OR AS A PART OF BROAD TOPIC	Social Science	History and Civic Education	Part of Many Subjects	Both
AGE AT FIRST LESSON	12-14 Years	Grade 8 - Age 14 Years	Grade 7 - Age 13 Years	12 Years
HOURS ALLOCATED	Institutional Decision	4-10 Hours	6-12 Hours	No Data
AREA OF STUDY	Social Sciences	History / Social Studies / Civics	History / Religion / Psychology / Philosophy / Sociology / Ethics	History / Civics / Theology / Psychology / Philosophy
TEACHER TRAINING	Several Over the Year	Several Programs	Several Training Seminars	No Data
NATIONAL HOLOCAUST DAY	April 19th	May 5th	January 27th	January 27th
NATIONAL HOLOCAUST MEMORIAL / MUSEUM	"Fundacion Memoria del Holocausto—Buenos Aires Shoah Museum—Since 1993"	Not Been Established	"Public Institution of the Jasenovac Memorial Area"	Danish-Jewish Museum
STUDENTS VISITING THE MEMORIAL / MUSEUM	May 2005 - 1,709	2004 - Jan-Sep - 81,708	1,000 in 3-Month Period	No Data

INTERNATIONAL MOBILE STUDENTS (1975-2005)

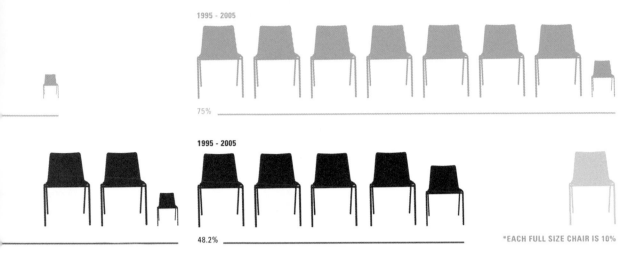

1995 - 2005

75%

1995 - 2005

48.2%

*EACH FULL SIZE CHAIR IS 10%

	FRANCE	GERMANY	ISRAEL	UK	US
	Mandatory Teaching	"Standing Conference of the Ministries of Education and Cultural Affairs"	Yes Since 1982	Statutory Subject in the English National Curriculum	No National Curriculum but State Initiatives
	100%	100%	100%	100%	In Schools In 24/50 States
	Independent Subject	Sub-Topic	Both	Sub-Topic	Sub-Topic
	10-11 Years	12 Years	Preschool, 5 Years	13/14 Years or Earlier	11 Years
	6-12 Hours	16-20 Hours	20-30 Hours	Varies	20-40 Hours
	History / German / Literature / Music / Philosophy	History / Civics / Literature / Religious Instructions	History / Music / Literature / Computer / Theology / Drama / Psychology / Sociology	History / Theology / Literature / Citizenship / Science / Art / Music / Drama	Social Science / Literature/ Philosophy / History /Government / Psychology / Religion
	None	Several, Also In-Service	Several	Several Options	Several Options
	January 27th	January 27th	Nisan 27th = April / May	January 27th	Nisan 27th = April / May
	None	100 Memorial Museums	Yad Vashem	Hyde Park, London	Yes
	0	No Data	100,000	25,000 Per Year	125,000

DESIGN: EVERETT PELAYO

3 UK ARCHAEOLOGY POST GRAD-UATE AND MASTER COURSES (2008-2009)

	% STUDENTS FROM OUT-SIDE UK	EXPENDI-TURE PER STUDENT	TUITION FEES: HOME STUDENTS	TUITION FEES: OVERSEAS STUDENTS
BIRMINGHAM	9%	3	4,200	9,450
BOURNEMOUTH	35%	9	3,800-8,000	7,500
BRADFORD	30%	6	3,960	8,500
BRISTOL	51%	4	3,950	10,200
DURHAM	36%	4	3,996	10,150
LAMPETER	2%	3	3,300	9,744
LEICESTER	4%	5	3,300	9,050
LIVERPOOL	20%	4	3,300	9,100
OXFORD	46%	10	3,390	11,750
SHEFFIELD	38%	4	3,300	9,920
SOUTHAMPTON	43%	3	3,300	9,380
TEESSIDE	15%	6	3,950	8,250
UNIV. COLLEGE LONDON	49%	10	3,300	12,940
YORK	42%	4	3,300	9,510

4 INTERPRETATION OF RELIGIOUS TEACHING BY RELIGIOUS BELIEFS IN THE US (2007)

THERE IS ONLY ONE TRUE WAY TO INTERPRET THE TEACHING OF MY RELIGION
THERE IS MORE THAN ONE WAY **NEITHER / BOTH EQUALLY / DON'T KNOW**

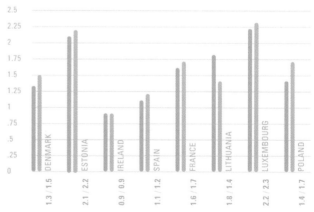

PROTESTANTS
31% 64% **5%**

CATHOLICS
19% 77% **5%**

JEWS
6% 89% **4%**

MUSLIMS
33% 60% **7%**

BUDDHISTS
5% 90% **6%**

ALL RELIGIOUS GROUPS
27% 68% **5%**

5 DISTANCE EDUCATION: % OF POSTSECONDARY INSTITUTIONS OFFERING COURSES (US; 2006-2007)

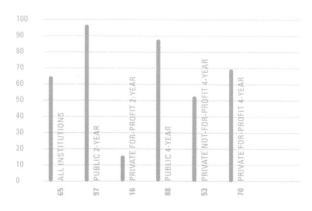

ALL INSTITUTIONS — 65
PUBLIC 2-YEAR — 97
PRIVATE FOR-PROFIT 2-YEAR — 16
PUBLIC 4-YEAR — 88
PRIVATE NOT-FOR-PROFIT 4-YEAR — 53
PRIVATE FOR-PROFIT 4-YEAR — 70

6 AVERAGE NUMBER OF FOREIGN LANGUAGES LEARNED BY PUPILS WORLDWIDE 2002 & 2005

DENMARK 1.3 / 1.5
ESTONIA 2.1 / 2.2
IRELAND 0.9 / 0.9
SPAIN 1.1 / 1.2
FRANCE 1.6 / 1.7
LITHUANIA 1.8 / 1.4
LUXEMBOURG 2.2 / 2.3
POLAND 1.4 / 1.7

Education

Education facilitates the transmission of knowledge, experience, and skills from one generation to another, and hence also of the heritage, memory, and identity of a society as understood in this volume. However, such is the grip both real and imagined of globalization today that educational institutions, particularly at the secondary and tertiary levels, particularly in Europe and the United States, now seek to globalize education as well (Hoelscher, forthcoming). The aim is not only to provide students with an international education, but also to enable them to transcend boundaries in an interdependent world, strengthening their competitive position in the marketplace and helping them cope with the demands of diversity and pluralism (Schuerholz-Lehr, 2007).

WHAT DO WE KNOW?

The education data suite examines how education shapes culture and collective memories in the context of globalization. The main findings include

- Absolute international student mobility, that is, the number of students studying outside their home country, has increased worldwide, but the growth in international student numbers has not kept pace with the dramatic overall increase in tertiary enrollment, resulting in a slightly lower share of international students between 1995 and 2005 (see data point 1).
- Studying history in schools is essential for many reasons: It helps students identify their own culture and understand societal changes to produce modern identity. Data point 2 concerns teaching about the Holocaust, an issue that is central to memory issues in the West. It shows that in Germany teachers allocate 16 to 20 hours on average to teach the Holocaust as a subject, while in Israel that time is nearly doubled. The first Holocaust lesson is taught to children at ages 11 to 13 years on average in most countries, while in Israel they start in preschool (see data point 2).
- Archaeology, which seeks to trace human cultures and origins and thus historical memory over time, seems to attract many international students despite high tuition fees for international students in the United Kingdom. Bristol University, for instance, admitted as many international students as British citizens in this discipline in 2008-2009, followed by University College London and Oxford, respectively (see data point 3).
- Religion plays an integral role in shaping societies and cultures, and religious teachings seem to have different degrees of openness toward alternative interpretations. While within a variance of religious traditions in the United States a majority thinks that there is more than one way to interpret their religion, Jews are the most tolerant. Protestants and Muslims seem to be slightly less liberal on this issue (see data point 4 and the suite on religion in this volume).
- Distance learning increases students' opportunities to access different countries and cultures. Distance learning has recently gained more attention due to new technologies that facilitate online degrees at a relatively low cost. In the United States, 97 per cent of public institutions, but only 16 percent of private 2-year

post-secondary institutions, offer college-level accredited distance learning educational courses (see data point 5).

- Speaking more than one language increases global understanding and cultural awareness. The average number of languages learned by students in public schools is higher for 2005 than for 2000. Poland experienced the highest percentage growth, while Lithuania experienced a slight decrease in the average number of languages learned by its students (see data point 6). A lack of motivation to speak another language in order to communicate globally is probably one of the reasons behind the lower figures for English-speaking countries (data for other countries are also available).

WHAT ARE THE ISSUES?

Globalization is a double-edged sword with respect to national education and culture, particularly in less developed countries. On one hand, it facilitates the spread of knowledge and improves understanding of cultural diversity. On the other hand, it arguably promotes dominant cultures of the well-established countries at the expense of others (Bakhtiari, 2006).

Political conflicts and societal anxieties over educational reform efforts in many countries will remain a barrier to promoting universal education systems that aim at balancing identity, memory, and heritage creatively at the national and international levels (see chapter by Wertsch and Billingsley in this volume).

According to Sutton (2005), global migration, the emergence of public policies that endorse public schooling, and the interdependence of societies fuel the need for intercultural education. Despite some promising features of the intercultural educational system, there are complications and challenges along the way. For instance, educators are challenged to balance local, national, and global knowledge and values in conveying curricula. But the question is: How prepared are the educators, the students, and the schools? International educational organizations, with the aid of local governments, might play an intermediary role between educators and students in transmitting intercultural knowledge within the curriculum through providing educators with the necessary training and skills.

Identity

GEOGRAPHICAL IDENTITIES

INTERNET IDENTITIES

MULTIPLE CITIZENSHIP

POPULAR CULTURE

IDENTITIES IN THE ECONOMY

RELIGION

Geographical Identities

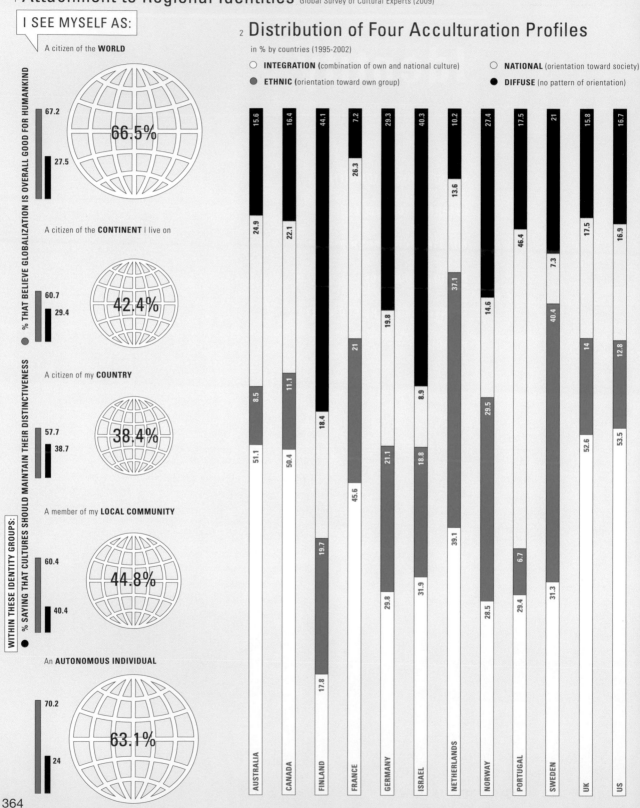

1

Attachment to Regional Identities Global Survey of Cultural Experts (2009)

I SEE MYSELF AS:

A citizen of the **WORLD**

66.5%

% THAT BELIEVE GLOBALIZATION IS OVERALL GOOD FOR HUMANKIND
67.2
27.5

A citizen of the **CONTINENT** I live on

42.4%

60.7
29.4

A citizen of my **COUNTRY**

38.4%

57.7
38.7

% THAT BELIEVE GLOBALIZATION IS OVERALL GOOD FOR HUMANKIND

% SAYING THAT CULTURES SHOULD MAINTAIN THEIR DISTINCTIVENESS

A member of my **LOCAL COMMUNITY**

44.8%

60.4
40.4

WITHIN THESE IDENTITY GROUPS:

An **AUTONOMOUS INDIVIDUAL**

63.1%

70.2
24

2 Distribution of Four Acculturation Profiles

in % by countries (1995-2002)

○ INTEGRATION (combination of own and national culture)   ○ NATIONAL (orientation toward society)

● ETHNIC (orientation toward own group)   ● DIFFUSE (no pattern of orientation)

Country	Diffuse	National	Ethnic	Integration
AUSTRALIA	15.6	24.9	8.5	51.1
CANADA	16.4	22.1	11.1	50.4
FINLAND	44.1	—	18.4	17.8 (19.7)
FRANCE	7.2	26.3	21	45.6
GERMANY	29.3	19.8	21.1	29.8
ISRAEL	40.3	—	8.9	18.8 (31.9)
NETHERLANDS	10.2	13.6	37.1	39.1
NORWAY	27.4	14.6	29.5	28.5
PORTUGAL	17.5	46.4	6.7	29.4
SWEDEN	21	7.3	40.4	31.3
UK	15.8	17.5	14	52.6
US	16.7	16.9	12.8	53.5

364

3 Regional Identification
% of respondents
within a cross-section of countries over time ● 1989 – 1993 ○ 1999 – 2004

WHICH IS MOST IMPORTANT: LOCALITY / REGION / COUNTRY / CONTINENT / WORLD ?

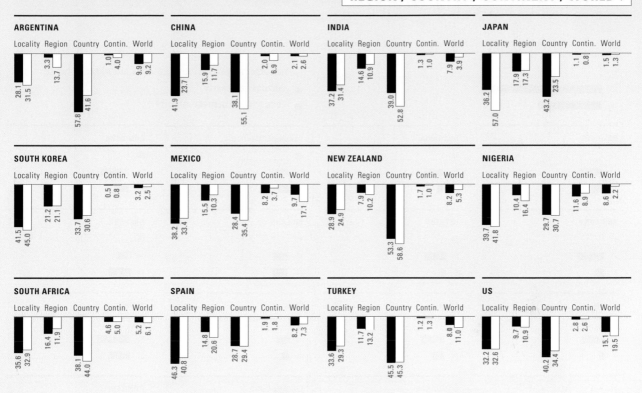

Country		Locality	Region	Country	Contin.	World
ARGENTINA	●	28.1	3.3	57.8	1.0	9.9
	○	31.5	13.7	41.6	4.0	9.2
CHINA	●	41.9	15.9	38.1	2.0	2.1
	○	23.7	11.7	55.1	6.9	2.6
INDIA	●	37.2	14.6	39.0	1.3	7.9
	○	31.4	10.9	52.8	1.0	3.9
JAPAN	●	36.2	17.9	43.2	1.1	1.5
	○	57.0	17.3	23.5	0.8	1.3
SOUTH KOREA	●	41.5	21.2	33.7	0.5	3.2
	○	45.0	21.1	30.6	0.8	2.5
MEXICO	●	38.2	15.5	28.4	8.2	9.7
	○	33.4	10.3	35.4	3.7	17.1
NEW ZEALAND	●	28.9	7.9	53.3	1.7	8.2
	○	24.9	10.2	58.6	1.0	5.3
NIGERIA	●	39.7	10.4	29.7	11.6	8.6
	○	41.8	16.4	30.7	8.9	2.2
SOUTH AFRICA	●	35.6	16.4	38.1	4.6	5.2
	○	32.9	11.9	44.0	5.0	6.1
SPAIN	●	46.3	14.8	28.7	1.9	8.2
	○	40.8	20.6	29.4	1.8	7.3
TURKEY	●	33.6	11.7	45.5	1.2	8.0
	○	29.3	13.2	45.3	1.3	11.0
US	●	32.2	9.7	40.2	2.8	15.1
	○	32.6	10.9	34.4	2.6	19.5

4a + 4b National vs. Religious Identity
in a Cross-Section of Countries (2006)

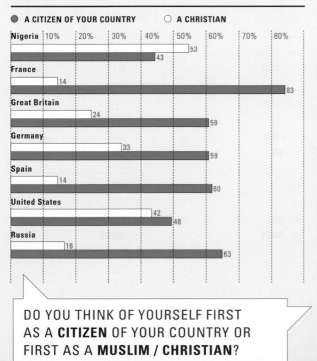

● A CITIZEN OF YOUR COUNTRY   ○ A CHRISTIAN

Country	A Christian	A Citizen
Nigeria	53	43
France	14	83
Great Britain	24	59
Germany	33	59
Spain	14	60
United States	42	48
Russia	16	63

DO YOU THINK OF YOURSELF FIRST AS A CITIZEN OF YOUR COUNTRY OR FIRST AS A MUSLIM / CHRISTIAN?

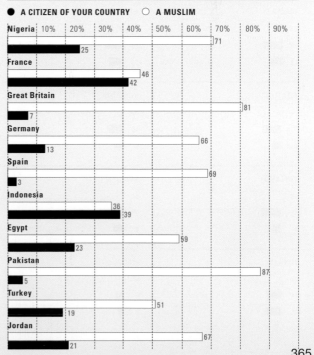

● A CITIZEN OF YOUR COUNTRY   ○ A MUSLIM

Country	A Muslim	A Citizen
Nigeria	71	25
France	46	42
Great Britain	81	7
Germany	66	13
Spain	69	3
Indonesia	39	36
Egypt	59	23
Pakistan	87	5
Turkey	51	19
Jordan	67	21

EUROPEAN UNION

42 ○ FREEDOM TO TRAVEL, STUDY AND WORK ANYWHERE IN THE EU
19 ● CULTURAL DIVERSITY
10 ● LOSS OF OUR CULTURAL IDENTITY

BELGIUM

42
22
10

BULGARIA

52
20
5

CZECH REPUBLIC

53
12
11

DENMARK

53
28
13

GERMANY

47
25
9

ESTONIA

70
21
4

IRELAND

44
14
14

GREECE

49
14
21

SPAIN

37
22
4

FRANCE

41
25
12

ITALY

33
13
8

CYPRUS

62
32
21

LATVIA

56
9
5

LITHUANIA

56
18
6

LUXEMBOURG

56
28
7

HUNGARY

38
14
4

MALTA

51
19
12

NETHERLANDS

49
17
12

AUSTRIA

46
23
18

POLAND

57
12
7

PORTUGAL

32
17
8

ROMANIA

47
16
8

SLOVENIA

52
19
12

SLOVAKIA

61
18
9

FINLAND

58
18
7

SWEDEN

56
23
9

UK

25
12
20

CROATIA

33
11
23

TURKEY

24
14
15

MACEDONIA

57
8
6

Geographical Identities

One of the most important dimensions of identity is probably the attachment to specific places, be it a region, a whole country, or even the whole world. Places give us some idea of "belonging," a *"Heimat"* or "home," where we trace our roots (see Warnier chapter in this volume). However, in times of increased mobilization (e.g., in and out migration; see the Migration suite) of global networks enabled by information and communication technologies, the scope and content of this spatial identity is bound to change. This suite presents data from different surveys and research-based sources, delving into the relationship between geographically bound identities and globalization.

WHAT DO WE KNOW?

Data point 1 displays results from a survey conducted with over 200 cultural experts from all over the world (Anheier & Hoelscher, 2010). First, it became apparent that most of the experts do not identify themselves with a single geographic location; instead, they hold multiple attachments. "Patchwork- identities" (Keupp, 1999) are widespread and seem to be no problem in people's minds. Interestingly, on the one hand, national identity, often seen as the most important of such identities, acquired the lowest figure within the expert sample. On the other hand, being a world- citizen and being an autonomous individual elicited the most responses. There are other issues and problems that became visible and were interconnected with these identities. While the majority of respondents viewed globalization as an overall benefit for humankind, those who see themselves as world- citizens and autonomous individuals supported this perspective the most. However, others were more supportive of the view that cultures should maintain their distinctiveness. Understandably, the more attached someone is to smaller geographical units, the more she or he opposes the merging of cultures. If it is true that national identities are decreasing in significance, then the question is whether they are being replaced by something else. While it is often claimed that regional identities are becoming more and more important, the European context is specific in that it offers a transnational alternative with strong political institutions. Europeans were asked what the European Union (EU) means to them, and they mainly highlighted "freedom to travel, study and work anywhere in the EU" (data point 5). While in most countries more people perceive the EU as bringing "cultural diversity," there are the interesting exceptions of Greece, United Kingdom, Croatia, and Turkey, where more people view the EU as leading to a loss of their cultural identity.

Looking at different levels of regional units, a pattern becomes visible across countries as different as Argentina, China, Nigeria, and Spain (data point 3): People mainly identify themselves with either their locality or their country. It should be noted that, while for data point 1 people were asked about each level separately and therefore could choose more than one level as most important, in this case respondents had to rank the levels. Figures for attachment to their continents are low for all countries, and only slightly higher in African countries, such as Nigeria. Though the data also allow comparison over a timespan of more than 12 years, no clear global trend is evident.

As mentioned, migration is a growing global phenomenon (see also the data about OECD Expatriates in the Identities in the Economy suite). But how do people cope with relocation (see chapters by Ang and Thomas in this volume)? Data point 2 presents the distribution of four different acculturation profiles within 12 countries. In the Anglo-Saxon countries and France, a large proportion of immigrants fit the "integration" profile, trying to combine their old and new identities. In Sweden, Norway, and the Netherlands, an "ethnic" profile predominates, in which immigrants demonstrate a clear orientation to their own ethnic group, endorsing a differentialist attitude. In Portugal, one finds a large proportion of immigrants who feel like they belong to their new home country. In Finland and Israel, and to some extent in Germany, no dominant integration profile can be identified. However, geographically based identities are only one part of the story. Religion (see the Religion suite) is an important factor as well. Data point 4 shows, for two religions, whether people feel primarily attached to their country or to their religion. Overall, while Muslims in most countries (except Indonesia and France) feel significantly more attached to their religion, Christians generally feel more attached to their country. The interesting exceptions with high levels of religious attachment of Christians are Nigeria and the United States (although in the latter case still a majority feels attached to the country).

WHAT ARE THE ISSUES?

Looking at the ranking of geographical identities alone (see data point 3), global identities are definitely not dominant. However, within certain (elite) sub-groups, transnational identities are already replacing traditional national and regional ones. The same is true for the growing number of people worldwide who have had the experience of migration, with its blending of old and new identities. Additionally, with regard to other dimensions of identity formation, geographically based identities, although often within the focus of empirical analyses, seem to be less relevant than, for example, religious-based identities, at least for certain groups. It seems that there are good reasons to give up "methodological nationalism" (Rössel, forthcoming) and putting more emphasis on globalized identification processes.

Internet Identities

₁ Internet Penetration Rates and Internet Users by World Region (2009)

- ● INTERNET PENETRATION RATES (IN %)
- ○ INTERNET USERS COMING FROM THIS WORLD REGION (IN %)

COUNTRIES BY COLOR:
AUSTRALIA / OCEANIA
MIDDLE EAST
AFRICA
LATIN AMERICA / CARIBBEAN
NORTH AMERICA
EUROPE
ASIA

₃ Geo-Location of Phishing Lures and Web Hosts (SEPT 2009)

- ○ CURRENT PROPORTION OF PHISHING LURES
- ○ CURRENT PROPORTION OF PHISHING WEBHOSTS

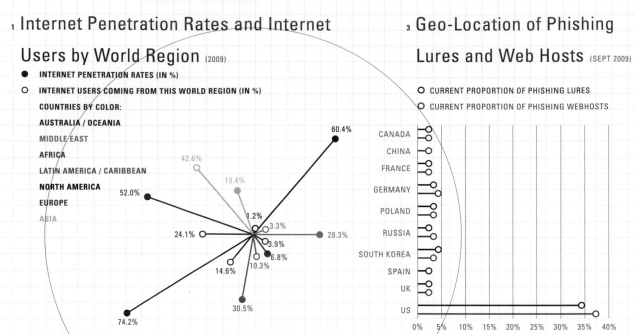

₂ Reasons US Social Network Users Joined a Social Network by Generation

(MAY 2009)

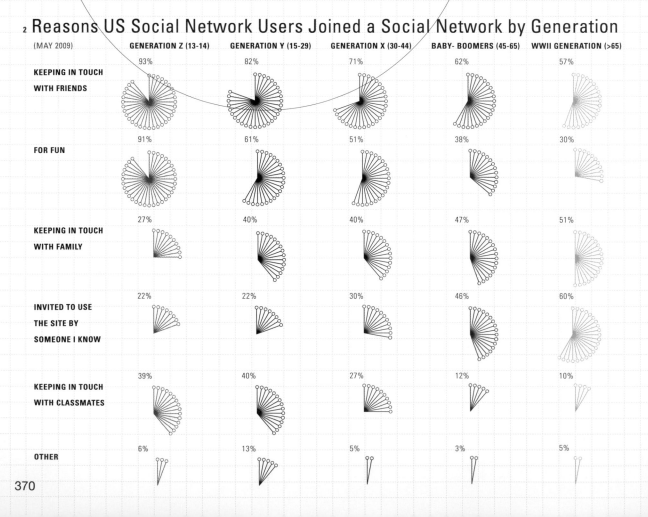

370

₄ Growth of Massive- Multiplayer Online Role-Playing Games (MMORPGs)

(1998 - 2008)

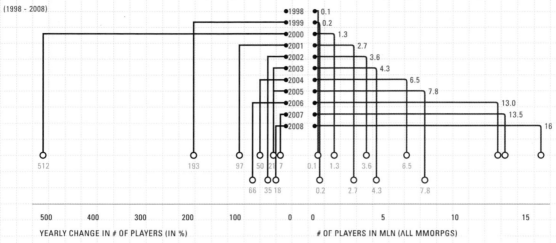

1998	0.1
1999	0.2
2000	1.3
2001	2.7
2002	3.6
2003	4.3
2004	6.5
2005	7.8
2006	13.0
2007	13.5
2008	16

512   193   97 50 21 7   0.1 1.3   3.6   6.5
                        66 35 18   0.2   2.7   4.3   7.8

500   400   300   200   100   0   0   5   10   15

YEARLY CHANGE IN # OF PLAYERS (IN %)   # OF PLAYERS IN MLN (ALL MMORPGS)

₅ Online Dating

PEOPLE IN USA, WHO HAVE BEEN IN A LONG-TERM RELATIONSHIP WITH OR MARRIED SOMEONE THEY
MET THROUGH A DATING WEBSITE (BASED ON INTERNET USERS WHO HAVE USED AN ONLINE DATING WEBSITE, N = 518)

| TOTAL | MALE | FEMALE | 18-29 | 30-49 | 50-64 | 65+ |
| 17% | 15% | 20% | 11% | 24% | 18% | 11% |

₆ Top 10 Most Bought Avatars in Second Life BY SELECTED SUBCATEGORIES

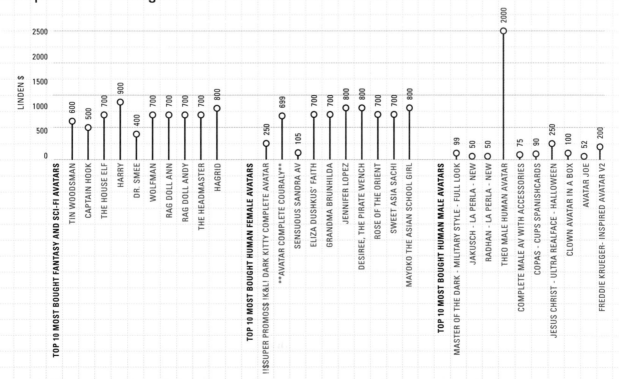

LINDEN $

TOP 10 MOST BOUGHT FANTASY AND SCI-FI AVATARS
- TIN WOODSMAN — 600
- CAPTAIN HOOK — 500
- THE HOUSE ELF — 700
- HARRY — 900
- DR. SMEE — 400
- WOLFMAN — 700
- RAG DOLL ANN — 700
- RAG DOLL ANDY — 700
- THE HEADMASTER — 700
- HAGRID — 800

TOP 10 MOST BOUGHT HUMAN FEMALE AVATARS
- !!SUPER PROMOSS !K&L! DARK KITTY COMPLETE AVATAR — 250
- **AVATAR COMPLETE COURALY** — 699
- SENSUOUS SANDRA AV — 105
- ELIZA DUSHKUS' FAITH — 700
- GRANDMA BRUNHILDA — 700
- JENNIFER LOPEZ — 800
- DESIREE, THE PIRATE WENCH — 800
- ROSE OF THE ORIENT — 700
- SWEET ASIA SACHI — 700
- MAYOKO THE ASIAN SCHOOL GIRL — 800

TOP 10 MOST BOUGHT HUMAN MALE AVATARS
- MASTER OF THE DARK - MILITARY STYLE - FULL LOOK — 99
- JAKUSCH - LA PERLA - NEW — 50
- RADHAN - LA PERLA - NEW — 50
- THEO MALE HUMAN AVATAR — 2000
- COMPLETE MALE AV WITH ACCESSORIES — 75
- COPAS - CUPS SPANISHCARDS — 90
- JESUS CHRIST - ULTRA REALFACE - HALLOWEEN — 250
- CLOWN AVATAR IN A BOX — 100
- AVATAR JOE — 52
- FREDDIE KRUEGER- INSPIRED AVATAR V2 — 200

DESIGN: ROXANE ZARGHAM

371

Internet Identities

"In the physical world [...] the norm is: one body, one identity. The virtual world is different. It is composed of information rather than matter." (Judith S. Donath, 1999)

"Cyberspace appears as a place in which individuals can put aside many of the inequalities of offline life." Therefore, real and online identities are not necessarily similar: The "identity fluidity [of the Internet] supports the masquerades and experiments of avatars, the ability to change gender [and] the ability to contact experts" (Jordan, 1999: 87).

WHAT ARE INTERNET IDENTITIES?

Identities are formed through individual or collective experiences. The Internet is an excellent tool for exchanges between like-minded people (see chapter by Schiff in this volume). Its influence on identity is quite ambivalent: On the one hand, free access to heterogeneous information can lead to the dissolution, reconstruction, or disruption of existing identities (see chapter by Boswell in this volume). On the other, it virtually brings together people's memories, hobbies, and preferences leading to identity continuity (see chapter by Volcic in this volume). In short, the medium is the message, meaning that the technical conditions of the Internet superimpose specific restrictions, but simultaneously offer opportunities for newly generated identities outside the boundaries of a nation-state (McLuhan, Fiore & Agel, 2001, and chapter by Ang in this volume).

WHAT DO WE KNOW ABOUT INTERNET IDENTITIES?

*   Data point 1 provides a snapshot of worldwide Internet usage. Asia constitutes 42.6 per cent of worldwide Internet users, but the Internet penetration rate shows that only 19.4 per cent of all Asians are connected to the World Wide Web. North America marks a stark contrast to Asia: While North Americans account for only 14.6 per cent of worldwide Internet users, the region has by far the highest Internet penetration rate in the world, with 74.2 per cent.
*   Identity-building processes take place at every stage in life, but particularly during childhood and adolescence. The Internet clearly has a great influence on young people. Data point 2 gives a glimpse of the reasons why different generations in the United States join Web 2.0 applications. The younger the respondents, the more likely they are to use the Internet as a tool to keep in touch with friends.
*   Phishing lures and phishing web hosts are globally quite dispersed, but locally cumulated at the same time (see data point 3).
*   Massive- Multiplayer- Online- Role- Playing- Games (MMORPGs) "allow thousands of gamers to play in the game's evolving virtual world at the same time via the Internet" (Webopedia.com, 2010). Between 1998 and 2008, the number of online role-players increased from 75,000 to 16 million (see data point 4). Players are able to choose from a wide variety of virtual characters called *avatars* and upgrade them, for example, with weapons, and interact with other avatars in different communities.

- Partnership is an integral part of identity. In this context, online dating services are quite popular. Among 30- 49- year- olds, for example, 24 per cent of online dating service users found a long-time partner or spouse (see data point 5). Opinions about online dating are quite positive: 48 per cent of all males and 41 per cent of all females believe that online dating is a good way to meet potential partners (Pew Internet and American Life Project, 2005).
- Second Life, online since 2003, is one example of a virtually organized world developed by the company Linden Lab. Second Life has its own currency, the Linden $ (L$), which can be bought with real currency and can be adapted to the virtual market economy. Currently (April 2010) , 1,000 L$ can be exchanged for 2.69 US$ (XCHange4LS, 2010). Data point 6 shows how much Second Life users are willing to pay for a virtual avatar. The cost of the top 10 most popular science fiction and fantasy avatars ranges between 400 and 900 L$; the top 10 female avatars, between 105 and 800 L$; and the top 10 male avatars, between 50 and 2000 L$.

WHAT ARE THE ISSUES AND TRENDS?

Virtual identities offer the opportunities discussed above, but they also come with challenges like abuse for mobbing and criminal activities. As many transactions on the Internet are anonymous, identity theft or negation is one of the biggest concerns (see Javelin Strategy & Research, 2010, and chapter by Boswell in this volume).

The eminent "capacity of the Internet for socialization"– through e-mails, discussion forums, chat rooms, and online games – is a primary reason for the excessive amount of time people spend having real-time interactions, exacerbating the risk of "social isolation and functional impairment of daily activities" (Byun et al., 2009: 203). A comparison of Internet addiction prevalence surveys from different countries and times shows huge differences in addiction rates— from 0.3 per cent in the United States (2006) to 10.6 per cent in Switzerland (1996) (Show & Black, 2008). However, these numbers are not easily comparable owing to challenges in data collection and biases in the definition of concepts.

Multiple Citizenship and Naturalization

₁ Countries According to Their Status of Legal Recognition of Dual Citizenship

₂ Frequency of Multiple Citizenship in Different Countries (2002–2008)

COUNTRY (YEAR; MAINLY CENSUS DATA COLLECTION)

- 2.8% CANADA (2006)
- 2.0% GERMANY (2007)
- 1.4% LATVIA (n.a.)
- 6.6% NETHERLANDS (2008)
- 1.2% POLAND (2002)

₃ Citizenship Tests in Different Countries

(1997 –2009)

CANDIDATES THAT PASSED THE CITIZENSHIP TEST IN %

- 97% AUSTRALIA 2008
- 30% CANADA 2007
- 73% CANADA 1997
- 99% GERMANY 2008
- 84% US 2007 (old test)
- 94% US 2007 (new test)
- 97% DENMARK 2007
- 46% NETHERLANDS 2006

₄ Number of Countries That Introduced Legislation That Allows for Dual Citizenship

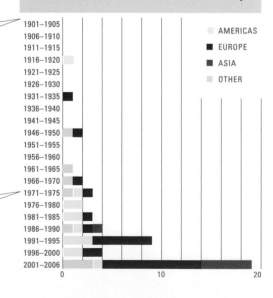

- AMERICAS
- EUROPE
- ASIA
- OTHER

5 Familiarity With the Term "Citizen of the European Union" (2002 AND 2007)

THE MAASTRICHT TREATY (1992) INTRODUCED THE CITIZENSHIP OF THE EUROPEAN UNION, WHICH COMPLEMENTS THE NATIONAL CITIZENSHIP OF EVERY CITIZEN OF AN EU MEMBER STATE. IT IS ASSOCIATED WITH SPECIFIC RIGHTS, SUCH AS FREEDOM OF MOVEMENT AND WORK OR THE RIGHT TO VOTE IN LOCAL AND EUROPEAN ELECTIONS.

ARE YOU FAMILIAR WITH THE TERM "CITIZEN OF THE EUROPEAN UNION"?

UNITED KINGDOM
2002: 42% never heard the term
2007: 25% never heard the term

ESTONIA
2002: n/a
2007: 5% never heard the term

NETHERLANDS
2002: 33% never heard the term
2007: 32% never heard the term

ITALY
2002: 26% never heard the term
2007: 8% never heard the term

GREECE
2002: 43% never heard the term
2007: 18% never heard the term

6 Attitudes of Germans and Foreigners Toward Naturalization (1996 AND 2006)

- **1.** GERMANS (NATIVE) 2006
- **2.** GERMANS (NATIVE) 1996
- **3.** GERMANS (NATURALIZED) 2006
- **4.** GERMANS (NATURALIZED) 1996
- **5** FOREIGNERS 2006
- **6** FOREIGNERS 1996

ANSWER SCALE:
1.00 = NOT IMPORTANT
7.00 = VERY IMPORTANT

HOW IMPORTANT IS IT THAT A PERSON, WHO WANTS TO ACQUIRE GERMAN CITIZENSHIP...

ACCEPTS FREE DEMOCRATIC ORDER
1 — 6.4
2
3 — 6.1
4
5 — 6.0
6

IS A MEMBER OF A CHRISTIAN CHURCH
1 — 2.4
2 — 2.09
3 — 2.3
4 — 2.4
5 — 2.15
6 — 1.96

KNOWS THE GERMAN LANGUAGE
1 — 6.3
2 — 5.2
3 — 6.1
4 — 5.2
5 — 5.8
6 — 5.4

IS ABLE TO EARN A LIVING
1 — 6.0
2 — 5.7
3 — 5.6
4 — 5.6
5 — 5.5
6 — 5.4

ADAPTED TO THE WAY OF LIFE
1 — 5.7
2 — 5.0
3 — 5.3
4 — 5.3
5 — 5.0
6 — 4.7

IS OF GERMAN DESCENT
1 — 3.4
2 — 4.5
3 — 3.3
4 — 5.2
5 — 3.0
6 — 3.6

DID NOT COMMIT A CRIME
1 — 6.4
2 — 6.1
3 — 5.9
4 — 5.8
5 — 5.9
6 — 5.6

LIVED IN GERMANY FOR A LONG TIME
1 — 5.0
2 — 5.4
3 — 5.0
4 — 5.0
5 — 5.0
6 — 5.3

WAS BORN IN GERMANY
1 — 3.5
2 — 4.8
3 — 2.8
4 — 3.8
5 — 3.0
6 — 3.9

DESIGN: ROXANE ZARGHAM

Multiple Citizenship

There are numerous ways through which people obtain more than one citizenship. If someone is, for example, born in a country that emphasizes the *ius solis* (right of ground) principle, he or she automatically gains the right to acquire the citizenship of this country. When the child's parents are citizens of another country – as might be the case with a family that immigrated recently – and their country of origin follows the *ius sanguinis* (right of blood) principle, the child has the right to obtain this second citizenship as well. More than two citizenships are possible when the parents themselves are bi-national. Political reconstruction, territorial changes, and wars can also lead to cases of multiple citizenship.

WHAT ARE THE TRENDS?

Whereas in the first half of the 20th century multiple citizenship was largely seen as a threat to the unity of nation-states, an increasing number of countries have introduced legislation that allows for multiple citizenship since then (see data point 4). It has to be kept in mind, however, that often a gap has existed and still exists between the *de jure* legal resistance against multiple citizenship and the de facto implementation of related laws. It seems that reliable data on multiple citizenship and the number of multiple citizens specifically are lacking mainly because states and national statistics tend to repress the existence of a presumably increasing number of multi-national citizens. Blattner, Erdmann & Schwanke (2009) summarize existing studies on multiple citizenship legislation on a global level (see data point 1). The few existing statistics on the numbers of multi-national citizens indicate that they form a very limited percentage of the given population – between 1.2 per cent in Poland and 6.6 per cent in the Netherlands (see data point 2). Although no exact data for the United States exist, Renshon (2001) concludes that a large share of immigrants legally admitted into the United States between 1961 and 1997 came from countries that allow multiple citizenships.

Survey data from Germany indicate a change in attitude toward the terms of naturalization (see data point 6). Naturalization law was changed in 2000 to turn away from the emphasis on descent. Accordingly, by 2006 the population attached less importance to this criterion, and more to the acceptance of the free democratic basic order, language proficiency, and other efforts to adapt, than in 1996. Additionally, the introduction of a citizenship test in 2008 was appraised positively by the majority of the German population (Worbs, 2009).

As of late 2007, countries that had introduced citizenship tests included the United States, Canada, the United Kingdom, Germany, the Netherlands, Denmark, Latvia, Lithuania, Estonia, and Australia; some others (e.g., France) were discussing the possibility of doing so (Wright, 2008). Most candidates pass the tests, as official numbers demonstrate (data point 3; figures on Canada and the Netherlands are from non-official studies). Nevertheless, present studies indicate that naturalization numbers fell considerably after tests were introduced in the Netherlands, Austria, and Denmark – excluding those who are not educated (de Hart, 2008).

Whereas the citizenship of the European Union can be seen as a new and supranational model for citizenship and citizen identity, many Europeans are not aware of their citizenship (see data point 5).

WHAT ARE THE ISSUES?

Multiple citizenship poses fundamental questions, for example, regarding military service, suffrage, diplomatic protection, travel regulations, work, taxes, and social benefits (see chapters by Ang and Thomas in this volume). Different political interests prevail regarding emigrants from and immigrants to a given country. Whereas countries with large groups of emigrants such as Hungary are often interested in keeping up strong ties to those groups for political and economic reasons, and therefore facilitate multiple citizenship in this respect, their policy toward multiple citizenship of immigrants tends to be more restrictive – although Blattner et al. (2009) observe a trend toward more symmetric regulations.

Citizenship tests are a controversial issue. On one hand, they can be seen as having positive effects on the integration of immigrants, who learn their rights and duties, as well as improve their language abilities. Those are prerequisites for participation in politics, civil society, and everyday life. On the other hand, it can be argued that testing fees, requirements of language proficiency, and intellectual abilities in general disadvantage less-educated immigrants and therefore camouflage specific immigration policy interests. Insofar as attitudes to basic rights of the given country and security issues are concerned, the reliability of the test results can be questioned, as in most cases the answers can be learned by heart. As regards content, the tests often deal with national heritage, myths, and symbols, implying a stress on assimilation instead of multiculturalism.

If multiple citizenship, with all its negative and positive implications, is an indicator of a changing relationship between national and individual identities, to what extent is this change caused by globalization? Are citizenship tests, then, an attempt by some traditional immigration countries to regain state control over citizens' national identities? How does multiple citizenship affect identities on the individual level? Does it really threaten national loyalty, democratic participation, or equal rights and duties of citizens?

POPULAR CULTURE

1. TOP TEN POPULAR SONGS 15 COUNTRIES AND HOME COUNTRIES OF ARTIST/S* (OCTOBER / NOVEMBER 2009)

US

US	10

UK

US	4
UK	3
FRANCE	1
COLOMBIA	1
AUSTRALIA	1

GERMANY

US	7
GERMANY	1
FRANCE	1
COLOMBIA	1
NORWAY	1

ITALY

ITALY	4
US	3
UK	1
COLOMBIA	1
AUSTRALIA	1

SPAIN

SPAIN	4
US	3
CANADA	1
FRANCE	1
SWEDEN	1

AUSTRIA

US	3
UK	3
AUSTRIA	1
GERMANY	1
FRANCE	1
COLOMBIA	1
NORWAY	1

SWEDEN

SWEDEN	5
US	4
UK	1
FRANCE	1
BARBADOS	5

NORWAY

NORWAY	5
US	4
UK	2
FRANCE	1
BARBADOS	1

NETHERLANDS

NETHERLANDS	6
US	1
UK	1
FRANCE	1
BELGIUM	1
ROMANIA	1

AUSTRALIA

US	5
UK	2
AUSTRALIA	2
GERMANY	1
FRANCE	1

CZECH REPUBLIC

FRANCE	2
CZECH REPUBLIC	1
US	1
CANADA	1
UK	1
BELGIUM	1
ROMANIA	1

SWITZERLAND

US	4
UK	2
CANADA	1
FRANCE	1
COLOMBIA	1
NORWAY	1
BELGIUM	1

NEW ZEALAND

US	8
UK	2
NEW ZEALAND	1
FRANCE	1
BARBADOS	1

2. MOST POPULAR NATIONAL AND INTERNATIONAL TV SERIES OF THE YOUTH (13 - 17) IN SELECTED COUNTRIES (2005)

SWEDEN	FRIENDS 28.8%	SIMPSONS 19.8%	SEX AND THE CITY 9%	OZ 8.1%	BIG BROTHER (NATIONAL TV SERIES) 8.1%	NATIONAL 18.9%
GERMANY	SIMPSONS 11.5%	SEX AND THE CITY 8.8%	FRIENDS 8%	GUTE ZEITEN, SCHLECHTE ZEITEN (NATIONAL TV SERIES) 7.1%	KING OF QUEENS 6.2%	NATIONAL 31%
AUSTRIA	SIMPSONS 23.5%	SEX AND THE CITY 11.8%	MALCOLM IN THE MIDDLE 11.8%	FRIENDS 8.4%	GILMORE GIRLS 8.4%	NATIONAL 11.8%
SLOVAKIA	FRIENDS 20%	ALIAS 10.5%	SIMPSONS 8.4%	STARGATE 4.2%	GILMORE GIRLS 3.2%	NATIONAL 7.4%
TURKEY	AVRUPA AKASI (NATIONAL TV SERIES) 19.7%	KURTLAR VADISI (NATIONAL TV SERIES) 18.4%	BIR ISTANBUL MASALI (NATIONAL TV SERIES) 9.2%	SEINFELD 7.9%	SOUTH PARK 6.6%	NATIONAL 51.2%
INDIA	FRIENDS 8.5%	JASSI JAISI KOHI NAHI (NATIONAL TV SERIES) 8.5%	C.I.D. 8.5%	FEAR FACTOR 6.4%	SMALL WONDER 3.2%	NATIONAL 29.8%

*THE TV SERIES IS PRODUCED IN THE CURRENT HOME COUNTRY OF RESPONDENTS

FRANCE

FRANCE	4
US	4
CANADA	1
UK	1
GERMANY	1

CANADA

US	5
CANADA	2
UK	1
IRELAND	1
GERMANY	1

3. % FEMALE FANS IN THE 20 MOST POPULAR SOCCER CLUBS IN EUROPE

CLUBS	%
GALATASARAY ISTANBUL	
AC MAILAND	
FC CHELSEA	
FENERBAHÇE ISTANBUL	
FC SPARTAK MOSKAU	
FC DINAMO MOSKAU	
ZENIT ST. PETERSBURG	
JUVENTUS TURIN	
ZSKA MOSKAU	
REAL MADRID	
AJAX AMSTERDAM	
INTER MILAN	
MANCHESTER UNITED	
ARSENAL LONDON	
FC BAYERN MÜNCHEN	
OLYMPIQUE MARSEILLE	
WISLA KRAKAU	
OLYMPIQUE LYON	
FC LIVERPOOL	
FC BARCELONA	

4. TOP 10 U.S. METROPOLITAN AREAS RANKED BY THE ESTIMATED PERCENTAGE OF GAY, LESBIAN, OR BISEXUAL ADULTS (2005)

METRO AREA (IN %)
LARGEST CITY (IN %)

2005 TOP TEN METROPOLITAN AREAS

	METRO / CITY
HARTFORD - WEST HARTFORD - EAST HARTFORD	5.6 / 6.8
ORLANDO - KISSIMMEE	5.7 / 7.7
MINNEAPOLIS - ST. PAUL - BLOOMINGTON	5.7 / 12.5
DENVER - AURORA	5.8 / 8.2
AUSTIN - ROUND ROCK	5.9 / 4.8
TAMPA - ST. PETERSBURG - CLEARWATER	5.9 / 6.1
PORTLAND - VANCOUVER - BEAVERTON	6.1 / 8.8
BOSTON - CAMBRIDGE - QUINCY	6.2 / 12.3
SEATTLE - TACOMA - BELLEVUE	6.5 / 12.9
SAN FRANCISCO - OAKLAND - FREMONT	8.2 / 15.4

5. CENSUS OF REAL (2000) AND VIDEO-GAME CHARACTERS (2006) IN THE US, BY RACE AND AGE

REPRESENTATION BY RACE

WHITE 80 /	
BLACK 10.7 /	
HISPANIC 2.7 /	
BI-RACIAL 1.4 /	
NATIVE AMERICAN 0.1 /	
ASIAN / PACIFIC ISLANDER 5.0 /	

REPRESENTATION BY AGE

CHILDREN 3.5 /	
TEENAGERS 7.8 /	
ADULTS 86.9 /	
ELDERLY 1.7 /	

■ CHARACTERS IN GAMES (%)
% OF PEOPLE IN 2000 US CENSUS

6. LOVE PARADES BY YEAR, LOCATION, MOTTO AND PARTICIPANTS (1989 - 2009)

YEAR, LOCATION, AND MOTTO	PARTICIPANTS
1989, BERLIN (FRIEDE, FREUDE, EIERKUCHEN)	
1990, BERLIN (THE FUTURE IS OURS)	
1991, BERLIN (MY HOUSE IS YOUR HOUSE AND YOUR HOUSE IS MINE)	
1992, BERLIN (THE SPIRIT MAKES YOU MOVE)	
1993, BERLIN (THE WORLDWIDE PARTY PEOPLE WEEKEND)	
1994, BERLIN (LOVE 2 LOVE)	
1995, BERLIN (PEACE ON EARTH)	
1996, BERLIN (WE ARE ONE FAMILY)	
1997, BERLIN (LET THE SUNSHINE IN YOUR HEART)	
1997, SYDNEY	
1998, BERLIN (ONE WORLD ONE FUTURE)	
1999, BERLIN (MUSIC IS THE KEY)	
2000, BERLIN (ONE WORLD ONE LOVEPARADE)	
2000, LEEDS (RADIO ONE - ONE LOVE)	
2001, BERLIN (JOIN THE LOVE REPUBLIC)	
2002, BERLIN (ACCESS PEACE)	
2002, MEXICO CITY	
2003, BERLIN (LOVE RULES)	
2004, SAN FRANCISCO	
2005, SAN FRANCISCO	
2005, SANTIAGO (SAL A LA CALLE Y BAILA)	
2006, BERLIN (THE LOVE IS BACK)	
2006, SAN FRANCISCO (AS LOVEFEST)	
2006, SANTIAGO (EL BAILE ES DE TODOS)	
2007, ESSEN (LOVE IS EVERYWHERE)	
2007, CARACAS (LIVE THE LOVE!)	
2007, SAN FRANCISCO (AS LOVEFEST)	
2008, DORTMUND (HIGHWAY TO LOVE)	
2008, ROTTERDAM (OLYMPIC EDITION)	
2008, SAN FRANCISCO (AS LOVEFEST)	
2008, CARACAS (KEEP THE LOVE ALIVE!)	
2009, SAN FRANCISCO (AS LOVEVOLUTION)	

379

Popular Culture

Today's pop cultures and subcultures deeply affect the process of identity formation. Traditional identification models such as profession, religion, class, and region appear to exert decreasing influence in the context of an increasing demand for personal flexibility. Pop cultures and sub-cultures not only serve as markers of distinction from others through – sometimes deviant – lifestyles, but also, supported by new media technologies, allow individuals to connect to like-minded people who share a culture worldwide. Sub-cultures can be characterized as groups of people who have something in common, such as problems, interests, or practices, which "distinguishes them in a significant way from the members of other social groups" (Thornton, 1997: 2). Popular cultures were often seen "as a form of liberation from the top-down strictures of high-culture." Today, the term connotes the idea of being well-liked or widely liked (Jenkins et al., 2002: 27).

WHAT DO WE KNOW ABOUT POP CULTURES AND SUBCULTURES?

The data suite sheds light on how popular cultures and sub-cultures express cultural identities in the context of globalization.

- Data point 1 shows the home countries of artists for the top 10 most popular songs in 15 countries. Overall, a remarkable global influence of artists located in the United States can be observed. However, some countries, like Spain or France, show high numbers of national artists in their top 10 list.
- Data point 2 compares the proportion of youth-preferred national TV programs, produced in the respondents' home country, and international TV series in six countries. The percentage of national TV series in Europe ranges between 7 per cent (Slovakia) and 51 per cent (Turkey), while the proportion of national TV series in India is around 30 per cent. Critical studies about the diffusion of American TV program exports label the dominance of its series in the importing countries as "cultural imperialism" (Dorfman and Mattelart, 1975). However, some studies show how the reception of TV series differs significantly across countries (Katz & Liebes, 2005: 4 & Curtin, 2008).
- Associating with other fans helps one to discover that "certain aspects of the self [...] can be shared unashamedly with others," because the chosen "life trajectory overlaps significantly" with that of others (Thompson, 1995: 224). Transnational connections between fans result from emotionally enhanced relationships in foreign countries, which lead to further transnational networks (Roose, 2010: 433p). Data point 3 provides a glimpse of the gender balance in the top 20 soccer fan clubs. While soccer is often perceived as a male domain, the proportion of female fans ranges from 22 per cent (FC Barcelona) to 54 per cent (Galatasaray Istanbul).
- Sexual orientation, especially if non-heterosexual, has a strong impact on a person's identity. While in some countries gays, lesbians, and bisexuals are still persecuted, even in liberal societies they often see themselves as victims of prejudice. Interesting in this context is the world map from the International Lesbian, Gay,

Bisexual, Trans and Intersex Association (ILGA) that depicts the actual state of homophobia as well as lesbian and gay rights (ILGA, 2010). Data point 4 underlines that the San Francisco metropolitan area in California is relatively more hospitable to gays, lesbians, and bisexuals than other regions.

- Data point 5 contrasts the representation of video game characters with that of real people in the 2000 United States population census. While whites and adults are overrepresented in the video games analyzed, African Americans, Hispanics, children, and elderly people are under-represented. As many of these games are distributed worldwide, the over-representation of White characters is likely to appear even larger on a global scale. However, it would be interesting to determine whether the over-representation of certain ethnic groups is correlated with the countries in which the games are produced.

- Data point 6 depicts the globalization of the "street demonstration" Love Parade that has taken place almost every year in Germany since 1989. It also serves as an indicator for the popularization of Techno, an originally sub-cultural variation of electronic music. As some Techno DJs and their success in the charts brought the music style into the mainstream in the mid-1990s, visitor figures rose enormously. The Love Parade began as a "small insider party" (Robb, 2002: 136), but 18 months later, "rave went over-ground in Germany with the degeneration of the underground" (Reynolds, 1998: 387). Since its introduction to Sydney, Australia in 1997, the Love Parade has become a global event.

WHAT ARE THE ISSUES AND TRENDS?

Many roots of pop cultures can be found in sub-cultures. Sub-cultural styles trickle up into the mainstream of popular culture through processes of commercialization, mostly via corporations, particularly in the cultural industry. Music-based sub-cultures are particularly vulnerable to this process. What may be considered as a sub-culture at a specific time, for example, gothic, punk, hip-hop, and rave cultures, may soon come to represent the mainstream taste (Blair, 1993), raising fears of a sell-out and the erosion of (artistic) authenticity (see volume 3 of this series).

Identities in the Economy

1 Top 15 Global Brands 2009 (According to Interbrand and Millward Brown)

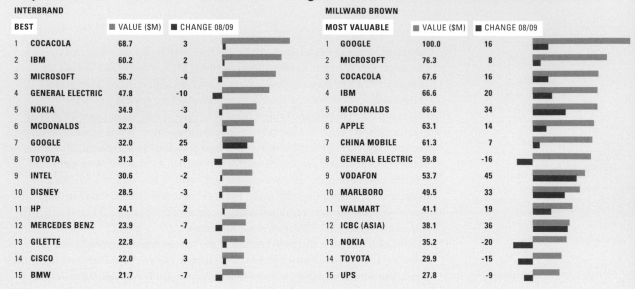

INTERBRAND				MILLWARD BROWN		
BEST	VALUE ($M)	CHANGE 08/09		MOST VALUABLE	VALUE ($M)	CHANGE 08/09
1 COCACOLA	68.7	3		1 GOOGLE	100.0	16
2 IBM	60.2	2		2 MICROSOFT	76.3	8
3 MICROSOFT	56.7	-4		3 COCACOLA	67.6	16
4 GENERAL ELECTRIC	47.8	-10		4 IBM	66.6	20
5 NOKIA	34.9	-3		5 MCDONALDS	66.6	34
6 MCDONALDS	32.3	4		6 APPLE	63.1	14
7 GOOGLE	32.0	25		7 CHINA MOBILE	61.3	7
8 TOYOTA	31.3	-8		8 GENERAL ELECTRIC	59.8	-16
9 INTEL	30.6	-2		9 VODAFON	53.7	45
10 DISNEY	28.5	-3		10 MARLBORO	49.5	33
11 HP	24.1	2		11 WALMART	41.1	19
12 MERCEDES BENZ	23.9	-7		12 ICBC (ASIA)	38.1	36
13 GILETTE	22.8	4		13 NOKIA	35.2	-20
14 CISCO	22.0	3		14 TOYOTA	29.9	-15
15 BMW	21.7	-7		15 UPS	27.8	-9

2 Share of Employees with Job Tenure 10 Years and Over (2000-2008)

FOR SELECT EUROPEAN COUNTRIES (%)

	2000	2001	2002	2003	2004	2005	2006	2007	2008
CZECH REPUBLIC	20.4	19.9	19.7	19.0	18.9	18.8	18.7	18.8	18.6
FRANCE	20.4	20.5	21.2	21.7	21.8	21.8	22.1	22.0	21.9
GERMANY	20.4	20.1	20.6	20.7	21.0	20.8	21.0	21.2	21.3
ITALY	20.0	20.3	21.1	21.4	21.8	21.6	21.8	22.0	21.8
NETHERLANDS	19.9	19.8	20.6	21.1	21.3	21.4	21.5	21.5	21.4
POLAND	21.6	21.7	21.9	21.8	21.6	21.5	21.5	21.4	21.6
SWEDEN	20.6	21.1	22.0	22.5	22.6	22.4	22.6	22.7	22.7
UK	18.4	18.7	19.6	19.8	20.0	20.1	20.2	20.3	20.3

3 Company Rankings by Students 2009

OF FOREIGN COMPANIES IN TOP 10 OF WHERE STUDENTS WOULD LIKE TO WORK

AUSTRIA	9	NETHERLANDS	5	
CHINA	4	POLAND	10	
DENMARK	2	RUSSIA	5	
GERMANY	3	SOUTH AFRICA	6	
INDIA	7	SWEDEN	4	
ITALY	6	UK	5	
JAPAN	3	US	2	

Importance of Work and Leisure Time in Different Countries Over Time

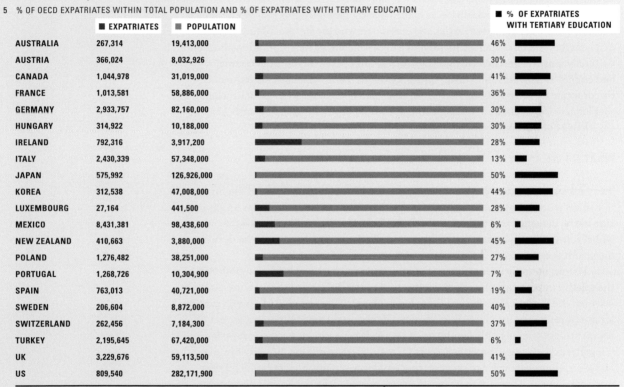

	WAVE	LT	W			WAVE	LT	W			WAVE	LT	W	
CHILE	2	2.1	1.3		JAPAN	2	2.0	1.8		SOUTH AFRICA	2	2.0	1.4	
	3	1.7	1.4			3	1.7	1.6			3	2.0	1.3	
	5	1.7	1.5			5	1.7	1.6			5	1.9	1.3	
CHINA	2	2.5	1.5		POLAND	2	1.9	1.3		SPAIN	2	1.8	1.4	
	3	2.4	1.4			3	2.0	1.4			3	1.9	1.5	
	5	2.4	1.7			5	1.9	1.6			5	1.7	1.7	
INDIA	2	2.4	1.2		RUSSIA	2	2.0	1.8		USA	3	1.7	1.7	
	3	2.7	1.2			3	2.1	1.7			5	1.8	2.0	
	5	2.3	1.4			5	2.0	1.7						

YEARS OF WAVE 2 = 1989-1993 3 = 1994-1999 5 = 2005-2008   SCALE FROM 1 (VERY IMPORTANT) TO 4   ■ LEISURE TIME (LT;MEAN)   ■ WORK (W;MEAN)

OECD Expatriates, 2004

% OF OECD EXPATRIATES WITHIN TOTAL POPULATION AND % OF EXPATRIATES WITH TERTIARY EDUCATION

	■ EXPATRIATES	■ POPULATION		% OF EXPATRIATES WITH TERTIARY EDUCATION
AUSTRALIA	267,314	19,413,000		46%
AUSTRIA	366,024	8,032,926		30%
CANADA	1,044,978	31,019,000		41%
FRANCE	1,013,581	58,886,000		36%
GERMANY	2,933,757	82,160,000		30%
HUNGARY	314,922	10,188,000		30%
IRELAND	792,316	3,917,200		28%
ITALY	2,430,339	57,348,000		13%
JAPAN	575,992	126,926,000		50%
KOREA	312,538	47,008,000		44%
LUXEMBOURG	27,164	441,500		28%
MEXICO	8,431,381	98,438,600		6%
NEW ZEALAND	410,663	3,880,000		45%
POLAND	1,276,482	38,251,000		27%
PORTUGAL	1,268,726	10,304,900		7%
SPAIN	763,013	40,721,000		19%
SWEDEN	206,604	8,872,000		40%
SWITZERLAND	262,456	7,184,300		37%
TURKEY	2,195,645	67,420,000		6%
UK	3,229,676	59,113,500		41%
US	809,540	282,171,900		50%

Total Worldwide AD Spending 2008 in $US

TOP 12 ADVERTISERS

	US		ASIA		EUROPE		LATIN AMERICA	
PROCTER & GAMBLE CO. (US)	3.4		19.3		35.5		3.0	
UNILEVER (UK/NETHERLANDS)	7.5		13.7		25.4		5.6	
L'OREAL (FRANCE)	8.0		5.3		24.6		1.0	
GENERAL MOTORS CORP. (US)	22.3		1.6		9.7		1.3	
TOYOTA MOTOR CORP.(JAPAN)	10.2		12.4		7.5		0.7	
COCA-COLA CO.(US)	4.4		6.8		12.4		1.7	
JOHNSON & JOHNSON (USA)	14.2		3.0		7.0		0.6	
FORD MOTOR CORP (US)	10.1		1.1		10.3		1.7	
RECKITT BENCKISER (UK)	5.4		2.0		13.8		1.1	
NESTLE (SWITZERLAND)	6.2		2.3		12.3		1.3	
VOLKSWAGEN (GERMANY)	2.9		1.3		17.1		1.2	
HONDA MOTOR CO. (JAPAN)	8.3		10.2		2.7		0.4	

■ SPENDING (100M US$)

Identities in the Economy

Several scholars have emphasized the strong cultural foundations of economic transactions (e.g., Hoelscher, 2006; Hofstede, 2001; House et al., 2004). This is one of the reasons why identities play an important role in the globalized economy. International corporations create brands that have global appeal because these brands improve their bargaining powers in negotiating with suppliers, help attract investors and employees, and ensure corporate stability and profitability (see chapter by Jiménez Lopez in this volume). Global brands, which are internationally famous, are often standardized and perceived by consumers worldwide as high in quality. However, this also often implies resistance from globalization critics and consumers who prefer local brands (Bauer et al., 2009: 58). The corporate identity of internationally active corporations is often culturally sensitive and diverse especially when they operate in different countries and employ expatriates from different backgrounds. Personal identity is influenced by corporate identity and can, therefore, be shaped in the context of globalization. As Hannerz (1992) pointed out, migrating for work purposes can significantly shape the identity of the employee (see chapter by Boswell in this volume).

WHAT DO WE KNOW?

Two rankings illustrate the economic importance of brands (data point 1). The figure illustrates the value of a brand to a company. This value can be identified as an expression of the influence that products like Coca-Cola, Google, or Microsoft have on global culture. There are usually significant investments associated with the development of successful global brands (data point 6).

People, not only as consumers, but also as producers, have different opinions on the relative importance of work and leisure. Between the 1989-1993 and 2005-2008 waves of the World Values Survey, there has been a global trend toward a preference for leisure time (data point 4). Work is considered the second most important aspect of life on average (trailing only family), with relatively little variance across countries. Globalization ideology sometimes takes increasingly dynamic job mobility for granted. However, empirical evidence suggests that employee retention seems to be increasing (data point 2). Thus, for most people, work-related identities are not necessarily becoming more heterogeneous, but rather are specific to one or a few firms.

In many countries, graduating students prefer to join large international high-profile organizations than local companies (data point 3). The reasons for such preferences might include different perceptions of the quality of trans-national companies, or the congruence of a firm's culture with the national culture and/or personal identity. OECD figures relating to the percentage of expatriates within selected countries' total population (data point 5) indicate the number of flexibly mobile workers from different cultures (see also the Migration and Diaspora Suite). Clearly, the level of economic development is not the only factor attracting people to the various countries, as differences within rich countries (e.g., between Luxembourg and Japan) as well as within poorer countries (e.g., Hungary and Mexico) are remarkable.

WHAT ARE THE ISSUES?

When it comes to global branding, marketers are confronted with the challenge of producing an attractive global product that can also be easily accepted at the local level. A key avenue of research regarding corporate identities is to examine how they vary across regions and adjust their corporate policy to the host country and how they are influenced by globalization.

Some researchers claim that work is losing its importance for human identity (e.g., Beck, 2000, or Sennett, 1998). However, most data contradict this extreme perspective (Doherty, 2009). Still, an interesting issue is the extent to which globalization alters work-related identity qualitatively and how it varies across countries. When it comes to expatriates, an important challenge is how to balance a win-win situation among migrants, host country, and worker's home country while avoiding the "brain drain,' in other words, the migration away from their own countries of highly skilled and educated people (Dumont & Lemaitre, 2005: 17f). Pohlmann (2009) shows that there is no significant management brain drain among the United States, Germany, and East Asia, since there are no significant markets for management talent among those regions. Expatriates often experience a sense of alienation, particularly when they face ethnic or other more subtle forms of discrimination in the host country (see chapter by Ang in this volume).

RELIGION

1. WORLD'S MOST VISITED RELIGIOUS DESTINATIONS IN MLN (2009)

BRAZIL

APARECIDA DO NORTE — 8

ITALY

THE VATICAN / ST. PETER'S BASILICA, VATICAN CITY — 18

PADRE PIO SHRINE — 7

BASILICA OF ST. FRANCIS — 4.5

POLAND

JASNA GÓRA — 4.5

ISRAEL

JERUSALEM — 2

PORTUGAL

FÁTIMA — 4.5

SAUDI ARABIA

MECCA AND MEDINA — 2.1

INDIA

SABARIMALA — 10

VARANASI — 1.3

FRANCE

NOTRE DAME CATHEDRAL — 13

SACRÉ COEUR BASILICA, MONTMARTRE — 10.5

LOURDES — 5

MEXICO

OUR LADY OF GUADALUPE SHRINE — 20

2. RELIGIOSITY IN DIFFERENT COUNTRIES (2008)

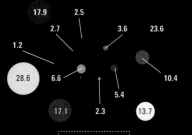

A CONVINCED ATHEIST

17.9 · 2.5 · 2.7 · 3.6 · 23.6 · 1.2 · 28.6 · 6.6 · 5.4 · 10.4 · 17.1 · 2.3 · 13.7

NOT A RELIGIOUS PERSON

60.3 · 37.3 · 62.1 · 36 · 41.3 · 19.5 · 24.4 · 26.7 · 16.6 · 40.9 · 67.4 · 9.3 · 10.8

BRAZIL
ITALY
ARGENTINA
INDIA
US
CANADA
UK
FRANCE
VIETNAM
SOUTH KOREA
HONG KONG
JAPAN
CHINA

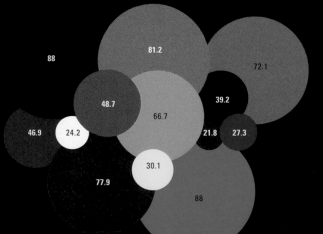

A RELIGIOUS PERSON

88 · 81.2 · 72.1 · 48.7 · 66.7 · 39.2 · 46.9 · 24.2 · 21.8 · 27.3 · 30.1 · 77.9 · 88

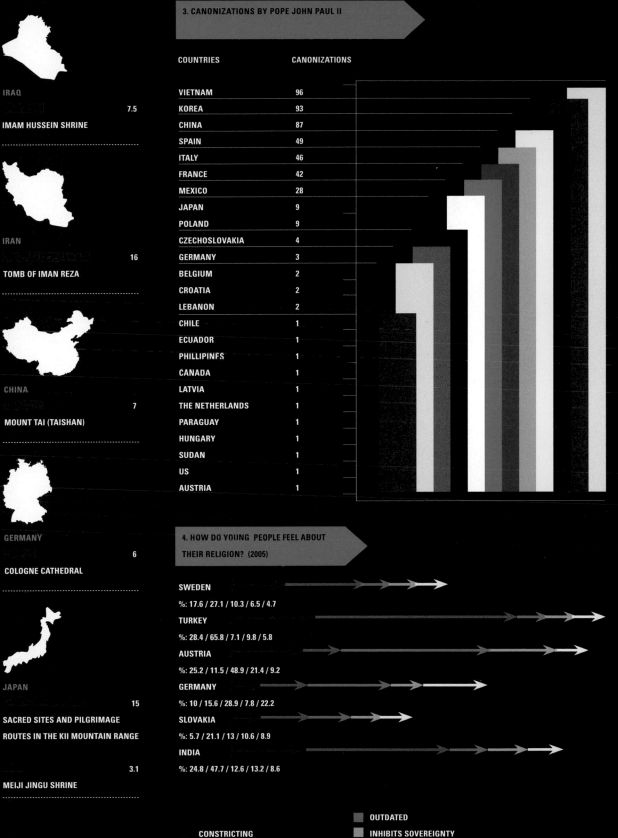

IRAQ
7.5
IMAM HUSSEIN SHRINE

IRAN
16
TOMB OF IMAN REZA

CHINA
7
MOUNT TAI (TAISHAN)

GERMANY
6
COLOGNE CATHEDRAL

JAPAN
15
SACRED SITES AND PILGRIMAGE
ROUTES IN THE KII MOUNTAIN RANGE

3.1
MEIJI JINGU SHRINE

COUNTRIES	CANONIZATIONS
VIETNAM	96
KOREA	93
CHINA	87
SPAIN	49
ITALY	46
FRANCE	42
MEXICO	28
JAPAN	9
POLAND	9
CZECHOSLOVAKIA	4
GERMANY	3
BELGIUM	2
CROATIA	2
LEBANON	2
CHILE	1
ECUADOR	1
PHILLIPINES	1
CANADA	1
LATVIA	1
THE NETHERLANDS	1
PARAGUAY	1
HUNGARY	1
SUDAN	1
US	1
AUSTRIA	1

4. HOW DO YOUNG PEOPLE FEEL ABOUT
THEIR RELIGION? (2005)

SWEDEN
%: 17.6 / 27.1 / 10.3 / 6.5 / 4.7
TURKEY
%: 28.4 / 65.8 / 7.1 / 9.8 / 5.8
AUSTRIA
%: 25.2 / 11.5 / 48.9 / 21.4 / 9.2
GERMANY
%: 10 / 15.6 / 28.9 / 7.8 / 22.2
SLOVAKIA
%: 5.7 / 21.1 / 13 / 10.6 / 8.9
INDIA
%: 24.8 / 47.7 / 12.6 / 13.2 / 8.6

CONSTRICTING

PRETENDS GOOD GENERALITIES

OUTDATED

INHIBITS SOVEREIGNTY

STILL UP-TO DATE

YEAR	TOTAL	RELIGIOUS	RELIGIOUS-CULTURAL	CULTURAL
1989	3,268	2,730	414	49
1990	4,918	2,359	2,086	256
1991	7,274	3,668	3,214	357
1992	9,764	5,269	3,943	537
1993	99,436	53,659	40,155	5,469
1994	15,863	9,637	5,655	554
1995	19,821	11,882	7,323	616
1996	23,218	15,532	6,786	899
1997	25,179	17,163	7,247	767
1998	30,126	20,109	8,209	1,808
1999	154,613	115,016	36,370	3,199
2000	55,004	36,131	16,479	2,389
2001	61,418	38,987	17,107	5,324
2002	68,952	45,627	18,353	4,972
2003	74,614	52,145	17,346	5,123
2004	179,944	134,330	35,528	10,086
2005	93,924	35,456	49,977	8,491
2006	100,377	41,793	49,726	8,858

Religion

In relation to the interactions between cultures and globalization, religion often plays an important role. Religious belief and practice have not disappeared (as was assumed by early secularization theory), but instead they have come center stage in public debate. The topic is, likewise, closely connected to the key topics dealt with in this volume and can be interpreted and analyzed from the perspective of diverse disciplines. Defining religion has always been a precarious endeavor. While some scholars strive to create a definition that is mostly connected to the *Zeitgeist*, others try to conceive religion as an open concept and consider that "scientific theories only obtain their relevance within the context of cultural discourses" (Kippenberg & Stuckrad, 2003: 20). Furthermore, different world regions have differing notions of religion and of its place in political and cultural life. Certainly, it can no longer be considered anywhere as an "autonomous province of human experience" (Kippenberg & Stuckrad, 2003: 13), but rather a vital and crucial cultural element in everyday life. In combination with identity, which can be characterized as a generated problem of modernity and post-modernity (Baumann, 1995), religious identity is under permanent construction and deconstruction, and is subject to theoretical controversy, even as regards religious heritage, e.g., rituals, a realm that till recently was considered solid and unalterable (Kreinath, Snoek, & Stausberg, 2006).

WHAT DO WE KNOW?

Religion encompasses a huge diversity of cultural and social heritage in the general sense of the term and is a source of cultural identification, but the processes of "religious socialization and identity formation have changed" (Kippenberg & Stuckrad, 2003: 136). Individualization processes and numerous forms of cultural contacts have brought about new hybrid and syncretic religions. Within almost every religious context there are pilgrimages to sacred places. Pilgrimages can be identity-establishing: For example, the fifth pillar of Islam, the Hajj, which stands for the traditional pilgrimage to the holy city of Mecca, is an obligation that every Muslim should accomplish if he or she can afford it financially and physically. In recent years one can observe a growing number of pilgrims to Mecca (Ministry of Hajj, Kingdom of Saudi Arabia) as shown in Table 1:

Table 1: Pilgrims to Mecca over the Years (Source: Ministry of Hajj. Kingdom of Saudi Arabia, n.d.)

1996	1997	1998	1999	2000	2001	2002	2003	2004	2005	2006
1,865,234	1,942,851	1,832,114	1,831,998	1,839,154	1,913,263	1,994.760	2,041.129	2,012,074	2,164,469	2,130,594

Among Christians pilgrimages are popular as well; in Europe the Way of St. James still attracts thousands each summer. In Mexico, the Our Lady of Guadeloupe Shrine is visited by even more people than the Vatican and St. Peter's Basilica (data point 1). But motivations have changed in subtle ways (data point 5): Over the years, people have begun choosing to make a pilgrimage not only for religious but also for cultural reasons. Paulo Coelho's book *The Pilgrimage* (2004 [1987]) illustrates the hybridity of religious motives. Thus religious destinations today attract a substantial number of visitors for reasons that are at once religious, cultural, social, or individual.

The main route of the Way of St. James, the Camino Frances, was designated as a World Heritage Site (WHS) in 1993 (see also the suite on World Heritage Sites). Indeed the World Heritage List clearly displays a certain Christian hegemony, judging from the number of monuments of that religion (see Table 2). One of the reasons is probably the much higher number of adherents to Christianity (2.1 billion), compared with other religions (1.5 billion to Islam, 900 million to Hinduism, 394 million to Chinese traditional religion, and 376 million to Buddhism (Adherents, 2005; see also the Data Suite on New and Syncretic Religions in the previous volume, *Cultural Expression, Creativity and Innovation*). Another reason is that most World Heritage Sites are located in Europe and North America, where Christianity is the majority religion (see the World Heritage Sites Suite).

Table 2. World Heritage Sites of Religious Structure, by Religion (2009)

Christian	Buddhist	Indigenous	Islamic	Hindu	Bahá'i Faith
103	24	19	18	8	1

Canonizations under Pope John Paul II (data point 3) reveal a rather political aspect of religion, in this special case Catholicism. The procedure of canonization can be interpreted and analyzed as a "repersonalization of charisma" (Bienfait, 2006: 1). Considering the large number of persons canonized in Asian countries, this Catholic function can be used for attracting people in countries where this denomination is a minority religion (data point 2).

WHAT ARE THE ISSUES?

Perceptions of religion differ tremendously worldwide. This is exemplified by the differences in attitudes of young people toward religion (data point 4). While in some countries a permanent decline of religious adherents or church goers can be observed (secularization), others are experiencing constant growth of membership in the world religions, mainly for demographic reasons (*Foreign Policy*, 2007). Religion will remain an ever-present element in the discourse on cultures and globalization, though in different forms, whether in Northern Ireland or in Iraq or Lebanon. In terms of heritage, for example, it can be linked to conflict (see the chapter by Croissant and Chambers). In terms of identity, it will be interesting to examine new forms of hybridity (see, e.g., the works of Christopher Helland [2005] on the topic of online religion) or innovations or processes of dynamization on behalf of religious institutions. However, not only religious heritage but also religious identities are under permanent contest, as the head scarf conflict in some European countries bears witness.

References

*Numerals Refer To Datapoints

Heritage

WORLD HERITAGE SITES

1a UNESCO World Heritage Centre. (2009). *World Heritage List*. Retrieved July 7, 2009 , from http://whc.unesco.org/pg.cfm?cid=31&l=en&&&mode=table

1b UNESCO World Heritage Centre. (2009). *World Heritage List*. Retrieved July 7, 2009 , from http://whc.unesco.org/pg.cfm?cid=31&l=en&&&mode=table

2 UNESCO World Heritage Committee. (2009). *Thirty third session*. Retrieved August 9, 2009, from http://whc.unesco.org/en/sessions/33COM/

UNESCO Institute for Statistics. (2009). *UIS statistics in brief*. Retrieved April 20, 2009, from http://stats.uis.unesco.org/unesco/tableviewer/document.aspx?ReportId=143

Frank, S. (2006). *Eurostat statistics in focus — Science and technology. R&D expenditure in Europe*. Retrieved September 1, 2009, from http://epp.eurostat.ec.europa.eu/cache/ITY_OFFPUB/KS-NS-06-006/EN/KS-NS-06-006-EN.PDF

The European Commission. (2008). *The 2008 EU industrial R&D investment scoreboard*. Retrieved October 10, 2009, from http://iri.jrc.ec.europa.eu/research/scoreboard_2008.htm

3 UNESCO World Heritage Centre. (2007). *Periodic report and action plan Europe 2005-2006*. Retrieved August 22, 2009, from http://whc.unesco.org/documents/publi_wh_papers_20_en.pdf

4 UNESCO World Heritage Centre. (2007). *World heritage – Challenges for the millenium*. Retrieved October 10, 2009, from http://whc.unesco.org/documents/publi_millennium_en.pdf

5 UNESCO World Heritage Centre. (2007). *Periodic report and action plan Europe 2005-2006*. Retrieved August 22, 2009, from http://whc.unesco.org/documents/publi_wh_papers_20_en.pdf

6 ICOMOS. (2004). *The world heritage list: Filling the gaps — An action plan for the future*. Retrieved October 10, 2009, from http://whc.unesco.org/uploads/pages/documents/document-273-1.pdf

DIGEST: WORLD HERITAGE SITES

Der Spiegel. (2009, November 30). Wetterfühlig. *Der Spiegel 49/2009*, 71.

UNESCO. (1972). *Convention concerning the protection of world cultural and natural heritage*. Retrieved January 9, 2010, from http://whc.unesco.org/archive/convention-en.pdf

UNESCO World Heritage Centre. (2002). *World heritage manuals 1. Managing tourism at World Heritage Sites: A practical manual for World Heritage Site Managers*. Retrieved January 9, 2010, from http://whc.unesco.org/uploads/activities/documents/activity-113-2.pdf

UNESCO World Heritage Center. (2010). *About*. Retrieved February 3., 2010, from http://whc.unesco.org/en/about/

LEGAL + POLITICAL FRAMEWORKS

1 UNESCO (United Nations Educational, Scientific and Cultural Organization). (n.d.). *Conventions*. Retrieved November 23, 2009, from http://portal.unesco.org/en/ev.php-URL_ID=12025&URL_DO=DO_TOPIC&URL_SECTION=-471.html

2 UNESCO (United Nations Educational, Scientific and Cultural Organization). *Legal instruments*. Retrieved November 23, 2009, from http://portal.unesco.org/la/convention.asp?KO=13055&language=E

3 ICOMOS (International Council on Monuments and Sites). (2008). *The World Heritage List: What Is OUV? Defining the outstanding universal value of cultural World Heritage Properties*. Retrieved October 7, 2009, from http://www.international.icomos.org/publications/monuments_and_sites/16/pdf/Monuments_and_Sites_16_What_is_OUV.pdf

4   ICOM (International Council of Museums). (2009). *Agreement of dealers in art, antiques, and antiquities to object-ID standards.* Retrieved October 10, 2009, from http://icom.museum/objectid/

5   Grasstek, V. (n.d.). *Treatment of cultural goods and services in international trade agreements.* Retrieved November 23, 2009, from http://www.unescobkk.org/fileadmin/user_upload/culture/Cultural_Industries/Singapore_Feb_05/Treatment_of_cultural_goods_and_services_GRASSTEK.pdf

DIGEST: LEGAL + POLITICAL FRAMEWORKS

Hoelscher, M. (2011). Generation, Sixty Eight. In H. K. Anheier & M. Juergensmeyer (Eds.), *Encyclopedia of global studies.* London: Sage.

ICOMOS. (2008). *The World Heritage List: What is OUV? Defining the outstanding universal value of cultural World Heritage Properties.* Available from http://www.international.icomos.org/publications/monuments_and_sites/16/pdf/Monuments_and_Sites_16_What_is_OUV.pdf

Isar, Y.R. (2008) The Intergovernmental Policy Actors, in H. K. Anheier & Y. R. Isar (Eds.), *The Cultural Economy, (The Cultures and Globalization Series, Vol. 2)*. London and Thousand Oaks: Sage.

UNESCO. (2009). Cultural property: Its illicit trafficking and restitution. Retrieved January 16, 2010, from http://portal.unesco.org/culture/en/ev.php-URL_ID=35252&URL_DO=DO_TOPIC&URL_SECTION=201.html

MUSEUMS

1   BodyWorlds. (n.d.). *Past exhibitions.* Retrieved October 6, 2009, from http://www.bodyworlds.com/en/exhibitions/past_exhibitions.html

Willkommen, H. (2004). *Bundesverband der Körperspender e.V.* Retrieved October 6, 2009, from http://www.koerperspender.de/

Truly Unusual. (2006, November 21). *Unusual art made from the dead.* Retrieved October 6, 2009, from http://www.trulyunusual.com/wards/showthread.php?t=6471&p=6628#post6628

'Body Worlds' attracts 338,000 visitors to museum. *Business Journal of Milwaukee.* (June 3, 2008). Retrieved October 6, 2009, from http://jacksonville.bizjournals.com/milwaukee/stories/2008/06/02/daily12.html

Discovery Place. (2007-08). *Circus: secrets of science under the big top.* Retrieved October 6, 2009, from http://www.discoveryplace.org/assets/pdfs/2009_annual_report.pdf

LuMrix.com. (n.d.). *Body worlds.* Retrieved October 6, 2009, from http://www.lumrix.net/medical/anatomy/body_worlds.html

2   Exhibition attendance figures 2008. *The Art Newspaper.* (April 2009). Retrieved September 27, 2009, from http://www.theartnewspaper.com/attfig/attfig08.pdf

3   Exhibition attendance figures 2008. *The Art Newspaper.* (April 2009). Retrieved September 27, 2009, from http://www.theartnewspaper.com/attfig/attfig08.pdf

4   European Group on Museum Statistic. (n.d.). *Percentage of people, who visited at least once a museum / gallery.* Retrieved September 27, 2009, from http://www.egmus.eu/index.php?id=88&L=STIL=

5   Osservatorio Ecomusei. (n.d.). *Europa.* Retrieved October 6, 2009, from http://www.osservatorioecomusei.net/start.php?PHPSESSID=5070aee803c8579e92060770936defba&stat=&ris=h&mf=em_europa

Osservatorio Ecomusei. (n.d.). *Mondo.* Retrieved October 6, 2009, from http://www.osservatorioecomusei.net/start.php?PHPSESSID=5070aee803c8579e92060770936defba&stat=&ris=h&mf=em_mondo

6   Exhibition attendance figures 2008. *The Art Newspaper.* (April 2009). Retrieved September 27, 2009, from http://www.theartnewspaper.com/attfig/attfig07.pdf

Le Louvre. (n.d.). Retrieved September 27, 2009, from www.louvre.fr/llv/commun/home.jsp?bmLocale=en

Centre Pompidou. (n.d.). Retrieved September 27, 2009, from www.centrepompidou.fr

Modern Tate. (n.d.). Retrieved September 27, 2009, from www.tate.org.uk/modern

British Museum. (n.d.). Retrieved September 27, 2009, from www.britishmuseum.org

The Metropolitan Museum of Art. (n.d.). Retrieved September 27, 2009, from www.metmuseum.org

National Gallery of Art Washington. (n.d.). Retrieved September 27, 2009, from www.nga.gov

Vatican Museums. (n.d.). Retrieved September 27, 2009, from http://mv.vatican.va/3_EN/pages/MV_Home.html

National Gallery. (n.d.). Retrieved September 27, 2009, from www.nationalgallery.org.uk

Musee d'Orsay. (n.d.). Retrieved September 27, 2009, from www.musee-orsay.fr/en/home.html

Museo Nacional del Prado. (n.d.). Retrieved September 27, 2009, from www.museodelprado.es

DIGEST: MUSEUMS

Becker, H. (1982). *Art worlds*. Berkeley: University of California Press.

Hall, S. (1997). *Representation: Cultural representations and signifying practices*. London: Sage.

ICOM (International Council of Museums). *Definition of a museum*. (n.d.). Retrieved January 21, 2010, from http://icom.museum/definition.html.

Le Louvre. *La fréquentation du musée du Louvre*. (n.d.). Retrieved January 21, 2010, from http://www.louvre.fr/mediarepository/ressources/sources/pdf/RA03frequentation_v2_m56577569830541189.pdf

Pieterse, J. N. (2005). Multiculturalism and museums: Discourse about others in the age of globalization. In G. Corsane (Ed.), *Heritage, museums and galleries* (pp.163-183). London: Routledge.

Stam, D. C. (2005). The informed muse: The implications of "the new museology" for museum practice. In G. Corsane (Ed.), *Heritage, museums and galleries – an introductory reader* (pp. 54-70). Routledge: London.

Waltl, C. (2006). *Museums for visitors: Audience development – A crucial role for successful museum management strategies*. Retrieved February 14, 2010, from http://www.intercom.museum/documents/1-4Waltl.pdf.

INTANGIBLE HERITAGE

1   UNESCO (United Nations Educational Scientific and Cultural Organization). (2009). *Endangered languages statistics*. Retrieved October, 22, 2009, from http://www.unesco.org/culture/ich/misc/UNESCO-EndangeredLanguages-Statistics-20090217.xls

2   City of Blumenau. (2009). *Blumenau online*. Retrieved December 16, 2009, from http://www.guiadeblumenau.com.br/indexe.htm

Octoberfest Celebrations. (2009). Retrieved December 16, 2009, from http://en.wikipedia.org/wiki/Oktoberfest_celebrations#cite_note-2

3   UNESCO (United Nations Educational Scientific and Cultural Organization). (2009). *Index translationum - world bibliography of translation*. Retrieved December 8, 2009, from http://portal.unesco.org/culture/en/ev.php-URL_ID=7810&URL_DO=DO_TOPIC&URL_SECTION=201.html

4   National Environment Management Authority, Transboundary Environmental Project. (2007). *Preservation and maintenance of biological diversity related knowledge of indigenous diversity and local communities with traditional lifestyles boni*. Retrieved October 15, 2009, from www.terranuova.org/file_download/49

5   WIPO (World Intellectual Property Organization). (2009). *Statistics on patents*. Retrieved December 17, 2009, from http://www.wipo.int/ipstats/en/statistics/patents/

6   UNESCO (United Nations Educational Scientific and Cultural Organization). (2006). *Masterpieces of the oral and intangible heritage of humanity proclamations 2001, 2003 and 2005.* Retrieved November 3, 2009, from http://unesdoc.unesco.org/images/0014/001473/147344E.pdf and http://www.unesco.org/culture/ich/index.php?pg=00011

DIGEST: INTANGIBLE HERITAGE

American Association for the Advancement of Science. (2008). *Traditional knowledge under threat: Faulty laws, lack of trust stymie promising advances.* Retrieved May 26, 2010, from http://www.eurekalert.org/pub_releases/2008-11/bc-tku110708.php

Centre for International Research and Advisory Networks. (2001). *Indigenous knowledge and development monitor.* Vol. 9. Retrieved May 26, 2010, from http://www.iss.nl/ikdm/IKDM/IKDM/pdf/0701.pdf

Haspelmath, M. (2009). *Sprachen der Welt.* Leipzig; Max-Planck-Institut für evolutionäre Anthropologie. Retrieved February 6, 2010, from http://www.uni-leipzig.de/-muellerg/su/haspelmath.pdf

Summer Institute of Linguistics. (2010). *Ethnologue. Languages of the world.* Retrieved February 6, 2010, from http://www.ethnologue.com/

UNESCO. (2003). *Convention for the safeguarding of intangible cultural heritage.* Retrieved January 16, 2010, from http://unesdoc.unesco.org/images/0013/001325/132540e.pdf

WIPO. (2009). *Intellectual property and traditional cultural expressions/folklore.* Retrieved January 18, 2010, from http://www.wipo.int/freepublications/en/tk/913/wipo_pub_913.pdf

World Bank. (2004). *Indigenous knowledge. Local pathways to global development.* Retrieved November 20, 2010, from http://www.worldbank.org/afr/ik/iknotes.htm

TOURISM

1   World Heritage Sites. (2009). *One million visitors or more.* Retrieved August 17, 2009, from http://www.worldheritagesite.org/tags/tag352.html

3   WTTC (World Travel & Tourism Council). (2009). *Real travel & tourism activity growth 1989 - 2009. Personal travel & tourism.* Retrieved October 12, 2009, from http://www.wttc.org/eng/Tourism_Research/Tourism_Impact_Data_and_Forecast_Tool/index.php

WTTC (World Travel & Tourism Council). (2009). *Real travel & tourism activity growth 1989 - 2009. Business travel & tourism.* Retrieved October 12, 2009, from http://www.wttc.org/eng/Tourism_Research/Tourism_Impact_Data_and_Forecast_Tool/index.php

4   UNWTO (United Nations World Tourism Organization). (n.d.). *Tourism highlights 2009 edition.* Retrieved December 3, 2009, from http://www.unwto.org/facts/eng/pdf/highlights/UNWTO_Highlights09_en_HR.pdf

2, 5 + 6   EU (European Commission). (2009). Survey on the attitudes of Europeans towards tourism. Analytical report. *Flash Eurobarometer 258.* Retrieved November 20, 2009, from http://ec.europa.eu/public_opinion/flash/fl_258_en.pdf

DIGEST: TOURISM

Cole, S. (2007). Beyond authenticity and commodification. *Annals of Tourism Research 34 (4),* 943-960

Guttentag, D.A. (2009). The possible negative impacts of volunteer tourism. *International Journal of Tourism Research, 11 (6),* 537-551

Kirtsoglou, E., & Theodossopoulos, D. (2004). "They are taking our culture away": Tourism and culture commodification in the Garifuna community of Roatan. *Critique of Anthropology, 24 (2),* 135-157

Mercer. (2009). *Gesetzlicher Urlaubsanspruch: Deutschland Schlusslicht in Europa.* Retrieved January 19, 2010, from http://www.mercer.de/summary.htm?siteLanguage=1000&idContent=1360495

Nypan, T. (2003). *Cultural Heritage Monuments and Historic Buildings as value generators in post-industrial economy. With emphasis on exploring the role of the sector as economic driver.* Retrieved November 20, 2009, from http://www.riksantikvaren.no/Norsk/Publikasjoner/Andre_utgivelser/filestore/IICH.PDF

Richter, L. K. (2005). The politics of heritage tourism development: emerging issues for the new millennium. In G. Corsane (Ed.). *Heritage, Museums and Galleries. An introductory reader* (pp. 243-271). London and New York: Routledge.

UNWTO. (1995). *Collection of tourism expenditure statistics. Technical manual No 2*. Retrieved January 19, 2010, from http://pub.unwto.org/WebRoot/Store/Shops/Infoshop/Products/1034/1034-1.pdf

Wearing, S., Stevenson, D. &, Young, T. (2010). *Tourist cultures. Identity, place and the traveller.* London: Sage.

Wearing, B. &, Wearing, S. (2001) Conceptualizing the selves of tourism. *Leisure Studies 20* (2), 143-159

Zins, A. (2004). *Bedeutung und Entwicklung der Tourismuswirtschaft.* Retrieved January 19, 2010, from http://tourism.wu-wien.ac.at/lehrv/lven/04ss/gk1/c1folien_ss04_s2.pdf

SUSTAINABILITY

1   European Commission. (2009). *Agriculture and rural development*. Retrieved December 12, 2009, from http://ec.europa.eu/agriculture/quality/door/list.html?locale=en

2   UNESCO. (2009). *Memory of the world project*. Retrieved December 16, 2009, from http://portal.unesco.org/ci/en/ev.php-URL_ID=17534&URL_DO=DO_TOPIC&URL_SECTION=201.html

3   IUCN (The International Union for Conservation of Nature). (2009). *IUCN Red List of threatened Species*. Retrieved April 20, 2010, from www.iucnredlist.org

4   World Values Survey. (2009). *Values Surveys Databank, environment, human & nature (2009)*. Retrieved December 12, 2009, from http://www.worldvaluessurvey.org/

5   Abdallah, S., Thompson, S., Michaelson, J., Marks, N., & Steuer, N. (2009). *The (un-) Happy Planet Index 2.0. Why good lives don't have to cost the Earth*. Retrieved December 15, 2009, from http://www.happyplanetindex.org/learn/download-report.html

DIGEST: SUSTAINABILITY

Abdallah, S., Thompson, S., Michaelson, J., Marks, N. &, Steuer, N. (2009). *The (un)Happy Planet Index 2.0. Why good lives don't have to cost the Earth*. Retrieved December 15, 2009, from http://www.happyplanetindex.org/learn/downloadreport.html

IUCN Standards and Petitions Working Group. (2008). *Guidelines for using the IUCN Red List categories and criteria*. Version 7.0. Prepared by the Standards and Petitions Working Group of the IUCN SSC Biodiversity Assessments Sub-Committee in August 2008. Downloadable from http://intranet.iucn.org/webfiles/doc/SSC/RedList/RedListGuidelines.pdf

Lowenthal, D. (1994). Identity, heritage and history. In J. R. Gillis (Ed.), *Commemorations. The politics of national identity*. Princeton, NJ: Princeton University Press.

Marquardt, E. (2005). *Visiotype and Stereotype*. Cologne: Halem.

INTERNATIONAL ORGANIZATIONS + HERITAGE

1   UIA (The Union of International Associations). (2008). *Number of international organizations by subject group: 1992-2007*. Retrieved September 30, 2009, from www.uia.org

2   UIA (The Union of International Associations). (2008). *Areas of concern of leading people in international organizations, by subject: 2007*. Retrieved September 30, 2009, from www.uia.org

3   Global Heritage Fund. (2009). *Annual report 2007-2008*. Retrieved October 10, 2009, from www.globalheritagefund.org

4   UIA (The Union of International Associations). (2008). *Leading people in international organizations – languages: 2007*. Retrieved September 30, 2009, from www.uia.org

5   *iCSO System*. (2009). Data retrieved October 20, 2009, from http://esango.un.org/civilsociety

6   UNESCO (United Nations Educational, Scientific and Cultural Organization). (2009). *List of NGOs maintaining official relations with UNESCO*. Retrieved October 29, 2009, from http://erc.unesco.org/ong/ONGlist_p.asp

DIGEST: INTERNATIONAL ORGANIZATIONS + HERITAGE

Anheier, H. K. &, Isar Y. R. (Eds.). (2008). *The cultural economy. The Cultures and Globalization Series 2*. London: Sage.

Anheier, H. &, Themudo, N. (2002). Organizational form of global civil society: Implications of going global. In M. Glasius, Helmut K. Anheier, &, M. Kaldor (Eds.), *The Global Civil Society Yearbook (pp. 191-216)*. Oxford: Oxford University Press.

Taylor, P. J. (2005). Leading world cities: Empirical evaluations of urban nodes in multiple networks. *Urban Studies, 42* (9), 1593–608.

Tunbridge, J. (1984). Whose heritage to conserve? Cross-cultural reflections on political dominance and urban heritage conservation. *Canadian Geographer, 28* (2), 111 – 204.

United Nations Permanent Forum on Indigenous Issues. (2010). *Fact sheet*. Retrieved February 7, 2010, from http://www.un.org/esa/socdev/unpfii/documents/5session_factsheet1.pdf

United Nations Declaration on the Rights of Indigenous Peoples. (2007). Retrieved February 5, 2010, from http://www.un.org/esa/socdev/unpfii/documents/DRIPS_en.pdf

World Monuments Fund. (2009). *Annual report*. Retrieved May 30, 2010, from http://www.wmf.org/sites/default/files/annual_report/2009-Annual-Report-WMF_0.pdf

Memory

MEMORIALIZATION

1   360travelguide.com. (n.d.). *Public holidays in India*. Retrieved April 18, 2010, from http://www.360travelguide.com/India/holidays.asp

Gill, K. (n.d.). *Public holidays in the United States*. Retrieved April 18, 2010, from http://uspolitics.about.com/od/usgovernment/a/public_holidays.htm

Zhao, S. (n.d.). *China public holidays 2009 coming out*. Retrieved April 18, 2010, from http://chinahighlightstravel.blogspot.com/2008/12/china-public-holidays-2009-coming-out.html

Australian Government. (n.d.). *Public holidays*. Retrieved April 18, 2010, from http://www.australia.gov.au/topics/australian-facts-and-figures/public-holidays

2   *List of eponyms of airports*. (n.d.). Retrieved April 18, 2010 from http://en.wikipedia.org/wiki/List_of_eponyms_of_airports

3   European Central Bank. (n.d.). *National Sides*. Retrieved April 18, 2010, from http://www.ecb.europa.cu/euro/html/index.en.html

4   Light, D. (2004). Street names in Bucharest, 1990-1997: Exploring the modern historical geographies of post-socialist change. *Journal of Historical Geography, 30*, 154-172.

5   Geographical Renaming. (n.d.). Retrieved April 18, 2010, from http://en.wikipedia.org/wiki/Geographical_renaming

Branford, B. (2005, May 26). *City names mark changing times*. Retrieved April 18, 2010, from http://news.bbc.co.uk/2/hi/africa/4579905.stm

DIGEST: MEMORIALIZATION

Anderson, B. (1991). *Imagined communities: Reflections on the origin and spread of nationalism*. London and New York: Verso.

Levy, D. &, Sznaider, N. (2002). Memory Unbound: the Holocaust and the Formation of Cosmopolitan Memory. *European Journal of Social theory, 5,* 87-106.

CONTESTED MEMORIES

1   ABC News/Washington Post. (2009, April 5). *Most back outreach to Muslim nations, but suspicion & unfamiliarity persist*. Retrieved April 18, 2010, from http://abcnews.go.com/images/PollingUnit/1088a5ViewsofIslam.pdf

2   Pew Research Center for the People & the Press. (2004, March 16). *A year after Iraq war; mistrust of America in Europe ever higher, Muslim anger persists*. Retrieved April 18, 2010. from: http://people-press.org/reports/pdf/206.pdf

3   Freedom House. (2009). Freedom of the press 2009. Retrieved April 18, 2010, from http://www.freedomhouse.org/uploads/fop/2009/FreedomofthePress2009_tables.pdf

4   Rummel, R. J. (1992). *Nazi genocide and mass murder*. New Brunswick: Transaction.

5   Gallup. (2006). *Religion*. Retrieved April 18, 2010, from http://www.gallup.com/poll/1690/Religion.aspx

   Newport, F. (2007). *Majority of Republicans doubt theory of evolution*. Retrieved April 18, 2010, from http://www.gallup.com/poll/27847/Majority-Republicans-Doubt-Theory-Evolution.aspx

6   Croissant, A., et al. (2009). *Kulturelle Konflikte seit 1945. Die kulturellen Dimensionen des Konfliktgeschehens*. Berlin: Nomos.

DIGEST: CONTESTED MEMORIES

Brown, D., Scheflin, A., &, Hammond, C. (1998). *Memory, trauma treatment and the law*. New York: W. W. Norton.

Halbwachs, M. (1992). *On collective memory*. Chicago: University of Chicago Press.

Rummel, R. J. (1994). *Death by government*. Retrieved November 16, 2009, from http://www.hawaii.edu/powerkills/DBG.CHAP2.HTM

Tajfel, H., &, Turner, J. C. (1986). The social identity theory of intergroup behavior. In S. Worchel & W. G. Austin (Eds.), *Psychology of intergroup relations*, (pp. 7-24). Chicago: Nelson-Hall.

GLOBAL COLLECTIVE MEMORIES

1   Liu, J. H., Paez, D., Slawuta, P., Cabecinhas, R., Techio, E., Kokdemir, D., et al. (2009). Representing world history in the 21st century: The impact of 9/11, the Iraq war, and the nation-state on dynamics of collective remembering. *Journal of Cross-Cultural Psychology, 40*(4), 667-692.

2   Jennings, M. K., & Zhang, N. (2005). Generations, political status, and collective memories in the Chinese countryside. *Journal of Politics, 67*(04), 1164-1189.

3   Liu, J. H., Paez, D., Slawuta, P., Cabecinhas, R., Techio, E., Kokdemir, D., et al. (2009). Representing world history in the 21st century: the impact of 9/11, the Iraq war, and the nation-state on dynamics of collective remembering. *Journal of Cross-Cultural Psychology, 40*(4), 667-692.

4   Schuman, H., & Rodgers, W. L. (2004). Cohorts, chronology, and collective memories. *Public Opinion Quarterly, 68*(2), 217-254.

5   Liu, J. H., et al. (2005). Social representations of events and people in world history across 12 cultures. *Journal of Cross-Cultural Psychology, 36*(2), 171-191.

6   Ellermann, H., Glowsky, D., Kromeier, K.-U., & Andorfer, V. (2008). How global are our memories? An empirical approach using an online survey. *Comparativ, 18*(2), 99-115.

DIGEST: GLOBAL COLLECTIVE MEMORIES

Schuman, H., Akiyama, H. &, Knäuper, B. (1998). Collective memories of Germans and Japanese about the past half-century. *Memory, 6* (4), 427-454.

Zerubavel, E. (1997). *Social mindscapes. An invitation to cognitive sociology*. Cambridge (MA) & London: Harvard University Press.

PLACES

1   U.S. Census Bureau. (n.d.). State & county quickfacts. Retrieved April 18, 2010, from http://quickfacts.census.gov/qfd/states

2   Statistisches Landesamt Berlin. (n.d.). *Statistiken*. Retrieved April 18, 2010, from http://www.statistik-berlin.de/zsp-jahr/jdb4.asp

3   Foreign Policy. (2008, October 15). *The 2008 global cities index*. Retrieved April 18, 2010, from http://www.foreignpolicy.com/story/cms.php?story_id=4509&page=1

4   NAAB (National Architectural Accrediting Board). (n.d.). http://www.naab.org/news/results.aspx

5   United Nations. (2008). *Creative Economy Report 2008*. Retrieved April 18, 2010, from: http://www.unctad.org/en/docs/ditc20082cer_en.pdf

6   JTB Corporation. (2008, October, 17). *JTB survey of wedding honeymoon intentions*. Retrieved April 18, 2010, from: http://www.jtbcorp.jp/en/press_release/pdf/release20081017.pdf

DIGEST: PLACES

Cattani, G., & Ferriani, S. (2008). A core/periphery perspective on individual creative performance: Social networks and cinematic achievements in the Hollywood film industry. *Organization Science, 19,* 824-844.

OTIS College of Art and Design. (2008). *Report on the creative economy of the Los Angeles region*. Los Angeles: Los Angeles County Economic Development Corporation. Retrieved from http://www.culturela.org/press/Economic_Report_OTIS_2008.pdf

Power, D. (2002). "Cultural Industries" in Sweden: An assessment of their place in the Swedish economy. *Economic Geography, 78,* 103-127.

Throsby, D. (2008). Globalization and the cultural economy: a crisis of value? In H. Anheier &, Y. R. Isar (Eds.), *The cultural economy* (pp. 29-42). London: Sage.

MEDIA

1   Wikipedia: Multilingual ranking October 2008. (2008). Retrieved April 18, 2010, from http://en.wikipedia.org/wiki/Wikipedia:Multilingual_ranking_October_2008

2   IMDB (Internet Movie Database). (n.d.). *Top rated "history" titles*. Retrieved April 18, 2010, from http://www.imdb.com/chart/history

3   Listophobia (n.d.) *10 largest libraries of the world*. Retrieved April 18, 2010, from Listophobia web site: http://listphobia.com/2009/08/06/10-largest-libraries-of-the-world/

TenMojo. (n.d.) *Top Ten List on the ten largest libraries of the World*. Retrieved April 18, 2010, from http://www.watchmojo.com/top_10/lists/knowledge/libraries/libraries_largest.htm

Lovett, H. (2010). *World's greatest libraries: past and present*. Retrieved April 18, 2010, from http://www.findingdulcinea.com/features/arts/literature/Worlds-Greatest-Libraries-Past-and-Present.html

LOC (Library of Congress). (n.d.) *About the collections*. Retrieved April 18, 2010, from http://memory.loc.gov/ammem/about/about.html

Deutsche National Biblioteck. (2010). *Welcome to the German National Library*. Retrieved April 18, 2010, from http://translate.google.com/translate?hl=en&sl=de&u=http://www.d-nb.de/&ei=rqrPSrGGOIjWtAO6x9XJBQ&sa=X&oi=translate&resnum=1&ct=result&ved=0CBMQ7gEwAA&prev=search%3Fq%3Ddeutsche%2Bbibliothek%26hl%3Den

British Library. (n.d.). *Explore the world's knowledge*. Retrieved April 18, 2010, from http://www.bl.uk/index4.shtml

4   MOAH (Museum of American Heritage). (n.d.) *Information storage timeline*. Retrieved April 18, 2010 from: http://www.moah.org/exhibits/archives/brains/timeline.html

Dunn, J. (n.d.). *Historical papyrus*. Retrieved April 18, 2010, from http://www.touregypt.net/featurestories/papyrus.htm

History of Science. (n.d.). *From cave painting to the internet*. Retrieved April 18, 2010, from http://www.historyofscience.com/G2I/timeline/index.php?era=2009

OSTA (Optical Storage Technology Association). (n.d.). *Understading CD-R & CD-RW*. Retrieved April 18, 2010, from http://www.osta.org/technology/cdqa13.htm

DVD Demystified. (n.d.). *DVD frequently asked questions (and answers)*. Retrieved April 18, 2010, from http://www.dvddemystified.com/dvdfaq.html

Conway, P. (1996). *Preservation in the digital world*. Retrieved April 18, 2010, from http://www.clir.org/pubs/reports/conway2/

5   Europeana. (n.d.). *Think culture*. Retrieved December 4, 2009, from http://www.europeana.eu/portal/brief-doc.html?start=1&view=table&query=*%3A*

LOC (Library of Congress). (n.d.). *Codes for the representation of languages*. Retrieved April 18, 2010, from http://www.loc.gov/standards/iso639-2/php/code_list.php

6   UNESCO (United Nations Educational Scientific and Cultural Organization). (n.d.). *Memory of the world*. Retrieved April 18, 2010, from http://portal.unesco.org/ci/en/ev.php-URL_ID=28984&URL_DO=DO_TOPIC&URL_SECTION=201.html

DIGEST: MEDIA

Charness, N., & Holley, P. (2004). The new media and older adults: Usable and useful? *American Behavioral Scientist, 48*.

Chun, W., & Keenan, T. (Eds). (2006). *New media, old media: a history and theory reader*. New York: Routledge

Hartley, J. (2002). (Ed). *Creative industries*. Cambridge, MA: Blackwell. 416-433

Southwell, B., &, Mira L. (2004). A pitfall of new media? User controls exacerbate editing effects on memory. *Journalism and Mass Communication Quarterly, 81:* 643-56

MIGRATION AND DIASPORA

1   United Nations Statistics Division. (2006). *Native and foreign-born population by age, sex and urban/rural residence: each census, 1985 – 2004* [Excel file]. Retrieved December 12, 2009, from http://unstats.un.org/unsd/demographic/products/dyb/dybcens.htm

OECD (Organisation for Economic Co-operation and Development). (2007). *International migration database*. Retrieved December 12, 2009, from http://stats.oecd.org/Index.aspx?DataSetCode=MIG

United Nations Population Division. (2008). *International migrant stock: The 2008 revision*. Retrieved December 12, 2009, from http://esa.un.org/migration/index.asp?panel=1

2   United Nations Population Division. (2008). *International migrant stock: The 2008 revision*. Retrieved April 20, 2010, from http://esa.un.org/migration/index.asp?panel=1

3   Dumont, J. C., & Lemaître, G. (2005). Counting immigrants and expatriates in OECD countries: A new perspective. *OECD Social Employment and Migration Working Papers, 25*.

4 + 5 World Bank. (2008). *World Bank staff estimates based on the International Monetary Fund's Balance of Payments Statistics Yearbook 2008*. Retrieved April 20, 2010, from http://siteresources.worldbank.org/ INTPROSPECTS/Resources/334934-1110315015165/ RemittancesData_July09(Public).xls

6 Rosenfeld, M. J. (n.d.). *A figure and worksheet describing the increasing percentage of American couples that are interracial, by several definitions of interracial*. Retrieved April 20, 2010, from http://www.stanford.edu/-mrosenfe/Rosenfeld_pct_interracial.xls

7 MyVisaJobs. (n.d.). *Top 1000 H1B visa and green card sponsors (2000-2009)*. Retrieved October 12, 2009, from http://www.myvisajobs.com/Top_Visa_Sponsors.aspx

DIGEST: MIGRATION AND DIASPORA

Berry, J. W. (2001). A psychology of immigration. *Journal of Social Issues, 57* (3), 615-631.

Hall, S. (2003). Cultural identity and diaspora. In J. E. Braziel & A. Mannur (Eds.). *Theorizing diaspora: A reader* (pp. 233-246). Malden: Blackwell.

Internal Displacement Monitoring Centre. (2008). *Internal displacement: Global overview of trends and developments in 2008.* Retrieved March 22, 2010, from http://www.internal-displacement. org/idmc/website/resources.nsf/%28httpPublications%29/06053610 27488A28C12575A90042305B?OpenDocument.

EDUCATION

1 UNESCO (United Nations Educational Scientific and Cultural Organization) (2009). Global education digest 2009 comparing education statistics across the world. Retrieved August 6, 2009, from http://www.uis.unesco.org/ template/pdf/ged/2009/GED_2009_EN.pdf

2 Berman, J. E. (2001). *Holocaust remembrances in Australian Jewish communities 1945-2000*. Western Australia: University of Australia Press.

USHMM (United States Holocaust Memorial Museum). (2006). *Austria- Holocaust education report*. Retrieved April 18, 2010 from: http://www.holocausttaskforce.org/ education/holocaust-education-reports/austria-holocaust-education-report.html

USHMM (United States Holocaust Memorial Museum). (2005). *Denmark-Holocaust education report*. Retrieved April 18, 2010 from: http://www.holocausttaskforce.org/ education/holocaust-education-reports/denmark-holocaust-education-report.html

3 Archaeology postgraduate and master's courses 2008-09. (2009, February 17). *The Guardian*. Retrieved September 16, 2009, from: http://www.guardian.co.uk/education/table/2009/ feb/17/postgraduate-masters-tables-archaeology

4 PEW Forum. (n.d.). *Interpretation of religious teachings*. Accessed April 18, 2010, from http://religions.pewforum.org/maps

5 Institute of Education Sciences. (2008). *Distance education at degree-franting postsecondary institutions: 2006–07*. Retrieved November 10, 2009, from http://nces.ed.gov/pubSearch/ pubsinfo.asp?pubid=2009044

6 Eurostat. (2008). *Europe in Figures*. Retrieved April 18, 2010, from http://epp.eurostat.ec.europa.eu/cache/ITY_ OFFPUB/KS-CD-07-001/EN/KS-CD-07-001-EN.PDF

DIGEST: EDUCATION

Bakhtiari, S. (2006). Globalization and education: Challenges and opportunities. *International Business & Economics Research Journal, 5.*

Hoelscher, M. (Forthcoming). 'Universities and higher learning'. In M. Juergensmeyer & H. K. Anheier (Eds.), *Encyclopedia of global studies*. London: Sage.

Schuerholz-Lehr, S. (2007). Teaching for global literacy in higher education: How prepared are the educators? *Journal of Studies in International Education, 11.*

Sutton, M. (2005). The globalization of multicultural education. *Indiana Journal of Global Legal Studies, 12*(1), 97-108.

Identity

GEOGRAPHICAL IDENTITIES

1 Anheier, H., & Hoelscher, M. (2009). *The global cultural futures network expert survey*. Conducted February 2009.

2 Phinney, J. S., Berry, J. W., Vedder, P., & Liebkind, K. (2006). The acculturation experience: Attitudes, identities, and behaviors of immigrant youth. *Immigrant youth in cultural transition. Acculturation, identity, and adaptation across national contexts*. Mahwah and London: Lawrence Erlbaum Associates.

3 World Values Survey. (2009). *Official aggregate v.20090901, 2009*. Retrieved December 1, 2009, from http://www.worldvaluessurvey.org/

4 The PEW Research Center. (2006). *Pew global attitudes project*. Retrieved October 15, 2009, from http://pewglobal.org/datasets/

5 European Commission. (2009, September). *Eurobarometer 71*. Retrieved December 15, 2009, from http://ec.europa.eu/public_opinion/archives/eb/eb71/eb71_std_part1.pdf

DIGEST: GEOGRAPHICAL IDENTITIES

Anheier, H. K., & Hoelscher, M. (2010). Creativity, innovation, globalization: What international experts think. In H. K. Anheier & Y.R. Isar (Eds.), *Cultural Expression, Creativity and Innovation* (pp. 421-433). London: Sage.

Keupp, H. (1999). *Identitätskonstruktionen: Das Patchwork der Identitäten in der Spätmoderne*. Reinbek bei Hamburg: Rowohlt.

Rössel, J. (forthcoming). Methodological Nationalism. In H. K. Anheier & M. Juergensmeyer (Eds.), *Encyclopedia of global studies*. London: Sage.

INTERNET IDENTITIES

1 Internet World Stats. (2009). *Internet penetration rates and internet users by world region*. Retrieved November 17, 2009, from http://www.internetworldstats.com/stats.htm

2 Inside Network. (May 2009). *New study shows how different generations use Facebook*. Retrieved November 17, 2009, from http://www.insidefacebook.com/2009/07/30/new-study-shows-how-different-generations-use-facebook/

3 Symantec. (2009, October). *State of phishing: A monthly report*. Retrieved November 17, 2009, from http://www.symantec.com/content/de/de/about/downloads/PressCenter/PhishingTrends_Okt2009.pdf

4 Mmogchart.com. (n.d.). *An analysis of MMOG subscription growth*. Retrieved December 12, 2009, from http://www.mmogchart.com/downloads/

5 Pew Internet & American Life Project. (2005, December 8). *September 2005 - Online dating*. Retrieved December 12, 2009, from http://www.pewinternet.org/Shared-Content/DataSets/2005/September-2005--Online-Dating.aspx

6 Second Life. (n.d.). *Browse category - Complete fantasy and sci-fi avatars*. Retrieved December 12, 2009, from https://www.xstreetsl.com/modules.php?name=Marketplace&CategoryID=341&&sort=popularity&dir=desc

Second Life. (n.d.). *Browse category - Complete human female avatars*. Retrieved December 12, 2009, from https://www.xstreetsl.com/modules.php?name=Marketplace&CategoryID=12&sort=popularity&dir=desc&page=1

Second Life. (n.d.). *Browse category - Complete human male avatars*. Retrieved December 12, 2009, from https://www.xstreetsl.com/modules.php?name=Marketplace&CategoryID=11&&sort=popularity&dir=desc

DIGEST: INTERNET IDENTITIES

Byun, S., Ruffini, C., Mills, J., Douglas, A., Niang, M., Stepchenjova, et al. (2009). Internet addiction: Metasynthesis of 1996-2006 quantitative research. *Cyber Psychology & Behavior, 12* (2), 203-207.

Donath, J. S. (1999). Identity and deception in the virtual community. In Smith, M.A., & Kollock, P., *Communities in Cyberspace* (pp. 29-59). London: Routledge.

Javelin Strategy & Research. (2010, February). *2010 Identity fraud survey report. Consumer cersion. Prevent – detect – resolve.* Retrieved May 21, 2010, from https://www.javelinstrategy.com/uploads/files/10 04.R_2010IdentityFraudSurveyConsumer.pdf.

Jordan, T. (1999). *Cyberpower – The culture and politics of cyberspace and the Internet.* London: Routledge.

McLuhan, M., Fiore, Q., & Agel, J. (2001). *The medium is the massage. An inventory of effects.* Corte Modero, CA: Gingko Press.

Pew Internet and American Life Project. (2005). *Online dating extension.* Retrieved May 21, 2010, from http://www.pewinternet.org/Shared-Content/Data-Sets/2005/September-2005--Online-Dating.aspx.

Show, M., & Black, D.W. (2008). Internet addiction. Definition, assessment, epidemiology and clinical management. *CNS Drugs, 22*(5), 353-365.

Webopedia.com. (2010). *MMORPG.* Retrieved February 17, 2010, from http://www.webopedia.com/TERM/M/MMORPG.html. XChange4LS. (2010). Retrieved January, 22, 2010, from http://www.xchange4ls.com/index.php?gclid=CNupuN7r354CFYcVzAodHj-Dxg&lang=en.

MULTIPLE CITIZENSHIP

1 Blattner, J. K., Erdmann, S., & Schwanke, K. (2009). Acceptance of dual citizenship: Empirical data and political contexts. *Working Paper Series "Glocal Governance and Democracy", 2.* Retrieved July 20, 2009, from http://www.unilu.ch/files/Acceptance-of-Dual-Citizenship-wp02.pdf

2 Statistics Canada. (2007). Detailed country of citizenship (203), single and multiple citizenship responses (3), immigrant status (4A) and sex (3) for the population of Canada, provinces, territories, Census Metropolitan Areas and Census Agglomerations, 2006 Census - 20% Sample Data. Retrieved August 11, 2009, from: http://www12.statcan.ca/english/census06/data/topics/RetrieveProductTable.cfm?ALE VEL=3&APATH=3&CATNO=&DETAIL=0&DIM=&DS=99 &FL=0&FREE=0&GAL=0&GC=99&GID=837928&GK=NA &GRP=1&IPS=&METH=0&ORDER=1&PID=89450&PTYP E=88971&RL=0&S=1&SUB=0&ShowAll=No&StartRow=1&Te mporal=2006&Theme=72&VID=0&VNAMEE=&VNAMEF=

Statista. (2009). *Haben Sie neben der deutschen eine zweite Staatsangehörigkeit?* Retrieved October 9, 2009, from http://de.statista.com/statistik/diagramm/studie/102342/umfrage/vorhandensein-einer-zweiten-staatsangehoerigkeit/

Office of Citizenship and Migration Affairs (n.d.). *Statistics on dual citizenship.* Retrieved October 5, 2009, from http://www.pmlp.gov.lv/en/statistics/dual.html;jsessionid=E4F920ACED2 90E7E1056D4C44B64BF73

Statistics Netherlands. (2008, December 16). *Nearly 1.1 million dual nationalities in the Netherlands.* Retrieved July 20, 2009, from: http://www.cbs.nl/en-GB/menu/themas/bevolking/publicaties/artikelen/archief/2008/2008-2640-wm.htm

GUS (Główny Urząd Statystyczny). (2003). *Raport z wyników Narodowego Spisu Powszechnego Ludności i Mieszkań 2002.* Retrieved July 20, 2009, from http://www.stat.gov.pl/cps/rde/xbcr/gus/PUBL_raport_z_wynikow_nsp_ludnosci_i_mieszkan_2002.pdf

3 Department of Immigration and Citizenship. (2009). *Australian citizenship test: Snapshot report.* Retrieved November 16, 2009, from http://www.citizenship.gov.au/__data/assets/pdf_file/0011/213140/citz-test-snapshot-report-jun09.pdf

Ipsos News Center. (2007). The Dominion Institute national citizenship exam survey of 2007. Retrieved November 16, 2009, from http://www.ipsos-na.com/news/pressrelease.cfm?id=3552

Migration info. (2009). *Deutschland: Einbürgerungstest wird fast immer bestanden.* Retrieved November 16, 2009, from http://www.migration-info.de/mub_artikel.php?Id=090101

Ny i Danmark. (2007, June 14). *97 procent bestod indfødsretsprøven.* Retrieved November 16, 2009, from http://www.nyidanmark.dk/da-dk/Nyheder/Pressemeddelelser/Integrationsministeriet/2007/Juni/97_procent_bestod_indfoedsretsproeven.htm

Gaouette, N. (2007, September 28). Government unveils new citizenship test. *Los Angeles Times.* Retrieved November 16, 2009, from http://articles.latimes.com/2007/sep/28/nation/na-citizenship28

De Hart, B. (2008). *Recent trends in European nationality laws: a restrictive turn?* Retrieved July 31, 2009, from http://www.europarl.europa.eu/document/activities/cont/200807/20080702ATT33276/20080702ATT33276EN.pdf

De Hart, B. (2008, April). *Recent trends in European nationality laws: A restrictive turn?* Retrieved July 31, 2009, from http://www.europarl.europa.eu/document/activities/cont/200807/20080702ATT33276/20080702ATT33276EN.pdf

Renshon, S. A. (2001, October). *Dual citizenship and American national identity.* Retrieved July 22, 2009, from http://www.cis.org/articles/2001/paper20/renshondual.pdf

Worbs, S. (2009). Bekenntnis zur Demokratie, Straffreiheit und Sprachkenntnisse wichtiger als Abstammung: Einstellungen zum Erwerb der deutschen Staatsangehörigkeit. *Informationsdienst Soziale Indikatoren, 42,* 11-14.

Wright, S. (2008). Citizenship tests in Europe: Editorial introduction. *International Journal on Multicultural Societies, 10.* Retrieved July 28, 2009, from http://unesdoc.unesco.org/images/0016/001607/160772m.pdf

4 Brøndsted Sejersen, T. (2008). I vow to thee my countries. The expansion of dual citizenship in the 21st century. *International Migration Review, 42,* 523-549(3)

5 Gallup Organization. (2008). European union citizenship: Analytical report. *Flash Eurobarometer, 213.* Retrieved August 10, 2009, from http://ec.europa.eu/public_opinion/flash/fl_213_en.pdf

6 Worbs, S. (2009). Bekenntnis zur demokratie, straffreiheit und sprachkenntnisse wichtiger als Abstammung: Einstellungen zum Erwerb der deutschen Staatsangehörigkeit. *Informationsdienst Soziale Indikatoren, 42,* 11-14.

DIGEST: MULTIPLE CITIZENSHIP

Blattner, J. K., Erdmann, S., & Schwanke, K. (2009). Acceptance of dual citizenship: Empirical data and political contexts. *Working Paper Series "Glocal Governance and Democracy", 2.* Retrieved July 20, 2009, from http://www.unilu.ch/files/Acceptance-of-Dual-Citizenship-wp02.pdf

POPULAR CULTURE

1 Charts & Ratings. (n.d.). *Music charts: Album charts.* Retrieved November 2, 2009, from http://allcharts.org/music/

2 Benard, C. & Schlaffer, E. (2005, May). *Global Kids: Modernisierung und Geschlechterrollen aus der Perspektive von Jugendlichen im Zeitalter der Globalisierung.* Retrieved November 2, 2009, from http://www.frauen-ohne-grenzen.org/files/downloads/GK-FB-internationaler_Vergleich.pdf

3 *Sport Market.* (n.d.). Retrieved December 16, 2009, from http://www.sportundmarkt.de/fileadmin/images/Upload_User/Online_Sales/Auszuege__Football_Top_20_2009_.pdf

4 Gates, G. (2006, October). *Same sex couples and the gay, lesbian, bisexual population: New Estmates from the American Community Survey.* Retrieved December 16, 2009, from http://www.law.ucla.edu/williamsinstitute/publications/SameSexCouplesandGLBpopACS.pdf

5 Marks, P. (2009, September 22). *Video games need a more diverse cast of characters*. Retrieved November 2, 2009, from http://www.newscientist.com/article/dn17819-video-games-need-a-more-diverse-cast-of-characters.html

6 *Love parade*. (n.d.). Retrieved November 2, 2009, http://en.wikipedia.org/wiki/Love_Parade

DIGEST: POPULAR CULTURE

Blair, M. E. (1993). Commercialization of rap music youth subculture. *Journal of Popular Culture*, 27(3), 21-33.

Curtin, M. (2008) 'Spatial Dynamics of Film and Television'. In Anheier, H. and Isar, Y.R. (eds.) *The Cultural Economy. The Cultures and Globalization Series, 3*. London: SAGE Publications.

Dorfman, A. & Mattelart, A. (1975). *How to read donald duck: Imperialist ideology in the disney comic*. New York: International General.

ILGA (International Lesbian, Gay, Bisexual, Trans and Intersex Association). (2010). *Lesbian and gay rights in the world*. Retrieved May 21, 2010, from http://ilga.org/ilga/en/article/1161.

Jenkins, H., McPherson, T. & Shattuc, J. (2002). Defining Popular Culture. In H. Jenkins, T. McPherson, & J. Shattuc, (Eds.), *Hop on pop: The politics and pleasures of popular culture* (pp. 26-42). Durhamm: Duke University Press.

Katz, E. & Liebes, T. (2005). *The export of meaning: Cross-cultural readings of "Dallas"*. Cambridge: Polity Press.

Reynolds, S. (1998). *Energy flash: A journey through rave music and dance culture*. London: Picador.

Robb, D. (2002). Techno in Germany: Its musical origins and cultural relevance. *GFL Journal, 2/2002*, 129-149. Retrieved January 21, 2010, from http://www.gfl-journal.de/2-2002/robb.pdf.

Roose, J. (2010). Fans und Globalisierung. In J. Roose, M. Schäfer, & T. Schmidt-Lux (Eds.), *Fans. Soziologische Perspektiven* (pp. 415-436). Wiesbaden: VS Verlag für Sozialwissenschaften.

Thompson, J.B. (1995). *The media and modernity: A social theory of the media*. Palo Alto, CA: Stanford University Press.

Thornton, S. (1997). General Introduction. In K. Gelder & S. Thornton, (Eds.), *The subcultures reader* (pp. 1-7). London: Routledge.

IDENTITIES IN THE ECONOMY

1 Interbrand. (2009). *Best global brands 2009*. Retrieved December 12, 2009, from http://www.interbrand.com/images/studies/-1_BGB2009_Magazine_Final.pdf

Millward Brown. (2009). *100 most valuable global brands 2009*. Retrieved December 12, 2009, from http://www.millwardbrown.com/Sites/Optimor/Media/Pdfs/en/BrandZ/BrandZ-2009-Report.pdf

2 *OECD Stats Extract*. (n.d.). Retrieved December 12, 2009, from http://stats.oecd.org/Index.aspx

3 UNIVERSUM. (n.d.). *Student survey*. Retrieved April 12, 2010, from http://universumglobal.com/IDEAL-Employer-Rankings

4 World Values Survey. (2009). *Official aggregate v.20090901*, 2009. Retrieved December 12, 2009, from http://www.worldvaluessurvey.org/

5 OECD (United Nations Educational, Scientific and Cultural Organization). (2005). Counting immigrants and expatriates in OECD countries: A new perspective. *Trends in International Migration: SOPEMI 2004 Edition*. Retrieved December 12, 2009, from http://www.oecd.org/dataoecd/46/33/37965376.pdf

6 *AdvertistingAge*. (2009). Retrieved December 12, 2009, from http://adage.com/images/random/datacenter/2008/globalmarketing2008.pdf

DIGEST: IDENTITIES IN THE ECONOMY

Bauer, H. H., Exler, S., Maurer, S., & Langenbein, M. (2009). Die Image- und Präferenzwirkung globaler Marken und ihre Determinanten. *Marketing: Zeitschrift für Forschung und Praxis, 31*, 57-79.

Beck, U. (2000). *The brave new world of work*. Cambridge: Polity.

Doherty, M. (2009). When the working day is through: The end of work as identity? *Work, Employment and Society, 23* (1).

Dumont, J.-C., & Lemaitre, G. (2005). Counting immigrants and expatriates in OECD countries: a new perspective. *OECD Social, Employment and Migration Working Papers No. 25.*

Hannerz, U. (1992). *Cultural complexity*. New York / Chichester : Columbia University Press.

Hoelscher, M. (2006). *Wirtschaftskulturen in der erweiterten EU. Die Einstellungen der Bürgerinnen und Bürger im europäischen Vergleich*. Wiesbaden: VS Verlag.

Hofstede, G. (2001). *Culture's consequences: Comparing values, behaviors, institutions, and organizations across nations* (2nd ed.). Thousand Oaks: Sage.

House, R. J., Hanges, P. J., Javidan, M., Dorfman, P. W., & Gupta, V. (Eds.). (2004). *Culture, leadership, and organizations. The GLOBE Study of 62 Societies*. Thousand Oaks: Sage.

Pohlmann, M. (2009). Globale ökonomische Eliten - Eine Globalisierungsthese auf dem Prüfstand der Empirie. *Kölner Zeitschrift für Soziologie und Sozialpsychologie*, 61, 513-534.

Sennett, R. (1998). *The corrosion of character: The personal consequences of work in the new capitalism*. New York: Norton.

RELIGION

1 Forbes Traveler. (2009). *World's most visited religious destinations*. Retrieved August 15, 2009, from http://www.msnbc.msn.com/id/22264757

2 *The World Values Survey(2005 &2008), the fifth wave of the WVS 2005-2008*. Retrieved October 15, 2009 from http://www.worldvaluessurvey.org/

3 Bienfait, A. (2006). Zeichen und Wunder. Über die Funktion der Selig- und Heiligsprechungen in der katholischen Kirche. *Kölner Zeitschrift für Soziologie und Sozialpsychologie 58 (1)*, 1-22.

Den Katolske Kirke. (2005). *Statistikk over pave Johannes Paul IIs helligkåringer*. Retrieved August 15, 2009, from http://www.katolsk.no/info/jp2/stat.htm

4 Benard, C., & Schlaffer, E. (2005). *Global kids. Modernisierung und Geschlechterrollen aus der Perspektive von Jugendlichen im Zeitalter der Globalisierung*. Retrieved August 30, 2009, from http://frauen-ohne-grenzen.org/files/downloads/GK-FB-internationaler_Vergleich.pdf

5 *Pilgerstatistiken bis 2009*. (2009). Retrieved August 15, 2009 from http://www.jakobus-info.de/jakobuspilger/statik05.htm

DIGEST: RELIGION

Adherents.com. (2005). *Major religions ranked by the number of adherents*. Retrieved February 23, 2010. from http://www.adherents.com/Religions_By_Adherents.html

Baumann, Z. (1995). *Life in fragments. Essays in postmodern morality*. Oxford: Blackwell.

Bienfait, A. (2006). Zeichen und Wunder. Über die Funktion der Selig- und Heiligsprechungen in der katholischen Kirche. *Kölner Zeitschrift für Soziologie und Sozialpsychologie, 58 (1)*, 1-22.

Coelho, P. (2004 [1987]). *The pilgrimage. A contemporary quest for ancient wisdom*. New York: Harper Collins.

Foreign policy. (2007). *The list: The world's fastest-growing religions*. Retrieved August 15, 2009, from http://www.foreignpolicy.com/story/cms.php?story_id=3835

Helland, C. (2005): Online religion as lived religion. Methodological issues in the study of religious participation on the Internet. *Online – Heidelberg Journal of Religions on the Internet 1.1*. Retrieved March 1, 2010, from http://archiv.ub.uni-heidelberg.de/volltextserver/volltexte/2005/5823/pdf/Helland3a.pdf

Kippenberg, H. G. & Stuckrad, K. (Eds.). (2003). *Einführung in die Religionswissenschaft. Gegenstände und Begriffe*. München: C.H.Beck.

Kreinath, J., Snoek, J. & Stausberg, M. (Eds.). (2006). Theorizing rituals. Issues, topics, approaches, concepts: 1. *Numen Book Series: Studies in the history of religions vol. 114.1*. Leiden et al: Brill Academpic Publishers.

Ministry of Hajj. Kingdom of Saudi Arabia (n.d.). *Hajj and Umrah Statistics*. Retrieved August 15, 2009, from http://www.hajinformation.com/main/l.htm

INDEX

Abatwa community, 163–4
Abhisit Vechachiwa, 151–4
Abu Simbel, 44
acculturation, 356, 364, 368
Adams, William M., 125
advertising expenditure, 383
Aegis Trust, 247–9
Africa, indigenous peoples in, 96–8, 101
Africa 2009 programme, 45
African Diaspora Heritage Trail, 84
Aga Khan Trust for Culture and Development
      Network, 73–4
Agier, M., 103
Ahmadinejad, Mahmoud, 338
Ahtisaan, Martti, 6–7
aid programmes, 71, 74–5, 79, 243
airports, naming of, 332, 334
Aksum obelisk, 58
Alexander, Jeffrey, 243
Al-Khiyam Prison Museum (APM), 66–7
Allison, Anne, 276–7
Álvarez, Magdalena, 109
America, indigenous peoples in, 98–101
Anderson, Benedict, 36
Angkor, 75–6
Anthes, Bill, 279
anti-Semitism, 254
Anucha Paepornworn, 152
Appadurai, Arjun, 9, 32
archaeology, 360–1
architectural heritage, 48, 347–8
Archivo del Duelo project, 106, 108–11
Argentina, 59, 116, 121, 203–4
art, definitions of, 264–6
Ashplant, T.G., 158
Ashton, Paul, 88–9
Ashworth, G., 86, 131
assimilation, 87, 377
Assmann, A., 8–9
Assmann, Jan, 34
AT Kearney (company), 348
Augé, Marc, 27
Auschwitz, 46, 57, 178
Australia, 87–9
authenticity, 49–50, 139–45
      and sacred heritage, 143–4
      and the World Heritage Convention, 142
authorised heritage discourse (AHD), 79, 87
autochthonous peoples *see* indigenous peoples
avatars, 371–2

Bach, J., 192
Bahia, 77–8
Balkin, Amy, 133

Ballé, Catherine, 217
Ballykilcline, 90
Bamiyan Buddhas, 55–7
Bangkok, 348
Banja Luka, 181
Barcelona Museum for the History of Immigration, 88
Bartlett, Frederic, 29–30, 34
Basso, Keith H., 130–1
Bastide, François-Régis, 263
Beck, Ulrich, 288
Becker, H., 312
Belgrade, 183, 193–4
Benbassa, E., 254
Benjamin, Walter, 236
Bennett, Jill, 248
Bennett, Tony, 213, 220
Bergen conference on authenticity (1994), 141
Berger, P., 252–3
Berlin, 25, 182, 346, 348
Bertilsson, U., 142
Bhabha, Homi, 218–19
Bharucha, Rustom, 10
Bienfait, A., 390
Bijelo Dugme (band), 197
Birmann, Dominik, 263
Biya, Paul, 98
Blackmore, Kara A., 72
Blattner, J.K., 376–7
Blom, Michael, 184
'Body Worlds 1' exhibition, 313
Bolin, Robert, 130
Borges, Jorge Luis, 27
Borobodur Temple, 44
Botswana, 15, 158–61, 167
boundary disputes, 149
Bourdieu, Pierre, 43
Bowornsak Uwanno, 152
Boyer, P., 289
Boym, Svetlana, 182, 191–3
branding *see* global brands
Braziel, J.E., 357
Brazil, 77
Brijuni islands, 187
British Museum, 25, 59
Brno, 184
Brown, David, 149
Brown, Ewart, 84
Brown, Jacqueline, 85
Browne, Sir Thomas, 281
Bucharest, 180, 182, 333–4
Budapest, 180–4
Buenos Aires, 116, 121
Bunzl, M., 254
Burri, Alfredo, 128

Buruma, Ian, 16
Byun, S., 373

call centres, 172–3
Cambodia, 15, 59, 75, 148–55
Cameroon, 98
Camino Frances, 390
Canclini, García, 291
canonizations, 388, 390
capital flows, 73
capitalism, 274
Carver, Martin, 165
Castro-Gómez, S., 80
Catanese, Brandi Wilkins, 85
Catholic Church, 179
Cati (company), 196
Cattani, G., 349
Ceausescu, Nicolae, 182
celebrity culture, 55
Chang, Anita, 130
Charnvit Kasetsirl, 154
Chase, S.E., 255
Chavez, M., 171
Chen, Chia-Li, 214
Cheney, Lynne, 32
Chernobyl, 128
Chifley, Ben, 88
Child, Brian, 125, 127
Chile, 118, 123
China and Chinese communities, 84–5, 80, 90–1, 129, 340,
    343–4, 348
Choay, Françoise, 4
Cisic, Rusmir, 120
Cité Nationale de l'Histoire de l'Immigration, Paris, 88, 214,
    216–19
citizenship, 292, 374–7
city life, 236, 347–8
civil society organizations, 139–40, 289
civil war, 53
Clark, Nigel, 132–3
Cleere, Henry, 142
Clifford, James, 86, 213
climate change, 132–3, 283; *see also* global warning
Clinton, Bill, 60
Cobh Heritage Centre, 214
Coelho, Paulo, 389
cognitive structures, 31
Cohen, R., 171
coinage, 332–4
Cole, S., 321
collective identity, 140, 189
collective memory, 5–9, 12, 29–35, 115, 190, 193, 200, 239,
    252–5, 260–1, 282, 289
  of the family, 252
  global, 340–4
  strong and *distributed* accounts of, 31–2
commemorative activity, 10
commodification, 13
'common memory' (Margalit), 190
communism and cultural production, 177–85
companies as potential employers, students' rankings of, 382, 384
Connerton, P., 63, 158
'conscience heritage', 121

Constitution Hill, South Africa, 122–3
contemporary arts, 200–9, 279
conventionalization, 30
Cooper, Fred, 274–5
cosmopolitanism, 291
cosmopolitanization of memory, 335
Côte d'Ivoire, 97
Council of Europe, 178, 180
couple identity, 252–5, 260–1
  of Arab-Jewish couples in France, 254–5
Crang, M., 288
Crawford, B., 103
creativity, concept of, 201–2
creolization, 169–75, 357
CRIC project, 65
Croatia, 191
Csikszentmihalyi, M., 201
cultural assets, 273–4
cultural capital, 43
cultural conflicts, 337
Cultural Development Association, 97
cultural diversity, 273, 276, 367
Cultural Diversity Convention, 40–1
cultural heritage, 65–6, 70–81, 229, 328
  destruction of, 53–5, 58–61
  and the environment, 124–33
  in post-communist transition, 178–80, 185
  see also intangible cultural heritage
cultural identity, 367
  definition of, 357
cultural landscapes, 46–7
cultural life-scripts, 34
cultural logics, 34
cultural production under communism, 177–85
cultural property, 41, 50
cultural relativism, 269
cultural resource management (CRM), 79
cultural rights, 10
cultural trade 47, 306–7
culture, concept and definitions of, 2–3, 42
Cunningham, Stuart, 126
Curie, Marie Sklodowska, 218
Cyprus, 55

Dah Theatre, 193–4
dating, online, 371, 373
Davis, F., 190
Davis, Mike C., 129
de Certeau, Michel, 34
deforestation, 127
democides, 337, 339
Democratic Republic of Congo (DRC), 246
Denitch, B., 188
Depardon, Raymond, 213
Derrida, Jacques, 284
Detienne, M., 98
deWaal, Thomas, 35
Diamond, Jared, 125
Dias, Nelia, 217
diasporas, 13, 82–93, 210–20, 290, 356–7
  and the myth of return, 90–1
  and national heritage, 87–90
  and transnational heritage, 91–2

digital divide, 353
Dinçer, I., 226
displacement, 86, 93
distance learning, 361–2
Donahoe, B., 100
Donath, Judith S., 372
Donne, John, 283
Donnersmarck, Florian Henckel von, 63
Doss, Erika, 26
Downs, Lila, 205
Dresden, 64
Dubrovnik, 178, 180–1
Dunhuang caves, 58

earthquake damage, 129–30
eco-tourism, 157–60, 165
Ecuador, 5, 206
educational characteristics of populations, 354, 356
educational systems, 290, 358–62
Edwards, Jack, 53
Einstein, Albert, 343
El País (newspaper), 56
Eldem, Nezih, 229
Ellis Island, 88, 214–16, 219
English, J., 43
English Heritage, 76
environmental issues, 124–33, 283
    physical and developmental, 125
epistemic communities, 39
Erdmann, S., 376
Eruzun, Cengiz, 228–9
Escuela Mecánica de la Armada, 121
Estonia, 26–7, 34
Ethiopia, 58
ethnic cleansing, 236
European Union, 65, 179–80, 243, 325, 366–7, 377
Europeana project, 353
EUSTORY network, 6–7
evolution, perceptions of, 337, 339
expatriates, 383–5

family relationships, 252–3
Faramond, Guy de, 263
Faruk Bey, 231–2
Feld, Steven, 130–1
Feldman, Allen, 245, 249
feminism, 242
Ferguson, J., 97
Ferriani, S., 349
fetishization, 5
films, historical, most popular, 350, 352
First World War, 58, 343–4
Fo Angwafo III, 97
football clubs, popularity of, 379
foreign-born populations
    by region and country, 354, 356
    in US cities, 346, 348
forgetting, 27–8
    types of, 158
Fortuyn, Pim, 111
France, 28, 47, 63, 216–19, 254–5
Francis, Michael, 163–4
Franco, Francisco, 58, 61, 108

Franco-Prussian War (1870–71), 58, 242–3
Franklin, A., 288
French Revolution, 217, 245, 343
Frigolé, Joan, 108
Fuentes, Carlos, 207

Gabric, Blasko, 195
Galapagos Islands, 127
Galeano, E., 61
Gamio, Manuel, 99–100, 199–200
Gandhi, Mahatma, 98, 122
Ganin, Dmitry, 26
Garcia Canclini, N., 201
Garuba, Harry, 166
Gautier, Théophile, 224
Gbagbo, Laurent, 97
Gdansk, 184
Gellner, Ernest, 32, 290
genocide, responses to, 245–50
geographical identities, 364–8
Germany, 243
    Bremerhaven Museum, 91
    Documentation Centre and Museum of Migration, 88
    naturalization in, 375–6
Gernika, 56–7, 64
Geschiere, Peter, 97, 101
Ghibellina, 128
Giant's Causeway, 64
Gielen, Albert, 184
Giesen, Bernhard, 243
Gillis, John R., 245–6
Gilroy, Paul, 86, 92
Giuliani, Carlo, 111
global brands, 382, 384–5
global cities, 347–8
Global Heritage Fund (GHF), 329
global warming, 124, 132, 283, 325
globalization, 9–10, 17, 40–1, 47, 53–4, 80, 82, 88, 96,
    124–5, 132–3, 139–40, 144–6, 175, 199, 201, 204, 209,
    213, 253, 281, 283, 288, 291, 293, 316–17, 348–9, 362
    cultural, 1–2, 84
    definition of, 1
    of heritage funding, 70–3
    of indigenous peoples movement, 101–2
    vis-a-vis national narratives, 35–6
'glocalization', 43, 201
Godnic, Ivo, 196
Goethe, Johann Wolfgang von, 284
Goody, J., 288–9
Gothenburg, 264–6
Graeber, D., 174
Groys, Boris, 184
Guatemala, 35–6
Guernica, 56–7
Guevara, Ernesto ('Che'), 202–4
Gulag history, 116–17

Hagens, Gunther von, 313
Hajji, Ismael, 218
Halbwachs, Maurice, 5–6, 29, 60, 157, 190, 252–3, 338
Hall, C. Michael, 126
Hall, Stuart, 3, 10, 219–20, 312, 357
Hamilton, Paula, 83

Handler, Richard, 11
Hanim, Mehves, 234
Hanim, Neyyire, 234
Happy Planet Index (HPI), 323–4
Hardt, M., 80
Harrison, Simon, 276
Harrow, Kenneth, 246–7
Hawass, Zahi, 25
Hedsved, Julia, 265
Held, D., 1
Hélys, Marc, 263
heritage
  concept and definitions of, 1–2, 4, 39–44, 86–7, 282
  conservation of, 3, 11, 14, 70–1, 77–80, 125, 127
  construction of, 123
  as a cultural process, 143
  as a democratic process, 121
  funding of, 70–3
  indicator suites on, 288–9
  political economies of, 70–81
  sustainability of, 324–5
  see also cultural heritage
'heritage expert' role, 146
Heritage Foundation, 42
heritage sites
  contested nature of, 120
  see also World Heritage sites
heritage studies, 27–9
Hinchcliffe, Steve, 127
hip-hop music, 348
Hirohito, Emperor, 242
historical consciousness, 32
history, pupils' study of, 361
Hitler, Adolf, 33, 343
Hobsbawm, E., 66
Hofer, Johannes, 190
Hokusai, Katsushika, 275–6
holidays, 318–20, 332, 334
Holocaust, the, 6, 243, 246, 335, 338
  teaching about, 358, 361
Holocaust Centre, UK, 249
Houphouet-Boigny, Felix, 97
Howard, Peter, 125
human rights, 14, 114–16, 245, 249, 274
Human Rights Watch, 246
Huntimgton, S.P., 292
hurricane damage, 129–30
Hussein, Saddam, 58
Huyssen, Andreas, 4, 6, 9–11, 27, 215, 239, 246
hybrid identities, 92

identity
  concept of, 1, 9–11
  indicator suites on, 290–2
  see also collective identity; couple identity; cultural
    identity, geographical identities; hybrid identities;
    Internet identities; 'memorable identities'; national
    identity; religion and religious identity
identity formation, 131
identity politics, 139–40
Idia, Queen, mask of, 59
India, 6, 48–9, 75, 91
'indicator suites', 2, 287 et seq

indigenous artists, 279
indigenous peoples (IPs), 13–14, 61, 95–104, 328–9
  representative organizations for, 327
information storage
  digitalization of, 352–3
  life expectancy of, 351–2
information technology, 277–9; see also Internet resources
innovation, 349
intangible cultural heritage (ICH), 3–4, 17, 47–9, 200, 209,
    273–4, 278, 288, 314–17
Intergovernmental Panel on Climate Change, 132
International Centre for the Study of the Preservation
    and Return of Cultural Property (ICCROM), 45–6, 50,
    144, 308
International Council on Monuments and Sites (ICOMOS),
    39, 43, 49–50, 140
International Council of Museums (ICOM), 312
International Court of Justice, 150
International Network for Traditional Architecture Building
    and Urbanism (INTBAU), 50
International Organization for Migration (IOM), 89
international organizations, work of, 326–9
International Union for the Conservation of Nature (IUCN),
    44, 324
Internet identities, 370–3
Internet penetration, 370–2
Internet resources, 29, 206–7, 291
InterSOS, 66
Iran, 61
Iraq, 56–8, 336, 338
Ireland, Republic of, 90
Ise Jingu shrine, 49
Israel, state of, 83, 85, 361
Istanbul, 16, 222–9, 231–6
  Chamber of Architects, 228–9
'ivory tower' metaphor, 17, 284
Iwabuchi, Koichi, 276

James, William, 27
Japan, 16–17, 239–43, 275–7, 347, 349
Jenkins, H., 277, 380
Jewish people, 83, 85
job tenure, 382
John Paul II, Pope, canonizations by, 388, 390
Jokilehto, Jukka, 142
Jones, Andrew, 128
Jordan, T., 372

Kaczyński, Jaroslaw, 53
Kaczyński, Lech Aleksander, 53
Kagame, Paul, 250
Kandy Temple of the Sacred Tooth Relic, 140, 143–5
Kasit Piromya, 153
Keane, J., 74
Keesing, R., 11
Kellner, H., 252–3
Kemal, Yahya, 223–5
Kennedy, Roseanne, 248
Kentsel Tasarim Rehberleri, 229
Khmer civilization, 149
Khmer Rouge, 59
Kippenberg, H.G., 389
Kirchner, Nestor 121

Kirshenblatt-Gimblett, Barbara, 4, 48, 111
Kirtsoglou, E., 321
kiwi bird, 127
Klimova, Barbara, 184
Kong, Lily, 2–3
Korda, Alberto, 203
Körningh, Johan Ferdinand, 263
Koselleck, Reinhard, 8
Kosovo, 181
Kurin, R., 43
Kurosawa, Akira, 241

Lähde, Ville, 132–3
Lambek, M., 174
languages, 317, 327
    pupils' learning of, 360, 362
'late photography', 56
Latin America, 206–9
    heritage, memory and identity in, 199–201
Lebanon, 66–7
Lefebvre, Henri, 214
leisure time, 383–4
Lemaire, Raymond, 141
Lo Morne village, 171–2
Lenin, Vladimir, 58
Levy, D., 335
Levy, Leon, 281
Lhasa, 80
libraries, 350, 352
lieu de mémoire, 128, 182; see also sites of memory
Lithuania, 181–2
living heritage, 143–5
Lopez Caballero, P., 99
Lorca, Federico Garcia, 28
Los de Abajo (group), 208
love parades, 379, 381
Lowenthal, David, 27, 49, 83, 89, 130, 142
Lubianska, Dorota, 265
Ludwig Museum of Modern Art, 180–1

Macedonia, 3–4
Macfarlane, Robert, 133
McIntosh, R.J., 157
McKibben, Bill, 125–6
Madagascar, 169–70, 173–5
Madame Butterfly, 275
Madrid bombings (2004), 14, 58, 106–10
Magar, Valerie, 76
Mahalhäes, Marta de, 78
Maison des Esclaves, 55
Mandela, Nelson, 122, 165–6
Manich Jumsai, 151
Mannur, A., 357
Margalit, A., 190
Margry, Peter Jan, 106–7
Maronite communities, 55
Márquez, García, 56
marriage, 252–3, 355
Martin-Barbero, Jesus, 201
Masjid, Babri, 26
massive multiplayer online role-playing games
    (MMORPGs), 371–2
material culture, 3

Matos, Baptistade, 218
Matsuura, Koichiro, 47
Mauritius, 169–75
Maya communities, 35–6
media, old and new, 352
'mediated action', 29, 31, 34, 56–7
'memorable identities', 157, 159
Memoria Abierta project, 116, 121
memorialization, 119–21, 128, 249, 289, 332–5
    definition of, 334
memorials and memorial practices, 14, 26, 58–65, 106–11
memory, 27–33
    concept of, 6
    construction of, 246
    contested, 289, 336–9
    cosmopolitanization of, 335
    culture of, 239–40
    diasporic, 356
    as distinct from history, 32–3
    distributed, 31
    indicator suites on, 289–90
    lack of specificity in, 30
    social nature of, 219
    see also collective memory
memory studies, 157–8
Merkel, Angela, 63
Mexico City, 208
Mexico City Declaration, 42
migration flows, 102–3, 131–2, 290, 348, 354–7, 368, 385;
    see also museums of migration; students, international
    mobility of
Mihelj, S., 189
Millennium Development Goals, 71
Mink, Louis, 32
Mishra, Sudesh, 86
Misztal, Barbara, 219
Mkomazi game reserve, 127
mnemonic tools, 31–3
modernity and modernization, 274–5
Moenjodaro, 44
Mogao Caves, 58
Monet, Claude, 275
Mongin, Olivier, 222
Monsiváis, Carlos, 202
Montebello, Philippe de, 281
monuments, 6, 26–7, 48
moral relativism, 240
Moravia, Alberto, 54
Morrison, Chandra E.F., 202–4
Mostar bridge, 120
Mulata Library, 205–6
multiculturalism, 87–8
Murambi memorial, Gikongoro, 247–8, 250
'museumization', 5
museums, 16, 25, 41, 57, 129, 178, 180, 288, 310–13
    definition of, 312
    of migration, 13, 88–91, 213–20
    role of, 217, 220
Myers, Norman, 127

Nagorny Karabakh, 35
names of countries and territories, changes made to, 333–5
Napier, Susan, 275–7

Napoleonic War, 33–4
Nara conference on authenticity (1994), 141–3
narrative, 30–5
    specific or schematic, 33–5
nation-states, role of, 3, 12, 32–5, 42, 82–3, 86–8, 91–2,
    121–2, 209
national identity, 367
National Mall, Washington DC, 26
National Museum of Beirut (NMB), 66–7
nationalism, 32, 86–7
    transnational, 92
Native Americans, 98–9, 101, 216
natural disasters, 57, 129–30
naturalization, attitudes to, 375–6
Negri, A., 80
Nehru, Jawaharlal, 40
Neisser, Ulric, 130
neo-liberalism, 15, 75, 177, 179
Nerval, Gérard de, 224
Netherlands, the, 128
Neues Museum, Berlin, 25
'Never Again' ethic, 115–17, 119, 246, 250
new museology, 313
New Orleans, 129
New York
    Lower East Side Tenement Museum, 116, 120
    Metropolitan Museum of Art, 281
    Museum of Modern Art (MOMA), 207
New Zealand, 127
Nicholson, Emily, 126–7
Nietzsche, Friedrich, 27
Nigeria, 59
Nkosi, Tshepo, 122
'no-go' areas along national borders, 64
Noppodon Pattama, 153, 155
Nora, Pierre, 44, 56, 67, 128, 290
North Atlantic Treaty Organization (NATO), 34, 243
Northern Ireland, 165
nostalgia, 182, 187–93, 197, 222–3
    medical view of, 190
    modernist variant of, 192
    private and collective, 190–1
    restorative and reflective, 191
    see also 'Yugo-nostalgia'
Novelo, Victoria, 111
Novick, Peter, 32–3

Object-ID standards, 305, 308
Okavango Delta, 159–60
Old Fort prison, 122
Olick, Jeffrey, 31
Oliver-Smith, Anthony, 130
Olympic Games, 73
Ong, W.J., 288–9
oral history, 48
Organization for Economic Cooperation and Development
    (OECD), 226
Orser, Charles, 90
Ortayli, Iber, 227–8
Oyama, Susan, 125, 133

Page, Stephen J., 126
Pakistan, 6

Pamuk, Orhan, 16, 222–4, 227
Panofsky, Erwin, 284
Papantia Flyers, 208
Papayannis, Thymio, 125
Pejić, Bojana, 183
Peleggi, Maurizio, 127
Pelourinho, 77–8
Percy, Walker, 124
Perm-36 Gulag Museum, 116–17, 120
Picasso, Pablo, 56
Pieterse, J.N., 312
pilgrimages, 388–9
Pinochet, Augusto, 118
place, sense of, 131
pluralism regarding heritage, 89
Poland, 53
Pollock, Jackson, 125
popular culture, 291–2, 378–81
post-conflict societies, 242–3
post-modernism, 16
post-socialism, 191–2
Powell, Colin, 338
Prague, 184
Preah Vihear Temple, 148–55, 348
press freedom, 336, 339
prisons as heritage, 165–7
Propp, Vladimir, 34
public-private partnerships, 76
Pündük, Şükrü, 229
Putin, Vladimir, 27

Radstone, S., 157
Rajoelina, Andry, 174
Rancière, Jacques, 267
Ravalomanana, Marc, 174
refugees and refugee camps, 103, 354, 356
relativism, see cultural relativism; moral relativism
religion and religious identity, 292, 336, 338–9, 360–1, 365,
    368, 386–90
remembering as a process, 12, 29–30
remittances, 355, 357
Renan, Ernest, 6
Renshon, S.A., 376
return
    of art and artifacts to their places of origin, 25, 41
    of diasporic communities, 90–1
Ricœur, Paul, 28
Riga, 181
Robben Island, 46, 159, 164–6
Rock Hospital, 181–2
Rogers, Peter J., 127
Rom Bunnag, 152
Romero, Margarita, 123
Rosario, 202–3
Rosetta Stone, 25
Rummel, R.J., 339
Rushdie, S., 172
Russia, indigenous peoples in, 100–1
Rwanda, 17, 245–50

Saami language, 262–3
sacred heritage, 144–5
Sadoon, Karim Ali, 265

St Louis Art Museum, 25
Sakalava people, 174
Salvador, 77
Samak Sundaravej, 150–3
San Agustin Center for the Arts (CASA), 204–5
San ethnicity, 163–4
San Francisco Museum of the African Diaspora
    (MoAD), 85
Sánchez-Carretero, Cristina, 106–7
Sankuyo village, 160–3
Santino, Jack, 106
Sarajevo, 196
Sarkozy, Nicolas, 63
Schacter, Daniel, 30
Scheuchzer, J.J., 190
Schiff, Brian, 31
Schwanke, K., 376
Second Life, 373
Second World War, 33, 58, 240, 343–4
sectarianism, 283
Seeman, Sonia, 225
Sellars, Richard West, 126
Sen, Amartya, 9
September 11th 2001 attacks, 56, 109–11, 290, 308,
    343–4, 349
Serbia, 193
Servole, Fanny, 217
Šešić, Milena Dragićević, 194
sexual orientations, 379–81
Seychelles, 170
Shanghai Expo (2010), 73
'shared memory' (Margalit), 190
Sharp, L., 174
Sheail, John, 126
Shelley, Percy Bysshe, 281
Shepherd, Robert, 79–80
Shonibare, Yinka, 279
Shopes, Linda, 83
Silk Road, 76
Simma, Asa, 263–4
Singapore Chinese Heritage Centre, 85
sites of conscience, 14
    coalition of, 114–19
    core policies for, 119–23
    definition of, 115–19
sites of memory, 171; see also lieu de mémoire
Sivaram, M., 151
Skopje, 195–6
Slapsak, S., 195
slavery and the slave trade, 85, 122, 174, 215–16
Smith, Joe, 132–3
Smith, Laurajane, 79, 87, 143
Smith, Rogers, 35
Snowy Mountains hydro-electricity scheme, 87–9
Sobukwe, Robert, 166
social identity theory, 338
social networking, 370
socialist regimes, ending of, 191–2
'soft power', 74
Somchai Wongsawat, 152
songs, popularity of, 378, 380
Sontag, Susan, 8, 56
Sørensen, M.L.S., 65, 131

South Africa, 15, 122–3, 158–9, 164–7
Spain, 14, 61–3, 88–9, 131
Spanish Civil War, 28, 53, 59, 61, 108
Srebrenica, 60
Sri Lanka, 143–5
Stalin, Joseph, 26, 58
Stanford, Lois, 130
Steinberg, Ted, 129
Stevens, Mary, 89
Stewart, S., 190
Stockholm Museum of History, 264
Stone Town, 71–2, 173
Stovel, Herb, 141–2
streets, naming of, 333–4
Stuckrad, K., 389
students, international mobility of,
    359, 361
sub-cultures, 380–1
Sugar, Janos, 184
'suitcase narrative' of migration, 86
Sulukule district, 16, 222, 225–9
sustainability, 288, 322–5
    of development, 200
    of heritage, 324–5
Sutton, M., 362
Sweden, 262–4
Sznaider, N., 335

taboos, 160–2, 167, 174
Tahan, Lina G., 66–7
Tallinn, 2
Tangshan museum, 129
Tanpinar, Ahmet Hamdi, 16, 222–5, 228
Tantan, Saadettin, 225
Tanzania, 127, 170, 173
Taylor, Charles, 89
Taylor, Diana, 248
Tel Aviv Museum of the Jewish Diaspora (Ben
    Hatefuthsoth), 85
television series, most popular, 378, 380
Teotihuacan, 278–9
Teresa of Calcutta (MotherTeresa), 343
territorialization, 102–3
textbooks, 33
Thailand, 15, 127, 131, 148–55
Thaksin Shinawatra, 150–1, 155
theatre of commemoration, 17, 245–50
Theodossopoulos, D., 321
Thomas, Julie, 16
Thongchai Winichakul, 152, 154
Thornton, S., 380
Throsby, David, 43, 349
Tibet, 79–80
Tito, Josip Broz, 183, 187–9, 195–6
    memorial website for, 195
Togno, Barthelemy, 218
Toledo, Francisco, 204
Tölölyan, Kachig, 82
Tomasson, Torkel, 263
Tomlinson, J., 291–2
Toninato, P., 171
totems, 160–2, 167
Toubon, Jacques, 217

tourism, 3–4, 13, 15, 57, 76, 80, 175, 180, 288,
    318–21
  classifications of, 320
  in southern Africa, 153–67
'Tower of Babel' metaphor, 17, 281–3
translation of languages, 284, 317
transnational companies, 139
Trouillot, Michel Rolph, 33
True, Marion, 25
truth and reconciliation commissions (TRCs), 58, 61–3, 66,
    165, 243, 283

Ugresic, D., 189, 194
United Nations
  Declaration on the Rights of Indigenous Peoples (2007),
      13, 95, 101–2, 104, 329
  Permanent Forum on Indigenous Issues, 101, 328
United Nations Educational, Scientific and Cultural
    Organization (UNESCO), 4, 11–12, 39–44, 49–50,
    58, 72–3, 80, 84, 88–9, 132, 140, 169, 171, 174, 178,
    226–9, 232–3, 273, 282, 329
  Convention on the Illicit Import, Export and Transfer of
      Cultural Property (1970), 308
  Convention on Intangible Cultural Heritage (2003),
      141, 200
  Convention on the Protection and Promotion of
      the Diversity of Cultural Expressions (2005), 144,
      208, 308
  Convention on the Protection of World Cultural and
      Natural Heritage (1972), 141, 308
  Convention for the Safeguarding of Intangible Cultural
      Heritage (1973), 160, 308, 316
  Memory of the World project, 322, 325, 351, 353
  signatories to treaties, 304–5
  Universal Declaration on Cultural Diversity
      (2001), 273
United Nations World Tourist Organization
    (UNWTO), 320
United States Environmental Protection Agency, 283
Universal Declaration of Human Rights (1948),
    96, 104

van Dijck, J., 9
Varro, G., 254
Venice, 44
Venice Charter (1964), 49–50, 141–3
Vergès, F., 171
video games, characters in, 379, 381
Viejo-Rose, Dacia, 63–4
Vienna, 183–4
Vigotsky, L.S., 201
Villa Grimaldi, 118–19, 123
Vilnius, 181–2
Viollet-le-Duc, Eugène, 49
Virilio, Paul, 213–14
'voicing', 262
Volcic, Zala, 182
von Droste, B., 142

Waller, Tony, 107
Wanwipa Charoonroj, 152

war
  and the creation of heritage, 57–8
  remembrance of, 60
  winners and losers in, 239
  see also civil war
war crimes, 246
Warner, Langdon, 58
Warren, Kay, 36
Washington consensus, 97, 103
Watersnoodmuseum, 128–9
weapons of mass destruction in Iran, belief in, 336, 338
Wearing, S., 321
Webmoor, Timothy, 278–9
Weisman, Alan, 127
Wertsch, James V., 31, 253
White, Hayden, 32–3
Whiting, Dean, 144
Wijesuriya, Gamini, 143
wilderness areas, 125–6, 133
Williams, Paul, 214
Williams, Raymond, 42, 124
Willoughby, W.C., 160
Woodward, Christopher, 128
World Bank, 76, 97
world figures and world events, perceived importance of,
    340–2
World Heritage Alliance, 76
World Heritage Committee, 45–6, 49–50, 308
World Heritage Convention, 40, 142, 298
World Heritage sites, 12, 45–6, 64, 71–2, 75, 77, 90–1,
    126–7, 133, 140–1, 148, 150, 153, 163, 166, 172–3,
    288, 298–302, 305, 308, 318, 390
World Monument Forum (WMF), 329
World Values Survey, 384
Wright, Susan, 42

Yai, Olabiliy Joseph, 85
Yelvington, K.A., 171
Yemen, 74
Younes, Rola, 266–9
Young, James E., 60
Yúdice, G., 75
'Yugo-nostalgia', 193–7
'Yugoland', 195
Yugoslavia, former territory of, 180–3, 187–97
  disintegration of, 189
Yusoff, Kathryn, 132–3

Zafinfotse, 174
Zagreb, 184
Zambrano, M., 171
Zanzibar, 71–2, 169–70, 173, 175
Zao Wou-ki, 85
Zapata, Emilio, 99
Zapatero, José Luis Rodriguez, 61
Zapatista movement, 206
Zerubavel, E., 253–4, 343
Zeuschel, Obilot, 265
Zionism, 83
Zorbas, Eugenia, 246
Zulu culture, 163